Rights and Duties of Directors 2015

Rights and Duties of Directors 2015

by

Martha Bruce FCIS
Director, Bruce Wallace Associates Limited

Bloomsbury Professional

Bloomsbury Professional Ltd, Maxwelton House, 41–43 Boltro Road, Haywards Heath, West Sussex, RH16 1BJ

This is the 14th edition of this work.

© Bloomsbury Professional Ltd 2015

Bloomsbury Professional is an imprint of Bloomsbury Publishing Plc.

A CIP Catalogue record for this book is available from the British Library.

ISBN: 978 1 78043 207 6

Typeset by Phoenix Photosetting, Chatham, Kent
Printed and bound in Great Britain by CPI Group (UK) Ltd, Croydon, CR0 4YY

Preface

Rights and Duties of Directors is a broad, practical guide for directors that has been written to help them understand the full extent of their duties. These derive from a considerable number of sources including the Companies Acts and core corporate legislation; employment, competition, consumer protection, health and safety and environmental legislation; codes of practice; best practice guides; and, for listed public companies, the UK listing regime and the UK Corporate Governance Code. Whilst it is not possible to cover each area in detail, the book provides directors with concise, key, up-to-date information and practical advice about what is required across all the areas, the intention being to put directors in a more informed position about the whole spectrum of duties arising from their appointment.

This 14th edition has been updated to include the many changes in legislation and best practice that have come into effect over the last year, as set out on the back cover. This includes in particular, the requirement for a strategic report and changes to the directors' remuneration report in companies' annual accounts; requirements of the 2014 UK Corporate Governance Code; and changes to the competition and consumer protection regimes.

To put the facts into a real-life context, illustrations have been given of instances where failure to observe requirements and ride roughshod over law and best practice have resulted in directors being disqualified or held personally liable for their wrongdoing. Information has also been included about regulatory fines and other penalties incurred by companies as a consequence of directors failing to observe their duties.

An important point to note is that there is no grace period for a new appointee to get up to speed with the responsibilities of the director's role. From the moment a director is appointed he is accountable for his actions, or lack of them, and no allowance is made for the director who did not know or was not aware that what they were doing was wrong or not enough. Then, on an ongoing basis, directors face the demanding task of staying up to date with the many changes to their responsibilities, otherwise they risk being called to account for something they or their companies have either done which is no longer permitted or have omitted to do and which is now required.

This in itself is all quite a challenge and this book is written and kept up to date to try and make the director's task a little easier.

The excerpts from the Listing Rules have been reproduced with the kind permission of the Financial Conduct Authority. The readers who need to consult the rules should refer to The Listing Rules which are available from the Financial Conduct Authority. Crown copyright is reproduced with the permission of the Controller of HMSO. ICSA Guidance Notes are reproduced by kind permission of the copyright holder, the Institute of Chartered Secretaries and Administrators. For more information on a wide number of Guidance Notes please refer to the frequently updated Guidance section of their website at www.icsa.org.uk.

Whilst every effort has been made to ensure the accuracy of the contents of this book, neither the author nor the publisher can accept responsibility for any loss arising to anyone relying on the information contained herein. The user is recommended to seek appropriate professional advice and guidance as to the applicability of the content of this book to any particular matter or circumstance.

Given the areas it covers, updating this book each year always takes a considerable amount of time and I would like to thank those around me for their continued patience and support.

Martha Bruce, FCIS
January 2015

About the author

Martha Bruce FCIS is a Chartered Secretary providing company secretarial advice and services to both private and public companies. For many years she was an executive director of David Venus & Company Limited and she is now a director of Bruce Wallace Associates Limited. Martha has held appointments as named secretary and consultant to an extensive portfolio of companies in all areas of industry and commerce, ranging from small private and unquoted public companies, to those that are fully listed. She also has extensive experience in the provision of trade mark, health and safety and employment advice and services to clients.

Martha's company secretarial career began in 1988 when she started working at Morgan Grenfell. She qualified as a Chartered Secretary whilst working for Chantrey Vellacott, joined David Venus & Company in 1992 and left there in 2012 after many enjoyable years and a successful sale to set up a new business.

As well as providing practical advice to help directors fulfil the daily challenges running a company presents, Martha has also written a number of books on the subject and has been a presenter at seminars for many years.

Contents

Table of Cases

[All references are to paragraph number]

S

Table of Statutes

[All references are to paragraph number]

Companies Act 2006 – *contd*

s 250 .... 1.10
251 .... 1.35
260 .... 8.30, 8.40
(3) 8.40
261, 262 .... 8.30, 8.40
263 .... 8.30, 8.40
(2)(a)–(c) 8.40
264–269 .... 8.30, 8.40
273 .... 6.12
275 .... 6.12, 6.21.3; App 3, App 4
275(4) .... App 4
276 .... 6.12, 6.31; App 3
282, 283 .... 8.25
288 .... 8.21.1.4
291(3)(b) 8.21.1.4
292(2) 8.22
293 .... 8.22
296 .... App 20
297 .... 8.21.1.4
302 .... 8.22
303 .... 8.21.1.1, 8.22
304 .... 6.11.7, 6.13.2
(1)(a), (b) 8.22
307 .... 8.23.2.1, 8.23.2.2
(1) 6.31; 8.23.2.1
(2)(a), (b) 8.23.2.1
(6)(a), (b) 8.23.2.2
307A 8.23.2.1
310 .... 8.23.1
311 .... 8.23
(3) 8.23
311A 8.24
312 .... 6.11.7; 8.23.2.3; App 19
314 .... 8.22
315 .... 8.23.2.3
316 .... 8.22
318 .... 8.26.1
319A 8.26
321 .... 8.26.2
323 .... 8.26.3
324 .... 8.10, 8.23, 8.26.3
(2) 8.23
327 .... 8.26.3
334 .... 8.21.1.3, 8.23.2.1
335 .... 8.23.2.1
336 .... 8.21.1.1
(3), (4) 8.21.1.1
337(2) 8.23.2.2
339 .... 8.23.2.3
341(1), (1A) 8.26.2
355 .... 6.28; 8.26.5; App 4
(2) 6.43

Companies Act 2006 – *contd*

s 356 .... 6.28
358 .... App 4
(2) .... App 4
360 .... 8.23.2.1
Pt 14 (ss 362–379) 7.25
s 362–365 .... 7.25
366 .... 7.25
(2)(b)(i), (ii) 7.25
367 .... 7.25
(5) 7.25
368–376 .... 7.25
377 .... 7.25
(1) 8.23
378, 379 .... 7.25
382 .... 7.14, **7.15.2**
(1) **7.15.1**
(2) .... **7.15.1**; App 14
(3)–(6) **7.15.1**
383 .... 7.14, **7.14.4**, **7.15.2**
(3) .... App 14
384 .... 7.14
385 .... **7.17**; 8.0
386 .... 7.11, **7.15.2**; App 3
387 .... 7.11
388 .... App 3, App 7
(1)(b) 3.130
389(4) 7.11
393 .... 7.13
394 .... 7.12, **7.15.2**; App 3
394A 7.12, **7.14.6**
394B, 394C **7.14.6**
396 .... 7.12
398 .... **7.14.4**
399 .... 7.12; App 3
400, 401 .... **7.14.5**
409–411 .... 7.13.8
412 .... 7.13.8
(5), (6) 7.13.8
413 .... 6.94; 7.13.8
(1), (2) 6.94
(8) 6.94
414 .... **7.16**; App 3
(4), (5) **7.16**
414A(5), (6) 7.13.3
415 .... 7.13.1
(5) 7.13.1
416 .... 7.13.1; 14.10
417 .... 7.13.3
418 .... 7.13.1
419 .... **7.16**; 11.10
(1), (3) 7.13.1
419A **7.16**

Table of Statutory Instruments

[All references are to paragraph number]

Table of European and International Legislation

[All references are to paragraph number]

1 The nature of office of director

1   The nature of office of director

Definition   1.10

The Companies Act 2006 (CA 2006) does not specifically define what a director is, although s 250 provides that the term includes 'any person occupying the position of director, by whatever name called'. Thus a director is recognised by his function, regardless of the title or name bestowed upon him. A company may therefore describe its directors as governors, trustees or council members, without affecting their legal status as directors. Similarly a person carrying out the function of a director will be deemed to be a director, notwithstanding that he has not been formally appointed (see paras **1.35**, **1.36**, **1.51** and **1.52**).

Whilst not legally defined, directors are responsible for leading the companies to which they are appointed by directing, overseeing, supervising, governing and controlling how their companies are run. The director's role will therefore involve evaluating options and making decisions on the company's direction and strategy, organisation, administration, regulation, governance and systems of control. The directors together determine the company's strategy and plans for how it will be achieved and review performance against those plans, making changes as necessary.

Requirement for directors   1.20

Every private company is required by CA 2006 s 154 to have at least one director whilst a public company must have at least two directors. Although one company may be appointed director of another company, at least one of the company's directors must be a natural or actual person (CA 2006 s 155).

In addition, where a company's Articles state that a higher minimum number of directors than this is required, or place a limit on the maximum number of directors that may be appointed, then those provisions must be observed. For example, the Model Articles for a private company state the minimum required is one director, but Table A reg 64 requires a minimum of two directors unless the shareholders have passed an ordinary resolution stating otherwise.

In the event that the number of directors appointed inadvertently falls below the required minimum, the directors remaining in office could find themselves liable for the debts of the company. It is therefore important the situation is immediately rectified and that any decisions made whilst the company had insufficient directors are ratified by the properly constituted Board.

Types of director   1.30

As set out below, there are many different names given to the different types of director. However, it is important to note that, regardless of the name ascribed to that type of director or whether or not the person has been properly appointed, a person 'occupying the position of director' and performing the director's function shares the same duties and responsibilities.

Executive director   1.31

Full-time working directors are often described as 'executive' directors, as they carry out extensive executive management functions within the company and are involved in managing operations, finance, marketing and human resources on a day-to-day basis. When a person is appointed as a full-time working director, he will usually enter into a service contract with the company at the same time as his formal appointment to the Board. Typically such contract will require that person to devote his full attention, or certainly a substantial part of his attention, to managing the company, and the matters usually included in the service contract are set out in **APPENDIX 1**.

However, whilst a director might be referred to as a finance director or marketing director, the director's duties are much wider, extend to the whole business and are not restricted to the director's own function. The unitary nature of the UK Board system and the directors' shared responsibility for decisions made by the Board on all matters is often not fully appreciated when executives are appointed to the Board and needs to be brought to their attention.

Many Boards appoint a chief executive office ('CEO'). The CEO is the most senior executive director and, in addition to the duties shared by all directors, is responsible for leading the executive directors and for proposing and delivering the company's strategy. The CEO will hold detailed meetings with the executive team and be responsible for communicating the executive director's views and conclusions from these meetings to the Board. In addition the CEO has a responsibility to ensure the views and any directions or requirements agreed by the Board are communicated to the company's employees and are effectively implemented. In particular the CEO must ensure that appropriate standards of governance are implemented and observed throughout the company. Consequently, an executive director who is appointed CEO takes on a very pivotal role requiring, amongst other things, a very high standard of communication skills.

Many Boards also appoint either a finance director ('FD') or chief financial officer ('CFO'). It is the FD or CFO's role to ensure that sufficiently high-quality financial information is presented to the Board for it to monitor and review the financial position of the Company.

Non-executive director   1.32

In contrast, a director who is not an employee of the company and is required to devote only part of his time to the affairs of the company as an adviser or supervisor may be referred to as a 'non-executive' director. Neither the term 'executive' nor 'non-executive' are recognised by CA 2006, but both are commonly used in practice.

A non-executive director has the same statutory duties and obligations as any other director and non-executive directors participate fully in the joint deliberations of the Board, but do not have any executive function or involvement in the company's management. The terms of their appointment are usually set out in a letter of engagement, an example of which is given in **APPENDIX 2**. It is important that the engagement letter states the minimum time required to be devoted to dealing with the company's affairs and that the non-executive director agrees to this from the outset.

However, the court may apply different standards when determining the level of skill and standard of duty of care that a non-executive can be expected to demonstrate. For example, in *Re Peppermint Park Ltd* [1998] BCC 23 the judge took account of the directors' relative responsibilities and a director who occupied a non-executive role was disqualified for a significantly lesser period than the director who effectively controlled the company. In *Re Stephenson Cobbold Ltd* [2001] BCC 38 the court refused to disqualify a non-executive director as, although he was a cheque signatory, he was not involved in deciding which creditors should be paid where preferential treatment had been given.

It is widely recognised that non-executive directors have a key role in ensuring that the companies to which they are appointed have an effective system of corporate governance and are appropriately directed and controlled. The main and supporting principles of A.4 of the UK Corporate Governance Code (which, whilst they only apply to companies with a premium listing of equity shares, comprise sound guidance on the key components of effective Board practice relevant to all companies) are more specific and state that the non-executive directors should:

- constructively challenge and help develop the Board's proposals on strategy;

- scrutinise the performance of management in meeting strategic goals and objectives;

- monitor reporting of performance;

- question the integrity of financial information and the robustness of controls and the company's risk management processes;

- determine remuneration of the executive directors; and

- be involved in determining appointments and removals from the Board and overall succession planning.

Undoubtedly non-executive directors have an important role to play in bringing independence and an outside objectivity into the Board's decision-making process. It is important the non-executive directors openly and constructively question, challenge and debate matters with the executive directors before decisions are reached to ensure, amongst other things, that all options, outcomes and risk arising from that decision have been fully considered.

The effectiveness of and need for non-executive directors initially came under a great deal of scrutiny following a number of large-scale corporate collapses and 'scandals' such as Enron, Marconi, Worldcom, Railtrack, Equitable Life and Independent Insurance. These caused shareholders, institutional investors and others to question the effectiveness of non-executive directors and why they were not aware of alleged mismanagement and corporate wrongdoing or the extent of the companies' problems. The worldwide 'credit crunch' and near collapse of many banks in the UK and other jurisdictions in 2008 has caused the effectiveness of non-executives to be examined further.

It is therefore essential that non-executive directors ensure they are in possession of sufficient information and can commit sufficient time to make a contribution to strategy and to fulfil their corporate governance responsibilities to monitor and challenge executives. They must insist upon sufficient and timely receipt of information if informed debate is to be achieved at Board meetings.

Judgment handed down by the Grand Court of the Cayman Islands in *Weavering Macro Fixed Income fund (in liquidation) v Stefan Peterson and Hans Ekstrom* is worthy of note as, amongst other things, it addresses governance of hedge funds and the standards expected of non-executive directors. In this particular case standard form minutes of Board meetings had been produced for a period of some six years and there was no evidence that the non-executive directors had received or requested any information necessary for them to fulfil their duty to supervise the hedge fund. As a consequence of their failure to perform their duties, an award of $111m for damages was made against Messrs Peterson and Ekstrom.

The Higgs Review examined the role and effectiveness of non-executive directors and, more recently, the Walker Review looked in detail at corporate governance and the balance of skills, experience and independence required on UK company Boards. Whilst many of the good practice recommendations from the Higgs and Walker Reviews were incorporated into the UK Corporate Governance Code, the Higgs Review itself has now been replaced by the FRC's Guidance on Board Effectiveness, more explanation of which is given in **CHAPTERS 2** and **10**.

When determining whether to appoint someone as a non-executive director, the Board needs to consider the contribution they will make, and ensure that the person has appropriate skills, experience and knowledge, knows the commitment required of them, and is not overstretched by other non-executive or executive directorships. In particular, the Tyson Report into recruitment and development of non-executive directors concluded that UK companies would benefit from greater diversity amongst non-executive directors and by adoption of a more far-reaching, rigorous and transparent recruitment process that looks beyond the usual candidates for appointment. This view and the need for diversity is supported and endorsed by the UK Corporate Governance Code as well as the review by Lord Davies into women on Boards, and is explored further in **CHAPTER 2**.

Independent non-executive director   1.33

An independent non-executive director is a non-executive director who has no ties or connections with the company, other than by virtue of the directorship. Independence amongst some or all non-executive directors is considered important from a governance perspective, the reason being that it allows them to question and challenge executive directors freely, without restrictions that might be faced by those who have other ties, connections or business relationships with the company.

Indeed the UK Corporate Governance Code requires that at least half the Board, excluding the chairman, of a company with a premium listing of equity securities be made up of independent non-executive directors. Smaller listed companies below the FTSE 350 are required to have at least two independent non-executive directors.

Whilst determination of a non-executive director's independence of character and judgment is made by the Board, the UK Corporate Governance Code lists specific relationships and circumstances which could affect a director's judgment and cause his independence to be questioned, namely:

- employment by the company or group within the last five years;

- existence of a material, direct or indirect, business relationship with the company within the last three years;

- receipt of remuneration in addition to directors' fees or a pension or participation in a share option or performance-related pay scheme;

- close family ties with any of the company's directors, senior employees or advisers;

- existence of directorships in other companies or involvement in other bodies linked to directors of the company;

- appointment in order to represent a significant shareholder; or

- service on the Board for more than nine years.

The Board's determination of a director's independence has to be explained in the listed company's annual report and accounts and, whilst the UK Corporate Governance Code makes clear that it is for the Board to determine whether a non-executive director is independent, in practice where any of the circumstances set out immediately above apply, no matter what justification and clarification is given by the Board, this will most likely cause concern amongst the various shareholder institutions that make voting recommendations to shareholders (including IVIS, RREV, NAPF, ABI, PIRC, Hermes, Manifest and others). This can cause a problem as an 'against' or 'abstain' recommendation on a resolution, say a particular director's election or re-election to the Board, could cause the resolution to fail.

The UK Corporate Governance Code also requires the Board of a company with a premium listing of equity securities to appoint a senior independent director (commonly referred to as the 'SINED') from amongst the independent non-executive directors. In addition to all other duties as a director, the SINED's role would also usually involve:

- acting as a sounding board, providing support, and working closely with the chairman;

- meeting at least annually with the non-executive directors to appraise the chairman's performance and where there is a dispute, disagreement or a difference in opinions between the chairman and CEO take the lead in mediating and resolving the matter to restore stability;

- ensuring succession planning for the chairman is addressed; and

- being available to shareholders and other non-executives to address any concerns or issues they have which have not been adequately addressed by the chairman through the normal channels of communication.

The SINED can also be key to resolving difficult Board issues such as a dispute between the chairman and CEO or, conversely, too close a relationship between them; lack of support for the strategy being recommended by the chairman and CEO; or concern that succession planning is receiving too little or no attention.

It is expected that these additional responsibilities and any others that are agreed would be set out in the SINED's letter of engagement to ensure clarity and avoid any confusion about what the role entails.

Alternate director   1.34

Whilst there is no provision in CA 2006, it is common in practice for a company's Articles to provide each director with the right to appoint an 'alternate' (Table A reg 65, and see para **3.10**). Where the Articles permit the appointment of an alternate director, the provisions should be carefully considered as they can differ considerably from company to company. For example, whilst Table A provides that a person put forward as an alternate director must be either an existing director or a person approved by the Board, it is not uncommon to give directors the power to appoint any person without the need for Board approval. The Articles will also state the manner in which the appointment shall be made and how it will cease, which is usually by written notice from the appointor director.

It should be noted that whilst there is no right to appoint an alternate director contained in the Model Articles for a private company, this right is included in the Model Articles for a public company.

An alternate director will be subject to all statutory obligations and responsibilities of other directors, and accordingly he must complete and sign a form of appointment which is submitted to Companies House, have his details entered in the register of directors and observe requirements to disclose any interest in shares, transactions and so forth (as set out in **CHAPTER 6**).

The alternate director may be restricted by provisions in the company's Articles which may provide, for example, that an alternate be appointed merely to attend and vote at meetings in the appointor's absence. An alternate director is not entitled to receive remuneration by virtue of his office and the appointment will automatically terminate when the appointor ceases to be a director.

Shadow director   1.35

A shadow director is defined by CA 2006 s 251 as 'a person in accordance with whose instructions or directions the directors are accustomed to act'. This does not include a person giving advice in a professional capacity such as an accountant, solicitor or tax specialist unless the advice and direction they are giving goes beyond their area of expertise.

There will have been no formal appointment as a director and often the person wants to remain in the 'shadows' without seeking formal appointment.

For example, behind the formally appointed Board there may be a controlling shareholder, secured creditor or banker, on whose instructions the Board is accustomed to act. Where this is the case and such person has the powers of a director without being formally appointed, he is likely to be considered a shadow director. Case law has also helped to clarify what constitutes a 'shadow' director as follows:

- influence must be exerted by the person over the majority of Board members (*Re Unisoft Group Ltd (No 3)* [1994] BCC 766);

- a company, including a parent company, in certain circumstances where influence is exerted (*Re Hydrodam (Corby) Ltd* [1994] 2 BCLC 180, [1994] BCC 161);

- *Secretary of State for Trade and Industry v Deverell* [2000] 2 All ER 365 widened the definition of 'shadow director' by establishing that the Board does not have to be subservient or surrender its discretionary powers to such person, the person merely has to exercise his influence over the affairs of the company. In this particular case it was held that an individual whose advice had been followed by the Board in respect of a wide range of issues over a long period of time was a shadow director and could be subject to disqualification proceedings.

CA 2006 provides that a shadow director shall be subject to the same rules as an appointed director and accordingly the same statutory obligations which apply to appointed directors apply also to shadow directors (see paras **6.61**, **6.70**, **6.80** and **6.91**). In addition shadow directors may find themselves caught by the wrongful trading provisions of the Insolvency Act 1986 (IA 1986). These provisions are designed to ensure that persons controlling companies but avoiding actual appointment as directors do not evade their legal duties and responsibilities. Shadow directors may be subject to disqualification proceedings where their conduct is considered to have been 'unfit' within the terms of the Company Directors Disqualification Act 1986 (CDDA 1986) or where they have failed to meet obligations required of them by virtue of their involvement with the company as a shadow director (see para **5.54**). By way of example, in *Yukong Line Ltd of Korea v Rendsburg Investment Corp of Liberia, The Rialto (No 2)* [1998] 2 BCLC 485, it was considered that a shadow director could be in breach of fiduciary duties as a director.

De facto director   1.36

A de facto director is a person who has not been formally appointed to the Board or whose appointment was improper who nevertheless holds himself or herself out as a director, occupies the position of director and deals with matters that could only be properly discharged by a director. In *Re Hydrodam (Corby) Ltd* [1994] 2 BCLC 180, [1994] BCC 161 the judge described a de facto director as a person who assumes to act as a director, is held out by the company as a director and who claims or purports to be a director 'without being validly appointed.

Although in some cases it is difficult to prove that a person has been acting as a de facto director and to determine the extent of their actions in this regard, a de facto director can be liable for disqualification as a director (see para **5.54**). They are also subject to the same statutory duties and responsibilities as the directors who have been properly appointed.

It is also important to note that a person acting in a professional capacity or a substantial investor taking an active part in running the affairs of a company may be considered a de facto director and consequently could be subject to disqualification (see the UKLI case example in para **5.53.4**).

Associate director   1.37

It is not uncommon for companies to give senior executives titles such as 'associate director' or 'assistant director', 'group divisional director', 'regional director', 'director of finance', 'facilities director', or 'sales director' and so forth (together referred to as 'associate directors') in recognition of their seniority and status, without appointing them as directors of the company. Associate director titles have no particular standing in law and are used generically as courtesy titles to senior executives without offering them a seat on the Board.

There are dangers attached to conferring such titles on people who do not have the powers of directors, and caution should be exercised with this practice as such a person may be considered a de facto director (para **1.36** above) and be liable for breaches of duties conferred on the directors. At the same time, if that person is held out as a director or as holding an executive position without formal appointment, he may inadvertently exceed the intended extent of his authority and commit the company to contracts which are beyond his power and such contracts would normally be enforceable against the company.

By way of example, in *SMC Electronics Ltd v Akhter Computers Ltd* [2001] 1 BCLC 433 an employee who was not a director was given the title of 'Director of Power Supply Unit Sales' and was accustomed to describing himself as a director on the company's notepaper. The employee entered into a contract which the company was unable to repudiate, in part due to the director being known and described as a director from which a third party would reasonably assume he had authority to enter into such a contract.

Authority must be provided in the Articles for the title of associate director to be bestowed upon a person and it is important that provisions in the Articles also make it clear that a person with such title is not a member of the Board and is not entitled to attend and vote at Board meetings. Where the Articles permit appointment of associate directors, they must also specify that the Board has authority to define and limit their powers. It is also important to ensure that individuals with these titles know not to hold themselves out as directors and make clear the limit of their powers to third parties.

Managing director   1.38

It is usual for provisions in the Articles to permit the Board to appoint one of the directors as managing director and to delegate all or any of its powers of management to such appointee (Table A regs 84 and 72 and article 5 of the Model Articles). Where a managing director is appointed, it is important to note that he is only permitted to exercise those powers specifically conferred on him by the Board; he does not have any powers merely by virtue of his appointment (*Mitchell & Hobbs (UK) Ltd v Mill* [1996] 2 BCLC 102). Appointment and delegation of powers to the managing director is made by simple resolution of the Board and the appointment can be revoked by the Board at any time.

Although the Articles empower the directors to manage and exercise all the powers of the company, it is unusual for the Board of Directors even of a large company to meet more than once or twice each month. Consequently, the managing director is often delegated authority to manage and take decisions on the day-to-day running of the company. Such authority is likely to allow the managing director to enter into contracts and agreements on behalf of the company either generally or limited to specific transactions. Similarly, the managing director may be specifically authorised by the Board to approve final details of agreements considered and approved in principle by the Board.

Except where a company has an executive chairman or a CEO, the managing director is usually the most senior executive of the company and, as such, has overall responsibility for the company's operations. Appointment of a managing director is more common in small public and private companies than in larger public and listed companies, which would tend to appoint a CEO, and often each trading subsidiary company in a group structure would have an appointed managing director.

Specific responsibilities delegated by the Board to the managing director will usually include matters such as:

- developing and implementing operational plans, policies, processes and procedures to enable the company to achieve the strategic goals set by the Board;

- putting in place effective systems of control and risk management;

- taking appropriate and timely corrective action where problems are identified and informing the Board of any significant changes to operations as a result;

- monitoring operational and financial performance against plans, targets and budgets;

- achievement of performance targets;

- building an effective executive management team;

- monitoring actions and performance of executive directors; and

- maintaining a dialogue with the chairman of the Board and representing the company to customers, suppliers and institutions, etc.

It should also be noted that the managing director will often be excluded from the requirement to retire by rotation (Table A reg 84).

Nominee director   1.39

It is not uncommon for a class of shareholders, debenture holders or a major creditor to have authority, either expressed in the company's Articles or in a supplementary agreement such as a shareholders' agreement, to appoint or remove a director to ensure they have representation on a company's Board. Whilst in principle there is nothing wrong with appointing a nominee director, that person must be left to exercise his judgment to promote the success of the company without any direction or instruction as to how to act or vote by the appointor (*Boulting v Association of Cinematograph, Television and Allied Technicians* [1963] 2 QB 606, 626, CA). The nominee director must not put the appointor's interests before those of the company (*Scottish Co-operative Wholesale Society Ltd v Meyer* [1959] AC 324, HL).

Failure to observe common law and statutory duties attributed to the office of director may render the nominee director liable for disqualification, in the same way as any director. In *Official Receiver v Brady* [1999] BCC 258 two limited companies were disqualified from acting as directors where their conduct was found 'unfit' when acting as nominee directors on behalf of various individuals.

Similarly an individual who accepted appointment as a nominee director of 1,313 companies was found to be 'unfit' and disqualified for 12 years (*Official Receiver v Vass* [1999] BCC 516).

Furthermore, directors should be aware of an interesting development in Ireland with the introduction of the Companies (Amendment) (No 2) Act 1999 which, subject to certain exceptions, prohibits an individual from holding more than 25 directorships at any particular time. Whilst this does not affect companies in the UK, it has undoubtedly been brought into effect to reduce the number of nominee directorships. CA 2006 has addressed this to some extent by requiring all companies to have at least one natural person as director.

Eligibility   1.40

Before a person can be appointed to the Board, the directors must ensure that such person is 'eligible' to hold the position. Surprisingly, CA 2006 does not lay down qualifications which make a person eligible or ineligible to hold office as a director save that CA 2006 s 157 requires the person to be at least 16 years old.

In general most legal and natural persons can hold the position, unless that person is:

- an undischarged bankrupt who does not have leave of the court to act (CDDA 1986 s 11);

- subject to a disqualification order or has given a voluntary disqualification undertaking and does not have leave of the court to act (CDDA 1986, as amended by Insolvency Act 2000 (IA 2000) ss 2–5);

- prohibited for failing to pay amounts owing under a county court administration order (CDDA 1986 s 12);

- director of an insolvent company and the proposed appointment is for a company with a 'prohibited' name (IA 1986 s 216);

- secretary of the company and the appointment is as sole director; or

- the auditor of the company.

In some instances provisions in the company's Articles set out more detailed criteria which must be met before a person can be appointed a director or which would specifically exclude them from appointment. Such provisions in the Articles are individual to the company concerned, but some exclusions found commonly in practice (derived from Table A to CA 1985 and the Model Articles) include where:

- a bankruptcy order has been made against the person;

- the person is suffering from mental disorder; and/or

- the person has entered into an arrangement with his creditors generally.

The company's Articles may contain a share qualification requirement, where to be eligible for appointment as a director the person must hold a specified number of shares in the company. Share qualification requirements are most often found in residents' management companies, formed for administration of a residential housing development.

Such eligibility requirements in a company's Articles not only prevent a person being appointed a director in certain circumstances, but, should they fall foul of any of them once they have been so appointed, will usually require the director to vacate office. Similarly, where the director is subject to a disqualification or bankruptcy order, he is not by operation of law entitled to hold the position of director and would be required to vacate his office forthwith.

In addition to an individual's own eligibility, consideration also needs to be given to the composition of the Board as a whole to ensure the most appropriate person is appointed to further enhance the range and balance of skills, experience, knowledge and independence already possessed by the existing directors on the Board. This is explored in more detail in **CHAPTER 2**.

Appointment of directors   1.50

Appointment of first directors   1.51

In practice the first directors of the company are appointed by the subscribers to the Memorandum. When the subscribers deliver the Memorandum to the Registrar of Companies prior to incorporation, they must ensure that it is accompanied by a statement of proposed officers setting out details of the first directors (CA 2006 s 12). This statement must be signed by those named therein indicating their consent to act as directors. Such persons are deemed, on registration of the company, to have been appointed and any purported appointment by other means, such as naming a director in the Articles, is not valid unless that same person is named in and has signed the required statement.

Subsequent appointments   1.52

Once the company has been incorporated, the manner in which subsequent appointments are made is based upon provisions in the company's Articles which may, for example, permit:

- the directors to appoint a director to fill a casual vacancy or as an additional director (Table A reg 79 and article 17(1)(b) of the Model Articles);

- the members to appoint a director by ordinary resolution (Table A reg 78 and article 17(1)(a) of the Model Articles);

- appointment by notice in writing from the holding company where the company is a wholly owned subsidiary.

The authority for appointment will be inferred on the members where subsequent appointments are not mentioned or otherwise delegated by the Articles. Although unlikely, where the Articles delegate the power of appointment exclusively to the directors the members have no such power to do so in general meeting as this would be usurping the directors' powers. However, when only limited power has been conferred on the directors, the members retain their power to appoint.

Where the Articles permit directors to be appointed by the company in general meeting, they will state the procedure to be followed. For example, Table A reg 76 permits a director to be appointed at a general meeting where either he is recommended to the members by the directors or where written notice has been received from a member, entitled to vote at the meeting, of his intention to propose the appointment. It is common for these provisions, or a modified version of them, to be adopted in the company's Articles.

It should also be noted that under Table A, if the number of directors in office falls below the number required to constitute a quorum, the remaining director or directors may act (notwithstanding that there is no quorum) to appoint new directors or convene a general meeting to appoint a new director but for no other purpose (reg 90).

The procedural requirements for appointment of directors are set out in para **6.10**, as are requirements for retirement of directors by rotation, their removal and resignation.

Re-election   1.53

Directors should be aware that, whilst there is no such requirement in CA 2006, a company's Articles may require a director to offer himself for re-election by the members at the AGM following his appointment and periodically thereafter, usually at three-yearly intervals. This is now less common for private limited companies as there is no longer any statutory requirement for them to hold an AGM, but re-election may still be required for larger private companies and public companies. The specific requirements and frequency of re-election will be detailed in the Articles.

In addition the UK Corporate Governance Code requires all directors of FTSE 350 companies to offer themselves for re-election annually. Whilst when this was initially proposed the requirement was the subject of considerable concern that it might lead to a lack of stability and continuity on Boards, there has been no evidence of this and the principle is largely being adhered to.

Composition of the Board   1.60

There has been considerable focus in recent years on what makes an effective Board and how to enhance and achieve effective decision-making. Whilst there is no 'one size fits all' solution, and each company must face and address many complex and inter-related circumstances and factors, few would dispute that composition of the Board is doubtless one of the key factors that contributes to an effective Board.

Indeed, the UK Corporate Governance Code states as one of its main principles that the Board and any committees of the Board should have an appropriate balance of skills, experience, independence and knowledge amongst the members of the Board or committee.

In many ways the requirement to achieve an appropriate 'balance' on the Board or committee is no different to what is required in any group, save that the expectations are higher and the consequences of failure greater. In order to generate different ideas, look at things and analyse proposals from different perspectives, challenge what is being presented and draw on past experiences and skills, but still maintain cohesion and a balanced perspective, it is important to have a diverse mix of individuals. This might be diversity in terms of psychological type, personal attributes and character, gender, background, nationality, or experience. Social psychologists studying groups and how they operate identified that members of a group often seek to conform and to gain a sense of unanimity, cohesiveness and belonging ('Groupthink': Irving Janus 1972). It is believed 'groupthink' is behind the many bad judgments and decisions made by what would otherwise appear to be very intelligent groups and it is more likely to occur where there is similarity in type of group member, little change in membership, an overbearing leader who discourages divergent views, inadequate information and pressure for quick decisions. It is possible that all or some of these factors and characteristics might be found at Board level.

The need for greater diversity on Boards has received particular attention in recent years, which is not surprising given that many Boards are comprised of like-minded men of a similar age, from similar educational and social backgrounds. To improve diversity, initially there was a call for Boards to use outside external recruitment organisations and rely less on the 'old school' network to replace out-going directors. The Higgs review recommended more women on Boards, then the Tyson Report called for directors to be appointed from more diverse backgrounds to decrease the tendency for Boards to be comprised of like-minded individuals. More recently an independent review by Lord Davies (the 'Davies Report') concluded that gender-diverse Boards were more effective and desirable and FTSE 350 companies should be looking to increase female representation on their Boards. The main recommendations from the Davies Report include the following:

- Chairmen of FTSE 350 companies should set out and announce their aspirational goals for the % of women they aim to have on their Boards by 2013–2015 and FTSE 100 companies should aim for a minimum of 25% by 2015. Alongside this, CEOs are required to review and report on the percentage of women on executive committees.

- Each year quoted companies should disclose the proportion of women on the Board, in senior executive positions and employed by the company. The Department of Business included this recommendation in their consultation on narrative reporting and disclosure is required in the strategic report (para **7.13.3**).

- Amendment of the UK Corporate Governance Code to strengthen the principles and improve disclosure on boardroom diversity. The Code has since been amended for accounting years beginning on or after 1 October 2012 to require disclosure in the annual report and accounts of the work of the nominations committee and its search, nomination and appointment processes; a summary of the Board's policy on diversity (including gender); measurable objectives for implementing the policy; and progress against those objectives (B.2.4). The Code has also been amended to require board evaluation to include consideration of the balance of skills, experience, independence and knowledge of the company on the Board, its diversity (including gender), how the Board works and other factors relevant to Board effectiveness (B.6).

In contrast to a number of EC countries which have statutory quotas for the minimum number of women required on Boards, the Davies Report favoured a voluntary, business-led approach in the UK and, from the subsequent reports issued by Lord Davies in March 2012 and 2013 tracking the progress of his recommendations, statistics available on the BIS website and the six-monthly monitoring reports published by Cranfield School of Management, this appears to be working. Whilst clearly there is still a long way to go, progress is now being made and the number of directorships held by women in the FTSE 100 and FTSE 350 have significantly increased over the last year.

Whilst the recommendations from the Davies Report are directed at listed companies seeking to comply with the UK Corporate Governance Code, it is clear that diversity (including gender) in Board composition would benefit the vast majority of companies.

Succession planning   1.70

Neither companies nor their directors stand still and it is very important that Board composition and succession planning are reviewed on a formal basis, taking account of the needs of the Company going forward, each director's length of tenure and the need to refresh membership of the Board, as well as feedback from the Board evaluation process. Clearly it is important to have an appropriate level of stability and continuity in a company and an organised approach to succession planning can help avoid situations where the company's chairman, CEO and finance director announce with little advance warning that they intend to leave at or around the same time. Such substantial change is likely to cause concern amongst a company's employees and shareholders and the resulting uncertainty, unrest and publicity could be very damaging. By conducting formal succession planning at least once a year it is more likely these situations can be pre-empted, enabling implementation of more orderly solutions and for directors' changes to be carefully planned around each other to ensure, as far as possible, they do not coincide.

Succession planning is important not only for the Board, but also for Board committees and senior executives who will be in the frame for appointment as executive directors. It might be, for example, that a senior executive might be suitable for appointment to the Board provided improvements are made to the person's skills and abilities and the succession plan would give an indication of the timescale within which these need to be achieved. Training and personal development programmes can then be put into place to ensure the senior executive is ready for appointment to the Board at the appropriate time.

In a listed company the nomination committee, with the involvement of the chairman, would usually be responsible for recruitment of directors and succession planning. In smaller, unlisted companies such matters would normally be addressed by the Board or by an ad hoc committee of the Board formed for the purpose.

The existing Board's composition needs to be taken into account when considering succession planning and what skills, experience, background, characteristics, etc are required of the new appointee to complement and further improve the existing balance of skills, experience, knowledge, independence and diversity on the Board (see para **1.60**). Feedback from the Board evaluation process (see para **2.80**) will be important as there might be particular areas of concern that could be addressed by well-timed and careful recruitment of a replacement director.

Consideration also needs to be given to the challenges faced by the company in light of decided strategy. It might be, for example, that the Board is gearing the company up for an acquisition or listing, in which case appointment of an independent non-executive director with corporate finance experience is considered necessary and desirable. Alternatively, it might be that the new director is also to join the audit committee in which case recent, relevant financial experience is needed. Non-executive directors are usually engaged for a limited term given the need to preserve their independence (see para **1.33**) and consequently they need to be periodically replaced, and their maximum length of tenure needs to be added into the succession planning process.

Once the company's succession plan has been determined, parts will need to be distilled out into action plans for managing succession of particular roles. A detailed and agreed specification of the required role is essential, setting out what skills, knowledge, experience and personal attributes are required of the replacement. Decisions will need to be made about who will lead and who will be involved in the process. For example, whilst it will usually be led by the chairman, the head of HR, company secretary, CEO, or certain executive directors might each be involved and responsible for different stages of the process. However where it is the chairman's succession, the senior independent directors will usually lead the process.

The need for and timing of additional nomination committee meetings (or Board meetings, depending on how succession is being addressed) will need to be considered, planned and organised. In addition the timetable, allowing time for handover and to restart the process if initial candidates are not suitable, and need for and timing of public announcements must be determined. Given the length of time that recruitment would normally take it is important to identify and put dates to key milestones in the process and to determine how to monitor and report progress against them. This is important to ensure an appointee is lined up, ready for succession, at the appropriate time.

The form the recruitment process will take is important as, in the interests of achieving diversity, it is important to go beyond the usual known channels and executive search agencies and headhunters will need to be given a brief detailing what is required of them and the breadth of search they are required to undertake. Where it is thought the replacement will come from the company's senior executive, such agency might be required to undertake a benchmarking exercise.

Whilst clearly the nominations committee and Board have responsibility for ensuring the new director will make a positive contribution to the company, the incoming director shares this responsibility and must make sufficient enquiry to be satisfied that he can make the required commitment before accepting the appointment.

Induction and training   1.80

It is well recognised that, to be successful, directors need more than just business knowledge. It is therefore recommended that at the time of a director's appointment, consideration be given to formal induction of the new director to ensure that the appointee makes an effective contribution to the Board at the earliest opportunity and fully understands what is required of him. This is particularly important given the increasing focus on Board performance and ongoing evaluation and training (see para **2.80**).

What is included in a director's induction will vary considerably from company to company and from director to director, depending on their previous experience, background and knowledge. For example if the appointment is the director's first directorship, he might need the induction to cover the requirements arising from holding such position generally in terms of the statutory statement of general duties and obligations (see **CHAPTER 4**) for the director and what matters the director needs to disclose to the Board, etc. It might be the director's first appointment to an FCA-regulated or listed company and his induction needs to focus on these requirements, including obligations arising from the FCA Handbook, UK Corporate Governance Code, Listing Rules and Disclosure and Transparency Rules, etc. In contrast, the newly appointed director might be fully aware and completely up to date with these duties, but still need to be advised of the company's own policies, procedures, internal control and risk management systems which would also be achieved through induction. Induction might include a tour of the company's operations, meetings with senior management and executives and meeting with major shareholders, particularly important for non-executives to broaden their understanding of the company's business and the environment and constraints within which it is operating. It might even include newly appointed non-executive directors 'partnering' with executives for a period of time and spending time with senior managers to get a more in-depth understanding of the company's key activities and challenges faced.

To assist Boards, the Institute of Chartered Secretaries and Administrators (ICSA) has produced a guidance note on 'Induction of Directors', contained in **APPENDIX 32**. The emphasis of the guidance note is to determine the level of the director's previous knowledge and adjust what information is included in the induction accordingly, with particular care not to overwhelm the newly appointed director with information and documents. Information can always be 'drip fed' to the director in a structured fashion, over an agreed period of time, allowing for questions and feedback.

Whilst the need for formal induction is self-evident in any company to ensure all Board members know what is required and expected of them, the UK Corporate Governance Code (relevant for companies with a premium listing of equity securities) specifically states that all directors should receive induction on joining the Board and that the chairman is responsible for ensuring this is arranged.

On an ongoing basis consideration should be given to how best to keep the Board up to date with changes affecting the company and the directors' duties and responsibilities to the company and wider stakeholder group. This might take the form of periodic information updates, targeted technical notes and bulletins, Board presentations and/or individual training sessions for directors on specific subjects. It is likely that the findings from the Board evaluation (see para **2.80**) will provide important input into identifying training needs for the Board and individual directors. Directors' own needs might be different, for example as a result of membership of different committees, or the Board as a whole might need updating due to a change in the company's circumstances.

As with induction, the UK Corporate Governance Code sets out requirements in relation to training and requires directors of companies with a premium listing of equity securities to regularly update their skills, knowledge and familiarity with the company's operations and market. Whilst the Code states that the chairman should regularly review and agree each director's training and development needs with them and make sure appropriate resources are made available, clearly directors have an individual responsibility to refresh their skills and knowledge so they are able to fulfil the role required of them.

2 Directors, the Board and the company secretary

2 Directors, the Board and the company secretary

The role of the Board and power to act   2.10

A company is a separate legal entity and clearly it is incapable of acting on its own and can operate only through its directors and officers. In practice the Articles of Association usually entrust the directors to manage the company and its business by providing them with full authority to exercise the company's powers to achieve this.

Regulation 70 of Table A provides that 'the business of the company shall be managed by the directors who may exercise all the powers of the company'. In Table A the extent of this authority is tempered by a further provision that the authority is subject to provisions of the Companies Acts, Memorandum and Articles and special resolutions of the members. Where this 'tempering' clause is not included, the directors have full power to manage the company subject to the company's constitution (*Automatic Self-Cleansing Filter Syndicate Co Ltd v Cunninghame* [1906] 2 Ch 34, CA).

Similarly, article 3 of the Model Articles states that 'subject to the articles, the directors are responsible for management of the company's business, for which purpose they may exercise all the powers of the company'. In addition article 4 permits shareholders to direct the directors, by special resolution, to take or refrain from taking specific action.

However, it is important to note that in general law the directors do not have the power to act individually on behalf of the company; they must act collectively as a unitary Board (*Re Haycraft Gold Reduction and Mining Co* [1900] 2 Ch 230). This means that decisions must be made by the Board as a whole, although it is usual for the Articles to permit the Board to:

- appoint one or more of its number to the office of managing director or any other executive office and delegate certain tasks and functions to such persons (reg 84 and article 5 of the Model Articles); and

- delegate any of its powers and duties to a committee consisting of one or more directors (reg 72 and article 5 of the Model Articles). Further guidance on the role of the directors as a unitary Board is contained in the supporting principles to provision A1 of the UK Corporate Governance Code, which state that the Board's role is to:

- provide entrepreneurial leadership to the company, whilst having in place prudent and effective controls to assess and manage risks;

- determine the company's strategy and ensure there are sufficient financial and human resources in place to achieve strategic goals and objectives;

- review management performance;

- set the company's values and standards and ensure all obligations to shareholders and others are understood and met.

Where the directors act within their delegated authority, the company is bound by the acts of the directors under the normal rules of agent and principal. If the director has not been given executive power by the Board or the Articles he has, in principle, no power or right to bind the company. However, even where the director exceeds his or the company's powers, in these situations the law usually allows third parties to enforce any such contracts entered into by the director on behalf of the company. Indeed CA 2006 s 40 provides that the powers of the directors to bind the company shall be deemed free from any limitations under the company's constitution and the validity of such contract will not be called into question. This protects third parties entering into transactions with the company in 'good faith' where the directors have exceeded their authority.

However, directors should be aware that this protection is only for third parties and does not prevent a member of the company bringing a restraining action in respect of an act carried out beyond their authority, unless that act is necessary to fulfil a legal obligation. For example, in *EIC Services v Phipps* (2003) All ER (D) 257 (Mar), Ch D, the court determined that a bonus issue of fully paid shares to shareholders who only owned partly paid shares without shareholders' approval was not void but irregular and a breach of the directors' authority. Such breaches of authority can be redressed by relying on s 40 (formerly CA 1985 s 35A), in this case rendering the allotments valid.

The directors can only be delegated powers of the company and they have a duty to check the company's Memorandum and Articles of Association to see whether there is any limit to the company's capacity that does not allow for or permit certain transactions. Such limitations are likely to be stated in the company's objects clause, if there is one, which whilst historically was embodied in the Memorandum may now be in the Articles. The validity of any act or contract which is outside the company's powers or capacity shall not be called into question on the grounds of lack of capacity in the company's Articles and it shall remain enforceable against the company (CA 2006 s 39(1)).

However, where the transaction or agreement concerned is with a director or a person connected with him, the company could choose to void the transaction, save where it is no longer possible to pay back money or pass assets back to the company; the company has been indemnified for any loss or damage arising from the transaction; others acquired 'bona fide' rights as a result of the transaction and would be adversely affected or the company has ratified the transaction after the event (CA 2006 s 41(4)).

Board effectiveness and decision-making   2.20

It is surely every director's desire to be part of an effective Board that makes well-informed and high quality decisions which move their company from strength to strength. However, the factors that make for an effective Board are many and complex, and have been the subject of much research and debate in recent years. In many ways Board effectiveness represents the coming together of all the strands and themes of corporate governance thinking.

In March 2011 the FRC issued Guidance on Board Effectiveness to encourage Boards to think more carefully about how they could improve their effectiveness, taking account not only of the structure of decision-making and reporting processes but also of the Board's behaviour, director's roles and the quality of support received. The FRC's Guidance makes no attempt to list the characteristics of an effective Board as clearly there is no 'one size fits all' approach and there are many inter-related, contributing and moving factors the importance and balance of which will vary from Board to Board.

However, the FRC's Guidance does state that an effective Board will develop and promote the company's vision and strategy, desired culture, values and behaviours and, in order to do this:

- provide direction for management;
- demonstrate ethical leadership and display and promote behaviour consistent with the company's culture and values;
- promote a performance culture and drive value creation, without excessive risk-taking;
- make well-informed, high-quality decisions with full understanding of the company's business;
- create a framework to enable the directors to fulfil their statutory and legal obligations;
- be accountable, particularly to capital providers; and
- give careful consideration to governance arrangements and evaluation of the Board's effectiveness.

As detailed in para **1.60**, it is clear that composition of the Board and the need for diversity to broaden perspectives, stimulate discussion and avoid a tendency towards 'groupthink' is a key factor contributing to Board effectiveness. Indeed, it has been suggested that perhaps there has been a tendency for some boards to become a little too comfortable, making directors reluctant to initiate challenging discussion and debate. Where this situation exists, the skills of the chairman will be called upon to encourage communication and debate between the directors, whilst keeping the Board cohesive (see para **2.30** below).

It is also important for members of the Board to fully understand what is expected from them in their respective roles, whether as chairman, an executive director, CEO, FD, independent non-executive or SINED as the requirements are all important and very different (paras **1.31**, **1.32**, **1.33** and **2.30**). It is therefore important this is made clear during directors' induction. For example an executive director will have detailed knowledge of how ideas and proposals being put to the Board can be implemented in practice, whereas an independent non-executive director might be able to draw on experience gained elsewhere and bring this into the discussion, the result of which might be to refine the decision reached.

Clearly the quality and timing of information, reports and proposals provided to the Board also has an important bearing on the Board's ability to make informed decisions. In public companies provision of this information will usually be facilitated by the company secretary, who will also provide support to the Board generally and assist the chairman with governance matters. This might, for example, include providing advice about director's conflicts of interest and the need to be excluded when certain decisions are made. The company secretary will also often support the Board by leading or facilitating directors' induction, training and board evaluation all of which are important to achieving an effective Board.

In addition, it is important that the actual process for making decisions is sound, appropriate for the company and well thought through. Indeed, the FRC's Guidance on Board Effectiveness states that good decision-making can be facilitated by:

- ensuring high-quality documentation is provided to the Board, so the Board can see the process that has been followed, who has been involved, the factors and alternatives considered, and how the suitable options have been analysed, evaluated and selected culminating in a recommendation to the Board;

- seeking expert opinions where necessary;

- allowing sufficient time and encouraging debate and challenge of proposals, particularly where they are significant for the company;

- ensuring timely closure; and

- making sure the actions required following the meeting, timescales and responsibilities are clear.

Boards would benefit from reviewing past decisions, their success and how they were reached to see whether any improvements are needed to the decision-making process. This is particularly relevant at the moment given the very tough economic environment, where there is little room for error in decisions made. This could be included in the Board evaluation process, or be carried out as a separate exercise. This might be done where, for example, there has been a large capital outlay to determine whether the project was a success, achieved its objectives and was, therefore, the best use of the company's resources.

Appointment and role of the chairman   2.30

Whilst there is no requirement at company law for a company to appoint a chairman, the directors are normally authorised by the company's Articles to appoint one of their number as chairman and it is usual practice for them to do so.

Details of the role, requirements and responsibilities of the chairman will largely be set out in the company's Articles and would normally include:

- responsibility for running and managing the Board, setting the agenda of meetings, ensuring timely, accurate and adequate information is provided on matters to be considered at the meeting, that there is sufficient time for adequate discussion and decision-making and that meetings are properly conducted;

- presiding as chairman of general meetings and ensuring that such meetings are properly convened and conducted from a procedural perspective, for example in relation to notice given, conduct of voting, rights of proxies, demands for a poll, etc;

- communicating effectively with shareholders, major investors and others; and

- ensuring executive directors are aware of their wider responsibilities and that appropriate induction and ongoing training are arranged for all directors. In addition to many of the points listed above, the UK Corporate Governance Code and the FRC's Guidance on Board Effectiveness make clear the key role the chairman has in creating and leading an effective Board. Whilst this guidance only directly applies to companies with a premium listing of equity securities, it contains principles of good corporate governance relevant to most companies.

It is well recognised that the chairman is fundamental to promoting and encouraging good boardroom behaviour and an open and accepted culture of challenge and debate amongst directors, essential requirements for an effective Board. Consequently greater emphasis is being put on the importance of the chairman in this respect. To help achieve this the FRC's Guidance on Board Effectiveness lists a wide range of matters which the chairman would usually be responsible for, namely:

- demonstrating ethical leadership;

- setting the Board agenda, primarily focused on strategy, performance, value creation and accountability, and ensuring that issues relevant to these areas are reserved for decision by the Board and are not delegated;

- ensuring a timely flow of high-quality information;

- making certain that the Board determines the nature, and extent, of the significant risks the company is prepared to take in implementing its strategy, and that directors are able to operate effective oversight of this;

- considering succession planning and composition of the Board on a regular basis;

- making certain that the Board has effective decision-making processes and sufficiently challenges and debates major proposals;

- ensuring the Board's committees are properly structured with appropriate terms of reference;

- encouraging all Board members to engage in and contribute to Board and committee meetings by drawing on their skills, experience, knowledge and, where appropriate, independence;

- promoting and fostering a relationship founded on mutual respect and open communication between the non-executive directors and the executive team;

- developing productive working relationships with all executive directors, the CEO in particular;

- providing support and advice;

- consulting the senior independent director on Board matters in accordance with the UK Corporate Governance Code;

- taking the lead on issues of director development, including through induction programmes for new directors and regular directors' performance reviews;

- acting on the results of Board evaluations; and

- ensuring effective communication with shareholders and other stakeholders and, in particular, that all directors are made aware of the views of those who provide the company's capital.

From the list set out above it is clear that the chairman has a key and pivotal role in achieving an effective Board and the behaviour he or she demonstrates is fundamental and underpins how the Board will operate and behave. This, in turn, will have a knock-on effect through the company.

The UK Corporate Governance Code also requires that the chairman satisfies the 'independence' criteria on appointment (see para **1.33**) and that he was not previously CEO of that same company, unless major shareholders have been consulted and the reasons for the appointment are fully explained in the annual report.

Matters reserved for the Board   2.40

As explained in para **2.70**, the company's Articles will usually permit the Board to delegate its powers. This is important because no matter how effective the Board, time will not usually allow the directors to have hands-on involvement with every aspect of a company's business. It may therefore be necessary to delegate responsibility for certain tasks to the executive managers or other suitably experienced and qualified persons within the company.

Having said this, there are certain matters which should in the interests of the company only be determined by the Board, either because this is a legal requirement or because the transaction or matter will or could have a significant impact on the company. An example of what these might comprise is set out below:

- strategy, business plans and budgets;
- major changes to corporate, management or capital structure;
- extension or change to business activities in terms of nature and area;
- approval of accounts and financial statements;
- proposed dividend payments;
- internal controls and risk management;
- significant or prolonged capital expenditure;
- formal shareholder communication;

- Board appointments and changes;

- composition of committees and terms of reference;

- remuneration policy and non-executive director's remuneration;

- delegation of authority and approval of Board policies;

- evaluation of Board, committees' and directors' performance.

To assist directors, the ICSA has produced a guidance note on 'Matters Reserved for the Board', an extract of which is reproduced in **APPENDIX 33**. However, the size of the company will have an important impact on this list and what matters are reserved for the Board and it is quite feasible that, for example, in a small company the directors will have hands-on day-to-day involvement with all aspects of a company's business and Board meetings can be held on short notice should there be any matter requiring Board approval, whereas in a large company this is not feasible and more decisions might be delegated, making the list of 'Matters Reserved for the Board' much shorter.

Board meetings   2.50

Apart from the need to keep minutes of all meetings of the Board, statutory provisions are silent on the requirement to hold meetings of the Board and how such meetings are conducted. Similarly, the Articles usually give the directors a large degree of freedom to call and conduct meetings as they consider necessary. For example, Table A and the Model Articles permit directors to regulate their affairs as they think fit and give them discretion to make further rules. In practice what tends to happen is that large private and public companies hold regular, scheduled and very formal Board meetings, which are necessary to consider the many facets of their operations. These will usually be planned a year or so in advance and be timed to coincide with known key reporting and approval dates. Small companies, on the other hand, might hold more unscheduled informal meetings, but formal meetings only very infrequently if at all. In smaller companies with one or two directors, it might well be the practice to conduct formal business by resolution in writing.

Obviously there may be unscheduled matters that require consideration and approval by the Board in a year which were not known about or anticipated when the timetable of meetings was drawn up. Where this is the case additional interim Board meetings can be called and, whilst all directors need to receive notice of the meeting, it is possible they might not all be able to attend. Where this is the case often their views and input will be sought in advance and be communicated by another director at the meeting.

A director has a general duty to attend Board meetings when he can, but he does not need to attend every meeting (*Re City Equitable Fire Insurance Co Ltd* [1925] Ch 407, CA). However, the Articles may contain a provision for removal as a director where a person fails to attend meetings for a specified number of consecutive months without permission of the Board (Table A reg 81). Clearly this is based on the premise that the director cannot be involved in and responsible for management of the company if he is never able to attend Board meetings and consequently cannot be involved in the joint deliberations of the Board.

Notice   **2.51**

The procedure for convening a Board meeting will usually be laid down in the Articles. Table A reg 88 and article 9 of the Model Articles provide that a director may, and the secretary at the request of a director shall, at any time summon a Board meeting by giving notice. Regulation 88 goes on to provide that it shall not be necessary to give notice of a Board meeting to any director for the time being absent from the UK. Where Board meetings are held at regular, predetermined intervals and at a fixed venue, then notice is not necessary.

Directors must observe any provisions in the Articles which specify the form and length of notice required for Board meetings. Article 9(2) of the Model Articles, for example, states that the notice must indicate the proposed time and date of the meeting, where it is to take place and, if the directors will not be in the same location, what arrangements have been made for those in different locations to communicate with each other.

If the Articles, like Table A, are silent on the matter, then 'reasonable' notice must be given to all directors. What is reasonable depends upon the circumstances giving rise to the need for a meeting and the normal practice of the company. In determining what is reasonable, it is fair to assume that directors of a large public company based at different locations would receive written notice well in advance of the meeting whereas directors of a small private company may, if they are all present, convene a meeting on the spot or with only a few minutes' notice (*Browne v La Trinidad* (1887) 37 Ch D 1, 57 LJ Ch 292, CA). Directors should be aware that where less notice than usual is given it may invalidate the meeting (*Re Homer District Consolidated Gold Mines, ex p Smith* (1888) 39 Ch D 546).

In practice notice of Board meetings takes the form of an 'agenda' listing the matters for consideration at the meeting. It will usually be accompanied by the various reports, proposals, papers and financial information to be considered at the meeting and be circulated sufficient time in advance to allow detailed review by the directors. The practical benefit of this is that the directors come to the meeting informed, prepared and ready to participate in discussion and debate, which is effective use of what is usually limited time available.

Attendance and quorum   **2.52**

Directors should be aware that all directors are entitled to attend and, in principle, vote at Board meetings in the absence of contrary provisions in the Articles. A director cannot lawfully be excluded from a Board meeting (*Pulbrook v Richmond Consolidated Mining Co* (1878) 9 Ch D 610).

The directors will need to check the quorum requirements in the Articles and, where they are silent, a majority of directors will constitute a quorum unless the Board's normal practice is a different number (*York Tramways Co v Willows* (1882) 8 QBD 685, CA). Where the Articles adopt provisions of Table A, reg 89 states that the quorum may be fixed by the directors at any number, including one, and unless so fixed shall be two. Since a private company may have only one director, then a sole director can constitute a quorum. Article 11 of the Model Articles, in contrast, states that the quorum must never be less than two directors but it could be more.

Directors must be aware that they cannot hold a valid meeting in the absence of an effective quorum and before proceeding to consider the business of the meeting they must check whether any of those present are prevented from being counted in the quorum and voting, for example on matters in which they have a conflict of interest (regs 94 and 95, article 14 of the Model Articles and see para **6.63**). In *Colin Gwyer v London Wharf* [2003] 2 BCLC 153 it was held that, although two directors were present at the meeting, one director had interests that precluded him from voting and being counted in the quorum and the meeting was therefore inquorate.

In the event that the meeting becomes inquorate when it addresses a certain item of business, to resolve the deadlock the directors may need to either appoint additional directors or call a general meeting, by ordinary resolution, to amend or remove the prohibition in the Articles on voting (reg 96 and article 11(3) of the Model Articles).

Directors of companies with a premium listing of equity shares should note that the UK Corporate Governance Code requires a statement to be made in the annual report and accounts not only of how many Board and committee meetings have been held, but also of the individual attendance by directors. A director who has failed to attend almost all Board and committee meetings might, unless there is a full explanation of justified, extenuating circumstances, find a lack of appetite amongst shareholders to vote in favour of his re-election.

Conduct and voting   **2.53**

As mentioned above, statutory provisions are silent on how Board meetings are conducted as are, most often, the company's own Articles. However, it is well recognised that appropriate boardroom behaviour is fundamental to achieving high standards of corporate governance and this point was specifically raised in the Walker Review (see para **10.13**). In response the ICSA conducted research on appropriate boardroom behaviours and has drawn up a guidance note (090928) on Board meeting etiquette (available at www.icsa.org.uk). The guidance note specifies types of behaviour appropriate at Board and committee meetings including, for example, the need for directors to dedicate their attention to the meeting and matters discussed and to switch off phones and other wireless devices that might otherwise distract them.

The directors will normally be authorised by the Articles to elect one of their number as chairman of their meetings and to appoint a substitute chairman in his absence (reg 91 and article 13 of the Model Articles). The chairman has responsibility to ensure the proper conduct of the meeting and to preserve order whilst at the same time ensuring that all sides of an argument are considered.

Questions arising at a Board meeting will normally be decided by a simple majority and each director usually has one vote. Where there are equal votes for and against a particular course of action the chairman may have a casting vote, although this right does not arise under common law and must be stated in the company's Articles (reg 88 and article 13 of the Model Articles). Depending on the circumstances and matters under consideration, caution needs to be exercised by the chairman in deciding whether to exercise the casting vote.

Directors must also be aware that it is open for the Articles to specify different voting rights or procedures and they need to be fully conversant with the relevant provisions to ensure that business is properly conducted at their Board meetings.

Individually a director has a duty not to allow any conflict between his own personal interests and those of the company and accordingly he must disclose the nature of any interest in a contract or proposed contract with the company and, if required, abstain from voting on the matter (CA 2006 s 177; see para **6.61**). It is important that the director's disclosure is recorded in the minutes of the meeting.

Directors should also be aware that the Articles may provide that a resolution signed by all the directors has the same validity as if passed at a meeting of the directors (reg 93). Where the company has a single director, the written resolution procedure is recommended as a means of recording formal resolutions.

Minutes   **2.54**

CA 2006 s 248, reinforced by Table A reg 100, requires minutes to be kept of all Board meetings, which includes meetings held by telephone or via other electronic media, and meetings of the company's managers. It is usual for this duty to be delegated by the directors to the company secretary. In addition, article 15 of the Model Articles goes a little further and states that such written record of any unanimous or majority decision must be kept for at least ten years from the date of the decision.

Directors must ensure that all decisions taken at the meeting are recorded in the minutes, with a short narrative to establish how a decision was reached and the key factors considered where necessary. Readers should refer to para **4.20.2** which sets out the directors' duty to promote the success of the company and to have regard to six key factors when making decisions and the effect this may have on what is recorded in the minutes of the meeting.

In practice the minutes are often recorded, prepared and circulated by the company secretary to the directors in draft for consideration and are then presented at the next Board meeting for signature by the chairman as a correct record of what was decided.

Directors should be aware that whilst the minutes are evidence of proceedings, should they be incomplete or inaccurate they are not conclusive, and where decisions were made at the meeting but not recorded in the minutes they may be proved by alternative means (*Re Fireproof Doors Ltd* [1916] 2 Ch 142). Furthermore, the production of standard form minutes is not sufficient to demonstrate directors have fulfilled their duties to supervise a company where there is no evidence of any reporting or supervisory functions and oversight having been carried out (see the *Weavering* case in para **1.32**).

Finally, directors should be aware that, if requested, they must make the Board minutes available to the auditors for inspection (CA 2006 s 499).

Meetings by telephone   **2.55**

There is no specific statutory provision, but many companies have amended their Articles to allow directors to hold meetings by telephone or via similar electronic media, such as video conferencing, which removes the need for them to be together in one place at a given time. The Articles may contain provisions permitting the directors to hold meetings by conference telephone connections or allowing the chairman to determine the directors' views in a series of telephone conversations, by telex, email or by facsimile.

Whilst many companies' Articles permit directors to hold meetings by telephone, they require directors to be deemed present to be able to speak and be heard by the other directors at the 'meeting'. Consequently, unless the Articles specifically provide, a series of telephone calls on a one-to-one basis stretches the common law meaning of a 'meeting' too far and is unlikely to be permitted. The same might also be said of 'instant messaging'.

However, article 10 of the Model Articles states that how the directors communicate with each other is irrelevant provided they can communicate information and their opinions on a particular matter to the other directors.

Committees of directors   2.60

The company's Articles will usually empower the directors to delegate their powers to committees consisting of one or more directors and to impose regulations and rules by which the committees must operate (articles 5 and 6 of the Model Articles). The directors have no powers of delegation unless specifically provided in the Articles which will determine, amongst other things, how and to what extent the directors' powers can be delegated.

Regulation 72 deals with such delegation and the conduct of meetings of committees of the directors. There is no objection in law to a committee of one person only (*Re Fireproof Doors Ltd, Umney v Fireproof Doors Ltd* [1916] 2 Ch 142, 85 LJ Ch 444). If reg 72 applies that person must be a director and where there are other members of the committee who are not directors, they would not have a right to vote unless the Articles otherwise provide.

It is important for directors to note that where power of delegation to committees is contained in the Articles, third parties shall not be prejudiced by a countermanding of acts properly carried out by the committee and they will be presumed to have been validly exercised in favour of a third party (*Totterdell v Fareham Blue Brick and Tile Co Ltd* (1866) LR 1 CP 674, 35 LJCP 278).

Furthermore the directors must ensure that the Board resolution establishing a committee is carefully drafted so that the committee's status and functions are clearly defined. Terms of reference setting out the committee's structure, membership, constitution, role and requirements for meetings and other matters would usually be determined and approved by the Board to ensure the extent of delegation, functions and required composition of the committee are clear. Such terms of reference would usually include:

- details of and requirements for membership;
- determination of how meetings are to be conducted in relation to the quorum, frequency, giving of notice and recording of minutes;

- duties of the committee; and

- the authority of the committee.

Any limitation of the powers delegated by the Board, ie where the committee is to 'make recommendations to the Board' rather than making and implementing decisions itself, needs to be stated in the terms of reference.

Committees frequently found in companies' management structures include remuneration, audit, risk, nomination, share allotment, reserving and standing committees and also ad hoc committees set up to consider specific issues such as safety, fund-raising, marketing, environmental issues, acquisitions or disposals, etc (see **CHAPTER 10** for corporate governance recommendations and membership requirements).

Whilst members of more routine standing committees tend to be appointed in person, it is not uncommon for committees comprising, for example, 'any two directors' to be formed with power delegated by the Board to finalise terms and complete a specific transaction. This might include, for example, final approval of annual or interim accounts or of an agreement all of which had been seen by the Board and approved in near final form. Being able to form a committee in this way is particularly useful where, due to constraints of time and logistics, it is not possible to hold a further full meeting of the Board.

As is the case with Board meetings, minutes must be kept of all meetings of the committee and, unless the Articles or the Board in the terms of reference state otherwise, the committee may appoint and remove one of their number as chairman. Furthermore, unless specified otherwise in the Articles, the committee should apply the same rules as regards the length and manner in which notice is given as applied by the Board.

However, it is important to note that whilst the directors may be entitled to delegate specific tasks and functions to a committee in the manner described above, overall responsibility cannot be delegated. Indeed, in *Re Barings plc, Secretary of State for Trade and Industry v Baker (No 5)* [1999] 1 BCLC 433 at 486, the judge concluded that whilst directors may be entitled to delegate particular functions to those below them, delegation does not absolve the directors from responsibility. It is therefore essential for the directors to ensure that the delegated functions are being carried out properly by:

- delegating to appropriate persons;

- checking, supervising and controlling the delegated functions;

- ensuring any systems implemented are appropriate and working correctly.

Any delegation of powers by the directors to a committee can be revoked by the Board at any time for whatever reason by assuming the powers previously delegated and recording the decision in the minutes.

The Board and the company secretary   2.70

As mentioned at the beginning of **CHAPTER 6**, the directors may, and in most cases do, delegate many tasks of a technical, administration and legal compliance nature to the company secretary. In many companies the company secretary plays a very central role. As well as dealing with many of the routine aspects of the directors' duties (such as maintenance of the statutory books, submission of documents to Companies House, preparation and retention of minutes of meetings, etc), the secretary is an essential part of the company's management and is frequently the directors' first port of call for advice, whether of a technical, legal, compliance, management or administrative nature.

Indeed, the importance of the company secretary is endorsed in the UK Corporate Governance Code which, in provision B.5.2, requires that:

- all directors should have access to the advice and services of the company secretary, who is responsible to the Board for ensuring that Board procedures are followed and that applicable rules and regulations are complied with;

- under direction of the chairman, the company secretary is responsible for ensuring good information flows within the Board and its committees and between senior management and non-executive directors;

- the company secretary facilitates the induction of new directors and assists with the professional development of existing directors; and

- the company secretary is responsible for advising the Board, through the chairman, on corporate governance matters.

In addition the FRC's Guidance on Board Effectiveness goes a little further and states that the company secretary should ensure high-quality information is presented to the Board and its committees, be involved in giving or arranging directors' induction and training and for advising and periodically reviewing Board governance matters.

The role of the company secretary varies tremendously from company to company but in all cases the company secretary is there to support and assist the directors. It would be fair to say that the company secretary is ideally placed to observe and protect the interests of the company as a whole by:

- advising the directors and reminding them of the requirement for them to act, and be able to demonstrate that they have acted, in the interests of the company;

- reminding the Board of their obligations towards shareholders, employees, creditors and other stakeholders and the implications of any decisions made;

- ensuring high standards of Board governance and adherence to best practice recommendations;

- ensuring proper compliance with requirements of all statutory, Stock Exchange and other regulatory bodies (where applicable);

- interpreting the implications of all decisions of the Board;

- ensuring decisions of the Board are recorded and implemented;

- informing directors of their obligations for disclosure.

Directors should, however, be aware that where any of their duties are delegated to the company secretary, liability for fulfilling those duties remains with the directors. With this in mind, whilst directors do in practice delegate many facets of their role to the company secretary, who understandably has a more thorough and detailed knowledge of legislation in certain areas, they must periodically check that the company secretary is carrying out his tasks satisfactorily and that all legal requirements are being met.

Board evaluation   2.80

Given the role of the Board in leading, directing and controlling the company for which it is responsible and that the extent to which it is successful in doing this can vary tremendously, it is important for the Board to consider and evaluate the effectiveness of its own performance. Undoubtedly the majority of directors recognise that shareholders have the power to remove some or all of the directors of their company from office or not to reappoint them when they retire by rotation (where applicable). Such decision is frequently judged according to the performance of the company, by whatever means it is measured.

The need for evaluation of a Board's performance was initially addressed in the Higgs Review and the need for formal Board evaluation is now a main principle of the UK Corporate Governance Code. The Code requires:

- the Board to undertake a formal and rigorous annual evaluation of its own performance and that of individual directors and committees of the Board (B.6 of the Code);

- evaluation of Board performance for a FTSE 350 company to be carried out externally at least once every three years (B.7 of the Code);

- individual evaluation of each director, which should identify whether he contributes effectively to the Board and the extent of his commitment. The Code also goes further and requires the chairman to act on the results of performance evaluation;

- that the chairman's performance be evaluated by the non-executive directors; and

- that the annual report should contain a statement from the Board on how performance evaluation has been conducted.

The directors of listed companies need to comply with the requirements of the UK Corporate Governance Code and, consequently, a review of the process, method and reporting requirements for evaluating Board performance will be required.

Even where a company is under no obligation to comply with the UK Corporate Governance Code, the benefits of conducting an evaluation of Board performance as a means of determining whether individual directors and the Board are doing what is required of them effectively and, insofar as they are not, to identify areas where improvement is needed, is self-evident. Indeed most executives who have reached Board level will have pursued careers during which their individual and group performance are regularly and actively evaluated and assessed and, where necessary, performance training and development programmes put in place to help them improve and move to the next level – the Board. It is therefore extremely important to continue the evaluation and development process for the Board and its members given the importance of decisions made by the Board and the disastrous effect a poorly performing Board or series of bad decisions can have on the success and future of a company.

In terms of what form the Board evaluation process should take and what matters should be covered, there is no prescribed system to be followed and it is very much for the chairman, directors and Board of the company to determine what is needed. Certainly from a corporate governance perspective there is now much greater emphasis on the actual behaviour demonstrated by directors and their Boards and on the distinction between the roles of the chairman, CEO, executives, non-executives and SINED, etc and therefore this behaviour will need to be assessed to know where improvements and help are needed. It might be, for example, that some Board members do not fully understand their roles and responsibilities and what is expected and required of them and further training for individual directors in these areas is needed.

41

The FRC's Guidance on Board Effectiveness, whilst not intending to be exhaustive or prescriptive, lists some areas that a Board evaluation might cover, including:

- Board composition and whether the mix of skills, experience, knowledge, and diversity amongst Board members is sufficient given current and future issues and challenges for the company;

- whether the purpose, direction and values of the company are clear and have been effectively communicated and whether the leadership is appropriate to ensure they are achieved;

- succession, training and development plans and means of implementation;

- operation of the Board;

- roles of the individual members of the Board, their effectiveness, how they work together and communicate;

- effectiveness of the executive and non-executive directors;

- quality, timing and sufficiency of Board papers, reports and presentations;

- Board behaviour and quality of consideration, discussion and debate of proposals before decisions are reached;

- effectiveness of Board committees and how they report and interact with the Board;

- quality of support provided to the Board and directors by the company secretarial team;

- determination of authority for decision-making and how clearly these requirements and the process have been communicated;

- effectiveness of the risk management and control process; and

- shareholder and stakeholder communication.

This is very much a list of some areas the Board evaluation might cover and a company's Board has complete discretion to add to or remove from the list as it considers appropriate.

It should also be noted that there is increasing recognition of the importance of relationships between directors, the mix of character types and behavioural dynamics on Board performance and a thorough evaluation will review these as well as the areas listed above.

However, caution needs to be exercised to ensure that 'boiler-plate' evaluation and reporting do not become the norm as this is not in the spirit of the UK Corporate Governance Code and is unlikely to identify issues relevant to an individual Board which, once addressed, will help enhance performance.

There are many different approaches to Board evaluation and they may be conducted in a number of different ways: internally, externally, by questionnaire, interviews with directors individually, or any combination of these approaches. Whatever the approach, the one thing that is clear is that unless a formal assessment is carried out it is very easy for problems to go unrecognised or not acknowledged for a considerable time, which is of no benefit to the directors, the Board or indeed the company. At best it might mean under-performance and at worst a corporate disaster, far too many of which have been seen in recent years.

For example, Board evaluation might identify that the quality of papers presented to the Board is poor, they lack detail and are received only a few hours before Board meetings. By identifying the problem and giving opportunity and incentive to improve the Board are less likely to reach an ill-informed or hasty decision they might later regret. Similarly, the Board evaluation might identify a fundamental lack of consideration of key risks and controls for the business and prevent the company sauntering towards a disaster the Board had no idea was on the horizon.

As mentioned above, FTSE 350 companies are now required by the UK Corporate Governance Code to carry out an externally facilitated Board evaluation at least once every three years. This obviously gives opportunity for a fresh, objective and independent evaluation by a third party which can bring benefits, not only in terms of external validation but also from an unaffected outsider reviewing performance from a different perspective. Whilst there was some concern initially, most now recognise the benefit of having a confidential external Board evaluation which often, because of the independence of the assessors, reveals more than obtained by one conducted internally.

Disagreements amongst directors   2.90

Where a director considers that a course of action decided by the Board is potentially damaging or improper, he should make sure his objection is brought to the attention of the Board and discussed. If that does not resolve the matter then further discussion with the chairman or senior independent director might be appropriate. If it is still unresolved, depending on the nature of the matter, the director may have a duty to act in the interests of the company and the members as a whole and take one or more of the following steps:

- make a formal objection to the Board with the aim of reversing the decision;

- resign, although this is unlikely to be considered an adequate discharge of his duties where the company is insolvent;

- appeal to the members and remain in place to attempt to bring about an improvement;

- where he is also a member, apply to the court for an order where the company's affairs have been conducted in a manner unfairly prejudicial to any of the members (see para **8.30**);

- apply to the Secretary of State for an investigation into the affairs of the company (see para **6.130**).

The dissenting director must select the appropriate course of action based upon the nature and scale of his dissatisfaction with the affairs of the company.

3 Directors' rights

3 Directors' rights

The rights of directors are mainly derived from provisions in the company's Articles of Association, as the Companies Acts provide little guidance as to which actions are within the directors' powers and, on the whole, place more emphasis on imposing restrictions on the rights and powers of directors rather than defining what they are.

Where the company has adopted Table A reg 70 or articles 3 and 4 of the Model Articles, they provide that the business of the company shall be managed by the directors who may exercise all the powers of the company, with the proviso that this authority is subject to the provisions of the Act, the Memorandum and the Articles and to any direction given by special resolution. This is important as, whilst the directors have authority and a right to manage the company generally, such rights may be tempered or altered by statutory provisions and decisions of the shareholders. At the same time, they have a common law duty not to abuse their position.

An extensive range of rights may be given to the directors by provisions in the Articles, which should be considered closely by a director following his appointment. The huge variety of permutations could not possibly be considered within the scope of this book and this chapter concentrates mainly on the provisions of Table A and the Model Articles, adopted by a vast number of companies. The company's own Articles may adopt, exclude or vary such rights and should be referred to individually to determine the actual provisions relating specifically to that company.

Back in 2003, the Higgs Report, and more recently the FRC in its 'Guidance on Board Effectiveness', recommended that a prospective director should carry out due diligence on a company and ensure they are committed and able to fulfil the role before accepting appointment as a non-executive director. This is important as a director's reputation can be irreparably damaged when tarnished by association with a large-scale corporate collapse or corporate wrongdoing. A prospective director should therefore carry out examination of the company's records and processes to satisfy himself that the company's affairs have been conducted properly and also to ensure he feels they will fit in well, be able to meet the time commitment needed and provide valuable contribution to the Board.

With this in mind the ICSA has provided a guidance note (030723) on 'Due Diligence for Directors'. This contains example questions to be asked about the company's business, governance arrangements and investor relations matters, suitability for the role and structure of the Board, and risk management and internal controls.

Whilst the ICSA's guidance note is aimed at non–executive directors, prospective executive directors should also go through a similar due diligence exercise. Often there is too little emphasis on the responsibilities being assumed when appointed as a director and the focus remains on the executive director's management role. Perhaps if more was appreciated about the wider role of a director at this stage, there would be more scrutiny of the Board and governance arrangements before accepting appointment.

It should also be noted that, unless stated, directors' rights detailed in the following paragraphs are rights conferred on the Board of Directors as a whole and directors must exercise those rights and powers collectively (not individually) through the authority and joint deliberations of the Board (*Re Haycraft Gold Reduction and Mining Co* [1900] 2 Ch 230). This is discussed in more detail in para **2.10**.

Appointment and resignation of officers   3.10

To avoid the need to hold a general meeting, it is usual for the Articles to provide directors with the right to appoint directors to fill vacancies arising during the year and to appoint additional persons as directors up to any maximum number fixed by the Articles (reg 79). Such appointments will be subject to approval of the members at the next annual general meeting (AGM), discussed in para **6.11.5**.

At the same time, and notwithstanding restrictions in any contract of service which is likely to exist, each director individually has the right to resign by tendering his resignation to the company. There may be any number of reasons for resignation but, as the judge commented in *Re a Company (No 004803 of 1996)* (1996) Times, 2 December, Ch D, where there has been a parting of the ways and the director's fellow directors clearly take no account of his opinion, resignation would be considered appropriate and advisable. Similarly, a director who is unable to carry out his role and duties should resign. The Articles will usually require the director to give reasonable notice of his resignation, but in the absence of any such provision a director can resign without the need for notice (*OBC Caspian Ltd v Thorp* 1998 SLT 653, OH).

Should the shareholders seek, for whatever reason, to remove a director before the expiration of his period of office, he has the right to receive notice of the intended resolution to remove him, to make written representations to the shareholders and to attend and speak on the matter at the shareholders' meeting (see para **8.23.2.3**). This right may be exercised where, for example, the director considers a full account of the events giving rise to the resolution have not been disseminated to shareholders or where he feels removal will not promote the success of the company.

As well as their own resignations and appointments, the Articles usually provide directors with the right to:

- appoint and remove the company secretary (reg 99 and now embodied in CA 2006);

- individually, appoint another director as their alternate (or any other person approved by resolution of the directors) to attend and vote at meetings of the Board on that particular director's behalf and to revoke the appointment by notice in writing to the Board (reg 65);

- appoint or remove the chairman of Board meetings (reg 91 and article 12 of the Model Articles);

- appoint one of their number as managing director and other directors to executive positions and delegate specific functions to such directors (reg 84 and article 5 of the Model Articles). Where a director has been appointed managing director, he shall be entitled to exercise the powers of the Board;

- appoint an agent to act on behalf of the company (reg 71 and article 5 of the Model Articles);

- delegate some of their executive functions to committees set up for whatever purpose the Board considers fit (reg 72 and article 5 of the Model Articles). This right is frequently exercised where it is not feasible, necessary or indeed appropriate for the full Board to meet and consider certain matters. Indeed, recommendations based upon good 'corporate governance' encourage implementation of remuneration, nomination and audit committees (see **CHAPTER 10**). There may be other matters specific to the company which the directors decide to delegate to a committee, such as allotments of shares, litigation matters or employee communication and relations issues, etc (see para **2.60**);

- authorise use of the company seal (where there is one).

The Articles might also permit the rest of the Board, usually by unanimous consent, to remove a director from office where, for example, he has not attended Board meetings for a specified number of months.

Meetings of directors

3.20

Clearly directors are entitled to receive notice of directors' meetings unless they waive their right to receive notice not more than seven days after the meeting was held (article 9(3) of the Model Articles). The Articles may provide that a director's right to receive notice is suspended where the director is absent from the UK, although with today's technology and use of electronic mail to provide an instant means of communication, such an exclusion may be difficult to justify in future. Indeed, whilst it is included in reg 88, no such provision is contained in the Model Articles adopted by companies since 1 October 2009, reflecting a change in perception of acceptable practice.

It is usual for the Articles to allow the directors to decide the manner in which their meetings are conducted and to permit any director (or the secretary at the request of a director) to call a meeting (reg 88 and article 9 of the Model Articles). Where the Articles, like Table A, provide this general authority but are silent on specifics such as the frequency of meetings, quorum requirement, period of notice, etc, these can be determined by the Board. Where the length of notice is not fixed by the Articles, the general law that it must be reasonable having regard to all circumstances must be observed.

In practice, small companies, depending on the scale of operations, tend not to set out in detail the business to be conducted at Board meetings, whereas large companies are on the whole more formal and the secretary will prepare and distribute agendas setting out the business for consideration at the meeting. In the latter case the agenda may be accompanied by Board papers and supporting documents which need to be considered prior to the meeting.

The Articles will usually provide that the chairman will preside over meetings of the directors and all directors have a right to vote at the meeting unless they are interested in any item of business under consideration. Although not in Table A, the Articles may state that, having disclosed his interest to the meeting, such director may vote on the matter under consideration. Having said this, the particular circumstances will need to be considered as in many instances voting would not be appropriate or best practice.

Resolutions are usually passed by simple majority and, unless restricted by the Articles or a shareholders' agreement, directors will usually have the right to one vote each. The chairman might also have the right to exercise a 'casting vote' where there is an equality of votes by the directors on any matter stated in the Articles (article 13 of the Model Articles).

In addition, provided the company's Articles contain the necessary provisions, the directors have the right to delegate powers to committees and a director who is a member of such committee will have rights in relation to that committee, for example to receive notice and attend meetings of the committee (para **2.60**). However, a director who is a member of a committee must be aware that he can only act within the constraints of the authority delegated by the Board, usually specified in 'terms of reference' for the committee approved at a Board meeting.

Calls on partly paid shares   3.30

Subject to the terms of allotment, Table A reg 12 provides directors with the right to make, cancel or postpone a call on members for unpaid amounts on partly paid shares held by them. Understandably the directors cannot exercise this right where the terms of the allotment provide for payment on pre-determined dates, but where a call has been made and is not paid within the required period, they are entitled to charge interest on the amount of the call outstanding (reg 15).

In the event that a shareholder fails to pay the amount required by the call, the directors have the right to impose a 'lien' on the shares for the amount outstanding and ultimately to sell the shares (regs 9 and 10). Similarly, reg 19 permits the directors to forfeit such shares where a call is not paid and either sell, re-allot or otherwise dispose of the shares as they consider fit.

No such provisions are contained in the Model Articles.

Transfer of shares   3.40

Regulation 24 permits the directors to refuse to transfer shares to persons of whom they 'do not approve' where the shares are not fully paid, and they may also refuse to register a transfer of a share or shares subject to a lien. Article 25(5) of the Model Articles permits the directors to refuse to register a transfer, provided they return the transfer and issue a notice of refusal to the transferee.

Further rights to refuse to transfer shares may be contained in the company's Articles. Where the directors exercise this right for the benefit of the company, the court is unlikely to intervene (*Village Cay Marina Ltd v Acland* [1998] BCC 417). In practice, the Articles of private companies provide detailed pre-emption provisions requiring a member who wishes to sell his shares to offer them first to other members of the company, thereby avoiding this problem.

It should be noted that where the directors refuse to register a transfer of shares, as permitted by the company's Articles, they must notify the transferee of the refusal as soon as possible, but in any event within two months of the transfer being lodged (CA 2006 s 771). Failure to do so may cause the court to decide that the directors' power of refusal has been lost and order that the transfer be registered (*Re Inverdeck Ltd* [1998] BCC 256).

It is also important to note that the directors' right to refuse a transfer request should only be exercised for the proper purpose it was intended and not in a manipulative manner.

Allotment of shares   3.50

The mechanics for allotting shares are discussed in **CHAPTER 8**, and suffice here to say that, provided the directors are authorised by provisions in the company's Articles or by ordinary resolution of the members, they have the right to allot shares.

The directors' right to allot shares may be tempered by certain conditions in the Articles or the resolution, for example, they may state that shares may only be allotted pursuant to a rights issue or up to a specified maximum number. Certainly for public companies in the past, such authority has remained valid for a period of 18 months or only until the next AGM at which it would ordinarily be renewed (see para **8.11.1**).

Meetings of shareholders   3.60

It is usual for the Articles to provide the directors with the right to convene general meetings of the members, whether such meeting be an AGM of a public company to consider ordinary and special business of the company or a general meeting to consider special items of business, as discussed in para **8.21.1**. In addition, the Articles may provide the directors with the following rights in respect of general meetings:

- to receive notice of general meetings (reg 38);

- to attend and speak at general meetings and, where relevant, class meetings even where the director is not himself a member (reg 44 and article 40 of the Model Articles);

- it is usual for the chairman of the Board to have the right to chair general meetings and, if he is not present, for any other director nominated by the directors to do so or, if there is only one director present at the meeting, for him to have the right to chair the meeting (reg 42 and article 39 of the Model Articles). During the meeting the chairman will take the members through the business under consideration by proposing resolutions, regulating the voting, declaring resolutions carried and closing or adjourning the meeting; and

- two directors may demand a poll (article 44 of the Model Articles).

Rights in relation to contracts 3.70

In pursuance of the authority provided by the Articles to manage the company, the directors have the right to act as agents and enter into contracts and arrangements with third parties on behalf of the company, and CA 2006 s 44(3) states that directors are authorised signatories of the company. The Board may delegate this right to enter into contracts to one or more directors, either generally or for specific contracts or transactions up to a specified monetary limit and this is quite common in practice.

Before directors exercise this right, they should check provisions in the Memorandum and Articles of Association to ensure that they are acting within the company's objects and within their own powers. For example, a director must only enter into an agreement for the company to borrow money or accept a bank overdraft facility where the company's objects authorise such transaction and any limitation on borrowing set out in the Articles is not exceeded. A director must also ensure, to avoid any personal liability, that any third party involved is aware that the director is acting as an agent for the company.

In addition, where the transaction involves the director or is one in which the director has an 'interest', he must ensure that he observes his duties of disclosure required by CA 2006 ss 177 and 182 (see paras **6.60** and **6.80**). The Articles may provide that, having made full disclosure, the director is entitled to be interested in such contract without having to account to the company for any benefits received.

Payment of dividends 3.80

CA 2006 does not specify who shall declare a dividend and there is no requirement for a dividend to be approved by shareholders in a general meeting. This being the case, provided there is nothing to the contrary in the company's Articles, the directors could declare an interim or final dividend under their general powers.

However, this practice is not commonplace and a company's Articles would usually contain provisions determining how dividends are to be declared, making a distinction between requirements for interim and final dividends. Articles usually provide that:

(a)   a final dividend can only be declared by the members of the company at the end of or after the accounting year to which it relates (reg 102 and article 30(1) of the Model Articles). The amount of the final dividend is recommended to the shareholders by the directors and, whilst only the members can approve payment, it is usual for the Articles to provide that they cannot increase the dividend to an amount which exceeds that recommended to them by the directors; and

(b)   for shareholders to receive a return on their investment on a more timely basis and more than once a year, the directors can declare payment of interim dividends during the year (reg 103 and article 30(1) of the Model Articles).

Where the Articles require members to approve payment of a final dividend and the company is a private company which is no longer required to hold an AGM, a general meeting would need to be held to obtain the required approval. Alternatively, the dividend could be declared an interim dividend.

The directors' right to declare interim dividends and recommend a final dividend can only be exercised where the company has sufficient distributable profits as required by CA 2006 Part V (see para **7.24**). Another important point to note is that the directors have a converse right not to declare a dividend where, for example, they determine excess profits need to be retained by the company to fund future growth and expansion plans without need to revert to borrowing.

Contract of service and remuneration – executive directors   3.90

Table A regs 82 and 83 provide that directors have the right to receive remuneration at a rate agreed by ordinary resolution of the members and to be reimbursed for all travelling, hotel and other expenses properly incurred in attending meetings.

The wording of article 19(1) of the Model Articles is slightly different and states that the directors are entitled to such remuneration as decided by the directors for their services as directors and any other services they undertake. Article 19(2) specifies that the remuneration can be in any form and include payment of a pension, allowance or gratuity, or any death, sickness or disability benefit.

In *Hutton v West Cork Rly Co* (1883) 23 Ch D 654, CA it was established that directors are not entitled to payment unless express provision is made in the Articles. Today it would be extremely rare for a trading company's Articles to be silent on directors' remuneration. Similarly, where remuneration must be agreed by members in general meeting, it is important that approval is obtained properly as, if it is found the resolution was not valid, the directors may be required to refund any money received. This was the decision in *Re J Franklin & Son Ltd* [1937] 4 All ER 43.

The Articles may specify an upper limit on total remuneration paid to all directors which, if in force, must be observed and not exceeded. Alternatively, a resolution could be put to the shareholders to amend the Articles by increasing the limit if considered beneficial and appropriate.

Furthermore, where a director has been appointed to an executive position, it is usual that he will be provided with a service contract setting out his individual rights relating to employment as an executive. Such contract would include normal employment rights relating to salary, holidays, sickness, entitlement to notice on termination and discipline and grievance procedures as well as those specific to his office. For example, a director's remuneration may include more than basic salary and additional entitlements, such as share options, payment of fees, pension contributions and participation in any profit-sharing scheme, must, for the avoidance of doubt, all be specified in the contract. **APPENDIX 1** sets out key provisions to be considered when drafting and entering into the service contract.

All this said, a surprising number of directors do not have a service contract, which makes determination of the director's rights in a dispute difficult. As well as simplifying dispute resolution, another important reason for a director to have a service agreement is to ensure that the company provides professional indemnity insurance on his behalf to pay any legal costs or awards of damages arising as a result of the director's negligence, breach of duty or trust as, without insurance, the director cannot be indemnified and may be exposed to personal liability. The reader is also referred to para **6.100**, where the other side of the contract, relating to directors' duties, is discussed.

It should be noted that a service contract that cannot be terminated by the company before two years, or can only be terminated in certain circumstances, may not be granted unless the contract is approved by ordinary resolution of the members (CA 2006 s 188). Where such approval has not been obtained, the term in the contract regarding termination shall be construed as meaning that the company may terminate the contract at any time on 'reasonable' notice.

HMRC has made it clear that directors working pursuant to a contract of employment on a daily basis in their own companies are to be regarded as employees and must receive the minimum wage. Whilst it is unlikely that a director would receive wages less than the statutory minimum, if he does for any reason (ie in the early stages of a new venture, where the company is struggling and in financial difficulties, or where the practice has been to pay a low wage and receive the remainder by way of dividend, etc) tax must still be paid as if the minimum wage had been paid for the hours worked.

As mentioned above, an executive director employed by the company benefits from being able to enjoy employments rights, including the right not to be unfairly dismissed. However, in most instances, the executive director's service contract will be carefully worded to ensure that employment would be deemed to automatically terminate when he ceases to be a director (*Cobley v Forward Technology Industries plc* (2003) All ER (D) 175), and vice versa.

Letter of appointment – non-executive directors   3.100

By the very nature of their employment, non-executive directors are not employed by the companies of which they have been appointed directors, and it is therefore not appropriate for them to enter into a service contract. However, it is still important that the terms of their appointment are formally recorded, usually in the form of a letter of appointment or engagement. Some parts of the letter will detail the non-executive director's rights, for example to receive remuneration, be included in the directors' and officers' insurance policy, or seek professional advice.

Guidance on the role of the non-executive director is contained in the FRC's Guidance on Board Effectiveness (see paras **1.32** and **1.33**). Some of the original points from the Higgs Guidance, including a sample letter of appointment for a non-executive director, have been developed into more detailed guidance notes by the ICSA, which recommends that the letter should include details of:

- the expected term of appointment and notice provisions;
- the role and what is required;
- the expected time commitment in order to fulfil the role;
- fees payable to the non-executive director;
- requirements in relation to permitted outside interests and disclosure of such interests;
- any confidentiality restrictions;
- induction and information to be provided following appointment;
- the review process in relation to the performance of individual directors, the Board and its committees;
- any directors' and officers' indemnity insurance;
- the process to follow in seeking independent professional advice; and
- details of any requirements and payments in relation to appointments to committees of the Board.

An example is set out in **APPENDIX 2** and, in many instances, the example will contain considerably more detail than companies and non-executive directors have been accustomed to in the past. However, this level of detail is considered 'best practice' as it sets out quite clearly the nature of the relationship, specifically what is expected of the non-executive director and the non-executive director's rights. As is evident from the list of details above, many matters dealt with in the letter give the director rights to receive information and pay, for example, or to be treated in a certain way, so should be examined carefully.

Compensation   3.110

Breach of the director's contract by the company clearly gives the director a right to bring action for damages for breach of contract. It should also be noted that it may also bring about a right to compensation for unfair dismissal and possibly claims based on discrimination, depending on the circumstances of the dismissal.

However, where compensation is paid for loss of office which is not part of an award for damages made by the court and is not required by a clause in the service contract, such payment must be approved by the members in general meeting (CA 2006 s 217). A company may not lawfully make any payment to a director by way of compensation for loss of office or as consideration for retirement unless particulars of the proposed payment have been disclosed to all members and the proposal has been approved by them. It is important to note that, should approval fail to be obtained, the recipient is liable to refund the amount received and the directors responsible for making the payment are also liable for any loss to the company.

Indemnity   3.120

CA 2006 s 232 provides that any provision, for example in the company's Articles or in any contract between the company and a director, which purports to indemnify the director against any liability arising from his negligence, default, breach of duty or breach of trust is void.

However, CA 2006 ss 233 and 234 provide that directors have the right to effect insurance against such claims and that the directors may be indemnified out of the assets of the company against qualifying third-party indemnity claims where they are found not guilty of the offence or acquitted, or where relief is granted to the director by the court where the director has acted honestly and reasonably and ought fairly to be excused. Such relief is not given easily, as illustrated in *Re Duckwari plc* [1997] 2 BCLC 713, where the Court of Appeal confirmed that whilst relief was available for a default under CA 1985 s 320 (since repealed) the request for grant was declined.

Increases in the potential for legal action against directors in recent years, most notably derivative actions, has led to the emergence of sophisticated directors' and officers' indemnity policies ('D&O policies') to cover directors and officers for loss arising from claims of 'wrongful trading' in their capacity as directors, including costs of attending regulatory investigations. Taking just one example, the directors of Equitable Life were sued collectively for £3.3 billion for not running the company effectively.

D&O policies are now fairly commonplace, particularly in public companies, large private companies with significant outside shareholder interests and those with business activities conducted in the United States, and indeed many see them as an essential feature of the company's insurance protection portfolio. The policy may be taken out by the company for all its directors, or by an individual director in respect of all of his directorships. Those who opt for a personal policy consider it beneficial as there is no opportunity under the policy for a conflict of interest with the company, an insurer acting for the company, or fellow directors; and the indemnity limit is not eroded by defending other directors claiming under the policy. Through the D&O policy, directors can protect themselves against personal liability for claims made by the company; shareholders; creditors, including the bank; liquidators, administrators and receivers; regulators; and government agencies, etc. Such claims may arise for any number of reasons, possibly corporate failure attributed to the directors' actions or following a merger or takeover where the directors were considered to have a conflict of personal interest which influenced their decision on the outcome.

Directors clearly have much to gain from effecting such insurance and exercising their right to be included from appointment, and there are also considerable benefits to the company, as once the D&O policy is in force the Board is likely to have a more balanced attitude to risk rather than taking a less risky, conservative approach given concern about their potential personal liability.

Such policies can be tailored to suit the particular directors' requirements and, whilst there is no standard wording for this type of policy, it would usually indemnify the director for any loss suffered, including payment of damages and legal costs, in his capacity as director arising from a breach of duty (statutory or otherwise), breach of trust, neglect, error, misleading statement, breach of authority or wrongful trading, and against costs incurred where subject to investigation or disqualification proceedings. Many choices will need to be made about what is included in the D&O policy such as the level of excess and overall indemnity limit required; whether the cover is worldwide, including defence costs in the USA; what type of costs are covered (for example costs of investigations, surveillance, counterclaims, travel costs, bail bonds and extradition defence). It is also important for the director to determine whether the policy provides for payment of living costs (in the event his assets are frozen) and whether emergency legal funding will be provided so a director can immediately commence legal and expert defence in response to a personal liability claim without many months of delay.

However, D&O policies will exclude loss arising from actual dishonesty, fraud and malicious conduct and loss attributed to wilful misconduct. It is not surprising therefore that there has been a great deal of press coverage about insurers avoiding classes of cover in relation to corporate collapse based on alleged non-disclosure and misrepresentation of financial information.

A director should review the company's D&O policy to ensure it is adequate prior to or on appointment and, unless he has a personal policy, ensure he is included.

It is likely that large-scale corporate collapses will cause further hardening of the D&O policy insurance market and an increase in premiums, and particular care must be taken to study the exclusion clauses in the policy to ensure that all required risks are covered. For example, fines, penalties and punitive damages levied by regulators or criminal courts, loss of earnings, personal injury and property damage, pollution and environmental liability and claims made by one insured under the policy against another insured are commonly excluded. Similarly, an existing standard policy may not have been extended to encompass the whole range of liability now imposed on directors (eg in terms of fines under FSMA 2000 for breaches of the Listing Rules and misstatements in listing particulars, health and safety or environmental breaches) and the policy should be examined to determine whether any extra cover needs to be arranged.

The ICSA has produced a Guidance Note, 'Directors' and Officers' Insurance', to draw directors' attention to some of the key issues when selecting a policy.

Access to information and accounting records   3.130

CA 2006 s 388(1)(b) provides directors with the right, individually or together, to inspect the company's accounting books and records. Similarly, case law established a director's right to inspect and take copies of documents necessary to enable him to perform his duties (*Conway v Petronious Clothing Co Ltd* [1978] 1 All ER 185).

Furthermore, in order for directors, and particularly non-executive directors who are not involved on a daily basis with the company, to be able to make informed decisions about the strategic direction of the company they need and have a right to obtain appropriate information on which to base their decisions. Many companies routinely produce detailed Board packs which are distributed to directors prior to Board meetings. With this in mind, it is important for directors to determine what information they require and for the executive directors and management team to ensure that it is collated, interpreted and disseminated. Such information would commonly include financial performance figures as well as information on project development, the market, competitors, employees and technical advances, etc. In the event that information requested by non-executive directors is not forthcoming or there is resistance in its preparation, this should be investigated by the Board, as this in itself may be cause for concern.

Pensions to former directors   3.140

Table A reg 87 allows the directors to pay benefits, gratuities, insurance or pensions to any ex-director, member of his family or any of his dependants and to contribute to any fund and pay premiums for provision of such benefit.

Obviously the requirements of the CA 2006 should be observed before such payments are made as they may, for example, require prior approval of the members. A pension paid to a director in respect of past services is, however, exempt from the members' approval requirement (CA 2006 s 220(1)(d)).

Service address   3.150

Since 1 October 2009 directors and company secretaries have had the right to disclose a service address for the purposes of the public record that is different from their home address, thus enabling them to protect details of their home addresses. Full details about the service address and the director's rights to restrict access to his home address are set out in para **6.11.3**.

4 Statutory statement of directors' general duties

4.10   **To whom duty is owed**

4.20   **General duties**

      4.20.1   Act within powers

      4.20.2   Promote the success of the company

      4.20.3   Exercise independent judgment

      4.20.4   Exercise reasonable care, skill and diligence

      4.20.5   Avoid conflicts of interest

      4.20.6   Not accept benefits from third parties

      4.20.7   Declare interests in transactions or arrangements

           4.20.7.1   Proposed

           4.20.7.2   Existing

4.30   **Common law origins**

      4.30.1   Fiduciary duty

           4.30.1.1   Duty to act in good faith

           4.30.1.2   Duty to exercise powers for a proper purpose

           4.30.1.3   Conflict of interest

           4.30.1.4   Secret profits

      4.30.2   Duty of skill and care

           4.30.2.1   Degree of skill

           4.30.2.2   Attention to the business

           4.30.2.3   Reliance on others

4 Statutory statement of directors' general duties

CA 2006 ss 170–181 sets out the statutory statement of directors' general duties. This statement has been introduced not only to provide greater clarity about what is required of directors and to make the law more accessible and easier for directors to understand, but also to make developments in the law on directors' duties more predictable.

The statutory statement does not cover all the duties that a director may owe to the company. Many duties are imposed elsewhere in legislation, such as the duty to keep accounting records and to protect the health and safety of employees, etc, and these are covered in other chapters of this book.

The statutory statement of general duties comprises seven duties which are based on, but replace, certain common law rules and principles owed by directors to the companies to which they are appointed. Whilst the common law rules and principles have been repealed, they remain important to the interpretation and application of the statutory general duties (CA 2006 s 170) (see para **4.30**).

The requirements of the statutory statement of duties extend to de facto, de jure and shadow directors and, in some instances, to former directors of a company.

To whom duty is owed   4.10

It was a fundamental principle of common law that in general, directors' duties are owed to the company as a whole and not to individual members (*Percival v Wright* [1902] 2 Ch 421 and *Peskin v Anderson* [2001] 1 BCLC 372). This principle has been preserved by CA 2006 s 170(1).

However, directors must be aware that in certain circumstances their duties are owed to a wider audience and, where relevant, consideration should be given to the following:

- the interests of employees where they are in the best interest of the company (*Hutton v West Cork Rly Co* (1883) 23 Ch D 654). Furthermore, directors must take account of the interests of the company's employees as required by CA 2006 s 172. This is particularly important where all or part of a company's business is sold or closed down. In such circumstances, for example, the directors might be permitted, provided they have requisite power conferred on them by the members in general meeting or by the Memorandum and Articles, to make provisions for employees out of distributable profits to fulfil this duty;

- the interests of the company's creditors. It was held in the case *Lonrho Ltd v Shell Petroleum Co Ltd* [1981] 2 All ER 456, [1980] 1 WLR 627, HL that the interests of the company 'are not exclusively those of the shareholders but may include those of its creditors'. This is reinforced by provisions of IA 1986, whereby a director has a duty to take every step he would be expected to take to minimise any loss to creditors from the moment it becomes apparent that the company cannot avoid insolvent liquidation;

- where the directors have specifically undertaken to act as the shareholders' agents, a duty will be owed to these shareholders (*Allen v Hyatt* (1914) 30 TLR 444).

In addition, companies have been put increasingly under pressure from the likes of the Department for Business, Innovation and Skills (BIS), the Association of British Insurers (ABI), major pension funds, institutional investors and the public generally to take account of their wider 'corporate social responsibilities', some of which has been encompassed in the factors to be taken into account when directors are making decisions (para **4.20.2**). It is clear that by addressing these issues and applying high standards, the company may benefit by improving its image, finding recruitment and retention easier and also gaining business from customers who want to deal with companies who have genuine concern about and are taking action in respect of corporate social responsibility.

General duties   4.20

The statutory statement requires directors, individually, to perform the following seven duties:

Act within powers   4.20.1

A director must act within his powers under the company's constitution and only exercise his powers for the purpose for which they were conferred (CA 2006 s 171). This is largely a restatement of well-recognised common law principles.

Promote the success of the company   4.20.2

A director must 'act in a way he considers, in good faith, would be most likely to promote the success of the company for the benefit of its members as a whole' (CA 2006 s 172). This duty applies to all a director's actions, not just those exercised at Board meetings.

In response to concern about how 'success' would be interpreted (as it is different from the known common law requirement of acting in the best interests of the company), the Government confirmed it will usually be taken to mean a 'long-term increase in value' of the company.

It should be noted that where the purpose of the company is not for the benefit of the members, it is the directors' duty to instead achieve the stated purpose (CA 2006 s 172(2)). Furthermore, where a company is insolvent, or approaching insolvency, then the directors have a duty to act in the interests of the company's creditors rather than the members (CA 2006 s 172(3)).

When making decisions, CA 2006 s 172(1)(a)–(f) requires directors to ensure that they have regard to:

- the likely consequences of the decision over the long term;

- the interests of employees;

- the impact on the community and environment;

- the need to foster business relationships with suppliers, customers and others;

- the need to act fairly between members; and

- the need to maintain a reputation for high standards of business and conduct.

This requirement formalises the need for directors to consider and balance the interests of the company's members with those of other 'stakeholders' when deciding what actions should be taken to promote the success of the company. It is quite likely that there will be conflicts in the factors to be considered and there may be negative effects on some, considered a necessary effect of 'promoting the success of the company'.

A great deal of concern has been expressed about this duty and its implications. However, given that the interests of employees, customers, the environment, and suppliers, etc are to an extent already intrinsically linked in the commercial environment, it is probable that many directors were already instinctively giving thought to these matters when making decisions, although this may have been in a less formal manner.

The directors must decide, using their own business judgment in good faith, what weight is given to the factors set out in CA 2006 s 172(1) (see the list above).

It is important for directors to note that it is not intended that these requirements would delay the decision-making process or create the need for a paper trail of factors considered when making decisions, although there might be situations where this is appropriate. Neither is it intended, or appropriate, that minutes of the company's Board meetings record whether each factor was considered. The minutes should only reflect and record those factors considered key to the decision being made.

From a practical perspective most decisions (certainly in larger companies) taken by the company's directors follow a detailed review and proposal process and are supported by background papers or briefing notes. It is therefore important that, as well as the directors considering the factors set out in CA 2006 s 172 in whatever manner they determine appropriate, the factors are also properly considered when the background papers are prepared and recommendations are made to the Board by the management or executive team. The directors therefore have a duty to ensure that such persons are fully aware of the requirements of CA 2006 s 172 and that all relevant matters are taken into account and evaluated when making a proposal.

Exercise independent judgment   **4.20.3**

A director must exercise independent judgment (CA 2006 s 173). This duty largely codifies the requirement in common law for directors to exercise their powers independently, without subordinating their powers to the will of others and without fettering their discretion.

A director is still able to seek advice where appropriate, which might include advice from the appointers where the director is acting as a nominee. The director must, however, exercise his own judgment when making the final decision.

However, a director's duty to exercise independent judgment is subject to restrictions contained in any agreements entered into by the company or in the company's constitution, including resolutions of the shareholders (CA 2006 s 173(2)).

Exercise reasonable care, skill and diligence   **4.20.4**

A director must exercise such reasonable skill, care and diligence as would be exercised by a reasonably diligent person with:

- the general knowledge, skill and experience that could reasonably be expected from a person carrying out the director's functions; and

- the director's actual general knowledge, skill and experience (CA 2006 s 174).

This two-step test is not new as it largely mirrors the common law standard and tests already laid down in IA 1986 s 214.

Avoid conflicts of interest   **4.20.5**

A director has a statutory duty to avoid any situations in which he has, or could have, a direct or indirect interest that conflicts, or could conflict, with the interests of the company (CA 2006 s 175). This duty applies in particular to the exploitation of any property, information or opportunity regardless of whether the company could take advantage of it. It applies to a conflict of duty, as well as a conflict of interest and includes the interests of 'connected persons'.

This is increasingly being referred to as a 'situational conflict' and includes circumstances where, for example, a director is involved with a competitor, major shareholder, customer or supplier, is an adviser to the company or a competitor, is a trustee of the company's pension scheme, or owns property adjacent to the company's premises. This list is not exhaustive and there may be other circumstances giving rise to a situational conflict.

Each individual director must determine his own situational conflicts and seek to avoid them. However, in some instances, avoidance might not be possible or even beneficial to the company, in which case the director must immediately notify the company of the situational conflict and seek prior approval of the circumstances and the existence of the situational conflict. Thereafter the director must also advise the company of any change in the nature of a previously notified conflict.

Provided a public company has the requisite provisions in its Articles of Association, the Board may authorise a conflict of interest notified to it by a director.

Where a private company was incorporated before 1 October 2008, authorisation may be given by the directors provided a resolution to this effect has been approved by the shareholders or the company's Articles of Association have been amended to include such authority. For any private company incorporated on or after 1 October 2008, authorisation may be given by the Board provided there is no provision stating otherwise in the company's Articles of Association.

Where a public company does not have the required provision in its Articles, or a private company incorporated before October 2008 has not passed the necessary shareholders' resolution or amended its Articles, approval by the shareholders of any director's conflict situations will still be needed. For many companies it would be costly, time-consuming, inconvenient and impractical to arrange shareholder meetings to approve such matters and most companies have ensured the directors have been given the necessary authority.

Authorisation of a conflict of interest is only effective if the quorum requirement for the meeting at which it is to be approved is met without including the relevant director, or would have been authorised without including the relevant director's votes. A transaction which has been validly authorised by the directors, as permitted by the company's Articles or resolution of the shareholders, does not need further authorisation by a company's shareholders (CA 2006 s 180(1)).

Authorisation by the directors of a company under s 175 cannot be retrospective and only applies to the actual conflict situation, and not to a breach of duty. This means that where a conflict situation had been validly authorised this does not absolve the director from his duties to act in a way he considers most likely to promote the success of the company (CA 2006 s 172).

A problem which many directors who have conflicts of interest may encounter relates to the receipt of confidential information. Where there has been a valid authorisation of the conflict, and the director receives confidential information as a result of that conflict, he can be excused from having to disclose that information to the company. Alternatively, the director may be excused from the whole or part of any Board meeting at which the matter giving rise to the conflict is being discussed.

Companies must consider directors' conflicts on a case-by-case basis and approval be given only in accordance with the general directors' duties as set out in CA 2006, in particular the need to promote the success of the company. However, the Board must consider what course of action it would take should an actual conflict (ie a specific transaction, contract or arrangement, see para **4.20.7**) arise after authorisation of a potential situational conflict has taken place. There are three options which a company could consider:

(1)   exclude the director from receiving information and discussing the matter;

(2)   exclude the director from the Board in relation to the matter; or

(3)   require the director to resign.

Companies should maintain a register of situational conflict authorisations, containing details of the nature of the conflict, when it was approved, any limitations or restrictions that apply and when the authorisation will expire. In order to do this, documentation recording the director's situational conflict should include:

(1)   details of the matter which has been authorised;

(2)   the duration of the authority (subject to, say, annual review) and a statement that the authority can be revoked at any time;

(3)   set out the circumstances when the director must refer back to the Board for the authority to be reviewed;

(4)   where appropriate, provisions stating that the director may not receive information relating to the conflict or participate in Board discussions in relation to the matter;

(5)   where appropriate, provisions stating that where the director obtains information as a result of the conflict he will not be obliged to disclose that information to the company or to use the information in relation to the company's affairs. It may also be useful, if another company is involved in the conflict, to ascertain if they have allowed the same provision.

As those sections of CA 2006 relating to conflicts of interest came into force on 1 October 2008, there will inevitably be overlap with situations that may have been authorised prior to the implementation date and those which occur after the implementation date. It is recommended that, to remove any uncertainty, the prior situations be authorised again to ensure compliance with CA 2006 s 175.

Companies vary in their approach to gathering information and encouraging directors to disclose the existence of any situational conflicts. Many carry out a formal annual or six-monthly review, often using a questionnaire for completion by each director, which is then considered by the Board. It is also usual practice to remind directors at the beginning of each Board meeting of the need for them to disclose any interests they might have in matters on the agenda for discussion, which also might help identify additional situational conflicts they need to notify.

Directors should note that, as recently clarified in *Killen v Horseworld Ltd* [2012] EWHC 363 (QB), a director's duty to avoid a conflict of interest continues after he resigns. In this particular case Killen became aware of a media broadcasting opportunity whilst still a director of Horseworld, which he exploited for himself after he had resigned. Killen was ordered to pay Horseworld all profits received as a consequence of exploiting the opportunity.

Disclosure of a director's conflict of interest and approval by the Board can also provide solid defence against derivative action (see para **8.40**).

Not accept benefits from third parties   4.20.6

A director has a statutory duty not to accept a benefit from a third party which is given because of the position held by the director or because of anything the director has done in his capacity as a director (CA 2006 s 176). Similarly a director has a responsibility under the Bribery Act 2010 not to give or receive anything that might be considered to constitute a bribe.

In brief, acceptance of benefits is not subject to any 'de minimis' limit under CA 2006 and is only permitted where the matter is approved by the company's members or it can reasonably be regarded that it will not give rise to a conflict of interest with the company.

Given the questions this raises with regard to corporate hospitality and gifts, companies would be well advised to consider their policies on this and to ensure that all directors are given guidance and are fully informed about what is acceptable. This will very much depend on the type of business the company is in and what is industry practice and the accepted norm. Timing of the receipt of corporate hospitality is also important, as it might be appropriate to decline if in the midst of contract or supply negotiations. Again, the duties and restrictions in relation to hospitality and gifts derive not only from CA 2006, but also from the Bribery Act 2010 (**CHAPTER 13**).

Maintenance of a register to record benefits offered, their approval and details of receipt will help to demonstrate compliance with this duty.

Declare interests in transactions or arrangements　　　　　**4.20.7**

Proposed　　　　　**4.20.7.1**

A director has a statutory duty to disclose any direct or indirect interest he has in a proposed transaction or arrangement with the company (CA 2006 s 177). This duty largely reflects the position in CA 1985 s 317 (now repealed) and provisions in the Articles of most companies.

The director will need to disclose the nature and extent of his interest to the other directors either at a meeting of the directors, by notice in writing to the directors or, alternatively, by a general notice made to the directors (s 177(2)). For the purposes of s 177 a director is treated only as having knowledge of matters of which he ought to reasonably be aware and a declaration is not required where a director is not aware of his interest or where the director is not aware of the transaction or arrangement in question (s 177(5)). Declarations of interest under s 177 are not required in the following instances:

(1)　　where it cannot be reasonably be regarded as likely to give rise to a conflict of interest;

(2) where the directors are already aware of it (for the purposes of s 177 they are treated as being aware of any situation which they should reasonably be aware of); or

(3) where it concerns terms of the director's service contract that have already been, or are to be considered at a Board meeting or by a committee of the Board appointed for this purpose as per the company's Articles of Association.

A director making a declaration under s 177 must state the nature and extent of the interest, and the declaration must be made to the Board prior to the company entering into the transaction or arrangement (s 177(4)).

A company's Articles must be checked to ensure that once an interest has been declared, the director may be included in the quorum and is able to participate in voting. Notwithstanding what it says in the company's Articles, there might be situations where it is advisable for a director not to participate in discussion and decisions reached on a matter in which he or she has an interest.

It will be beneficial for companies to keep records of directors' interests, whether they are required to or not, to demonstrate and monitor the disclosures made.

Existing   **4.20.7.2**

In addition, CA 2006 s 182 requires directors to declare to the company any interest, whether direct or indirect, they have in an existing transaction or arrangement, save where a director has already made a declaration under s 177 (para **4.20.7.1**). Declarations under s 182 may be made either at a meeting of the Board, by written notice under s 184 or by giving a general notice under s 185 and must be made as soon as practicable.

As under s 177, where a declaration has been made but becomes inaccurate or incomplete, a further declaration is required from the director.

The same principles apply under s 182 as under s 177 in respect of the directors being treated as aware of matters which they ought to reasonably be aware, without actual notification.

As with proposed transactions or arrangements, a company's Articles must be checked to ensure that once an interest has been declared, the director may be included in the quorum and able to participate in voting. Again, there might be circumstances where, although entitled to participate, it would be better practice for a director to be excluded from discussion and decisions made on the matter.

As detailed above, it is beneficial for companies to keep records of directors' interests, whether required to or not, to demonstrate and monitor disclosures received from the directors.

Common law origins   4.30

It has long been established in common law that a director owes two types of duty to the company: a 'fiduciary duty' and a 'duty of skill and care'. Whilst the statutory statement has replaced the common law rules and principles, they remain important for interpretation and application of the general duties (see para **4.20**). For this reason it is important that directors understand the common law principles from which the statutory statement is largely derived.

Common law required directors operating and making decisions as a Board to:

• act in good faith in the best interests of the company;

• use powers conferred on them for the proper purpose; and

• exercise whatever skill they possess, and reasonable care, when acting in the company's interests.

Furthermore, an individual director was not permitted to allow his personal interests to conflict with those of the company nor derive any personal profit from his position beyond that which the company paid him.

Fiduciary duty   4.30.1

An individual director was required to act in good faith in his dealings with or on behalf of the company and to exercise the powers conferred on him and fulfil the duties of his office honestly.

Duty to act in good faith   4.30.1.1

Directors acting as a Board have a duty to act in good faith in what they consider to be the best interests of the company (*Re Smith and Fawcett Ltd* [1942] Ch 304 at 306, CA). They must not use their powers for the benefit of third parties or themselves. It is likely that, provided the director's motives were honest and he genuinely believed the action taken was in the best interests of the company, such director would not normally be subject to claims that he should have acted differently.

The duty is subjective and, taking the judge's comment in *Re Smith & Fawcett Ltd* [1942] 1 All ER 542, CA that 'directors must exercise their discretion bona fide in what they consider – not what a court may consider – is in the interest of the company, and not for any collateral purpose', the court will usually allow directors absolute discretion, interfering only where they believe no reasonable director would consider the action taken to be in the best interests of the company. However, in *Knight v Frost* [1999] 1 BCLC 364 where a company lent money without the directors checking that a commercial rate of interest was charged, it was held that action could be brought against the directors for failing to act bona fide in the interests of the company.

Where a director is found to have acted honestly but not in the best interests of the company, he is in breach of duty. In *Re W & M Roith Ltd* [1967] 1 All ER 427 a director in poor health who entered into a service contract providing for a generous widow's pension in the event of his death was held not to be acting bona fide in the interests of the company and the contract was void. Similarly in *J J Harrison (Properties) Ltd v Harrison* [2001] 1 BCLC 158 a director who bought land from the company without informing his fellow directors of the planning status, failing to obtain market value for the land and using company resources to obtain planning permission for his own benefit, was considered to be in breach of his duty to act in the best interests of the company and required to account for the profits.

Duty to exercise powers for a proper purpose   **4.30.1.2**

A company's Memorandum and Articles, relevant shareholders' resolutions and Board minutes will determine the powers conferred upon directors and the context in which they can be reasonably exercised. Any director who exercises these powers over the company's assets other than for the purpose intended or for the benefit of the company as a whole will be liable for a breach of duty as follows:

- In general, directors have authority to issue shares to raise capital needed by the company and are not allowed to use these powers for any other purpose, such as preventing the majority of the members from exercising their constitutional rights. For example, in *Punt v Symons & Co Ltd* [1903] 2 Ch 506 the directors issued shares to five additional members to secure approval of a special resolution concerning their own position. The court ruled that this was not a bona fide exercise of their power for the advantage of the company as a whole.

- Even where they are acting in good faith in the interests of the company as a whole, the directors must still use their powers for the purposes for which they were intended. In *Hogg v Cramphorn Ltd* [1967] Ch 254 the directors issued shares with special voting rights to the trustees of a scheme set up for the benefit of the company's employees in order to forestall a takeover offer. It was held that although the directors had acted in good faith they had breached their duty to the company by making improper use of their power to issue shares.

In certain circumstances, where there is no question of insolvency of the company, these breaches of duty can be ratified after the event by the members in general meeting. This was permitted in *Bamford v Bamford* [1970] Ch 212, where the Court of Appeal held that the improper issue of 500,000 shares by the directors to defend a takeover bid could be ratified by the shareholders and therefore no challenge could be made to the directors' actions. However, shareholders cannot ratify a breach of duty by the directors where the company is insolvent.

Conflict of interest   **4.30.1.3**

A director must not put himself in a position where there is an actual or potential conflict between his personal interest and his duty to the company. A conflict of interest will arise where the director seeks to exploit the assets or opportunities of the company for his own benefit. The effect of this at common law is that a director may not enter into a valid contract (other than a service contract) with the company, directly or indirectly, unless the company gives its approval in general meeting, or the Articles permit such transaction.

In *Aberdeen Rly Co v Blaikie Bros* (1854) 2 Eq Rep 1281, HL the railway company agreed to buy iron chairs from a partnership of which its chairman was managing partner and it was held that, as this was not disclosed, the company was entitled to avoid the contract irrespective of its merits. Similarly in *Knight v Frost* [1999] 1 BCLC 364, a director was liable to compensate the company for making a loan to reduce his own personal liability when the company was insolvent.

Strict application of this principle in all circumstances would often work to the detriment of companies and it is established that disclosure by the director of his interest may validate the contract. In practice, in most companies provisions in the Articles render contracts in which a director is interested enforceable subject to disclosure by the director of his interest to the Board. For example, reg 85 of Table A specifically permits a director to have an interest in a contract 'subject to the provisions of the Act and provided that he has disclosed to the directors the nature and extent of any material interest'.

CA 1985 s 317 imposed a requirement, which cannot be waived by the Articles, for a director to disclose to the Board any interest he may have in a contract with the company. Such disclosure must be made to the full Board, not at a committee meeting (*Guinness plc v Saunders* [1990] 2 AC 663, HL).

By extension, a director must not 'fetter his discretion' to act in the best interests of the company by, for example, a contract with an outsider. Whilst the director is not under an obligation to refrain from competing with his company or even from becoming a director in a rival company (provided that he makes disclosure to the Board as above), care must be exercised to ensure that he does not subordinate the interests of the one company to those of the other (*Scottish Co-operative Wholesale Society Ltd v Meyer* [1959] AC 324, HL). Directors should also be aware that a member or members of the company may make application to the court for protection against unfair prejudice where they consider the company's affairs have been conducted in an unfairly prejudicial manner.

In *Ball v Eden Project Ltd* [2002] 1 BCLC 313, a director who registered the trademark 'The Eden Project' in his own name for his own benefit was found to be in breach of his fiduciary duty to the company. Also in *Bhullar v Bhullar, Re Bhullar Bros Ltd* (2003) All ER (D) 445 (Mar), the Court of Appeal ruled that availability of a property for sale next to the company's grocery business should have been notified to the company before being acquired by a separate company owned and controlled by some of the company's directors and shareholders only. As the directors had breached their duty to communicate information about availability of the property to the grocery company, the Court of Appeal determined that the property be transferred to the company at purchase price.

In certain circumstances a contract which is voidable by reason of a director's interest can be ratified by the company in general meeting (*North-West Transportation Co Ltd v Beatty* (1887) 12 App Cas 589).

Secret profits   **4.30.1.4**

A director's fiduciary position precludes him from taking a personal profit from any opportunities that result from his position as a director, even if he is acting honestly and for the good of the company. Any profit arising in such circumstances must be repaid to the company unless it has been previously disclosed and authorised by the shareholders. This applies whether the profit arises from a contract with the company or a third party.

In *Regal (Hastings) Ltd v Gulliver* [1942] 1 All ER 378, HL, it was established that, even if the director's profit would not have accrued to the company, he must still account for it if the opportunity to make it arose through his directorship. In this case the House of Lords held that Regal (now controlled by a new Board) was entitled to recover the personal profit made by the former directors, because the opportunity to make the profit arose only through knowledge they had gained as directors. A similar decision was reached in *Gencor ACP Ltd* [2000] 2 BCLC 734, in which the court found that the mere fact a director makes a secret profit from a corporate opportunity renders him liable to account to the company.

Although it is not a defence that the directors acted honestly and in good faith, the company in general meeting can often ratify the directors' actions and allow them to keep the profit. In Regal the directors had the necessary majority, and would have been protected by resolution of the shareholders, but because they were acting in good faith did not realise approval was necessary.

However, in *Cook v Deeks* [1916] 1 AC 554, directors who personally acquired a contract they had a duty to acquire for the company were not allowed to ratify their action by resolution in general meeting. They had directly deprived the company of an opportunity to make profit, and in such circumstances it seems unlikely that directors would be permitted to vote on their majority shareholdings where they have committed fraud on the minority by misappropriating company assets.

More recently, in *Towers v Premier Waste Management Ltd* [2011] EWCA Civ 923 a director of the company borrowed equipment from a customer for his own personal use on a property renovation project. He did not disclose this private arrangement to the Board and the company took action against him on the basis that he had breached his fiduciary duties and made a secret profit. The action was a success and the director was ordered to pay the company the market rate for hiring the equipment in recognition of the personal benefit he obtained.

It should also be noted that a director cannot escape his duty to account for a personal profit by resigning before he takes it and that, even where the company could not have benefited from the contract, the director is liable to give up the profit (*Industrial Development Consultants Ltd v Cooley* [1972] 2 All ER 162).

Duty of skill and care   4.30.2

The directors' fiduciary duties impose on them a largely negative obligation to do nothing which conflicts with the company's interests. At the same time, when they are acting in the company's interests, they are expected to exercise whatever skill they possess and reasonable care.

Case law has long established that a director must attend diligently to the affairs of the company and that in performing his duties he must display the 'reasonable care … an ordinary man might be expected to take in the same circumstances on his own behalf' (*Re Brazilian Rubber Plantations and Estates Ltd* [1911] 1 Ch 425).

The leading case on the nature and extent of the duty of skill and care is *Re City Equitable Fire Insurance Co Ltd* [1925] Ch 407, CA ('City Equitable'), in which the personal liability of other directors for the managing director's misappropriation of £200,000 of the company's assets was questioned. This case established three basic principles as follows:

- a director is not an expert, and need only display skills he actually possesses. He is not expected to exercise a level of skill he does not have;

- a director need not devote his continuous attention to the business;

- a director is entitled, in the absence of suspicious circumstances, to rely on the experience and expertise of his co-directors and other officers of the company.

Despite the passage of time, City Equitable remains the leading authority, and the extent to which its principles hold good is considered in the following paragraphs. In some ways the principles can be criticised as more relevant to the Victorian gentleman director rather than today's full-time executive director.

Degree of skill   **4.30.2.1**

The level of skill required of a director based on the City Equitable case is subjective and implies that he would not be expected, merely by virtue of his office, to possess any particular skills. His performance is judged by the way he applies any skills which he actually has.

The most concerning limitation of this subjective test is that it exonerates the incompetent but honest director from his actions on the basis that he can do no better. In reality, and given the company's power to remove a director by ordinary resolution of the members, such person is unlikely to remain a director of the company for long.

Two developments since City Equitable have introduced the concept of 'objective' tests for the level of skill required of a director, as follows:

(1)   The existence of a service contract between the director and the company, where the director is under a contractual obligation to fulfil specific tasks within the company based upon his expertise, knowledge and experience. The director may have experience and expertise relevant to the business as a whole or to certain specialist functions such as accounting, financing, marketing, etc and would be required to display an objective level of skill implied in such contract. As an example of this, in *Bairstow v Queens Moat Houses plc* [2000] 1 BCLC 549 the court held that an executive director is expected to bring to his work a level of competence commensurate with his responsibilities and for which he is paid substantial remuneration.

(2)   IA 1986 s 214: this provides that where a company is insolvent, a director faces personal liability for wrongful trading if he does not display both the

general knowledge, skill and experience that he actually has and also that which might reasonably be expected of someone carrying out his function within the company. There are signs that the 'reasonable director' standard introduced by s 214 is influencing the courts in their consideration of directors' conduct in companies which are going concerns (*Re D'Jan of London Ltd* [1993] BCC 646). This standard is also influencing the court in determining whether conduct of a director is unfit for the purposes of disqualification, as seen in *Re Landhurst Leasing plc* [1999] 1 BCLC 286 (see para **5.53.1**).

For example, in *Dorchester Finance Co Ltd v Stebbing (1977)* [1989] BCLC 498 it was held that two non-executive directors, both experienced accountants, had been negligent in their duties as directors in signing blank cheques at the request of the one full-time director. In considering a director's duties and the level of skill and care required, it was held that no distinction was to be drawn between executive and non-executive directors, the test being dependent upon the directors' knowledge and experience. The directors were accountants by profession and were expected to exercise their knowledge, skill and experience and perform to a higher standard in relation to the company's finances. A similar decision was reached in the case *Re Continental Assurance Co of London plc* [1996] BCC 888 (see para **5.53.1**).

Attention to the business   **4.30.2.2**

It was held in *City Equitable* that 'a director is not bound to give continuous attention to the affairs of the company. His duties are of an intermittent nature'. This dictum is clearly more appropriate to the circumstances of a non-executive director and refers specifically to attendance at Board meetings. An executive director's service contract normally requires that he devotes his full attention to the business of the company.

Clearly the size and nature of a company's operations will determine the matters which are attended to by the directors personally. In a small family-owned and run company they will be very different to those which concern the directors of a large multinational organisation. In the latter case the scale of operations makes it impossible for the directors to attend to many matters personally, and the need for effective delegation and supervision becomes essential.

Reliance on others   **4.30.2.3**

Generally, a director is entitled to rely on his fellow directors and officers of the company. Thus in *Dovey v Cory* [1901] AC 477, HL it was held that a director was entitled to rely on a subordinate 'put in a position of trust for the express purpose of attending to the detail of management' and was not liable for any loss resulting from wrongful acts committed by that person.

Similarly, in *City Equitable* it was held that 'in respect of duties ... that may properly be left to some other official, a director is, in the absence of grounds for suspicion, justified in trusting that official to perform such duties honestly'. Thus in this case the directors were entitled to sign cheques which appeared to be properly authorised although subsequently put to an unauthorised use.

The absence of suspicious circumstances was also relied on in *Huckerby v Elliott* [1970] 1 All ER 189, in which a director failed to enquire whether a gaming licence had been obtained but had no grounds for suspicion.

Directors may also rely on the opinions of outside experts, and in fact may be negligent if they do not obtain an outside opinion in appropriate circumstances (*Re Duomatic* [1969] 2 Ch 365). In *Coulthard v Neville Russell* [1998] 1 BCLC 143, CA it was held that auditors had failed to exercise their duty of care, not only to the company but also to its directors, to advise them that payments and other financial arrangements amounted to unlawful financial assistance for the purchase of own shares.

It is important to note that directors cannot absolve themselves entirely of responsibility by delegation to others. For example, in *Re Bradcrown Ltd* [2001] 1 BCLC 547, a finance director who relied solely on professional advice received without making his own independent judgment was found to be unfit, although the fact he had taken professional advice was a mitigating factor. Ignorance is not a defence and directors are expected to exercise their judgment and to delegate and supervise activities in such a manner as to uncover any unauthorised or unapproved actions. Furthermore, in *Re Barings plc, Secretary of State for Trade and Industry v Baker* [1998] BCC 583 at 586, when making a disqualification order the judge held that whilst directors may be entitled to delegate functions, the high level of responsibility associated with their office requires them to supervise the delegated functions, even where they trust the competence and integrity of those below them.

5 Breach of duty by a director

5 Breach of duty by a director

A director or directors who have breached their statutory duties may face removal from office, imposition of civil and criminal penalties, personal liability for their acts or omissions or, to protect the public interest, may be liable for disqualification from holding office as a director, unless they give a voluntary disqualification undertaking. Each of these is discussed in the following paragraphs and serves to emphasise the importance to directors of fulfilling their duties.

The director who fails in his duties to the company may have unlimited liability for any loss suffered by the company, even if he himself has not made any personal gain, and may be accountable to third parties for any loss or damage suffered by them as a result of the director's acts, omissions or information supplied by them.

Whilst a company is permitted to effect insurance to indemnify directors against certain liabilities (see para **3.120**), subject to CA 2006 s 1157 (where the court can grant relief where it determines the director acted honestly and fairly and ought to be excused), any other attempt by the company to exempt the directors, whether by provision in the Articles or a contract with them, from liability for negligence, default, breach of duty or breach of trust in relation to the company is void.

Courts do not accept ignorance of duties as a defence and, indeed, specifically stated in the case *Grupo Torras SA v Al Sabah (No 5)* [2001] 1 CLC 221 that foreign individuals who accept directorships in UK companies must familiarise themselves with the obligations arising from these appointments by English law.

Dismissal of the director   5.10

Where the members of the company become aware and are concerned that a director is not carrying out his duties in relation to the company and its affairs, they may consider it necessary to seek to remove the director from office to protect the company, either financially or otherwise (CA 2006 ss 168 and 169). The members may consider that decisions made by the director generally were not in the best interests of the company or that he failed to fulfil specific duties required of him and, for example, did not keep thorough and accurate accounting records, persistently failed to submit documents required by Companies House or failed to ensure that a safe working environment was provided for employees. Alternatively, they might determine that the director's conduct or public image does not lend itself to promoting the interests of the company or they might be concerned that association with the director could damage the company's reputation. Whatever the circumstances, the members have power to remove a director by ordinary resolution, as set out in para **6.11.7**.

Breach of general duties   5.20

Where a director breaches the requirements of the statutory statement of general duties (see **CHAPTER 4**), CA 2006 s 178 states that the consequences would be the same as if the common law rule or equitable principle had been breached. The director will, therefore, be liable to civil action instigated by the party, most often the company, to whom the duty is owed for any loss suffered, undisclosed profit made or advantage taken. The company may consider it appropriate that the director's breach of duty be ratified after the event, permissible in certain circumstances, or may take legal action to obtain:

- an injunction to restrain the director and prevent him from carrying out or continuing the action constituting the breach of duty in the future;

- an award of damages where the director's action is considered negligent;

- restoration of the company's property, provided it does not prejudice an innocent third party, where the director's fiduciary duty has been broken and assets have been misappropriated;

- an account of profits made by the director;

- rescission of a contract in which the director has an undisclosed interest; or

- dismissal of the director (see para **5.10**).

The decision in *Philip Towers v Premier Waste Management Ltd* [2011] EWCA Civ 923 is a salutary reminder to company directors that the courts will strictly enforce their fiduciary duties to the company, which are now contained within the statutory statement of general duties. In this case, Mr Towers was required to account to the company for the personal benefit he had received by way of a loan of equipment free of charge from one of Premier Waste Management's customers. Mr Towers was ordered to pay the company just under £8,000, equating to the benefit he had received, for breaching his duty not to make a secret profit. Despite having opportunity Mr Towers had not advised the Board of the arrangement, hence it was undisclosed, unapproved and 'secret' and considered irrelevant that the company had not suffered any actual loss.

A director's duty to exercise skill and care in carrying out his duties is commonly called into question in respect of statements and information issued on behalf of the company to third parties. These statements may appear in brochures, accounts, circulars, prospectuses and offer documents, etc. Where the purpose of such statements is to entice third parties to acquire securities of the company or in any way deal or contract with it and they are found to contain inaccurate, misleading, false or unsubstantiated information, the directors themselves may be liable for their breach of duty in giving the mis-information (FSMA 2000 s 90). If the misstatements are made as a result of careless omission or neglect, the directors may face a civil claim for negligence. Alternatively, where there is evidence of intentional fraud or recklessness in compiling the information, the directors may be liable for criminal penalties.

Most importantly, a director cannot shelter under the protection of a company where he commits wrongful acts in the course of his duties and, where he is found guilty of fraud, misrepresentation, deceit or other tort, he will be personally liable alongside the company. Where a director is found to have abused his position as 'trustee' of the company's assets and has misapplied them in any way, provisions of IA 1986 s 212 permit the liquidator to pursue the director for restoration of the company's property or payment of the money involved or compensation. Furthermore, where, in the course of winding up it transpires that the company's business has been conducted with intent to defraud creditors, itself considered as misapplication of funds, the court may impose personal liability on those directors party to the fraud for all debts and liabilities of the company, without limitation.

The following cases are important as they illustrate the way in which directors could be considered to have breached their general duties under CA 2006 s 170.

(1)   In *Roder UK Ltd v Titan Marquees Ltd* [2011] EWCA Civ 1126, two directors who had given false, reckless and deceitful statements to one of the company's creditors, reassuring them that they would receive payment, were held personally liable for the company's debt to the creditor.

(2)   In *MacPherson v European Strategic Bureau Ltd* [2000] 2 BCLC 683, the court concluded that the directors were in breach of their fiduciary duties as the unlawful payment of certain creditors had no discernible benefit to the company. It is important to note that there had been no breach of CA 1985 s 263, now repealed, but reliance on these technical rules provided no protection to the directors whose actions (including payment to themselves) did not stand up to the broader fiduciary duty test.

(3)   In *Colin Gwyer & Associates Ltd v London Wharf (Limehouse) Ltd* [2002] EWHC 2748 (Ch), [2003] 2 BCLC 153 the High Court ruled that a director who showed 'wilful blindness' to creditors and the company's

interests was in breach of his fiduciary duty. In this case the company was insolvent and the interests of creditors were not taken into account when a settlement to benefit one particular shareholder was agreed.

(4) In *Item Software (UK) Ltd v Fassihi* [2002] EWHC 3116 (Ch), [2003] 2 BCLC 1 the Chancery Division held that a director has an additional duty to disclose a breach of duty. In this case a director did not disclose his interest in an arrangement under discussion, as he was trying to divert business to his own company. This constituted fraudulent concealment and the company was entitled to recover damages from the director in respect of the contract that was, as a result, lost by the company.

(5) In *British Midland Tools v Midland International Tooling* [2003] All ER (D) 174 (Mar) the High Court held that directors had breached their fiduciary duties where they knew that a potential competitor was trying to poach members of the company's workforce and they did nothing to prevent it during the period in which they remained directors before they left to join the competitor.

It should also be noted that a director's inactivity may be a breach of duty and is unlikely to be a defence, as a director has a duty to participate in decision-making by a company and to challenge others on the Board. In *Lexi Holdings plc (in administration) v Luqman* [2009] EWCA Civ 117 the managing director had fraudulently taken almost £60m out of the company through fictitious directors' loans, false facility letters and misapplication of bank accounts and the company's two other directors were found to have breached their fiduciary duties by failing to be involved, investigate and challenge the managing director about his actions.

Two interesting cases outside the UK serve to further illustrate that, regardless of jurisdiction, directors must play an active role in overseeing and controlling how the companies to which they are appointed are run. First is the judgment handed down by the Grand Court of the Cayman Islands in the *Weavering Macro Fixed Income Fund (in liquidation) v Stefan Peterson and Hans Ekstrom* case (see para **1.32**), where awards for damages totalling $111m were made against two non-executive directors for failing to fulfil their duty to supervise the hedge fund. The second is the Federal Court of Australia's judgment in *Australian Securities and Investments Commission v Healey (No 2)* [2011] FCA 1003 in which the CEO was ordered to pay AUS $30,000 plus a share of costs; the CFO was disqualified for two years; and six non-executive directors were ordered to share the costs of the case for breaching their duties by failing to exercise the level of care and diligence expected of a reasonable person when reviewing and approving Centro Group's financial reports. Significant deficiencies in Centro Group's financial reports were not questioned by the directors, despite all of them being aware of a number of liabilities which had been omitted or classified incorrectly in the accounts.

Where there has been a breach of duty, the court has power pursuant to CA 2006 s 1157 to exempt a director from action for negligence, default, breach of duty or breach of trust where it considers that he acted honestly and reasonably having regard to all the circumstances. However, relief is not always forthcoming. For example, in *Globalink Telecommunications Ltd v Wilmbury Ltd* [2002] EWHC 1988 (QB), [2002] BCC 958 a nominee director on instruction from his principal, who was an undischarged bankrupt, negotiated an agreement to sell the company's assets whilst the other directors and shareholders were out of the country. The nominee director applied for relief under s 727 (now repealed and replaced by s 1157) but it was not granted as it was considered that he had not acted honestly and reasonably, as he did not have authority to negotiate agreements without his fellow directors.

Breach of statutory duties   5.30

The many statutes which impose duties on directors each contain provisions detailing sanctions that can be imposed if such duties are breached, together with those persons who can enforce them. CA 2006 itself contains some 250 offences, the majority of which are 'summary offences' and, as such, would be brought before and considered by magistrates and consequently result in a fine rather than a custodial sentence.

Unless specifically stated in the relevant statute, criminal liability for acts of the company rests with the company and not the directors. Having said this, in many sections of CA 2006 where duties are imposed on the company (eg for allotment of shares) subsections exist making 'every officer of the company who is in default' (meaning any officer of the company who knowingly and wilfully authorises or permits the default, refusal or contravention) accountable for the offence. The nature of accountability will be specified in the relevant section and may be a fine, imprisonment or both and, whilst other persons holding office in the company may be similarly liable for the offence, the directors are inevitably first in line for any action because of their position of control over management of the company. This includes 'shadow' and 'de facto' directors.

Some requirements under CA 2006 are the responsibility not of the company but of the directors; for example, responsibility for delivering annual accounts to Companies House. In these instances the directors are directly liable for their failure to comply, and the penalties and action to be taken are as stated in CA 2006. Indeed, in *Re Westmid Packaging Services Ltd* [1998] 2 BCLC 646 at 654, CA, the judge said 'any individual who undertakes the statutory and fiduciary obligations of being a company director should realise that these are inescapable personal responsibilities'.

A director may be held liable for offences committed under other statutes, such as the IA 1986 (fraudulent and wrongful trading), the Health & Safety At Work etc Act 1974 (HSWA 1974) (health and safety in the workplace), the Consumer Protection from Unfair Trading Regulations 2008 (SI 2008/1277) (unfair trading practices and making misleading trade descriptions to consumers), the Bribery Act 2010, and the Proceeds of Crime Act 2002 (giving or receiving of bribes or failure to implement adequate procedures to prevent bribery within organisations), and the Theft Act 1968 (theft and fraud offences), etc (see **CHAPTERS 9, 11, 12** and **13**). For example, in the Mabey & Johnson case summarised in para **13.64.4**(1) Messrs Mabey and Forsyth were successfully prosecuted and given prison sentences for allowing UN sanctions to be breached.

It should also be noted that a director may face penalties for failing to observe a legislative requirement relevant to his particular company's business and activities. For example, should the company be involved in gaming activities and breach the requirements of the Gambling Act 2005 the directors may be prosecuted in addition to the company where the offence occurred with their consent or connivance or was the result of their negligence. The penalty in this instance might involve a fine or imprisonment but, as the offences under the Gambling Act 2005 are largely summary offences, is unlikely to result in disqualification.

Personal liability   5.40

Directors must be aware of the possibility that they may incur personal liability for their acts or omissions in managing the company.

On the whole, directors are considered to be acting as 'agents' for their company and, as long as they make it clear to a third party that the transaction is with the company and not the directors themselves, they will not incur personal liability should any breach of contract or tortious act be committed by the company. However, directors may incur personal liability where they have personally guaranteed the company's obligations under a contract or arrangement or have failed to make clear to the third party that they are acting as an agent for the company.

The other probable development worth noting is the change proposed in the Small Business, Enterprise and Employment Bill, currently on its passage through Parliament, in which it is proposed that the Secretary of State will have authority to pursue directors who have been disqualified for 'compensation orders' on behalf of specific creditors, such as HMRC, or creditors generally. This will mean that a director could also be pursued for a monetary claim as a consequence of the actions or inactions that gave rise to disqualification.

Third parties 5.41

As illustrated in the table below, there are an extensive range of circumstances where directors may find themselves personally liable to third parties for loss resulting from a breach of duty or statutory offences committed by them.

Offence committed	Statutory provision/case example
(a) Making false or misleading statements or omitting information from listing particulars or a prospectus	FSMA 2000 s 90(1) for any resultant loss
(b) Irregularities in allotments	CA 2006 s 579(3)
(c) Fraudulent trading	CA 2006 s 993
(d) Failure to observe shareholders' rights of pre-emption	CA 2006 ss 563(2) and 568(4)
(e) Failure to obtain a trading certificate for a public company before entering into a transaction with a third party	CA 2006 s 767
(f) Where, in winding up the business of the company, it becomes apparent that it has been conducted with intent to defraud	IA 1986 s 213
(g) Where guilty of 'wrongful trading'	IA 1986 s 214 (*Official Receiver v Doshi* [2001] 2 BCLC 235, where a director responsible for wrongful trading was ordered to make an appropriate contribution to the company's assets)
(h) Where a director of an insolvent company carries on business using a prohibited name	IA 1986 s 217 (*Thorne v Silverleaf* [1994] 1 BCLC 637, [1994] BCC 109, CA)
(i) Non-payment of betting or gaming duties by the company	Betting and Gaming Duties Act 1981 (*Customs and Excise Comrs v Hedon Alpha Ltd* [1981] QB 818, [1981] 2 All ER 697, CA)
(j) Fraudulent evasion of VAT	FA 1986 s 14 (*Customs and Excise Comrs v Bassimeh* [1995] STC 910)

Offence committed	Statutory provision/case example
(k) Making a dishonest declaration or failing to register for VAT	FA 1986 s 13(1) (*Stevenson and Telford Building & Design Ltd v Customs and Excise Comrs* [1996] STC 1096, CA)
(l) Employing illegal immigrants and overstayers	Asylum and Immigration Act 1996
(m) Deliberately driving the company into liquidation to avoid NI debts	Proceeds of Crime Act 2002
(n) Knowingly giving preference to a creditor on a winding-up	IA 1986 ss 238–240 (*Re Living Images Ltd* [1996] 1 BCLC 348, [1996] BCC 112)
(o) Acting as a director whilst disqualified	CDDA 1986 s 15
(p) Health and safety offences	Health and Safety at Work etc Act 1974 (*R v Rollco Screw and Rivet Co Ltd* [1999] 2 Cr App Rep (S) 436, CA where directors were fined for asbestos contamination)
(q) Authorising payment of an illegal dividend	*Bairstow v Queens Moat Houses plc* [2000] 1 BCLC 549
(r) Paying a loan to a director without disclosing the loan to the shareholders and obtaining their approval	CA 2006 s 213
(s) Bribing, being bribed or bribing a foreign official	Bribery Act 2010 ss 2 and 10

It should also be noted that:

- Directors who fail to make their capacity as an 'agent' for the company clear when contracting with a third party may find themselves liable where the company defaults.

- Under the Social Security Act 1998 directors may be personally liable for unpaid National Insurance contributions where the company is insolvent and the directors are found to have acted fraudulently or negligently.

- Where a director knows, or ought to know, that a company is insolvent but gives false representations to a customer stating the contrary in order to secure further business, the director could be held personally liable for the tort of deceit (*Lindsay v O'Loughnane* [2010] EWHC 529 (QB)).

Regulators   **5.42**

There are many regulators, for example the Environment Agency, Health and Safety Executive, Pensions Regulator and FCA (formerly FSA) that may impose fines and penalties on directors as well as on the companies for which they act in respect of both their actions and inactions where they fall short of what is required by the regulator. A simple search through the various regulators' websites will reveal many such examples. By way of illustration, the enforcement notices section of the FSA's website (now the FCA) sets out numerous instances where significant fines have been imposed on directors of companies involved in the provision of regulated financial services for matters such as lack of appropriate supervision, mismanagement and misreporting figures in published annual accounts. By way of example:

- the Environment Agency fined Glazewing Ltd £3,600 for supplying soil contaminated with plastics, insulation foam, metals, cables and household waste to be spread on farm fields when it should have gone to landfill and it was ordered to pay full Environment Agency costs of £4,718 by Norwich Crown Court (Environment Agency notice, 21 November 2014);

- the FCA fined Barclays Bank £37.7m on 23 September 2014 for failing to adequately protect clients' safe custody assets worth £16.5bn;

- the FSA's fines in March 2012 of £400,000 on the finance director of Cattles plc and of £200,000 on the finance director of its subsidiary, Welcome Financial Services Limited, for publishing misleading information to investors;

- the FSA's fine in January 2012 on Mr Einhorn and his company Greenlight Capital Inc of £7.2m for engaging in market abuse and trading on inside information.

The FCA also has power to ban a regulated person from performing any function in relation to the regulated activity, which has been exercised on many occasions to protect the public. In addition, the FSMA 2000 made it possible for the UK Listing Authority (UKLA) to fine directors personally for breaches of the Listing Rules and the Disclosure and Transparency Rules (see para **9.40**) and not just the company which has primary responsibility for compliance. Whilst this authority is now exercised by the FCA, one such example is the FSA's £210,000 fine on Sir Ken Morrison for failing to notify the market of his own transactions in shares of in Morrisons in the manner required by the Disclosure and Transparency Rules (para **9.47**).

The company   5.43

Directors may also be required to account to the company, as opposed to a third party, for any loss or damage suffered by their failure to observe their duties to the company, eg:

(1)   where the directors authorise a loan to a director contrary to provisions of CA 2006 s 197, they are likely to face civil action for restitution of money (CA 2006 s 213) as well as criminal liability for their actions. It was held in *Currencies Direct Ltd v Ellis* [2002] 1 BCLC 193 that a loan to a director could be recovered where it had not been properly disclosed and approved by the shareholders of the company;

(2)   as well as being liable to a fine or conviction (CA 2006 s 183(2)), they would be held liable to repay monies to the company for contracts involving substantial property transactions and in which they failed to disclose their interest (CA 2006 s 195(3));

(3)   to compensate the company where, in the course of a winding up, it is apparent that they have misappropriated any of the company's money or property (IA 1986 s 212(3));

(4)   where a company has been fined for anti-competitive practices, it might bring a case against the directors on the grounds that they had breached their contracts and their fiduciary duties to the company. In *Safeway Stores Ltd v Twigger* [2010] EWHC 11 (Comm), [2010] All ER (D) 90 (Jan) the company brought a claim against the directors for anti-competitive practices in relation to sale of dairy products.

A director can also be guilty of theft from the company and of fraud and deceit.

The imposition of personal liability on directors in given circumstances emphasises the need for them to be conversant and compliant with their duties to avoid accounting financially for their acts or omissions.

Disqualification   5.50

In every compulsory liquidation, the Official Receiver has a duty to investigate the affairs of the company, the causes of its failure and the conduct of the company's directors and to report any unfit conduct by the directors to the Secretary of State with a view to bringing disqualification proceedings. Similarly when a company goes into creditors voluntary liquidation, has an administration order made against it, or an administrative receiver is appointed or a company is wound up by the court, the office-holder is required by the CDDA 1986 to report any unfit conduct to the Secretary of State.

Details of directors' disqualification orders and the penalties imposed on directors by the courts are frequently reported in the press and elsewhere. Although provisions enabling courts to disqualify persons from acting as directors have been in force for many years, courts are now imposing severe penalties on directors who fail to meet their statutory obligations and directors' actions are increasingly subjected to closer scrutiny. Directors need to ensure that they are fully aware of the precise nature of their obligations so that their conduct in managing the company cannot be called into question nor lead to personal liability or disqualification.

Figures published by the Insolvency Service for its 2013/14 financial year show that 1,208 directors were disqualified as a result of disqualification orders and voluntary disqualification undertakings, with an average length of disqualification period of 6.2 years. The number has increased slightly from 2012/13, and serves to demonstrate that the Secretary of State's calls for tougher sanctions on directors who fail to meet their duties are being put into effect and they do face a very realistic threat of disqualification, the effects of which will be substantial.

Obviously we are in difficult economic times and Insolvency Service statistics show the most common reason for disqualification is conduct rendering the directors unfit by, for example, failing to account for and pay Crown debts, irregular accounting matters, transactions to the detriment of creditors, criminal matters, misappropriation of assets and breach of statutory obligations. There were also a few disqualification orders made for trading whilst insolvent and trading through 'phoenix' companies.

The Insolvency Service operates a disqualified directors 24-hour enforcement hotline and encourages members of the public to name disqualified directors who are blatantly continuing to act as directors despite disqualification orders made against them. Furthermore Companies House has a register of disqualified directors on its website (www.companieshouse.gov.uk) in an attempt to publicly 'name and shame' offenders.

Legislation   **5.51**

The law regarding disqualification of directors is consolidated in CDDA 1986 and allows for either:

- automatic disqualification as an outcome of defined events or occurrences; or

- application to be made to the court for a disqualification order to be brought.

Where a director has failed to meet obligations required by other legislation, such as CA 2006, FSMA 2000, IA 1986, HSWA 1974 or the Enterprise Act 2002 (EnA 2002), an application may be made for a disqualification order. The application will be made under the relevant section of CDDA 1986 for decision by the court.

Furthermore, where a person is an undischarged bankrupt (CDDA 1986 s 11) or has failed to pay under a county court administration order (CDDA 1986 s 12), he is prohibited (rather than disqualified) from acting as a director. It was held in *R v Brockley* [1994] 1 BCLC 606, CA that persons adjudged bankrupt must ensure that the bankruptcy order has been discharged before they engage in any prohibited activities in relation to management of a company.

A person may also be prohibited by IA 1986 s 216 from being a director of a company with a 'prohibited' name, meaning the exact or a similar name of a company that has gone into insolvent liquidation in the last 12 months.

Often the action for disqualification follows conviction for other offences. For example, on 13 September 2010 Mr Mulholland of BI Industries (Holdings) was convicted of one charge of theft under the Theft Act 1968 and eight charges of fraudulently removing funds contrary to the IA 1986 (BIS, 13 September 2010). After further investigation he was disqualified from acting as a director for 14 years under the CDDA 1986.

Directors should note that BIS has been consulting on extending the reach of the CDDA 1986 to require courts to take account of any misconduct overseas when deciding whether or not to disqualify a director in the UK. BIS is also considering whether to extend provisions of the CA 2006 to prevent those restricted from acting as directors overseas from being appointed directors in the UK.

Implications of a disqualification order   5.52

Once disqualified, the person who is the subject of the disqualification order may not, without leave of the court, be a director of a company, act as receiver of a company's property or as an insolvency practitioner, or directly or indirectly be concerned with or take part in the promotion, formation or management of a company (CDDA 1986 s 1). These same restrictions apply where a person has given a voluntary disqualification undertaking (CDDA 1986 s 1A).

To act in contravention of a disqualification order is a criminal offence and is punishable by legal process, the penalty for which is up to two years' imprisonment or an unlimited fine.

In illustration, a director, Mr Welbourn, was sentenced to two years' imprisonment at Lincoln Crown Court after pleading guilty to two counts of fraudulent trading and one count of managing a company while disqualified as a director (Insolvency Service, press release, 23 April 2012). Mr Welbourn admitted that from 2003 to 2010, despite having been disqualified as a director in 2008, he deceived creditors by running a series of haulage companies which were only kept afloat using some £300k of employees' income tax and National Insurance contributions. Mr Welbourn's sentence comprised 15 months for two counts of fraudulent trading (see para **5.53.4**), and nine months for managing a company whilst disqualified as a director. Disqualified directors should take heed of the Investigation Officer's comment in the case that 'This sends out a clear message that the Department for Business, Innovation and Skills will take action against disqualified directors'.

Grounds for disqualification 5.53

The grounds for disqualification under CDDA 1986 are many and varied but normally involve culpable mismanagement. When the court is deciding whether a person's conduct, whilst a director or shadow director of a company, makes him unfit to be involved in the management of a company the court will consider the matters set out in Sch 1 Parts I and II to CDDA 1986 (see **APPENDIX 3**) to determine whether there has been any breach of the director's duties in respect of the Companies Acts and Insolvency Acts.

An increasing number of applications for disqualification, coupled with substantial fines, are being made where directors have failed to meet their obligations required by statutes other than the Companies Acts, such as the HSWA 1974 and EnA 2002, etc. Understandably the courts have adopted the view that, where risks to the health and safety of those in the workplace resulting from the director's negligence are high, the penalties should be equally severe and disqualification is applicable.

Application for disqualification is made under the relevant section of CDDA 1986 and, depending on which section applies, disqualification may be automatic, as an outcome of certain defined events, or discretionary (ss 2–5).

Disqualification for unfitness where company is insolvent 5.53.1

Pursuant to CDDA 1986 s 6, the court is obliged to make a disqualification order against a director where a company is or has been insolvent and the court is satisfied that the director's conduct makes him 'unfit' to be involved in management of a company. Figures issued by the Insolvency Service for the financial year 2008/09 show that there were 1,024 disqualification orders brought by the disqualification service under CDDA 1986 s 6. The minimum period for disqualification for unfitness is two years and the maximum period 15 years, which is reserved for particularly serious cases.

Craig Whyte, the ex-chairman of The Rangers Football Club plc, was disqualified as a director for 15 years with effect from 21 October 2014 for failing to promote the success of the company and to avoid his own conflict of interest (Insolvency Service, press release, 30 September 2014). He was disqualified for the harm he caused by using cash to fund purchase of the company's own shares, when it was needed for investment; his lack of regard for proper corporate behaviour, by repeatedly failing to consult other directors on important decisions, meaning his behaviour and decisions went unchallenged; and causing the company to disregard its tax obligations. He also caused the subsidiary, Tixway UK Ltd, to fail to maintain adequate accounting records. Through his behaviour he clearly breached his statutory duty to ensure the company was run properly, for the benefit of the creditors, shareholders and football fans, and paid the penalty of disqualification from acting as a director until October 2029.

Mr Abdulkadir Aydin, sole director of Goldtrail Travel Ltd, was disqualified on 8 May 2013 by the High Court in London for the maximum period of 15 years for gross mismanagement of the company's affairs (Insolvency Service, press release, 10 May 2013). Goldtrail Travel collapsed and went into administration in July 2010 with debts of over £2m, 23,000 holidaymakers were left stranded and another 110,000 people suffered ruined holiday plans. Goldtrail Travel's failure cost the CAA's Air Travel Trust and ATOL approximately £20m, of which nearly £6m was for repatriation alone. Investigation by the Insolvency Service, assisted by a number of law enforcement bodies and regulatory agencies including SOCA and the CAA, found numerous instances of mismanagement by Mr Aydin. These included involvement in secret share sale agreements for personal gain contrary to CAA licensing requirements, providing inaccurate information to the CAA, receipt of commission personally for purchase of airline tickets with no benefit to the company, and unexplained payments totalling over £6m to Turkish companies owned by his family, some of which were made in the week leading up to the company being placed in administration.

In another case Mr Mario Rea, director of DMR Assets Limited, was disqualified for seven years in proceedings brought by Airdrie Sherrif Court under CDDA 1986 s 6(1) for financial irregularities involving failure to explain receipts into and payments from the company's accounts of substantial amounts of money prior to the company being placed in administration (Insolvency Service, press release, 21 December 2011 and Issue 27034 of the Edinburgh Gazette, Notice 194). In the absence of explanation, the transactions were considered to be detrimental to creditors, who were owed some £3m.

In *Re Structural Concrete Ltd* [2000] 26 LS Gaz R 35, Ch D (Blackburne J) it was held on appeal that a deliberate policy by the directors of withholding Crown debts to finance the company's business was misconduct for which the director who had day-to-day control of these matters was disqualified for four years and the other directors were disqualified for two years.

In *Official Receiver v Doshi* [2001] 2 BCLC 235, a director of an insolvent company was disqualified for 12 years for unfitness resulting from false invoicing and evading VAT.

A director can also be found unfit for failing to act. For example:

- in *Re Galeforce Pleating Co Ltd* [1999] 2 BCLC 704 a director who was inactive but continued to receive remuneration without carrying out the duties reasonably expected of him was found to be unfit and disqualified;

- in *Re Bradcrown; Official Receiver v Ireland* [2002] BCC 428 it was found that a director who exercised no independent judgment and relied solely on professional advice and the controller of the company when a complex demerger of business was agreed, resulting in liquidation, was found to be unfit and disqualified for two years.

Furthermore, a shadow director can be disqualified for unfitness (*Re Tasbian Ltd (No 3)* [1991] BCC 435) as can a company acting as a director of another company (*Official Receiver v Brady* [1999] BCC 258 in which two companies acting as directors of other companies were disqualified for the maximum 15-year period).

Conviction of an indictable offence   5.53.2

The court *may* make a disqualification order against a person who has been convicted of an indictable offence in connection with the promotion, formation, management or liquidation of a company or with the receivership or management of a company's property (CDDA 1986 s 2). The offence must have some bearing on the management of a company and where the director is convicted summarily the maximum period of disqualification is five years and in other cases is 15 years (CDDA 1986 s 2(3)). By way of example, two directors of Blue Index, Messrs Sanders and Swallow, and Mr Sanders' wife Miranda were sentenced for insider dealing contrary to s 52 of the Criminal Justice Act 1993. Mr Sanders, the driving force behind the criminality, was sentenced to four years in custody and disqualified as a director for five years as his actions were calculated acts of dishonesty making him unsuitable to be involved in the management of a company (FSA, press release, 20 June 2012).

Similarly, conduct which amounts to performance of duties in an unlawful manner such as carrying on insurance business without the required authorisation may result in disqualification under this section of CDDA 1986.

Persistent breaches of statutory obligations   **5.53.3**

A disqualification order may be made against a person for a maximum of five years for persistent breaches of statutory obligations, such as failure to submit annual accounts, returns or any other document required to be submitted to the Registrar of Companies (CDDA 1986 s 3). On 24 March 2011 the DTI accepted a nine-year disqualification undertaking from Mr Dobbin, a director of Timber Frame Homes Ltd, which went into liquidation in 2008 owing £400k to creditors. The unfit conduct demonstrated by Mr Dobbin included financing the business by withholding payment of Crown debts, persistently failing to submit annual returns and accounts and failing to pay dividends as required by the company's articles which all were in breach of the leave to act he had previously been granted (Northern Ireland Executive, news release, 14 April 2011).

Fraudulent trading   **5.53.4**

A disqualification order may be made against a person where, in the course of winding up a company, a person appears guilty of an offence under CA 2006 s 993 for deliberately intending to defraud creditors, or where that person has committed some other fraud or breach of duty whilst an officer of the company (CDDA 1986 s 4). For example:

- in *Secretary of State for Business, Innovation and Skills v Nadhan Singh Potiwal* [2012] EWHC 3723 (Ch) a director was disqualified for 13 years for causing the company to participate in transactions linked to VAT fraud and wrongfully claim over £2.6m of VAT. Whilst disqualification proceedings were commenced by the Insolvency Service at the High Court in Manchester, on 5 March 2013 Mr Potiwal dropped his defence and gave a disqualification undertaking not to promote, manage, or be a director of a limited company until 2026;

- six directors of UKLI Ltd, a company involved in a £70m land-banking scam, vastly inflating the value of land it sold to people, have been disqualified for a total of 41 years. Whilst five of the directors gave disqualification undertakings in 2010 agreeing not to act as directors for a total of 29 years, a sixth, Mr Chohan, chose to defend court action brought by the Insolvency Service. Unfortunately for Mr Chohan the investigation found he had acted as a director despite not being formally appointed; operated a collective investment scheme without the required FSA regulation; advanced unsecured loans exceeding £12m to other businesses owned, controlled or connected with him; and made dividend payments to himself of over £1m which the company could not afford. As a consequence on 25 March 2013 he was given a 12-year disqualification order by the High Court in London (Insolvency Service, press release, 2 April 2013);

- on 21 December 2011 Mr Yaqub, a director of property company Maple Grow Ltd, was disqualified as a director for 15 years by Birmingham City Court for a property scam whereby mortgage loans of £3.8m were obtained on six properties when Mr Yaqub and other directors knew they were worth less than £1m (Insolvency Service announcement, 21 December 2011). Four other directors gave voluntary disqualification undertakings totalling 32 years (para **5.60**);

- a six-year disqualification undertaking was accepted from Mr Mullan, a director of the company Irish Polymers Ltd, for unfit conduct involving allowing the company to continue to trade at the expense of creditors, failing to file accounts and annual returns and permitting payment to be made to a directors in preference to creditors (Northern Ireland Executive Press Release, 17 December 2010); and

- as well as being imprisoned for periods of eight and seven years respectively, Messrs Shepherd and Scott were disqualified as directors for periods of 15 and ten years and a third director also received a prison term for conducting online ticket fraud through the Xclusive group of companies. The companies involved failed to supply over £5m of tickets sold for the Beijing Olympics and other summer music events and, given their involvement in this fraudulent trading as well as money laundering, both were considered totally unfit to be in control of a company. Confiscation orders were also made against them for a total £1.75m (Serious Fraud Office, press release, 11 July 2011).

The lengthy disqualification periods being applied reflect the serious nature of these cases. In many instances the directors' unfit conduct has caused substantial loss and financial hardship to others and it is expected that the Insolvency Service and courts will continue to pursue and apply stiff penalties for those who offend in order to protect the public going forward.

Disqualification on summary conviction   **5.53.5**

Where an individual has been convicted of a summary offence as a consequence of continuous failure to meet his statutory obligations to file returns, accounts or other documents, he *may* be the subject of a disqualification order (CDDA 1986 s 5) for a maximum period of five years. The failure must have been persistent and have given rise to a number of convictions or default orders in the previous five years (CDDA 1986 s 5(3) and (4)).

Public interest   **5.53.6**

Pursuant to CDDA 1986 s 8, the Secretary of State has complementary powers to apply to the court for a disqualification order where it appears to be in the public interest that such an order be made. This may occur following a report by his inspectors or from information or documents obtained under sections of CA 1985 or FSMA 2000. There is no requirement for the company to be insolvent before such application is made and the maximum period for disqualification is 15 years. Consideration may be given to Sch 1 to CDDA 1986 (see **Appendix 3**) when determining whether a director's conduct makes him unfit to be involved in the management of a company.

In the case *Re Looe Fish Ltd* [1993] BCLC 1160 investigation by the DTI (since renamed BIS) revealed that a director had used his power to allot shares in the company to keep control of the company. The director was disqualified for two and a half years, as use of his power in this manner was a clear breach of his duty.

Directors guilty of FSA breaches may be disqualified, as was the case in *Secretary of State for Business, Innovation and Skills v Aaron* [2009] EWHC 3263 (Ch). Two directors were disqualified for mis-selling financial investments to consumers and for failing to keep proper records as it demonstrated a lack of commercial probity, which the public needed to be protected against.

Wrongful trading   **5.53.7**

A disqualification order may be made under CDDA 1986 s 10 for a maximum period of 15 years against a director of a company in insolvent liquidation where the director has allowed the company to continue trading whilst insolvent. In this instance the director will also be required to make a contribution to the company's assets for insolvent trading pursuant to IA 1986 s 214 (see para **14.53**).

In *Secretary of State for Trade and Industry v Creegan* [2002] 1 BCLC 99 the Court of Appeal clarified that both elements of the 'wrongful trading' test, namely that a company is trading whilst insolvent and there is no reasonable prospect that it will be able to meet creditors' claims, must be present to constitute unfitness for the purposes of disqualification.

Competition infringements   **5.53.8**

EnA 2002 added ss 9A–9E to CDDA 1986. Section 9A requires that the court must make a disqualification order against a person where the company of which he is a director commits a breach of competition law and the court considers that the director's conduct makes him unfit to be concerned in the management of a company. In this instance, the orders are called competition disqualification orders ('CDO').

Application for disqualification may be made by the Office of Fair Trading (OFT) or a specified regulator, and the maximum period of disqualification is 15 years (CDDA 1986 s 9A(9)).

It is worth noting that a director may be liable to disqualification where he had reasonable grounds to suspect a breach of competition law and did nothing about it, or ought to have known that the company's conduct infringed competition law. Consequently, directors need to know what protections are in place in their companies to prevent price-fixing, market-sharing, limitation of production, bid-rigging and other anti-competitive behaviour, and to monitor performance to identify any possible breaches.

In August 2010 the OFT published revised guidance on 'Director Disqualification Orders in Competition Cases' from which it is clear that the OFT will actively seek to disqualify a director not only where they uncover evidence that the director was responsible for a breach of competition law but also where the director ought to have known about the breach. Ignorance of a situation or a lack of knowledge of a practice being followed will not be an excuse, as all directors have a duty to make sure they know and fully understand their responsibilities under competition law and to make sure appropriate policies, control measures, monitoring and review processes are in place to prevent infringements.

The first convictions for a cartel offence since criminal prosecution powers were given to the OFT under EnA 2002 were secured on 10 June 2008 when three UK businessmen were sentenced to imprisonment for two and a half to three years for cartel offences and disqualified from acting as company directors for periods of between five and seven years. Messrs Whittle, Brammar and Allison pleaded guilty at Southwark Crown Court to dishonestly participating in a cartel to allocate markets and customers, restrict supplies, fix prices and rig bids for the supply of marine hose and ancillary equipment (*R v Whittle, Brammar, Allison* [2008] EWCA Crim 2560).

These first criminal prosecutions send a clear message to individuals and companies about the seriousness with which UK law views cartel behaviour. The OFT has announced it will actively seek to investigate and prosecute individuals for competition infringements, as well as continuing to fine the companies concerned. As the company fines process is not perceived as sufficient deterrent, the OFT has also announced a likely increase in arrests of executives whilst investigations of possible offences are carried out and in the deployment of CDOs as sanctions on offending directors.

In addition, as identified in para **5.60**, instead of applying for a CDO, the OFT may accept a voluntary disqualification undertaking from a person.

Obtaining leave of the court to act   **5.53.9**

Pursuant to CDDA 1986 s 17 a director who is the subject of a disqualification order may apply to the court for leave to act as a director or to be involved in the management of a company. Whether or not the court grants leave to act depends on the director's behaviour and the circumstances giving rise to his disqualification as well as the overriding need to protect the public. A wealth of cases concerning leave of the court to act continues to develop, a very small sample of which is set out below to illustrate how the court derives its decision.

- In *Re Britannia Home Centres Ltd* [2001] 2 BCLC 63, the court queried the wisdom of allowing a disqualified director leave to continue to act as director of a one-man company.

- In *Re China Jazz Worldwide plc* [2003] EWHC 2665, a director was granted leave to act as director of another company on the basis that his disqualification was not for more than five years, he had not acted dishonestly and the other company needed his services and had procedures in place to ensure proper accountability.

- In *Secretary of State for Trade and Industry v Barnett* [1998] 2 BCLC 64 it was held that, whilst the director had not acted dishonestly, two of the companies in which he was involved had collapsed at the expense of creditors. It was therefore not considered appropriate for the court to grant leave to act.

- In *Re Barings plc, Secretary of State for Trade and Industry v Baker (No 5)* [1999] 1 BCLC 262 leave of the court to act as an unpaid non-executive director was granted where fellow directors submitted affidavits to the court stating that they valued the director's advice and expertise in company management. The court decided that the need for the director to act was balanced with the need to protect the public. Leave was granted on the condition that the director continued in a non-executive capacity and did not enter into an employment contract or receive director's fees from the company concerned.

- In *Secretary of State for Trade and Industry v Rosenfield* [1999] BCC 413 leave of the court to act was granted as failure to do so may have resulted in serious consequences for employees of the company concerned. In granting leave to act, the court required the production of quarterly accounts and the appointment of a person with financial expertise to the Board.

- In *Shuttleworth v Secretary of State for Trade and Industry* [2000] BCC 204 the High Court granted leave for a disqualified director to take part in the management of a company in circumstances where the disqualification resulted from inadequate management rather than dishonesty or a lack of probity and the new company to which the individual was seeking appointment as a director was unlimited.

However, it should be noted that severe penalties will be applied where a director breaches the terms of a disqualification order. For example, Mr Boll, a disqualified director who breached his disqualification undertaking, was sentenced to six months in prison and made the subject of a ten-year disqualification order. Mr Boll pleaded guilty to acting as a director of JP Diamonds Ltd contrary to CDDA 1986 s 13 as he was subject to a 14-year disqualification undertaking imposed in 2007. This prohibited him from acting as a director or being involved in the management of any company without leave of court which he failed to obtain (Insolvency Service, press release, 8 October 2012).

Disqualification of shadow and de facto directors   5.54

It is important to note that disqualification orders have been successfully brought against shadow directors where their conduct rendered them unfit to be involved in management of a company. In *Secretary of State for Trade and Industry v Deverell* [2001] Ch 340 and *Secretary of State for Trade and Industry v Jones* [1999] BCC 336 it was held that persons found to exercise a real influence over the companies' affairs as shadow directors could be disqualified.

Furthermore, de facto directors can be disqualified as unfit under CDDA 1986 s 6 where the court is satisfied that the person was, or has been, a director, in fact, if not in name, of a company which has become insolvent and that the director's conduct renders him unfit to be involved in management of a company: *Re Sykes (Butchers) Ltd (in liquidation), Secretary of State for Trade and Industry v Richardson* [1998] 1 BCLC 110. Similarly, in *Secretary of State for Trade and Industry v Jones* [1999] BCC 336 a management consultant was found to be a de facto director and subject to disqualification.

In *Secretary of State for Trade & Industry v Hall and Nuttall* [2006] EWHC 1995 (Ch) two persons who were de facto directors of 42 insolvent companies were found guilty of misfeasance and breaches of their duties as directors in causing the payment of unlawful dividends totalling £13m.

Voluntary disqualification undertaking   5.60

The idea of accepting a voluntary undertaking by a person not to act as a director or be involved in the management of a company as an alternative to pursuing costly and often prolonged formal disqualification proceedings was first addressed and successfully applied in *Re Carecraft Construction Co Ltd* [1994] 1 WLR 172, in which the director reached agreement with the Secretary of State to proceed to court on the understanding that a disqualification order would be made for an agreed period. The procedure established by this case has been applied in many subsequent cases, and statistics published by the Insolvency Service for 2013/14 show that some 80% of disqualifications secured in the period were by way of disqualification undertaking from the individuals concerned.

The need for a 'fast track' process was further addressed in ss 5–8 of the Insolvency Act 2000, which amended provisions of the CDDA 1986. The amended provisions permit a director of an insolvent company, who recognises and accepts there are grounds for his disqualification, to give a voluntary undertaking to the Secretary of State not to act as a director or be involved in the management of a company.

The Secretary of State will consider the offer to give a disqualification undertaking and, where he considers the director's conduct in relation to the company makes him unfit to be involved in management of a company and that it is in the public interest that he should accept the undertaking instead of proceeding or applying with an application for a disqualification, he may accept the undertaking (CDDA 1986 ss 7(2A) and 8(2A)). Account will be taken of the matters for determining unfitness, detailed in Sch 1 to CDDA 1986 (see **APPENDIX 3**), when the Secretary of State is considering whether to accept the undertaking (CDDA 1986 s 9(1A)).

As well as giving a voluntary disqualification undertaking, the director must provide a 'statement of unfitness' setting out the director's own admission of events and conduct that he considers makes him unfit. This requirement was clarified by the Court of Appeal in *Secretary of State for Trade and Industry v Davies* [2001] All ER (D) 27 (Sep), CA.

The voluntary undertaking has the same legal effect as a disqualification order as set out in para **5.52**, but is intended to save the time and money often necessary when obtaining a disqualification order. This is particularly important where the company is insolvent and funds are to be recovered from directors for payment to creditors, etc (see para **5.40**).

The maximum period for which a disqualification undertaking may be given is 15 years and the minimum period is two years (CDDA 1986 s 1A(2)).

This relatively straightforward procedure, whilst being no less onerous on a director than a disqualification order, undoubtedly has a number of discernible advantages where a director recognises his past conduct renders him liable for disqualification, including:

- the speed with which a voluntary undertaking can be agreed with the Disqualification Unit minimises the time, money and resources that would otherwise be expended in defending court action;

- by reaching early agreement, disqualification will take effect sooner and consequently expire at an earlier date; and

- there is less potential for adverse publicity than were protracted court action to commence.

Such benefits accrue not only for the offending director as, by obtaining a voluntary disqualification undertaking from a director in a relatively short space of time, the Secretary of State will have more time to consider other cases. Another significant benefit is that directors who are unfit are brought to account and disqualified earlier, which is undoubtedly in the public interest. Indeed, figures published by the Insolvency Service for its 2011/12 financial year show that of 1,151 directors disqualified, 80% were achieved by way of voluntary undertakings.

In one high-profile example, Peter Ridsdale, former chairman of Leeds United, Barnsley and Cardiff City football clubs, gave a voluntary undertaking to be disqualified from acting as a company director and from managing or in any way controlling a company for seven and a half years, following an investigation by the Insolvency Service into his conduct as a director of WH Sports Group Ltd (WHSG) (Insolvency Service, press release, 3 October 2012). The investigation found that he acted improperly and in breach of his duties to WHSG by causing payments for invoices raised by WHSG to be paid into his personal bank accounts to the detriment of WHSG and its creditors; failing to disclose these transactions to WHSG's liquidator; and failing to ensure that WHSG complied with its statutory obligations to make corporation tax, PAYE and National Insurance contributions and VAT returns and payments to HMRC when due.

Ratification of breaches of duty   5.70

The company has power in certain circumstances, whether by resolution of the director or members, to ratify a director's breach of duty after the event, for example where:

- shares were allotted for an improper purpose;

- the director failed to disclose his interest in a contract;

- the director's personal profit or advantage from a transaction was not disclosed;

- the director's duty of skill and care was not exercised, provided it was not fraudulent;

- the act was outside the company's powers.

However, breaches cannot be ratified where they infringe shareholders' rights, are fraudulent or dishonest, or involve a secret profit being made by a director at the direct expense of the company.

6 Statutory duties of directors

6 Statutory duties of directors

Historically the general duties required of directors were set out in common law, augmented by an extensive range of specific duties imposed by statute. Following the enactment of CA 2006 ss 170–177 directors' general duties are now codified in statute.

In addition to these codified general duties under CA 2006 (detailed in **CHAPTER 4**) there are other statutory duties which a director has to the company. These are broadly based to take account of the many aspects of the director's role and, whilst those relating specifically to his office are covered extensively in CA 2006, many other statutes impose duties on directors to protect employees, shareholders, customers, creditors and the environment. Directors may find themselves liable for offences, committed by them directly or by the company, which have been caused by their consent, connivance or neglect.

This chapter concentrates largely on duties imposed by CA 2006. Those duties placed on directors by other statutes, together with their non-statutory obligations, are discussed in detail in subsequent chapters.

Duties for directors arising from CA 2006 can be broadly divided into those of an administrative and compliance nature and those which restrict the directors' activities and require them to disclose certain information as follows:

Administrative/compliance matters	Restrictions and disclosure requirements
● Appointment and removal of company officers	● Disclose interests in contracts and other transactions
● Maintaining the company's statutory books and records	● Disclose interests in shares and debentures (listed companies only)
● Preparation and submission of forms and returns to the Registrar of Companies	● Restrictions on property transactions
● Filing of annual accounts	● Loans to directors
● Retaining records and company documents for specified periods	● Service contracts

Administrative/compliance matters	Restrictions and disclosure requirements
• Display and use of the company name	• Takeovers and mergers
• Indemnity insurance	• Investigations

Whilst many of these are duties for which the company as a whole is responsible, the directors, by virtue of their position and the authority they have as policy-makers, are ultimately responsible for ensuring compliance. Often directors choose to delegate responsibility for these matters to, for example, the company secretary, professional adviser or a designated legal or secretariat department. However it is important to note that they remain ultimately responsible for compliance and any breach, for which the company and those directors in default will be liable to a fine and possibly a daily default fine for continued contravention. Furthermore, the directors may face disqualification for their acts or omissions and, where a serious breach of duty has occurred, be liable to imprisonment. They must, therefore, ensure that any persons to whom they delegate responsibility for carrying out these duties have the necessary experience, qualifications and knowledge to discharge the duties delegated to them satisfactorily.

Appointment and removal of company officers   6.10

The directors, by virtue of their position in the company and their overall knowledge of legislative requirements, have a duty to shareholders and others who have dealings with the company to ensure that officers required by statute are appointed and approval of these appointments, or any change thereto, is obtained in the correct manner. As discussed below, all companies are required to have a director or directors, public companies must have a company secretary and all companies, subject to certain exemptions, an auditor. These appointments are made or changed by a simple resolution of the Board.

Directors   6.11

Appointment   6.11.1

As discussed in para **1.52**, the appointment of a director subsequent to incorporation can, subject to provisions in the company's Articles, be made either by resolution of the directors or the members (Table A regs 78 and 79 or for companies who adopt the Model Articles under CA 2006, article 17 for private companies limited by shares and guarantee companies and article 20 for public companies).

Once appropriate approval to the appointment has been obtained at a meeting of the directors or a general meeting, the directors must ensure that the following procedural requirements are carried out:

- Companies House must be notified of the appointment on prescribed form AP01 (or AP02 for a corporate director) within 14 days which means that, at the time of appointment or immediately thereafter, the director must be provided with this form to complete the required details and sign to confirm his consent to act. However, signature of the Companies House form alone is not in itself conclusive evidence of consent to act if the person did not know what they were signing (*Re CEN Connections Ltd* [2000] BCC 917). The director must also be made aware of his duty to inform the Registrar of Companies of any change in his personal details (CA 2006 s 167(1)(b)).

- Details of the appointment must be entered in the Register of Directors and Register of Director's Residential Address (paras **6.11.3**, **6.21.1** and **6.21.2**).

- Specimen signatures must be supplied to the bank if the director is to be a signatory to the account and, in any case, they need to be notified of the appointment.

- The newly appointed director must be requested to disclose any interest he may have in shares of and contracts with the company at the time of his appointment and ensure that he is aware of his continuing obligation to notify the company of any changes in interest (paras **6.60–6.80** below).

- It may be appropriate for the director to have a service contract. Where the contract proposed cannot be terminated before a term of two years, it will be necessary for this contract to be approved by ordinary resolution of the members and the directors must ensure that the necessary approval is obtained (para **6.104**).

- If appropriate, the company's insurance brokers will need to be notified of the appointment to include the new director in any professional indemnity policy or directors' and officers' indemnity policy, etc, that may be held by the company (paras **3.120** and **6.120**).

The above matters also need to be considered for appointment of an 'alternate director' where permitted by the Articles (para **1.34**). The directors will need to check the required method of appointment, which for a company which has adopted Table A is by notice in writing from the director making the appointment as approved at a meeting of the directors (reg 68). For companies adopting the Model Articles under CA 2006 this provision is contained in article 25 of the public company Model Articles and is not contained in the Model Articles for private companies limited by shares or guarantee companies.

In addition, the duty to notify Companies House of the appointment (para **6.31**) and make an entry in the Register of Directors (para **6.21**) must not be overlooked.

It should also be noted that it is now permitted for a director's form of appointment to be submitted to Companies House electronically in which case the director must confirm his 'consent to act' by providing three items of personal information (see para **6.31**).

Eligibility   **6.11.2**

Directors have a responsibility, when appointing or laying before the members a resolution to appoint another person as a director, to check that the person is eligible for appointment in terms of the requirements set out in para **1.40** and, at the same time, ensure that:

- where the Articles of a public company permit a director to be appointed by the members, the resolution for their appointment must be proposed and voted on as a separate resolution (CA 2006 s 160);

- any provision in the Articles for a maximum number of directors is not exceeded by the proposed appointment;

- where there is a share qualification in the Articles requiring directors to hold a specified number of shares in the company, the director being appointed has already obtained the required shares, or that he does so within two months of his appointment, or such shorter period as specified in the Articles. The directors must check the situation, as if at the end of the period the director has not obtained the required number of shares he must vacate the office and, if he continues as a director, will be liable to a fine;

- that the proposed director satisfies the minimum age requirement for appointment (as set out in para **1.40**).

Service address   **6.11.3**

Directors and company secretaries are able to use a service address for the purpose of the public record, restrict access to details of their residential address and suppress availability of residential address details on documents and records at Companies House. This enables directors not only to protect their privacy, but also to preserve a greater degree of separation between their work and home lives.

A director or company secretary is able to use any address as a service address without need to demonstrate a threat of serious violence or intimidation, as was required under the old 'confidentiality order' regime.

The service address could continue to be the director or secretary's residential address or, alternatively, be changed to his usual office address, the company's registered office or any other suitable address.

However, an important point to note is that it must be possible to physically 'serve' documents at the chosen address and, where required, for delivery to be acknowledged by, for example, obtaining a signature. This is particularly important as, where it becomes evident to the Registrar of Companies that documents cannot be effectively served on the director at the service address, the Registrar has power to restore the director's residential address to the public record.

The choice of a suitable service address is therefore important, as in ensuring there is an effective system or procedure for dealing with official correspondence received to avoid it being lost in the 'ether', or the filing records of a large office.

The director's or secretary's address recorded in a company's registers of directors and secretaries and appearing on the public record at Companies House immediately prior to 1 October 2009 is deemed to be the service address, save where one has already been granted under a confidentiality order. In this case, the existing service address automatically became the service address.

For new directors and secretaries appointed after 1 October 2009, the service address will need to be recorded in the relevant register of directors and secretaries and be notified to Companies House.

It is expected that many directors will take advantage of being able to register a service address, although they might choose to wait until they move house before doing so where they would not be able to suppress details of their current home address appearing on the public record (para **6.11.4** below).

Residential address   **6.11.4**

The director's residential address must be notified to Companies House, but will not form part of the public record. In addition, where a director's service address is the same as his residential address, nothing on records available from Companies House will show this is the case.

Unless the service address is a director's home address, the residential address will be protected information, and restrictions on use and disclosure will apply. This means that a company must not use or disclose protected information about one of its directors unless: communicating with the director; sending particulars to the Registrar in compliance with a requirement of the Companies

Acts; it is required to do so under court order where, for example, effective service of documents has not been possible at a director's service address; or consent has been obtained from the director.

Similarly, the Registrar must not use or disclose protected information unless communicating with the director or required to do so under court order. The Registrar will, however, be permitted to disclose protected information to a specified public authority in response to receipt by the Registrar of a statement confirming that the information will only be used for performance of that authority's public function. These public authorities might include the FCA, HSE, Charities Commission, or HMRC amongst others.

Additionally the Registrar may disclose protected information in response to a request from a credit reference agency, subject to satisfying certain conditions based on data protection principles and provided the director does not already have a service address under the existing confidentiality order regime. The credit reference agency must deliver a statement to the Registrar confirming that the information will only be used by it to assess a director's financial standing; in connection with money laundering requirements and the need to verify a director's identity; to conduct conflict of interest checks required by enactment; or to provide information to a public authority or other credit reference agency which has satisfied the relevant conditions and requirements.

Since October 2009 a person who is, or is to become, a director can apply, in prescribed form and on payment of a single fee, to the Registrar to stop protected information being disclosed by the Registrar to a credit reference agency. This can be done under s 243 of the Act. To be successful the director must be able to demonstrate in the application that either he, or any person living with the director, will be at serious risk of violence or intimidation as a result of the directorship; or he has been or is employed by a relevant organisation (which includes the police, armed forces and so on). Where the application is successful, the Registrar will be required to refrain from disclosing protected information to a credit reference agency. This restriction will remain in place indefinitely, unless revoked.

However, where a director had a confidentiality order in place immediately prior to 1 October 2009, he was automatically treated as if a successful s 243 application had been made restricting the Registrar from disclosing protected information to a credit reference agency.

In addition, where desired, an application under s 1088 of the Act can be made to the Registrar for the director's residential address to be made unavailable on the register. A fee is payable, the amount of which will depend on the number of documents on which the address is to be suppressed.

This is only possible where the address was placed on the register on or after 1 January 2003, and, for the application to be successful, a director must be able to demonstrate either serious risk of violence or intimidation or employment by a relevant organisation. The s 1088 grounds will also, on application, be deemed satisfied where the director has already successful made a s 243 application. In addition, where a director has a confidentiality order in place immediately prior to 1 October 2009, he will be automatically treated as if a successful s 1088 application had been made without need for application by the director.

The director must disclose the service address that is to replace the residential address and, where successful, the s 1088 restriction will continue indefinitely unless revoked by the Registrar.

Retirement and rotation   **6.11.5**

Although there is no general requirement in CA 2006 for directors to retire by rotation at each AGM, it is usually included in the company's Articles (Table A regs 76–79 or, for public companies who have adopted the Model Articles under CA 2006, it is contained in article 21). Having said this, a company such as a small private limited company where the directors and shareholders are one and the same may choose to exclude the retirement and rotation provisions where they do not consider them necessary.

Directors need to check the requirement for retirement by rotation when planning the AGM and the items of business to be included in the notice sent to shareholders. The directors will need to consult provisions in the Articles to determine if any procedures must be followed and whether any directors, such as the managing director or chairman, are excluded from the requirement to retire by rotation. For example, the provisions of Table A to CA 1985 require:

- all directors to retire and offer themselves for reappointment at the first AGM of the company (reg 73);

- at subsequent AGMs, new directors to retire and offer themselves for reappointment at the AGM following their appointment (reg 79); and

- one third of *existing* directors to retire by rotation at each AGM (reg 73). The directors will need to refer to minutes of previous AGMs to determine when each of them was reappointed, as those who have been longest in office are required to retire by rotation. In the event that the directors were all reappointed on the same day, the directors to retire by rotation at the next AGM shall be determined by lot (reg 74).

Where the resolution for a director's reappointment is approved the director shall continue in office, but where the resolution is not approved he shall retain office only until the end of the AGM at the latest (reg 80).

For those companies who have adopted the Model Articles under CA 2006 similar provisions are contained in article 21 of the Model Articles for public companies:

- all directors to retire and offer themselves for reappointment at the *first* AGM of the company;

- at subsequent AGMs, *new* directors to retire and offer themselves for reappointment at the AGM following their appointment; and

- directors who were not appointed or reappointed at one of the preceding AGMs must offer themselves for reappointment.

It should be noted that the UK Corporate Governance Code requires all directors of companies within the FTSE 350 to offer themselves for re-election each year and any company not doing so must explain its reasons for not observing this provision.

The directors have a duty to ensure that, where required, the directors to retire are determined in accordance with methods outlined by the company within an ordinary resolution or the provisions contained in the Articles. Where a company has no such provisions in its Articles, the company may pass an ordinary resolution to determine the means for choosing which directors are to retire by rotation (reg 78).

This information must then be communicated to members in the notice of the AGM. The members will, quite rightly, be relying on the directors to ensure that any regulations of the company concerning retirement by rotation have been complied with at the AGM.

Cessation of appointment   6.11.6

Directors should be aware of circumstances under which they, or any of them, would no longer be entitled to hold office and their appointment must be terminated. These circumstances may include the following:

- events specifically contained in the Articles. For example, Table A reg 81, article 18 of the Model Articles for private or guarantee companies, and article 22 of the Model Articles for public companies require a director to vacate office if he becomes bankrupt, suffers from mental disorder or is absent from meetings of the directors without consent of the Board.

Other circumstances may be included in the Articles, such as failure to take up a share qualification or revocation of a director's appointment by a class of shareholders or by a holding company where the Articles empower them to do so;

- there are certain requirements in legislation for the office of director to be vacated where certain events occur, such as the director being made bankrupt or disqualified by the court (CDDA 1986).

In addition to the above where a director is required to vacate office, he has a right to resign at any time, and the method by which he must notify the company of his resignation will be contained in the Articles (reg 81 of Table A or article 18 of the Model Articles for private or guarantee companies, or article 22 of the Model Articles for public companies) (para **3.10**).

In any event where a director resigns or is required to vacate office, the directors have a duty to ensure that the following procedures are carried out to record and disclose the change correctly:

- hold a meeting of the directors to record the resignation or report the reason why the director is required to vacate office;
- submit form TM01 to Companies House to report the resignation;
- record the resignation in the Register of Directors and update the Registers of Directors and Directors' Residential Address (para **6.21**);
- notify the company's bank and insurers, where relevant, of the change;
- arrange for the company stationery to be reprinted where directors' names are disclosed (para **6.52**);
- ensure that where a minimum number of directors is required by provisions in the Articles and this resignation causes the number to fall below the minimum, an additional director is appointed without delay.

Removal by members   **6.11.7**

The members of a company may, at any time before the expiration of his period of office, and notwithstanding anything in the Articles or any service agreement with the company, remove a director from office (CA 2006 ss 168 and 312). The Articles cannot exclude this provision but they may permit removal by alternative means, such as by majority vote of fellow directors.

As removal of a director is, in most circumstances, a contentious matter and represents a parting of the ways between the director concerned and the members of the company, the remaining directors have a duty to the members to ensure that the correct procedures are followed for removal to ensure that there is no recourse by the director so removed at a later date.

Consequently, subject to any specific provisions in the company's Articles, the directors must ensure that the following procedures are followed when removal of a director is proposed:

- that special notice is received by the company from a member, detailing his intention to move a resolution to remove a director, at least 28 days before the meeting at which they require the resolution to be proposed;

- where it is received in time, the directors should (although there is no statutory obligation) include the proposed resolution in the notice of the next AGM. Alternatively, the members may requisition the directors to hold a general meeting to consider the resolution, in which case they must convene a general meeting within 21 days of receiving the requisition on special notice (CA 2006 s 304, as discussed in para **8.22**);

- a copy of the special notice must be sent to the director who is to be removed and, where he wishes to exercise his right to make written representations to the members and attend and speak at the general meeting on the resolution for his removal, the directors must ensure that he is permitted to do so (CA 2006 s 169). If the company feels that the written representations contain defamatory material, it may apply to the court to obtain permission for it not to be required to circulate such material;

- if the ordinary resolution to remove the director is approved, the directors must ensure that the procedures detailed in para **6.11.6** are followed.

Whilst the ability of shareholders to remove a director ensures that ultimately shareholders have control over the directors, the shareholders are in many ways reliant on the directors to ensure that, when they exercise this right, the necessary procedures are followed.

In addition, the directors should communicate with the shareholders to ensure that they are aware of the possible consequences of removing a director, such as a potential claim by the director for compensation for breach of his service contract or a petition to the court for a just and equitable winding up (more relevant to 'quasi partnerships' than public companies). The directors may also need to advise the shareholders where provisions in the Articles give the director, who is also a shareholder, weighted voting rights where a resolution is proposed to remove him (*Bushell v Faith* [1970] AC 1099, HL).

Company secretary   **6.12**

The directors of a public company must ensure that there is a secretary of the company and that the person appointed as secretary has the requisite knowledge or qualifications to fulfil the position satisfactorily (CA 2006 s 273). This may be demonstrated where the person either:

- appears to the directors to have the requisite knowledge and experience to discharge the functions of secretary of the company; and

- holds any one or more of the following qualifications:

  - held the position of secretary in a company other than a private company for at least three out of the five years immediately preceding their appointment;

  - is a member of any of the following institutes:

    Chartered Accountants in England and Wales, Scotland or Ireland;

    Chartered Association of Certified Accountants;

    Chartered Secretaries and Administrators;

    Chartered Institute of Management Accountants;

    Chartered Institute of Public Finance and Accountancy;

  - is a barrister, advocate or solicitor;

  - is considered by the directors as capable of discharging the duties required satisfactorily, as demonstrated in previous positions held or by membership of another body or institute not mentioned above.

Private companies are no longer required to have a company secretary, provided the company's Articles do not contain provisions requiring anything to the contrary.

As mentioned in para **2.70**, the directors may delegate certain duties and responsibilities to the company secretary where the company has one and, in these circumstances, they must be confident that the person appointed is capable of such tasks. In addition, the company secretary should be able to advise the directors on detailed provisions of the Companies Acts and associated legislation and provide advice of a technical and compliance nature to the directors.

Where a company has a company secretary, it is usual for the directors to have authority to appoint or remove the company secretary by a resolution approved at a Board meeting (for companies who have adopted Table A this is contained in reg 99). Similarly, the secretary may resign by notice in writing to the company. When an appointment or resignation is made, the directors have a corresponding duty to notify Companies House and update the Register of Secretaries in the manner as detailed in paras **6.21.3** and **6.11.5** subject to using different forms for Companies House purposes (CA 2006 ss 275 and 276).

Auditors   **6.13**

Every company, except private companies exempt from the audit requirement and dormant companies exempt pursuant to CA 2006, must appoint an auditor (CA 2006 ss 485 and 489). See para **7.16** for details of the exemptions.

Directors must ensure that the auditors' statutory right of access to the company's books, accounts, vouchers and associated documents is observed and that they supply such information to the auditors as they consider necessary for the performance of their duties. Any officer who knowingly or recklessly makes a statement to the auditors which is misleading, false or deceptive is guilty of a criminal offence (CA 2006 ss 499 and 500).

Appointment   **6.13.1**

The directors have responsibility and authority to appoint the first auditors by resolution approved at a Board meeting and to fill any casual vacancies that may arise from time to time (CA 2006 ss 485(3) and 489(3)). The members may also appoint an auditor by ordinary resolution (CA 2006 ss 485(4) and 489(4)).

When appointing an auditor, the directors must ensure that the person or firm they are considering for appointment is appropriately qualified and is an eligible member of a recognised supervisory body (CA 2006 s 1217).

Under CA 2006 a private company (unless they are exempt under CA 2006 ss 477 and 480) must appoint an auditor for each accounting period.

Where the auditor is appointed by the directors, the auditor needs to be reappointed by ordinary resolution of the shareholders. Where a private company no longer holds an AGM, this can be done by way of written resolution. Subject to this initial reappointment by the members, thereafter the auditor of a private company may be 'deemed' to be reappointed for subsequent accounting periods (CA 2006 s 487(2)). The members can, however, prevent the deemed reappointment by petitioning the company. This involves the requisite percentage of shareholders (usually 5%) giving notice to the company that they do not wish the auditor to be reappointed (CA 2006 s 488).

However, if a private company had dispensed with the obligation to appoint auditors annually pursuant to CA 1985 s 379A they remain able to rely on this dispensation despite the elective regime being repealed under the CA 2006.

Public companies must (unless exempt) also appoint an auditor for each financial year of the company (CA 2006 s 489). There can be no deemed reappointment of the auditors of a public company. They must be reappointed at each general meeting at which accounts are laid before the members (CA 2006 s 491(1)(b)).

Under CA 2006 s 492, if the auditors of a company are appointed by the directors, their remuneration must be determined by the directors. Similarly, if the auditors of a company are appointed by the shareholders, their remuneration must be determined by the shareholders.

The directors must be aware that, where there has been a change in auditor at any point during the year, they must ensure that 'special notice' of the proposed resolution for reappointment of the auditor appointed to fill the casual vacancy arising at the general meeting is given and that copies of the special notice are sent to the members as well as to the previous auditor (CA 2006 s 511).

Directors of listed companies should also be aware that the UK Corporate Governance Code recommends that the audit committee is made responsible for overseeing and managing the relationship with the company's external auditors (see para **10.23.1**).

Resignation   **6.13.2**

An auditor has the right to resign by sending notice in writing to the company at its registered office at any time, together with a statement listing any circumstances that should be brought to the members' or creditors' attention or, in the absence of any such circumstances, a statement to that effect. Once notification has been received, the directors have certain procedural duties they must carry out to ensure that the resignation is recorded correctly and rights of the auditors are observed. These are as follows:

- A copy of the resignation must be submitted to Companies House within 14 days of receipt (CA 2006 s 517).

- They must check that within 28 days from the date on which the notice of resignation was deposited with the company the auditor has submitted to Companies House a statement of circumstances, or a statement that there are no circumstances in connection with the resignation that need to be brought to the attention of members or creditors (CA 2006 s 521).

- Where the statement contains circumstances that the auditor considers members should be made aware of, the directors must ensure that a copy of the statement is sent to shareholders and all persons entitled to receive copies of the accounts within 14 days of receipt (CA 2006 s 520(2)).

- Where the directors believe the statement has been issued for purely defamatory purposes, they may make application to the court to restrain publication and must notify the auditors if such application has been made (CA 2006 s 520).

- On receipt of a signed requisition from the resigning auditors, the directors must, within 21 days of receipt of the requisition, convene a general meeting to consider the circumstances of the auditors' resignation (CA 2006 s 518(2)). The general meeting must be for a date not more than 28 days after notice is given.

- The auditor may require the directors to circulate a written statement to members prior to the requisitioned meeting or, alternatively, to circulate such statement before the AGM at which his appointment would otherwise have expired (CA 2006 s 304).

Failure by the directors to observe the rights of resigning auditors or to send information to Companies House concerning their resignation within specified time periods will result in liability for a fine or daily default fine.

Removal   **6.13.3**

A company may remove its auditors from office by ordinary resolution of which 'special notice' has been given (CA 2006 s 510, see para **8.23.2.3** for explanation of 'special notice'). The directors must ensure that a copy of the special notice is sent to the auditors to be removed and to the incoming auditors where their appointment is to be considered at the same meeting. The auditors must also receive notice of and be permitted to attend and speak at the meeting at which their removal is proposed.

The directors must also ensure that they observe the auditors' rights discussed in para **6.13.2** and, where the resolution for their removal is approved, notify Companies House within 14 days.

It should also be noted that where an auditor has been removed and a new auditor is appointed to fill the vacancy, special notice must be given of the resolution proposing appointment of the incoming auditor at the next general meeting at which accounts are approved.

Maintenance, inspection and disclosure of
information in statutory books   6.20

The term 'statutory books' is frequently used to refer to a company's minute books and registers, the size and complexity of which normally depends on whether the company is public or private, the size of its share capital, the number of shareholders and directors, the size of the company, the volume of movement in share ownership and level of trading activity. Details and extracts from them are the source of most information supplied to Companies House for public record (**APPENDIX 4**).

There are various alternatives available to directors when considering how best to maintain the statutory books and registers, as follows:

(1)   The directors of many smaller, family-owned and run companies frequently choose to maintain the statutory books themselves. This is particularly cost-effective and practical where few changes in statutory matters are anticipated during the year.

(2)   Alternatively, as occurs in many instances, the directors may employ their accountants, solicitors or a specialist firm of chartered secretaries to maintain their statutory books.

(3)   An increase in the volume of compliance work necessary for a larger private company, group of companies or public company in many cases warrants a specialist secretariat department to undertake these tasks, as can be seen with many listed companies.

(4)   They may deal with the majority of statutory matters in-house and engage a share registration agent purely to maintain the company's share registers.

(5)   As permitted by CA 2006 s 1148, they may maintain the company's statutory registers in computerised form, which is permissible provided information can be extracted and printed in legible form when required. A wide range of dedicated computer systems are available to directors which vastly speed up and reduce the administrative burden of statutory compliance matters, particularly now that it is possible to generate and file many forms electronically direct from such systems. Use of computers in maintaining statutory records has provided large-scale benefits to directors and has taken the tedium out of many of the updating tasks. At the same time computer systems enable increased use of information stored to produce useful and meaningful management reports and can be used to check that compliance matters have been carried out.

Subject to restrictions identified in the following paragraphs, a public or private company shall make its statutory records available for inspection as set out in

APPENDICES 4 and **5**. A person may also request a copy of a company record in hard copy or electronic form.

The statutory books are required to be maintained and available for inspection at the company's registered office or such other location as advised to Companies House. The latter is referred to as a 'single alternative inspection location', as permitted by CA 2006 s 1136 and the Companies (Company Records) Regulations 2008 (SI 2008/3006). A single alternative inspection location might, for example, include a transfer office where maintenance of the company's register of members has been outsourced to a share registrar.

It should be noted that where a company is incorporated in England and Wales, the registered office, or single alternative inspection location notified for the statutory books, must be within England or Wales and similar rules apply for a company registered in Scotland.

Failure to maintain the required registers or to disclose information contained therein will be an offence for which every officer of the company in default, including the directors, will be liable.

An additional requirement for directors to note is that any person who deals with the company in the course of business may make a written request for the company to provide him with details of the registered office, any place at which statutory records are kept for inspection and what records are kept at that place. The directors must ensure that the requested information is provided within five working days of receipt of the request or be liable to a fine (Companies (Trading Disclosures) Regulations 2008, regs 9 and 10).

Directors and secretaries   **6.21**

Whilst historically details of a company's directors and company secretary were recorded in one register, three separate registers are now required.

Directors   **6.21.1**

Every company is required to maintain a register of directors at the registered office or other single alternative inspection location. This register must be available for inspection by the shareholders or members of the public (CA 2006 s 162 and **APPENDIX 4**).

The directors must ensure that the register contains the following information for each person appointed as well as the date and nature of their appointment:

- full name, including any former names or names by which he was known for business purposes within the previous 20 years;

- service address (para **6.11.3**);

- nationality;

- date of birth;

- business occupation (if any);

- the country, state or part of the UK in which the director is usually resident.

In particular, it should be noted that given the register of directors and register of secretaries are open to public inspection, it is the service address that must be recorded for a director or secretary in these registers, not his home address.

Where a director or secretary is happy for his home address to remain the service address then the entry in the registers of directors can merely state that the address shown complies with the requirement of CA 2006 to show a service address. For new directors and secretaries appointed on or after 1 October 2009, just the service address needs to be recorded in the relevant register of directors or secretaries.

Whilst maintenance of the register of directors is a routine compliance matter, it should attract no less attention from the directors. This is highlighted in *Re Bath Glass Ltd* (1988) 4 BCC 130, where the decision to disqualify the director was, in part, for failure to maintain the register of directors.

Any change concerning the directors, whether it is a resignation, appointment, change of address or other particulars, must be recorded in the register and be notified to Companies House (see para **6.31**).

Residential address   **6.21.2**

It is necessary to record a director's usual home address in a separate register of directors' residential address as this information is restricted and the register is not open to inspection by the public (CA 2006 s 165). There is no corresponding requirement for company secretaries, as only the secretary's service address needs to be recorded. Any change in the address must be noted in the register and advised to Companies House (para **6.31**).

If a director's residential address is the same as his service address (and it does not just state that it is 'the company's registered office' in the register of directors), the register can merely record this fact.

More detail about the director's service address and residential address are set out in paras **6.11.3** and **6.11.4**.

Secretaries   **6.21.3**

A separate register of a company's secretaries is required (CA 2006 s 275). The register must contain details of the secretary's name, and any former names used for business purposes in the last 20 years, service address (see para **6.11.3**) and dates of appointment and resignation. Where a corporate secretary is appointed, details of the place of incorporation and registered number must also be recorded.

The register of secretaries must be open for inspection, kept at the company's registered office or 'single alternative inspection location' and be updated to record any changes.

Members   **6.22**

Every company must maintain a register containing details of the names, addresses and number of shares held by each member of the company (CA 2006 s 113).

The directors must ensure that the register is available for inspection at the registered office or such other place as notified to the Registrar (CA 2006 s 114).

Under CA 2006 s 116 the register of members must be open for inspection to the members of the company without charge and to the public on payment of a prescribed fee. Copies of the register of members or a particular part of it may also be requested by any person, and such copies may be provided upon payment of a prescribed fee.

A person wishing to inspect or copy the register of members must provide a request to the company containing their name and address (and, if the request is from an organisation, it must include the name and address of the individual responsible), the purpose for which the information will be used and whether the information will be disclosed to a third party and, if so, the name and address details of those persons or organisations to whom the information will be disclosed and the purpose for which it is required.

Where a company receives a valid request it must either comply with it and provide the information within five working days or, within the same period of time, make application to the court not to comply. Neither the company nor the directors have power to simply not comply.

If the directors believe that the information obtained will be used for an 'improper purpose' an application can be made to court, and the court has power to relieve the company of its obligation (CA 2006 s 117). For further information the ICSA has produced a Guidance Note, 'Access to the Register of Members: The Proper Purpose Test', which can be downloaded from the ICSA website.

Directors should note that failure to provide a copy of the Register of Members without an order from the court is a fineable offence (CA 2006 s 118).

It is also important for directors to ensure that only required information is recorded in the Register of Members and, for data protection reasons, no other personal details (such as dividend mandate and bank account instructions) are recorded in that part of the register made public.

Allotments and transfers   **6.23**

Whilst there is no statutory requirement in CA 2006 to maintain registers of allotments and transfers of shares, it is both usual and important for such registers to be kept and updated so as to provide explanation and details of changes recorded in the register of members. It is also helpful when addressing shareholder queries and when completing share details on the annual return each year.

Where these registers are maintained, the directors do not have to make them available for inspection nor provide copies to members or non-members if requested.

Directors' interests in shares   **6.24**

Following repeal of the requirements contained in CA 1985 ss 324 and 325, there are no longer any statutory requirements for directors to disclose their interests in a company's shares or debentures or for companies to maintain a register of directors' interests. However, as notification of directors' interests is still required for companies whose securities are listed on the Official List, AIM and PLUS Market, the information will still need to be maintained by these companies in an appropriate manner, which might involve use of a register (see paras **6.70–6.72**).

Register of interests disclosed (public companies)   **6.25**

Every public company is required to maintain a register of interests in the company's shares disclosed to it in response to a notice issued by the company to a person it believes is interested in the company's shares (or had an interest within the last three years).

Where it appears that a member of the company has acquired an interest, the directors of a public company may, either on their own initiative or in response to receipt of a member's requisition (CA 2006 s 803), issue notice to the person who is the subject of investigation requiring them to supply details of their interest in the company (CA 2006 s 793).

Any information about interests in shares received in response must be recorded in the register of interests within three days of receipt (CA 2006 s 808).

The register of interests disclosed must be kept at the company's registered office or such other location at which the company keeps records available for inspection and as notified to the Registrar of Companies (CA 2006 s 809).

The register of interests disclosed must be available for inspection by any person without charge, subject to satisfaction of the 'proper purpose' test.

A person seeking to review this register must make a request to the company containing their name and address, purpose for which they require the information and details of whether the information will be disclosed to another person (CA 2006 s 811).

Directors should also note that, in addition to the requirement to maintain and update the register, where the directors have issued a notice requiring information about interests in shares at the request of the members, they have a duty to report the outcome of the investigation (CA 2006 s 804). The report must be available for inspection no more than 15 days after completion of the investigation. If all of the requested information has not been obtained within a period of three months, a report must be prepared containing the information which has been received by the company. Further reports must be prepared every three months until such time as the investigation is concluded. The members of the company who submitted the request under CA 2006 s 803 must be advised within three days of a report being prepared, notifying them that such a report has been prepared and where it is available for inspection (CA 2006 s 805).

Where a member fails to reply to a s 793 notice, the directors must ensure that they pursue the company's right to receive a reply by either:

- exercising any express provision that the company may have in its Articles permitting restrictions to be imposed on a member's shares (known as 'disenfranchisement') by removal of a member's right to attend and vote at general meetings, transfer their shares and receive payment of dividends in respect of those shares. Such restrictions cannot be imposed unless permitted by the Articles; or

- applying to the court pursuant to provisions contained in CA 2006 s 794(1) for an order imposing restrictions on the shares contained in CA 2006 s 797 which include removal of the member's right to transfer shares, vote, receive any shares pursuant to a 'bonus' issue and receive income on the shares. Ultimately, the court may order that the shares be sold.

Debenture holders   **6.26**

Whilst there is no statutory obligation to maintain a register containing details of debenture holders, where a number or series of debentures are issued such register will assist the directors to keep accurate and reliable records and ensure that no details are mislaid with the passage of time.

Where the directors consider it necessary to maintain a register of debenture holders, statutory regulations determine that it must be kept at the registered office, or at such other location as the company keeps records available for inspection and as notified to the Registrar of Companies (CA 2006 s 743). Furthermore, members and the public have the right to inspect and receive copies of the register of debenture holders, in accordance with provisions contained in **APPENDIX 5**.

Mortgages and charges   **6.27**

The Companies Act 2006 (Amendment of Part 25) Regulations 2013 (SI 2013/600) changed the requirements for charges created on or after 6 April 2013 and imposed a new registration regime.

Where charges, fixed or floating, are created over a company's property or undertaking, CA 2006 s 859P requires the company to keep a copy of every instrument creating, amending or varying a charge available for inspection (save where the charge is contained in a series of debentures, in which case a copy of one debenture is sufficient). These instruments must be kept at either the company's registered office or the single alternative inspection location (see para **6.20**), whichever is notified to Companies House as the place for inspection (CA 2006 s 859Q).

The information kept by the company about mortgages and charges must show the registered name and number of the company clearly and, for each charge, detail the name of the person holding the charge, the property charged, the date the charge was created, whether it is a fixed or floating charge, what property is subject to the charge and the obligations secured by the charge. Once the charge has been registered (see below), Companies House will issue a certificate of registration of the charge which should be kept with the other documents.

The directors must ensure that this information is available for inspection without charge by any member or creditor of the company and by other persons subject to payment of the prescribed fee (CA 2006 s 859Q(4) and see **Appendix 5**). Where the parties agree, the inspection may be carried out by electronic means and the directors should be aware that failure to make the information available, or to prohibit inspection, is an offence for which any officer in default will be liable to a fine (CA 2006 s 859Q(6)).

The directors must also ensure that Companies House is notified in the manner and using the forms prescribed by Companies House when a charge is created or when an existing charge is amended, varied or satisfied (see para **6.31** and **Appendix 6**). Failure to register the charge at Companies House within 21 days of the charge being created will render the charge void and the money secured by it becomes immediately repayable (CA 2006 s 859H).

It is important for the directors to ensure that requirements in respect of charges are observed, as not only is the information about charges important for suppliers, customers, creditors and any persons dealing or considering entering into contracts with the company to enable them to determine the extent to which the company's property has been charged and whether the company will be able to satisfy its debts and carry on trading in the event the charges are enforced; but also to ensure the money or facilities secured by the charge do not need to be repaid earlier than planned, as this could threaten the success of the company. It is therefore very important for directors to ensure that, as required by CA 2006 s 859L, Companies House is notified when a charge is fully or partly satisfied as this could have a positive and beneficial effect on the company's credit status. A certificate of satisfaction will be issued by Companies House which should be retained.

Minute books   6.28

Every company is required to keep minutes of all general meetings and directors' meetings (CA 2006 ss 248 and 355). For companies who have adopted Table A, this statutory requirement is reinforced by reg 100, which requires a record to be kept of all appointments of officers by the directors and all meetings of members, directors, committees of directors and holders of any class of shares.

The directors should ensure that minutes kept are accurate, precise and in no way ambiguous as, once signed by the chairman, they are evidence (unless proven to the contrary) of the proceedings and decisions made at the meeting (CA 2006 ss 249 and 356). It has been confirmed in *R v Kingston Crown Court* [2001] EWHC Admin 581, [2001] 4 All ER 721 that there is nothing inherently wrong with using pre-prepared minutes provided they reflect business conducted at the meeting. However, caution should be exercised with regard to the use of pre-prepared minutes as they do not in themselves demonstrate that the directors have fulfilled their duties (see the *Weavering* case para **1.32**).

Many companies keep separate minute books for minutes of meetings of the members and the directors and any committee of the directors. The reason for this is that whilst the directors must ensure that the books containing minutes of general meetings are kept at the registered office (or such other place as permitted and notified to Companies House) and are available for inspection by members, there is no statutory requirement regarding the location or right of the members to inspect minutes of meetings of the directors or any committee of the directors.

As well as their right to inspect minutes of general meetings, members are also entitled to request that a copy be sent to them and the directors must ensure that this request is met within 14 days of receiving the request. They may impose a charge for the provision of a copy.

In practice the directors' minute book is likely to be kept at the registered office, place of business or location where meetings are held and decisions made, as it may be required for reference purposes.

Whilst the members do not have the right to inspect directors' minutes, the auditors are entitled to inspect them, based upon statutory provisions contained in CA 2006 ss 498 and 499. Inspection of Board minutes will be conducted as a routine part of the audit process. Furthermore, directors have a common law right to inspect minutes of previous Board meetings, provided in *McCusker v McRae* 1966 SC 253.

Documents, forms and returns for submission to Companies House   6.30

Filing requirements in general   6.31

In addition to their responsibility for maintaining the statutory books and registers of the company, the directors have a corresponding duty to ensure that key changes in the company's location, structure, management and constitution are notified to Companies House within specified time periods.

Most of the events that need to be notified are triggered by changes made in the registers, or location of them, which the directors have responsibility to maintain. Routine and sometimes frequent changes and events which occur and need to be notified to Companies House include the following:

- *Change in location of the registered office.* Prior notice of the change must be given on the prescribed form where practicable, but in any event not more than 14 days after the change (CA 2006 s 87). The directors should note that the change in registered office is only effective once it has been notified to Companies House and that notice on a company, such as a county court judgment, may be validly served at the old registered office address up to 14 days after the change.

- *Allotments of shares.* Details of the number of shares, names of holders and the date of allotment must be notified on the prescribed form within two months of the allotment taking place (CA 2006 s 554).

- *Increases in authorised share capital.* The ordinary resolution passed by the members approving the increase, together with a statement of capital, must be submitted within 15 days of the resolution being passed. However, for some companies, the concept of having an upper limit on share capital no longer applies.

- *Purchase by a company of its own shares.* Where approval of the members has been obtained, a copy of the special resolution recording approval must be filed at Companies House within 14 days. The prescribed form, recording details of the shares purchased and the date the purchase took effect, must be submitted within one month (CA 2006 s 307(1)).

- *Alterations to the share capital.* Any consolidation, conversion or subdivision of the share capital must be notified to Companies House on the prescribed form within one month of the change or alteration (CA 2006 s 619, 621 or 689).

- *Changes in directors and secretaries.* An appointment, resignation or change of address or other details must be notified on the prescribed form, which depends on the nature of the change, within 14 days of the change occurring (CA 2006 ss 167 and 276).

- *Certain ordinary resolutions* (such as removal of a director or auditor and the granting authority to directors to allot shares) *and all special resolutions* passed by members of the company must be submitted within 14 days of approval by the members (CA 2006 s 30).

- *Creation of a charge over a company's assets* must be notified by giving a statement of particulars within 21 days of creation of the charge and providing a certified copy of the instrument creating or evidencing the charge (CA 2006 ss 859(1) and (2) and 859A(4)). Such information is important and time-critical for creditors and those dealing with the company.

- *Alteration to Articles of Association.* Where a company amends its Articles, it must send a copy of the amended Articles to Companies House within 15 days of the amendment taking effect (CA 2006 s 26(1)). Where Companies House becomes aware that this has not been done, a default notice will be issued and, if the company fails to comply within 28 days, it will be liable to a £200 fine for the default (CA 2006 s 27).

For a complete list of forms to be submitted to Companies House and their required filing periods, directors should refer to the Schedule contained in **APPENDIX 6**. Information in the Schedule illustrates how extensive their duties are in terms of filing requirements, which is based on the need to ensure that the public record is kept up to date at all times, which Companies House is strict to enforce.

Failure to fulfil any of the above filing requirements will render the directors and every officer of the company in default liable to a fine and, for continued contravention, to a daily default fine. Consequently they must ensure that, where a change is recorded in the company's statutory books, if necessary it is notified to Companies House.

Many forms can now be WebFiled and companies with approved software packages are able to submit an increasing number of forms electronically and to incorporate companies electronically. Directors must ensure that the authentication codes issued by Companies House permitting electronic filing and establishing authenticity of the documents submitted are kept confidential and only made known to those persons authorised to submit documents electronically to Companies House.

In addition, where a prescribed form concerning a director's appointment is submitted electronically, the director being appointed must confirm his 'consent to act' by providing three items of personal information to Companies House. Such items may include place or date of birth, telephone number, house or flat number or name, National Insurance number, passport number, eye colour or his mother's maiden name or father's first forename.

Companies House is encouraging greater use of electronic filing, not only because it reduces the burden and cost of administration at Companies House once documents are submitted, but also because of the greater security it gives companies. With this in mind, companies are able to use the PROOF (PROtected Online Filing) service provided by Companies House to prevent fraudulent paper filings. There is now an electronic opt-in facility for this service and Companies House has indicated that it will be moving away from acceptance of hard-copy documents towards electronic and WebFiled documents only.

Annual returns **6.32**

Every company must file an annual return form each year signed by a director or the secretary of the company (CA 2006 s 854). It is effectively a 'snapshot' of the company made up to a specific date showing details of the company's:

- name and registered number;

- registered office address (and the location of the register of members and debenture holders where different from the registered office);

- principal business activity (using standard industry classification codes);

- secretary's details (full name and home address only);

- directors' details (full names, service addresses, occupations, dates of birth, nationalities);

- summary details of issued share capital;

- shareholder details.

CA 2006 ss 116–119 allow companies to restrict access to the register of members and consequently annual returns are similarly restricted in terms of what information is shown about a company's shareholders. In addition the Companies Act 2006 (Annual Returns) Regulations 2011 (SI 2011/1487) changed the details that must be shown about shareholders in annual returns as follows:

(1)   where the company's shares have not, at any time, been admitted to trading on a relevant market it must provide a 'full list' of all shareholders in the first annual return following incorporation and in every third annual return prepared thereafter. The details required include the names of members and number of shares held by each of them. There is no requirement to show the addresses of the members. Details of shares transfers made during a year must be included in the annual returns prepared in intervening years;

(2)   where the company's shares have been admitted to trading on a relevant market, it must provide the names and addresses of shareholders who hold 5% or more of the company's issued share capital as at the made up date of the return every year and include details of share transfers during the year, but there is no requirement for a full list of shareholders every third year; or

(3)   where the company's shares have been admitted to trading on a relevant market throughout the return period and DTR5 applied throughout the return period, shareholder details do not have to be provided (see

para **9.43**). The rationale behind this distinction is that where a company has to comply with the disclosure requirements of DTR5, there is little benefit including this information once a year as it will soon be out of date.

The directors must ensure the information disclosed on the form is correct and that the form is signed and returned to Companies House within 28 days of the 'return date' shown. This date is either the anniversary of incorporation where it is the first annual return, or the anniversary of the date shown on the previous year's return.

Failure to submit the return within the required period is an offence for which the company, its directors and the secretary are liable to prosecution. Initially a default notice will be issued by Companies House to the company and, if no response is received, letters will be sent to the directors warning them of the possibility of criminal proceedings for their default. Failure to comply with the notice within the time period specified may lead to prosecution of the directors. Alternatively Companies House may conclude that the company is no longer trading and initiate proceedings to strike the company off the register of companies.

Directors should note that the Government is also considering further changes to the annual return as part of the ongoing Company Law Review and 'Red Tape Challenge' with the aim of making it quicker and easier to complete and file especially where there have been no changes during the year. In particular, the Government has announced that requirements for statements of capital will be simplified across the board, including in annual returns, when a suitable legislative vehicle is available.

Annual accounts   **6.33**

The directors of every company, even where the company is dormant or has ceased trading, have a statutory duty to prepare and submit accounts and reports to Companies House (CA 2006 s 441). The directors' duties in relation to preparation of accounts and their required form and content are discussed in detail in **Chapter 7**, suffice to say here that the directors are required to approve and sign the accounts, circulate them to the members and lay them before the company in general meeting for adoption (unless the company is a private company and is not required to hold an annual general meeting, see para **8.21.1.1**). Following this, the accounts must be submitted to Companies House.

The directors are required to deliver the accounts and reports to Companies House within the period specified in CA 2006 s 442 as follows:

- private company: nine months from the end of the accounting period;

- public company: six months from the end of the accounting period;

- new private company: 21 months from the date of incorporation, or three months from the end of the accounting reference period (whichever expires last);

- new public company: 18 months from the date of incorporation, or three months from the end of the accounting reference period (whichever expires last).

Where the directors fail to ensure that the accounts and reports are delivered to Companies House within the relevant period above, each person who was a director at the time will be guilty of an offence and liable to receive a criminal record and fine of up to £7,500 (CA 2006 s 451).

In addition, where a company's accounts and reports are delivered to Companies House after the required filing period, the company will be subject to a civil penalty as determined by the Secretary of State through regulation (CA 2006 s 453). The size of penalty payable is determined according to the type of company and how late the accounts are submitted. The table below sets out current late filing penalties.

Length of period late	Public company	Private company
Not more than 1 month	£750	£150
More than 1 month but less than 3	£1,500	£375
More than 3 months but less than 6	£3,000	£750
More than 6 months	£7,500	£1,500

In particular, directors should note that where accounts are submitted late by a company and the company fails to file accounts on time the following year, the fine will double.

In addition, where a company files defective accounts very close to the filing deadline and they are rejected, Companies House no longer has power to grant a filing extension. If they are not rectified and resubmitted before the end of the filing period, a late filing penalty will be payable.

Consequently the directors have a personal responsibility to ensure that accounts are submitted and may be liable for summary prosecution if they fail to submit them on time. Where the accounts are not submitted within the required period, Companies House will notify the directors of their responsibility and, if no response is received, will commence legal proceedings against the directors and the company.

When preparing accounts for submission to Companies House, directors should note that to prevent rejection they must state the company's number in a prominent position (either on the balance sheet, profit and loss account, directors' report, directors' remuneration report or auditor's report), be on A4 size plain white paper (of between 80–100gsm) in portrait format, have a matt finish, be printed clearly and legibly in black type or ink, be an original and not have shaded areas or any photographs. Whilst in previous years accounts containing graphs have been rejected, this is no longer the case and, in response to a requirement of the Directors' Remuneration Report Regulations 2002, accounts containing line graphs will be accepted. Each of these presentational points is important to ensure that the accounts can be easily scanned onto the image database at Companies House.

Retention and disposal of records   6.40

Statutory provisions set out in the Companies Acts and other associated legislation, such as the Taxes Management Act 1970 (TMA 1970), the Insolvency Regulations and the Health and Safety Regulations, require private and public companies to retain certain documents and records either indefinitely or for specified periods of time (the 'minimum retention period'). Directors are responsible for implementing policies and procedures to ensure that these requirements are met.

Whilst it is essential that directors ensure that minimum retention periods are observed, realistically it is not possible for a company to retain all old files and records as storage space is costly and limited. Consequently directors must balance the need to reduce the volume of documents placed in storage with the need to ensure that documents are retained for at least their minimum retention period.

The table in **APPENDIX 7** provides an indication of statutory and recommended retention periods for documents which directors would be well advised to consult before making any decisions to retain or destroy documents.

Minimum retention periods   6.41

Minimum retention periods for many documents or classes of documents are specified, or implied, by statutory provisions and there is a legal obligation not to destroy documents before the specified period has elapsed.

Where a minimum retention period applies, the directors must ensure that the document to which it relates is retained and placed in storage until this period has elapsed. However, these statutory periods are a 'minimum' requirement and other obligations, such as tax investigations and the need for assessments, are frequently more onerous and require documents to be retained for longer.

Although specific requirements must be examined before documents are destroyed, as a general guide any documents relating to accounts, taxation, VAT, personnel and employee details, share registration and health and safety matters have minimum retention periods that must be observed.

Limitation periods   **6.42**

A further consideration is that past records and documents may be required as evidence in legal proceedings that the company, at the time under consideration, discharged its duties satisfactorily. Where this is relevant, documents should be kept until the period within which legal proceedings can be brought has expired (the Limitation Act 1980 (LA 1980), as amended). In brief, these are as follows:

(1)   product liability action must be brought within ten years of the date of supply;

(2)   action for breach of contract must be commenced within six years of the breach (or 12 years where the contract is under seal or executed as a deed);

(3)   claims for personal injury must be brought within three years of either the cause of injury, or when the plaintiff becomes aware of injury;

(4)   claims for negligence not in respect of (3) above may be brought up to three years after the damage or loss is discovered.

The need to reproduce documents as evidence in legal proceedings to defend the company's position should be considered when selecting the appropriate manner in which documents are stored, ie original copy versus optical storage techniques. For example, CA 2006 s 1135 permits a company's records to be kept in hard copy or electronic form, provided copies can be produced in hard form when required. However, other transactions may need to be evidenced in writing, such as dispositions of land, transfers of shares, hire purchase agreements and contracts of guarantee. In the latter case, directors must ensure that original documents are kept indefinitely.

A further consideration is that, whilst the courts in most cases accept copies of documents reproduced from a storage medium such as microfilm, microfiche, computer or optical disk as admissible evidence in legal proceedings (Civil Evidence Act 1995 (CEA 1995) ss 8 and 9) where they believe they can be relied upon as accurate, there may be specific requirements for evidence in civil and criminal proceedings and consultation with legal advisers will be necessary before any relevant original documents are destroyed.

With this in mind, directors should also note that all original documents submitted to Companies House as required by CA 2006 are saved where submitted electronically and scanned where submitted by hard copy, indexed and stored without any alteration. Consequently the electronic image would be admissible as secondary evidence, subject to provisions on authentication contained in CEA 1995. Furthermore, 'certified copies' from Companies House are as valid as the original documents.

Other considerations 6.43

When making decisions to reduce the volume of documents placed in storage, or when drafting policies or procedures to be followed by others in the company, directors must be simultaneously aware of requirements other than those based on provisions in the Companies Acts, as these may require documents to be kept for longer than the minimum statutory period. Some such considerations are as follows:

(1)   commercial and operational reference purposes;

(2)   retention periods implied or specified in the company's Articles of Association. For example, Table A reg 108, article 33 of the Model Articles for private and guarantee companies and article 75 of the Model Articles for public companies require unpaid dividends to be retained for 12 years after the date of payment, which by implication requires documents relating to such dividends to be retained for the same period. However, where there is no such provision in the Articles, the time limit to recover dividends is six years (LA 1980 s 5) and it may be considered appropriate to dispose of dividend records and papers after the lesser amount of time;

(3)   under CA 2006 s 355(2) copies of all minutes and resolutions of a company's members must be kept for at least ten years from the date of the resolution, meeting or decisions (as appropriate);

(4)   HM Revenue and Customs (HMRC) is permitted under normal circumstances to raise tax assessments at any time up to six years after the event (TMA 1970 s 34);

(5)   where HMRC suspects that a taxpayer has avoided payment of tax by negligence, they may extend the period for raising an assessment by six years or, where it suspects fraud or wilful neglect, it may raise an assessment at any time after the event (TMA 1970 ss 36 and 39);

(6)   companies registered for VAT are required to keep records, accounts and related documents for at least six years after the event (Value Added Tax Act 1994 s 58 and Sch 11 para 6(3)). These records are permitted to be retained on microfilm, computer or similar storage medium;

(7)   PAYE employment records must be retained for three years after the end of the tax year to which they relate (reg 97 of the Income Tax (Pay As You Earn) Regulations 2003 (SI 2003/2682)). It should be noted that this requirement also needs to be balanced against the restriction of the DPA 1998 that personal data should not be kept longer than strictly necessary for the intended purpose;

(8)   documents relating to calculation and payment of National Insurance contributions must be retained for a minimum of three years (2001/1004, as amended, and Sch 1 para 32(5)).

The directors, once they have considered all possible requirements for documents and determined which documents to move to storage, must ensure the archive system is clearly and accurately indexed, as documents are retained on the assumption that they may be required at a later date and it is futile to retain such documents where indexing is inefficient and documents cannot be traced and recalled when needed.

Where the directors are in any doubt as to the requirements for any documents, they should ensure that they are not destroyed until specialist advice has been sought from either the company secretary, legal adviser, auditor, or HMRC, depending on the nature of documents.

As mentioned above, the directors of many companies formulate policies and procedures to be followed to ensure that others within the company, to whom they are likely to delegate responsibility for document retention and storage, are aware of legal and commercial requirements and follow a reasoned and informed process when deciding which documents to keep and which to destroy.

APPENDIX 8 contains a diagrammatic representation of the decision process for disposal or retention of documents which may assist the director in adopting a systematic and consistent approach to review of documents for retention or disposal. Directors should also be aware that it is not a one-off decision, but that documents in storage must be periodically reassessed to make space for more records which need to be archived.

Display of company name and other details   6.50

Choosing a company name can be a complex and protracted process, involving statutory and commercial as well as marketing considerations. It is important to check that, not only is the company name not already in use on the companies' register but also that there are no registered or unregistered trademarks using the same name.

CA 2006 Part 5 and the Company and Business Names (Miscellaneous Provisions) Regulations 2009 (SI 2009/1085) must be consulted as they set out important provisions regulating a company's registered name.

CA 2006 s 69 has, in many ways, simplified the process for objecting to a proposed company name, as it permits any person or organisation that can demonstrate it has goodwill in that same name and which is identified with them to make application to the Company Names Adjudicator objecting and requesting that the name be changed. Prior to this, more protracted and expensive action would have been necessary, relying on being able to demonstrate 'passing-off' and/or trademark infringement. Indeed since the Company Names Adjudicator issued its first signed order on 9 January 2009, ordering 'Coke Cola Limited' to change its name and pay £700 to Coca-Cola, there have been approximately 220 signed orders which can be seen on the IPO's Company Names Tribunal website (www.gov.uk/government/organisations/company-names/tribunal). Recent examples include:

- Zurich Partners Limited and Security Zurich Limited being ordered to change their names on 27 March and 20 February 2013 as a result of successful applications by Zurich Insurance Co Limited;

- UK Rolls Royce Global International Holdings Limited being ordered to change its name on 25 February 2013 as a result of a successful application by Rolls-Royce plc; and

- Virgin Ventures being ordered to change name on 11 March 2013 as a result of a successful application by Virgin Enterprises Limited.

Company name   **6.51**

Once a company has been successfully incorporated, every company is required by the Companies (Trading Disclosures) Regulations 2008 (SI 2008/495) and the 2008 Amendment Regulations to clearly display the company name, as follows:

(1)   At the company's registered office, every office and premises in which business is carried on, and at any location where the company keeps available for inspection any company records (para **6.20**). However, companies that have been dormant since incorporation are exempt from this requirement, as are premises that are primarily used as living accommodation (ie a director's home address where this is also the registered office); the offices of an insolvency practitioner, administrator

or administrative receiver for a company in liquidation or administration; and where the premises concerned are not the registered office nor an inspection place and there is a risk of violent activity being attracted by display of the company's name.

In addition, the company's name does not need to be displayed at any office where business is carried out if all the directors have been granted a s 243 restriction (see para **6.11.4**).

The company's name must be displayed in characters that can easily be read, continuously displayed and in such position that it can be seen by a visitor to the premises (even outside business hours). If a location is shared by six or more companies then it is permissible for display of the company names to rotate, save that each name must be displayed for a minimum continuous period of 15 seconds in every three minutes.

(2)   On all business letters, notices and official publications, order forms, endorsements, bills of exchange, promissory notes, cheques and orders for money or goods signed on behalf of the company, and on all demands for payment, receipts, invoices and credit notes issued by the company and on all other forms of business correspondence and documentation.

Failure to comply with these requirements will render the company and its officers liable to a fine. Furthermore, the officer who signed such cheque, promissory note, bill of exchange or order for money or goods may be liable to a fine and be ordered to account to the holder for the amount concerned if the company fails to honour the payment (see para **5.40**).

(3)   On any applications for licences to carry on trade or activity.

(4)   On the company's website.

(5)   Where the company has a common seal, the company name must be engraved in legible characters. Liability to a fine is imposed on the company and officers for failure to show the company name correctly.

With increasing use of email as a means of communication, reg 1(2)(d) has confirmed that emails will be treated in the same way as paper-based communications. Consequently, directors must ensure that any business letters, order forms or company documents sent electronically comply with the requirements set out above.

Failure to comply with these regulations without reasonable excuse renders the company and every officer in default liable to a fine (reg 10, as permitted by CA 2006 s 83).

It should also be noted that there are potential commercial consequences of default to the extent that, if a company is bringing legal proceedings where it is enforcing its rights under a contract which was made at the time when the company was in breach of the regulations, then the court has power to dismiss the proceedings, if it is considered equitable to do so, if the defendant can show that: (i) he has a claim against the company arising out of the contract, which he is unable to purse due to the company's breach of the regulations; or (ii) the defendant has suffered financial loss in connection with the contract by reason of the company's breach of the regulations.

Directors should note that there is now also a trading disclosure regime for overseas companies that have registered an establishment in the UK. The requirements are set out in the Overseas Companies Regulations 2009 (SI 2009/1801) and they closely adhere to what is needed for display of the company name by a UK company as set out above.

Information on company documents and websites   **6.52**

The directors must also ensure that pursuant to the Companies (Trading Disclosure) Regulations 2008 the following information is given on all business letters, order forms, invoices, receipts, payment demand notices and websites (regs 7 and 8):

- any trading name under which business is conducted (as well as the registered company name);

- place of registration, ie England and Wales, or Scotland, etc;

- company's registration number;

- address of the registered office at which documents may be served. Where this is the same as the place of business the address need not be repeated but a statement to that effect must be made on the document. Directors should note that where any change is made to the location of the registered office, the new address must be displayed on documents within 14 days of the change;

- where the company is an investment company, a statement of this fact must be made;

- where the company is a charity and no indication is given in the company name by use of the words 'charity' or 'charitable', then a statement must be made to that effect;

- where a director's name is given on letters and other documents, the names of every director must be shown. It is important that directors are aware of this requirement when considering the use of personalised stationery and the need to reorder stationery every time the directors change. They should also note that the disclosure requirement for all directors' names includes 'shadow' directors;

- where the company chooses to include details of its share capital on documents, it must state it is the issued and fully paid share capital;

- where the company is exempt from use of the word 'limited' in its name, this must be stated;

- if applicable and the company is not a public company, a statement that the company is a community interest company.

A company is also required to state its VAT number on all VAT invoices and receipts and to post it clearly on the company's website (regardless of whether the website is used for e-commerce transactions).

In practice, much of the information listed above would appear as a pre-printed footnote on headed paper, company documents and emails and the directors must ensure that, before such documents are reordered and reprinted, they are checked thoroughly to ensure that none of the statutory information has changed, been omitted or printed incorrectly.

With regards to a company's website, this information can be included and displayed in a number of ways; the important point to note is that it must be posted clearly and be easy to find. Use of footnotes on all or most website pages, supported by more detailed information in contact and legal disclosure pages is quite common.

Email correspondence   **6.53**

As a minimum the company's registered name must be disclosed in all emails but, as most emails comprise business correspondence, the requirements set out in para **6.52** should be observed. Typically this information will appear in standard, boilerplate form at the end of all emails.

Directors' interests in transactions and arrangements   **6.60**

Disclosure to the Board of Directors   **6.61**

CA 2006 ss 177 and 182 together require directors to declare any interest they have in a proposed or existing transaction or arrangement with the company. This duty to disclose 'transactional conflicts' is largely a restatement of CA 1985 s 317, with which directors will be familiar and it is also covered in para **4.20.7**.

Any direct or indirect interests held by the director must be disclosed, together with the interests of any 'connected persons' and the declaration must state the nature and extent of the director's interest. Direct or indirect interest includes transactions or arrangements described in CA 2006 s 197(4) (such as loans or quasi-loans), covered in detail in para **6.90**.

Unless there is anything to the contrary in the company's Articles, a declaration of a proposed or existing transactional conflict may be made at a meeting of the Board or alternatively by notice in writing to the directors, in which case it will be deemed to form part of the proceedings at the next Board meeting. The declaration may be specific or take the form of a 'general notice' of interest in any transaction or arrangement with a body corporate, firm or person.

Declaration by a director of a proposed transactional interest must be made prior to the company entering into the transaction or arrangement. Declaration of an interest in an existing transaction or arrangement must be made as soon as practicable and specimen wording for recording such disclosure is contained in **APPENDIX 9**.

The purpose of CA 2006 ss 177 and 182 are twofold, principally to ensure that all other directors are aware or reminded of the director's interest and to give them an opportunity to consider the matter in light of the requirement that a director must not put himself in a position where there is a conflict between his personal interests and his duty to promote the success of the company. At the same time, a director is prohibited from making a secret profit arising from a contract with the company.

For the director who has such interest, failure to disclose the interest in a proposed or existing contract or transaction is an offence for which a fine can be imposed (CA 2006 ss 178 and 183). At the same time any profit arising in such circumstances must be repaid to the company (*Regal (Hastings) Ltd v Gulliver* [1942] 1 All ER 378).

It is also important for the Board of Directors to note that failure to record that the director's declaration of interest has been made exposes the company and every officer in default to a fine.

The following points need to be considered by the director when making disclosure:

- provisions apply to directors of all private and public companies;
- 'shadow directors' must declare their interest by notice in writing to the directors (CA 2006 s 187(3)) as, by inference, a shadow director will not be present at a meeting of the directors;

- a director must disclose his interest at the earliest opportunity, which will be either:

  - at the first meeting convened to consider a proposed contract; or

  - at the first meeting after a director becomes interested in an existing contract;

- disclosure of the interest must be made at a meeting of the full Board of Directors. Notification at a committee meeting is not considered sufficient, as determined in *Guinness plc v Saunders* [1990] 2 AC 663;

- general notice of a director's interest in any existing or future contracts with a particular firm or company may be given where the interest arises from the director being a member of that firm or company (CA 2006 s 177). Where general notice has been given, the need for disclosure at subsequent meetings to discuss such matters is waived provided the declaration has not become inaccurate or incomplete, in which case a further declaration must be made.

Once disclosure has been made, a transaction is not voidable by virtue of the director's interest and the director is not required to account for any benefit gained from the transaction where his interest has been duly notified.

Whilst failure by a director to declare an interest in a contract can render the contract voidable at the option of the company, if the company does not avoid the contract, it remains enforceable (*MacPherson & Torevell v European Strategic Euro Ltd* [1999] 2 BCLC 203). Furthermore, the contract can only be voidable where the parties can be restored to their original position, which was not the case in *Craven Textile Engineers v Batley Football Club Ltd* [2001] BCC 679, CA, where services had already been supplied.

It is also important to note that, even where the director is the sole director of a company, his interest in any contract must be disclosed formally and recorded in the minutes of a Board meeting (*Neptune (Vehicle Washing Equipment) Ltd v Fitzgerald* [1995] 1 BCLC 352).

Once the director has disclosed his interest in the transaction the Articles may, depending on the nature of his interest, permit the director to vote on the matter (for companies which have adopted Table A please refer to reg 94) or they may prohibit the director from being counted in the quorum of the meeting and voting on the resolution. Companies which have adopted the Model Articles will need to refer to article 14 for private companies or companies limited by guarantee or article 16 for public companies. In either case, notification of the director's interest needs to be recorded in minutes of the meeting (**APPENDIX 10**).

Disclosure in accounts   **6.62**

Companies must disclose information about directors' interests in contracts and arrangements in their annual accounts, save those that qualify as small or medium-sized companies as they are now exempt from this requirement (the Small Companies and Groups (Accounts and Directors' Report) Regulations 2008 (SI 2008/409) and the Companies Large and Medium-sized Companies and Groups (Accounts and Reports) Regulations 2008 (SI 2008/410)).

Disclosure and the Articles of Association   **6.63**

Disclosure requirements of CA 2006 ss 177 and 182 cannot be abrogated by provisions in the Articles of Association but, once disclosure has been made, many companies' Articles provide that the director may:

- be party to or interested in any transaction with the company (Table A reg 85); and

- be an officer, employee or in any way be interested in another company conducting transactions with the company.

It is normal practice for a company's Articles to provide that, subject to certain exceptions, a director cannot be counted in the quorum nor permitted to vote when considering matters in which he has declared an interest (Table A regs 94 and 95 and, for companies which have adopted the Model Articles, article 14 for private companies and article 16 for public companies). However, it is necessary to consult the Articles to determine the circumstances in which such 'exceptions' apply and the director could vote.

Rule 11.1.7(4)(a) of the Listing Rules requires that listed companies ensure that where a director or a person connected to a director has an interest in a transaction (making it a related party transaction) the director does not vote in relation to the contract, arrangement or proposal in which he has such interest.

Directors' interests in shares and debentures   **6.70**

There is no longer any statutory requirement for directors and shadow directors to disclose to the company their interest in shares in and debentures of the company or any holding or subsidiary company within a group structure. However, directors should note that for those companies with securities listed on the Official List, AIM and PLUS Market, this information is still required (see paras **6.71**, **6.72** and **6.73**).

Disclosure requirements: public listed companies   **6.71**

Fully listed companies   **6.71.1**

Under the Disclosure and Transparency Rule ('DTR') 3.1 where the shares or debentures are listed on a recognised investment exchange (for this purpose the Official List), a person discharging managerial responsibility ('PDMR'), which includes a director, and any persons connected to the PDMR, must notify the company in writing of any movement in their interests in shares of the company within four business days of the transaction.

The notification by the PDMR must include the:

- name of the PDMR (and, where relevant, the connection person);
- reason for the requirement to notify;
- name of the company;
- where applicable, the nature of the financial instrument;
- date and place of the transaction; and
- price and volume of the transaction.

The company must then notify the Regulatory Information Service of the movement as soon as possible and, in any event, by the end of the next business day (DTR 3.1). This must include any information notified by the director, together with the date disclosure was made to the company.

The company is also required to notify the Regulatory Information Service of any interest held by a person 'connected' with a director (explaining the nature of the connection and disclosing the information listed immediately above) as well as details of the grant of any option to acquire listed securities to a director or connected person and any acquisition, disposal, exercise or discharge of or dealing with any such option.

Furthermore, dealings by directors of listed companies in their own company's securities are regulated by the Listing Rules compiled by the London Stock Exchange. These require, amongst other things, that the Board adopt and adhere to requirements of the Model Code when dealing in the company's securities (**APPENDIX 22** and para **9.47**).

AIM companies   **6.71.2**

AIM Rule 17 requires an AIM company to announce any deals by directors without delay and Schedule 5 to the AIM Rules requires the disclosures to include:

- the director's identity;

- the date the disclosure was made;

- the date of dealing;

- the price, amount and class of securities;

- the nature of the transaction; and

- the nature and extent of the director's interest in the transaction.

Where the transaction has taken place in a 'close period' or concerns a related financial product, additional disclosures would be required.

ISDX Growth Market   **6.71.3**

A company whose shares have been admitted to the ISDX Growth Market is required by rule 46 of the ISDX Growth Market Rules to ensure that a deal by a director, member of his family, or a connected person is announced as soon as possible. The announcement must contain details of the following:

- the name of the person who has the obligation;

- the nature of the transaction;

- the resulting number of voting rights held by the notifying person;

- the date of the transaction;

- the date on which the company was notified;

- the number and class of securities concerned;

- where relevant, the name of the family member or connected person;

- the price paid for the shares; and

- any other information required under a DTR notification.

Recording directors' interests   **6.72**

As detailed in para **6.24**, companies are no longer required to maintain a register of directors' interests. However for those companies listed on regulated exchanges such as the London Stock Exchange, this information is required.

Therefore directors should maintain up-to-date information regarding directors' interests. It is likely this will take the form of a register of directors' interests, in which changes can be easily recorded.

Disclosure in audited accounts   6.73

Previously companies were required to disclose in the audited accounts the existence and extent of any directors' and their families' interests (CA 1985 Sch 7 Part I). Whilst this requirement was repealed by CA 2006, under the Listing Rules (LR 9.8.6R) a public listed company must still provide details in the annual report of any interests held by directors or their connected persons in the company's shares.

Companies with securities listed on the Official List are required to disclose the following information on directors' interests in their audited accounts:

- a statement setting out all the directors' interests during the period under review (including interests of 'connected persons');

- details of any options held by directors at the end of the year in the capital of the company and any company in the group;

- distinction between interests they have which are 'beneficial' and 'non-beneficial' in securities of the company;

- changes in interests between the end of the financial year and a date not more than one month prior to the notice of the meeting at which the accounts will be approved, or a statement that no changes have occurred.

This information is usually disclosed in the directors' report.

Substantial property transactions   6.80

A director or a person connected with a director of a company or of its holding company may not enter into any arrangement to acquire from or transfer to the company a substantial non-cash asset without obtaining approval for the transaction from the members by ordinary resolution (CA 2006 s 190(1)). A company can enter into a substantial property transaction which is conditional on member approval being obtained. Should the required approval not materialise, the company would not be liable under the contract. In general, approval is required for acquisitions and disposals for valuable consideration, gifts and voluntary dispositions where the value of the 'non-cash asset' is greater than £5,000. Where the asset concerned is valued above £5,000 and is greater than 10% of the company's net asset value or £100,000 (whichever is the lower), such transaction requires approval.

A 'non-cash asset' is defined in CA 2006 s 1163 as any property or interest in property other than cash (for these purposes cash also includes foreign currency) and includes discharge of a person's liability and creation of an interest in property such as a lease.

The restriction on substantial property transactions extends to persons connected with a director and to shadow directors. It should be noted that where a director or connected person is a director of the holding company, additional approval of the members of the holding company must also be sought.

Under CA 2006 non-cash assets forming part of a series of transactions or arrangements must be aggregated, in order to determine if the relevant thresholds have been exceeded. *Micro Leisure Ltd v County Properties and Developments Ltd (No 2)* 1999 SLT 1428, OH clarified that the relevant value of a non-cash asset acquired from a company by a director is the value to the director (or person connected) and not the market value of the asset.

Exemptions from approval   6.81

Circumstances in which approval of the shareholders to the transaction is not required are as follows:

- the company is not a UK registered company;

- the transaction involves a non-cash asset valued at less than £5,000;

- where the non-cash asset is more than £5,000, but is not as much as £100,000 and does not amount to more than 10% of the company's net asset value;

- the arrangement is between a wholly owned subsidiary and either the holding company or a fellow wholly owned subsidiary;

- it is part of an arrangement where the company is in administration or is being wound up (except a members' voluntary winding up);

- the company is listed on a recognised investment exchange and the transaction has been effected by a director or a person acting on behalf of the director as an independent broker.

Whilst such transactions do not require approval of the shareholders by ordinary resolution in general meeting, the director will nevertheless be obliged to notify his interest to the Board and approval must be formally recorded in the minutes of the Board's meeting (see para **6.61**).

Disclosure requirements   6.82

As set out in para **6.62**, small and medium-sized companies are now exempt from providing details of substantial property transactions in their accounts.

Contravention of s 190   **6.83**

Where requirements of CA 2006 s 190 are contravened and a transaction does not receive the necessary approval, the director or connected person and any other directors who authorised such arrangement or transaction are liable for the following:

- to account to the company for any direct or indirect gain made from the transaction (CA 2006 s 195(3)(a)); and

- to jointly and severally indemnify the company from any loss or damage resulting from the transaction (CA 2006 s 195(3)(b)).

Section 190 is largely concerned with preventing acquisitions of non-cash assets at an inflated price and disposals under their true value and to protect the company from conflicts of interest. Although directors are not relieved from their duty imposed by s 190, where advance approval was not obtained, the transaction can be affirmed or ratified by members in general meeting within a reasonable period thereafter (CA 2006 s 196).

In *British Racing Drivers' Club Ltd v Hextall Erskine & Co* [1996] 3 All ER 667, Ch D the importance of obtaining prior approval was highlighted. The company purchased shares in a motor retail business in which its chairman was a director and substantial shareholder. The solicitors acting for the company failed to advise the Board that the purchase was a 'substantial property transaction' requiring approval of the shareholders and mentioned only that the directors' interest needed approval of the Board. In action brought against the solicitors, the court held that the solicitors had been negligent in their advice as, had the matter been put before shareholders, it would not have been approved.

Re Duckwari plc [1997] Ch 201 involved sale of a property by a person connected with a director without prior approval of the shareholders. In this case the connected person was required to pay the difference between the market value at the time of sale and the actual price paid. The case was further examined (*Re Duckwari plc (No 3)* [1999] Ch 268) by the Court of Appeal, which confirmed that the indemnity to be paid was limited to the loss arising from acquisition of the property.

Loans to directors   **6.90**

Directors are required to make best use of the company's assets and have a duty to ensure that they do not abuse their position by borrowing money from the company for their own personal gain. Statutory obligations place restrictions on loans to directors, which they must ensure are observed, and at the same time create a requirement for directors to disclose details of any such loans in the company's annual accounts.

Directors who fail to observe the restrictions and disclosure requirements are guilty of an offence and render themselves liable to a fine or imprisonment.

Members' approval   **6.91**

Loans generally   **6.91.1**

The general prohibition on loans to directors was abolished under CA 2006 and replaced, generally, with the requirement for shareholder approval for all companies (CA 2006 s 197(1)).

Provided the transaction has been approved by a resolution of the members of the company it may make a loan to a director of the company or of its holding company (provided the members of the holding company have also approved the transaction) or give a guarantee or provide security, in connection with a loan to such director. 'Related arrangements' entered into by another person are also covered by this requirement for members' approval (CA 2006 s 203(1)).

The resolution to approve the transaction must be accompanied by a memorandum setting out the nature of the transaction, the loan amount and purpose for which it is required and the extent of the company's liability in respect of the loan (CA 2006 s 197(3) and (4)).

However, it should be noted that approval by the members is not required where the company is an overseas company or a wholly owned subsidiary of another corporate body (CA 2006 s 197(5)).

Additional public company requirements   **6.91.2**

In addition all public companies and companies associated with a public company must make sure that approval is obtained from the company's members (and the members of the holding company where the director is also a director of the holding company) before:

(i)   making a quasi-loan to a director of the company or its holding company or giving a guarantee or providing security in connection with the loan (CA 2006 s 198(1)–(3));

(ii)   making a loan or quasi-loan or guarantee or security in connection with such loan or quasi-loan available to a person 'connected' with a director (CA 2006 s 200(1)–(3) and see full definition in the **GLOSSARY**);

(iii)   entering into a credit transaction as creditor for the benefit of a director of the company or of the holding company or give a guarantee or provide security in connection with such credit transaction.

As described in para **6.91.1**, the members must be provided with a memorandum setting out the key terms of the transaction.

It should also be noted that members' approval is not required where the company is an overseas company or a wholly owned subsidiary of another body corporate (CA 2006 ss 198(6), 200(6) and 203(5)).

Exceptions   6.92

There are certain exceptions to the requirement for members' approval in CA 2006 ss 197, 198, 200 and 201 (see para **6.91**) as follows:

(i)   expenditure on company business by the director to enable him to properly perform his duties or for the purposes of the company, provided such expenditure does not exceed £50,000 (CA 2006 s 204);

(ii)   expenditure defending criminal or civil proceedings in connection with the director's alleged negligence, default, breach of duty or breach of trust or in connection with an application for relief provided the monies are repaid in the event the director is convicted and judgment is against him or the court does not grant relief (CA 2006 s 205);

(iii)   where the director is provided with funds to meet expenditure incurred defending himself against regulatory action or investigation in connection with the director's alleged negligence, default, breach of duty or breach of trust (CA 2006 s 206);

(iv)   where for the purposes of CA 2006 ss 197, 198 and 200 the value of the transaction in totality (including other relevant transactions) does not exceed £10,000 (CA 2006 s 207(1));

(v)   where for the purposes of CA 2006 s 201 the value of the credit transaction in totality does not exceed £15,000 (CA 2006 s 207(2));

(vi)   the transaction is intra-group, to an associated body corporate (CA 2006 s 208); and

(vii)   where the company is a money-lending company and the transaction is entered into in the ordinary course of the company's business and the amount and terms of the loan or quasi-loan are no more favourable than would be offered to others.

Penalties for non-compliance   **6.93**

Directors have a duty to ensure that when any loan, quasi-loan or credit transactions are proposed, such transactions are permitted within the provisions of CA 2006 ss 197–214. Where a transaction is entered into in contravention of these sections, any director of the company (and of the holding company, where applicable) who was involved in or authorised the transaction is guilty of an offence and is liable to account to the company for any direct or indirect gain made from the transaction and to indemnify it against any loss or damage suffered (CA 2006 s 213(3)).

However, where a director can demonstrate that he took all reasonable steps to secure compliance or that he did not know the relevant circumstances of the contravention he may be relieved of personal liability.

Disclosure requirements   **6.94**

Disclosure of transactions described in CA 2006 ss 197–214 must be made in the notes to the company's audited accounts and, where the company is part of a group, in the group accounts (CA 2006 s 413).

A company must disclose details in the notes to its own accounts of any advances and credits granted by the company to its directors and of any guarantees entered into by the company on behalf of its directors. A parent company that prepares group accounts must disclose details of advances and credits granted by the company to the directors of the parent company by the company or any subsidiary and any guarantees entered into on behalf of the directors of the parent company, by the company or any subsidiary in the notes to the group accounts (CA 2006 s 413(1) and (2)).

The details to be disclosed include:

- where the company has given an advance or credit, the company must include details of the amount, the interest rate, the main conditions and any amounts which have been repaid;

- where the company has given a guarantee, the company must include the main terms, details of the maximum liability which may be incurred by the company (or subsidiary), the amount paid by the company and any liability which may be incurred by the company (or subsidiary) by fulfilling the guarantee. This includes any loss incurred as a result of enforcement of the guarantee;

- the total amounts (for all directors and connected persons) of the amounts outstanding and repaid of any advances and credits and the maximum liability for the company and any amount already incurred by the company for all guarantees;

- where the company is a banking company or holding company of a credit institution, they need only state the details in respect of an amount of an advance or credit or the maximum amount of liability which may be incurred by the company (or subsidiary).

These details must be included in the accounts for any person who was a director at any time during the financial year for which the accounts are applicable, and total amounts must be declared (CA 2006 s 413(8)).

Service contracts   6.100

An executive director is an employee of the company and therefore, as detailed in paras **3.90** and **11.21** needs to be issued with a written contract setting out the terms under which he has been engaged. For an executive director this usually takes the form of a service contract which, in addition to the usual employment provisions, will contain specific requirements arising from his appointment to the Board. The basic contents of a director's service contract are discussed in para **3.90,** and **APPENDIX 1** contains a checklist of matters to consider for inclusion. The service contract will also usually contain a statement of the director's general duties, for example to:

- promote the success of the company;
- carry out specific tasks as assigned to him by the Board of Directors;
- devote time and attention to the company during agreed hours; and
- observe all competition and confidentiality restrictions.

In addition, the service contract should detail those requirements which relate to the executive director's executive function. For example, the finance director would have certain financial reporting obligations, in particular to provide high quality financial information to the Board; and the CEO would be responsible for delivering strategy and implementing appropriate standards of governance. These responsibilities should be specified in the director's service contract.

It is also recommended that the need for the director to attend Board meetings and any requirement to participate in committees of the Board or to serve on subsidiary company Boards is made clear in the contract, with an indication of the likely time commitment required from the director to fulfil these obligations.

Negotiating terms   6.101

Drafting the exact terms of the contract is a complex task and expert advice may need to be sought to ensure that the contract is in accordance with legal requirements and accurately records all matters agreed.

In terms of the negotiating process, whilst the appointment needs to be approved by the Board, it is recommended that negotiation of the terms in an executive director's contract is carried out by a remuneration committee comprised of non-executive directors (para **10.23.4**). By their very nature, non-executive directors are outside and slightly remote from the company's business and therefore have a degree of independence, putting them in a good position to challenge proposals and ensure there is no bias in favour of the director to the detriment of the company and its shareholders. Delegating negotiation to a remuneration committee in this way is an important means of avoiding speculation that a director exercised undue influence over the Board when agreeing the terms of his or her own contract. However, not all companies have a remuneration committee and, in any event, it is important to remember that a director should not be involved in the Board's consideration and approval of the terms of his or her own service contract.

Remuneration   6.102

Without doubt determining the appropriate level of a director's remuneration is extremely difficult given the need to attract, motivate and retain top calibre candidates, whilst at the same time not paying more than is necessary or awarding salaries that are considered excessive or over-generous. Considerable concern has been expressed about the scale of salaries being paid to executive directors in some high-profile, listed companies, as evidenced by almost daily reports in the press and also by an increase in the number of shareholders voting against companies' remuneration reports at their AGMs.

Recent developments concerning executive directors' remuneration and reporting requirements are detailed in **Chapters** **7** and **10**, save to say here that it is extremely important that the director's rights in respect of remuneration are clearly set out in the director's service contract. This should cover all fixed and variable elements of the director's remuneration; from base pay, to annual bonus, long-term incentives, share schemes and pension entitlement, etc. These details needs to be entirely clear, not only to avoid the time and costs of resolving discrepancies in the year ahead, but also to ensure they achieve the desired effect of retaining and motivating the executive director to achieve results.

Termination provisions   6.103

Even though when negotiating terms appointment for a new director, resignation or dismissal of the executive and termination might seem very remote, it is extremely important that termination provisions are decided at the outset when the director's service contract is being drawn up.

For some years now termination provisions in directors' service contracts, particularly in public companies, have been the subject of considerable concern and controversy as, although ultimately the company has power to remove a director by ordinary resolution approved in general meeting (CA 2006 s 168), the potentially high costs of compensation to be paid for termination before expiry of the contract term can act as a significant deterrent to the company exercising its power in this way.

There continue to be numerous cases reported in the press of outgoing directors receiving substantial amounts of compensation for termination of office, even where termination was as a result of poor performance by them personally or as a consequence of the company failing. Amongst these was the former chief executive of the Royal Bank of Scotland, who stepped down after the bank had to be bailed out by the Government and, whilst he waived receiving a pay-off which included a year's salary, he was able to draw a generous six-figure, yearly pension. Similarly outrage expressed over the £1.32m severance package paid by the BBC Trust to the outgoing director general of the BBC, which was double the contractually required sum, has prompted the new director general to propose introduction of a £150k cap on severance payments (*Telegraph*, 25 April 2013). There is wide recognition large severance payments for directors who have failed to perform is unjust, unacceptable, and risks undermining the credibility of a company's policy on directors' remuneration.

'Fat cat' payments to under-performing directors have been recognised as a problem for some time and back in 2003 BIS produced a consultation paper, 'Rewards for Failure: Directors' Remuneration – Contracts, Performance and Severance' to consider the need for further measures to ensure that compensation reflects performance and to establish a framework to allow shareholders to participate in the process more effectively. There were some 112 responses to the consultation paper, the majority of which thought there was no justification for further legislation in this area and considered corporate governance best practice principles with the 'comply or explain' approach to be the most effective means of control. A subsequent report, 'Rewards for Failure', from the House of Commons Trade and Industry Committee, concluded that a company must carefully consider the way in which executive's contracts are constructed but that legislative solutions to issues of concern would be premature and inflexible. In more recent years there have been further reviews and consultations, including the FSA, Walker, Turner and the European Commission (see **CHAPTER 10**), and the majority view of the respondents is that whilst companies need some form of guidance on how to avoid excessive payments to departing directors, legislation is not the way forward, as companies need flexibility in order to judge and determine what is best for them.

Corporate governance initiatives have attempted to limit a company's exposure to large-scale severance payments by recommending that directors' service contracts should be limited to one year, but they have not yet been universally applied and many institutional investors believe more could be done to avoid making large, undeserved severance payments. To try and address this, in 2002 the Association of British Insurers (ABI) and the National Association of Pension Funds (NAPF) jointly issued a statement of best practice on executive contracts. This was subsequently updated in February 2008 and 2013.

The statement is on the ABI website (www.abi.org.uk) and consists of eight sound commercial principles to discourage large-scale payouts to directors of failing companies, including:

- Notice periods: Boards should consider making directors' contracts with a shorter notice period than the standard 12 months.

- Severance payments: responsibility outlined for remuneration committees to justify severance payments and not to reward failure.

- Contract terms: remuneration committees should ensure that policy and objectives on directors' contracts are clearly stated in the remuneration report.

- Pensions: the importance for remuneration committees to regularly review pensions to ensure that unmerited payments do not occur in the event of severance.

- Executive commitment: Boards should ensure that executives show leadership by aligning their financial interests with those of the company.

The statement is a very useful tool for assisting companies to decide and apply termination provisions for executive directors and senior employees.

The ABI and NAPF particularly emphasise the role and importance of the remuneration committee when determining the company's needs and objectives and on being able to justify a director's severance terms to shareholders, employees and other stakeholders especially where the company is failing, share price tumbling and large-scale job cuts are being made.

Other practical points raised by the ABI and NAPF include the following:

- When drafting contracts, Boards should take account of all material commitments the company would face in the event of severance for failure or under-performance.

- The Board should consider the possibility of serious reputational risk by having to make and disclose large payments to executives who have failed to perform.

- Clear performance objectives should be set for executives.

- Phased payments of compensation are considered preferable to one-off lump sums, which can be reduced or stopped where the executive secures another job.

- Pension enhancements should not be granted to departing executives if they cannot be justified to shareholders.

Whilst this guidance has no legal basis, the ABI and the NAPF expect that their members will take compliance into account when deciding whether or not to vote in favour of the directors' remuneration report. Indeed, as noted in para **6.102**, an increasing number of shareholders are registering their dissatisfaction by voting against the remuneration report.

Finally, when determining a director's service contract the UK Corporate Governance Code (provision D.1.4) specifically requires the remuneration committee to consider what the compensation commitments would be in the event of early termination with a view to not rewarding poor performance and of mitigating loss and reducing compensation where possible.

Requirement for approval of service contracts   **6.104**

In general, the Board of Directors is able to negotiate the terms and conditions of a director's service contract without referring the matter for approval by the members. Any requirement in the company's Articles for approval of a service contract must be observed, as failure to observe such requirements may result in the contract being unenforceable. Importantly, in *UK Safety Group Ltd v Heane* [1998] 2 BCLC 208 a director's service contract was only made known to and approved by the remuneration committee, rather than the full Board as required by the Articles. The contract was held to be not binding and the company could not enforce restrictive covenants contained in the contract.

Having said this, CA 2006 s 188 requires that where a service contract is under consideration for a term exceeding two years, the directors must obtain prior approval of the contract from the shareholders by ordinary resolution approved in general meeting. This requirement for approval by the members does not apply where the company is a wholly owned subsidiary of another body corporate (CA 2006 s 188(6)).

Directors should be aware that this requirement for prior approval also applies to contracts which permit the director, at his option, to extend the contract (CA 2006 s 188(3)).

Failure to obtain shareholder approval will render void any term exceeding two years and the company will be able to terminate at any time, subject to giving reasonable notice (CA 2006 s 189)).

In addition, the UK Corporate Governance Code recommends that Boards should work towards setting notice periods on service contracts at one year or less and such agreements should not exceed one year's duration without approval of shareholders.

The aim of obtaining shareholder approval is two-fold: to ensure that not only are shareholders aware of the company's liability should any terms of service contracts be breached but also, at the same time, to restore shareholders' control over the company's financial commitments under long-term contracts.

Inspection of service contracts   **6.105**

Under CA 2006 s 188(5) a proposed service contract, or a memorandum containing its terms, must be available for inspection by members at the registered office of the company at least 15 days before the meeting at which approval is sought and at the meeting itself.

Provisions contained in CA 2006 ss 228 and 229 place a duty on directors to ensure that, once approved, any service contract or, if not in writing, a memorandum of terms, with a company or a subsidiary must be available at the registered office of the company or such other inspection place is notified to the Registrar of Companies for inspection by any member of the company without charge. The contract must also be kept available for inspection until 12 months after expiry or termination. This will enable members to determine the financial obligations of the company and potential compensation payable on termination of any director's service contract.

Statutory provisions are further enhanced by Stock Exchange requirements for listed companies as illustrated in the table following:

CA 2006 requirements	Additional Stock Exchange requirements
• Each written contract of service and any variation thereto shall be available for inspection for not less than 15 days prior to the meeting at which it is proposed for approval and at the meeting by any member free of charge (s 188(5)).	• From the date of notice of the AGM copies of service contracts must be available for inspection by members during normal business hours up to close of the meeting.
• Copies of the contracts shall be kept at either the registered office, or other location as notified to the Registrar of Companies (ss 228 and 299).	• Copies must be available at the location of the AGM for at least 15 minutes prior to and during the meeting.
• The Registrar must be notified of the location or any change in the location of the service contracts unless they have at all times been kept at the registered office.	• Notice convening the AGM must contain a note either that service contracts are available for inspection or that no such contracts exist.
• The directors must make sure that such documents are open to inspection by members of the company without charge (s 229(1)). A member is also entitled to a copy within seven days of making the request, upon payment of a prescribed fee (s 229(2)).	• A statement must be made in the directors' report to the annual report and accounts of either the unexpired term of service contracts of any director proposed for re-election at the AGM or that no such contracts exist.

Directors should note that any failure to make service contracts available for inspection or to keep copies at the appropriate location will expose the company and every officer in default liable to a fine for non-compliance with their statutory obligations (CA 2006 ss 228 and 229). This is important as at least one listed company has failed to make the directors' service contracts available at its AGM in the past causing some embarrassment and generating unwelcome press coverage.

Given that it is now possible for a director to file a service address at Companies House in order to prevent his home address appearing on the public record, where a director has registered a service address which is different to his residential address, it is essential that the residential address remains confidential.

Careful consideration should therefore be given as to where else it is disclosed. Ordinarily a service contract would contain details of a director's residential address, therefore before making it available for inspection either the director's consent to the disclosure of this 'protected information' must be obtained or the address must be removed or scored out. This is particularly important for listed companies which are more likely to receive public scrutiny.

Payment for loss of office   6.106

A company may not make a payment to a director of the company for loss of office unless the payment has been approved by the members of the company (CA 2006 s 217). Such payment might be as compensation for loss of office or be paid to the director to secure his resignation or retirement and includes any payments made to a connected person. Where payment is proposed to a director of the company's holding company for loss of office, the payment also needs to be approved by the members of the holding company.

The requirement for members' approval does not apply where the company is a wholly owned subsidiary of another body corporate (CA 2006 s 218(4)).

Furthermore, approval by the members is not required:

(i)   where the payment is made in good faith to comply with a legal obligation or to pay damages for breach of such obligation, is made by way of settlement or compromise for termination of the person's office or employment or is made by way of pension for past services (CA 2006 s 220); or

(ii)   where the amount or value of the payment (together with any other relevant payments for loss of office) does not exceed £200.

Where the requirement for members' approval applies but is not observed, civil consequences apply and the recipient is deemed to be holding the payment on trust for the company and any director who authorised the payment will be jointly and severally liable to indemnify the company against any loss resulting from the payment (CA 2006 s 222).

Takeovers and mergers   6.110

Directors must be aware that when they are considering making an offer to acquire or merge with another company or are evaluating an offer that has been received, they have an overriding obligation to observe their statutory duties to the company and to act honestly, and seek to promote the success of the company to which they have been appointed (**CHAPTER 4**).

The directors also have a duty to ensure that any information or representations provided during the takeover or merger process are correct, up to date and accurate, or risk action for fraudulent misrepresentation. In *Erlson Precision Holdings Ltd v Hampson Industries PLC* [2011] EWHC 1137 (Comm) the parent company, Hampson Industries, and its CEO, who was also a director of the subsidiary being sold, were found guilty of fraudulent misrepresentation for providing misleading forecasts and failing to advise the buyer that the subsidiary had lost one of its main customers immediately prior to conclusion of the sale. As a consequence the buyer, Erlson Precision Holdings, was entitled to rescind the share purchase agreement.

There are also a number of specific additional requirements concerning takeovers and mergers which stem not only from statutory provisions, including the FSMA 2000 (as amended) and CA 2006, but also from the Takeover Code, which the directors must ensure are observed. In addition to these, where the OFT considers a merger might decrease competition, the matter might be referred to the Competition Commission (para **13.62.2**).

FSMA 2000   **6.110.1**

Restrictions concerning information disseminated to the market about a proposed takeover or merger of a public company are contained in FSMA 2000, s 397 including the provisions that:

- no person carries out an act or engages in conduct to create a false impression of the market or value of shares to induce them to buy or sell such shares; and

- no false, misleading or deceptive statement is made to induce a person to buy or sell their shares or refrain from doing so.

Breach of FSMA 2000 requirements is a criminal offence.

CA 2006   **6.110.2**

Whilst the Panel on Takeovers and Mergers has long been established and responsible for administering and issuing the Takeover Code and for supervising and regulating takeovers and other matters to which the Code applies, it now also has statutory functions set out in CA 2006, Part 28, Chapter 1. The Panel is the supervisory authority responsible for regulating takeovers and mergers by and of companies which are registered in the UK, Channel Islands and Isle of Man where they have securities admitted to trading on a regulated market or multilateral trading facility in the UK (including the main market and AIM), or on any Stock Exchange on the Channel Islands or Isle of Man.

The Panel's remit also extends to certain unlisted public companies, and to Societas Europaea where the Panel considers their place of central management and control is in the UK. However, the Takeover Code only applies to private companies where, in the previous ten years, the company's securities were admitted to the Official List, dealings or the price of dealings in the company's shares were published for a continuous period of six months, any securities were subject to a marketing arrangement, or they were required to file a prospectus for the issue of securities with the Registrar of Companies or to have the prospectus approved by the UKLA.

The Panel is required to determine the rules regulating takeovers, mergers and other matters involving a change of ownership or control of a company (CA 2006 s 943). Such rules include the provisions set out in the Takeover Code.

The Panel has authority to require the production of information under CA 2006 s 947 and the directors must provide information and assistance to the Panel in a timely, open and cooperative way and correct or update the information provided where necessary. Failure to comply with a written request for information or documents constitutes a breach of the Takeover Code.

Where the Panel is satisfied a person has or is reasonably likely to contravene a requirement of the Takeover Code (in relation to offer document or response document rules), the Panel has enforcement powers and may give such direction it considers necessary to restrain a person from acting or doing a particular thing in breach of the rules in order to secure compliance with the rules (CA 2006 s 953). The Panel also has power to make compensation rulings for payment of monies to the holders of securities disadvantaged by conduct of a takeover and, if necessary, to seek enforcement through formal court process (CA 2006 s 955).

The Panel also has certain disciplinary powers that may be exercised in connection with breaches or alleged breaches of the Code. These include the ability to:

- issue disciplinary actions and proceedings;

- issue a private or public statement of censure;

- suspend or withdraw any exemption, approval or other special status the Panel may have previously granted to a person, or impose conditions that must be fulfilled for such status to remain;

- report the offender's conduct to a regulatory or professional body (in the UK, the FCA); or

- publish a Panel Statement indicating the offender which, in the UK, has the effect of preventing a person authorised under the FSMA 2000 from acting or continuing to act in connection with the transaction.

Takeover Code   6.111

The Takeover Code has been devised to ensure fair treatment of all shareholders in a takeover or merger and comprises general principles as well as more precise rules governing the manner in which a takeover or merger (including a statutory merger or scheme of arrangement) is carried out. The directors must ensure these general principles and rules are observed.

The eleventh edition of the Takeover Code, published on 20 May 2013 is available from www.thetakeoverpanel.org.uk. A number of reforms were made to the takeover process in 2011, to:

- increase protection for offeree companies against 'virtual bid' periods;

- strengthen the position of the offeree company;

- increase transparency and improve the quality of disclosure; and

- provide greater recognition of the interests of offeree company's employees.

To achieve these objectives, the tenth edition of the Code was amended to:

- require potential offerors to clarify their position within a shorter four-week period;

- prohibit deal protection measures and payment of inducement fees, except in certain limited cases;

- allow an offeree company's Board more scope in the factors it takes into account in giving its opinion and recommendations on the offer;

- require the disclosure of all offer-related fees;

- require the disclosure of the same financial information regarding an offeror and the financing of an offer irrespective of the nature of the offer;

- improve the quality of disclosure by offerors and offeree companies in relation to the offeror's intentions regarding the offeree company and its employees; and

- improve the ability of employee representatives to make their views known.

These changes have been preserved in the eleventh edition of the Code and they aim to address concerns expressed by many about the ease with which hostile takeover offers have tended to succeed and how the outcome of an offer can be unduly influenced by short-term investors. There was particular concern about the hostile bid by Kraft Foods to acquire Cadbury in 2010 with which took almost 170 days to complete as Kraft took maximum advantage of each deadline, prolonging the process. Such delays not only extend the period of uncertainty for the offeree company which can be damaging in itself, but also place unnecessary strain on management time and resources often to the detriment of the offeree's business. This has been addressed by shortening a number of deadlines and time limits.

General principles   **6.111.1**

The six general principles of the Takeover Code which directors must ensure are observed in a takeover or merger situation are as follows:

(1)   shareholders of the same class must be treated equally and, in particular, be protected should someone acquire control of the company;

(2)   shareholders must be given sufficient information and time in which to reach a decision and, in particular, directors of the company being acquired must give their views on the effects the bid will have on employees, employment conditions, and locations of places of business;

(3)   the Board of the offeree must act in the interests of the company as a whole and not deny the holders of securities opportunity to consider the merits of a bid;

(4)   a false market must not be created in securities of the offeror, offeree or any company concerned with the bid;

(5)   directors of the company making the offer should only announce the offer when they are confident it can be implemented and the consideration be met in cash or as otherwise intended; and

(6)   the offeree company must not be hindered in the conduct of its affairs for longer than is reasonable by a bid.

These broad principles set the standard of commercial behaviour expected.

Rules   **6.111.2**

In addition to the general principles, the Takeover Code contains detailed rules set out in Sections D to R (inclusive) on the conduct of a takeover or merger.

These rules set down the framework for how a takeover or merger is to be conducted and cover requirements including the need for secrecy of price-sensitive information; timing of announcements; restrictions on share dealing; mandatory and voluntary offers; conduct and timings; issue of information; profit forecasts; asset valuations; and post-offer restrictions, etc. The rules need to be consulted in detail by directors of both the company making the offer and the company which is the subject of the offer to ensure that all procedural requirements are met in 'spirit' as well as by the letter.

Of particular note is the requirement in Rule 2.2 for announcement about the offer where:

- a firm intention to make an offer is notified by an offeror to the offeree company's Board, regardless of the Board's feelings about the offer;

- the offeror has acquired an interest in such number of shares as to give rise to an obligation to make a mandatory offer under Rule 9.1; or

- there has been an approach by a potential offeror, the consequence of which is market speculation, rumour or untoward share price movement in which case announcement of the offeror's intention to make an offer is necessary to restore order to the market.

Copies of all announcements need to be made available to the Panel, shareholders and employees or, where they exist, employees' representatives of the offeree and offeror companies. Explanation of the implications of the offer must also be given.

Where the offeror's 'intention' to make an offer has been announced, Rule 2.6 states that the offeror then has 28 days (unless extended by the Takeover Panel) in which to announce either a firm intention to make an offer or to clarify that it will not be making an offer. Where the offeror has withdrawn, it will be restricted in making another offer or dealing in the offeree company's securities for a period of six months.

Rules 3.1 and 3.2 require the Boards of the offeree and offeror companies to obtain competent, independent advice on any offer, the substance of which must be reported to the company's shareholders. It should be noted that certain 'success fee' arrangements are considered to create a conflict of interest and affect determination of an adviser's independence.

Rule 4.1 prohibits dealing in securities by any person who has access to price-sensitive inside information before an announcement about the offer is made, which is consistent with the prohibition in the Criminal Justice Act 1993 (CJA 1993). The directors must therefore make sure that all those with access to such information are aware of these dealing restrictions.

Rule 9 requires that if a person or persons acting in concert acquire an interest in shares of a company which carry 30% or more of the voting rights of the company, such person or persons shall be required to make an offer to acquire the remaining equity shares of the company. Many listed companies actively monitor their share dealing to determine whether there is evidence of any stake building.

Rule 19 sets out detailed requirements about the conduct of an offer and information issued, in particular the need to obtain Panel clearance before information is published. This rule also makes clear that the directors of the offeror and offeree, as applicable, are expressly responsible for the information given in documents and advertisements issued to shareholders concerning an offer. Rule 19.2 specifically requires that all documents and advertisements issued in connection with an offer contain a responsibility statement confirming that the directors accept responsibility for information disclosed and that to the best of their knowledge and belief the information is correct and does not omit anything likely to affect the substance and meaning of the information. It is therefore essential that the directors ensure high standards of care and accuracy are applied when the information is collated and that all statements, statistics, forecasts, views and trends, etc are fully supported and can be verified.

Rules 21 requires that, without shareholders' consent, the Board must not take any action to frustrate an offer or do anything so as to deny shareholders the opportunity to consider the merits of the offer.

Unless consent is obtained from the Panel, offer-related fee arrangements are prohibited by Rule 21.2. These include any agreement, arrangement, commitment, or inducement with a financial or economic benefit between the offeror and offeree and any persons acting in concert with them.

Rule 24.1 requires the offer document to be sent by the offeror to the offeree company's shareholders, persons with information rights and employees within 28 days of the announcement of a firm intention to make an offer (unless the Panel have granted an extension). The offer document is very detailed and contains all the information about the offer, consideration, acceptance, event timings, continued trading of securities, and of all fees and expenses connected with the offer and financing the offer, etc. In addition the offer document must also explain the offeror's strategic plans and the implications these will have for the offeree's employees, their terms of employment and where work will be carried out.

The offer document must also disclose information about the offeror directors' own interests in securities of the offeree; their share dealings during the 12-month period leading up to the offer (Rule 24.4); and how their emoluments will be affected by the transaction (Rule 24.5).

Within 14 days of the offer document being issued, the offeree company's Board must send a circular to its own shareholders. Rule 25 requires that the circular contains the offeree company Board's view on the offer and the offeror's plans for the company and its employees as well as information about the directors' own interests, dealings and service contracts. The circular must also contain details of all fees and expenses connected with the offer and, where there is one, have the employee representatives' opinion on the offer appended to the circular.

In addition, it should be noted that shareholders of the offeree company, persons with information rights and employees/employee representatives of the offeree company have the right to see or be sent information in connection with the offer, as set out in Rules 2.12, 20.1, 23.1, 24.15, 25.1, 30.2, 30.4, 32.1, and 32.6(a), and the directors must ensure these requirements for information are fulfilled. Similarly the Panel and all advisers to the offer have the right to be sent information and documents.

Whilst it is common practice for a committee of the Board to be formed to deal with an offer, this does not detract from the Board's ultimate responsibility. This is specifically addressed in Appendix 3 to the Takeover Code which makes clear that the whole Board remains responsible and must ensure proper arrangements are in place to ensure the takeover is conducted in an orderly fashion and in accordance with the Code. Copies of all documents and advertisements must be shown to each director and approved before they are made public, to ensure that they are in agreement with the information contained therein. All directors must be kept up to date, Board meetings be held as needed, opinions of advisers be available and sought as necessary and those to whom the Board has delegated responsibility be able to justify actions taken and proposed pursuant to the offer.

Payments to directors   6.112

Directors, when recommending a takeover or plan for a merger to shareholders, must ensure that they do so observing their duty to seek to promote the success of the company. The advice they give must be in their capacity as directors, taking into account the interests not only of shareholders but also employees and creditors, and under no circumstances should their personal interests influence their decisions.

As a safeguard against the difficulties of disregarding personal interests, the directors are required to obtain shareholder approval for certain payments as follows:

- where payment as compensation for loss of office is to be made to a director on a takeover, this must first be approved by the members. The directors must ensure that a memorandum setting out the particulars, including the amount of the proposed payment, are sent to the relevant shareholders. Neither the person making the offer nor any associate of his are entitled to vote on the resolution (CA 2006 s 219). Payment made without approval will be deemed to be held 'in trust' for persons who have sold their shares as a result of the offer and the expenses incurred by the director to whom the payment was made (CA 2006 s 222(3));

- where the proposal is for property of the company to be transferred as compensation for loss of office, particulars must be disclosed to and approved by members (CA 2006 s 218). Payment made without approval will be deemed to be held 'in trust' for the company and be repayable by the director (CA 2006 s 222(1)).

Failure by the director, or by any person properly instructed by him, to comply with these disclosure requirements may lead to imposition of a fine. Any payment received by a director without required approval will be deemed to have been received 'in trust' for members who sold their shares pursuant to the offer (CA 2006 s 222). Also, any director who authorised the payment will be jointly and severally liable to indemnify the company for any loss resulting from the payment.

The director is likely to be required to repay any money or property received to the members and bear the costs of distribution personally.

Dissenting minority shareholders   6.113

Where an offeror has acquired or contracted to acquire 90% of the shares in the target company, he may give notice to the remaining minority that he desires to acquire their shares by compulsory purchase, which he is entitled to do (CA 2006 s 979). Similarly, the shareholders originally failing to accept the offer may, by notice in writing, require the offeror to acquire their shares (CA 2006 s 983).

In both cases notice must be given by the offeror, within one month of the 90% threshold being reached, notifying shareholders either of their right to be bought out or the offeror's right to purchase their shares. The directors must ensure that:

- the terms offered are the same as those in the original offer or such terms as are agreed between the dissenting shareholders and the offeror;

- where the offeror is exercising his right to acquire shares, the directors must place monies remitted to the company by the offeror in payment for such shares in an account where it is held in trust for those shareholders and register the offeror as the holder of the shares (CA 2006 s 981(9)).

The directors therefore have a duty to protect the interests of dissenting minorities and ensure that they are treated on terms equally favourable to those offered to shareholders in agreement with the offer and that they are advised of their rights of acquisition.

Listing particulars   6.114

Listed companies involved in a takeover are required to submit the offer document to the UKLA for approval, and the directors must ensure that this document has been prepared in an acceptable format and contains information prescribed by the rules for listed companies.

Directors need also to be aware that where consideration for the takeover or merger consists of securities for which listing will be sought, listing particulars may be required by the UKLA (see para **9.20**). The directors will need to consult the UKLA rules for listed companies relevant in a takeover bid to determine whether full listing particulars are required or summary particulars are sufficient.

In either case they will normally be required to be published and circulated to shareholders at the same time as the offer document. Where the offer is revised, listing particulars will need to be revised, or supplementary listing particulars be prepared, and circulated to shareholders at the same time as the revised offer document.

Directors' and officers' indemnity insurance   6.120

Under CA 2006 (s 232) a company cannot indemnify a director (to any extent) from liability as a result of negligence, default or breach of duty and any provisions contained in a company's Articles of Association to that effect, are void. However, provided the company's Articles of Association permit, a company may effect insurance to indemnify directors and officers against any liability incurred in respect of negligence, default, breach of duty or breach of trust which may occur whilst fulfilling their role as directors or officers of the company (CA 2006 s 233 and see para **3.120**).

Disclosure of information during an investigation   6.130

Directors should be aware that the Secretary of State has power to investigate the affairs and membership of a company and, where the company is subject to investigation, they and all officers and agents of the company have a duty to cooperate with the investigation (CA 2006 s 1035)). These statutory powers of investigation are conferred on the Secretary of State to act as a deterrent and discourage malpractice by the directors and shareholders of a company.

The Secretary of State *must* appoint inspectors to investigate a company's affairs when ordered to do so by the court and has *discretion* to appoint inspectors where:

- application has been made by the company or a prescribed minority of members requesting investigation and the Secretary of State considers there are sufficient grounds to justify such investigation (CA 1985 s 431);

- it appears that the company's affairs have been conducted with intent to defraud creditors and others or for a fraudulent, unlawful or prejudicial purpose (CA 1985 s 432);

- the company was formed for fraudulent or unlawful purposes (CA 1985 s 432);

- it appears that those involved in formation of the company or management of its affairs are guilty of fraud, misfeasance or misconduct towards the company or the members (CA 1985 s 432);

- evidence suggests the members have not been given all the information they might reasonably expect to receive (CA 1985 s 432).

In addition, it should be noted that the Secretary of State has power, pursuant to authority in CA 1985 s 442 (as amended by CA 2006 s 1035), to investigate the membership of a company where there is an apparent need to determine the persons interested in or controlling the company or where insider dealing is suspected (see para **6.133**).

The outcome of an investigation may lead to civil or criminal proceedings for a breach of duty or other statutory offences, a petition for the company to be compulsorily wound up or a petition for relief by minority shareholders.

Requisition and seizure of documents   6.131

Once inspectors have been appointed, it is the duty of the directors, officers and agents of the company to provide all assistance they could reasonably be expected to give to assist the investigation. This includes producing documents for the inspectors and attending before them to give evidence when they require (CA 1985 s 434(1)). Where the directors, or any of them, do not cooperate with the investigation and withhold information, the inspectors have power to enforce this duty and require them to produce documents, including those in non-legible form, attend before them and otherwise provide assistance (CA 1985 s 434(2), introduced by CA 1989).

The Secretary of State may at any time, where he considers it necessary, direct a company to produce certain documents for inspection, take copies of such documents and require any past or present officers of the company to provide an explanation of the documents (CA 1985 s 447). He also has power, once a warrant has been issued, to enter and search a company's premises where it is believed documents have been withheld or where there is concern that if production of documents was requested they would be hidden, tampered with or destroyed (CA 1985 s 448).

Failure to cooperate   **6.132**

Any person who fails to comply with a requisition to produce information, provide an explanation or statement of circumstances, or who intentionally obstructs the inspectors' right to search the company's premises conferred by a warrant is guilty of an offence and liable to a fine (CA 1985 s 447(6)). For persistent failure to cooperate and answer questions, directors will be held in 'contempt of court' and punishment will be at the discretion of the court (CA 1985 s 436).

In *Re an inquiry into Mirror Group Newspapers plc* [2000] Ch 194, [1999] All ER (D) 255 a director refused to cooperate with DTI Inspectors investigating the affairs of the company. The inspectors commenced proceedings as if the director had been guilty of contempt of court and it was held that, subject to certain steps being taken by the inspectors, the director was not entitled to refuse to answer questions.

As well as the duty to supply information requested, directors should be aware that any attempt to destroy, mutilate or falsify documents of a company or make false entries in any document or book of account is an offence. Where found to be guilty, such person will be liable to a fine, imprisonment, or both (CA 1985 s 450).

Similarly, a person who makes a false statement, or provides a false explanation of events, is guilty of an offence and will be liable to a fine, imprisonment or both (CA 1985 s 451).

Investigation of insider dealing   **6.133**

Dealing by an individual in a company's securities where that person has 'insider information' likely to affect the price of those securities is an offence pursuant to CJA 1993 (see para **9.60**). Under CJA 1993 it is an offence for persons to deal in securities of the company where:

- they are or were during the last six months a director, officer or employee or had a business relationship with the company ('connected person') which allowed them access to unpublished price-sensitive information;

- they obtain confidential price-sensitive information from such connected person; or

- they are contemplating, or have received information from another party that they are contemplating, a takeover of the company.

It is also important to note that any person who has access to such price-sensitive information is prohibited from offering 'tips' or in any way advising or procuring other persons to deal in the company's securities.

Where the Secretary of State believes there to have been a contravention of CJA 1993 s 52, he may appoint inspectors to establish whether any such contravention has occurred (FSMA 2000). The powers that the inspectors (usually from the FSA's enforcement and financial criminal division) have in terms of investigation are similar to those provided by Companies Act provisions, although the penalties for failure to comply with requests by the inspectors may be more severe, as follows (CJA 1993 s 178):

- cancelling any authorisation the company or individual may have to carry on investment business;

- restricting or limiting their authorisation in a prescribed manner;

- prohibiting certain specific types of business or transactions; or

- prohibiting dealings or business with certain identified persons.

On receipt of the inspector's report, the Secretary of State may instigate criminal proceedings (see para **9.60**) or apply for a disqualification order against the director or directors concerned.

Given the severe penalties imposed for insider dealing, directors must ensure that they (as well as any employees who may have access to restricted information) observe strict rules of confidentiality and take particular care not to discuss the company's results or future prospects with persons outside the company.

Investigation into proceeds of crime   6.134

The Proceeds of Crime Act 2002 (POCA 2002) has expanded investigatory powers to allow the director of the Assets Recovery Agency or any constable, customs office or accredited financial investigator to issue:

(1)   production orders to obtain material known to be in existence relating to a known account;

(2)   search and seizure warrants to search premises and seize documents;

(3)   customer information orders to search accounts in financial institutions;

(4)   account monitoring orders for future transactions; and

(5)   disclosure orders requiring documents and information to be disclosed relating to an investigation.

A person found guilty of prejudicing an investigation by, for example, destroying or concealing documents required by an order, could face up to five years in prison. Directors must therefore ensure that any order is complied with to its full extent.

Furthermore, regs 36–41 (inclusive) of the Money Laundering Regulations 2007 (SI 2007/2157) have given officers of HMRC authority to enter premises, inspect and if required take copies of the records of any business, observe the carrying on of business or professional activity, require an explanation from any person on the premises in connection with the records and if the case so relates, and to inspect any money found on the premises. Such powers are only in respect of matters subject to the Money Laundering Regulations 2007. Regulation 40 provides that the court may issue an order, for failure to allow access to and inspection of premises, comply with an order for recorded information or with an order to present information removed from the premises.

7 Accounting and financial responsibilities of directors

7 Accounting and financial responsibilities of directors

Accounting duties of directors   7.10

In fulfilment of their role as managers and custodians of a company's assets, directors have responsibilities in relation to maintaining accounting records, preparing, approving and filing accounts of the company. These are discussed below, noting that the form and content of narrative reporting in companies' accounts has been subject to substantial change.

Maintaining accounting records   7.11

The directors are responsible for maintaining detailed accounting records so that at any time they are able to demonstrate and explain the financial position of the company and determine what transactions have taken place (CA 2006 s 386). More specifically, directors have a duty to:

- keep accounting records, which must be sufficient to record and explain transactions and provide a reasonably accurate picture of the financial position of the company at any time;

- provide information from which to compile the balance sheet and profit and loss account, comprising the annual accounts, as required by CA 2006;

- keep records of all money received and paid out on a daily basis;

- maintain records of assets and liabilities;

- carry out an end of year stocktake and keep a statement of stock levels held (where applicable to goods);

- where goods are sold other than in the normal course of retail business, details of the buyers and sellers must be kept in order to be able to identify them.

Failure to maintain adequate accounting records is a criminal offence will cause every officer in default, including the directors, to be liable to a fine, imprisonment for up to two years, or both (CA 2006 s 387).

Directors must ensure that they have sufficient information to enable them to manage the company's business effectively. For this purpose they will require detailed accounting records from which management information and reports can be compiled, ongoing assessments of profitability be made, cash resources be managed and projections, forecasts and budgets be calculated, which may extend beyond statutory requirements for accounts and records. These accounting records must then be kept for at least three years by a private company and six years by a public company, although many companies will keep them a lot longer.

The directors must ensure that systems are established to provide them with required information, that such systems are adequately controlled and that they can be used to provide regular and timely information as required.

Two cases involving disqualification of directors highlight the importance of maintaining accounting records and that BIS will prosecute those that fail to observe their duties in this respect. In the first, Mr James Patrick Lloyd, sole director of Quality Building Developments Ltd, an electrical and heating installation company, pleaded guilty to failing to keep proper accounting records and explain £1.1m withdrawn from the company, for which he received a four-month suspended prison sentence (Insolvency Service, press release, 13 February 2013). The company went into liquidation in September 2009 with total debts of £269,612 and initial investigation by the Insolvency Service, followed by full criminal investigation by BIS, revealed that the company had no accounting records at all for three years, there were no Construction Industry Scheme records and had not kept any details of wages paid to subcontractors.

In the second case, *Re Pamstock Ltd* [1994] 1 BCLC 716, directors were disqualified for failure to maintain adequate accounting records and for operating systems of management which made it impossible to determine the financial condition of the company. Consequently the financial health of the company could not be monitored and it continued to trade some time after trading should have ceased.

The accounting records must be kept at the company's registered office or such other place as the directors consider appropriate and shall be open for inspection by the company's officers at any time. Furthermore, as discussed in para **6.41**, accounting records must be retained for a minimum statutory period of three years for a private company and six years for a public company, although directors would be well advised to consider other requirements for accounting records before they are destroyed (**APPENDIX 7**). Where found guilty of failing to take sufficient measures to ensure accounting records are retained or by acting deliberately to defraud, the officers concerned will be liable to a fine, imprisonment, or both (CA 2006 s 389(4)).

Preparation of the accounts   **7.12**

CA 2006 s 394 requires the directors of every company to prepare accounts for each financial year, save where the company is a dormant subsidiary and qualifies for exemption under s 394A (see paras **7.14.5** and **7.16.1**).

Under CA 2006 s 396, accounts prepared under CA 2006 must comprise a balance sheet as at the last day of the relevant accounting period and a profit and loss account (the date being determined by the company's accounting reference date). Both the balance sheet and profit and loss account must give a true and fair view of the affairs of the company. Similarly, the requirements of the accounting standard under which the accounts have been prepared must be observed. These might, for example, include International Accounting Standards ('IAS'), UK GAAP or US GAAP.

The basic accounting principles required to be used remain the same as they were under Schedule 4 to CA 1985. As the directors are responsible for preparing the accounts, they must be aware of and ensure that these principles are observed in preparation of the accounts:

- *Going concern basis*: In preparing the accounts the company must (as long as it is applicable) be treated as if it will continue business and operations on the same scale for the foreseeable future.

- *Consistency*: Accounting policies must be applied consistently from one financial year to the next to allow comparisons to be made between figures in one year and the next.

- *Prudence*: Requiring the value of any item to be determined on a 'prudent basis' by taking account of actual profit realised before the end of the financial year and any liabilities or losses which have arisen or are likely to arise in that period, provided the directors are aware of them before the accounts are signed.

- *Accruals*: Any income and charges must be taken into account in the financial period to which they relate, without regard to when they are paid or received.

- Individual determination of any assets or liabilities in the balance sheet.

Where a company is part of a group, there is an obligation for the parent company to provide consolidated accounts for the group as well as individual accounts for the company (CA 2006 s 399). These accounts must comprise a consolidated profit and loss account and consolidated balance sheet and comply with the principles listed above. However, there are certain exceptions to the general requirement for group accounts which the directors need to be aware of which might apply (see para **7.14.3**).

Content of the accounts 7.13

In addition to the profit and loss account and balance sheet required by CA 2006 s 393, the company's report and accounts must include narrative reports comprising a directors' report, strategic report (which replaced the business review), separate corporate governance statement, going concern statement, remuneration report, notes to the accounts and an auditors' report.

DTR 4.1.5 also requires the annual financial report of a listed company to include a management report and directors' responsibility statement.

These requirements are detailed below and summarised in **Appendix 13** by type and size of company.

In the last year a number of fundamental changes have been brought into effect to improve the form and content of narrative reporting in companies' accounts after much discussion and formal consultation. These take into account consensus from initial and further consultations conducted by BIS on 'The Future of Narrative Reporting' and 'A Long-Term Focus for Corporate Britain', which evidenced widespread support by companies, shareholders, institutions and shareholder advisory bodies for changes to the reporting framework so that readers of companies' annual reports are able to find the information they require more easily without being overwhelmed by the volume of information.

The changes have overhauled the way annual reports are prepared and presented and have introduced a new, clearer, structure for reporting. Some of the previous disclosures required in the annual report have fallen away, as has the requirement for the business review and SFS (both replaced by the strategic report), and the remuneration report in its current form.

Overall, the changes aim to create more clear, concise, useful and meaningful annual reports.

Directors' report 7.13.1

All companies must prepare a directors' report each year in accordance with the requirements of CA 2006 s 415 and include the information required by CA 2006 s 416 as well as Sch 5 to the Small Companies' and Groups (Accounts and Directors' Report) Regulations 2008 (SI 2008/409) and Sch 7 to the Large and Medium-sized Companies and Groups (Accounts and Reports) Regulations 2008 (SI 2008/410), which expand on the requirements under CA 2006.

However, directors should note that the Companies Act 2006 (Strategic Report and Directors' Report) Regulations 2013 (SI 2013/1970) took effect in October 2013, removing and amending some of the directors' report disclosure requirements. The amendments were made to address concerns about duplication and remove the need for information that was not found particularly useful.

Directors should also note that whilst BIS did consult on replacing the directors' report with an annual directors' statement, this has not been implemented.

In brief, the directors' report for all companies (save where specific exemptions are claimed) should contain details of:

(1)   names of directors who held office during the year;

(2)   amounts, if any, of any dividends recommended by the directors;

(3)   save where not material to determination of the company's financial position, potential risks to the company and financial risk management objectives and policies for financial instruments;

(4)   important post-balance sheet events of the company (and subsidiaries);

(5)   likely future developments of the company (and subsidiaries);

(6)   research and development by the company (and subsidiaries);

(7)   existence of any branches of the company outside the UK;

(8)   where the average number of employees exceeds 250 during the year:

(a)   the company's policy on employing and continuing to employ disabled people, and on their training, career development and promotion;

(b)   the extent of employee involvement, which should contain details of the manner in which information concerning employees is communicated to them, procedures used to consult employees and steps taken and arrangements in place to encourage involvement of employees with the company's performance, such as an employee share scheme. Although BIS consulted on removing the requirement for this disclosure, it was retained as a means of promoting and encouraging employee engagement;

(9)   political donations or political expenditure incurred by the company and its subsidiaries where it exceeds £2,000 in aggregate;

(10)   exposure to price, credit, liquidity or cash flow risk save where not material to assessment of the company's financial position;

(11)   any information included in the strategic report that would, otherwise, have been required in the directors' report; and

(12)   any qualifying indemnity provisions for the benefit of directors.

In addition, where some of the information required in the strategic report (see para **7.13.3**) is disclosed in the directors' report, this will need to be stated.

A small company (see para **7.14.1**) is entitled to omit much of the information from the directors' report and in fact only has to include items 1 and 8(a) listed above, but where the small company exemption is claimed, this must be stated in a prominent position in the report, usually just above where it is signed. If the accounts are group accounts, this must also be stated in the directors' report.

Directors' reports for listed companies are also required by Part 6 of Schedule 7 to the Large and Medium-sized Companies and Groups (Accounts and Reports) Regulations 2008 (SI 2008/410) (amended by the Companies Act 2006 (Strategic Report and Directors Report) Regulations 2013 (SI 2013/1970) to contain information as at the end of the year on the following matters:

(a) the structure of the company's capital, including the rights and obligations attaching to the shares and, where there are two or more classes, the percentage of the total share capital represented by each class;

(b) restrictions on the transfer of securities in the company;

(c) in the case of any person with a significant direct or indirect holding of securities in the company, such details as are known to the company of the identity of the person, the size of the holding, and the nature of the holding;

(d) in the case of any person holding securities carrying special rights with regard to control of the company, the identity of the person, and the nature of the rights;

(e) where the company has an employees' share scheme, and shares to which the scheme relates have rights with regard to control of the company that are not exercisable directly by the employees, how those rights are exercisable;

(f) restrictions on voting rights;

(g) agreements between holders of securities that are known to the company and may result in restrictions on the transfer of securities or on voting rights;

(h) rules that the company has about appointment and replacement of directors, or amendment of the company's Articles of Association;

(i) the powers of the company's directors, including in particular any powers in relation to the issuing or buying back by the company of its shares;

(j) significant agreements to which the company is a party that take effect, alter or terminate upon a change of control of the company following a takeover bid, and the effects of any such agreements;

(k) agreements between the company and its directors or employees providing compensation for loss of office of employment in the event of a takeover; and

(l) as far as it is practical to obtain, the annual quantity in tonnes of carbon dioxide emissions created by the company's operations and activities and also from the electricity, heat, steam or cooling means purchased by the company.

In addition, listed companies must also disclose the following information in their accounts and this often appears in the directors' report:

- directors' interests in shares and share options and changes from the beginning to the end of the year;

- a statement that the directors have made enquiries and conducted a review and consider that the company will continue in operational existence for the foreseeable future (alternatively disclosed in a separate 'going concern statement'; see para **7.13.5**);

- a report on compliance with principles of the UK Corporate Governance Code and the effectiveness of the company's internal controls (alternatively disclosed in a separate corporate governance statement; see para **7.13.4**).

When finalised, the directors' report must be approved by the Board of Directors and either a director or the secretary of the company be authorised to sign it (CA 2006 s 419(1)). The report must also contain a statement confirming that each director believes and has taken all steps necessary to check that the auditors have received all information relevant to the audit.

The copy submitted to Companies House must bear an original signature, whilst copies sent to members and others entitled to receive accounts must have the name of the person who signed the report printed thereon. Failure to comply with these requirements will render the company and any officer guilty of an offence and liable to a fine (CA 2006 s 419(3)).

Where the directors fail to prepare a directors' report, or the contents do not comply with the requirements of CA 2006 ss 416–418 and the regulations detailed above, all directors who were in office immediately before the period for laying and delivering accounts shall be guilty of an offence and liable to a fine for the offence (CA 2006 s 415(5)).

Statement of directors' responsibilities for accounts 7.13.2

Directors of companies with a premium listing of securities are required by SAS 600 and provision C.1.1 of the UK Corporate Governance Code to include a statement in the annual report and accounts, usually immediately before the auditors' report, explaining their responsibility for preparing the annual report and accounts. Directors must ensure that this statement details their responsibility to:

- prepare accounts which give a true and fair review of the company's state of affairs;

- select suitable accounting policies and apply them consistently;

- make judgments that are prudent and reasonable;

- state whether applicable accounting standards have been followed, subject to any material departures disclosed and explained in the notes to the accounts (applies to large companies only);

- maintain proper accounting records, safeguard assets of the company and take reasonable steps to prevent and detect fraud or other irregularities; and

- (where there is no separate going concern statement) to prepare accounts on a going concern basis unless it is not appropriate.

This statement should also make clear that the directors consider the report and accounts, taken as a whole, are fair, balanced and understandable and provide such information as is necessary for shareholders to accurately assess the company's performance, business model and strategy. Example wording for this statement is set out in **APPENDIX 12**.

For a listed company, DTR 4.1.5 also sets out requirements in relation to the responsibility statement and, for each person making the statement, it must state that the person:

- confirms that to the best of his knowledge the financial statements have been prepared in accordance with relevant accounting standards and give a true and fair view of the assets, liabilities, financial position and profit or loss of the company (and group, when consolidated accounts are prepared); and

- believes, to the best of his knowledge, that the management report (see para **7.13.7**) includes a fair review of the performance and development of the business and its principal risks and uncertainties.

The example statement for a listed company in **APPENDIX 21** would usually be made by the directors after consideration and approval of the annual accounts.

Strategic report (replaced the business review)   **7.13.3**

Directors should note that the Companies Act 2006 (Strategic Report and Directors' Report) Regulations 2013 (SI 2013/1970) took effect in October 2013, replacing the business review with the strategic report.

Consequently, all companies, unless entitled to exemption as a small company, now need to produce a separate strategic report in their annual accounts in place of the business review (CA 2006, new Chapter 4A). It is intended that by including a separate report in this way, company strategy will be more prominent in reporting and the same will be achieved for diversity, human rights and remuneration. In turn, the information will help the company's members assess whether the directors have been effective in fulfilling their duty to promote the success of the company (para **4.20.2**).

The aim of the strategic report is that it will, in a concise and clear manner:

- provide insight into the company's business model, overall strategy and objectives;

- describe the company's principal risks and how they might affect prospects and strategy; and

- provide analysis of past performance.

The strategic report must contain a fair review of the company's business and a description of the principal risks and uncertainties it faces. The review must embrace a balanced and comprehensive analysis of the development and performance of the company's business during and at the end of the financial year and include analysis of such financial and non-financial indicators as are necessary and appropriate (including environmental and employee matters) to understand the development, performance or position of the company's business. Medium-sized companies do not, however, have to analyse and report information on non-financial key performance indicators.

Where necessary to understand the development, performance or position of a quoted company's business, the strategic report must include analysis of the main trends and factors likely to affect the future development, performance and position of the company's business. This might include information on environmental matters (including the impact of the company's business on the environment), employees, and social, community and human rights issues as well as policies implemented by the company in relation to these matters.

The quoted company's strategic report must also contain a description of the company's strategy and business model, as well as a breakdown of the number of persons by gender employed and at senior manager and director level as at the end of each financial year.

Once prepared, the strategic report needs to be approved by the Board and signed on behalf of the Board by a director or the company secretary. Failure to provide a strategic report is an offence, punishable by a fine of any director in office who failed to take steps to ensure it was provided (CA 2006 s 414A(5) and (6)).

Whilst for small companies and many non–quoted medium/large companies the changes are relatively minimal, they are more significant for quoted companies and many conducted a full review of changes to reporting requirements and how they could be implemented.

In addition, the Companies Act 2006 (Strategic Report and Director's Report) Regulations 2013 replaced the need for summary financial statements with the option for companies to send the strategic report, plus supplementary information (s 426), to shareholders in place of the full annual report. Previous elections by shareholders to receive the summary financial statement will continue to apply to the strategic report.

New s 426A requires the supplementary information referred to in s 426 to state:

(1) that the strategic report is only part of the company's annual report and accounts;

(2) how a person can obtain a full copy of the company's annual report and accounts;

(3) whether the auditor's report on the annual accounts was unqualified or qualified and, if it was qualified, set out the report in full together with any further material needed to understand qualification by the auditor; and

(4) whether the auditor's statement on whether strategic report and directors' report were consistent with the accounts was unqualified or qualified and, if it was qualified, set out the qualified statement in full together with any further material needed to understand the qualification.

In addition, in the case of a quoted company, the supplementary information must also contain a copy of that part of the directors' remuneration report which sets out the single total figure table in respect of the company's directors' remuneration in accordance with the requirements of Schedule 8 to the Large and Medium-sized Companies (Accounts and Reports) Regulations 2008 (SI 2008/410).

Separate corporate governance statement ('SCGS')   **7.13.4**

Whilst all companies, whether quoted or unquoted, which do not qualify as small or medium-sized companies (see **APPENDIX 14**) are required by CA 2006 ss 446 and 447 to prepare a SCGS within the report and accounts, CA 2006 s 472A makes clear it is the statement required by the FCA's Disclosure and Transparency Rules ('DTRs') rules 7.2.1–7.2.11, and this in turn only applies to companies with securities that are fully listed. As stated above, the SCGS must be made in accordance with DTRs 7.2.1–7.2.11 and needs to contain the following:

- reference to the corporate governance code the company is obliged or chooses voluntarily to apply (for example, the UK Corporate Governance Code, in para **10.50**) or information about corporate governance practices applied beyond the requirements of UK legislation;

- state where such corporate governance code is available and the extent and reasons for any departure by the company from the code;

- where the company has decided not to apply a provision of a code, explanation of the reasons for the decision must be given;

- a description of the main features of the company's internal control and risk management systems in relation to financial reporting;

- information on share capital, voting and other rights attaching to shares; significant shareholders; rules on appointment of directors; and rules on amendment of the company's articles as required in the Large and Medium-sized Companies and Groups (Accounts and Reports) Regulations 2008 (SI 2008/410), provided the company is subject to that part of those regulations; and

- details of the composition of the company's administrative, management and supervisory bodies and how they operate.

The SCGS takes the form of narrative explaining how the main principles of the UK Corporate Governance Code have been applied, as well as a statement of whether the company has complied with the best practice provisions of the UK Corporate Governance Code for the whole accounting period and reasons for any areas of non–compliance.

The information required in the SCGS can either be:

(1)   included in the directors' report;

(2)   set out in a separate report published together with the annual accounts; or

(3)   made publicly available on the company's website, provided reference to the website and where the information can be found is made in the directors' report.

The SCGS must be approved on behalf of the company's directors and be signed by a director or the company secretary. A copy of the SCGS must also be submitted to the Registrar of Companies as part of the statutory accounts.

In addition the SCGS must be reviewed by the auditors, who must state whether in their opinion the company has complied with the provisions of the UK Corporate Governance Code and the requirements of DTRs 7.2.5 and 7.2.6.

Going concern statement **7.13.5**

Directors of listed companies should be aware that C.1.3 of the UK Corporate Governance Code and LR 9.8.6R(3) require inclusion of an explicit, written statement from the directors in the annual report that they are satisfied that the company's business will continue as a 'going concern' for a period of at least 12 months. This statement needs to be prepared in accordance with the FRC's 'Going Concern and Liquidity Risk: Guidance for Directors of UK Companies 2009' (www.frc.org.uk/publications) and be disclosed in the business review section of the directors' report with such supporting information or qualification as considered necessary. The FRC's guidance seeks to clarify the process the directors should follow when making the going concern assessment, the period to be covered and disclosures required on going concern and liquidity risk.

The going concern statement should only be made after the directors have conducted a rigorous assessment of the company's position and ability to continue taking into account all relevant factors including, for example, the nature of the company's business, market and competition, opportunities, risks and uncertainties.

The statement needs to stand up to close scrutiny as it must be reviewed by the auditors who, if they have any doubts about the company's ability to continue in operational existence as a going concern, would be required to issue a 'qualified' audit report emphasising a matter they have concerns about or indicating disagreement with the directors' assessment. Additional disclosures might need to be made to address the auditor's concerns.

Directors should note that the Sharman Report recommended that an auditor be required to provide an explicit statement that it is satisfied with the disclosures made by the company and robustness of the going concern assessment process and conclusions drawn. Particular concerns were raised in the report that too much emphasis was being placed on merely supporting information in the annual report and determining liquidity. Having considered information in the report, in February 2013 the FRC published draft proposals for 'Implementing the Recommendations of the Sharman Report' for consultation. As well as refocusing attention on the need for more continual assessment and broader consideration of stewardship and solvency issues, the guidance suggests the auditor should draw attention to any concerns about the going concern statement in the auditor's report to the accounts. The period for consultation has now closed, and the outcome from the FRC is awaited. Whilst the requirement for a going concern statement is directed at listed companies, directors of AIM, PLUS-quoted, and large private and unquoted public companies would be well advised to determine appropriate going concern review procedures, even if they decide not to include any explanation or narrative in the annual report.

Directors' remuneration report   **7.13.6**

Quoted companies must also prepare a directors' remuneration report for each financial year (CA 2006 s 420). The requirements of the form, content and approval of the directors' remuneration report changed substantively in October 2013 when the Enterprise and Regulatory Reform Act 2013 (ERRA 2013) and the Large and Medium-sized Companies and Groups (Accounts and Reports) (Amendment) Regulations 2013 (SI 2013/1981) came into effect.

The changes were made to address what are considered excessive levels of remuneration paid to executive directors, improve transparency by requiring more information to be disclosed on directors' remuneration and increase the level of control that shareholders can exert over remuneration. The package of measures are aimed at improving good pay practice and governance by increasing the level of transparency and strengthening shareholders' voting powers, whilst not enabling shareholders to micro-manage a company's decisions around pay.

Since October 2013 the content of the directors' remuneration report has needed to comply with the requirements of Schedule 8 to the Large and Medium-sized Companies and Groups (Accounts and Reports) (Amendment) Regulations 2013, which require the report to contain the following:

- A statement from the chairman of the remuneration committee, highlighting key points and messages and issues for the year on remuneration, explaining the context in which decisions were made and any significant changes during the year.

- An annual remuneration report showing how the directors' remuneration policy was actually implemented, updated each year and subject to an annual advisory only vote at the AGM.

  The annual remuneration report must detail how the directors' remuneration policy (see below) was implemented during the year, what actual payments were made to directors and how they were determined, including a single total remuneration figure for each director in table format with breakdowns of salaries and fees, taxable benefits, pension related benefits, bonuses and options, etc. The report must also include information on total pension entitlements, variable pay awards, payments made to past directors, payments for loss of office, statements of directors' holdings and share interests, a comparison of remuneration with total shareholder return in graph format, details of the CEO's remuneration (or such other comparison as the company considers appropriate) in table format, directors' remuneration relative to retained profit, dividends, tax and the overall wage bill in graph form, any matters the Board considers relevant to determination of remuneration, and the result of shareholder voting on the previous directors' remuneration report.

- The directors' remuneration policy, comprising a forward-looking statement of the company's remuneration policy, detailing the key factors taken into account when setting the policy. This report must identify the key elements of pay, information on service contracts, the approach and principles applied when making exit payments and any other material factors taken into account when determining the pay policy. A table is required with accompanying notes setting out the key elements of remuneration including information on how the policy supports the company to achieve stated short- and long-term strategy and objectives, the performance criteria, how all the elements of pay operate and what arrangements are in place for awarding over-performance and clawing back remuneration for under-performance, and the maximum potential remuneration that can be achieved. The policy should also contain explanation of whether, and if so why, the directors' remuneration is any different from that of other employees. A statement of the principles of the company's approach to remuneration of new directors is required, detailing the various elements that would be included in the package and maximum salary award. Similarly an outline of the key elements in directors' service contracts and letters of appointments is required together with description of the obligations these place on the company. There must be a chart setting out the fixed and variable elements of pay, with an indication of the planned and maximum amounts payable. The loss of office payment policy must be shown, indicating lengths of contracts, notice periods and termination payments, and statements must be made about directors' remuneration policy relative to pay and contracts of all employees within the company as a whole and to shareholders' views.

The ERRA 2013 introduced new CA 2006 s 439A, requiring a binding shareholder vote on the directors' remuneration policy every three years. Whilst the director's remuneration policy only strictly needs to be included in directors' remuneration report in a year when the company intends to propose the policy to shareholders for approval at the general meeting at which the accounts are to be laid before the members (which will be once every three years, or where a change in policy is proposed), it is generally accepted that it will be useful for the policy to be included in the directors' remuneration report even in years when it is not to be put to the vote.

Where the directors' remuneration policy is not produced in the annual report and accounts for a particular year, shareholders should be informed where they can obtain a copy of the last version approved by shareholders, normally from the company's registered office or website. However, it is difficult to see companies not including the directors' remuneration policy in each year's annual report and accounts, since cross-referencing without it will be very difficult.

Once the remuneration policy is approved, payments to directors by way of remuneration or for loss of office can only be made within the limits of the approved policy unless a new policy is approved by shareholders or their consent to a specific deviation is obtained (new CA 2006 ss 226B and 226C). Where consent to a deviation is being sought, the resolution must be accompanied by a note or memo explaining why, how and the reasons for the proposed deviation from approved policy.

These revised regulations aim to remove some of the complexity around reporting of directors' remuneration and improve the quality of disclosures, making it much easier to see what directors are being paid overall and to determine the rationale applied by the company and the link between pay and performance.

Of particular note is inclusion of the provision that any pay or benefits granted in breach of the approved directors' remuneration policy (or without having obtained specific consent to a deviation as set out above) will be deemed to be held on trust and be recoverable from the receiving director. In addition, the directors who allowed the unauthorised payments will be jointly and severally liable to indemnify the company (new CA 2006 s 226E).

These changes to remuneration reporting are significant, hence the FRC's Financial Reporting Lab set up a project team to work with listed companies to develop example formats. In addition, further guidance can be found in the GC100 and Investor Group's 'Directors' Remuneration Reporting Guidance'.

Management report   **7.13.7**

The management report required as part of the annual financial report of a listed company by DTR 4.1.5 must include a fair review of the company's business and detail the principal risks and uncertainties facing the business going forward (DTR 4.1.8). In particular, it must:

(1)   contain a balanced and comprehensive analysis of development and performance of the company during the year and its position at the end of the year;

(2)   be consistent and appropriate for the size and complexity of the company's business;

(3)   include analysis using financial and non–financial 'key performance indicators' to the extent necessary to help understanding of development and performance;

(4)   give an indication of any important events since the end of the financial year, likely future development, R&D activity, provide information about purchases of own shares and (where applicable) about the use of financial instruments.

Additional disclosures and notes   **7.13.8**

Directors must be aware that they have a corresponding duty to inform the company of information required to be disclosed in the notes to the accounts and to ensure that the required disclosures are made.

CA 2006 ss 412 and 413 require disclosure of the following information on directors' remuneration, advances, credit and guarantees in the notes to the accounts:

●   the aggregate amount of gains made on exercise of share options;

●   the aggregate amount of benefits receivable or received by directors under long–term incentive schemes;

●   (including entitlement to emoluments waived), pensions of past and present directors, any compensation paid to directors for loss of office;

●   any advances or credits granted in favour of directors or connected persons and details of any agreements to enter into such arrangements or agreements;

●   any guarantees entered into by the company, or any subsidiary company, on behalf of the directors.

It is the duty of any director, or past director who ceased to be a director less than five years previously, to notify the company of matters relating to himself and his remuneration which need to be disclosed. Failure to fulfil this obligation is an offence, for which a fine may be imposed (CA 2006 s 412(5) and (6)).

Failure by directors to make the required disclosures may be picked up by the auditors when conducting their audit of the company's books and records and, where they consider information has not been disclosed as required by the Act, they are required to make a statement in their audit report of the required particulars (CA 2006 s 498).

CA 2006 ss 409–413 also require disclosure of information about related undertakings, off balance sheet arrangements, advances, credit, guarantees and employee numbers and costs.

Under the CA 2006 the Secretary of State also has authority to make provision by regulations about information to be disclosed in the notes to the accounts. The information required to be inserted into the notes of the accounts is currently contained in the Small Companies and Groups (Accounts and Directors' Report) Regulations 2008 (SI 2008/409) and the Large and Medium-sized Companies and Groups (Accounts and Reports) Regulations 2008 (SI 2008/410). These regulations expand those requirements under CA 2006. These regulations require disclosure of additional information either in the accounts or within the notes to the accounts, unless there is a reason for exemption. The required information for small companies and groups includes:

- the aggregate amount of dividends either liable to be paid or paid by the company together with amounts set aside or proposed to be set aside from the company's reserves;

- disclosure of accounting policies;

- the aggregate number and value of shares allotted and if there is more than one class, details of each class and information if the shares are redeemable;

- the value of fixed assets at the beginning and end of the financial period and details of any acquisitions, disposals, transfers or revisions in value of fixed assets;

- details of any listed investments and the aggregate market value of those investments;

- where the company has any financial instruments and they have been valued to show their fair value (assets or liabilities) details must be given of the assumptions made, changes in value and any terms and conditions which may affect determination of value;

- where a company has any investment property or living animals and plants, details of the valuation models must be shown. Where the item is investment property, comparable amounts must be shown, using either historical cost accounting rules or the actual differences between those amounts and the amount shown in the balance sheet;

- where amounts have been transferred to or from reserves, to any provisions for liabilities or from any provision for liabilities other than the purpose for which it was established, the details of the amounts must be disclosed;

- details of any debts which are payable other than by instalments and fall due within the period of five years from the financial year end must be stated and, where debts are repayable in instalments, the amounts which fall due for payment after the current financial period. Details must also be provided of any fixed cumulative dividends which are in arrears:

- details must be given of any charge that exists over the company's assets;

- particulars of any asset where the purchase price of production cost has been determined for the first time;

- information to supplement the profit and loss account;

- particulars of turnover, expressed as a percentage of turnover, attributable to geographical markets outside the UK;

- particulars of extraordinary income or charges during the year; and

- the basis of any foreign currency translation into sterling.

Companies required to observe the Large and Medium-sized Companies and Groups (Accounts and Reports) Regulations 2008 (SI 2008/410) must observe additional requirements to those contained in the Small Companies and Groups (Accounts and Directors' Report) Regulations 2008 (SI 2008/409). Whilst the requirements listed in the bullet points above still apply, the required disclosures are generally more detailed and the following additional information is also required:

- the amount of any provision for deferred tax must be stated separately from any other tax provision;

- repayment details for all loans, advances and liabilities;

- details of all debt and other fixed-income securities;

- details of any subordinated liabilities that exceed 10% of liabilities;

- particulars of guarantees and other financial instruments;

- contingent liabilities of group undertakings;

- distinction between listed and unlisted transferable securities;

- aggregate amount of property (excluding land) leased by the company to other persons;

- explanation of any sundry assets and liabilities; and

- details of any unmatured/forward transactions outstanding at the balance sheet date.

In addition, LR 9.8.4 and LR 9.8.6 specifically require that the audited financial statements of listed companies also contain the following additional information:

- an explanation of any difference of 10% or more on previously forecast results;

- a statement of the amount, if any, of interest capitalised and details of any related tax relief;

- details of any waiver by directors of their emoluments in the current or future accounting periods;

- details of any waiver of dividends by shareholders relating to the current or future accounting periods;

- a statement of director's interests (disclosed pursuant to DTR 3.1.2) and details of any change in those interests between the beginning and end of the period and details of any right to subscribe for shares or debentures. Distinction must be made between beneficial and non-beneficial interests and the information must be updated to within one month of the date of the notice of the AGM;

- a statement of information concerning major interests in shares as at a date not more than one month prior to the date of notice of the AGM (DTR 5) or a statement that there are no such interests;

- details of any shareholder approval given for purchase of the company's own shares and of any purchases made during the period;

- details of allotments for cash, including the names of allottees and market price of shares at the time of issue (other than pro rata allotments to existing shareholders);

- details of any undertaking given by the parent company (if any) where a placing was made during the period;

- particulars of any significant contracts in which a director is or was materially interested;

- particulars of any significant contracts made with a controlling shareholder during the period;

- details of any small related party transactions during the period;

- details of long-term incentive schemes (if any);

Auditors' report   **7.13.9**

Unless specifically exempt from the obligation to appoint auditors (discussed in paras **7.14.5** and **7.16**), the accounts must include a statement from the auditors as to whether the balance sheet, profit and loss account and any group accounts give a true and fair view of the state of affairs and profit and loss for the year and whether, in their opinion, the accounts have been properly prepared in accordance with the Act (CA 2006 s 495).

The auditor must state in his report whether:

(1)   the information in the directors' report is consistent with the accounts;

(2)   if the company is quoted, in his opinion the audited part of the directors' remuneration report has been properly prepared; and

(3)   the information in the separate corporate governance statement (see para **7.13.4**), if required, complies with the DTRs.

The auditors' report must state the name of the auditor and be signed and dated (CA 2006 s 503). Where the auditor is a firm, the report must be signed by the senior statutory auditor in his own name, for and on behalf of the firm.

For listed companies, auditors are also required to review the directors' statement of compliance against principles of the UK Corporate Governance Code (para **10.12**) and internal controls (para **10.22**). The outcome of the auditors' review would usually form part of the auditors' report.

It is now acceptable for a copy of the auditors' report (rather than a signed copy) to be submitted to Companies House, the members and any other person entitled to receive the accounts (the Companies Act 2006 (Amendment) (Accounts and Reports) Regulations 2008 (SI 2008/393)).

The directors have a duty to ensure that the requirements concerning the auditors' report are met, as failure to do so could render the company and any officers in default liable to a fine (CA 2006 ss 505 and 507).

It must be emphasised that the directors have a duty to ensure that the auditors are permitted access to all books and records required to audit the accounts satisfactorily and are provided with any information and answers to questions they may raise. This is an essential duty, as the auditors are required to make a statement in the auditors' report if they have not been provided with all the necessary information and answers to questions necessary to conduct the audit, or they consider proper accounting records have not been kept, or the required disclosures by directors have not been made.

Accounting exemptions   7.14

Directors should be aware that, subject to meeting necessary qualifying criteria, certain private companies may qualify for exemptions in preparation of their accounts.

To qualify for very small, small or medium-sized company or group exemptions (discussed below), the company or group must satisfy at least two of the criteria contained in **Appendix** **14** (CA 2006 ss 382, 383, 465 and 466). Directors must be aware that where the company satisfies these criteria, but is either a public company, banking or insurance company, an authorised person under FSMA 2000, a member of an ineligible group, an e-money issuer, a UCITS management company or a MiFID investment firm, the special provisions and exemptions discussed below do not apply and full accounts will be required (CA 2006 ss 384 and 467). A group is also ineligible if within the group there is a company that has been admitted to trading in an EEA state.

A further point is that where a small or medium-sized company is the parent company of a group, it cannot take advantage of the relevant exemptions unless the group as a whole qualifies as 'small' or 'medium-sized' respectively.

Groups of companies will be ineligible for these accounting exemptions, regardless of size, where the parent company is a public company, a banking or insurance company.

Very small companies (micro-entities)   **7.14.1**

For accounting years ending on or after 30 September 2013, a company that qualifies as a very small company, or a 'micro-entity', is permitted by the Small Companies (Micro-Entities' Accounts) Regulations 2013 (SI 2013/3008) to deliver just an abridged balance sheet to Companies House. Such company can also choose to file an abridged profit and loss account, directors' report, auditor's report and notes to the accounts with Companies House, or it may claim exemption as a small company.

Small companies   **7.14.2**

A small company may claim exemption from the requirement to deliver a profit and loss account, directors' report and full balance sheet to Companies House and instead it may deliver abbreviated accounts and a modified balance sheet and notes to the accounts prepared in accordance with the Small Companies and Groups (Accounts and Directors' Reports) Regulations 2008 (SI 2008/409).

However, where abbreviated accounts are delivered, the company is still under an obligation to prepare and audit a full set of accounts for shareholders in accordance with the requirements CA 2006 s 449. The Companies Act 2006 (Amendment) (Accounts and Reports) Regulations 2008 (SI 2008/393) allow for certain information, normally required in the notes to the accounts and the directors' report, to be omitted. For small companies preparing abbreviated accounts in accordance with CA 2006 no profit and loss account or directors' report need be filed and a summarised version of the balance sheet and notes to the accounts may be filed in accordance with the Small Companies and Groups (Accounts and Directors' Report) Regulations 2008 (SI 2008/409).

Where a small company takes advantage of these modifications and delivers abbreviated accounts to Companies House, a statement must be included in the balance sheet that the accounts have been prepared in accordance with provisions relating to small companies (CA 2006 s 444). In addition, a full audit report need not be delivered but a 'special audit report' is required, which must include a statement that the company is entitled to deliver abbreviated accounts and that they have been properly prepared (CA 2006 s 444(7)). This requirement for a special audit report will be waived where the company is exempt from appointing auditors (see paras **7.14.5** and **7.16**).

Medium-sized companies   **7.14.3**

Where the company qualifies as a medium-sized company, it is permitted to file an abbreviated profit and loss account and does not have to disclose details of profit and turnover in the notes to the accounts in accordance with the Large and Medium-sized Companies and Groups (Accounts and Reports) Regulations 2008 (SI 2008/410). A 'special audit report' may be delivered rather than a full audit report, but full audited accounts are required for the shareholders.

Small and medium-sized groups   **7.14.4**

Certain parent companies of small and medium-sized groups (which satisfy at least two of the criteria specified in **APPENDIX 14**) are exempt from obligation to prepare group accounts in accordance with criteria within the Small Companies and Groups (Accounts and Directors' Report) Regulations 2008 (SI 2008/409). However, parent companies that are subject to the small companies regime can opt to prepare group accounts as well as preparing individual accounts if desired (CA 2006 s 398).

In all other instances, and provided no other exemptions apply, those companies classed as medium-sized companies and groups must conform to criteria set out in the Large and Medium-sized Companies and Groups (Accounts and Reports) Regulations 2008 (SI 2008/410).

Where a small company has prepared individual accounts and is preparing group accounts for the same year, the group accounts need to comply with the provisions of the Small Companies and Groups (Accounts and Directors' Report) Regulations 2008 (SI 2008/409). In addition, the same disclosure exemptions that apply to small companies directors' reports and notes to the accounts apply (see para **7.14.1**). Where these exemptions are claimed, a statement must be made on the balance sheet that the group accounts have been prepared in accordance with provisions of CA 2006 s 383.

Group parent overseas   7.14.5

A company is exempt from the requirement to prepare group accounts where it is a subsidiary, the parent company is registered in an EEA State and the company's results are included in the parent's consolidated group accounts (CA 2006 s 400). This applies where the company is a wholly owned subsidiary of the parent undertaking and where the parent undertaking owns more than 50% of the allotted shares. However, shareholders may request the preparation of group accounts. To request preparation of group accounts application must be made to the company by holders of more than half the remaining allotted shares or of 5% of the total allotted shares in the company (CA 2006 ss 400–401).

Dormant companies   7.14.6

A company that has been dormant since incorporation or has been dormant since the end of the previous financial year, has had no significant accounting transactions during the year and qualifies as a small company (see paras **7.14.1** and **7.15**) can prepare and submit unaudited dormant company accounts. Whilst public companies were previously excluded, unless they are quoted companies, they may now qualify as dormant and claim exemptions in preparation of their accounts. However, as set out in para **7.15.1** certain types of company and activities undertaken by the company might exclude the company from taking advantage of the dormant company exemptions (CA 2006 ss 481 and 394B).

It is important to note that payments to the Registrar of Companies for change of name or re-registration fees, late filing penalties and annual return fees do not constitute 'significant accounting transactions' neither does payment for shares made by subscribers on incorporation of the company (CA 2006 s 1169). The benefits for the dormant company are that it is entitled to take advantage of a number of exemptions from preparation and submission of full audited accounts as follows:

(1)   no report of the auditors is required to be delivered to the members or to Companies House. Where it is not delivered, a statement must be made by the directors on the balance sheet that the company was dormant throughout the accounting period to which the accounts relate;

(2)   all exemptions that a small company is entitled to claim, as detailed in para **7.14.2**. A public company, however, may be required to deliver a directors' report and (where it traded the previous year) a profit and loss account.

The dormant accounts must contain statements which confirm that the company is entitled to the exemption, that an audit has not been requested by the requisite number of members and that the directors acknowledge their responsibilities in respect of the preparation of accounts as outlined under CA 2006.

The directors must still ensure that the dormant accounts are sent to members and others entitled to receive copies and are submitted to Companies House within the required filing periods.

The directors must ensure that these exemptions are claimed only whilst the company remains dormant and meets the qualifying criteria. As soon as this is not the case, then full audited accounts will be required unless other exemptions can be claimed.

Entitlement to these exemptions does not automatically terminate the appointment of an existing auditor, and it would therefore be advisable for the company to ask the existing auditors to resign to give effect to the termination.

Further, recent and significant changes brought into effect by the Companies and Limited Liability Partnerships (Accounts and Audit Exemptions and Change of Accounting Framework) Regulations 2012 (SI 2012/2301) permit dormant subsidiary companies to be exempt from the obligation to prepare and file accounts (new CA 2006 ss 394A and 448A).

Unless excluded (see para **7.15.1**) a dormant subsidiary company is exempt from the requirement to prepare individual accounts for a financial year if it complies with the criteria listed in para **7.15.1**(b) (save amending the parent undertaking guarantee which is to be given in accordance with CA 2006 s 394C).

Unless excluded (see para **7.15.1**) a dormant subsidiary company is also exempt from the obligation to file individual accounts for a financial year if it complies with the criteria listed in para **7.15.1**(b) (save amending the parent undertaking guarantee which is to be given in accordance with CA 2006 s 448C).

Whilst doubtless many dormant subsidiary companies will take advantage of these exemptions in order to save costs and time involved in preparing accounts, the directors do need to carefully evaluate whether these exemptions are appropriate by consulting and considering not only the company's articles but also any relevant commercial, finance, banking or regulatory restrictions that might make it difficult to take advantage of these exemptions.

Audit exemptions   **7.15**

Significant changes were made by the Companies and Limited Liability Partnerships (Accounts and Audit Exemptions and Change of Accounting

Framework) Regulations 2012 (SI 2012/2301) and now a company that qualifies as a small company, a dormant company or a 'qualifying subsidiary' in a financial year may (provided it is not excluded) be entitled to exemption from having its accounts audited that year (CA 2006 ss 477, 480 and 479A). However, it should be stressed that even where the company is able to claim exemption from having the accounts audited, the directors must ensure that:

- proper accounting systems are maintained, with adequate controls;

- the accounts prepared show a true and fair view and comply with provisions of CA 2006 in terms of form and content;

- a directors' report is prepared for a public company as required by CA 2006;

- the accounts (and directors' report where required) are submitted to Companies House within the period required for submission (see para **6.33**).

The directors must also ensure that the company is permitted to take advantage of the audit exemptions in CA 2006 and it is not prohibited by any provisions in the company's Articles of Association. The Articles must be consulted and, where for example Table A to the CA 1985 has not been adopted, they may need amendment. For example, Table A in Sch 1 to CA 1948 requires the appointment of auditors, and many companies have adopted detailed provisions for transfers of shares in their Articles which require independent valuation by the auditors. Where either of these provisions apply, the directors must ensure that special resolutions for amendments to the Articles are proposed to the members for approval before any audit exemptions are claimed.

Qualifying criteria   **7.15.1**

Directors should note that, notwithstanding the qualifying criteria set out below, certain companies are ineligible and may not dispense with the requirement to have their accounts audited. These include:

- public companies (where the small company exemption is claimed) and quoted companies (where the 'qualifying subsidiary' exemption is claimed);

- a bank, authorised insurance company, e-money issuer, UCITS management company and MiFID investment company (applied to all companies claiming exemption);

- a company that carries on insurance market activity (where dormant company exemption is claimed); or

- a special register body as defined in s 117(1) of the Trade Union and Labour Relations (Consolidation) Act 1992 or an employers' association as defined in s 122 of that Act or Article 4 of the Industrial Relations (Northern Ireland) Order 1992 (where the small company or 'qualifying subsidiary' exemption is claimed).

Subject to not being ineligible as set out above, the criteria in CA 2006 that must be satisfied for a small, dormant or 'qualifying subsidiary' company to qualify for exemption from audit includes the following:

(1) Small company: the company must qualify as a small company in accordance with provisions of CA 2006 s 382(1)–(6) (see para **7.14.1**). In addition, if the company is part of a group, the group must qualify as a small group and not be ineligible (see para **7.14.3**). Of particular note is the change in requirements so that now a company qualifies by satisfying any two of the balance sheet, turnover or maximum employee number criteria set out in **APPENDIX 14.**

(2) Qualifying subsidiary: the company must be a subsidiary of a parent undertaking established under the law of an EEA state and, where this is the case, exemption is conditional upon compliance with all of the following conditions:

  • all members of the company agree the exemption for the financial year;

  • the parent undertaking giving a guarantee for that year which, in accordance with s 479C, must guarantee all outstanding liabilities to which the subsidiary company is subject at the end of the financial year to which the guarantee relates until they are satisfied in full and be enforceable against the parent undertaking by any person to whom the subsidiary company is liable in respect of those liabilities;

  • the company being included in the consolidated accounts drawn up for that year (or to an earlier date in that year) by the parent undertaking and the parent undertaking disclosing in the notes to those accounts that the company is exempt from the requirements of CA 2006 relating to the audit of individual accounts; and

  • the directors delivering written notice of the members' agreement exemption, the parent undertaking's guarantee, a copy of the consolidated annual report accounts drawn up by the parent undertaking and the auditor's report on those accounts to the registrar on or before the date that they file the accounts for that year.

(3) Dormant company: the dormant company must be entitled to prepare accounts under the small companies regime (see para **7.14.1**), have been dormant either since incorporation or since the end of the previous accounting year and not be required to prepare group accounts.

If the above criteria are met, the company can claim exemption from the requirement to have audited accounts for that year, provided also that the statements set out in para **7.15.2** are made in the balance sheet, just above where it is signed (CA 2006, s 475(2) and (3)).

Form of accounts   **7.15.2**

The accounts must comply with provisions relating to small company accounts and may include an abbreviated balance sheet and modified notes to the accounts (see para **7.14.1**). The format and content of the accounts must be prepared in accordance with the Small Companies and Groups (Accounts and Directors' Report) Regulations 2008 (SI 2008/409). It should be noted that the directors have a duty to ensure that full accounts, are circulated to the members except that, where exemption from audit applies, no audit report is required (CA 2006 s 477).

Where a company takes advantage of the audit exemption, the directors are required to include statements on the balance sheet that:

- the company was entitled to claim exemption under CA 2006 s 477(1);

- no notice has been received from the holders of 10% or more of the issued share capital (of any class) requiring an audit to be conducted (CA 2006 s 477(5));

- the directors acknowledge their responsibilities to keep proper accounting records and prepare accounts that show a true and fair account of the state of affairs of the company (in accordance with requirements of CA 2006 ss 386 and 394);

- advantage has been taken of exemptions conferred by CA 2006 ss 382 and 383 and the Companies Act 2006 (Amendment) (Accounts and Reports) Regulations 2008 (SI 2008/393), relating to small companies and that the company, in the opinion of the directors, is entitled to those exemptions (required where abbreviated accounts and modified notes to the accounts are submitted to Companies House).

These statements must be signed by a director on behalf of the Board.

Approval of the accounts   **7.16**

When the accounts have been finalised, they must be approved by the Board of Directors and the balance sheet must be signed by a director on behalf of the Board (CA 2006 s 414).

Where accounts are approved but do not comply with the requirements of CA 2006 (or, where applicable, Article 4 of the IAS Regulations), every director who knew that they did not comply, was reckless as to whether they complied or failed to take reasonable steps to ensure that the accounts complied or prevent them from being approved, will be considered to have committed an offence and be liable to a fine (CA 2006 s 414(4), (5)).

Similarly, the directors' report (which now includes a business review for all companies, except small companies which are exempt) must also be approved by the Board and signed by a director or the secretary of the company (CA 2006 s 419), as must the separate corporate governance statement (SCGS) (CA 2006 s 419A) and the directors' remuneration report for quoted companies (CA 2006 s 422). As above, directors who approve a directors' report, SCGS or directors' remuneration report which does not comply with the CA 2006 commit an offence, for which they could be held liable.

It is now permissible for accounts submitted to Companies House and to members to be conformed copies, stating the names of the persons who signed without need for original signatures (see para **7.18.2**).

Circulation of the accounts   **7.17**

A company must send copies of its accounts and reports for each financial year to every member of the company, every holder of the company's debentures and every person who is entitled to receive notice of general meetings (CA 2006 s 423).

Where abbreviated or modified accounts have been prepared for the purposes of submission to Companies House, the directors must ensure that full accounts are circulated to members, unless the company is a listed public company and the members have agreed to be sent an SFS (soon to be replaced by the strategic report with additional information), as discussed in para **7.14**.

For companies which are unquoted as defined under CA 2006 s 385, the accounts and reports circulated must include the annual accounts, directors' report and the auditors' report for those accounts. A company is not required to include an auditors' report where it is eligible for audit exemptions.

The accounts and reports for quoted companies circulated must include the annual accounts, directors' remuneration report, directors' report, and auditors' report on the accounts.

For private companies which are not required to hold an AGM, the directors must ensure that copies of the accounts are sent to each person entitled to receive them no later than the end of the period allowed for delivering the accounts to the Registrar of Companies or (if earlier) the date on which the company actually delivers the accounts to the Registrar of Companies (CA 2006 s 423).

Where the company is a public company, the accounts must be circulated to those entitled to receive them at least 21 days before the date of the relevant meeting at which they will be laid before the members, usually the AGM (CA 2006 s 424(3)).

Under CA 2006 s 430 a quoted company must also publish its accounts on a website, which must be available for download free of charge. The accounts must remain on the website until the accounts for the next financial year are published. This same requirement also applies to AIM companies, in accordance with the AIM Rules.

Laying and delivering accounts   **7.18**

The directors of every company have a duty to lay the accounts before the members and deliver them to Companies House within a specific time period as discussed below. It is a criminal offence for the directors to fail to do so and it is important for directors to note that even where a company has been dissolved and Companies House decides not to prosecute, a private prosecution could be brought by, for example, a creditor and the directors could be fined and ordered to pay costs for their failure to file accounts.

Laying accounts before members   **7.18.1**

The directors of public companies have a statutory duty to lay the annual accounts, together with the directors' and auditor's reports thereon, before the company in general meeting (CA 2006 s 437). The accounts will normally be laid before the members at the AGM, but may be laid before the members at any general meeting convened for the purpose. The directors must ensure that the meeting is convened with the appropriate period of notice, ie 21 'clear days' for an AGM and for receipt of the accounts prior to the meeting, unless consent to a shorter notice period is approved by the members.

Private companies are no longer required by CA 2006 to hold an AGM each year or to lay accounts before their members. However, this might be required by a company's Articles which will either need to be amended or the requirements observed.

For those companies that are not required to hold an AGM, the time period by which the accounts must be distributed to the members is now linked to the actual delivery of the accounts to the Registrar of Companies (CA 2006 s 423) (as explained in para **7.17**).

It should also be stressed that whilst companies may be permitted to submit abbreviated or modified accounts to Companies House, this exemption does not release the directors from the obligation to circulate or lay full accounts before the members.

Delivering accounts to Companies House   **7.18.2**

The directors have a duty to deliver the annual accounts and reports to Companies House (CA 2006 s 441). Directors should be aware that failure to submit the accounts within the required period carries an automatic civil penalty payable by the company in default, which increases according to the lateness of the accounts when finally submitted (CA 2006 s 442). The scale of this penalty is discussed in para **6.33**. In addition, where directors are persistently in default for failure to file accounts and other statutory returns they may be liable to disqualification, as it is an indication that they are not fit to be involved in the management of a company. Persistent offenders also risk their companies being struck off.

There are numerous instances reported in the press of Companies House pursuing high-profile companies and individuals that persistently fail to file accounts each year. Recent examples include TweetDeck Limited, the online tool owned by Twitter, which was dissolved by Companies House on 7 May 2013 for failing to files accounts despite several warnings and sanctions from Companies House (*Telegraph*, 7 May 2013). Considerable adverse publicity was also generated around failure by Gordon Ramsay Holdings Limited and reports of court action for failing to file accounts (*Telegraph*, 1 October 2008). In *Secretary of State for Trade and Industry v Ettinger* [1993] BCLC 896, CA emphasises the seriousness with which the courts consider cases where the directors have persistently disregarded their duty to submit accounts to Companies House. In this case the directors were found to be unfit to be involved in the management of a company for failure to submit accounts and were disqualified for periods of three and two years. Furthermore, directors should note that a creditor successfully brought action against a director for failure to deliver accounts, after the company was dissolved, resulting in a fine and an order to pay costs (*The Papillon Centre (Watford) Ltd* (unreported, company dissolved 2003)).

The Registrar of Companies has specified the form in which the accounts are to be submitted, and the directors must ensure that the audited accounts are printed on A4-sized matt white, or near white, paper. If the accounts are submitted in a form different to this, they are likely to be rejected and returned to the company for amendment and resubmission.

Required period 7.18.3

The directors must ensure that the accounts, and the directors' and auditor's reports thereon, are laid and delivered within the period required by CA 2006 442 (see para **6.33**). Whilst there is a civil penalty payable by the company for failure to submit accounts in time (this tends to concentrate directors' minds on filing the accounts at Companies House), it should not be forgotten that the directors have a corresponding duty to lay the accounts and reports before the members within this same period. Failure to lay the accounts before the members is an offence, for which the company and the directors in office at the time will be liable to a fine.

Other financial responsibilities 7.20

As discussed above, an important function of the directors is to manage the company's finances. This is achieved in part by keeping thorough and accurate accounting records. The directors are then able, based on information extracted from management accounts, reports or other records, to make financial predictions on which to base their strategic decisions.

At the same time, the directors are required to observe a general duty to exercise skill and care, as well as specific statutory requirements, in relation to other financial matters relevant to the company. These duties are necessary to protect the interests of shareholders, creditors and other persons having dealings with the company.

Share capital 7.21

Essentially the share capital of a company (together with any profit available) is the amount that would be available for distribution to the company's creditors and other parties who have claims against the company should it be wound up. Once such lawful claims have been met, any share capital remaining would be available for distribution to the proprietors of the company.

As a consequence, the directors have a duty to ensure that any money brought into the company as share capital is done so correctly and that all statutory requirements concerning any reductions in share capital are observed.

Allotment of shares 7.21.1

Directors must ensure that any information provided to encourage investment in the company is accurate and does not contain any false or misleading statements. Where a director fails to observe this duty, he may be liable to civil action for deceit or criminal action for fraud. The latter may be brought where the director has knowingly made false statements and, in doing so, has manipulated the market (FSMA 2000 s 397). Directors should be aware that in such circumstances they may be required to indemnify anyone who suffers loss from their actions.

Having encouraged investment, the directors must observe and follow duties in relation to the procedures for allotting shares as detailed in para **8.11.2**. Where they have the necessary authority and are able to allot shares, the directors must ensure that the following restrictions of a financial nature are observed before any shares are issued:

- payment for shares issued must be received, which may be by money or money's worth, including goodwill and know-how (CA 2006 s 582);

- a public company may not accept an undertaking to provide work or services to the company in payment for shares (CA 2006 s 583);

- issue of shares cannot be made at a discount. The issue price of each share must be at least its nominal value (CA 2006 s 580);

- shares of a public company may not be issued unless payment is received for a minimum of one-quarter of the nominal value of each share and the whole of any share premium (CA 2006 s 586). This requirement does not apply where the shares are being allotted pursuant to an employee share scheme;

- where a public company makes an allotment of shares, the consideration for which will be satisfied by some means other than cash, the value of the consideration must have been independently valued and a report of the value be made to the company and to the allottee (CA 2006 s 593). The valuation report must have been prepared less than six months prior to the proposed allotment. In some circumstances the issue of shares in a takeover or merger may be exempt from this requirement for valuation, for example where it forms part of a share exchange;

- a public company may not issue partly paid shares for consideration other than cash where the undertaking to pay for the shares in full is at a time more than five years from the date of issue (CA 2006 s 587).

Once payment has been received and the shares have been allotted, the directors must ensure that the appropriate entries are made in the issued share capital and share premium accounts (where the price paid for the shares is in excess of the nominal value) and, where the shares are issued partly paid, payment in full is received at the relevant time.

Maintenance of capital (public company) **7.21.2**

On incorporation a public company must have a minimum issued share capital of £50,000 or €65,600 of which at least 25% of the nominal value of each share must be paid up together with the whole of any share premium (CA 2006 s 761 and s 763 and the Companies (Authorised Minimum) Regulations 2008 (SI 2008/729)). The directors of a public company must ensure that this minimum capital requirement has been met and, when the company needs to commence business and exercise borrowing powers, they are required to make a declaration stating compliance with this requirement to obtain a trading certificate (CA 2006 s 762). The Registrar will accept the statutory declaration as evidence that the minimum capital requirement has been met, but the directors should be aware that where this requirement has been contravened they may be liable to a fine and to account, jointly and severally, to any person who has suffered loss by entering into a transaction with the company in such circumstances. The application for a trading certificate must be made on Form SH50.

In the event that the net assets of a public company fall to half or less than half of the company's called up share capital the directors have a duty, within 28 days of becoming aware of the loss of capital, to convene an extraordinary general meeting for the members to consider the matter. This meeting must be held not more than 56 days thereafter (CA 2006 s 656). Where the directors fail to fulfil this duty they will be liable to a fine as well as being exposed to possible claims of trading whilst insolvent and or continuing to trade with intent to defraud creditors.

Purchase and redemption of shares **7.22**

Every private limited company with a share capital may issue shares which are liable to be redeemed (CA 2006 s 684). There is no longer the requirement for specific authority to issue redeemable shares to be contained within the Articles of private companies, although the Articles may restrict or prohibit the issue of redeemable shares. This does not, however, apply to public companies which still require provisions enabling the issue of redeemable shares to be contained in their Articles. A limited company may redeem and purchase its own shares from distributable profits or from the proceeds of a new issue of shares (CA 2006 s 692).

Directors should be aware that tight statutory controls are in place to protect the interests of creditors, as the redemption or purchase by a company of its own shares will result in a reduction of capital and essentially reduce the funds available to creditors were the company to be wound up.

The initial duty of the directors, of a private company, where a redemption or purchase of shares is proposed is to check the Articles to ascertain the terms and conditions of the redemption and/or purchase of own shares. For directors of public companies they must ensure that the Articles contain the required clause providing authority for redemption and/or purchase of shares. In the event that no such authority is contained in the Articles, the directors must convene a general meeting to approve a special resolution to amend the Articles to include such authority before the proposed redemption or purchase can be made, and suggested wording for the resolution to amend the Articles, if required, is contained in **APPENDIX 16**. In *R W Peak (Kings Lynn) Ltd* [1998] 1 BCLC 193, Ch a shareholder was restored to the register as it was held that purchase of his shares was void under CA 1985 s 143, as the company was not authorised to purchase its own shares by its Articles.

The directors have a duty to check that the following requirements can be or have been met before the redemption or purchase takes place:

(1)   the shares to be purchased must be fully paid (CA 2006 s 686);

(2)   there will be some non-redeemable shares left in issue after the transaction;

(3)   the redemption or purchase may be financed from distributable profits or proceeds of a fresh issue and private companies may, subject to restrictions discussed in para **7.22.3.3**, make payment out of capital (CA 2006 s 687). It should also be noted here that, as was established in the case *BDG Roof-Bond Ltd v Douglas* [2000] 1 BCLC 401, a company can pay for purchase of its own shares by a transfer of assets;

(4)   where the purchase or redemption meets certain criteria, it may not be regarded as a distribution for corporation tax purposes by HMRC and it may be necessary to obtain advance tax clearance from them and ensure that a return containing details of the purchase is submitted to them within 60 days of payment for the shares;

(5)   whether approval of the transaction by shareholders is required in terms of CA 2006 s 190 (see para **6.80**).

Redemption   7.22.1

Any redemption of shares must be made in accordance with specific provisions contained in the Articles or determined by ordinary resolution at the time the shares were issued as 'redeemable'. Directors must check whether such provisions exist. Where no such provisions exist the directors are able to set the terms and conditions of a redemption. It will then be necessary for the directors to ensure that the following procedure is followed when redeeming the shares:

Steps	Purpose
(1) Hold a meeting of the directors.	To resolve to approve the redemption pursuant to terms in the Articles (or ordinary resolution, as the case may be).
(2) Serve notice on the shareholders.	Notifying them of the proposed redemption (example wording of notice is given in **APPENDIX 17**). It should be noted that the terms of redemption may permit redemption at the request of shareholders, in which case they will serve notice on the company which the directors must then act upon.
(3) Request return of the share certificate from the shareholder.	The share certificate needs to be cancelled and a balance certificate may be required where redemption is for part of the holding only.
(4) Note details of the redemption in the Register of Members.	The issued share capital needs to be reduced by number of shares and their nominal value.
(5) Make the necessary accounting entries.	Reduce the issued capital by the nominal value of shares redeemed. Transfer that amount to the 'capital redemption reserve'. Check whether the share premium account or revaluation reserve is also affected by the transaction.
(6) Notify Companies House of the redemption.	Using form SH02 within one month of the redemption taking place.

The directors must ensure that, where the redemption is financed out of capital, additional procedures detailed in para **7.22.3.3** are followed.

Purchase of own shares 7.22.2

Under Chapter 4, Part 18 of CA 2006 and the Companies (Share Capital and Acquisition by Company of its Own Shares) Regulations 2009 (SI 2009/2022), purchase by a company of its own shares can only be made pursuant to a contract. This contract may be a contingent purchase contract where the company may be entitled or obliged to purchase the shares at a future date (CA 2006 s 696). The directors are responsible for drafting the contract, which must be placed before the members for approval by special resolution before it can be entered into with a shareholder or number of shareholders (CA 2006 s 695).

The directors must make a copy of this proposed contract available for inspection at the general meeting and for 15 days prior to the meeting (CA 2006 s 696). Other general procedural requirements which the directors have a duty to ensure are observed include:

Steps	Purpose	Additional requirements for directors to observe
(1) Convene general meeting.	● To approve the contract by special resolution and provide authority for purchase.	● The resolution for a public company must specify a date within five years when the authority will expire.
		● Where more than one class of shares exist, check requirements for separate class meetings.
		● Where shares for a quoted company are to be purchased through a recognised investment exchange (including AIM), directors must ensure that prior approval to the market purchase is obtained from the members by ordinary resolution (CA 2006 s 701). The resolution must be submitted to Companies House and state: (i) the maximum number of shares to be acquired;

Steps	Purpose	Additional requirements for directors to observe
		(ii) maximum and minimum prices to be paid for shares; and
		(iii) a date, no later than five years from the date of the resolution, on which authority will expire.
		• Directors should also consult requirements of the Stock Exchange Listing Rules and those of other bodies such as the Association of British Insurers to ensure that the proposed purchase meets any requirements they may have, ie requiring approval by special rather than ordinary resolution.
(2) Submit the special (and ordinary if relevant) resolution to Companies House.	• Required to file the return within 28 days.	• The resolution cannot be recorded as approved where it could not be passed without votes of the person whose shares are proposed for repurchase.
(3) Prepare and submit form SH03 to Companies House.	• Required within 28 days of purchase, setting out details of purchase.	• Stamp duty must be paid to HMRC calculated on the purchase price of shares.

Steps	Purpose	Additional requirements for directors to observe
		• Where advance HMRC clearance from duty has been obtained, a return containing details of the purchase must be made within 60 days of payment.
(4) Cancel share certificate and amend Register of Members.	• A stock transfer form is not required but records must be adjusted to reflect purchase.	• The shareholder may require a balance certificate where only part of their holding has been purchased.
(5) Make necessary accounting entries.	• Reduce the issued capital by the nominal value of shares purchased.	• Where a premium is paid, the share premium account or the revaluation reserve may be affected by the transaction.
	• Transfer that amount to the 'capital redemption reserve'.	
(6) Retain the contract of purchase for ten years.	• Members have the right of inspection for up to ten years.	
(7) Make disclosure in accounts	• Where purchase is made during the preceding financial year, disclosure must be made in the directors' report to the accounts (CA 1985 s 235 and Sch 7 Part II, applicable for financial years beginning	

Steps	Purpose	Additional requirements for directors to observe
	before 6 April 2008 and Regulation 10 Part 2 of the Large and Medium-sized Companies and Groups (Accounts and Reports) Regulations 2008 (SI 2008/410 or Schedule 5 Part 7 to the Small Companies and Groups (Accounts and Directors' Report) Regulations 2008 (SI 2008/409) for financial years beginning on or after 6 April 2008).	

Where the purchase is financed out of capital the directors have a duty to ensure that the procedures and requirements detailed in para **7.22.3.3** are observed.

It is important to note that where directors intend to submit a proposal to shareholders for the company to purchase its own listed securities, notification of the proposal must also be made to the Regulatory Information Service without delay, as must the decision made at the shareholders' meeting (Chapter 12 of the Listing Rules). Notification of actual purchases must be made as soon as possible and in any event no later than 7.30 am the next business day after the day the repurchase occurred. Furthermore, directors must determine in advance whether the circular to be sent to shareholders seeking their approval and setting out details of the repurchase requires prior approval of the Stock Exchange and whether the purchase is generally prohibited by Listing Rule 12.2 by virtue of being in a prohibited period (unless exempt).

Finance for redemption or purchase   **7.22.3**

Distributable profits   **7.22.3.1**

A public or private company may purchase shares out of distributable profits, in which case the directors must ensure that appropriate accounts and reports are prepared for them to be in a position to accurately determine the amount of profit available for the purchase. In any event, all prior year losses will need to have been paid off or satisfied for the company to have any distributable profits.

The case *BDG Roof-Bond Ltd v Douglas* [2000] 1 BCLC 401 has clarified that, provided it has sufficient distributable profits, a company can pay for its own shares by a transfer of assets.

Proceeds of a new issue   **7.22.3.2**

The purchase may be financed by the proceeds of a new issue of shares by a public or private company, in which instance the directors have a duty to check provisions regarding the allotment of shares and that there is sufficient authorised capital for a further issue of shares. The allotment can be carried out at the same time as the purchase and the directors must ensure that the necessary approval is obtained for the allotment (see para **8.11.2**). Any share premium on shares purchased from the proceeds of a new issue by a public company must still be paid for out of distributable profits.

Purchase out of capital   **7.22.3.3**

Private companies only, where authorised by their Articles, may make payment for shares to be redeemed or purchased by the company out of capital. Payment out of capital is subject to further procedural requirements over and above those contained in paras **7.22.1** and **7.22.2**. Directors have a duty to ensure that these additional requirements are observed to safeguard the interests of creditors. These are as follows:

- Payment may not be made out of capital unless all distributable profits have been exhausted and all proceeds from a new issue have been applied (CA 2006 s 710). The difference between the amount of money needed to make the payment and the amount to be made up from distributable profits together with proceeds of a new issue constitutes the 'permissible capital payment'.

- Any premium to be paid over the nominal value when the shares are purchased must be paid out of distributable profits unless the shares were initially issued at a premium, in which case the premium may also be paid from the proceeds of a new issue.

- 'Relevant accounts' made up to a date less than three months prior to purchase are required to enable the directors accurately to determine the amount of distributable profits and the permissible capital payment

(CA 2006 s 712(6)). These may be annual accounts or those prepared specifically for the purpose.

- Directors must make a statement, in which they declare the amount of permissible capital payment, that having enquired into the affairs and state of the company (including consideration of contingent or prospective liabilities) they do not consider there to be any grounds or circumstances in which the company would be unable to meet its debts and that the company will continue as a going concern for at least the next year (CA 2006 s 714). It should be noted that it is an offence for a director to make such declaration without reasonable grounds, punishable by up to two years' imprisonment. In addition, a director who signed the statutory declaration may be personally liable to the company's creditors where the company is wound up within a year of the purchase (IA 1986 s 76(2)(b)).

- The auditors must make a report, which must be attached to the directors' statement, that, having enquired into the affairs of the company and having checked the directors calculation of the permissible capital payment, they have not found anything to indicate that the directors' opinion and declaration is unreasonable (CA 2006 s 714(6)).

Once these requirements have been met and it has been determined that the required declarations and reports can be given, the directors must ensure that the following procedural requirements are met:

Steps	Purpose
(1) Convene general meeting.	• Payment out of capital must be approved by special resolution.
	• Must be arranged so that the special resolution is passed within one week of directors' statement being made.
	• Members must be able to inspect a copy of the declaration.
(2) Publish a notice in London Gazette (Edinburgh Gazette for Scottish company).	• Must be arranged within one week of passing special resolution to inform creditors of proposal. Specifically, notice must state:
	(a) that the special resolution has been approved;
	(b) the permissible capital payment;

Steps	Purpose
	(c) that the directors' statement and audit report are available for inspection at the registered office;
	(d) that creditors may apply to the court for an order prohibiting the payment within five weeks of the date of the special resolution.
(3) Publish notice in a national newspaper or send notice to all creditors (s 719(2)).	● To ensure that creditors are aware of proposal.
(4) Make payment for shares.	● Necessary after five weeks when it is known whether creditors have made an objection, but within seven weeks of approval of the special resolution.

The directors must ensure that where payment is proposed out of capital these requirements are observed. In particular they should note that, whilst with a purchase of shares out of capital the special resolution necessary to approve the payment may be proposed at the same meeting convened to approve a purchase contract, a redemption of shares does not require approval by shareholders unless payment is to be made out of capital.

Where a creditor or a member who did not originally vote in favour of the resolution objects to the proposed payment out of capital and a court order is received to cancel the purchase, the directors must immediately notify Companies House (using form SH15 or SH16) and within 15 days of the court order deliver an office copy to Companies House.

Provided redemption or purchase out of capital is approved and no objection is received from creditors, the directors must finalise the process by notifying Companies House, updating the Register of Members, cancelling share certificates and making appropriate accounting entries, etc, as outlined in paras **7.22.1** and **7.22.2**.

Financial assistance for acquisition of own shares   7.23

The prohibition on a company giving financial assistance for the purposes of the acquisition of a company's own shares or the shares of a holding or subsidiary company in the same group now applies only to public companies (CA 2006 ss 678 and 679).

Directors of public companies should be aware that the general prohibition on financial assistance extends to:

- gifting or lending money or entering into an agreement for provision of funds;

- providing a guarantee, security or indemnity for a loan or other agreement entered into by the person to effect the purchase. This is illustrated by the High Court's decision in the case *John Phillip Walter Harlow and Kirankumar Mistry v Paul Christopher Loveday and Royscot Trust plc* sub nom *In the Matter of Hill & Tyler Ltd (In Administration)* [2004] EWHC 1261 (Ch) that, where security was granted as a condition of a loan to a company to be used to assist the buyer acquire shares in that company, it constituted unlawful financial assistance;

- the release or waiver of an obligation to the company, the effect of which assists the purchase;

- assistance provided before, at the same time as or after the acquisition;

- assistance provided by any of the company's subsidiaries. This is illustrated by the Court of Appeal's decision in *Chaston v SWP Group plc* [2003] BCC 140, in which payment made by a subsidiary of the target group for accounting reports to facilitate the sale of the group was considered to be unlawful financial assistance.

If the directors of public companies permit shares to be acquired in circumstances where financial assistance is prohibited, they will be liable to a fine and imprisonment (CA 2006 s 680). Consequently directors have a duty, before issuing any shares, to check whether the acquisition will involve financial assistance. Where this is the case, the directors of public companies will need to study the requirements of CA 2006 s 682 in detail, as the transaction may fall within the exceptions and be permitted.

General exceptions   **7.23.1**

If the directors of a public company are able to demonstrate that the following circumstances apply to the acquisition of shares, then they may consider providing financial assistance (CA 2006 s 682):

- that the company has net assets which are not reduced by the giving of the assistance or to the extent that the net assets are reduced, the assistance is provided out of distributable profits;

- the company lends money in the normal course of business and the proposed loan is no different;

- that assistance is in good faith, and in the interest of the company or its holding company for the purposes of an employees' share scheme;

- that assistance is given for the purposes of or in connection with anything done by the company or a group company to facilitate the holding of shares in the company or its holding company by bone fide employees or ex-employees (or their spouses, civil partners, widows, widowers, surviving civil partners, minor children or stepchildren) of the same group; or

- the assistance is given to enable loans to be granted to employees (other than directors) of the company for them to acquire the fully paid beneficial interest in shares in the company or its holding company.

It must be possible to fund the acquisition out of distributable profits. By way of example, a gift would clearly reduce the net assets and it must be possible to finance this out of distributable profits, otherwise providing security on a loan or similar option may need to be considered. Directors have a duty to ensure that they accurately determine the amount of available distributable profits and will need to consult either the year end, interim accounts or management accounts prepared for this purpose.

Directors should also note that payment of a dividend which may subsequently be used to acquire shares, or the redemption or purchase of one class of shares followed by acquisition of shares in another class, are not considered financial assistance and are not prohibited (CA 2006 s 681).

Private companies   7.23.2

The need for the so-called CA 1985 'whitewash' procedure involving a statutory declaration of solvency by the company's directors, report from the auditors, forms for Companies House and approval by special resolution of the members in general meeting was repealed with effect from 1 October 2008 and a private company is now permitted to give financial assistance for the purchase of its own shares.

However, directors must still ensure they observe their duty to promote the success of the company when considering any decisions for the giving of financial assistance (CA 2006 s 172).

Dividends and distributions   7.24

Directors generally have responsibility for a company's dividend policy, and common practice is for the directors to be provided with authority in the

Articles to pay an interim dividend, whilst approval of the members is required for any final dividend which the directors recommend to them (Table A, Model Articles and see para **3.80**).

However, the Articles may contain more precise rules which the directors have a duty to consult and observe as well as stringent statutory provisions relating to payment of dividends, discussed in detail below.

Directors should be aware that where they pay an 'illegal dividend' they may be personally liable to repay the company (CA 2006 s 847). In *Re Loquitar Ltd: Inland Revenue Commissioners v Richmond* [2003] EWHC 999 (Ch), it was held that directors of the company who had received dividends and were aware they had been paid out on the basis of improperly drawn up accounts for which they were responsible, were holding such dividends on constructive trust for the company and were ordered to repay them. Furthermore, in *Bairstow v Queens Moat Houses plc* [2000] 1 BCLC 549, it was held that there had been a breach of trust as a reasonably diligent director should have been aware that dividends should not be paid out of capital. Consequently directors of public companies who authorise the payment of dividends otherwise than out of distributable profit may be personally liable to repay such sums to the company, whether or not they are recipients of the dividend. In the Queens Moat Houses case, the Court of Appeal ruled in favour of the company and increased the amount the former directors were required to pay from £26.9m to £79m (*Bairstow v Queens Moat Houses plc* [2002] BCC 91).

Requirements in Articles   **7.24.1**

Every company limited by shares has the power to declare a dividend, but no company is under an obligation to distribute profits unless the Articles specifically provide. Before declaring or paying a dividend, the directors must consult the Articles or Memorandum to determine:

- the manner in which the dividend is required to be approved for payment, ie by the directors or by the members as recommended to them by the directors. Where approval is required by the members, they may be restricted to declaring a dividend which is not more than the amount recommended for payment by the directors;

- if there are any rights attaching to a class of shares conferring entitlement to a fixed dividend, which may be cumulative. Where such rights exist, the directors must ensure that the dividend is paid to the holders of those shares accordingly;

- whether the Articles permit a dividend to be paid by distribution of assets subject to statutory restrictions detailed below.

Statutory requirements   **7.24.2**

A company may not make a distribution or pay a dividend unless there are sufficient 'distributable profits' available for the purpose (CA 2006 s 830) and a director has a duty to ensure any dividends paid comply with the requirements of the CA 2006. Where the directors make improper dividend payments based on defective accounts or where they believe such payments cannot be afforded by the company, they may be liable for disqualification (*Re AG (Manchester) Ltd; Official Receiver v Watson* [2008] BCC 497).

In addition, public companies can only make a distribution where the amount of net assets after deducting the distribution will be at least equal to the amount of the aggregate called-up share capital and undistributable reserves (CA 2006 s 831). Investment and insurance companies are subject to similar restrictions, which need to be consulted by the directors (CA 2006 ss 832–835).

The directors must ensure that accounts are prepared for them to determine accurately the amount of such profits available for distribution (CA 2006 s 836). These accounts, referred to as 'relevant accounts', may be either:

- the last annual accounts;

- interim accounts, normally prepared where the directors believe there to be more profits available for distribution than reflected in the annual accounts (CA 2006 s 838). Where a public company prepares interim accounts, the directors must ensure that they are prepared on the same basis as the annual accounts and, whilst they need not be audited, that a copy is submitted to Companies House before the dividend is paid (CA 2006 s 838);

- initial accounts, prepared where a company wants to make a distribution in its first accounting period before accounts have been laid before the members. Where the company is a public company, any initial accounts prepared must be audited and submitted to Companies House (CA 2006 s 839).

Directors should also be aware that where the audit report to the relevant accounts is qualified, they must obtain a statement from the auditors as to whether they, the auditors, consider the qualification is material to the proposed distribution (CA 2006 s 837(5)).

Once the directors have determined whether there are sufficient distributable profits to pay a dividend and have considered wider issues influencing payment of a dividend, such as the need for reinvestment in the company and capitalisation of profits, shareholder relations and any tax implications, etc they have a duty to ensure that payment is approved and the mechanics of payment are set up as follows:

Requirement	Explanation
(1) Obtain approval for payment of the dividend.	● Convene a Board meeting to approve the amount determined to be paid as an interim dividend.
	● Where a final dividend is proposed, the directors must hold a Board meeting to recommend the amount to be paid and convene a general meeting to obtain approval from the members.
(2) Decide the payment and record dates and calculate dividend amounts.	● To permit calculation of the dividend due to individual shareholders on the Register of Members at a specified 'cut-off' date.
	● Directors must observe any dividend rights attaching to a particular class of shares in their calculations.
(3) Arrange preparation and printing of dividend warrants.	● Consists of a cheque payable to each shareholder (in accordance with any mandate instructions received from them) with an accompanying tax credit voucher.
(4) Set up a separate dividend account with the bank (if necessary) and prepare a dividend list.	● To assist control of dividend payments and provides a means of retaining any unclaimed dividends for 12 years from date of declaration (required by Limitation Act 1980).
(5) Send cheques to shareholders.	● To facilitate payment.
	● Reconcile cheques presented for payment against the dividend list, as the account may be closed when all dividends have been claimed.

Distribution in specie   **7.24.3**

A private company may, where permitted to do so by provisions contained in the Articles (or Memorandum for companies incorporated prior to 1 October 2009), declare a dividend to be paid wholly or partly by the distribution of specific assets to the shareholders, such as shares of a subsidiary company (in a demerger) or the freehold or leasehold interest in property. Where such authority exists, approval of the members in general meeting will generally be required, based upon recommendations made by the directors.

Political donations 7.25

Payment of political donations is perfectly permissible, provided the provisions of Part 14 of CA 2006 ss 362–379 concerning political donations and expenditure are observed and directors ensure that:

(1) the payment is approved by ordinary resolution of the shareholders, unless the Articles or the directors determine that a special resolution or resolution passed by a percentage higher than an ordinary resolution is required (s 366(2)(b)(i));

(2) where the company is a subsidiary, the payment is also approved by the holding company in general meeting (s 366(2)(b)(ii));

(3) the resolution is expressed in general terms and not authorising particular donations or expenditure (s 367(5)); and

(4) the resolution gives authority for four years or less or such shorter period as the Articles or the directors determine (s 368).

Directors must be aware that failure to obtain shareholder approval cannot be ratified after the event and the directors may be liable to pay the company the amount of the political donation or expenditure, damages for loss or damage sustained by the company and interest on the amount (s 369). Furthermore, directors of a parent company are jointly and severally liable for breaches committed by subsidiaries both in the UK and outside. It is therefore imperative for directors to ensure they do not breach the prohibitions on political donations and expenditure. Furthermore, as set out in para **7.13.1** disclosure of amounts donated must be included in the directors' report to the audited accounts.

In addition, the directors must ensure that provisions and restrictions in the Bribery Act 2010 are observed when political donations are made (see para **13.64**). Timing, the amount of such payments, openness and transparency are all particularly important as the donation must not be considered to have been made in order to coerce or influence behaviour. For example, if a company is waiting for a decision on a significant award of work in the public sector, then a large donation whilst the decision is being made might be inadvisable.

Bank account 7.26

Pursuant to 'general powers' to manage the company's business contained in the Articles, one of the first things that the directors will need to do once a company has been incorporated and is ready to commence trading is to open a bank account for the company to be able to make and receive payments.

No director alone has authority to open an account; approval by the Board of Directors of the terms and conditions of operation of the account is required and the Board must provide authority to a director to proceed and open an account. All banks require their standard bank mandate form to be completed and signed for a company to open an account and the mandate is frequently in the form of draft minutes, emphasising the requirement for Board approval. The bank may also require sight of the company's original Certificate of Incorporation and Memorandum and Articles, or certified copies thereof, before opening an account.

Consequently directors have a duty to ensure that, before signing and returning the mandate form to the bank, they have approval of the Board and an additional signed copy of the mandate has been placed in the company's minute book as evidence of the Board's decision and approval for opening an account.

Where an overdraft facility needs to be arranged, banks will normally require security or collateral for this facility and the directors have a duty to ensure that they have the necessary authority, normally contained in the Articles, to borrow money and charge the company's assets before entering into such agreement.

As part of the directors' general duty to look after and protect the company's assets, they must give due consideration not only to opening but also operating the company's bank account:

- signatories must be chosen carefully to ensure adequate control of the account. Often companies will authorise a single signatory to sign cheques up to a small specified amount per cheque, above which two or more signatories are required;

- the frequency with which bank statements are required;

- reconciliation of the bank account needs to be conducted as part of the accounts control processes and should be carried out by a person other than an authorised signatory at appropriate intervals. Such reconciliation will normally form part of the management accounting process necessary for the directors to be aware of the company's financial position.

Directors must also ensure that the bank is kept advised of changes in directors, secretary, registered office, accounting reference date, auditors, etc, and that the bank mandate instruction is revised as soon as a person leaves and ceases to be eligible as a signatory.

Taxation (tax, NIC and PAYE records)   **7.27**

The directors of a company are responsible for arranging calculation of taxes due and payable by the company (and to some extent for employees also), filing returns and making payments to the relevant tax authority and the maintenance and retention of tax records generally. Normally tasks of computing tax and making returns will be delegated, but directors should be aware that such delegation does not in any way relieve them of ultimate responsibility for tax matters. Although directors may rely on fellow directors and officers of the company to an extent in dealing with day-to-day matters, they must ensure that tax matters are appropriately monitored, as they should not assume without question that such matters are being dealt with correctly.

Indeed there has been much publicity and controversy about the amount of tax being paid – or rather, not being paid – by a number of high-profile global companies, including Starbucks, Amazon, Google, Apple and Vodafone. Whilst it is recognised that the complex tax avoidance tactics deployed by these companies are not technically illegal as they have exploited tax loopholes, for example paying earnings through subsidiaries in jurisdictions with much lower tax rates or applying more favourable tax rates in jurisdictions where contract are negotiated, the whole affair has called into question the extent of a Board's responsibility. Whilst years ago it would have been to exercise powers in the best interests of the company for the benefit of shareholders, the directors' responsibility to 'promote success of the company' is now much wider and extends to other stakeholders and those affected by a company's activities (see **CHAPTER 4** for more detail). Without doubt it is quite a grey and difficult area, but directors do have a duty to not only comply with the law but also to ensure that ethical, right, fair and just decisions are made about how their companies operate. Many would argue that such aggressive tax avoidance, to the extent that no tax has been paid in the UK, is unethical, unfair and uncompetitive for tax-paying British businesses. Public outcry about these tactics has been considerable and prolonged, potentially damaging these companies' reputations and encouraging customers to switch to those that demonstrate more ethical practices and greater consideration for the countries in which they operate.

Timely and accurate tax compliance is essential for any company. The principal taxes for which the director is responsible include corporation tax, VAT, PAYE and National Insurance, all of which attract severe financial penalties where a company is late or inaccurate in making returns and paying tax due. Directors should be aware that in many instances interest may be charged on late payments or underpayments, which is automatically imposed, and it is therefore essential that errors are corrected without delay.

Whilst tax departments of the HMRC have the ability to instigate criminal action against those guilty of tax evasion, they will in most cases (except where the offence is blatant) pursue action for imposition of civil penalties where they only have to prove that 'on the balance of probabilities' an offence was committed.

Re Stanford Services Ltd [1987] BCLC 607, 3 BCC 326 illustrates the need for directors to keep records of VAT, PAYE and National Insurance contribution debts and to pay them periodically to the relevant tax department. In this case tax debts were not paid and instead were applied to finance the business. The court ruled that tax payments could not be withheld and, by using the money to finance the business, the directors were committing an offence by allowing the company to continue to trade whilst technically insolvent.

HMRC, Excise Departments and the Contributions Agency have merged, which should simplify taxation matters for directors, who will be able to deal with one organisation for all tax, National Insurance contributions, employee benefits and payroll matters.

Corporation tax   7.27.1

Corporation tax is levied on the profits, including income and chargeable gains arising from disposal of assets by the company, and is charged at the rate applicable to the financial year to which the company's accounts relate. The directors will need to ensure that required corporation tax returns are completed and HMRC's payment deadlines are observed to avoid any late payment penalties or fines.

PAYE   7.27.2

The PAYE tax collection system requires a company to calculate income tax due from employees on their pay and other taxable benefits, deduct this amount from payment made to employees and account for it directly to the HMRC. Directors have a duty to ensure that income tax is deducted from employees' salary payments and that the tax deducted is paid directly to HMRC at that time.

Failure to operate a PAYE system will result in liability to pay the tax due to HMRC plus the possible imposition of civil penalties which cannot necessarily be recovered from the employee. HMRC carries out PAYE audits and control visits periodically to recover shortfalls in the tax paid. The directors have a duty to make available records relating to calculation of pay, deduction of tax under PAYE and National Insurance contributions during such inspections.

National Insurance contributions   7.27.3

Directors will be aware that National Insurance (NI) is payable not only by employees on their income, normally collected from employees by the company's

PAYE system, but also by employers. A previous loophole, where companies could pay employees in shares, thereby avoiding their NI contribution, has been closed. Similarly, anti-avoidance measures were introduced by HMRC to prevent individuals avoiding income tax and NI by providing services to clients through their own one-man personal service companies and paying themselves a low wage supplemented by dividends.

Directors must ensure that when NI is collected from employees it is paid without delay to the Contributions Agency. Payment may also be made via the PAYE system to HMRC, who will account for payment accordingly.

Failure to pay NI is an offence for which the directors may be held personally liable. An order made under the Proceeds of Crime Act 2002 permits the court to freeze the assets of officers of companies which failed to pay NI. This power will be exercised where it is evident that the directors or officers of a company have intentionally, and for their own benefit, driven a company into liquidation to avoid accounting for NI debts.

VAT   **7.27.4**

The directors must ensure that HMRC is notified if the company's taxable turnover exceeds limits required for VAT registration on either historic results or according to future forecasts. At present a company is required to register for VAT purposes where taxable supplies have or are predicted to exceed £79,000 a year. The company must notify HMRC within 30 days of occurrence or the predicted occurrence.

Directors have a duty to be aware of and keep up to date with VAT registration requirements, as not only do the limits for registration vary, but other requirements may apply to the company as follows:

- a company which makes only exempt supplies is not entitled to register;

- where the registration limit is exceeded but supplies are wholly or mainly zero-rated, then the need to register is likely to be waived;

- the directors may choose to register the company for VAT where it is below the threshold but will benefit from being able to reclaim input tax on goods and services received.

Requirements once registered   **7.27.4.1**

Where the company has registered for VAT purposes, HMRC will prescribe VAT accounting periods, which are usually quarterly, and at the end of each period the company must make a return declaring the amount of output tax due to be paid by the company and the amount of input tax being reclaimed.

The directors must ensure that a note of the VAT number appears on all VAT invoices and demands for payment, receipts and credit notes and that the amount of payment attributable to VAT is shown separately. The VAT number must also appear on the company's website, if it has one.

HMRC has authority to make periodic checks on companies to ensure that they have been calculating VAT payments and amounts reclaimed correctly. The directors have a duty to ensure that a competent person is responsible for preparing the VAT returns and that adequate controls and checking procedures are put in place to ensure that accurate returns are submitted. *Dryer Co Ltd* (*Tax Journal*, 19 May 1994) emphasises that the responsibility of the company to submit accurate returns and errors cannot be attributed to an incompetent bookkeeper.

Accounting records for VAT inspection purposes must be kept for at least six years and be made available to HMRC inspectors during any visit they may make.

Penalties   **7.27.4.2**

Offences and defaults made in connection with VAT payments attract severe penalties which may be either criminal, where there has been deliberate tax evasion, or civil, where heavy penalties are levied by HMRC. Such offences and defaults include:

- failing to register;
- failure to submit a return on time;
- deliberate evasion of tax;
- failure to retain records;
- misdeclaration, including underpayment of output tax or claiming too much for repayment of input tax.

Directors should ensure that VAT accounting systems are in place to make sure that none of the above offences occur. Where such offences are made, they each attract a penalty on the company which may be fixed or increase proportionally according to the length of time the default exists. Directors should also note that a court has ability to make a director personally liable for the whole of a penalty imposed for VAT evasion by a company (*Customs and Excise Comrs v Bassimeh* [1995] STC 910). This decision will be made by the court where it appears that conduct giving rise to the penalty is attributable to a director (Finance Act 1986 ss 13 and 14).

Money laundering   7.28

Money laundering is the exchange of money or assets obtained by criminal activity for money or assets that are clean and have no obvious links to such activity.

The requirements that directors need to observe in relation to preventing money laundering are embodied in the Proceeds of Crime Act 2002 (POCA 2002), the Money Laundering Regulations 1997, CJA 1988, the Drug Trafficking Act 1994 and the Terrorism Act 2000 (TA 2000). POCA 2002 extended money laundering offences to include the proceeds of any crime or criminal activity, such as theft, burglary and tax evasion as well as drug trafficking, serious fraud and terrorism, etc.

Directors should be aware that it is an offence to:

- conceal, disguise, convert, transfer or remove criminal property;

- arrange or facilitate the acquisition or retention of criminal property;

- acquire, use or possess criminal property; or

- for persons who obtain information which leads them to suspect money laundering not to report their suspicions, irrespective of the amounts involved.

It is therefore important for directors to ensure that a formal process and procedures are implemented within the company to verify the identity of new clients and to facilitate the reporting of any suspicions that a new or existing client is engaged in laundering illegally acquired funds. To do this they need to appoint a money laundering reporting officer to whom employees are able to report any reasonable grounds for suspicion. The directors must also ensure that the money laundering reporting officer completes a suspicion transaction report to notify the National Crime Agency (NCA) of their concerns.

In addition, the Money Laundering Regulations 2007 (SI 2007/2157) ('the Regulations') place additional responsibilities on financial and credit businesses, accountants, estate agents, trust and company service providers, etc. These Regulations require:

(1)   stringent tests to ensure that businesses and firms which set up and manage trusts have not done so for criminal purposes;

(2)   due diligence for businesses ie customer relations must be monitored on an ongoing basis and where a trust exists the beneficial owner must be identified;

(3)   varying levels of customer due diligence and monitoring dependent on the type of business;

(4)   extra checks where a customer would be considered high risk, for example, someone not met face-to-face or a foreign head of state;

(5)   implementing a simple checking process for low risk customers, such as a company listed on a regulated market.

Suitable policies and procedures must be put in place to identify money laundering, ensure records are kept of client verification checks and train and inform employees about the requirements of POCA 2002 and TA 2000 (Regulations 19, 20(3) and 21).

In practical terms, the directors will need to determine guidelines for employees to follow in verifying the identity of new clients and reporting any suspicions about a client or a particular transaction. Such guidelines and procedures are likely to include:

●   identifying the person in the company (the money laundering reporting officer) with overall responsibility for following up and reporting suspicions of money laundering to whom employees should report *any* suspicious clients, events or transactions;

●   setting a monetary limit (which must be less than €15,000) below which transactions would not ordinarily be examined in detail, unless there are any suspicious circumstances, such as payment always in cash, only a post box address for contact, or where payment is made by cheque from a source other than the client;

●   determining a formal procedure for verifying the identity of a new client. Where the client is an individual, his identity can be confirmed by asking to see and recording details of his passport, driving licence, bank or building society passbook, mortgage statement, council tax bill, utilities bill or other official document. Where the client is a company, then a search of records at Companies House may be conducted (the procedure followed by banks when considering new account enquiries), details of VAT registration and tax reference numbers obtained and checked, references from the company's bank requested, a credit reference check obtained, etc;

●   deciding the manner and length of time for which evidence of verification details are kept;

- identifying circumstances to staff which could be considered suspicious and need to be reported.

Many of these procedures may well be carried out as standard practice to determine the person or company's credit status. The emphasis here is that the person or company's identity must be verified and any suspicious circumstances identified be reported.

Regulation 42(5) states that it is an offence to contravene the requirements, punishable by fines up to an amount the designated authority deems fit or up to two years imprisonment or both. Regulation 47 also goes on to state that an officer (which includes a director) as well as the body corporate may be liable for the offence where it is committed with their consent or connivance or arises due to their neglect. It is also a criminal offence not to report reasonable suspicion that someone is engaged in money laundering, punishable by up to two years' imprisonment, a fine or both.

Again, a scan through recent press reports will reveal a number of high-profile companies that have failed to observe requirements to identify and prevent money laundering. By way of example:

- HSBC's record fine of £1.2m agreed with US authorities for lack of adequate controls, the consequence of which was billions of US dollars created by drugs cartels and terrorists in the US and Mexico being laundered through the US banking system (similar claims have also since been made against HSBC by the Argentine tax authority); and

- the £4.2m fine by the FCA on EFG Private Bank for failing to exercise and maintain effective anti-money laundering controls for high-risk customers, despite having policies in place which were just not put into practice.

Indeed, a recent investigation by the FCA into a number of small companies found that many of them had failed to manage risks of financial crime effectively and most had significant weaknesses in their anti-money laundering systems and controls. In most cases, senior management was engaged and receptive to the need for anti-money laundering systems, but a lack of resource coupled with poor communication and knowledge meant this engagement did not result in any positive action. The FCA's findings are a salutary reminder of the need to be proactive and actually implement measures to prevent money laundering.

8 Directors' duties and the members

8 Directors' duties and the members

As discussed in **CHAPTER 4**, directors have extensive obligations to the company's members. These obligations originated from case law and are often referred to as common law duties, requiring the directors to act in good faith and in the interests of the company, as would a trustee, with a degree of skill and care that can reasonably be expected of them.

Whilst, as explained in **CHAPTER 4**, the statutory statement of directors' general duties contained in CA 2006 ss 171–177 has largely replaced the common law duties, they remain important for interpretation of exactly what is required by the statutory statement.

Whilst these obligations must be considered at all times, the duties discussed in this chapter go beyond this and examine actual actions required of the directors in respect of members.

It is fair to assume that the members will have only limited knowledge, if any at all, of statutory requirements and provisions in the company's Articles which dictate the manner and timing by which routine and non-routine decisions and statutory matters of a company are dealt with. Directors therefore have an important role in ensuring that any decisions which require prior approval of the members are proposed to members in general meetings and that any scheduled meetings, such as the annual general meeting (AGM), are convened within the required period and in a manner that complies with the company's Articles and provisions in CA 2006.

Directors have a duty to ensure that restrictions relating to changes in share ownership, which have been devised to protect shareholders' interests, are observed and that authority to waive or vary such restrictions is obtained in the correct fashion. When general meetings are convened, either by the directors or by requisition of the members, the directors must ensure that valid notice of the meeting is given to members, the appropriate resolutions are proposed for consideration and that any circulars, statements or supporting documents necessary to consider the resolutions are supplied at the same time as the notice. During the meeting the chairman, normally a director, must ensure that a quorum is present and that any requirements relating to voting, proxies, corporate representatives and the required majority of votes necessary to approve the resolutions in question are observed.

Provisions in CA 2006 recognise the need to protect members' interests and impose the requirement for significant business decisions to be made by a specified majority of members. However, directors must at all times remain aware that they have a duty to protect the interests of the minority shareholders when decisions and changes are proposed. Where such shareholders consider they have been treated in an unfairly prejudicial manner they may make application to the court to remedy the situation in a number of different ways, all of which may impose restrictions or duties on the directors (CA 2006 ss 994–999).

Directors also have a duty to communicate with members and by statute are required to notify them of specific events or circumstances, such as a serious loss of capital. However, the trend, especially amongst listed public companies, has been to improve and enhance communication with shareholders through circulars, announcements and use of the Internet and electronic media. Directors should be aware that under CA 2006 companies are able to communicate information by electronic means and, with agreement of the members, they are now able to use electronic communications for statutory purposes such as:

- sending accounts, directors' reports and auditors' reports to members and others rather than sending them by post. Furthermore, where a company and its shareholders agree, accounts and reports may be published on a website for a period of at least 21 days prior to the AGM. The publication of accounts and reports on a website is now compulsory for a quoted company (as defined under CA 2006 s 385);

- providing shareholders agree, giving notice of general meetings electronically, either by email or by posting on a website; and

- allowing members to appoint proxies or corporate representatives by email, notwithstanding anything to the contrary in the company's Articles.

These provisions are likely to have a significant effect on shareholder and member communications and have benefits not only to members in terms of the speed by which they receive information and greater flexibility and convenience by being able to access information and documents on a website when it suits them, but also for the company in printing and postage cost savings.

When considering their duties to members, directors should be aware that, in addition to statutory penalties which may be imposed where they take action and make decisions without requisite member approval, fail to convene required meetings, or omit to inform members of notifiable events, the company's members may express their dissatisfaction with the directors' conduct by removing them from office, not approving their reappointment at the next AGM or, amongst other things, by selling their shares. As a result, the directors have a vested interest in fulfilling their duties to members to secure their own position and, as demonstrated in **CHAPTER 9**, the power of the shareholders in this respect should not be underestimated.

Ownership of shares   8.10

A shareholder's relationship with a company is based on property rights, where he either owns a number of shares, or has the right to subscribe for or convert securities into shares. Based on this relationship, it seems logical that statutory provisions and a company's Articles provide shareholders with an element of protection and control over admission of new persons to membership and the issue of additional shares which would in effect dilute their interest in the company.

Directors have a duty to uphold shareholders' rights and must ensure that they have authority to allot or transfer shares and that any requirements, restrictions or procedures governing such transactions set out in the Articles or by statute are observed. A director who knowingly contravenes any of these requirements will be liable to civil liabilities and criminal penalties.

Directors need to be aware that shareholders' rights have been extended by CA 2006 (ss 145–153). These changes include:

- s 145 – provided there is a specific enabling clause in the company's Articles of Association, the company's shareholders may make certain of their rights available to another person;

- ss 146–151 – a member of a company whose shares are traded on regulated markets is able to nominate another person to enjoy information rights. That person will be entitled to receive copies of all communications that the company would send to its shareholders normally, the right to receive copies of accounts and reports and the right to request that documentation be sent them in either hard copy form or otherwise;

- s 152 – where a person holds shares on behalf of a number of beneficial owners, the rights over those shares may be exercised in different ways;

- s 153 – indirect investors may participate in certain situations requiring shareholders requisitions.

In addition, s 324 permits holders of more than one share to appoint multiple proxies who may attend, vote and speak at any general meeting even if the Articles of Association do not allow this.

Similarly, directors have a duty to shareholders when redeeming or purchasing shares in the company, discussed in para **7.22**.

When considering shareholders' rights, reference must be made by the directors to the class of shares and the rights that attach to it, details of which will be contained in the Memorandum or Articles of Association. Where the company has only one class of share in issue all shareholders' rights will be the same, but where there is more than one class of share each may confer different rights on the holders of those shares with regard to the following:

- entitlement to receive notice of, attend and vote at general meetings;
- entitlement to receive dividends or distributions of capital;
- pre-emption over shares in that class and other classes.

A final point that directors will need to check, particularly where there are a number of classes of shares, is whether there is any shareholder qualification that must be satisfied before a person or persons can be admitted to membership.

Issue of shares   8.11

Prerequisites for issue   8.11.1

Before directors are permitted to issue shares in the company they must address issues relating to availability of shares, authority for issue and rights of pre-emption of existing shareholders as follows:

(1)   *Authorised capital.* For companies incorporated prior to 1 October 2009, and which have retained provisions relating to authorised capital, the company must have a sufficient number of unissued shares remaining in the authorised share capital from which to make the proposed allotment.

Where the authorised share capital needs to be increased, the directors must ensure that the increase is approved by ordinary resolution of the members. This would normally be done by convening a general meeting to consider the matter. However, directors should note that the resolution may only be proposed where authority to make an alteration to the share capital is provided in the Articles (Table A reg 32). Where such authority is not specified, the directors will need first to propose a special resolution to members at a general meeting to amend the Articles to include authority, after which the ordinary resolution to increase the authorised capital may be proposed.

It is important to note that directors may have an additional duty under a company's share option scheme to keep available for issue sufficient unissued shares in the company's share capital to satisfy the exercise of subsisting options pursuant to the scheme.

The concept of a maximum cap on authorised capital was abolished with effect from 1 October 2009 and companies incorporated on or after 1 October 2009, or those which have passed a resolution removing the relevant provisions from their Memorandum and Articles will not need to consider this point.

(2)   *Authority to allot shares.* Since 1 October 2009, CA 2006 s 550 grants directors of a private company with only one class of shares authority to allot shares for an indefinite period of time. This is providing there are no restrictions contained in the company's Articles and the company's shareholders have not passed a resolution placing any restrictions on the issue of shares.

Companies incorporated prior to 1 October 2009 will need to pass an ordinary resolution in order to take advantage of the s 550 provisions.

For private companies incorporated prior to 1 October 2009 (who have not passed an ordinary resolution to take advantage of the provisions contained in s 550) or with more than one share class and public companies directors can only issue shares when they have authority to do so and they must check whether such authority has been provided either by the members in general meeting or provisions contained in the Articles. They must also determine whether the authority is valid at the date of the proposed allotment and for the number of shares proposed to be issued (CA 2006 s 551).

Where authority has not been provided, or has since expired, the directors must convene a general meeting to propose an ordinary resolution to the members to provide them with authority to allot shares. Many public companies renew this authority each year at the AGM as part of standard business.

The directors should ensure that the following requirements are met when proposing the ordinary resolution to members:

(a)   For private companies with more than one share class and unlisted public companies, the resolution must state the maximum number of shares to which authority applies and may remain in force for any period up to five years from the date of approval (CA 2006 s 551). As noted above, the directors of private companies with one share class may allot shares for an indefinite period (providing no restrictions exist in the Articles). Under CA 1985 it was possible for a private company (even one with multiple share classes) to elect that the authority be for an indefinite period (CA 1985 s 80A(2)) – where a company has passed this elective resolution prior to 1 October 2009, the resolution will remain valid, whether or not the company has more than one share class.

(b) For a listed public company (the majority of unlisted public companies follow suit), the resolution must state the maximum number of shares the directors are authorised to allot and the percentage this is of total ordinary share capital, calculated on figures not more than one month before. In practice and in accordance with recommendations of the ABI and the NAPF most public companies restrict renewal of authority to the lesser of the company's unissued ordinary share capital and one-third of the company's issued ordinary share capital. The time limit for the authority must be stated in the resolution and, whilst it can be expressed to last for anything up to five years, it is commonly expressed to expire at the next AGM or 15 months thereafter, whichever is sooner, as it is intrinsically linked to waiver of pre-emption rights. Having said this, changes in relation to waiver of pre-emption rights, detailed in clause (3) below, are affecting public companies and renewal of this authority for up to five years is being increasingly applied.

(3) *Rights of pre-emption.* Directors must be aware that statutory provisions apply to the allotment of shares requiring them to be offered first to existing members, in proportion to their current holdings, before they are offered to persons who are not members of the company (CA 2006 s 561). Directors must ensure that rights of pre-emption are observed for all issues of shares except where the provisions of s 560 do not apply, ie an issue of subscriber's shares on incorporation, a capitalisation issue, options exercised pursuant to an employee share option scheme, or an issue wholly or partly for consideration other than cash, such as a share-for-share exchange between companies on a takeover.

Statutory rights of pre-emption may be excluded or varied by a private company by provisions contained in the Articles (CA 2006 s 567). Such exclusion or variation is set out in the Articles, which the directors should review carefully when an allotment is proposed. They should ensure that any provisions contained in the Articles relating to pre-emption are applied rather than the statutory provisions.

Where the proposal is for shares to be offered other than to existing members, the directors will need to propose a special resolution for approval by members to disapply their statutory rights of pre-emption (CA 2006 ss 569–571). The proposal must be recommended by the directors who shall state their reasons for making the recommendation, the amount to be paid to the company for securities to be allotted and the director's justification of that amount (CA 2006 s 571). The directors' recommendation must accompany the special resolution and may appear in the notes to the notice, a separate letter or the directors' report to the accounts where proposed at the AGM. It is important to note that any person who knowingly or recklessly authorises or permits inclusion of any misleading, false or deceptive material in the statement will be liable to imprisonment, a fine, or both (CA 2006 s 572).

Alternatively, approval of a special resolution will be necessary to waive any pre-emption rights contained in the Articles. In a similar vein to the provisions of CA 2006 relating to directors authority to allot shares, private companies with only one share class may disapply pre-emption rights indefinitely. This is done by either the passing of a special resolution or the insertion of relevant provisions into a company's Articles.

It should be noted that, as standard procedure, many public companies automatically include a resolution for approval at the AGM to disapply these pre-emption rights. In the past, whilst limited companies were permitted to waive these rights for up to five years as permitted by statute, listed public companies were not permitted to waive them for more than 15 months at a time (Listing Rules, para 9.2). The Listing Rules have been amended (Amendment 11) to remove this time restriction, although directors should be aware that the ABI and NAPF advise their members to vote against such resolution where it seeks to waive rights of pre-emption for greater than 5% of the company's issued share capital.

Once the directors have checked the requirements and possible restrictions on an issue of shares thoroughly and are satisfied that they have, or have taken action to secure, authority to allot shares and there are sufficient shares in the authorised share capital and shareholders' rights of pre-emption have been observed or waived in the correct manner, they may proceed to offer shares to new or existing members.

They should be aware that where they knowingly approve or permit the issue of shares without being authorised to make an allotment, they will be liable to a fine (CA 2006 s 549(4) and (5)) and, where they fail to observe pre-emption rights of existing shareholders, may be liable to compensate the person whose rights were ignored for any loss, damage or expenses incurred as a result of the issue (CA 2006 ss 563 and 568). However, allotment of the shares will not necessarily be considered invalid.

Procedure for allotment **8.11.2**

Provided the directors are satisfied that they have authority to issue shares and shareholders' rights of pre-emption have either been observed or waived, they may proceed with the allotment as follows:

Procedure	Explanation
1	Hold a meeting of the Board of Directors to approve the allotment and authorise the issue of letters of application. At the same meeting any offer documents would need to be checked to ensure accuracy of statements made therein and be approved for issue.
2	Issue forms of application and accompanying offer documents to members.
3	Convene a further meeting of the Board of Directors once the closing date for application has passed to consider applications received, approve allotment of shares to those who have made application and payment and authorise the issue of share certificates to allottees.
4	Enter details of the allotments in the Registers of Allotments and Members.
5	Issue share certificates to allottees within two months of the date of allotment (CA 2006 s 769).
6	Within one month of the allotment complete, sign and submit a form of allotment (form SH01) to Companies House notifying the increase in issued share capital (CA 2006 s 555).

The above procedure for allotting shares that the directors must follow becomes more complex given any of the following circumstances:

(1)   *Offers of shares.* Where shares of a company are offered to the public, the directors must take account of stringent requirements of the Listing Rules, Prospectus Rules and FSMA 2000 which govern the manner and form in which shares are offered to the public. These regulations have been devised to protect the interests of the public as a whole (para **9.10**).

The directors will need to consult the relevant provisions in detail to ensure that any offer of shares complies. In general, these additional requirements relate to issue of any offer documents, the issue of and details contained in a prospectus and statement of a minimum amount required to be raised by the offer which, if not reached, would prohibit the issue of any shares. Directors duties relating to issue of a prospectus are discussed in more detail in paras **9.10, 9.20** and **9.30**.

Directors should be aware that, in light of provisions of the Companies Acts and FSMA 2000, they may be held personally liable for the accuracy of information given in documents encouraging people to invest in the company (*Hedley Byrne & Co Ltd v Heller & Partners Ltd* [1964] AC 465, HL).

(2) *Consideration paid for shares allotted.* Shares may be allotted for money or money's worth, or by way of capitalising a company's reserves (see points (3) and (4) below). They may not under any circumstances be allotted at a discount (CA 2006 s 580) and, where the company is a public company, the directors must ensure that at least one-quarter of the nominal value and the whole of any share premium is paid up (CA 2006 s 586).

Where shares of a public company are issued for payment other than cash, directors must ensure that the statutory requirement for an independent valuation report is met (CA 2006 ss 593, 596 and 1150). The report must confirm that the value of the consideration is not less than the nominal value and any premium of shares to be allotted. A copy of this report must be sent to Companies House with the return of allotment forms (CA 2006 ss 597 and 602).

A formal contract would normally be required where allotment is made for a non-cash consideration and the directors must ensure that the terms of such contract are approved at a Board meeting. A certified copy of the contract must be submitted to the Stamp Office for adjudication for stamp duty purposes and, when returned, be sent to Companies House at the same time as the form of allotment SH01 mentioned above.

(3) *Rights issue.* This involves the offer of shares to existing shareholders for cash, in proportion to their current shareholdings, and therefore does not require waiver or disapplication of pre-emption rights (unless shareholders have the right to renounce their rights, in which case the Articles should be consulted to ensure that the offer complies with requirements set out therein). Directors must ensure that any renunciation rights set out in the Articles are observed.

(4) *Bonus or capitalisation issue.* This involves the issue of shares to existing members pro rata to their existing holdings. The issue is funded by capitalising some or all of the company's distributable reserves which are allocated to shareholders as new shares credited as fully paid (or, very rarely, as partly paid). Directors will need to observe the procedure outlined in the Table above and, at the same time, have regard to the following additional requirements:

(a) the Articles must contain a provision to permit capitalisation of reserves. If no such authority exists, the directors have a duty, before any such bonus issue of shares is made, to propose a special resolution to the members that the Articles be amended to include such a clause;

(b) hold a Board meeting to approve the convening of a general meeting to recommend the bonus issue to members;

(c)   convene a general meeting for members to approve the bonus issue by ordinary resolution (a special resolution to amend the Articles would be proposed first, at the same meeting, if necessary);

(d)   submit signed copies of relevant ordinary and special resolutions to Companies House;

(e)   issue letters of allotment or renounceable letters of allotment, if appropriate;

(f)   submit form SH01 to Companies House to record the allotment of shares for consideration other than cash.

Partly paid shares   **8.11.3**

Where shares are issued as partly paid on application they may, and will commonly, have fixed dates for payment of the unpaid balance outstanding. Once such shares have been issued, the directors have a continuing obligation to ensure that instalments due are received at the appropriate time. In the event that payments for outstanding amounts due on shares are not received, the directors have a duty to ensure that their authority to impose restrictions over those shares, contained in the Articles, is exercised. These restrictions are likely to include the ability to impose a lien on the shares, withhold dividend payments and ultimately forfeit the shares where payment has still not been received. For companies incorporated prior to 1 October 2009 these provisions are contained Table A regs 8–22. However, there are no such provisions in the Model Articles and private companies limited by shares, incorporated after 1 October 2009, will need to ensure that relevant provisions are inserted into the Articles where partly paid shares are required to be issued.

Transfer of shares   **8.12**

As mentioned previously, shares are essentially property and as such may be bought and sold by members freely in the manner provided in the company's Articles (CA 2006 s 544). Directors maintain the Register of Members and, as an extension of this duty, are responsible for registering transfers and updating these records. In fulfilling this duty they must ensure that statutory requirements relating to the transfer of shares and provisions in the company's Articles and shareholders' agreement (if one exists) are observed.

It should be noted that where a director purchases shares from a member of the company a directors' duties as outlined under CA 2006 must be considered, and the director who is interested in the transaction must declare the fact to the Board of directors under s 177 and it might be appropriate, or indeed a requirement of the company's Articles of Association, that the interested director abstains from voting on the matter. The director under s 172 must have regard to the need to act fairly between the members of the company in any decision they make concerning the transfer of shares.

In addition, case law provides that full and frank disclosure of information relating to the finances of the company must also be provided to the member from whom the shares are being purchased (*Platt v Platt* [1999] 2 BCLC 745).

Documents required for transfer   8.12.1

Before proceeding to register a transfer, the directors must ensure that the stock transfer form submitted to them for registration is either in the form required by the Stock Transfer Act 1963, or such form required by the Articles (CA 2006 s 544 and Table A reg 23 or article 26 (private companies limited by shares) and article 63 (public companies) of the Model Articles).

They must check that the transfer has been properly executed by or on behalf of the transferor (or transferors where there is a joint holding) and has either been signed on the reverse as evidence of exemption from stamp duty, or bears a stamp given by HMRC showing that duty has been paid. Where the stock transfer has not been stamped and is not exempt from duty, the directors cannot register the transfer. Where they fail to observe this duty they are committing an offence and (in theory at least) will be liable to a fine for registering an invalid instrument of transfer (CA 2006 s 770). Furthermore it should be noted that under the Stamp Act 1891, s 17 (as amended), the Stamp Office can impose a fine of £300 for each occasion on which a stock transfer form has been registered without being correctly stamped. Accordingly, such transfers should be returned to the transferee to arrange for stamp duty to be paid. In *Elliott v Hollies Ltd* [1998] 1 BCLC 627 the court dismissed an application for a share register to be rectified by registering a stock transfer form which had not been properly stamped and where there were doubts concerning validity of the signature.

The stock transfer form must be accompanied by a share certificate, evidencing ownership of the shares, when submitted for registration and the directors are required to check that the certificate is valid, the owner of the shares and the transferor are one and the same person and the number of shares to be transferred are at least covered by the shares on the certificate. In the event that the existing member has mislaid his share certificate, the directors will need to issue a letter of indemnity which, once signed by the shareholder, can be accepted in place of a share certificate and is sufficient evidence of title. It is common practice for public companies to require such indemnities to be joined into by a bank or insurance company. Care must be taken when issuing indemnities for lost certificates, as illustrated in *Royal Bank of Scotland plc v Sandstone Properties Ltd* [1998] 2 BCLC 429 where issue of a duplicate certificate assisted a fraudster to transfer shares, although it was the forged stock transfer form which was the main concern in this offence.

The directors must ensure that, where a transfer form or any accompanying documents submitted for registration do not meet the criteria set out above, the request for transfer is rejected and documents are returned to the transferor, or person acting on their behalf, for correction.

Process for registering a transfer   **8.12.2**

The Articles of a company and the shareholders' agreement, where one exists, are likely to contain provisions concerning transfers of shares which the directors must consult before proceeding to register a transfer. For example, the Articles may require that the shares are offered to existing members before being transferred elsewhere. As mentioned above Table A regs 23–28, and article 26 (private companies limited by shares) and article 63 (public companies) of the Model Articles, specify the form the transfer must take and detail circumstances in which the directors have authority to refuse to register a transfer. For example Table A reg 24, prevents a transfer where there is a lien over the shares. Other Articles may contain pre-emption on transfer provisions similar to those for an allotment requiring that shares are offered to members pro rata to their existing shareholdings which must be either observed or waived by all such members. The Articles may also contain share qualification requirements, or prohibit the transfer of shares where they are not fully paid or the transferee is someone not approved by the directors.

Failure by the directors to ensure these provisions are observed before a transfer is registered may result in an order by the court for the register of members to be rectified (*Re TA King (Services) Ltd; Cottrell v King* [2004] BCC 307).

Once any special provisions in the Articles have been checked and compliance has been secured, the process by which the directors proceed and register a transfer is essentially as follows:

Step	Explanation
(1) Convene a meeting of the Board of Directors.	To approve the transfer and issue of a share certificate to the transferee.
	If empowered by the Articles they may refuse to register a transfer, in which case the following steps are not relevant. Under CA 2006 s 771, if a transfer is refused the company must notify the transferee of the refusal together with the reasons for doing so as soon as practicable, but within two months. The company will also be obliged to provide the transferee with further information regarding the refusal should the transferee reasonably request, but this does not include the provision of any copy Board minutes.
(2) Update the company's statutory records.	Record details of the transfer in the Register of Transfers and the Register of Members. The record date for the transfer should be the date, after stamp duty has been assessed, that entry is actually made in these registers (*Michales v Harley House (Marylebone) Ltd* [1997] 2 BCLC 166).
(3) Cancel and reissue share certificates.	The transferor's share certificate must be cancelled and a new certificate be issued in the name of the transferee within two months of registering the transfer (CA 2006 s 769). Where the share certificate submitted is for a greater number of shares than on the transfer, a balance certificate in the name of the transferor must be issued within the same time limit.
	The directors must ensure that the certificates are either executed as deeds, signed under the common seal of the company, or executed under the securities seal, if that is the normal practice of the company, before they are sent to members.
(4) Retain the transfer and cancelled certificate.	Normal practice is to retain such documents for at least 12 years after the date of transfer.

This procedure should be observed for all transfers of shares unless the shares changing hands are bearer shares where ownership is based on possession and changes are made simply when a share warrant is passed from one person to another.

Directors should also note that the requirement for transfers to be approved by the Board of public companies is generally not sought, as in practice the volume of transfers for registration and the fact that the share register is maintained by an outside Registrar makes the prior approval of transfers impractical. It is common practice, however, for transfer reports to be produced at periodic Board meetings for review. The directors will need to notify the Registrar of any shares on which restrictions have been imposed preventing transfer.

Transmission of shares 8.12.3

Whilst the end result of a transmission of shares is the same as a transfer by causing title to the shares to pass to another person, it occurs automatically in circumstances where the member either:

- dies – usually evidenced by an office copy of the death certificate and grant of probate (or a letter of representation where the person died intestate). Generally where the shares are held jointly, ownership passes to the other surviving joint holders and where the deceased was the sole member, title to the shares will pass to those appointed to administer the deceased's estate (either as executors or administrators); or

- is declared bankrupt – the Articles may provide that, on submission of a Bankruptcy Order, a shareholder's trustee in bankruptcy has the right to be registered as the member and receive dividends and other sums due on the shares; or

- becomes of unsound mind – subject to an Order of the Court of Protection (the Mental Health Act 1983).

Table A regs 29–31 and the Model Articles 27–29 (private companies limited by shares) and articles 65–68 (public companies) refer to the change of ownership on transmission of shares, and the directors must consult the Articles to determine whether Table A or the Model Articles apply or whether the Articles contain different provisions. For example, in some instances pre-emption rights in the Articles require that where a member dies the person entitled to those shares cannot be admitted as a member until the deceased member's shares have been offered to existing members of the company.

The Stock Exchange and the CREST settlement system 8.12.4

Listed companies with securities quoted on the main Stock Exchange market or on AIM are not subject to the procedures or restrictions mentioned above. Shares must be freely transferable on the market and, in many cases, the company's Register of Members will be maintained by a share registration agent and the directors will only be aware of share transactions after the event, in reports by the Registrar normally provided to coincide with Board meetings.

Since January 2000 it has been a condition for listing (Listing Rules, para 3.27) and there has been a continuing obligation (Listing Rules, para 9.39) that, subject to a limited number of exceptions, listed securities of a UK company must be eligible for electronic settlement through CREST. CREST is an electronic book entry and settlement system for corporate securities which does not require share certificates and stock transfer forms. However, before securities can be held in electronic form, the Uncertificated Securities Regulations 2001 (SI 2001/3755) require that either:

- the Articles of Association be amended by special resolution, approved by the members, to allow the company to dispense with issue of share certificates and permit transfer of shares electronically; or

- approval be obtained by Board resolution disapplying those Articles inconsistent with CREST. The resolution can only apply to one class of shares and the proposal must be notified to all shareholders in advance or, if not, within 60 days of passing the resolution.

Before joining CREST, the directors must ensure that approval has been obtained. In practice the majority of companies have obtained approval by Board resolution, which is evidently easier and less costly. Notification made to members can be timed for inclusion when mailing the annual accounts or interim statements and therefore not incur additional costs.

Companies using CREST now benefit from faster registration of transactions, immediate payment against settlement and a reduction in the generation and movement of paper between sellers, buyers, brokers, the Stock Exchange and registrars.

Meetings of members   8.20

The directors have a duty to ensure that no decisions are made or action taken on matters which are outside their authority and they should be aware of the risk of being held personally accountable for actions taken for which such authority has not been obtained.

With this in mind, they must be aware of circumstances which require approval of members and know whether it is appropriate and timely for them to be included in the business of a forthcoming AGM, or whether it is necessary to call a general meeting, class meeting or propose resolutions for approval by the members in writing. They have a duty to ensure that requirements contained in the Articles and CA 2006 relating to procedures by which meetings are convened, periods of notice given, number of members constituting a quorum, conduct of general meetings, voting and the approval of resolutions are observed without exception.

The circumstances above describe directors convening general meetings as and when they are necessary but, at the same time, they should also be aware of their duty to convene general meetings when requisitioned to do so by the members and the need to ensure that the appropriate resolutions are proposed to approve the matters under consideration.

In general terms, the duties of a director in relation to meetings can be divided into two:

- those required before the meeting, such as ensuring that the appropriate type of meeting is convened with sufficient notice and the correct type of resolutions are set out in the notice; and

- those required at the meeting, relating to quorum requirements, voting and recording approval of resolutions.

Both before and during the meeting, directors have an overriding duty to ensure that procedures prescribed in legislation and in the company's Articles are strictly observed and do not jeopardise the validity of decisions reached.

It should also be mentioned that, whilst the following paragraphs concentrate largely on the legal requirements for convening and holding general meetings, directors have responsibility for arranging the practical aspects of holding a general meeting, such as pre-booking the venue and ensuring that it is of sufficient size to accommodate members expected to attend, observing the need for security measures, preparing attendance sheets, voting cards, appointing scrutineers and a range of other matters. In practice these arrangements will more often than not be delegated to the company secretary but should nevertheless be closely supervised by the Board, with whom ultimate responsibility remains.

Duties prior to the meeting   8.21

Determine type of general meeting   8.21.1

Whilst general meetings are meetings of the members of the company, it is extremely unlikely that the members will be aware of requirements contained in CA 2006 or the company's Articles governing the manner in which such meetings are convened and held. The directors play an extremely important role in ensuring that general meetings are conducted in accordance with such requirements.

Annual general meeting   **8.21.1.1**

Under CA 2006 only public companies are obliged to hold an AGM each calendar year. The public company's AGM must be held within six months of its accounting year end.

Private companies are no longer required to hold an AGM, providing that the company's Articles do not state anything to the contrary. Wording in a private company's Articles stating that an AGM must be held within 15 months of the previous AGM would not be sufficient to require the company to hold an AGM in each year. A company's members can require a private company to hold a general meeting (CA 2006 s 303).

It should be noted that despite the fact that private companies are no longer required to hold AGMs under CA 2006, they must still provide all members, the holders of any debentures and every person entitled to receive notice of general meetings, with copies of the annual accounts and reports (CA 2006 s 423(1)). The time allowed for sending out copies of the annual accounts and reports is detailed under CA 2006 s 424(2). This section states that a private company must send, to the relevant parties, a copy of the annual accounts and reports not later than the date by which the accounts and reports must be received by the Registrar of Companies or the date on which the accounts and reports are actually delivered to the Registrar of Companies if earlier.

Although the shareholders, through general knowledge, may be aware that a public company must hold an AGM each year, they are unlikely to be aware of the timing for this meeting and the latest date that it can be held. The duty to convene and hold the meeting to comply with s 336 rests with the directors, who will be liable to a fine for failure to ensure compliance (CA 2006 s 336(3) and (4)).

Whilst CA 2006 requires a public company to hold one AGM each year, it does not specify the business to be conducted at the meeting and the directors will need to consult the Articles to determine whether there are any special requirements in this respect. Indeed, for companies which have adopted Table A reg 73, this requires directors to be reappointed at the AGM.

Nonetheless, there are standard items of business all or some of which would normally be considered at the AGM as follows:

- accounts are laid before the members;

- if required, approval of the directors' remuneration report;

- a final dividend declared by the directors may be proposed to the members for approval;

- reappointment of directors (if required by the Articles, usual business for a public company and annual re-election of whole Board required for FTSE 350 companies);

- auditors' reappointment and remuneration;

- resolution permitting general meetings, other than the AGM, to be held on just 14 days' notice (listed companies only);

- renewal of directors' authority to allot shares (normally included by public companies);

- waiver of pre-emption rights on allotments of shares (normally included by public companies);

- seek advisory approval of the directors' remuneration report (listed companies);

- seek a binding vote on the company's remuneration policy (listed companies at least once every three years, or where a policy change is proposed).

The accounts would normally be prepared to allow them to be laid before the members at the AGM but, in the event that it is not possible to finalise the accounts in time for consideration at the meeting, the directors should be aware that the AGM is still required to be held. In these circumstances it is likely that the AGM would be convened and, if there are no other items of business to be considered at the meeting, a resolution to reconvene the meeting when the accounts are available may be proposed. At the same time, the directors should also note that reappointment of auditors can only be considered at the general meeting at which the accounts are laid before the members.

Depending on the size of the company, the importance of the AGM as a means of communicating with shareholders will vary (see para **8.50**). For example, a small unlisted public company where the majority of shareholders are directors would have held an AGM to deal only with routine items of business (and are likely to have now dispensed with the need), whereas a large quoted company is more likely to use the opportunity as a forum to communicate with shareholders with whom they have little contact from one AGM to the next. In the latter case, where the large number of members makes convening a general meeting a costly and time-consuming exercise (although this will be helped by electronic communication), the directors should ensure that any matters that need members' approval are included in the notice and proposed at the meeting to negate the need to hold a separate general meeting later in the year. The ICSA provides further guidance, 'A Guide to Best Practice for Annual General Meetings'.

One of the key corporate governance recommendations is that companies make better use of AGMs to communicate with members and encourage their involvement with the company. It is difficult to say that this is being widely achieved when, according to a survey conducted by the ICSA, most companies could start and finish an AGM inside half an hour. The ICSA's best practice guide recommends that at least one executive gives an oral account to shareholders on operations and that a separate report on corporate social responsibility be put forward.

General meetings   **8.21.1.2**

Directors must be aware that a company can hold only one AGM each year, and all other meetings of the members, whether convened by the directors or requisitioned by the members, held in a year are general meetings. Matters that need consideration and approval of the members would normally, if timing permits, be included in the business of the AGM, but where this is not possible a general meeting would need to be convened to deal with matters as they arise during the year.

The period of notice required for a general meeting is discussed in para **8.23.2.1**, and the business to be conducted will be set out in the notice.

Class meetings   **8.21.1.3**

Where different classes of shares have been issued, in addition to the need to hold a general meeting, a separate meeting of the members of a particular class is required where the action proposed to be taken by the company would vary the rights of the holders of that class of shares (CA 2006 s 334). Generally, matters which are considered to affect class rights include proposals to reorganise the capital, change entitlement to dividends or distribution of capital on a winding up, and any alteration of voting rights or proposals to wind up the company.

Directors should also be aware that the Articles, shareholders' agreements or other relevant shareholders' documents, if any, may contain specific provisions in relation to the need for class meetings and they must ensure that they consult these documents to determine whether a class meeting is necessary.

Where, for example, the rights attaching to shares are changed by putting through amendments to a company's Articles of Association to remove the right of pre-emption on transfer that is approved only in general meeting without holding a class meeting, the variation may be considered void and in breach of the requirements of s 334 (*Re Smiths of Smithfield Ltd: Willow International Investments Ltd v Smiths of Smithfield Ltd* [2003] EWHC 568 (Ch)).

Resolutions in writing   **8.21.1.4**

There are circumstances where it is simply not possible or convenient for the directors of a private limited company to assemble the members of the company for a meeting. On these occasions the members of a private limited company, or holders of the class of shares concerned, are expressly authorised to approve resolutions proposed to them in writing without prior notice (CA 2006 s 288). Such resolutions are as valid as if they had been proposed at a general meeting, or class meeting, provided they are signed by all members who were, at the date of the resolution, entitled to attend and vote had a meeting been held.

The statutory authority cannot under any circumstances be applied to public companies, although their Articles may, and in many cases do, contain authority and a procedure for approval of directors resolutions in writing.

Directors of private companies should be aware that, whilst generally approval of all ordinary and special resolutions may be obtained by resolution in writing, they will need to convene a meeting where the proposal is either to remove a director (CA 2006 s 168) or remove an auditor (CA 2006 s 510) as these resolutions must be considered at a meeting to allow the parties concerned to make representations.

Once they have determined the suitability of the resolution for approval by resolution in writing, the directors of a private company may either follow the procedure as determined in the Articles, or the statutory procedure, and will need to:

(1)   prepare the written resolution for circulation to members. An example is given in **APPENDIX 20**. This may be one document which all members sign or several documents in like form which are individually signed and accurately set out the resolution (CA 2006 s 291(3)(b));

(2)   ensure that any documents required to accompany the resolution are circulated to members at the same time as the resolution in writing. For example, a directors' statement, audit report and draft purchase contract must be circulated where the resolution proposes purchase of own shares out of capital (CA 2006 s 718) and a written memorandum setting out the terms of a director's service contract where appointment is for a term exceeding two years (CA 2006 s 188). These requirements are summarised in **APPENDIX 18**;

(3)   ensure that the written resolution is signed by the required majority of members, being a simple majority for an ordinary resolution and 75% majority in favour by number of shares held for a special resolution. The resolution must be signed by the required majority of members within 28 days of the circulation date, failing which it will lapse (CA 2006 s 297);

(4)   when the written resolution has been signed by the required majority of members it must be entered in the minute book, in the same manner as if the resolution were minutes of a meeting, and the date of approval recorded be the date that the last member signed the resolution.

Directors of private companies are likely to consider use of the written resolution procedure where there are a limited number of members, where time to approve the resolutions proposed is restricted and where they are confident that sufficient of the members will agree the proposals.

Convening general meetings 8.22

The Articles of a company normally provide directors with the power to convene general meetings and, indeed, CA 2006 s 302 makes them responsible for holding AGMs within the required time period each year. The Board of Directors would normally hold a meeting to discuss the matter and, if a general meeting is considered necessary, authorise the secretary to issue notice of the meeting to members.

The directors should also be aware that the members of the company have the ability to convene a general meeting at any time by requisition in writing deposited at the registered office, to consider matters they have detailed in the requisition (CA 2006 s 303). Any provisions in a company's Articles which are contrary to this right will be overruled. A requisition received at the company's registered office by fax is a valid requisition (*PNC Telecom plc v Thomas* [2003] BCC 202).

On receipt of the requisition the directors must check that it has been made by members who, at the date when they deposit the requisition, either:

• hold not less than 5% of the paid-up share capital which carries the right to vote (this threshold is lowered to one-twentieth for a private company where there has been no exercise of the power in the last 12 months); or

• where the company does not have a share capital, represent not less than 5% of the total voting rights of all members.

The above percentage of 5% was decreased from 10% by the Companies (Shareholders Rights) Regulations 2009 (SI 2009/1632).

When the directors have determined that the requisition is valid and has been signed by all members party to it, they must proceed to issue notice of the general meeting. Notice must be issued within 21 days of receiving the requisition for a general meeting to be convened within 28 days of the day on which the notice is issued (CA 2006 s 304(1)(a) and (b)). Directors will need to check the Articles, as they may extend protection afforded to members beyond CA 2006 and reduce the period in which they must convene the general meeting.

Similarly, a member or members of the company who either hold not less than one-twentieth of the total voting rights, or who are not fewer than 100 in number and have each paid up on average £100 on their shares, may requisition the directors to circulate a resolution or statement (providing the statement is not inconsistent with the requirements of CA 2006, defamatory, frivolous or vexatious (CA 2006 s 292(2)) of not more than 1,000 words in length on the subject matter of the resolution to all persons entitled to receive notice and, in the case of a written resolution, every eligible member (CA 2006 ss 293 and 314). The cost of circulation must be paid by the requisitionists, unless the company resolves otherwise (CA 2006 s 316).

The meeting will be held at the appointed time, in accordance with provisions relating to general meetings discussed below, to consider the items contained in the requisition.

Notice of meetings 8.23

The directors have a duty to ensure that all members entitled to attend and vote at a general meeting or a class meeting are sent notice of the meeting, either by post or electronically by email or displayed on a website (having notified members, see para **8.50**). They should note that whilst the Articles may provide that accidental omission to give notice to a person would not invalidate proceedings of the meeting, such error would not instil confidence amongst the members that they have an efficient Board.

The directors must ensure that the notice given to members is in writing and contains the following information which, where not specifically mentioned in CA 2006, would normally be required by the company's Articles:

- the time, date and place at which the meeting is to be held (Table A reg 38/CA 2006 s 311);

- the general nature of the business to be conducted (Table A reg 38/ CA 2006 s 311). In practice, a notice will specify each resolution to be proposed for approval to enable members to decide whether to attend the meeting or how to instruct their proxy to vote;

- where the meeting is an AGM of a public company, this must be specified (CA 2006 s 377(1));

- authority under which the notice is issued, ie by the secretary by order of the Board;

- details of a member's right to appoint multiple proxies and where and by what date the proxy appointment must be notified (CA 2006 s 324(2)). CA 2006 s 324 permits a member of a company to appoint another person (or persons) as his proxy to attend, vote and speak at the general meeting. Whilst there is no requirement in CA 2006 for private and unlisted public companies to send proxy forms to members with the notice of meeting, it is usually required by a company's Articles;

- further notes may be required in the case of a public limited company, such as payment details where a final dividend is to be declared, or confirmation of the determination date may be given where shares are traded on CREST dematerialised settlement system. In the latter case the date given (which must not be more than 48 hours prior to the meeting) is in effect the cut-off date where members on the register at that time will be entitled to attend and vote at the meeting (required by reg 41 of the Uncertificated Securities Regulations 2001 (SI 2001/3755));

- a note of documents available for inspection at the meeting may also be required to be given, such as copies of directors' service contracts for a term of more than one year, or Memorandum and Articles;

- where notice is issued by a listed company and includes business other than ordinary business at an AGM (see para **8.21.1.1**) the Listing Rules require that the notice is accompanied by an explanatory circular.

Directors should be aware when preparing and issuing notices that, rather than stating at length the precise and often complicated wording of resolutions to be proposed, there is now an underlying trend for information in notices to be concise, easy to understand and intelligible. Similarly, many companies now provide detailed notes to the notice explaining why and for what purpose particular resolutions are being proposed. In some instances, for example for waiver of statutory pre-emption rights on an allotment of shares, an explanation from the directors is specifically required and frequently included in the notes.

In addition, CA 2006 s 311(3) requires that notice of a general meeting issued by a traded company also includes the following information:

- details of the website where required information about the meeting is disclosed (see para **8.24**);

- a statement clarifying that the right to vote is determined by reference to the register of members no more than 48 hours prior to the meeting (excluding non-working days from the calculation);

- details of the procedures members must adhere to in order to attend and vote at the meeting;

- a statement with details of how to appoint a proxy and the form to be used;

- if the facility is offered, details of how to vote electronically in advance of the meeting; and

- notification of the right that members have to ask questions relating to the business of the meeting.

These additional requirements only apply to quoted companies.

Entitlement to receive notice   **8.23.1**

As well as complying with requirements in the Articles stating who is entitled to receive notice of meetings, the directors must be aware of any statutory entitlement that other persons may have and ensure that notice is sent to them. The directors should consider the following issues before sending out notices of meetings:

- auditors have a statutory right to receive notice of and attend general meetings (CA 2006 s 502);

- members resident outside the UK, who have not notified an address within the UK at which to serve notice, may be excluded by the Articles from the right to receive notice;

- a director who is not a member is entitled to attend a general meeting or class meeting and must receive notice (CA 2006 s 310);

- a deceased member's representative or trustee in bankruptcy is entitled to receive notice (CA 2006 s 310);

- where a class of shareholders have restricted voting rights, the Articles will normally provide that they are not entitled to receive notice of general meetings, although the directors must remain aware of their right to attend a class meeting.

Once the directors have determined precisely who is entitled to receive notice, they must ensure that it is sent out or delivered to all such persons, together with any documents to be considered at that meeting which might, for example, include the annual report and accounts, or new Articles proposed for adoption, etc.

In addition, to allow members who are not able to attend to register their votes, a proxy form will need to be sent at the same time as notice of the meeting (see paras **8.23** and **8.26.3**). Whilst sending the proxy forms with the notice is not obligatory for private companies and unlisted public companies, it is good practice to do so. Where they are sent, they must be sent to all members.

Period of notice **8.23.2**

General requirements **8.23.2.1**

There are specified lengths required for the period between the day when members are notified of the scheduled meeting and the actual day the meeting is held. These are as follows:

Type of meeting	Length of notice
AGM (public company)	21 days (CA 2006 s 307(2)(a))
General meeting (public company)	14 days (CA 2006 s 307(2)(b))
General meeting (traded company)	21 days (CA 2006 s 307A), but can be reduced to 14 days where approved at the prior AGM and the facility to vote by electronic means is provided
General meeting (private company)	14 days (CA 2006 s 307(1))
Class meeting	14 days (CA 2006 ss 334, 335 and 307)

Listed companies are required to comply with the UK Corporate Governance Code requirement that notice be sent to shareholders not less than 20 working days before the AGM (provision D.2.4).

The required period of notice can be increased, but not reduced, by provisions in the company's Articles, with which the directors will need to consult and comply. They must ensure that notice is sent to those entitled to receive a copy at least the required minimum number of days before the meeting.

In addition, the Articles will normally define the number of days required for notice as clear days. The directors must be aware of any such provision, as in practical terms it will affect how they calculate the latest day on which notice must be sent out. The meaning of 'clear days' will be defined in the Articles. For example, Table A and CA 2006 s 360 excludes the day on which the notice is given (or deemed to be given) and the day of the actual meeting from the statutory period of notice, which means that this must be added on to the calculation of days' notice required specified in the table above. Consequently, where clear days notice is required, the notice must be sent out earlier to take account of the day of the meeting and date of posting.

Where the notice is posted to members, the Articles will usually contain a provision stating how long after being put in the post the notice is deemed to have been given, usually 24 or 48 hours after postage. Regulation 115 in Table A or s 1147 of CA 2006 states this period as 48 hours after the notice is posted. However, directors must give attention to practical matters, such as ensuring that first-class post is used for sending the notice (unless more than the minimum time has been allowed for notice). In addition, directors should be aware that recorded delivery is not recommended for sending notices as, on occasions where the package cannot be signed for, and is returned to the company unopened, notice cannot be deemed to have been served (*Re Thundercrest Ltd* [1994] BCC 857).

By way of example, a company incorporated prior to 1 October 2009 which has adopted Table A or a company employing the provisions of CA 2006 s 1147 would calculate the earliest date for a public company's AGM as follows:

Date of notice	–	1 May
Deemed date of service	–	3 May
21 days to run from	–	4 May
Expiry of 21 days	–	24 May
Earliest date of AGM	–	25 May

Consent to short notice   **8.23.2.2**

There are circumstances where the need for urgent business decisions makes it necessary for the directors to convene and hold general or class meetings without delay and with less than the recommended period of notice (CA 2006 s 307). In such circumstances it is possible for the directors to arrange for members to waive the required notice period, provided agreement is obtained from the percentage of members set out in the table below:

Type of meeting	Number of members required to agree to short notice
AGM (public company)	All members entitled to attend and vote (CA 2006 s 337(2))
General meetings (public company)	Members holding not less than 95% of shares having the right to vote (CA 2006 s 307(6)(b))

Type of meeting	Number of members required to agree to short notice
General meeting (private company)	Members holding not less than 90% of shares having the right to vote (CA 2006 s 307(6)(a))*
Class meeting	Members holding not less than 95% of the relevant class of shares having the right to vote

*Note: Or such other higher amount (not exceeding 95%) as specified by the company's Articles.

In practical terms, the directors can only take advantage of these provisions where the company has a relatively small number of members as, although the CA 2006 does not specify it as a requirement, it is important and recommended that for evidential purposes that agreement to a meeting being held on short notice is obtained in writing. The directors must check the signed agreements to ensure that the necessary percentage approval has been obtained before they proceed and hold the general or class meeting. Failure to do this may invalidate the proceedings conducted at the meeting.

Special notice **8.23.2.3**

Certain resolutions can only be considered at a general meeting where the company has received special notice to move the resolution (**APPENDIX 19**). Special notice can be given by one or more members and must be received by the company at least 28 days before the general meeting at which it is intended to be considered (CA 2006 s 312). Ordinary resolutions requiring special notice include:

- removal of a director (CA 2006 s 168(2));
- removal of an auditor or appointment of an auditor other than a retiring auditor (CA 2006 s 511(1) and s 515).

Directors must ensure that special notice has been given for the above resolutions and may include the resolution in the notice of the meeting, although they are not required to include the resolution unless it is accompanied by a requisition to that effect (CA 2006 ss 315 and 339, para **8.22**). Assuming they agree or have received a requisition, they must give notice of the resolution to members at the same time as notice of the meeting and not less than 28 days before the meeting. The director or auditor concerned must be sent a copy of the special notice and be allowed to make written representations on the matter for circulation to members (CA 2006 s 169 and s 511(3)).

Publication of information on website 8.24

A traded company is also required by CA 2006 s 311A to make sure the following information is made available on a website when a general meeting is being convened, namely:

(1)   details of the matters set out in the meeting notice;

(2)   the total number of issued shares over which shareholders can exercise voting rights (and, where applicable, by class);

(3)   the voting rights that can be exercised at the meeting (in total and, where applicable, by class); and

(4)   any statements, resolutions and matters of business received by the company from members once the notice is given.

Items (1)–(3) must be made available before or at the same time that notice of the meeting is given to members, and any information received relating to item (4) must be disclosed as soon as reasonably practicable. Provided the website clearly identifies the company it can be a hosted site, the information must continue to appear on the website for two years from when the meeting notice was given (or from when available on the website if earlier) and it must be possible to obtain hard copies of the information without payment of a fee.

Resolutions proposed 8.25

There are a number of different types of resolution which may be proposed to members for approval at general meetings, and the resolution required is generally determined by the nature of the business to be considered at the meeting. Resolutions differ in terms of the number of members who must give approval before the resolution can be considered passed.

Generally decisions which have a significant effect on members and the company as a whole require a greater number of votes in favour for their approval. This is logical, as decisions on more complex matters, where the implications might be far-reaching, need to be made by a significant majority.

The types of resolutions that are approved by members in general meeting are set out in the table below, with examples of circumstances where they should be proposed:

Type of resolution	Period of notice required	No of votes at meeting required to be cast in favour	Decisions requiring the resolution
Ordinary resolutions (CA 2006 s 282)	Determined by the type of meeting	Simple majority of total voting rights of eligible members present	• Routine business, where CA 2006 or Articles state that approval is required by 'members in general meeting', such as granting directors authority to allot shares (CA 2006 s 551), payment of a final dividend or capitalisation of reserves. • Certain ordinary resolutions such as alterations to the share capital and renewal of directors' authority to allot shares must be submitted to the Registrar of Companies within 15 days of being passed (CA 2006 s 30).
Special resolutions (CA 2006 s 283)	21 clear days' notice if being passed at an AGM or general meeting of a public company, otherwise 14 days	75% of total voting rights of eligible members present	• As required by the Act or Articles, which will state where a special resolution is required, such as to alter provisions in the Articles, change the company's name, re-register the company, waive members' pre-emption rights, make a reduction of capital, approval for a private company to purchase its own shares or ratify an act of the directors. • The notice must state resolution as a special resolution.

	• Must file a signed copy with Registrar of Companies within 15 days of being passed (CA 2006 s 30).

Notes:

(1)   'Members present' in this context means members present in person or by proxy who are entitled to attend and vote at the meeting.

(2)   Agreement to short notice for consideration of the resolutions may be obtained in a similar fashion as obtained for meetings being held at short notice (see para **8.23.2.2**).

Directors must ensure that they consult the Articles of the company and the requirements of CA 2006 to ensure that the appropriate resolution is included in the notice of the meeting. This is essential to ensure that the resolution is not invalidated by failure to give sufficient notice or by failure to obtain the required number of votes for approval of that type of resolution.

Directors should also note that where the resolution or resolutions concerned are passed as written resolutions, without need for a general meeting, requirements for filing a signed copy must be observed following the format set out in **APPENDIX 20**.

It should also be mentioned that the concept of 'extraordinary' resolutions was repealed by CA 2006. In most instances special resolutions should be substituted.

Duties at the meeting   8.26

The directors' role as advisers to the members continues while general meetings are being conducted. This is principally the role of the chairman and company secretary assisted by the remaining directors.

Together they need to ensure that business considered at the meeting is conducted in a manner that complies with requirements in the company's Articles and any relevant statutory provisions to ensure that the validity of the meeting and resolutions passed cannot be questioned. To achieve this in practical terms, the directors will need to check provisions relating to appointment of a chairman, quorum, voting rights and restrictions, method of voting and proxy appointments and ensure strict compliance by the meeting.

As well as acting as advisers, the directors have a duty similar to that of scrutineers, as they must monitor the business conducted, check that persons attending the meeting and voting are entitled to do so and ensure that the manner in which voting is conducted is appropriate. Whilst members will be aware of business to be considered at the meeting, by reference to the notice, they are not likely to be aware of technical and legal requirements dictating how the meeting should be conducted and will be reliant on the directors to provide advice and guidance.

With this in mind, in many instances, a chairman's script is prepared in advance of the meeting to help the chairman through the formal business of the meeting in the correct manner, but still allowing opportunity for questions and discussion which is important in terms of encouraging engagement by shareholders. Indeed CA 2006 s 319A gives members of a traded company the right to ask questions relating to the business of the meeting and they must be permitted to exercise this right.

Quorum 8.26.1

It is usual for the Articles of a company to provide that the chairman of the Board of Directors or, in his absence, another director, shall preside as chairman at general meetings. In addition, Table A regulation 43, article 39 (Model Articles for private company limited by shares), article 25 (Model Articles for private company limited by guarantee) and article 31 (Model Articles for public company) of the Model Articles state that where there are no directors present, the members may appoint a chairman for the meeting.

The directors have a duty to check and advise whether there are sufficient members present at the meeting to constitute a quorum. The quorum for general meetings is usually stipulated in a company's Articles (Table A reg 40) and, where no such provision has been made in the Articles, CA 2006 requires two members to be present personally to constitute a quorum, unless the company is a single-member company, in which case the sole member shall be a quorum (CA 2006 s 318). The Articles may contain special members' provisions to protect members' interests which must be checked before proceeding with the business of the meeting; eg joint venture companies may issue different classes of shares to major investors and the Articles may require at least one member from each class of shares to be present to constitute a quorum.

To check that the meeting is quorate, rather than counting heads the directors must be certain that the persons present are entitled to vote at and be included in the quorum of the meeting. This would normally be carried out by checking the attendance sheet completed as persons enter the meeting against entries in the Register of Members.

Where there is not a quorum, the directors must advise that the meeting cannot proceed and the Articles would normally provide the manner in which it should be adjourned. Table A reg 41, adopted by many companies prior to 1 October 2009, provides that where a quorum is not present within half an hour of the time appointed for the meeting, or if members leave during the meeting and it becomes inquorate, the meeting shall be adjourned to the same day the next week and at the same time and place or such other time and place as the directors determine. The provisions under the Model Articles are slightly different in that there is no specification to adjourn to the same day and time the following week.

Conduct of voting   8.26.2

Prior to a general meeting being held, the directors must ensure that they are aware of all provisions in the company's Articles and requirements of company law relating to voting rights and the manner in which resolutions are put to the vote. For example, where a special resolution for purchase of a company's own shares is under consideration, the member holding those shares should be excluded from voting as the resolution is not effective where the resolution would not have been passed if such person had not voted (CA 2006 s 698(3)).

Voting rights will be specified in the company's Articles and, where there is only one class of shares, will normally be pro rata to the number of shares held and, where it is a guarantee company, each guarantor would usually have one vote. Where there are two or more classes of share, the directors must check their entitlement to vote precisely, as different voting rights may need to be applied. They will also need to check whether any of the members present and intending to vote have any restrictions on their shares, eg where an amount has been called on partly paid shares but payment has not been met, then the shareholder's right to vote may be restricted as contained in Table A reg 57 and article 41 in the Model Articles for public companies.

At the meeting voting may be conducted by:

- *Show of hands.* This is the most straightforward means of voting and it is usual at general meetings, unless the Articles specify otherwise, for resolutions to be proposed for approval initially on a show of hands (Table A reg 46; article 42 (private companies limited by shares), article 28 (private companies limited by guarantee) and article 34 (public companies) of the Model Articles). Each member present and entitled to vote has one vote and shows whether they are voting for or against the resolution by raising their arm. When a show of hands has been requested, the directors must check the eligibility of those voting. Every proxy present who has been duly appointed by a member entitled to vote now also has one vote on a show of hands.

- *Poll vote.* On occasions where a decision cannot be reached on a show of hands (which may be the case where the matter is contentious or the overall opinion of the meeting is not clear or the required majority for approval cannot be obtained) then either the chairman or any member, or a number of members, may demand a poll. The directors must check specific requirements in the Articles to ensure that the manner in which the poll is requested is consistent with any provisions relating to a demand for a poll. Alternatively the vote could be carried out by poll without need for a show of hands, provided it is validly demanded.

For example, Table A reg 46 and article 44 (private companies limited by shares), article 30 (private companies limited by guarantee) and article 36 (public companies) of the Model Articles specify that a poll may be demanded by any of the following:

(1)   the chairman;

(2)   any two members with the right to vote at the meeting;

(3)   any member or members holding not less than one-tenth of the total voting rights of the company;

(4)   any member or members who hold shares conferring the right to vote and who have paid up an aggregate sum equal to at least one-tenth of the total sum paid up on shares conferring the right to vote (Table A reg 46/ CA 2006 s 321).

Proxies are entitled to demand or join in a demand for a poll.

Directors should be aware that best practice requires the chairman to exercise his right to call a poll where it is likely that the vote on a show of hands would have a different result to a poll vote which takes account of shareholders voting by proxy. The chairman is obviously in the privileged position of knowing proxy voting numbers in advance of the meeting and will know from the show of hands whether a poll vote is necessary.

The directors will need to assist the chairman during the meeting by checking that the poll has been validly requested and, once this has been determined, the poll vote may proceed. This would normally be done using voting cards which scrutineers (often the auditors) appointed by the directors, will check against the Register of Members to confirm that the number of votes each member has cast is correct. It should be noted that where a poll is validly requested by members, the chairman must comply with the request, unless he can persuade those shareholders to withdraw their request where he can establish that the voting position will not change on a poll.

Directors of listed companies should be aware that even where the vote is conducted on a show of hands, the chairman needs to announce on a website maintained by or on behalf of the company what proxy votes have been received for each resolution (UK Corporate Governance Code requirement). Even where proxy votes are announced in the meeting, best practice recommendations are such that companies also provide a written summary of proxy votes for shareholders to collect at the end of the meeting. This helps to show that the vote on a show of hands was consistent with the weight of shareholders' opinion, had a poll been conducted. Furthermore, PIRC (Pensions and Investments Research Consultants Ltd concerned with good governance) recommends that voting always be conducted by poll vote to take account of proxies received and that the results of the poll be notified to members. PIRC's recommendations are evidently being followed as a survey of proxy voting levels amongst the UK's top 350 listed companies found that 50% conducted a poll vote to take account of proxies received.

Where a quoted company conducts the vote at a general meeting by poll, the following information needs to be disclosed on a website maintained by or on behalf of the company:

- when the meeting was held;

- wording of the resolutions proposed; and

- the number of votes for and votes against each of the resolutions.

This is required by CA 2006 s 341(1) and, in addition, a traded company is required by CA 2006 s 341(1A) to also disclose the number of votes validly cast, what percentage of the company's issued share capital this represents and the number of abstentions. This information must be displayed within 16 days of the meeting or, if later, within a day of the result of the poll being declared.

Directors should be aware that concern has been expressed on occasion by shareholders of listed companies that votes submitted by proxy have gone missing and have not been counted. Where this is the case, shareholders can always request independent scrutiny of the voting process. This said, the more likely explanation is a disconnect between beneficial owners, asset managers and custodians, the result of which is that proxies simply fail to be submitted or are voted by someone else in a pooled account.

Proxies and corporate representatives   **8.26.3**

As stated in paras **8.23** and **8.23.1**, CA 2006 s 324 permits a member of a company to appoint one or more person as proxy. Prior to the meeting any proxy forms received need to be checked to ensure that the proxy appointments are valid and the forms have been received within the required time. CA 2006 s 327 requires proxy forms to be lodged with the company more than 48 hours prior to the meeting to which they relate, excluding from that calculation any days that are not working days. A company's Articles can reduce this period and could, for example, permit forms to be lodged right up to commencement of the meeting to which they relate. The Articles cannot, however, increase the 48-hour period stated in CA 2006. Usually, once the proxy submission deadline date has passed, the company or its registrars will prepare a list of final proxy voting figures for the company on each resolution so the directors have an indication of how proxy votes have been cast which it is important to know before the meeting commences.

Subject to the CA 2006 and notwithstanding what it states in the company's Articles, proxies can attend, speak, join in the demand for a poll and vote on a show of hands and poll at a general meeting. Subject to there not being anything contrary in the Articles, where multiple proxies have been appointed by a member, it is legitimate for each proxy to vote on a show of hands. Separate proxy forms should be completed for each proxy appointment indicating how many shares the proxy is entitled to vote on behalf of the shareholder.

The proxy appointment form will usually give members the option to appoint a person or persons of their own choosing as their proxy or, failing that, the chairman of the meeting. The directors should note that on a poll the proxy (whether it is the chairman or another appointee) has to actually vote by completing a poll card in respect of the shares over which he or she has been appointed proxy. Where an appointed proxy fails to attend the meeting, the shareholder's votes cannot be voted which is the reason many shareholders choose to appoint the chairman of the meeting.

CA 2006 allows proxies to be appointed by an electronic communication sent to an address notified by the company to shareholders for that purpose. The Listing Rules also allow listed companies to accept proxies notified in this way and they may also be notified through the CREST settlement system. Corporate and institutional investors are also entitled to appoint one or more corporate representatives to attend general meetings and vote on their behalf (CA 2006 s 323). The corporate representative is entitled to exercise all the same powers as an individual member at the general meeting and, where multiple corporate representatives have been appointed, any one of them is entitled to exercise the member's powers.

The position regarding corporate members' ability to appoint multiple corporate representatives was clarified under the Companies (Shareholders' Rights) Regulations 2009 (SI 2009/1632). Under regulation 6 of these regulations it clarified that corporate members may appoint multiple corporate representatives, providing they are appointed in respect of different shares.

Documents for inspection   8.26.4

Directors' service contracts for a listed company, or a summary of their terms, must be available for inspection for at least 15 minutes before the AGM and for its duration. Directors must therefore ensure that these documents are available as required.

Minutes and resolutions   8.26.5

The directors must ensure that minutes recording business conducted at a meeting are prepared and signed and together with any written resolutions passed are placed in the company's minute book (CA 2006 ss 248 and 355). These signed minutes and resolutions are evidence of the proceedings and must be retained for at least ten years from the date of the meeting, or in the case of a written resolution, from the date of the resolution. In addition, where certain types of ordinary resolutions and all special and extraordinary resolutions are approved, signed copies will need to be submitted to Companies House for which the directors will be responsible (para **8.25**).

Minority interest   8.30

General meetings are an important part of the company process whereby shareholders, who have the right to vote, are involved in making decisions. Directors must be aware that, whilst the general principle is that decisions are made by approval of the majority of members, directors who are the majority shareholders of a company have a duty not to abuse their position.

Directors must ensure that they strike a balance in the recommendations they make to members and the need to protect minority members' interests. For example, the recommendation to pay large and unjustified directors' bonuses may be considered unjust and detrimental to minority members who are not also directors.

In the event that a member or number of members consider the company's affairs to have been conducted in an unfairly prejudicial manner, they have a number of remedies available, all of which will involve scrutinising the directors' actions and the method by which decisions have been reached. Recourse available to members which the directors should be aware of includes:

- applying to court for permission to bring a derivative claim against the directors for breach of duty (CA 2006 ss 260–269). In order to gain permission from the court to bring a derivative claim against the directors of a company, the shareholders must prove that those directors who are in breach of duty control the majority of the shares held within the company (see para **8.40**);

- any member may petition the court for a just and equitable winding up in situations where the management of a company has broken down or opposing parties have reached an irresolvable deadlock (IA 1986 s 122(1)(g));

- a member may apply to the court for an order to relieve matters or reverse a decision which is found to be unfairly prejudicial to members generally or some part of them (CA 2006 ss 994–999).

Of these remedies, winding up the company is obviously a last resort. Statutory protection provided by CA 2006 ss 260–269 or 994–999 against unfair prejudice are the remedies which will be chosen in the first instance. However, protection provided by CA 2006 ss 260–269 has important ramifications for directors and have caused considerable concern, as former directors and shadow directors may have actions brought against them. Under CA 2006 s 994–999 the court has wide discretionary powers and may choose to:

- regulate the future conduct of the company's affairs;

- instruct that the act or omission considered prejudicial be stopped or carried out, as appropriate;

- authorise persons to take civil proceedings for a wrongdoing in the name of the company;

- require the company not to make any, or any specified, changes in its Articles of Association without permission from the court (CA 2006 s 996(2)(d));

- order that a member's shares be repurchased by the company or other members (CA 2006 s 996(2)(e)).

In *Re Brenfield Squash Racquets Club Ltd* [1996] 2 BCLC 184 the majority shareholder caused the company to enter into arrangements, including giving a bank guarantee, which had no benefit to the company and was to the detriment of the minority shareholder. The court held that appropriate relief for the minority shareholder was the sale of shares by the majority shareholder to the minority shareholder in accordance with the pre-emption clause in their shareholders' agreement. The majority shareholder was a company and a clause in the shareholders' agreement required sale of shares by the corporate shareholder to the other shareholder where it was unable to meet their debts.

The House of Lords provided guidance on what may constitute unfairly prejudicial conduct under CA 1985 s 459 (*O'Neill v Phillips* [1999] 2 BCLC 1).

The House of Lords clarified that a balance has to be struck between a person exercising his rights and powers embodied in the company's constitutional documents against any undertakings or agreements also made, which prohibit the act in question.

Remedies available under CA 2006 ss 994–999 are not automatically available where there has been a breakdown in trust and confidence between the parties.

Directors should also note that even where a company genuinely needs additional funds, to be raised by a rights issue, a minority shareholder unable to participate in the rights issue may be able to restrain the issue on the basis that his or her interest would be diluted (*Hall v Gamut Technologies Ltd* 1999 SLT 1276, OH). Consequently, all such issues must be considered and addressed by the directors before making a recommendation to the shareholders.

Derivative action   8.40

The common law principle established in *Foss v Harbottle* that where a wrong was done to a company by its directors only the company itself, and not the members, could bring action has been superseded by CA 2006 ss 260–269. A single member of a company may now make a derivative claim in respect of an actual or proposed act or omission involving negligence, default, breach of duty or breach of trust by a director (CA 2006 s 260(3)). A member may make a derivative claim even where he was not a member at the time the act or omission took place.

When these provisions first came into effect there was considerable concern that the volume of vexatious claims against directors for negligence or breach of trust would increase. However, these concerns have not been realised and there have been relatively few reported instances where derivative claims have been brought and the vast majority of claims brought have not been allowed by the court to proceed.

The potential for an increase in vexatious claims was anticipated at the outset and CA 2006 s 261 requires a member who wants to bring a derivative claim to apply to the court for permission to continue the claim.

Where it appears to the court that the application and the evidence filed by the applicant demonstrate a prima facie case, the claim will be allowed to proceed. Where not, the case will either be dismissed by the court or a consequential order be made for more evidence to be produced.

Permission will not be granted for the derivative action to proceed where the court determines:

- that a person acting in accordance with CA 2006 s 172 (duty to promote the success of the company) would not seek to continue the claim (CA 2006 s 263(2)(a)); or

- where the cause of the action arises from an act or omission which was authorised by the company before it occurred or subsequently ratified by the company once it had occurred (CA 2006 s 263(2)(b) and (c)).

In considering whether to give permission for the derivative action to proceed, the court must also take into account a number of discretionary factors, namely:

(i) whether the member is acting in good faith;

(ii) the importance that a person acting in accordance with s 172 (see above) would attach to continuing the claim;

(iii) whether the act or omission could be and is likely to be authorised or ratified by the company;

(iv) whether the company has decided not to pursue the claim; and

(v) whether the act or omission gives rise to a cause of action the member could pursue in his own right, rather than on behalf of the company.

In *Mission Capital plc v Sinclair* [2010] 1 BCLC 304 (Ch), heard in March 2008, the court exercised its discretion and refused permission for a derivative claim by two dismissed executive directors against the continuing directors to proceed. The basis of the refusal by the court was that a notional director seeking to promote the success of the company would not continue the claim (see (ii) above) and that the two directors could instead pursue action in their own right for unfair prejudice (see (v) above).

Similarly, in *Franbar Holdings v Patel* [2009] 1 BCLC 1 (Ch), heard in July 2008, whilst the court did not consider permission should be withheld based on the mandatory factors, permission was refused on the grounds set out in points (i) and (v) above.

However, in *Parry v Bartlett* [2011] EWHC 3146 (Ch) permission was granted for a shareholder to continue a derivative claim as there was strong evidence of a breach of duty in relation to distribution of the proceeds of sale of the company's only asset to the other 50% shareholder and the company was deadlocked, making it impossible for the breach to be ratified.

Whilst it appears from the case evidence to date that the court is adopting a restrictive approach when considering whether permission should be granted for a derivative claim to continue, especially where brought in conjunction with other claims, the ability for a member to bring a derivative action increases the opportunity for a director to be held to account for his or her negligence, breach of duty or breach of trust. The court may order the company to pay the costs of an unsuccessful claim where reasonably brought by a member.

Another important point to note is that formal disclosure and approval of a director's conflict of interest in a transaction can help secure refusal by the court for a derivative action to proceed. For example, in *Kleanthous v Paphitis* [2011] EWHC 2287, heard in October 2011, application by a shareholder for a derivative action was refused as all transactions concerned had been approved by the company's Board and the Board had also been made fully aware of and approved the particular director's conflict of interest that was being called into question. This matter involved a director of Rymans Group ('Rymans') pursuing acquisition of La Senza once Rymans had decided not to proceed, which a shareholder of Rymans claimed was a conflict of interest from which he received personal benefit.

Communication with members   8.50

An important principle for directors to remember is that they have been appointed by the members of the company to run the business on their behalf and it is very much in the directors' own interests to establish good relations with members who, in effect, have control of their future. Directors are accountable to members for progress of the company and have a duty to report to them on performance of the company. The power that shareholders can exert in this respect should not be underestimated, as demonstrated by reports of increasing 'shareholder activism' in **CHAPTER 9**.

Company law and the UK Listing Authority's regulations require that directors automatically send certain information to members, such as the annual report and accounts, interim statements (listed companies only), and notice and details of any resolutions to be proposed in general meeting. This will ensure that members are informed of the financial status and progress of the company and are aware of any proposed decisions that require their approval.

CA 2006 allows a company to send documents required to be sent to members to a member's nominated electronic address, to permit the company to place company information on a website accessible to members, and to accept proxies sent by email. Many companies have found that an increasing number of members are signing up to electronic communications, giving rise to large cost savings in terms of printing and mailing fees.

Subject to having authority in the company's Articles or to approval by resolution of the members, a company may now communicate with members by posting documents on its website. Before doing so, they must seek consent from members individually but, if no response is received, consent is deemed to have been given. The company must still notify members when it posts new documents on its website and this can be done by post or, where they have provided an email address, by electronic communication.

Many company directors recognise the value of good member relations and have established member communication policies which extend beyond the limits of compulsory information required to be sent to shareholders by the UK Listing Authority and statute. Such policies are supported and recommended as best practice by professional bodies such as the Institute of Chartered Secretaries and Administrators (ICSA), and the additional communication may take the form of:

- timely response to all shareholder enquiries by the executive who is best able to provide an answer;

- supply of quarterly financial reports;

- sending circulars to shareholders on plans, current developments, and strategy;

- ensuring that market information and reports reach the financial press;

- holding briefing meetings with institutional investors and analysts;

- holding information face-to-face meetings with substantial shareholders, discussion forums and conducting surveys;

- making information on the company's progress and development available through the internet and establishing this as a two-way channel of communication.

At the same time, directors of many companies have expanded the business conducted at the AGM beyond statutory requirements as they recognise the value of this meeting, not only for compliance, but also as a forum through which they can communicate details of the company's performance over the past year to members. Holding the AGM is an expensive and time-consuming business which they have found can be put to best use by:

- explaining items of business in the notice of the meeting clearly and minimising use of legal terms which serve to confuse;

- ensuring that accounts are not 'laid' before the meeting as a purely symbolic act, but are made part of the business of the meeting and discussed fully;

- encouraging constructive questions during the meeting;

- either as part of the meeting or before, giving oral, video or graphic presentations and reports on items such as the company's performance, market information and opportunities, new strategies and technological developments, etc which help to widen the shareholders' understanding of the company as a whole. It is also recommended that such presentations be combined with a question and answer session to encourage shareholder engagement;

- providing information in an appropriate form to specialist shareholder groups, for example by the use of Braille in printed documents, audio tapes, large print, etc.

Directors of listed companies should also be aware that the FRC's UK Corporate Governance Code requires:

(1) a dialogue with shareholders which the Board has a responsibility to make sure takes place; and

(2) that the Board use the AGM to communicate with investors and encourage their participation.

As set out in **CHAPTER 10**, the Board has to comply with the requirements of the UK Corporate Governance Code or explain where they have not done so.

Although the directors' duty to impart any additional information is not embodied in statute, as their appointment is secured by the members and a vote to confirm reappointment of some of their number is part of the business at each AGM (unless excluded), many would consider establishing good relations with shareholders of vital importance. As can be seen above, the value and importance of the AGM as a means of communicating with shareholders forms an integral part of corporate governance requirements and it is likely that there will be improvements, certainly amongst listed companies, both in the amount and means by which information is imparted to members.

However, a certain amount of caution needs to be exercised together with advance planning to ensure that no inside information is inadvertently communicated at the AGM without having been announced. It is therefore recommended that advance consideration be given to likely questions and appropriate answers. Arrangements should be made for any inside information that is to be discussed at the meeting to be included in an announcement at or before the time of the meeting. This would usually be done in the form of a trading update or statement.

It is also hoped that the Stewardship Code (see para **10.50**) will successfully enhance the quality of engagement between companies and their institutional investors by making institutional investors accountable, on a 'comply or explain' basis, for monitoring the companies in which they invest and having a clear voting policy. Whilst it remains to be seen whether their presence at AGMs will increase, it is at least expected that there will be an increased level of engagement with companies and in the submission of proxies to register their votes at general meetings.

9 Directors' duties in public and listed companies

9 Directors' duties in public and listed companies

A public company is not permitted to commence business or exercise any borrowing powers until a trading certificate has been obtained from the Registrar of Companies (CA 2006 s 761). To obtain a trading certificate a director, or the secretary, must make and submit to the Registrar of Companies a statutory declaration confirming that the nominal share capital is not less than the authorised minimum, presently £50,000, the amount of any preliminary expenses and details of any monies paid to the company's promoter and accompanied by a statement of compliance (CA 2006 s 762).

Where the company commences business without a trading certificate, the directors will be liable to a fine and be required to indemnify any party who has entered into a transaction with the company for any loss or damage suffered by them in that respect (CA 2006 s 767).

To raise sufficient share capital and be in a position to make the statutory declaration, the directors need to attract shareholders which a public company may do by offering shares to the public.

Any document offering a company's shares for sale to the public, unless exempt, constitutes a prospectus. Even prior to legislation and regulations in this area (which are explored in more detail below), case law established a person's right to recover damages suffered by reliance on a misstatement made encouraging them to invest (*Hedley Byrne & Co Ltd v Heller & Partners Ltd* [1964] AC 465, HL). In addition, a director may be held personally liable for a negligent or reckless misstatement made in a prospectus or listing particulars (*Derry v Peek* (1889) 14 App Cas 337).

Public issues   9.10

Listed and unlisted companies are now subject to the same listing and prospectus regime and, unless exempt, must comply with the requirements of the Financial Services and Markets Act 2000 (FSMA 2000) as amended by the Financial Services Act 2012, Prospectus Rules and Listing Rules. Section 85 of the FSMA 2000 requires a company to issue an approved prospectus whenever it makes an offer of transferable securities to the public in the UK.

Where the FSMA 2000 applies, directors must ensure that all statutory requirements are met when an offer is made to the public. Where a breach occurs, the directors may be liable for civil and criminal penalties punishable by fine and/or imprisonment (FSMA 2000 s 85 and PR1.2.1). Any person responsible for listing particulars is liable to pay compensation to a person who has acquired securities to which the particulars apply and has suffered loss as a result of a false or misleading statement made in the prospectus (FSMA 2000 s 90).

Whilst this chapter focuses on requirements for fully listed companies, where a company has securities listed on the Stock Exchange's Alternative Investment Market (AIM) or on ISDX's Main Board, they must adhere to provisions contained in either the AIM Rules for Companies or the ISDX Main Board Admission and Disclosure Standards (ISDX Rules), whichever is relevant. Unfortunately, the scope of this book does not permit coverage of each of these in detail and readers should specifically refer to provisions in the AIM Rules or the ISDX Rules where relevant to their company or situation.

Unlisted offers   9.20

Many offers of securities made in respect of securities which are neither to be admitted to official listing nor are the subject of an application for listing ('unlisted offer') do not fall within the scope of the FSMA 2000 s 85 or they fall within the exemptions. Directors need to give careful consideration to the exemptions set out below and determine if they apply to the company's proposed unlisted offer.

First, the directors need to determine whether or not the proposed offer constitutes an 'offer of transferable securities to the public'. FSMA 2000 s 102B states that this includes any communication made in whatever form and by any means which contains enough information about the securities being offered and the terms of the offer to enable a potential investor to decide whether to acquire shares pursuant to the offer.

Second, and assuming the offer does fall within the definition above, the directors need to determine whether the offer might be exempt from the requirement to produce an FSA-approved prospectus. The exemptions set out in FSMA 2000 s 86 (amended by the 2005 and 2011 Prospectus Regulations) are as follows:

(a)   the offer is made to or directed at only qualified investors;

(b)   it is made to fewer than 150 persons, other than qualified investors, in each EEA state;

(c)   the minimum consideration required pursuant to the offer is at least €50,000 or an equivalent currency amount;

(d)   the transferable securities are denominated in amounts of at least €50,000, or equivalent amount; or

(e)   the total consideration for securities in the offer does not exceed €100,000.

An approved prospectus is also not required for a public offer of any of the types of transferable securities listed in FSMA 2000 Sch 11A. Whilst most of the exemptions listed in Sch 11A have limited application and concern securities to be issued by governments' central banks, credit institutions, charities, housing associations and industrial and provident societies, there is an overall exemption threshold and an approved prospectus is not required where an offer seeks to raise less than €5,000,000 (or other, equivalent amount).

In addition, as permitted by FSMA 2000 s 85(5)(b), the Prospectus Rules contain further exemptions from the requirement to produce an approved prospectus. These are contained in PR1.2.2 and include where:

(1)   shares are offered in substitution for shares of the same class already issued, provided there is no increase in issued capital;

(2)   an offer is made in connection with a merger or takeover, provided a document equivalent to an approved prospectus is available;

(3)   shares are offered without charge to existing shareholders (ie bonus issues or scrip dividends, etc), provided a document is available with details of the number and nature of the shares and the reasons for and details of the offer; or

(4)   transferable securities are allotted, or to be allotted, to existing or former directors or employees by the employing company, provided a document is available with details of the number and nature of the shares and the reasons for and details of the offer.

The Prospectus Rules also contain further exemptions to the need for an approved prospectus in certain circumstances where application for admission to trading is made for shares that are already in issue (PR1.2.3). For example, where the share represent less than 10% of the number of shares of the same class already admitted to trading on the same regulated market over a 12-month period.

Before offering shares to the public, the directors must determine whether or not the offer is exempt from the requirement for a prospectus. It is important to note that where any of the above circumstances apply and a prospectus is not required, an offer document may still constitute a 'financial promotion' which cannot be issued unless the contents have been approved by a person authorised within the terms of FSMA 2000 s 21. These requirements must be checked carefully before any advertisement of the offer is made.

Where the FSMA does apply to the offer the directors must ensure that the requirements set out in para **9.30** are met.

Directors must ensure that the prospectus complies with requirements of the FSMA and Prospectus Rules in terms of the form, content and publication. This is particularly important as the directors, amongst others, are responsible for the prospectus and may be required to compensate a person for any loss or damage suffered by relying on information contained therein.

Listed offers   9.30

Where a public company makes an offer of transferable securities to the public and those securities are listed or are to be listed on the London Stock Exchange, the company must comply with provisions of FSMA 2000 s 85(1) and produce an approved prospectus. The offer may be by way of an offer for sale or subscription, placing, rights issue or open offer, etc.

Prospectus requirements   9.30.1

The Prospectus Rules set out the detailed requirements for the prospectus, including its form and content and means of publication.

FSMA 2000 s 87A sets out requirements for the general contents of a prospectus, as follows:

(1)   the prospectus must contain information about the assets, liabilities, financial position, profit and loss and prospects of the company and the rights of the transferable securities in the offer;

(2)   the information must be presented clearly and comprehensively so that it is easy to understand and analyse;

(3)   preparation of the information must take account of the particular nature of the securities being offered and of the company;

(4)   unless exempt, the prospect must include a summary of the essential characteristics and risks of the offer and the company. PR2.1.7 also requires that the summary includes a warning that any decision to invest should be based on consideration of the whole prospectus, in totality.

A prospectus may be drawn up as a single document or as separate documents. In the latter case, the separate documents must divide the information into a:

(a)   registration document, containing information about the issuing company;

(b)   securities note, containing information about the transferable securities being offered, and

(c)   summary (see sub-para (4) above).

The prospectus will need to include a table of contents and identify the risk factors linked to the company and securities being offered. Other information items and minimum information will also need to be included in the prospectus with reference to what items are required by the schedules and 'building blocks' in Articles 3 to 23 of the Prospectus Directive Regulations (PR2.3.1).

However, where the company making the offer for securities is concerned that disclosure of certain information might be contrary to public interest, seriously damage the interests of the issuer or is only of minor importance, the company can request permission from the FCA for it to be omitted (FSMA 2000 s 87B(1) and PR2.5).

Directors have a duty to ensure compliance with the requirements of FSMA 2000 and the Listing and Prospectus Rules, as they are responsible, with others, for the prospectus or listing particulars and may be required to compensate persons for any loss or damage suffered where they acquire shares on the basis of false or misleading information in the prospectus or where relevant information was omitted (FSMA 2000 s 90). Particular attention is necessary to ensure the information is correct and can be verified, validated and supported.

Once the prospectus has been drawn up approval must be sought, by application, from the FCA. The approved prospectus can then be valid for a period of up to 12 months, provided it is updated by approved supplementary prospectuses as necessary (PR5.1).

The prospectus must not be published until it has been approved by the FCA, but must be published as soon as practicable thereafter and no later than commencement of the offer or admission to trading (whichever is applicable). Publication may be by inclusion in a newspaper with suitably wide circulation; by making it available at the company's registered office and the offices of the regulated market, company's advisers and relevant financial intermediaries; inclusion on the company's (and others') website; and inclusion on the regulated market's website. Any investor can request a hard copy, which must be supplied. Also, on the day the FCA is to consider the listing application, it must also be provided with a shareholder statement and completed pricing statement (where relevant).

Listing application   9.30.2

Under FSMA 2000 s 75, where the company requires securities comprised in the offer to be admitted to the Official List the directors need to ensure that an application for listing is made in the manner prescribed by the Listing Rules. Chapters 3 to 8 of the Listing Rules set out detailed requirements and procedures for admission to the Official List and the FCA, acting as the UKLA, is responsible for admitting securities to the Official List whilst the London Stock Exchange will continue to admit securities to trading.

It is worth noting that the listing application process will involve a thorough review of the company's constitution, board composition, committee structure and governance arrangements, systems for risk management and internal controls, etc to ensure they are suitable for a listed company. Where necessary, changes will need to be made prior to listing and this change and move to a new and often unfamiliar regulatory environment can, in itself, be quite a challenging process perceptually for the Board. One example of a change that might be necessary where the company that is to be listed has a controlling shareholder, is an amendment to the company's Articles to provide that any resolution to elect or re-elect an independent director must be approved by the shareholders and by the independent shareholders, with the controlling shareholder abstaining (LR9.2.2E).

Directors must ensure that the following procedural requirements are met when the company is making a public offer of securities for which listing is sought:

- either a prospectus or listing particulars need to be prepared. A prospectus is required where securities are being offered for the first time for admission to the Official List and listing particulars are required on all other occasions. Whichever document is prepared (for the purposes of this chapter referred to collectively as 'listing particulars'), one copy must be submitted to UKLA for approval (together with the completed application for admission of securities to the Official List, any circular and written confirmation of the number of shares to be issued) by midday at least two clear business days before the FCA is to consider the application (Listing Rule 3.3.2 and FSMA 2000 s 75);

- on the day the FCA is to consider the listing application, they must also be provided with a shareholder statement and completed pricing statement (where applicable);

- admission only becomes effective once the FCA's decision to admit the securities to listing has been announced either through a Regulated Information Service ('RIS') or on a notice board approved by the FSA where electronic means of publication are not available (LR 3.2.7). Only then may the directors publish, advertise or circulate the listing particulars. Listing particulars must be published by making them available through an RIS, the company's registered office and the offices of any paying agent. Directors should be aware that it is an offence to offer the securities to the public before publication of the listing particulars and any contravention of this requirement will render the directors guilty of an offence for which they will be liable to a fine, imprisonment, or both (FSMA 2000 s 85(3)).

Directors must ensure that any information given in the listing particulars is presented in a form which is easy to analyse and understand. As with the prospectus, sufficient information must be given about the assets, liabilities, financial position, profits or losses and prospects of the company, together with the rights attaching to securities being offered, to enable a potential investor to make an informed assessment of the offer (FSMA 2000 s 80).

Verification process 9.30.3

Whether the offer is for listed or unlisted securities, the directors are responsible for the contents of the prospectus or listing particulars. It is therefore essential that directors follow some form of verification process to ensure that each of them is satisfied that:

- each statement of fact or opinion made is accurate and not misleading;

- no relevant information has been omitted;

- a true and fair description of the company's business and prospects is given; and

- the risks as well as benefits from investment are made clear.

The aim of this process is to work through the prospectus and any supporting notes and documents statement by statement to verify the relevant facts, identify and record any sources of evidence to support statements made and opinions expressed, ensure that all relevant information has been included and that any inferences drawn from the prospectus are justified.

It is important for directors of companies whose securities are fully listed or are to be fully listed to note the need to include a responsibility statement in the Listing Particulars, which the UKLA may require is adapted or extended to additional persons, accepting responsibility for information included (LR 4.2.13(1)(b)). Suggested wording for the statement is set out in **APPENDIX 21**.

The final form of the prospectus and the verification notes should be approved by the Board of Directors, normally at a verification meeting during which the final draft prospectus and supporting documents are examined and approved, before the prospectus is sent to UKLA.

Listed companies and continuing obligations   **9.40**

On an ongoing basis, companies with shares quoted on the London Stock Exchange must, in addition to legislative requirements, abide by the UKLA's Prospectus, Listing and Disclosure and Transparency Rules ('DTRs'), which have been devised to regulate and ensure smooth operation of the securities market. In particular, directors of a listed company should be aware that they are collectively, with other members of the Board, and individually responsible for the company's compliance with these Rules, not only when making application for securities to be listed but also on an ongoing basis once the securities have been listed.

The listed company regime is now split into two segments: premium and standard listing. Standard listed companies mainly have to comply with the Prospectus Rules and DTRs. Premium listed companies, being those on the FTSE 100, 250 and 350 Indexes, have to adhere to more stringent standards around due diligence, governance and regulation of the company's affairs.

In the interests of maintaining an orderly market the Listing Rules contain a list of continuing obligations which the directors must ensure are observed by the listed company (Chapter 9 of the Listing Rules). These requirements centre on the need to disclose information to the market, uphold shareholder rights and communicate information to shareholders and are detailed in the following paragraphs.

Similarly, directors of companies with shares quoted on AIM or the ISDX Main Board must comply with requirements specified in their respective Rules and Codes of Practice.

The importance of compliance with the Listing Rules is emphasised by the power possessed by the UKLA to refuse an application for listing, suspend listing of the company's securities, or cancel the listing of securities altogether where they or the Stock Exchange consider the company's obligations have not been met.

Furthermore, the FSMA 2000 sets out a broad range of enforcement powers for the FCA when requirements of the Listing, Prospectus or Disclosure Rules have been breached or when transparency rules and obligations or corporate governance rules have not been met. Directors should therefore be aware that where a breach has occurred, the UKLA may impose:

(1)   a suspension or discontinuance of listing (FSMA 2000 s 77);

(2)   financial penalties of an amount it considers appropriate on the company and on its current and former directors (FSMA 2000 s 91); and

(3)   public censures on the company, its directors and former directors.

Whilst primary responsibility for compliance is that of the company, directors can also be held individually liable for a breach. Moreover, directors who held office at the time of a breach may be called to account for their actions or inactions notwithstanding their subsequent resignation.

Whilst there are now numerous examples of companies being fined by the FCA for Listing Rule breaches, the FSA exercised its powers for the first time on 29 March 2004 when it fined Sportsworld Media Group plc for failing to announce a profits warning. The company was censured for breaching LR 9.2 and the company's former CEO was also fined £45,000 for knowingly committing the breach.

A more recent example is the £14m fine imposed by the FSA (now FCA) on Prudential plc on 27 March 2013 for failing to deal with the FSA in an open and cooperative manner, in breach of Listing Rule Principle 6. Another example is the FSA's £292,950 fine rendered on 26 April 2012 on Exillon Energy plc for breaching the requirements of LR11.1.11R by failing to identify and notify the FSA that £930,000 of related party payments had been made to its former chairman and beneficiary of the major shareholder. There are many other examples, details of which can be found in the Fines Tables on the enforcement and fines section of the FCA website. In the first half of 2013 alone FSA fines reached £153m.

Listing principles   **9.41**

As explained in LR7.1 and 7.2, the Listing Principles are designed to assist premium listed companies in identifying their responsibilities and obligations under the Listing, Prospectus, Disclosure and Transparency Rules. The rules are there to try and achieve a fair and orderly market and maintain market confidence. The principles, set out below, are intended to promote adherence to the 'spirit' as well as the letter of the Rules:

(1)   a listed company must take reasonable steps to enable its directors to understand their responsibilities and obligations as directors;

(2)   a listed company must take reasonable steps to establish and maintain adequate procedures, systems and controls to enable it to comply with its obligations, in particular with regard to timely and accurate disclosure of information to the market;

(3)   that the listed company acts with integrity and honesty towards holders and potential holders of listed securities;

(4)   that the company communicates information towards these holders in such a way as to avoid creation or continuation of a false market in the company's listed securities;

(5)   the holders of the same class of listed securities must be treated equally;

(6)   a listed company must deal with the FSA in an open and cooperative manner.

The FSA has power to sanction a premium listed company or its directors for a breach of the Listing Principles, even where no other breach of the Listing, Prospectus, or Disclosure and Transparency Rules has occurred.

Inside information   9.42

All listed companies must adhere to the requirements of the Listing Rules and Disclosure and Transparency Rules and announce any information that could lead to a substantial movement in the price of the company's listed securities.

Disclosure   9.42.1

As a general rule, directors must ensure that the company notifies an RIS of any inside information that directly concerns the company as an issuer (DTR 2.2.1). 'Inside information' includes information that is not generally available, relates directly or indirectly to the issuer and would, if made available, be likely to affect the price of the company's listed securities (FSMA 2000 s 118C).

In certain circumstances the directors may be permitted to delay disclosure of inside information in order to protect the company's legitimate business interests (DTR 2.5.1R). This might be, for example, where negotiations are under way and the outcome would be affected by public disclosure, or where the decisions or contracts to be made need approval by another body as well as the company.

However, delay in notifying the RIS is only permitted where it would not mislead the public and where the company can ensure confidentiality of the inside information and there are arrangements in place to ensure no leaks to the market. This needs to be carefully considered as it is only possible in certain, exceptional circumstances and FSMA 2000 s 90A has been amended to address unwarranted delays in making information public by extending coverage of liability to include paying compensation to those who suffered loss as a result of intentional delay in making information available.

Directors should also note that, in certain very limited circumstances, a company may make 'selective disclosure' of inside information before such time as the inside information is announced to an RIS (DTR 2.5.7G). The recipients must be bound by a duty of confidentiality to the company and might, for example, include the company's advisers or the advisers of other parties involved in negotiations, persons with whom the company is negotiating a commercial or financial investment transaction, employee representatives or trade union officials, major shareholders, lenders or credit-rating agencies. However, selective disclosure must always be carefully considered, as it is not justified in every circumstance. Obviously the more people who are aware of the inside information, the higher the risk of a leak to the market. Should inside information be leaked, this will immediately trigger the requirement for full public disclosure to an RIS.

Press speculation and market rumours about the company should be monitored as they may give rise to a disclosure obligation for the company (DTR 2.7).

Control and insider lists   9.42.2

Directors must ensure that appropriate arrangements are in place to make sure that only those persons who require the inside information in the exercise of their duties for the company have access to it. This means that means of security for the information must be implemented, whether electronically in terms of password restricted files and encrypted data or by means of a secure manual storage system. These are important practical considerations and persons who have access to this inside information must be placed under a duty of confidentiality to the company.

The listed company must ensure that it and any person working on its behalf draws up a list of any persons who have access to the company's inside information, whether on a regular or occasional basis (DTR 2.8.1). It is very important that the 'insider list' is kept kept up to date at all times and it must state why a person is on the list and be revised should a new person become an insider, an existing insider cease to be an insider or there be any change in the reason why a person is an insider. All insider lists must be kept for at least five years from the date they are drawn up or updated.

It is also important for the company to ensure that employees and others acting on its behalf or account who have access to inside information are aware of and acknowledge the legal and regulatory duties this places on them, in particular, restrictions on dealing in the company's listed securities and the need to keep the information confidential (DTR 2.8.9 and 2.8.9.10).

Notification to RIS   9.43

In addition to the disclosure obligations set out above, all listed companies must notify an RIS as soon as possible about any of the matters set out in the table below.

Inside information that is likely to be price sensitive would tend to include information about:

(1)   major new developments in the company's sphere of activity not already known in the public domain, where these developments and the effect they have on the assets and liabilities, financial position or general course of the company's business cause either:

   (a)   a substantial movement in the price of the listed securities; or

   (b)   a significant change in the company's ability to meet its obligations;

(2)   changes in the company's financial condition, performance or expectations of performance which are likely to cause substantial movement in the price of the company's listed securities;

(3)   details of any strategic developments or matters under negotiation where it is believed a breach of confidence has occurred or is likely to occur;

(4)   Board decisions on profits, decisions and other matters that require announcement;

(5)   shareholders' meetings, where information is to be disclosed to the holders of the company's listed securities which may cause a substantial movement in their price.

Disclosure is necessary for the UKLA to ensure that all users of the market have simultaneous access to the same information. In the event that the RIS is closed, the directors must arrange for notification to be made in at least two national newspapers in the UK and on two newswire services, and notify the RIS of the information for release as soon as it reopens.

Directors should note that it is expressly stated in LR 1.3.3 that information and forecasts made available to the RIS by a company must not be misleading, false or deceptive and must not omit anything likely to affect their meaning.

The table below lists briefly specific circumstances or events which need to be notified to the RIS and the timing required for notification. These are covered in detail in the Listing Rules and the Disclosure and Transparency Rules, to which readers are referred.

Events requiring notification to the RIS	Timing of notification
Board changes (LR 9.6.11–9.6.13) *(premium listed companies only)*	
(a) Appointment of a director	● Without delay and, at the latest, the end of the next business day after receipt of the information.
(b) Resignation of a director	● Notification must state the effective date of change and, where a director is appointed, whether the appointment is executive or non-executive and details of any specific functions or responsibilities.
(c) Any change in executive functions or responsibilities of a director	
Changes in capital (DTR 6.1.9–6.1.13 and LR 9.6.4)	
(a) Alterations to the capital structure	● Without delay, but may be postponed for a new issue until obligations of any underwriters have been determined.
(b) New issues of debt securities and guarantees and security over them	
(c) Changes in rights attaching to securities	
(d) Drawing or redemption of listed securities	
(e) Allotment of listed securities to the public and open offers to shareholders	
(f) Any change in the time for which 'temporary documents of title' are considered current	

Events requiring notification to the RIS	Timing of notification
(g) Issues of securities and the effect they will have on exercise of rights under options, warrants and convertible securities	
(h) The outcome of a new issue	
Major interests in shares (DTR 5)	
(a) Information disclosed to the company relating to major interests in shares and voting rights	• Without delay and, at the latest, the end of the next business day after receipt of the information. • Notification is deemed to have been given where information has been supplied to the Regulatory Information Service in fulfilment of requirements of the Takeover Code. • Must include the date information received by the company and date of the transaction giving rise to the interest.
(b) Any information obtained relating to beneficial ownership (CA 2006 s 793, see para **6.25**)	• Without delay and, at the latest, the end of the next business day after receipt of the information.
Interests of persons discharging managerial responsibility (including directors) and their connected persons in shares (DTR 3.1.2R)	
(a) Any information disclosed to the company relating to the PDMR's shareholding in own company.	• Without delay and, at the latest, the end of the next business day after receipt of the information.

Events requiring notification to the RIS	Timing of notification
(b) Information relating to any interest of a PDMR's 'connected person'	• Notification must include the date of notification, date of the transaction giving rise to disclosure, the reason for responsibility to notify, the price, amount and class of securities, nature of the transaction and extent of the PDMR's interest.
(c) Grant of any option relating to securities or the right to acquire or dispose of listed securities of the company to a director or connected person or any dealing with any such option or right	• Without delay and, at the latest, the end of the next business day after receipt of the information
Disposal of shares under a lock-up arrangement (or of any variation to the arrangement) (LR 9.6.16–17)	• As soon as possible
Shareholder resolutions (other than resolutions concerning ordinary business at the AGM) (LR 9.6.18)	• As soon as possible
Change of name (LR 9.6.19)	• As soon as possible
Change of accounting reference date (LR 9.6.20)	• As soon as possible
Decisions made by the Board of Directors relating to payment of a dividend (LR 9.7A.2)	• Must be notified as soon as possible after the decision made by the Board.
Total voting rights (DTR 5.6.1)	
(a) Total voting rights.	• At the end of each month during which an increase or decrease has occurred.
(b) Voting rights attached to shares held in treasury.	• At the end of each month during which an increase or decrease has occurred.
Classifying transactions (acquisitions and disposals by companies with a premium listing) (LR 10.2)	• As soon as possible once terms of transaction are agreed and becomes a realistic prospect.

Events requiring notification to the RIS	Timing of notification
This includes all transactions, whether classed by the UKLA as Class 3, Class 2 or Class 1 transactions. (Note: consideration is being given to deleting the Class 3 notification requirements in LR10.3 as covered by the 'price sensitive information' disclosure requirement in DTR 2.2R)	• Minimum notification must include details of the transaction, any securities issued, consideration given in an acquisition and how this is satisfied (or the value of net assets acquired, whichever is greater) and the effect of any disposal on the company. • Disclosure of a Class 2 transaction must also include details of key individuals and of any directors' service contracts. • In addition, a circular and prior shareholder approval will be required for Class 1 transactions.
'Related party' transactions (LR 11.1.7) (premium listed companies only) Transactions, arrangements or contractual arrangements with current or recent directors, substantial shareholders and their associates.	• As soon as possible once terms of transaction are agreed. • A circular containing details of the transaction and prior approval of shareholders are generally required. • Notification must contain the related party's details, details about the transaction and the information required for a Class 2 transaction.

Events requiring notification to the RIS	Timing of notification
Purchases of shares (LR 12.4.4) (premium listed companies only)	
Both the proposal by the Board to the shareholders and outcome of any purchases of shares by the company or any group company must be notified.	● Must be notified as soon as possible and, where a purchase takes place, no later than 7.30 am the business day following the purchase of shares (LR 12.4.6).
	● Notification must include the date of purchase, number of equity securities purchased and details of the highest and lowest price paid, if relevant.
Preliminary announcement of annual results (LR 9.7A1 (premium listed companies only)	
No longer compulsory, but company can choose to prepare.	● If a listed company prepares a preliminary statement of annual results, it must be published as soon as possible after approval by the Board.
Annual accounts (DTR 4.1.3)	● As soon as possible after approval by the Board and within four months of the end of the financial period covered by the accounts.
Half-yearly financial reports (DTR 4.2.2)	● As soon as possible after approval by the Board and within two months of the end of the financial period covered by the accounts.
Interim management statement (DTR 4.3.3)	● In a period between ten weeks after the beginning and six weeks before the end of the relevant six-month period and be made as soon as possible after Board approval.

Directors must take particular care when preparing, reviewing and approving information for release to the market via an RIS to ensure it is accurate, not misleading, false or deceptive, that nothing important to overall interpretation is omitted and that it is announced as soon as it needs to be. This is specifically required by both DTR 1.3.4 and LR 1.3.3. The scope of FSMA 2000 Sch 10A has been extended to include liability for any loss to those who not only acquire shares as a result of misleading information, but also to those who retain shares as a result.

Should the listed company fail to announce any of the required information set out above or fail to announce inside information as soon as required (see para **9.42**) the FCA has power to impose an unlimited fine on the company and its directors (FSMA 2000 s 91). Such breach could also give rise to regulatory action by the FCA for market abuse (see para **9.70**).

The listed company must also forward copies of all circulars, reports, notices, resolutions of general meeting (for non-ordinary business) and other documents to which the Listing Rules and Disclosure and Transparency Rules apply electronically to the FCA for publication through the document viewing facility at the same time as they are issued and announce, in the form of a Technical Note on the DTRs, through an RIS when this has been done (LR 9.6.1–9.6.3).

To assist listed companies the UKLA has provided some practical guidance on the identification control and dissemination of inside information which directors would be well advised to consider. Whilst it does not impose additional obligations to those set out in the Listing Rules and Disclosure and Transparency Rules, by following its suggestions the company is more likely to be considered to have complied with requirements of these rules.

The directors have overall responsibility for control and dissemination of inside information, although they would usually delegate execution of announcements. The UKLA recommends implementing a framework for handling inside information which may be price sensitive and the main recommendations are:

- that companies should have a consistent and predetermined procedure for determining what information is inside information and requires announcement;

- preparation and communication of a 'sensitivity list' setting out the types of information likely to be price-sensitive to avoid inadvertent disclosures, for example in response to questions at a company's annual general meeting;

- responsibility for communicating with analysts, investors and the press should be clearly defined, usually by delegation to a specific person or persons, and all other employees should be informed that they are prohibited from communicating price sensitive information outside the company;

- persons nominated to deal with communications must be appropriately trained in how to identify and handle inside information and how to handle external contacts;

- analysts, investors and the press should be informed who in the company is responsible for communications and the basics of the company's communications policy so, for example, they know that no comments will be made in response to market rumours, etc;

- companies must make arrangements to ensure inside information remains confidential until it is announced and be ready to make an announcement where there has been a leak and it has affected share price;

- providing scheduled regular updates on the company's trading prospects and position in the form of a trading statement;

- arranging for any price sensitive information that is to be discussed at the company's annual general meeting to be announced at or before the meeting.

It is important for directors to ensure that inside information which is price sensitive is handled correctly at all times as, whilst primary responsibility for compliance with these aspects of the Listing Rules rests with the company, the directors can also be held individually accountable for breaches of the rules. The Board retains overall responsibility for identification, control and dissemination of inside information even where it delegates the execution.

Communication with shareholders and others   **9.44**

Directors have responsibility for ensuring that shareholders receive notices of meetings and information about their entitlement to attend and exercise their vote at such meetings (consistent with requirements of CA 2006, detailed in para **8.23**) as well as information about payments of interest or dividends, issues of securities and any redemption or repayment of securities.

At the same time, they must notify a RIS of decisions made by the Board relating to dividends and profits and procure that two copies of circulars, notices, reports, announcements and resolutions (other than resolutions concerning routine business at the AGM) are sent to the FCA for publication through the document viewing facility either at the same time as they are issued or, in the case of resolutions, without delay after the meeting at which they are approved (see paras **9.41** and **9.43**).

Circulars   **9.44.1**

Notwithstanding a number of exceptions in the Listing Rules (such as listing particulars, annual accounts, interim reports and proxy cards) any information sent by the directors to holders of listed securities in the company will take the form of a circular. A company that has a premium listing of securities must ensure that any circular issued to the holder of its securities complies with the requirements of LR13 and has been approved by the FCA before it is circulated or made available to the public.

However, circulars covering matters listed in LR 13.2.2 and 13.8 do not require approval by the FCA. These include circulars in connection with a resolution to renew the directors' authority to allot shares, waive shareholders' rights of pre-emption, increase or reduce the share capital, propose a capitalisation issue, purchase of the company's own shares or payment of a scrip dividend, amendments to the constitution or an employee share scheme and certain notices of general meetings. Where the matter is to be considered at the company's AGM, the additional information required in the circular may be included in the directors' report to the accounts. Circulars that are sent for information only and are not requiring a vote from shareholders and those proposing a change of company name are also exempt. All other circulars to be issued by a company with a premium listing of securities require approval.

When drafting and approving the form and content of a circular, the directors must make sure the circular is drafted to provide:

- a clear explanation of the circumstances giving rise to the circular;

- a statement about why the circular is being sent and (if applicable) why the security holder is being asked to vote;

- sufficiently detailed information to allow an informed decision to be made where a decision is required;

- a header note explaining the importance of the document where voting or other action is required and advising the recipient to obtain professional advice to help them determine what action to take;

- a recommendation from the directors on which way to vote, if a vote is required;

- instructions to persons who have since transferred their securities to forward the circular to the agent who dealt with the sale for them to pass on to the purchaser of the securities;

- an explanation of what to do with existing documents of title where new securities are being issued in substitution for existing securities;

- where applicable, a statement that application has been or will be made for listing of the securities;

- a statement that any adviser named in the circular has given and not withdrawn their consent to inclusion of their name in the circular;

- no reference to any 'ex' benefit or entitlement unless it has been agreed with the relevant recognised investment exchange; and

- if the circular concerns cancelling listing, a statement confirming whether the company intends to cancel listing.

Directors should be aware that additional information may be needed and further approval be required depending on the matters being proposed in the circular. These requirements are set out in LR 13.5 to 13.8 and include where the circular contains certain pro forma financial information or where it concerns a Class 1 or related-party transaction or purchase by the company of its own shares. A further circular may also be needed if there are significant changes which would affect and influence the reader's determination of a reasoned decision.

Formal approval of the FCA is obtained by submitting two copies of the circular and any supporting documents to the FCA at least ten clear business days before the intended date of publication (LR 13.2.4).

The circular must be circulated as soon as possible after approval and a copy be sent to the FCA for publication through the document viewing facility at the same time as it is despatched to shareholders.

Financial promotions 9.44.2

FSMA 2000 s 21 (which needs to be read alongside FSMA 2000 (Financial Promotion) Order 2005, which is important for interpretation), prohibits a person in the course of business from communicating an invitation or inducement to engage in investment activity unless the communication is exempt or it is made or approved by an authorised person. There are criminal penalties for breaches of FSMA 2000 s 21 and an agreement entered into as a result of an unlawful communication may be unenforceable.

Directors should be aware that the financial promotion regime applies to a much wider set of activities and investments than the old 'investment advertisement' regime. Most importantly, whilst the company may not carry out an activity requiring authorisation, financial promotion restrictions may still apply to its communications, for example where the company invites persons to acquire or dispose of shares, and these must be made or approved by an authorised person.

Financial promotion restrictions apply to:

- 'real time' communications: such as personal visits, telephone calls or other interactive dialogue;

- 'non-real time' communications: such as communications by letter, email or that contained in a publication; and

- invitations or inducements: such as an invitation to treat, a direct offer, a prospectus with an application form or an online dealing facility.

Concern has been expressed that directors may be acting in breach of the FSMA 2000's financial promotions regime by making statements and responding to shareholders' questions at the AGM. The basis of the concern is that shareholders have not given their written agreement to receive unsolicited communications which could make them illegal. To avoid this, many companies are including wording in the notice of the meeting or displaying such at the meeting to the effect that, by attending, members are giving their agreement to receiving such communications.

General meetings and shareholder activism 9.44.3

Whilst requirements in respect of general meetings do not, specifically, come within the scope of the continuing obligations in the Listing Rules this section on communication with shareholders by listed companies would not be complete without mention of the importance of general meetings, particularly the AGM. As can be seen in para **8.50**, the directors of many companies have expanded the purpose of such meetings well beyond what is needed for pure statutory compliance purposes as they recognise that significant benefits can be gained by engaging with shareholders prior to, and at, such meetings and in using the meetings as a forum for communication. It is important that directors recognise the importance of actively engaging with shareholders by, for example, discussing announced plans and strategies with the shareholders and explaining how some of the decisions were reached and the constraints within which the company operates, etc. Such discussion might be held at the AGM or in advance of the meeting.

Alongside this, there has been a sustained call to institutional shareholders to take a more active interest and engage with the companies in which they have invested, culminating in introduction of the Stewardship Code, which aims to enhance the quality of their engagement with companies (**CHAPTER 10**).

In some instances it is important to seek shareholders' opinions, feedback and support for proposed strategy in advance of a meeting as the alternative might be confrontation and formal opposition at the general meeting. A prime example of this is executive directors' remuneration about which there has been a considerable amount of well-publicised unrest amongst the shareholders of large, high-profile, listed companies in recent years.

This unrest or expression of dissatisfaction is often referred to as 'shareholder activism'. The concept is not new and activism may take many forms, ranging from communicating shareholder concerns in the hope the Board will revise the proposals, voting against a resolution or resolutions proposed at a general meeting, requesting circulation of written statements in an attempt to influence other shareholders' voting decisions, requisitioning general meetings, selling shares, commencing derivative action, to lobbying government, etc.

Whatever form the activism takes it can be expected that once news about it reaches the public domain, it will receive considerable press coverage. As well as putting the company's directors and management under considerable pressure to address the issues whilst in the public eye and under close scrutiny, the negative publicity created could damage the company's reputation in the market and discourage potential investors from acquiring shares. Activism was probably at its peak in 2013, with numerous reports of a 'Shareholder Spring' hitting the headlines. It is fair to say that, whilst the message from shareholders remains as strong and unchanged, the mood is less volatile as shareholders and companies turn their attention to the many changes to reporting that have been brought into effect,

However, investors will still exercise their right to intervene in the management of listed public companies and speak out when they do not agree with the Board's policies and decisions. Issues over which shareholders have expressed concern about and engaged with companies recently include directors' remuneration, Board composition, takeover bids, share buy-backs and routine resolutions. Some recent high-profile examples of shareholder dissent expressed at AGMs in 2014 identified in the NAPF's report on the 2014 AGM season include:

- Directors' remuneration report – some 50% of the shareholders of Kentz Corporation, 45% at EasyJet, 31% at First Group and 17.39% at Lonmin voted against the remuneration report.

- Remuneration policy – approximately 50% of shareholders at Kentz Corporation also voted against the remuneration policy, as did 42% of shareholders at Hiscox, 41% at Standard Chartered, 40% at Sports Direct and 39% at Astra-Zeneca.

- Routine resolutions – 44% of investors at Astra-Zeneca voted against re-election of one of the directors, as did 33% of shareholders at SVG Capital.

It should also be noted that in recent years there have been numerous instances of lobbying for changes to strategy and structure (for example at Vodafone), and where special interest groups lobby for change (for example at Tesco, where shareholders lobbied for an improvement in the working conditions of Tesco's clothes manufacturers in Asia). Investors may also wish to pursue shareholder activism as a means of procuring a return of capital, increasing company efficiency by procuring the disposal of underperforming assets, or influencing the outcome of a takeover or other merger or acquisition activity. Whatever the driver, it is fair to say that shareholders are now less likely to tolerate actions and decisions taken by the Board that they consider are wrong and will not promote success of their companies.

Whilst traditionally discussion between shareholders and boards would have taken place behind closed doors out of the public domain, directors need to be aware that in this age where they fail to engage, investors are likely to publicise their concerns as a means of escalating external pressure to create change. Directors are therefore well advised to engage with their company's shareholders and to take heed of their concerns. Such engagement and dialogue is recommended at an early stage so concerns and issues are fully understood. This will enable the directors to give greater explanation of how a decision or strategy was derived and, where possible, seek resolution and support from the investors.

Often engagement is needed well in advance of the AGM or general meeting to ensure support for the resolutions to be proposed at the meeting is demonstrated in proxy forms submitted by institutional shareholders. With this in mind many companies hold a series of road shows for shareholders, brokers and analysts in the days following announcement of the company's results to address any concerns and ensure investors feel able to support the company's plans and strategy.

Directors of listed companies should note that following the suggestion in the Kay Review that there be an investor forum to promote engagement, the NAPF, ABI and IMA have announced that a working group will be established to look at improving long-term investment returns by developing collective engagement between shareholders and the companies in which they invest.

Financial disclosure obligations   9.45

Preliminary announcement of results   9.45.1

The Listing Rules no longer require premium listed companies to make a preliminary announcement of financial results, but where a company still chooses to make this announcement, the company must comply with the requirements of LR 9.7A.

Where a listed company prepares a preliminary announcement of results, it must ensure:

(1)   the preliminary results are notified to the RIS as soon as possible after approval by the Board;

(2)   the statement has been agreed with the auditors prior to publication.

(3)   it is in table format consistent with the layout of the annual accounts, including the items in the half-year report;

(4)   it gives details of any qualification or modification likely to be made by the auditors in the annual accounts;

(5)   it includes any additional information necessary for shareholders and others to assess the accounts.

Where a company decides not to issue a preliminary announcement of results, consideration will need to be given how otherwise to address the DTR's requirement to notify the market of inside information as soon as possible.

Audited financial statements   **9.45.2**

Directors must ensure that audited financial statements are published as soon as possible after approval and, in any event, not more than four months from the end of the accounting period to which they relate (DTR 4.1). The required content of the audited financial statements is detailed in **CHAPTER 7** and directors should note that, as well as sending a copy to Companies House, a copy must be also be sent to the FSA's National Storage Mechanism within the required time period.

Interim report   **9.45.3**

In addition to audited annual accounts, directors of companies with listed securities will be responsible for arranging and overseeing preparation of an interim report (or 'half-yearly financial report') on the activities and profit or loss made by the company in the first six months of each financial year (DTR 4.2.2). In fulfilling this responsibility, directors must ensure that:

● accounting policies and procedures applied in preparing the interim report are consistent with those applied to the audited accounts;

● a copy of the interim report, including the auditors' report, is sent to an RIS as soon as possible after approval by the Board;

● the interim report is published as soon as possible, and in any event within two months of the end of the period to which it relates; and

- copies are sent (by post or electronic means) to the holders of listed securities or, alternatively, a copy is published in at least one national newspaper.

The interim report must contain a condensed set of financial statements (comprising a condensed balance sheet and profit and loss account, explanatory notes and a cash flow statement), an interim management report and responsibility statements (DTR 4.2.3). Comparative figures for the corresponding period in the previous accounting year must also be provided.

The interim management report must include details of any important events that have occurred in the period and their impact on the results and a statement of the principal risks and uncertainties for the remaining second half of the financial year (DTR 4.2.7).

The responsibility statements must contain the same information as required at the full year (see **CHAPTER 7**) but in relation to the half year and the next six months.

Finally, directors should be aware that whilst there is no requirement in the Listing Rules for the interim report to be audited, it is recommended by the Auditing Practices Board and, where it is audited, the review report of the auditors and any qualifications made by them must be reproduced in full in the interim report and be included in the notification made to the RIS (DTR 4.2.9).

Interim management statements ('IMS')   **9.45.4**

A listed company whose home state is in the UK must make a public statement (the IMS) by its management during the first six-month period of the financial year and a further statement by management in the second six months of the year (DTR 4.3.2). These public statements must be made between ten weeks after the beginning and six weeks before the end of the relevant six-month period to which they relate (DTR 4.3.3).

The IMS must include an explanation of any material events and transactions during the relevant period and the impact on the company and its undertakings as well as a general description of the financial position and performance during the period.

However, where a listed company produces quarterly financial reports it will be considered to have satisfied the requirements of DTR 4.3.2 and no separate IMS will be required.

Issue 14 of the UKLA's Publication List (now replaced by the Primary Market Bulletin) gave practical guidance for directors on what is required of the IMS, which in brief includes:

(1)   companies are to use their own judgment on what needs to be reported, the content and form of the IMS;

(2)   the IMS is not intended to be onerous to produce or to be generic in form;

(3)   information in trading statements may be sufficient to meet the requirement for an IMS but might require inclusion of additional information;

(4)   the nature, scale and complexity should be taken into account as, provided full narrative and explanation of events is given, it might negate the need for additional financial data.

Dividends   **9.45.5**

Any decision to make a distribution or pay a dividend on listed securities must be notified to the RIS as soon as possible after the Board has approved the payment. Notification must contain details of the net amount to be paid per share, payment date and record date where applicable and any foreign income dividend election, together with any income tax treated as paid at the lower rate and not repayable (LR 9.7A.2).

Disclosure of directors' details   **9.46**

When a new director is appointed, a premium listed company must notify an RIS of the following information as soon as possible and, in any event, within five business days of the decision to appoint the person (LR 9.6.13):

(a)   the names of all publicly quoted companies of which the person was a director or partner in the previous five years, indicating whether the directorships are current or past;

(b)   any unspent convictions for indictable offences;

(c)   any bankruptcies or involuntary arrangements of the director;

(d)   any liquidations, administrations, receiverships, company voluntary arrangements or compositions or arrangements with creditors of companies in which the director held an executive role for 12 months prior to such events;

(e)   any compulsory liquidations, administrations or partnership voluntary arrangements of any partnership where the director was a partner for 12 months prior to such events;

(f)   receiverships of any asset of such person or of a partnership where he was a partner at the time or 12 months prior to the receivership; and

(g)   public criticisms made about the director by any statutory or regulatory bodies.

If there is no such information to be disclosed, there must be a statement to that effect. Furthermore any change in the information sent to an RIS must be advised as soon as possible after the change has occurred and any additional directorships a director accepts for another publicly quoted company must be announced.

An announcement to the RIS is required where there has been any change to the Board whether by appointment, resignation, removal or assignment of a different role or executive function to a director. The announcement of change must be made as soon as possible and no later than the end of the next business day following the decision or receipt of notice about the change. For a new director, the announcement must include the information set out in (b)–(g) above as well as the date of appointment, whether the person was appointed as an executive or non-executive director and whether they were assigned any specific function or responsibility (LR 9.6.11).

It should also be noted that changes to the Board of Directors of a subsidiary of a listed company might also need to be notified and announced where they are considered price-sensitive for the listed company.

Dealing in securities   9.47

Details of share dealings in shares of the listed company by 'persons discharging managerial responsibility' (which would usually include directors and senior management) and their 'connected' persons need to be announced as soon as possible and by no later than the end of the business day after receipt of the notification from the director by the company (DTR 3.1.4).

Directors should be aware that they (and other persons considered PDMRs) are personally required by DTR 3.1.2 to provide the company with this information (and details of any grant of options) as soon as possible and in any event no later than the fourth business day after they become aware of the event and change of interest.

In addition, directors and PDMRs of premium listed companies must be aware of and observe restrictions imposed by the Model Code on dealing in their company's securities, which are far more limiting than those embodied in statute (**APPENDIX 22**).

Whilst a company may have its own share-dealing policy, in which case it must be observed, the Model Code sets a minimum standard which must be followed. Restrictions embodied in the Model Code have been devised to ensure that directors and other PDMRs, and those connected with them, do not conduct any transactions in securities of the company during periods when they have access, or are deemed to have access, to inside information. In addition, any employee who has access to inside information and is included on the company's 'insider list' (see para **9.42**) by virtue of his position in the company must adhere to the Model Code.

In brief, the principles of the Model Code are as follows:

- a director must not deal in securities of the company on considerations of a short-term nature (the definition of 'securities' in this respect has been extended to include unlisted securities which are convertible into listed securities);

- a director must not deal in securities of the listed company during a close period. The close period is the period of 60 days immediately prior to announcement of the company's preliminary statement of annual results (where made) or prior to announcement of the annual accounts. For interim statements the close period lasts from the end of the half year until the results are announced and, if the company reports on a quarterly basis, for 30 days before the announcement of such quarterly results. The exception to this is the formulaic grant of options to directors under an employee share option scheme where the grant of options could not reasonably be made at any other time and failure to make the grant would indicate the company is in a prohibited dealing period;

- a director must not deal in securities at any time when he is in possession of unpublished inside information. This is a prohibited period. This might be, for example, when discussions are under way about an acquisition or merger or significant contract, etc;

- a director must not deal in securities without seeking prior clearance from the chairman for the transaction to proceed and such clearance must not be given where the company is in a prohibited or close period or when there exists any matter which constitutes unpublished inside information.

Listed companies may impose more rigorous restrictions on share dealings by directors if they wish, and directors must check any such restrictions in the company's share dealing policy before dealing in the company's listed securities.

Prohibition on dealing in share options 9.50

Where a company's securities are quoted on the London Stock Exchange, directors should be aware that it is an offence for them to buy options to deal in listed shares or debentures, or those of any company in the same group, through the market. Where found guilty of an offence under this section, the director will be liable for a fine, imprisonment, or both.

This does not prohibit a director from buying a right to subscribe for shares or debentures directly from the company or from being included in a grant of options pursuant to an employee share scheme.

Where a contravention is deemed to have occurred, the Secretary of State for Trade and Industry has authority to appoint inspectors to investigate the matter (see para **6.130**).

Insider dealing 9.60

Insider dealing involves the use of restricted information about a company by a buyer or seller of its securities to gain an advantage (CJA 1993 and see para **6.133**).

An individual (who may be a director, employee or any other person) who is in possession of information not available to the public which would have a significant effect on the price of the company's listed securities is prohibited from dealing in the company's securities. Importantly, it was clarified by the ECJ in *Spector Photo Group NV v CBFA* [2010] All ER (D) 125 (Feb) that if a person is in possession of inside information about the company he commits an offence merely by dealing in the company's securities whether or not the inside information was the reason for dealing. This therefore clarifies that a person should not deal when in possession of inside information.

Where the individual fails to observe this prohibition, he is committing a criminal offence and, if found guilty, will be liable to a fine, imprisonment, or both (CJA 1993 s 61).

Directors, by virtue of their position, will have unrestricted access to the company's financial records and detailed information about the company's progress, plans and developments well before any information is released to the public and be involved in making decisions affecting the future of the company. It is therefore essential that they observe restrictions on dealing in securities when they alone are party to this information to ensure that there is no contravention of insider dealing regulations. They must also ensure that they observe the requirements contained in the Model Code, which are more restrictive than legislation (para **9.47** and **APPENDIX 22**).

Directors also have an obligation to advise others of their obligations and the restrictions placed upon them in respect of insider dealing and to implement suitable procedures to ensure no dealing occurs whilst in possession of inside information (see para **9.42**).

Directors need to implement a policy for information flow to ensure that inside information is kept confidential and disseminated in a timely manner, in accordance with requirements of the Listing Rules (para **9.42**). In practice, responsibility tends to be delegated and restricted to a few key executive directors who communicate with the UKLA, London Stock Exchange, brokers and analysts. By establishing a formal arrangement for control of inside information and communication directors are able to ensure that inside information is kept confidential until the moment they are ready to make an announcement, reducing opportunity for insider dealing and for any damage to negotiations or discussions that are taking place.

The FSMA 2000 gave the FSA (now FCA) power to investigate and prosecute cases of insider dealing and, since this time, a considerable number of criminal prosecution charges have been brought against individuals for insider dealing and it has confirmed that it will be making greater use of its criminal prosecution powers to tackle insider dealing.

In order to prosecute insider dealing cases on criminal grounds, the FCA must be able to demonstrate that there is sufficient evidence of wrongdoing, the insider dealing act or actions were intentional and it is in the public's interest to prosecute. Alternatively, prosecution on civil grounds might be considered, in which case demonstration of intent is not necessary and the actions could be accidental.

Fines imposed by the FCA, introduced by the Penalties Policy in March 2010, are now more closely linked to income and can now be up to:

- 20% of the company's revenue generated by the product or business area linked to the breach in the relevant period; and

- 40% of the individual's salary and benefits (including bonuses) from their job relating to the breach in non-market abuse cases.

This demonstrates the FCA's commitment to stamping out insider dealing by imposing harder hitting financial penalties on firms and individuals who ignore the law and it is expected this will lead to a significant increase in the level of fines.

There are many examples of fines, disqualifications and prison sentences for insider dealing set out on the FCA website and in the wider press, a few of which are set out below by way of illustration.

- On 22 July 2014 Ian Hannan was fined £450,000 for engaging in two instances of market abuse by disclosing insider information in September and October 2008.

- On 7 March 2013 Paul Milsom, a senior equities trader, was sentenced to two years' imprisonment for disclosing inside information relating to forthcoming transactions over a prolonged period between October 2008 and March 2010. A confiscation order was also made in the sum of £245,000.

- On 10 March 2013 Richard Joseph, a former futures trader, was found guilty of six counts of conspiracy to deal as an insider between September 2007 and July 2008 and sentenced to four years' imprisonment on each count (to run concurrently). Mr Joseph had confidential and price-sensitive information about takeover bids for two investment banks which he attempted to pass secretly to another individual in exchange for payment.

- In February 2010 the FSA levelled its largest ever fine of almost £1m against the CEO of Genel Enerji for dealing in the shares of its joint venture partner, UK listed Heritage Oil Plc, on the basis of inside information.

- On 20 June 2012 Southwark Crown Court sentenced two directors of Blue Index and the wife of one director for insider dealing contrary to CJA 1993 s 52 in one of the biggest cases ever pursued by the FSA. Mr Sanders was sentenced to four years in custody and disqualified as a director for five years whilst his wife and his fellow director, Mr Swallow, were sentenced to ten months in custody. Confiscation and costs orders were to be dealt with at a later date. The case involved obtaining inside information about a number of mergers and acquisitions in listed US securities over an 18-month period. This information was used by the defendants themselves and to encourage clients of Blue Index to trade, generating approximately £1.9m profit for them and £10.2m for clients.

There are many other examples on the FCA's website and reported in the press.

Market abuse   **9.70**

Part VIII of FSMA 2000 (amended by the Financial Services and Markets
Act 2000 (Market Abuse) Regulations 2014 (SI 2014/3081)) contains
provisions prescribing 'market abuse', involving use of inside information and
manipulation of markets, as an offence (s 118). To protect the UK's prescribed
financial markets it also gives the FCA a broad range of enforcement powers
including the power to impose unlimited financial penalties or public censures
for breaches of the Listing Rules (s 123(1)). In its March 2010 Penalties Policy,
the FCA stated that a minimum fine of £100,000 would be made where
individuals were involved in serious market abuse cases.

The market abuse regime is intended to complement and not replace
existing criminal laws dealing with misconduct in financial markets, which
carry very severe penalties against someone found guilty. However, market
abuse has a much wider application than existing criminal law and applies
to anyone who participates in or whose conduct may affect the UK's
financial markets. For example, in circumstances where certain behaviour
might not constitute a criminal offence under CJA 1993, the FCA can still
seek to impose an unlimited financial penalty where it can be proven that
the behaviour constitutes market abuse. FSMA 2000 s 118 (as amended by
the Financial Services and Markets Act 2000 (Market Abuse) Regulations
2005 (SI 2005/381)) sets out seven broad types of behaviour that amount to
market abuse, namely:

(1) *Insider dealing.* Dealing on the basis of inside information (see para **9.60**).

(2) *Improper disclosure.* Where an insider discloses insider information to
     another person otherwise than in the normal course of employment,
     profession or duties.

(3) *Misuse of information.* This is use of information which is not generally
     available but which would be relevant to an investor's dealings in a
     particular investment and which is normally disclosed to the market. This
     offence is similar to the existing criminal offence of insider dealing and
     may, for example, include acting on information from a colleague about
     a possible takeover of a company when such information is generally not
     available in the public domain.

(4) *Manipulating transactions.* Effecting transactions or giving orders to trade to
     give a misleading impression of supply and demand to artificially inflate
     (or deflate) prices.

(5) *Manipulating devices.* Effecting transactions or orders to trade using
     fictitious devices or other form of deception.

(6)   *Creating a false or misleading impression.* This is behaviour likely to give a false or misleading impression as to the supply or demand, price or value of an investment. For example, by posting misleading information on internet bulletin boards and chat sites.

(7)   *Misleading behaviour and distortion.* This offence interferes with the normal process of supply and demand and therefore manipulates the market price of an investment. For example, where a person buys a large amount of a particular share near the end of the day with the purpose of artificially inflating the share price.

The FCA has produced a Code of Market Conduct which contains guidance on behaviour that may or may not amount to market abuse. It is important that this is read and understood by the directors so they can communicate key points within their companies as anyone who participates in, or whose conduct may have an effect on, the UK financial markets whether or not they intended to cause the abuse or whether they carried it out themselves or encouraged others to do so is subject to restrictions.

Directors should be aware that the FCA can take action against any market participant who abuses the market by, for example, misusing information and insider dealing, creating false and misleading impressions through artificial transactions and information released and who intentionally distorts the market. Such action may include investigation, a hearing, imposition of a civil fine with no upper limit specified, the ability to make a public statement and therefore 'name and shame', application for an injunction to prevent continued market abuse, requiring the person to give up profits made or losses avoided by the abuse or requiring the payment of compensation to victims. Some examples of FCA fines are set out in para **5.42**, and the FCA has also set up a market abuse hotline to encourage notifications of concerns by the public, which the FCA will then investigate.

The FCA has taken action against and imposed many fines when engagement in market abuse has been discovered and there are many examples on the FCA's website. By way of illustration, fines imposed by the FCA include the following:

●   On 28 January 2013 the Upper Tribunal (Tax and Chancery Chamber) confirmed the decision by the FSA (now FCA) on 31 August 2011 to fine Swift Trade Inc £8m for market abuse as a result of extensive manipulative trading which caused a succession of small price movements in securities and artificially raised their price.

●   13 March 2012 – the Head of European Credit Sales at Credit Suisse was fined £210,000 for improper market conduct.

- 9 November 2011 – a Dubai-based private investor, Mr Goenka, was fined $9,621,240 for manipulating the closing price of Reliance Industries' securities by carefully planning and timing a series of trades.

Consequently it is very important for directors to ensure there is no opportunity for market abuse to occur by persons within, advising or representing the company and that appropriate procedures and controls are in place addressing the requirements of the Code of Market Conduct to prevent and detect such abuse at the earliest opportunity.

10 Directors and corporate governance

10 Directors and corporate governance

Corporate governance is defined as 'the system by which companies are directed and controlled' and it forms a key and fundamental part of a director's role in managing a company. Whilst directors are, essentially, free to determine what policies, procedures, strategies, directions and controls are needed and appropriate for their own companies and how they are implemented, the requirements for listed companies are a little more prescriptive as explained below. High standards of corporate governance are desirable as it is widely recognised that they help to underpin, although obviously cannot guarantee, a company's long-term performance.

From a simplistic perspective, it seems obvious that a company has more chance of success if the directors have carefully thought through:

- what the company is trying to achieve and what needs to be done to get there – achieved through strategic planning, filtering down to detailed plans for particular parts of the business, for example human resources, marketing, research and development plans, etc.

- what risks might prevent a company achieving its strategic objectives and how can they be monitored, controlled, avoided or mitigated – achieved by thorough and wide-ranging assessments of possible risk and implementation of risk management systems.

- what review and internal control processes are necessary to ensure everything stays on track and, if not, identify when and what corrective action or measures are needed before damage is suffered to such an extent that it might prevent the company achieving its strategic objectives.

On this simplistic level, corporate governance does not appear complicated and is all about planning; anticipating opportunities and problems; having review and control processes in place; and determining whether performance is on track or whether mitigating or corrective action is needed. However, complexity is introduced given the vast number of factors that impact on a company's performance and how these can be captured by the corporate governance process.

In determining the appropriate corporate governance framework for their organisation, the directors must pay attention to the detail of how direction and control measures flow down through their companies and how reports are

321

generated, reviewed and flow up through the reporting framework. There has been considerable criticism of standards of corporate governance demonstrated by many large companies recently and one thing that is becoming increasingly evident is that the merest 'chink' somewhere in a company's corporate governance framework (where one small, but potentially significant, aspect is not being adequately monitored or checked) can have a disastrous effect. Take the Deepwater Horizon oil spill incident in the Gulf of Mexico and the damage to BP, not only in terms of cost, but also to the company's reputation (see **CHAPTER 12**). Many of the required protocols and assessment processes were in place at BP but, for a variety of reasons, they were not observed and the warning signs did not show up and were ignored until it was too late to avert the disaster. This represents a failure and breakdown in BP's systems of corporate governance and, sadly, BP are not alone as there are many other examples.

When determining what corporate governance measures are required and appropriate, all directors need to give consideration to legislative requirements and regulations, approved codes of practice and recommended industry best practice, and be able to respond to current experience and developments in their sector and the economy as a whole to ensure the company's measures and controls remain appropriate for them to manage the company effectively over time and not just at one historic point.

Directors of listed companies also need to take into account the requirements of the Disclosure and Transparency Rules, Listing Rules (covered in **CHAPTER 9**) and the UK Corporate Governance Code. The latter sets out recommendations for good practice which, as explained below, the directors of companies with a primary listing of securities must either ensure the company adopts and follows or be prepared to explain areas of deviation in the company's annual report. Decisions will also need to be made about matters such as composition of the Board and how to facilitate good quality decision-making; the company's principle risks and what identification, review and control measures are needed to avoid or mitigate the consequences; information and reporting requirements; and how to delegate authority and responsibility whilst ensuring accountability is retained.

Corporate governance recommendations and reviews   10.10

Quite rightly, corporate governance is a Board priority as directors are increasingly required to demonstrate and report to those with an interest in the company about the procedures, systems and controls they have put in place to achieve results, improve accountability and prevent malpractice or fraud. Clearly such prevention is difficult to achieve as, despite the numerous corporate governance reviews and refinements to the best-practice requirements described below, incidents of corporate malpractice and fraud continue to arise. Indeed the Walker Review was commissioned in 2009 to independently review governance of the UK's banks and other financial institutions following the near collapse of the banking industry, which was widely attributed to governance failings and excessive risk-taking. This was followed by reports of widespread phone-hacking at News Corporation and the' manipulation of the inter-bank lending rate by a number of well-known high street banks.

Summary of report recommendations   **10.11**

Over the years various recommendations have been made in reports, including the Cadbury Report, the Greenbury Report, the Hampel Report, the Turnbull Guidance, the Higgs Review, the Smith Report, the Walker Report and various FRC reviews, in an attempt to determine the best way for companies to be structured to achieve high standards of corporate governance and improve the way they are directed and controlled. Whilst the recommendations of these reviews are of particular relevance to listed companies, they may be applicable and should be considered by directors of all types of companies, listed or not.

The reviews and reports are summarised below, starting with the oldest and running through to the most recent:

Corporate governance report	Key recommendations in report
Cadbury Report	• Appointment of non-executive directors.
	• Appointment of an audit committee to achieve greater control of financial reporting.
	• Improving management of the Board.
Greenbury Report	• Appointment of a remuneration committee to determine directors' remuneration and other pay issues.
	• Appointment of a nomination committee responsible for appointments to the Board.
Hampel Report	• Consolidated recommendations of earlier reports into one combined code (now the UK Corporate Governance Code)
	• Improve communication with shareholders.

Corporate governance report	Key recommendations in report
	• Redress the balance between implementing controls and achieving business success by allowing companies discretion to apply corporate governance principles in the manner most suited to their organisation, and to explain deviations from best practice to shareholders through their annual accounts.
Turnbull Guidance (frc.org.uk) (review in 2004)	• Made directors, rather than operational managers, responsible for risk management and maintaining and reviewing a sound system of internal controls.
	• Adopting a risk-based approach to the internal control process.
	• Embedding controls in the company's operations, with procedures for identifying and reporting control weaknesses so that appropriate remedial action can be taken.
	• Contained guidance for directors on how to comply with the UK Corporate Governance Code's requirements to maintain a sound system of internal control, review effectiveness of the system and report to shareholders on the wider aspects of internal control.
Higgs Review (now replaced by the *FRC's Guidance on Board Effectiveness*)	• At least half of the directors on the Board, excluding the chairman, should be non-executive directors.
	• A non-executive director should normally serve only two three-year terms, with annual re-election after nine years.
	• A time commitment should be set for non-executive directors.
	• Non-executive directors should meet as a group at least once a year.
	• After ten years in office, a non-executive director ceases to be independent.
	• A full-time executive director should not take on more than one non-executive directorship.

Corporate governance report	Key recommendations in report
	• A senior independent director should be identified and available to communicate with shareholders.
	• No one non-executive director should sit on the audit, nomination and remuneration committees.
	• There should be a formal recruitment, retirement and executive development programme.
The Smith Report	• The audit committee should have at least three members, all independent non-executive directors.
	• At least one member of the audit committee should have significant, relevant and recent financial experience.
	• The role and responsibilities of the committee should be set out in written terms of reference, containing at least the requirements of the Combined Code (as amended).
	• The committee should be provided with sufficient resources to undertake its duties.
	• The chairman of the audit committee should attend and be available to answer questions at the AGM.
	• The committee should make recommendations to the Board concerning the external auditors' appointment, and monitor and review their independence.
Walker Review (financial sector focus, but many recommendations embodied in UK Corporate Governance Code)	• Improve and personalise director induction, training, development and awareness of business issues.
	• Provide dedicated support to non-executive directors and increase their time commitment.

Corporate governance report	Key recommendations in report
	• Strengthen the role of the chairman, clarify his time commitment and require his annual re-election.
	• Require externally facilitated performance evaluation every three years.
	• Require creation of a separate Board risk committee, chaired by an independent non-executive director, and appointment of a chief risk officer reporting to the Board.
	• Disclosure of remuneration of employees earning over £1m in the remuneration report.
	• At least half of expected variable remuneration should be on a long-term incentive basis with vesting deferred for up to five years and the ability to claw back awards in the event of irregularities.
	• Require the re-election of the remuneration committee chairman the following year if the remuneration report fails to secure 75% support from shareholders.

The UK Corporate Governance Code   10.12

The UK Corporate Governance Code ('the Code') sets out recommendations for how to achieve good or, indeed, best practice in relation to corporate governance. The Code comprises main principles, supporting principles and provisions relating to the governance of companies with premium listings of equity shares, and it is divided into sections covering leadership, effectiveness and accountability of the Board and its committees, remuneration and relations with shareholders. As explained in para **10.15.1**, companies with a premium listing of equity shares are required by the Listing Rules to either comply with the principles and provisions of the Code or to explain why they have not done so in the company's annual report and accounts. The Code is available from the FRC's website (www.frc.org.uk) and the requirements in relation to shareholders and institutional investors are addressed in more detail in the Stewardship Code (para **10.50**). The Code is the responsibility of the Financial Reporting Council ('FRC') which regulates and has responsibility for promoting high-quality corporate governance and reporting by UK listed companies, thereby encouraging investment. The Code has been updated on a number of occasions since it was first issued and, at present, the September 2014 version is in force. This version of the Code applies to financial years beginning on or after 1 October 2014.

Key amendments in the 2014 Code include:

- emphasis on the importance of embedding a governance culture within the organisation to drive behaviour, promote accountability and achieve high standards of governance. Amendments to the Preface of the 2014 Code emphasise that, to achieve this, companies need to demonstrate they have the right 'tone from the top' and Boards need to lead by example, thereby instilling high standards of governance throughout their companies as a matter of routine;

- a requirement for large corporates to focus on long-term sustainability and the position of the company. Indeed, the CEO of the FRC suggested that the recent changes are 'designed to strengthen the focus of companies and investors in the longer term and the sustainability of value creation';

- the requirement to assess the company's going-concern status for a period significantly longer than 12 months, although there is no suggestions that this should necessarily give rise to an extension of the going concern statement in the annual accounts;

- an increase in risk reporting by requiring companies to robustly assess principal risks and their impact on the long-term viability of the business and to confirm this in the annual report, with details of how they are being managed or mitigated;

- the need for executive remuneration to deliver long-term benefit to the company, for greater transparency around performance-related elements of pay, retention of minimum shareholdings, longer vesting periods and more substantial remuneration clawback provisions where directors underperform; and

- the need to announce the actions the board intends to take to understand the reasons behind a significant vote against a resolution put to the shareholders.

An observation made by the FRC when reviewing the Code in the wake of the global financial crisis (and in recommendations from the Walker Review) was that too much emphasis was placed on the letter of the Code rather than spirit. This was a concern as ticking the boxes and following the Code to the letter does not guarantee good governance: what is appropriate depends on the company's own circumstances.

A second observation at that time was that there was still significant room for improvement in relations, engagement and interaction between companies and their shareholders which are considered necessary in the interests of good governance. The FRC has sought to address this in revisions to the Code by placing greater emphasis on behaviours, roles, relationships and accountability of directors and their Boards, particularly on the role and importance of the chairman in achieving high standards of governance and an effective Board. The chairman is specifically responsible for many areas of compliance with the Code and is encouraged to report on how the principles relating to leadership and effectiveness have been applied in the annual report. It is hoped this will discourage 'boiler plate' disclosures and a box-ticking attitude to governance as this is of no benefit. Furthermore the chairman is responsible for ensuring there is communication and interaction with shareholders which, together with responsibilities now placed on investors to engage by the Stewardship Code, it is hoped will lead to a substantial improvement in shareholder engagement.

In addition the FRC has also issued 'Guidance on Board Effectiveness', 'Guidance on Audit Committees' and 'Guidance on Risk Management, Internal Control and Related Financial and Business Reporting' to assist companies and their Boards apply and implement the principles of the Code. These are available on the FRC's website (www.frc.org.uk) and are recommended reading.

The Walker Review   10.13

In February 2009 Sir David Walker was commissioned by the Government to conduct an independent review of the governance of the UK's banks and other financial institutions ('BOFI's) in light of the near collapse of the banking industry which, as widely reported, has been attributed to governance failings allowing excessive risk-taking. Whilst the review was specific to and focused on the financial sector, many of the best practice recommendations are relevant and applicable to companies with a primary listing of their securities and they have been included in the June 2010 Code. The full text of the final report can be found on the HM Treasury website (www.gov.uk/government/organisations/hm-treasury).

The Walker Review supports the 'comply or explain' approach and does not endorse further legislation, favouring instead behavioural change and improvement through better identification of best practice and encouraging a sense of ownership.

The main aim of the review was to determine how to minimise risky behaviour and improve how companies and shareholders communicate and interact.

Thirty-nine recommendations were made which fall under the following five main headings:

(1) Board size, composition and qualification;

(2) functioning of the Board and performance evaluation;

(3)   shareholders' engagement and communication (Stewardship Code);

(4)   governance of risk;

(5)   remuneration.

The most notable points in the review include:

(i)   provision of induction, training and development of directors;

(ii)   an increase in the non-executive directors' time commitment to their role to between 30–36 days per year;

(iii)   the need for the chairman to devote two-thirds of his time to the role and be subject to annual re-election;

(iv)   tougher selection criteria for non-executive directors, including an interview, as part of the FSA's authorisation process and a relaxation of the nine-year rule governing determination of independence;

(v)   institutional investors should sign up to a Stewardship Code, based on the Code on the Responsibilities of Institutional Investors prepared by the Institutional Investors Committee, overseen and monitored by the FRC;

(vi)   requirement for a separate risk committee, separate from the audit committee and chaired by an independent non-executive director;

(vii)   appointment of a chief risk officer to report directly to the Board;

(viii)   disclosure, by numbers within bands, of the remuneration of employees earning over £1m in the remuneration report;

(ix)   at least half of expected variable remuneration should be on a long-term incentive basis with vesting deferred for up to five years and the ability to claw back awards in the event of irregularities;

(x)   the chairman of the remuneration committee to stand for re-election the following year if the remuneration report is approved by less than 75% of votes cast.

Many of the recommendations from the Walker Review are embodied in the Code as they are relevant for the Boards of non-financial companies with a premium listing of equity securities.

Turnbull Guidance (for accounting years beginning before 1 October 2014)   **10.14**

First issued in September 1999, the Turnbull Guidance provides guidance to directors on the internal control requirements of the Code as it was considered there was a lack of clarity about what a Board needs to do to maintain a sound system of internal control, review effectiveness of the system and report to shareholders on the wider aspects of internal control. The Turnbull Guidance was reviewed in 2004 and found to be still fit for purpose and in need of little change. This was broadly the same conclusion drawn from a series of meetings orchestrated by the FRC in 2011, although some changes were considered necessary to reflect changes to the role of the Board set out in the June 2010 version of the Code. Further consultation has concluded that the Turnbull Guidance should be replaced by the FRC's Guidance on Risk Management, Internal Control and Related Financial and Business Reporting ('Risk Guidance') for financial years beginning on or after 1 October 2014.

The Turnbull Guidance established that responsibility for review of internal controls should be that of the directors, who could no longer leave risk management to the operation's managers.

In brief, the Turnbull Guidance set out the principle characteristics of a sound system of internal control and how effective review of such system can be achieved, as follows:

- responsibility for review of risk management procedures and internal controls should be that of the directors, although the audit committee may review financial controls and provide a focal point for wider control issues;

- internal control should take a risk-based approach. This involves conducting an assessment of risks the company faces, determining what control activities are required to avoid or reduce the impact of those risks and ensuring that appropriate and timely information is communicated to directors to enable them to monitor performance and respond rapidly where change is required;

- to be successful internal control needs to be embedded in the company's operations and, to ensure the system is not just left to run on its own, managers are required to report on specific areas assigned to them. This will ensure that emerging risks or changes to existing risks are identified and reported at the earliest opportunity;

- procedures and the frequency of reporting required should be communicated and agreed allowing for major control weaknesses to be reported immediately and, where significant, direct to management.

The aim of Turnbull's internal control system was to identify, avoid, manage or mitigate the risks to which the company is exposed, thereby safeguarding the company's assets and enhancing shareholder investment over time. Turnbull requires a company's directors to assess the internal and external risks to the company using a very broad approach, extending far beyond those which are purely financial. Whilst risk management and corporate governance were considered by many companies as separate issues, Turnbull recognised the importance of risk management within the corporate governance framework and how it is intrinsically linked with internal control.

However, the Turnbull Guidance purposely did not prescribe any best system for risk management and internal control in recognition that, in reality, what is appropriate depends to a large extent on a particular company's culture, objectives and business environment, etc., and no one system is suitable for all companies.

In addition, by not providing a model for companies to adopt and follow, the guidance encourages active consideration of internal control and risk management by the Board rather than a box ticking exercise to meet regulatory requirements, which is to be discouraged.

Corporate governance disclosures and compliance   **10.15**

Whilst adoption of the recommendations arising from the many corporate governance reviews and reports summarised in para **10.11** are essentially voluntary and the directors may exercise discretion as to the manner and extent to which they are implemented, many of the best-practice provisions have been adopted by the UKLA and incorporated into the Listing Rules. The consequence of this is that directors of companies with a premium listing of equity securities must ensure the recommendations are adopted or, in so far as they are not, be able to explain and justify the company's departure from what is considered best practice.

However, pressure from investor institutions and the need to maintain good shareholder relations have reinforced the need for directors of such companies to comply with the principles and provisions embodied in the Code as the likes of IVIS, PIRC and the ABI will expect compliance and, in many instances, have also issued their own standards and requirements for corporate governance which also have to be considered.

Whilst the directors of a company might give what they consider is an adequate explanation of a justified area of non-compliance with a Code provision or a requirement of PIRC or the ABI, their justification is not always considered sufficient and frustration and difficulties can occur where investors or the shareholder voting bodies do not share the directors' view. In these instances it is not uncommon to see a PIRC or the ABI make an 'abstain' or 'no' voting recommendation. Listed companies are keen to avoid this situation as many shareholders will simply follow such recommendation without looking at the company's explanation, jeopardising the success of a resolution. Indeed during the 2012 and 2013 AGM voting seasons there were numerous examples of shareholders voting against resolutions, most commonly those concerning directors' remuneration and the remuneration report.

It is therefore very important that the Board recognises the importance of explaining deviations from the Code. Such explanations need to be specific, clear, easy to understand, meaningful and convincing, avoiding standard 'boiler plate' disclosures which are not sufficient. Indeed, the publication by the FRC of a report of discussions between companies and investors on 'What Constitutes an Explanation under Comply or Explain' in February 2012 supports this and also makes clear the benefit of giving sufficient information and setting the context and historic background for the deviation; explaining the rationale for action taken; and describing what other mitigating actions are in place and why these are more suitable for the company. A case was also made for giving more explanation generally about the company's whole corporate governance framework and how it supports the business model, so shareholders have a better understanding of the need for deviations and how they fit into the company's overall corporate governance approach. These recommendations for better and specific explanations have, to an extent, been included in revisions to the Code.

Notwithstanding that the Code does not apply to all companies, the directors of many unlisted private and public companies choose to comply with the principles and provisions of the Code and to disclose the information required by the Code in their report and accounts on a purely voluntary basis. They do this where they consider the Code is applicable to their company and that it will help them to achieve and demonstrate high standards of governance.

Alternatively, the directors of smaller listed companies might seek to observe the 'Corporate Governance Guidelines for Smaller Quoted Companies' published by the Quoted Companies Alliance where they feel these are more appropriate to their company's own circumstances and requirements. Similarly, the directors of unlisted companies might observe the Institute of Directors' 'Corporate Governance Guidance and Principles for Unlisted Companies in the UK'. In any event these should be consulted as they represent a good starting point from which the directors can then develop their own thinking and determine appropriate corporate governance arrangements for their own organisations.

The disclosures specifically relating to corporate governance issues which the directors must ensure are made by the listed company can broadly be divided into disclosures connected with the:

- Listing Rules;
- Disclosure and Transparency Rules;

- the Code (statements of appliance and compliance with the principles); and

- Turnbull Report.(for accounting years commencing prior to 1 October 2014) and thereafter those contained in FRC's Guidance on Risk Management, Internal Control and Related Financial and Business Reporting ('Risk Guidance').

These are set out in Schedule B to the Code. There is some overlap between them which is highlighted below but it is important to note that whilst the Listing Rule disclosure requirements apply only to companies with a premium listing of equity securities, the Disclosure and Transparency Rule requirements apply where a company's securities have been admitted to trading on a regulated market which includes those with a standard listing.

The disclosures needed in the annual report and accounts, as identified below, can either be made in a separate stand alone 'corporate governance statement' or be included in the directors' report to the accounts.

Listing Rule disclosures   **10.15.1**

LR 9.8.6 requires the following information to be included in the reports and accounts of a company that has a premium listing of equity securities:

- a narrative statement of how the company has applied the main principles set out in the Code together with sufficient explanation to allow shareholders to evaluate how the principles have been applied; and

- a statement as to whether or not the company complied with the Code provisions throughout the whole accounting period and, where the company failed to comply with any of the provisions for part or the whole of the period, identify those provisions and give reasons for non-compliance.

No guidance is given on the form and content of the disclosures required in the 'comply or explain' statement, as it is not intended to be a standard or bland statement that can be applied to any company. The directors are responsible for formulating this statement once they have carried out a review of matters arising from the Code and it may either be made in a separate 'corporate governance statement or the directors' report (see para **7.13.4**). As set out in para **10.12** above any deviations from the Code must be very clearly explained with clear identification of the rationale for non-compliance and a description of relevant mitigating actions.

The directors must ensure that the review process, carried out at least once a year, is thorough in its findings as the corporate governance statement must be reviewed by the auditors and the auditor's report on the statement be included in the accounts.

The need for directors' responsibility, going concern and remuneration policy statements is dealt with in **CHAPTERS** **7** and **9**.

Disclosure and Transparency Rule disclosures 10.15.2

The disclosures required under the Disclosure and Transparency Rules ('DTRs') primarily concern financial reporting, internal control and risk management processes and the need for a 'comply or explain' corporate governance statement (DTRs 7.1 and 7.2 respectively).

Whilst DTR 7.2.2R specifically requires a corporate governance statement identifying the relevant corporate governance code for the company and explaining any areas of non-compliance, DTR 7.2.4G recognises that this requirement is met where the 'comply or explain' statements required by Listing Rule 9.3.6R have been included (see para **10.15.1**). This removes the need for any unnecessary duplication of information. The corporate governance statement required by DTR 7.2.2R may also be disclosed on the company's website, in which case this must be explained and a cross-reference be given in the accounts.

DTR 7.2.5R to DTR 7.2.10R require that the corporate governance statement contains:

- a description of the main features of the company's internal control and risk management systems relevant to the financial reporting;

- information, where necessary, required by Schedule 7 to the Large and Medium-Sized Companies and Groups (Accounts and Reports) Regulations 2008 (SI 2008/410), paras 13(2)(c), (d), (f), (h) and (i); and

- a description of the company's administrative, management and supervisory bodies and their committees including information about composition and how they operate.

However, these disclosure requirements are deemed satisfied where the company makes the relevant disclosures required by the UK Corporate Governance Code (see para **10.15.1**).

In addition DTR 7.1.5R requires disclosure of information about the body, usually the audit committee, responsible for monitoring the financial reporting process, effectiveness of internal control and risk management systems, the statutory audit and independence of the auditor. This must include details of the committee's composition and the FRC's Guidance on Audit Committees suggests further information that it could be beneficial to disclose.

Additional Code disclosures **10.15.3**

As well as the need to include a statement confirming whether the company has complied with the main principles of the Code (para **10.15.1**), the Code also lists a number of specific disclosures required in the annual report, including:

- a statement of how the Board operates, including a high level statement of what matters are reserved for decision by the Board and those delegated to management (A.1.1);

- the names of the chairman, the deputy chairman (if applicable), the chief executive, the senior independent director and the chairmen and members of the Board committees (A.1.2);

- the number of meetings of the Board and those committees and individual attendance by directors (A.1.2);

- explanation where a chief executive is appointed chairman (in the annual report following the appointment only) (A.3.1);

- the names and explanation of those non-executive directors determined independent by the Board (B.1.1);

- a separate section describing work undertaken by the nomination committee, including the process used for Board appointments and an explanation if neither external search consultant nor open advertising has been used for appointment of a chairman or a non-executive director. This section should now also include a description of the Board's policy on diversity, including gender, identify measurable objectives and progress made to achieving them (B.2.4);

- any changes to the other significant commitments of the chairman during the year (B.3.1);

- a statement of how performance evaluation of the Board, its committees and its directors has been carried out (B.6.1);

- identify the external facilitator of Board evaluation where applicable and disclose whether they have any other connection with the company (B.6.2);

- an explanation from the directors of their responsibility for preparing the accounts and a statement that they consider that the annual report and accounts, taken as a whole, is fair, balanced and understandable and provides the information necessary for shareholders to assess the company's position and performance, business model and strategy. There should also be a statement by the auditors about their reporting responsibilities (C.1.1);

- an explanation from the directors of the basis on which the company generates or preserves value over the longer term (the business model) and the strategy for delivering the objectives of the company (C.1.2);

- a statement from the directors that the business is a going concern, with supporting assumptions or qualifications as necessary, together with a statement that they consider it appropriate to adopt the going concern basis of accounting in preparing the accounts and identification of any material uncertainties to the company's ability to continue as a going concern for a period of at least 12 months from the date of approval of the financial statements (C.1.3);

- a report confirming that the Board has conducted a robust assessment of the principal risks facing the company, including those that would threaten its business model, future performance, solvency or liquidity, describing the risks and explaining how they are being managed or mitigated (C.2.1);

- explanation from the directors about how they have assessed the prospects of the company, over what period and why they consider that period appropriate and a statement from them whether they reasonably expect the company to continue in operation and meet its liabilities as they fall due over the period of their assessment, drawing attention to any qualifications or assumptions as necessary (C.2.2);

- a report confirming that the Board has conducted a review of the effectiveness of the company's risk management and internal controls systems, covering all material controls, including financial, operational and compliance controls (C.2.3);

- where there is no internal audit function, the reasons for the absence of such a function (C.3.6);

- where the Board does not accept the audit committee's recommendation on the appointment, reappointment or removal of an external auditor, a statement from the audit committee explaining the recommendation and the reasons why the Board has taken a different position (C.3.7);

- a separate section describing the work of the audit committee in discharging its responsibilities, including: the significant issues that it considered in relation to the financial statements, and how these issues were addressed; an explanation of how it has assessed the effectiveness of the external audit process and the approach taken to the appointment or reappointment of the external auditor, including the length of tenure of the current audit firm and when a tender was last conducted; and, if the external auditor provides non-audit services, an explanation of how auditor objectivity and independence is safeguarded (C.3.8);

- a description of the work of the remuneration committee as required under the Large and Medium-Sized Companies and Groups (Accounts and Reports) Regulations 2008 including, where an executive director serves as a non-executive director elsewhere, whether or not the director will retain such earnings and, if so, what the remuneration is (D.1.2);

- where remuneration consultants are appointed, they should be identified in the annual report and a statement be made as to whether they have any other connection with the company (D.2.1); and

- the steps the Board has taken to ensure the members of the Board, in particular the non-executive directors, develop an understanding of the views of the major shareholders about their company (E.1.2).

The annual report and accounts are usually sent to the company's members at the same time that notice of the AGM is issued, in which there will be resolutions to approve the reappointment of directors offering themselves for re-election at the AGM. Where this is the case, the Code requires such resolutions to be accompanied by:

- sufficient biographical details to enable shareholders to make an informed decision about the resolution (B.7.1);

- why the individual should be elected to a non-executive role (B.7.2); and

- for a non-executive director, confirmation from the chairman that having formally reviewed the individual's performance he or she continues to be effective, is committed to the role and is suitable for re-election (B.7.2).

The Code also requires that the following information is 'made available', which will usually be done by placing the information on a website that is maintained by or on behalf of the company:

- the terms of reference of the nomination, audit and remuneration committees, explaining their role and the authority delegated to them by the Board (B.2.1, C.3.3 and D.2.1); and

- the terms and conditions of appointment of non-executive directors (B.3.2).

Turnbull disclosures (for accounting years beginning before 1 October 2014)   **10.15.4**

Principle C.2.1 of the 2012 Code requires the Board for accounting years beginning before 1 October 2014 to review effectiveness of the company's risk management and internal control systems at least once a year and to report to shareholders that they have done so. The review should cover all material controls, including financial, operational and compliance controls. The Turnbull

Guidance builds on the requirements of the Code and disclosures made in the accounts must give meaningful and high-level information without creating any misleading impressions. The disclosures made by the directors must include explanation of:

(a)   the ongoing process for evaluating and managing the company's key risks and regular review by the Board;

(b)   how effectiveness of the internal control system has been reviewed, the role played by the audit committee, internal audit function, managers and others suitably placed;

(c)   whether any material losses were suffered and what remedial action or contingency plans were put into effect; or

(d)   where the directors are not able to make the disclosures in (a), (b) or (c) above, then explanation of why no such system has been implemented must be given.

As can be seen in para **10.22**, risk management and internal controls have been under considerable scrutiny given the 'credit crunch' and banking failures, which some have criticised as having arisen because of the opaque nature of risks and the very complex and split manner in which risks from often complicated derivative products were reported. The reporting of risks needs to be meaningful so that true interpretation of total risk can be drawn from information provided to the Board.

Indeed, the Walker Review has specifically addressed the governance of risks and, as set out in para **10.13**, specifically recommends that a separate Board risk committee is established, a chief risk officer is appointed to report to the Board and there should be a separate Board risk committee report in the company's annual report and accounts. Whilst the Walker Review is only of direct relevance for banking companies and financial institutions, some organisations (such as the ICAEW Foundation) believe the Code's provisions on risk are relevant and should be considered by other companies. The directors of companies outside the scope of the Walker Review may, therefore, find their companies' standards of governance are improved by drawing on some of the Walker Review's recommendations.

Risk disclosures (for accounting years beginning on or after 1 October 2014)   **10.15.5**

With effect from 1 October 2014 new and amended provisions comprised in C.2.1 to C.2.3. (inclusive) of the Code expand the risk disclosure requirements and require the board to robustly assess the company's principal risks and confirm this to shareholders in the annual report, together with a description of how such risks are being managed or mitigated and the Board's reasonable expectation of the company's continued viability.

For accounting years beginning on or after 1 October 2014, disclosures set out in the FRC's 'Guidance on Risk Management, Internal Control and Related Financial and Business Reporting' ('Risk Guidance') must be observed.

The assessment and processes set out in the Risk Guidance should be used to inform a number of distinct but related disclosures required in the annual report and accounts, namely reporting:

- the principal risks facing the company and how they are managed or mitigated;

- whether the directors have a reasonable expectation that the company will be able to continue in operation and meet its liabilities as they fall due;

- on the going concern basis of accounting; and

- on the review of the risk management and internal control system and the main features of the company's risk management and internal control system in relation to the financial reporting process.

Key corporate governance components   10.20

As mentioned in the beginning paragraphs of this chapter, the company's directors need to decide what policies, procedures, strategies, directions and controls are needed and appropriate to control and direct their own company. As a consequence, the corporate governance measures implemented will vary from company to company, although there are some key components relevant to all companies which are briefly set out below.

Effective Board   10.21

There has been considerable debate and discussion over the years about the characteristics of an effective Board and how to achieve consistently good quality and effective decision-making (para **2.20**). One thing that is clear is that there is no one-size-fits-all solution as an effective Board is derived from a combination of many inter-related factors.

Composition and structure   10.21.1

The issues around composition of the Board, balance, diversity, distinction of roles and succession planning, etc are set out in paras **1.60**, **1.70** and **2.20**, and these are all important for achieving high standards of corporate governance. Problems with any one of these factors can have a significant effect on standards of governance. Take succession planning, for example, which is important to ensure that:

- the ambitions and intentions of members of the Board are identified in terms of their length of service, amongst other things, to ensure that any changes of directors are carefully planned as far as possible so they do not coincide, thereby preserving continuity and minimising disruption at the company's most senior level – a failure in this respect could result in, say, the chairman, CEO and FD all planning to leave at the same time without the company being aware until they give notice which could have a significant impact on perception of the company's strategy and direction;

- decisions about who to involve in, how to conduct and when to start recruiting for a replacement are made at the appropriate time, which again is important for preserving continuity by having sufficient time for recruitment and handover as well as for drawing on an appropriately diverse candidate pool – insufficient time, identification of few suitable candidates or a lack of agreement amongst those involved in the selection process might mean a replacement is not found in time;

- the characteristics and skills required of a new director are properly considered and a detailed job specification and selection criteria are drawn up, taking into account not only the key skills and experience required for the particular role in question, but also the existing balance and structure of the Board as a whole and how this might be improved, say, by increasing diversity – without considering and formalising ideas about what skills, experience, and characteristics, etc are needed it will be difficult to assess suitability of candidates and make a reasoned judgment, the consequence of which might be a poor recruitment decision.

In terms of structure, again whilst the directors are free to determine what is suitable, the Code recommends a clear division of responsibilities at the head of the company and that no one has unfettered powers of decision. To comply with the Code:

(1) the roles of chairman (responsible for the running and leadership of the Board) and CEO (responsible for running the company's business) should be divided, clearly established, set out in writing and agreed by the Board;

(2) except in exceptional circumstances and with prior consultation with major shareholders, the CEO should not go on to be appointed chairman of the company and no one individual should have unfettered powers of decision;

(3)   the Board should be of an appropriate size and contain an appropriate balance of executive and non-executive directors (in particular, independent non-executive directors) to ensure that no individual or group dominates Board decisions;

(4)   except for companies below the FTSE 350, at least half of the Board, excluding the chairman, should comprise non-executive directors determined by the Board to be independent. A smaller company should have at least two independent non-executive directors. Criteria by which to judge the extent of independence are addressed in para **1.33**;

(5)   the Board should appoint one independent non-executive director as the senior independent non-executive director and that person must be available to shareholders.

Board structure and the factors set out above are clearly important elements of good corporate governance as a common feature in a number of corporate scandals including Enron, Parmalat and, more recently, News Corp, has been the over concentration of power in the hands of one individual. In News Corp, for example, Rupert Murdoch was chairman and CEO, the company had no truly independent non-executive directors and Mr Murdoch was known for his strength of character and views about being able to make his own decisions without having to consult committees and the Board. News Corp's well publicised current demise demonstrates the consequences of over dependence on one single individual and failing to implement a suitable structure.

Meetings   **10.21.2**

Clearly Board meetings need to be held as often as necessary to enable the Board to discharge its responsibilities for setting strategy as well as directing, managing and controlling the company. This requirement is recognised by the Code which also recommends as best practice that:

(1)   there is a formal schedule of matters to be determined by the Board and a statement about this is included in the annual report;

(2)   the chairman determines the Board agenda, allows adequate time for discussion of agenda items and encourages openness and debate; and

(3)   meetings are held periodically by the chairman with the non-executive directors, without executives present.

A list of the matters that might normally only be determined by the Board is set out in para **2.40** and **APPENDIX 33**. Consideration would also usually be given to expanding this out to determine when matters need to be formally reviewed and how to work this into the agenda and plans for scheduled meetings. For example, whilst setting the company's long-term strategy might only be considered in detail and determined, say, every three years, the setting and review of more detailed strategic plans and budgets for the operation are likely to be considered on at least a yearly basis. This will all need to be worked into the planned meeting timetable.

The pivotal role the chairman has in promoting and encouraging good boardroom behaviour and achieving an effective Board, necessary for good corporate governance, is detailed in para **2.30**. In most companies, how the Board operates and behaves in turn has a knock-on effect through the company. So if very high standards are required and demonstrated by the Board, this message is likely to permeate to all levels of the company.

Information and reporting   **10.21.3**

Formal consideration should be given by the Board to what information is required and the frequency and content of reporting in order that it can discharge its duty to oversee and control the company's business and performance. It is very important for the Board and its committees to receive suitable and sufficient information in a timely manner in order that informed decisions can be made about the company and how to best deploy its assets for maximum long-term benefit.

It is likely that the chairman will, as recommended by the Code, be instrumental in ensuring the Board receives the required information and that it is accurate, timely, clear and sufficiently comprehensive for the Board's purposes.

Particular attention should also be given to when the information is provided to ensure the directors have sufficient time in advance of meetings to review and consider it in detail and, if necessary, ask initial questions of the preparer, so each can attend the Board or committee meeting with a comprehensive understanding of the issues faced, ready to discuss and debate the matters on the agenda.

The Code also recommends that the advice and services of the company secretary (who should be well rehearsed in compliance rules) are available to Board members, particularly on matters of governance and that the chairman ensures there are good information flows amongst the Board and committees and between the executives and non-executive directors. Again, this free flow of information makes perfect sense in terms of improving understanding, ensuring transparency and encouraging openness and debate by the Board.

Development   **10.21.4**

It is recommended that all directors receive formal, tailored induction on joining the Board so they are fully aware of their duties and responsibilities and what is expected of them from day one of their appointment. As well as covering the matters set out in para **1.80** and **APPENDIX 32**, such inductions might also include the opportunity to meet the company's major shareholders, key executives and senior managers in the business and to visit operations. Once appointed the Code recognises the need for directors to keep updating their skills and knowledge on a regular basis, which is particularly important as the regulatory environment in which companies operate does not stand still and changes come into effect at an alarming rate.

The Code also recommends that directors' training and development needs are reviewed with the chairman and appropriate training is provided as necessary. This might take the form of individual training sessions or periodic updates and presentations to the Board or committees on particular matters relevant to the company's operations. It is also recommended that the directors are permitted to seek independent legal or professional advice at the company's expense in furtherance of their duties.

Performance evaluation **10.21.5**

Linked closely to the desire to ensure the Board is effective and to knowing and addressing the areas that need improvement, the Board should undertake a formal and rigorous annual evaluation of its own performance and that of its committees and individual Board members (para **2.80**). The chairman should act on the results of the evaluation, proposing new appointments or seeking resignations where considered necessary. To avoid any conflict of interest, the chairman's performance should be reviewed by the non-executive directors. Evaluation of Board performance for a FTSE 350 company should be carried out externally once every three years and the results of the internal or external evaluation be fed into identifying training and development needs.

According to statistics published in Grant Thornton's report 'Governance steps up a gear; December 2013', 94% of FTSE 350 companies carried out an externally facilitated Board review in the previous three years, and it is clear from the FRC's report on 'Developments in Corporate Governance 2013' (FRC's annual report for 2013) that directors, company secretaries, investors and independent reviewers generally consider the impact of board evaluations has been positive and that they have contributed to boards becoming more professional.

The company is also required to describe in the annual report how performance evaluation has been carried out and, if an external facilitator has been engaged, disclose the external facilitator's details.

Re-election **10.21.6**

The membership of a Board would usually need to be periodically refreshed to prevent it from becoming too cosy and lacking any form of constructive challenge, where members might have a tendency towards groupthink (para **2.20**). Recognising this need, the Code requires all directors of FTSE 350 companies to offer themselves for election at each AGM. Indeed, statistics in the FRC's annual report for 2013 show that all but two FTSE 350 companies put all directors up for election during 2012/13. In addition, 43% of small cap and fledgling companies put all directors forward for re-election even though the Code provision does not apply to them. The Code also recommends that where a non-executive director is to be reappointed for a term beyond six years, this should be subject to rigorous review and, where the term is in excess of nine years, the non-executive director be proposed for re-election each year.

Directors of companies outside the FTSE 350 would usually be re-elected at the first AGM following their reappointment and thereafter at intervals of no more than three years. Explanation of the proposal for election or re-election needs to be given in or alongside the notice of the meeting, including not only a summary of biographical information, but also confirmation that the director's performance remains effective and that he is committed to the role (see para **10.15.3**).

Risk management and internal control **10.22**

Directors will not be in any doubt about the importance, whatever the size of the company, of identifying, monitoring and as far as possible either avoiding or mitigating risks that might impact the company's performance or prospects. Failure to do so would effectively leave the success of a company to chance which is a luxury none can afford and no shareholders are likely to support.

In recent years there have been numerous reports of corporate governance and risk management failings with considerable costs and consequences for some very sizeable companies. Such examples include the:

- failing by Citiibank, HSBC, JP Morgan Chase, RBS and UBS AG to control business practices in their G10 Spot FX trading operations, resulting in manipulation of FX currency rates, for which they were fined a total £1.1 billion by the FCA in November 2014;

- manipulation of the London inter-bank offered rate ('LIBOR') by Barclays, RBS and UBS for which fines of £290m, £390m and £940m have been imposed respectively;

- weak risk management and seriously defective control processes at UBS. This meant a trader managed to carry out unauthorised trading for a prolonged period without being detected, for which UBS were fined £29.7m;

- catastrophic failure of HBOS due to ill-judged lending decisions, poor risk control and inadequate liquidity which it is believed would have caused the bank to fail, even absent of the banking crisis;

- lack of adequate controls at HSBC over bearer share company accounts making it possible for them to be used to launder Mexican drug money around the world; and

- £3m fine by the FCA on JPMorgan for systems and control failings and an order to tighten material risk controls.

There are numerous other examples in the enforcement section of the FCA website. Reporting incidents such as these has raised public awareness and considerable concern has been expressed about how it is possible for such problems and issues to go undetected, often for prolonged periods of time.

Whilst many of the points set out below focus on requirements for listed companies, the need for risk management and implementation of internal controls is common to all companies and must be addressed by the directors. Having said this, depending on the nature of a company's operations, the risk identification and management process may prove a lot simpler in a smaller organisation where the directors are much closer to operations and have a working knowledge of the risks and control issues. In large companies the risk assessment and risk management process will doubtless involve delegation of responsibility for much of the detail, for which the Board will retain responsibility.

The Board's duty to present a balanced and understandable assessment of the company's position and prospects was first established in the Cadbury Report and it is now included as a main principle in the Code. The Code also contains the requirement for the Board to determine the nature and extent of significant risks faced by the company as a consequence of the Board's approved strategy and to identify the level of risk they are willing to accept to achieve the strategy.

Directors are required to include a statement in the annual accounts, immediately preceding the audit report, explaining their responsibility for preparing accounts and commenting on the company's internal system of risk management and control. The requirement for an explanation of the basis on which the company generates or preserves value, how it is to achieve strategy and confirming that the company is a going concern has also been incorporated in the Code and directors of premium listed companies must ensure that this statement is included in the accounts.

These requirements mean the directors must now implement controls for all types of risk to which the organisation is exposed and actively review how effective such measures are in managing and responding to those risks. The Code also requires that directors of listed companies conduct such review at least once a year and report to shareholders on the effectiveness of the company's risk management, corporate reporting and internal control systems. The review must cover all aspects of corporate reporting, internal control and risk management including operational and compliance issues and not just purely financial matters.

For the vast majority of companies the need to manage and control risks has always been recognised and carried out, possibly informally at a more operational level, in order for companies to survive and overcome changes in their business environment.

The Turnbull Guidance (para **10.14**) made clear that:

(1)   the Board is primarily responsible for risk management and internal control and, whilst it may seek assurances and assistance from the management or operating team, the internal audit function, committees of the Board or other advisers, the Board must determine the appropriate system of internal control and risk management for the company; and

(2)   the Board is also responsible for reviewing the effectiveness of internal control and, whilst the directors may request reviews and reports from designated committees or the management team, the Board must review and consider the results and reach its own conclusions on effectiveness.

The Turnbull Guidance has been replaced for accounting years beginning on or after 1 October 2014 and companies must instead observe the requirements of the FRC's Guidance on 'Risk Management, Internal Control and Related Financial and Business Reporting' ('Risk Guidance').

The Risk Guidance clearly states that the Board has responsibility for an organisation's overall approach to risk management and internal control. The Board's responsibilities are:

●   ensuring the design and implementation of appropriate risk management and internal control systems that identify the risks facing the company and enable the Board to make a robust assessment of the principal risks;

●   determining the nature and extent of the principal risks faced and those risks which the organisation is willing to take in achieving its strategic objectives (determining its 'risk appetite');

- ensuring that appropriate culture and reward systems have been embedded throughout the organisation;

- agreeing how the principal risks should be managed or mitigated to reduce the likelihood of their incidence or their impact;

- monitoring and reviewing the risk management and internal control systems, and the management's process of monitoring and reviewing, and satisfying itself that they are functioning effectively and that corrective action is being taken where necessary; and

- ensuring sound internal and external information and communication processes and taking responsibility for external communication on risk management and internal control.

These responsibilities certainly make sense from an operational perspective. It is particularly important for the Board to promote and encourage the right culture and attitude within the company to ensure that the need to observe systems, procedures and control measures is recognised, understood and observed at all times and at all levels within the company without any temporary lapses. With this in mind it is important for directors to remember that whilst they might not be directly involved or responsible for the action resulting in loss or damage to the company, they will be held accountable if they failed to identify a potential risk, did not implement sufficient controls or failed to put in place appropriate reporting requirements from which it would have been apparent.

Adequate consideration must be given to the content and frequency of monitoring and reporting to ensure risks are identified, managed and mitigated as soon as they arise, thereby minimising any damage or adverse consequences for the company. Risk management and control systems must also be responsive to the need to change and adapt in light of the emergence of new risks and the experience of others. For example, recently there has been a shift in focus towards:

- companies identifying and managing show-stopping strategic risks, which alone or together could totally undermine the company's ability to achieve its strategic objectives or cause it to fail;

- recognition of the need to combine risks and risk events, as well as determining the net effect of each individually, so total potential exposure can be gauged;

- active consideration of potential reputational risks and the need for crisis management policies, given that in today's electronic world bad news is transmitted virtually instantaneously;

- recognition of risks presented by cyber crime and the scale of damage and disruption that could be caused; and

- identifying solvency and liquidity risks over a longer period, through the economic cycle, to give greater certainty to the company's going concern statement (consistent with the Sharman recommendations).

Directors need to consider how best to apply the recommendations of the Code and the Risk Guidance to their own organisations and put in place suitable and effective systems of control. They must also have regard to recommendations of the Walker Review and determine whether it is appropriate for the company to have separate audit and risk committees and to appoint a chief risk officer (para **10.13**).

Committees   10.23

As set out in para **2.60** a company's Articles will usually contain provisions allowing the directors to delegate their powers. This is important because as a company becomes larger and its operations and activities more complex, there might reach a point where it is no longer effective, feasible or appropriate for the Board to consider all aspects of development and control to the required level of detail. One way of addressing this limitation issue is through the use of committees and, at this stage, the Board might decide to establish certain committees and assign particular roles and responsibilities to those committees. Usually directors will be members of some committees, but not all of them, and are therefore able to better divide and use their time in the areas where they have more input and expertise. Once particular matters have been considered in detail by the relevant committee, they will be reported to the Board, often with a recommendation requiring decision by the Board.

Committees may be set up to assist the Board by dealing with and reporting on a whole variety of matters largely dependant on the company's operations. For example a mining company might have environmental or health and safety committees and a pharmaceutical company have an ethics and medical approval committee. In each case the members of these committees would need particular experience and knowledge to enable them to adequately consider the matters at hand and the manner in which decisions, recommendations and information are reported to the Board needs careful determination. Some of the usual committees that would be seen in most large companies, regardless of their sector, are set out below.

As detailed in para **10.15.3**, the Code requires the terms of reference for the audit, remuneration and nomination committees to be placed on a website (B.2.1, C.3.3 and D.2.1).

Audit committee   **10.23.1**

The Board of every company should consider whether introducing an audit committee would help it to more effectively manage and control the company. With some very small companies an audit committee might not be considered necessary, whilst other Boards might determine that not only is an audit committee essential but also that a separate risk committee is also needed (para **10.23.2**). The decision reached by the Board will, amongst other things, largely depend on the size, complexity and risk profile of the company.

Whether listed or not, from the Board's point of view it is widely recognised that the benefits of introducing an audit committee can be far reaching and the committee can:

- assist directors in meeting their statutory and fiduciary responsibilities for maintaining accounting records and preparation of the annual audited accounts;

- provide a mechanism to ensure that the Board focuses on key audit, accounting, risk management and internal control issues;

- provide an independent check on executive directors;

- introduce strong internal controls which will reduce the opportunity for fraud;

- improve the quality of communication between directors, internal and external auditors, and establish a forum for consideration of recommendations and any deficiencies in corporate governance that need to be addressed;

- increase public confidence in the validity and credibility of published financial statements and that adequate controls are in place.

The audit committee is generally considered an essential part of the reporting, risk management and internal control process. Many companies already operate with executive committees, and those formed to carry out administrative functions and recommendations initially set out in the Combined Code made establishment of audit committees a mandatory requirement for listed companies, save where they are able to explain why they do not need one. Provisions in the 2012 Code strengthened the role of the audit committee in terms of their responsibility for monitoring the integrity of financial reporting, reinforcing the independence of auditors and reviewing risk management and internal control systems as follows:

- extension of the audit committee's remit to include consideration of the annual report in its totality (narrative as well as figures) and advising the Board on whether it considers it is fair, balanced and understandable and discloses all information necessary for investors to be able to assess the company's performance, business model, strategy and prospects with sufficient certainty. Based on this assurance from the audit committee, the Board is required to disclose this information in the annual report and accounts;

- the requirement for more meaningful disclosures required from the audit committee, including identification of significant issues and how they have been addressed, key judgments made and more information about the external auditor and assessing their performance, length of tenure and the approach and frequency of retendering;

- the audit committee being required to report how it discharged its responsibilities to the Board and providing a more meaningful description of the committee's work in the annual report; and

- FTSE 350 companies required to put the external audit contract out to tender every ten years.

These changes were intended to go some way to addressing substantial criticism that many companies failed to provide key financial information or any indication of their sensitivities in their annual reports and accounts in the lead up to the global financial crisis. They also aimed to ensure the function and role of the audit committee met the expectations of the company's many stakeholders and readers of the accounts, as well as the public.

A further change introduced by the 2014 Code expanded the remit of advice provided by the audit committee to the board to include assessment of the company's position (C.3.4).

Headline changes include extending the audit committee's remit and making the disclosures it makes more meaningful and informative.

These changes followed consultation conducted by the FRC on the audit committee's role and retendering requirements, as set out in the consultation document 'Revisions to the UK Corporate Governance Code and Guidance on Audit Committees' in April 2012 (which itself included many of the recommendations in the FRC's earlier Guidance on Audit Committees and the discussion paper, 'Effective Company Stewardship – Enhancing Corporate Reporting and Audit').

Directors should be aware that provision C.3.1 of the Code requires the Board of a company with a premium listing of equity securities to establish an audit committee comprising at least three members that are independent non-executive directors (or in the case of smaller companies, below the FTSE 350, two). At least one of the members needs recent and relevant financial experience and, whilst for smaller listed companies it is considered acceptable for the chairman of the company to be a member of the audit committee, this is only permitted where the person is considered independent when appointed chairman and he is in addition to satisfying the required numbers of independent non-executive director members.

For the audit committee to operate efficiently the directors need to delegate responsibility and determine formal terms of reference outlining clearly the objectives, responsibilities, composition and authority of the committee. In particular the distinction between those matters where the committee has authority to make decisions and those where recommendations are required for consideration by the Board needs to be made clear. Specimen terms of reference determined by the ICSA which might be suitable for the company's use are contained in **APPENDIX 24**.

In practice, the audit committee is usually required by its terms of reference to:

- monitor the integrity of financial statements and any formal announcements relating to financial performance;

- review the company's accounting principles and the practices underlying them and the financial judgements made in the financial statements and associated announcements;

- monitor effectiveness of the internal audit function (where applicable);

- review the scope, results and cost-effectiveness of the audit, the objectivity of the auditors and their terms of engagement;

- liaise with the company's internal and external auditors;

- monitor and review effectiveness of internal financial controls, internal control and risk management systems;

- review performance of the external auditor and monitor the extent of their independence;

- make recommendations to the Board for the appointment, reappointment and removal of the external auditor and to approve their remuneration and terms of appointment;

- develop and implement a policy on engagement of external auditors for providing non-audit services;

- ensure arrangements are in place by which employees can raise concerns in confidence (commonly referred to as whistleblowing) about possible improprieties or wrongdoing within the company; and

- report to the Board on how the committee has discharged its responsibilities.

More information on the role and responsibilities of the audit committee is set out in Section C of the Code. In addition the FRC's 'Guidance on Audit Committees' aims to assist directors and their Boards in implementing the requirements of the Code with regard to the role and requirements of the audit committee. It is recommended that the directors of any company, whether listed or not, review the FRC's guidance in full before setting up an audit committee or contemplating becoming a member. Some key points from the FRC's guidance include:

- it is envisaged there would be no fewer than three formal meetings per year, to coincide with key financial reporting and audit cycle dates;

- at least one meeting should be held each year with the internal and external auditors without management present to give them opportunity to raise and discuss any areas of concern;

- sufficient resources must be provided to the audit committee with particular reference to planning and arranging meetings, timely provision of committee papers and the ability to seek expert advice when considered necessary;

- the audit committee should review all significant financial reporting (including financial statements, interim reports and preliminary announcements, etc), issues and judgements made and prepared by management and determine whether they are appropriate in light also of the external auditor's view;

- the audit committee should review the internal financial controls and, in the absence of a risk committee, the internal control and risk management system and any statements made about them in the annual report;

- that suitability of the company's whistleblowing arrangements, investigation and follow-up actions should be reviewed by the audit committee;

- where there is no internal audit function, the audit committee should consider whether there is a need for one on an annual basis and report to the Board on the continued suitability of existing arrangements; and

- that the company's relationship with the external auditor should be overseen by the audit committee, which shall recommend the auditor's appointment, reappointment or removal to the Board and approve their terms of engagement and remuneration.

The FRC's guidance emphasises the key role of the audit committee in ensuring shareholders are properly protected in relation to integrity of financial reporting and sufficiency of internal control and risk-management systems and that there are times when the audit committee must be prepared to take a robust stand on difficult issues. The Code also recommends that the Board delegates responsibility to the audit committee for overseeing and managing the relationship with the company's external auditors, by:

- making a recommendation to the Board about whom to appoint;

- approving their terms of engagement and remuneration;

- periodically reviewing the objectivity and independence of the external auditor;

- agreeing, with approval of the Board, the company's policy on employing former employees of the auditor;

- monitoring the audit firm's compliance with ethical guidance on the rotation of audit partners as well as the level of fees paid by the company as a proportion of that firm's total fee income; and

- developing and recommending to the Board the company's policy on non-audit services to ensure that they do not impair the auditor's independence or objectivity.

The disclosures around this responsibility and the company's relationship with the auditors will increase as envisaged in para **10.12**.

In particular, a separate section is now required in the annual report and accounts describing the work of the audit committee and how it has discharged its responsibilities. The report should identify the significant issues that the committee considered in relation to the financial statements and how they were addressed; explanation of how the committee assessed effectiveness of the external audit process and the appointment, reappointment and retendering of the external auditor; and, if the external auditor provided non-audit services, explanation of how their objectivity and independence were safeguarded.

In addition, where requested by the Board, the audit committee should provide advice on whether the annual report and accounts, taken as a whole, is fair, balanced and understandable and provides the information necessary for shareholders to assess the company's performance, business model and strategy.

Risk committee 10.23.2

Whilst not a requirement under the Code, the Walker Review recommends that the Board of a FTSE 100 listed bank or life insurance company establishes a risk committee separate from the audit committee (para **10.13**). This was considered necessary because of the complexity of risk-management issues faced by these companies which, it was considered, needed separate and dedicated focus.

The Walker Review recommends that the risk committee has responsibility for oversight and advice to the Board on the current risk exposures of the bank or financial institution and future risk strategy, including strategy for capital and liquidity management, and the embedding and maintenance throughout the organisation of a supportive culture in relation to the management of risk alongside established prescriptive rules and procedures. In preparing advice to the Board on its overall risk appetite, tolerance and strategy, the Walker Review recommends that the risk committee ensures that account has been taken of the current and prospective macroeconomic and financial environment drawing on financial stability assessments such as those published by the Bank of England, the FCA and other authoritative sources that may be relevant for the risk policies of the firm.

However, not every company will determine that a separate risk committee is necessary. As a starting point the Board should assess the company's existing risk management and control structure to determine if there are any perceived weaknesses or areas that could be improved. Consideration should also be given to the complexity of the company's operations and risk environment over the medium and long term to determine whether current arrangements, through the audit committee or the Board, will remain appropriate over time.

Assuming the Board determines that improvements will be gained by putting a separate risk committee in place, the responsibilities of the committee and how it will interact with other committees will need to be clarified. For example if there is an audit committee potential areas of overlap need to be addressed and made clear. The financial reporting risks might remain the responsibility of the audit committee, with input to the audit committee from the risk committee where relevant, and all other risks be overseen by the risk committee but this needs to be determined by the Board.

Again the Board will need to determine appropriate membership of the risk committee, bearing in mind recommendations of the Walker Review that the majority of members and the chairman should be non-executive directors, the finance director should also be a member, the chief risk officer (where there is one) be present at all meetings and the chairman of the audit committee also participate at meetings. It is recommended that meetings are held quarterly but, in any event, no less than three meetings per year.

The Board needs to determine the role of the risk committee and ensure this is clearly set out in the committee's terms of reference, an example of which can be found on the ICSA's website (www.icsa.org.uk, Guidance Note 101018). These duties might, for example, include:

- advising the Board about the company's overall risk appetite and the existing and future strategy;

- monitoring and advising the Board of exposure to risk;

- reviewing any risk limits breaches and reporting them to the Board;

- reviewing the risk assessment process to ensure it remains effective and able to identify, capture and control new and emerging risks;

- ensuring internal controls and the risk management system remain effective; and

- determining the structure and resourcing of the risk management function.

If it is decided that a risk committee is needed, consideration will need to be considered to also amending the terms of reference of other committees, such as the audit committee, to remove any overlap and make clear how the committees will work together.

Nomination committee   **10.23.3**

Whilst not applicable to all companies, the Code requires a formal, rigorous and transparent procedure for the appointment of new directors to the Board and that there is a nomination committee with clear terms of reference to lead the process for Board appointments and make recommendations to the Board. Example terms of reference compiled by ICSA are set out in **APPENDIX 31** and the company is required to make these available, usually through the website. Further requirements of the committee are that:

(1) the majority of members of the nomination committee be independent non-executive directors and the chairman is either a non-executive director or chairman of the Board (save that he would not be able to chair the committee when dealing with succession of the chairman);

(2) the procedure for the appointment of new directors must be formal, rigorous, transparent and based on merit against objective criteria for the role and capabilities needed, with due regard to achieving diversity on the Board;

(3) the requirements for a particular appointment should be formally determined in advance following evaluation of the Board and with particular regard to the balance of skills, independence, knowledge and experience required on the Board as a whole;

(4) no-one other than the chairman or committee members are entitled to attend meetings, but others can be invited to do so;

(5) committee membership should be periodically refreshed;

(6) the Board must ensure appropriate succession plans are in place for the Board and senior management;

(7)   terms and conditions of appointment of non-executive directors should be available for inspection;

(8)   all directors should be required to undertake that they will have sufficient time to attend to the company's affairs;

(9)   non-executive directors should be appointed for a specified term, subject to re-election, with rigorous review of continue appointment beyond six years;

(10)   the Board should not agree to a full-time executive director taking on more than one non-executive directorship or chairmanship of a FTSE 100 company.

Provision B.2.4 of the Code requires inclusion of a separate section in the annual report and accounts describing the work of the nomination committee. This should include description of the process used for Board appointments and the Board's policy on diversity, including gender, any measurable objectives that it has set for implementing the policy, and progress towards achieving the objectives. An explanation should also be given where neither an external search consultancy nor open advertising was used for appointment of the chairman or a non-executive director. Where an external search consultancy or external evaluator is used for Board evaluation, they should be identified in the report and a statement be made as to whether they have any other connection with the company.

It is unlikely that the Board of a small company would determine there is a need or a benefit from having a separate nomination committee, but it can be very beneficial in large companies particularly with reference to giving adequate consideration to succession planning (para **1.70**).

Remuneration committee   **10.23.4**

Whilst it may be addressed by the Board, and often is in small private companies, responsibility for determining the executive directors' pay is usually delegated to a remuneration committee. However it is addressed, it is essential that no director is involved in determining his own remuneration.

Directors should be aware that the Code recommends that whilst the Board or, where required by the company's Articles, the shareholders, shall determine remuneration of the non-executive directors, the remuneration of the chairman and executive directors should be determined by an independent remuneration committee.

Such committee should comprise at least three, or in the case of smaller companies (below the FTSE 350) two, independent non-executive directors.

This is a logical step in removing any potential for conflicts of interest that would be present should directors be involved in determining their own pay. To operate efficiently the directors must ensure that they have formally delegated responsibility for setting remuneration to the remuneration committee and that they provide the remuneration committee with detailed terms of reference setting out its responsibilities (see **APPENDIX 23** for ICSA's terms of reference). The company is required to make these terms of reference available, usually through the website. The remuneration committee will usually be responsible for:

- determining remuneration and rewards for the chairman, executive directors and senior management;

- monitoring and determining all executive benefits, including pensions and share options;

- appointing consultants and obtaining and monitoring internal and external information relating to remuneration;

- instigating studies of market position and comparative rates of pay;

- ensuring that the remuneration policy pursued attracts and motivates top quality executive personnel without paying more than is necessary; and

- generally overseeing executive remuneration to ensure the process is formal and transparent, following best-practice recommendations as far as practically possible.

As detailed in para **7.13.6** significant changes set out in ERRA 2013 will soon be taking effect, which will have an important impact on directors' remuneration. In the meantime the remuneration committee needs to consider the implications of these changes on the role of the committee and how it will address the new requirements for approval of remuneration policy, disclosure requirements and statements in the annual report and accounts.

Directors' remuneration   10.30

There has been considerable debate about how best to address what appear to be excessive levels of remuneration paid to executive directors, improve transparency by requiring more information to be disclosed on directors' remuneration and increase the level of control that shareholders can exert over directors' remuneration. The measures being implemented to address these concerns, improve pay practice and governance, increase the level of transparency and strengthen shareholders' voting powers are detailed in para **7.13.6.2**.

Amidst considerable public concern about the level and excesses of executive pay, determining what is appropriate and how it would be best structured is a very complex matter. Essentially the level of remuneration should be sufficient to attract, retain and motivate directors of the quality required to direct, lead and run the company successfully, but without paying more than is needed. Obviously this is difficult to determine and there are many widely publicised statistics that suggest remuneration for executive directors has continued to increase at an alarming rate that is out of step with their companies' performance and valuations. Figures from IDS, Office for National Statistics report, for example, that:

- in 2011 average pay for directors of top businesses in the UK rose by 50%, average pay for a director of a FTSE 100 company was £2.7m and bonuses rose by 23% from £737k to £906k; and

- in 2012 average pay for a FTSE 100 director rose seven times faster than average employee wage increases.

Looking at these statistics, the public outcry about the excesses of executive remuneration seems justified. On a positive note, findings from more recent surveys are promising as they indicate that remuneration committees are beginning to exercise restraint with regard to executive pay. For example, PwC's survey of large UK companies found that 81% of respondents expect executive bonuses to be the same or lower than 2012 and that over a third of companies responding planned to freeze salaries for executive directors in 2013. In addition from the Executive Directors' Remuneration Report published by Deloitte in September 2012, it appears that around one-third of directors of FTSE 100 companies will not receive any salary increases in 2013 and any increases that are awarded will be around a moderate 2.5%.

This indicates that companies are listening and adjusting in response to concern expressed by the investor community and public about excessive levels of directors' remuneration. Indeed, failure to listen can have disastrous effects and result intense media interest and speculation which in itself can be very negative and potentially damage the company's reputation and the perceived credibility of the Board. There were many examples of votes against directors' remuneration in the 2012 AGM season (dubbed the 'Shareholder Spring') including, amongst others, the vote by 11.6% of Prudential Plc's investors against the proposed £4.7m increase in the CEO's remuneration package and the vote against the CEO and finance directors' severance packages on takeover of Sportingbet by William Hill and GVC Holdings. Even in the 2014 AGM season there were a considerable number (see paragraph **7.13.6**).

Given these concerns, there was overwhelming support for the new remuneration reporting and approval regime set out in para **7.13.6** to increase transparency and allow shareholders to exercise greater control over the directors' remuneration policy.

The Code sets out detailed requirements in relation to directors' service contracts and key requirements for the remuneration policy. Recommendations in the Code recognise that sufficient remuneration must be offered to attract and retain directors and, at the same time, focus on the need for the remuneration committee to ensure these are not too onerous for the company in terms of actual remuneration paid, notice periods or compensation for loss of office.

This being the case, the Code requires that:

- performance-related elements form a significant proportion of a director's remuneration, are stretching and designed to promote sustained, long-term success (Schedule A to the Code);

- remuneration should reflect the time commitment and responsibilities of the role;

- remuneration for non-executive directors should not include share options but, if it does, shareholder approval should be sought in advance;

- compensation commitments in the event of early termination are carefully considered so as not to be too onerous on the company nor reward poor performance and seek to mitigate any loss suffered;

- notice or contract periods are set at one year or less;

- shareholders are invited to approve significant changes to long-term incentive schemes and any new schemes;

- consideration is given to pay and employment conditions elsewhere in the company, especially when deciding annual salary increases; and

- benchmarking is considered, bearing in mind the limitation that this can in itself cause an upwards ratchet.

The remuneration committee must obtain as much information and support, whether in the form of survey results or engagement of remuneration consultants, etc, as it considers necessary to make an informed decision which it believes will achieve the most successful outcome for the company.

Many companies use remuneration consultants and executive search agencies to help identify levels of pay within comparable companies, against which they then set their own remuneration benchmark in terms of whether they want to be at the high, middle or more conservative end of what is being paid to others. However, this methodology has come under some criticism and needs to be carefully exercised as there might be a tendency to chase the median, resulting in spiralling levels of pay.

In particular, the performance-related element of an executive director's remuneration is an important way to align directors' interests with those of the company's shareholders. The company should seek to determine a well thought through long-term plan, possibly with some short-term staged targets and rewards along the way. Directors should only be rewarded where agreed value-creation targets have been achieved.

Responsibility for setting the non-executive directors' remuneration generally resides with the directors, unless the company's Articles require otherwise, and the level of remuneration should reflect the time commitment and responsibilities of the role, including the non-executive director's membership of any committees.

Clearly, determination of the appropriate level and structure of remuneration is extremely important and needs careful consideration. With this in mind in 2011 the ABI issued Guidelines on Executive Pay (www.abi.org.uk) which, whilst aimed at fully listed companies, sets out a number of remuneration principles which are worth consideration even by non-listed companies. In particular the guidelines state that remuneration structures should not be overly complex; focus on long-term delivery of strategy and value creation; have an appropriate split between short-term and long-term targets and fixed and performance-related variable elements of pay; and avoid payments for failure to perform.

Key amendments in the 2014 Code relating to remuneration that need to be observed are set out in paragraph **7.13.6**. Of particular note is the need for the remuneration committee to avoid potential conflicts of interest when considering remuneration and the need for the committee chairman to maintain contact with principal shareholders about remuneration (supporting principle D.2).

Where applicable such additional requirements and restrictions in relation to determining executive remuneration must be observed.

Communication and relations with shareholders   10.40

Section E of the Code requires the chairman to ensure there is effective communication with shareholders, comprising a two-way dialogue, and that the Board uses general meetings to communicate with investors and encourage their participation. These responsibilities for the chairman and the Board are not new, but are now linked to the institutional shareholders' responsibilities in the Stewardship Code (see para **10.50**) to also commit to dialogue, communication and participation or explain why they have not done so.

The 2014 Code also contains a new provision requiring announcement where there is a significant vote by shareholders against a resolution, advising the actions the board intends to take to understand the reasons behind the vote (E.2.2).

More responsibility now rests with the chairman to make sure the whole Board is made aware and is fully advised of major shareholders' views about the company and of any issues or concerns they might have. This might involve holding meetings with shareholders, particularly for the CEO, finance director, SINED and other non-executive directors, or analyst's or broker's briefings and roadshows, etc.

It is fair to say that for some years larger listed companies in particular have been trying to use the AGM to communicate with shareholders but there has been a lack of interest by institutional investors who will rarely attend and in some instances even fail to vote on the resolutions put to the meeting. It is hoped the Stewardship Code will improve this situation and encourage greater participation (see para **10.50**).

The Stewardship Code   10.50

The UK Stewardship Code ('the Stewardship Code') was first issued by the Financial Reporting Council ('FRC') in July 2010 with the aim of enhancing the quality of engagement between institutional investors and companies to improve not only long-term returns to shareholders but also the standards of governance in companies in which institutional shareholders have invested. It represents formal recognition that institutional investors have a responsibility to monitor the workings of the companies in which they invest and to communicate and engage with them.

An updated version of the Stewardship Code was issued in September 2012 and key changes in the updated version include clarification of the meaning of 'stewardship' and how it relates to governance, the use of voting advisory services and the requirement to review compliance statements annually. The Stewardship Code is complementary to the UK Corporate Governance Code (the 'Code') and applies to firms that manage assets on behalf of institutional shareholders such as pension funds, insurance companies and investment trusts.

It is made up of seven principles and supporting guidance, in a similar fashion to the Code. The main principles state that institutional investors should:

- **Principle 1**: publicly disclose their policy on how they will discharge their stewardship responsibilities;

- **Principle 2**: have a robust policy on managing conflicts of interest in relation to stewardship and this policy should be publicly disclosed;

- **Principle 3**: monitor their investee companies;

- **Principle 4**: establish clear guidelines on when and how they will escalate their activities as a method of protecting and enhancing shareholder value;

- **Principle 5**: be willing to act collectively with other investors where appropriate;

- **Principle 6**: have a clear policy on voting and disclosure of voting activity;

- **Principle 7**: report periodically on their stewardship and voting activities.

As with the Code, the Stewardship Code should be applied on a 'comply or explain' basis. In practical terms this means the institutional investor publicly disclosing a statement on their website that contains:

- a description of how the principles of the Stewardship Code have been applied; and

- disclosure of the specific information listed under Principles 1, 5, 6 and 7; or

- an explanation if these elements of the Stewardship Code have not been observed.

The FRC recognises that not all parts of the Stewardship Code are relevant to all institutional investors and that small institutions may judge that some principles and guidance are disproportionate. In these circumstances, advantage should be taken of the 'comply or explain' approach and it should be set out why this is the case.

When a company publishes a statement of compliance with the Stewardship Code (or an explanation of non-compliance, depending on the circumstances) they should notify the FRC, who will retain on its website a list of those investors that have published such statement. The FRC also suggest that the statement should contain the name of an individual who can be contacted for further information as this helps promote communication and engagement by the companies in which they invest.

When the Stewardship Code was implemented there was considerable scepticism about whether it would achieve its aims or merely result in a public statement of support and a tick-box approach to compliance. However, there is evidence that this view is changing, prompted largely by the level of support seen from institutional investors.

In particular:

- the FRC publishes a list of institutional investors that have publicly reported the extent to which they follow the Stewardship Code, now in excess of 260. This includes numerous institutions, large asset managers, asset owners and service providers, smaller specialised investors, proxy voting agencies, investment consultants and UK pension funds;

- NAPF issued a public statement of support urging pension funds and asset managers to include stewardship in their investment manager review processes; and

- the FCA requires all member firms (excluding venture capitalists) that manage investments for professional clients (excluding individuals) to adhere to the Stewardship Code and publicly disclose the extent to which they comply.

Indications from the FRC's report 'Developments in Corporate Governance 2013' are that the market is willing to take on board the concept of stewardship. The FRC also found some evidence that investors were taking account of their stewardship responsibilities in their general contact with companies, even though it was clear there is a considerable way to go in the integration of governance and investment decision-making. In practical terms there is evidence that this is having a positive effect and engagement by shareholders is improving, as demonstrated by a larger percentage of shareholders casting their votes at general meetings. Whilst in the past there might have been an average of 50–60% of votes cast by shareholders of a listed company, this has increased certainly amongst FTSE 250 companies to more in the region of 80–90% of votes. It is also evident that shareholder engagement was instrumental in discouraging the G4S Board not to proceed with acquisition of the Danish company ISS; in changing the remuneration policy at Barclays; and improving the terms of Xstrata's merger with Glencore.

It has not been uncommon historically for an institutional shareholder's vote to fail to be submitted to the company due to a long and complex proxy voting chain. This has long been a frustration for companies. However, now the institutional shareholder's responsibilities are set out in the Stewardship Code and must be publicly reported on, there is less scope for such inefficiency and lack of accountability in proxy submission. This in turn links into the Association of Investment Companies' Code of Corporate Governance ('AIC Code') which requires investment companies to determine what is required of investment managers in terms of voting and engagement, and this must be set down formally and adherence be monitored.

EU corporate governance regime   10.60

An effective corporate governance framework is essential for success of the internal market as it will give companies and customers confidence to conduct business with those from other European countries, confident that appropriate corporate governance arrangements are in place to ensure they are competitive and sustainable into the future.

However, the financial crisis, problems of excessive risk-taking in credit institutions and many incidents of corporate wrong-doing and failings that have emerged since have showed up potential flaws in current corporate governance practice in the UK, causing the European Commission ('EC') to question the validity of the current approach based on Codes, soft law and the principle of complying or explaining any deviations from what is considered best governance practice. In particular, debate was sparked about whether there was a need for more prescriptive regulation.

As a result, on 5 April 2011 the EC published a Green Paper on the EU corporate governance framework launching public consultation and a process of reflection on possible ways to modernise and improve effectiveness of the existing company law and corporate governance framework and regimes across Europe. The Green Paper focused on three areas:

- **Board of Directors**: the need to have high-performing effective Boards to challenge the executive management, which include in their memberships non-executives with diverse views, skills and appropriate professional experience, who have sufficient time to dedicate to the companies. The role of the chairman and the Board's responsibilities for risk management were also considered.

- **Shareholders**: shareholder engagement is essential to hold management accountable for its performance. Shareholders should be encouraged to avoid short-term profits and take greater interest in sustainable returns, long-term performance and be more active on corporate governance issues.

- **Comply or explain**: the Green Paper explored how the regime could be improved, as often the explanations of departures from Code requirements were not considered satisfactory. This examination was particularly relevant to the UK where the 'comply or explain' regime is still considered to work very well, giving companies and their Boards a desired degree of flexibility.

The EC published the results of the consultation on the 2011 Green Paper, from which it was evident that the majority of respondents were in favour of new measures to modernise the company law and corporate governance framework.

Respondents supported the 'comply or explain' approach, which they consider offers an appropriate degree of flexibility. Many other points were raised, for example, on diversity and gender balance, distinction between and clarification of directors' functions, external evaluation of the Board, greater disclosure of directors' remuneration, putting the remuneration report to the vote and greater responsibility by the Board for risk management arrangements, etc and, as seen throughout this book, these are already being debated and addressed at national level in the UK.

However, it should be noted that whilst there was continued support for the 'comply or explain' approach and many respondents were generally against the imposition of compulsory rules, there was a call for improvements and more detailed explanation of departures from the Code as well as better monitoring of the explanations given by shareholders, Boards, auditors and market specific monitors. The FRC has addressed this by initiating discussion and seeking feedback on what constitutes a meaningful explanation, sufficient for shareholders' needs (para **10.15**). The FRC's report entitled 'What Constitutes an Explanation under "Comply and Explain"?' was issued in February 2012 and provides important guidance for directors.

Towards the end of 2012 the EC launched an action plan which sets out initiatives the EC intends to take to modernise company law and the corporate governance framework, focussed in three key areas: enhancing transparency; engaging shareholders; and supporting companies' growth and competitiveness.

The EC's main initiatives are summarised at the end of the action plan and include, amongst others, initiatives to improve:

(1)   disclosure of the Board's diversity policy and risk management arrangements;

(2)   visibility of shareholdings;

(3)   quality of corporate governance reports, particularly explanations of non-compliance with corporate governance best practice;

(4)   transparency of directors' remuneration policies and individual remuneration awards, granting shareholders the right to vote on remuneration policy;

(5)   regulation of proxy advisors who exert substantial influence over voting by large institutional investors, given concern about their lack of transparency in methods used to prepare their advice and possible conflicts of interest;

(6)   shareholder oversight of related party transactions;

(7)   disclosure of voting and engagement policies.

From this list it is evident that much progress has already been made by the UK on points (1), (2), (4), (6) and (7) and the main area of focus now is on improving the quality of disclosures made by companies of the reasons and underlying factors where they do not comply with corporate governance best practice provisions.

11 Directors' duties and employment issues

11 Directors' duties and employment issues

Whilst employees essentially sell their labour to companies in exchange for a salary and other benefits, the rights and duties contained in present day employment protection legislation extend well beyond the bounds of their contractual relationship with the company. Indeed, many provisions of the Employment Act 2002 (EA 2002) have a significant impact on employment matters.

Directors are of course responsible for ensuring that the company complies with requirements of employment legislation but, where they fail in any respect, a claim made by an aggrieved employee will be against the company and not the director, who has the protection of limited liability. However, where the directors are considered by the shareholders to have acted in a fraudulent or negligent manner in breaching requirements of employment legislation, the company may make a claim against them for failure to act in the best interests of the company and to attend diligently to its affairs. Such counterclaim may be for a contribution to, or an indemnity against, any financial penalty imposed on the company for the breach.

More specifically, CA 2006 s 172(1) places a duty on directors to have regard to employees' interests when making decisions. This duty is owed by the directors to the company and is enforceable by the company in the same manner as any other fiduciary duty owed to the company.

In practical terms, the directors must ensure that they act in a way likely to promote the 'success of the company for the benefit of its members as a whole' in their treatment of employees throughout the span of their relationship with the company, which means that they must ensure that:

- an employment contract or written particulars of employment are provided and terms of the contract are observed (para **11.20**);
- there is no discrimination in the workplace on any grounds;
- employees' statutory rights are observed;
- a safe and healthy work environment is provided;
- employee rights on a transfer of undertaking are observed;
- required insurance policies are effected and maintained;
- illegal immigrants are not employed; and
- employees are of a legal age.

Failure to meet the requirements of legislation in these areas may result in a claim against the company for unfair dismissal, injury arising from work, or breach of contract terms, etc, all of which would be likely to involve direct or indirect costs to the company in the form of damages, taking up management time, by attracting bad publicity or damaging the company's reputation. Indeed statistics published by the Employment Appeal Tribunal reveal that there were 186,300 claims made to it by aggrieved employees in the year to 31 March 2012, covering some 321,800 complaints. Although a considerable number of claims are usually withdrawn or settled before a tribunal hearing, dealing with a claim in the first place can take up a significant amount of time which could be much better spent on directing and managing the company's operations.

Indeed, the majority of directors and those in managerial positions recognise that by rewarding employees (through a combination of security and good working conditions), the company is more likely to achieve a high level of productivity coupled with harmonious employee relations, desirable from a commercial perspective. Many companies have adopted government-supported staff motivation and training schemes such as Investors in People in recognition of the benefits such initiatives provide to the company.

Furthermore, directors must be aware that common law applies 'vicarious liability' to companies for actions by employees carried out in the course of their work which result in injury to third parties. The company could therefore be liable for acts of race or sex discrimination, harassment, victimisation and abuse and or for accidents which occur between employees or are caused by them, even where there is no prior knowledge by the company as employer that such acts took place. For example, in *Wallbank v Wallbank Fox Designs Ltd* [2012] EWCA Civ 25 the Court of Appeal held that the employer was vicariously liable for substantial injury caused to the company's managing director in a violent assault by a worker in their factory. This emphasises the need for directors to not only address employment protection, codes of conduct and associated matters at a managerial level, but also to ensure the company's philosophy and requirements for treatment of such matters are communicated to employees and adhered to by them at all times.

Directors of large companies will usually have employment professionals within their organisation who have expertise in this area and can advise on human resources, personnel and employment matters. Where this is the case, the directors will be able to delegate day-to-day responsibility for such matters to these specialists, whilst retaining overall responsibility for the company's treatment of employees and the procedures and controls in place. Directors of smaller companies, on the other hand, are unlikely to have access to such internal resource and are likely to be more closely involved in day-to-day employment issues and so must ensure so keep up to date with current requirements and changes in best practice. Such directors must also recognise the limits of their knowledge and, where appropriate, engage and consult with outside specialists and use all available information resources, such as the Advisory Conciliation and Arbitration Service (Acas).

Requirements of CA 2006   11.10

Provisions in CA 2006 s 172(1) require directors to regard the interests of employees in the management of the company and performance of their functions, which, as mentioned above, in practice, it would be difficult not to consider if the company is to attract and secure a workforce.

In addition, unless entitled to the small company exemption, the business review contained in the directors' annual accounts must contain a fair review of the company's business and descriptions of the main risks and uncertainties, which may include employment matters, for example where a company operates in areas where there is political unrest. Furthermore, a quoted company must, as far as is necessary to understand the development, performance and future of a company, include information about the company's employees. This includes the requirement to disclose relevant policy information and analysis of how effective such policies are with reference to identified and measurable key performance indicators. This is likely to include the company's policies on employment, training, promotion, advancement of disabled persons, etc.

Where the required disclosures are not made in the directors' report to the accounts, the directors in office immediately before the end of the accounting period in question will be guilty of an offence and liable to a fine (CA 2006 s 419).

Contracts of employment   11.20

Directors must be aware that the Employment Rights Act 1996 (ERA 1996), as amended by EA 2002, requires the employer to provide a written statement of basic terms and conditions of employment to all employees who will be working for eight or more hours a week and be employed for more than a month.

Contents   11.21

The statement must be provided within two months of the employee commencing employment and, if an employer fails to comply with this requirement, an employment tribunal has power to award two weeks' pay to the employee for non-compliance.

As a minimum, the statement of particulars must contain the basic information shown in **APPENDIX 25** (ERA 1996 s 1). This statement of basic terms must be consistent with the terms of employment offered on recruitment and, at the same time, comply with minimum statutory requirements for notice of termination, statutory sick pay, maternity pay and redundancy payments, etc.

The written statement must also specify disciplinary rules and to whom an employee can apply if he has a grievance or is dissatisfied with a disciplinary decision, or advise the employee where these rules and policies can be found.

Whilst many employers limit information in the employment contract to the statutory minimum, in many instances they are extended, particularly for senior staff, managers and executives.

Additional provisions in the employment contract need careful consideration, as they habitually increase the employee's benefits and, at the same time, increase the restrictions on them. Wording of clauses for inclusion in the employment contract need careful drafting as, for example, a clause stating that an employee's pay would be reviewed annually may inadvertently give the employee a contractual right to a pay increase each year (*Clark v BET plc* [1997] IRLR 348) and a clause imposing a penalty on an employee might not be upheld (*Giraud UK Ltd v Smith* [2000] IRLR 763, where a clause requiring payment to the employer for unworked notice was not enforceable).

The drafting of a non-standard employment contract would normally be considered on an individual basis in liaison with the employee, by either the Board or senior management with advice and assistance from employment professionals. Non-standard clauses might include:

- confidentiality requirements;

- restrictive covenants, such as prohibiting the employee from working for a competitor for a given amount of time. Restrictive covenants must be tailored to the particular circumstances, should be based on the realities of the individual's role and must be limited to what is strictly necessary to protect the employer's legitimate interests. The length of time for which such 'non-competition' clauses or restrictive covenants apply should be carefully considered and must be reasonable in relation to its duration, area and terms (in *Associated Foreign Exchange Ltd v International Foreign Exchange (UK) Ltd* [2010] EWHC 1178 (Ch) it was considered longer than necessary and was not upheld). If the clause is drafted too widely it is likely to be considered unnecessarily restrictive and unenforceable (*WRN Ltd v Ayris* [2008] EWHC 1080 (QB) in which non-dealing and non-solicitation covenants were considered too wide and could not be enforced wide). As a practical point, it is a good idea to get the employee to take legal advice about the effect of any restrictive covenants and to obtain written confirmation that they have done so and consider the terms of the covenants to be fair;

● garden leave provisions;

● fringe benefits;

● mobility requirements;

● exclusivity of service agreement;

● definition of the ownership of any inventions, patents and copyright developed during employment.

Once the contract terms are finalised, the contract is usually signed by the employer and the employee to confirm that both parties agree to adhere to the terms and conditions detailed in the document. The directors then have a duty to ensure that terms in the contract, as well as any statutory requirements relating to employees' rights, are observed and adhered to by the company and the employee. Failure by an employer to observe a contractual arrangement, eg by reducing contractual bonus payments would be considered a breach of the employment contract (*Attrill v Dresdner Kleinwort Ltd* [2012] EWHC 1189 (QB)) as would failure to make payment in lieu of notice where an employee is dismissed summarily unless loss of the right is specifically stated in the employment contract (*T & K Home Improvements v Skilton* [2000] IRLR 595, EAT).

Furthermore, it is important that employment contracts are periodically reviewed over the duration of the relationship with the employee. This is important not only to ensure the contracts comply with current law and practice and do not contain any inconsistencies, but also to make sure that provisions which might be appropriate given an employee's progression towards seniority (such as enhanced restrictive covenants and confidentiality requirements) are included.

Change of contract terms   **11.22**

A change to an employment contract can be made at any time by agreement between the employee and the employer and a written statement setting out full details of the change must be supplied to each employee affected within a month of the change, although failing to do so will not necessarily invalidate the change.

If consent from an employee to a change in their contract is not forthcoming, it cannot be imposed unilaterally and it is not, for example, sufficient to notify employees of a change via a staff noticeboard (*Kerr and Park v Sweater*

Shop (Scotland) Ltd [1996] IRLR 424). The directors would need to consider whether it was appropriate to terminate the employee's contract and offer him a new contract incorporating the new terms. Directors should be aware that by taking this course of action they would be breaching the terms of the employee's existing contract and it is likely to result in a claim for damages for wrongful or unfair dismissal. The particular circumstances of each case will need to be considered, although generally such action should be avoided.

Furthermore, where an employer's breach of contract is of sufficient materiality to be repudiatory, it may justify a claim for unfair dismissal. For example, in *Hilton v Shiner Ltd* [2001] IRLR 727, an employee was successful in bringing a claim for constructive dismissal against his employer who had demoted him, when they suspected his honesty, to a job that did not involve handling money as an alternative to dismissal. The employee did not consent to the demotion which, as it was material, was considered a breach of contract. It is advisable to obtain written confirmation from the employee indicating his consent to the change. However, in most circumstances continuing to work for the employer implies that he has agreed to the change, although there are exceptions to this (*Aparau v Iceland Frozen Foods* [1996] IRLR 119, EAT).

Handbook and policies   11.30

From a practical perspective directors must ensure that their companies' employees know what is expected of them in terms of performance and behaviour and what they can expect from the company in return. A great many employment problems stem from a mere lack of understanding and difference in expectations, which can be avoided by good, clear, written communication. Even a small company will benefit from a concise employment handbook setting out what an employee must do when they are sick or would like to take holiday, what form performance reviews will take and how training and development needs will be addressed, and how the company will support equal opportunities, etc.

The handbook might be longer and more complex in a larger company and be supported by numerous other standalone policies such as those addressing use of email, social media and the Internet; corporate hospitality, anti-bribery and corruption; whistleblowing; equal opportunities; discrimination, anti-harassment and bullying; and maternity and paternity leave, etc. Implementation of these policies will help ensure employees know what behaviour is expected of them and the consequences of should they breach the requirements. In addition they should identify the channels an aggrieved employee can use to raise a complaint and the approach the employer will take to try to resolve matters.

Once reviewed and endorsed by senior management and the Board, these policies and procedures should be communicated to employees. This can be done by a variety of methods including use of email, the company's intranet, newsletters or as part of employee induction packs and periodic training programmes. Communication should be ongoing, with periodic refreshers given to employees and others such as contractors and suppliers where appropriate.

Once written and issued the employment handbook and supporting policies should not be historic documents left on a shelf. They should be written in such a way that they are useful, informative and frequently used for reference by employees and employers to check employment requirements.

Provisions in the employment handbook are not normally contractual and can therefore be varied by employers and, indeed, it is important for the employer to keep the handbook and accompanying policies up to date as legislation, employment practices and the environment in which the company operates change frequently and the policies need to adapt accordingly. For example, the company's email and Internet provisions might to be reviewed and expanded to ensure internal rules on employees using Facebook and other social media both in and outside work are clear. Indeed, recognising the complexities in this area, Acas have published guidelines for employers specifically on use of social media.

Dismissal   11.40

Directors must be aware that they may dismiss an employee from working for the company where there is a valid reason sufficient to cause dismissal, but the employee's treatment must be fair and employees have statutory rights to protect them from unfair dismissal which must be observed (ERA 1996 s 94). Subject to having been employed by the company for two years, an employee who has been dismissed can request a written statement of the reasons for dismissal.

Quite rightly, gone are the days of calling someone in to address aspects of their performance or unacceptable behaviour, dismissing them on the spot and marching them off the company's premises with their final pay cheque and P45 in hand. As detailed below, it is necessary for a careful and considered formal approach to be taken to disciplinary action and, if necessary, dismissal, and for the process and actions taken to be evidenced in writing. Without this, even if the reason for dismissal is considered fundamentally fair, the employment tribunal might determine the process that was followed was unreasonable.

Unfair dismissal   11.41

With effect from 6 April 2012, an employee who has been employed for at least two years and considers himself to have been unfairly dismissed may make application to an employment tribunal disclosing details of the complaint for consideration (Unfair Dismissal and Statement of Reasons for Dismissal (Variation of Qualifying Period) Order 2012 (SI 2012/989)). For employees engaged prior to 6 April 2012, a one-year qualifying period applies.

However, directors should be aware that if an employee is dismissed for a reason connected with maternity (ERA 1996 ss 108(3) and 109(2)), for refusing to forgo a right conferred by the Working Time Regulations 1998 (SI 1998/1833), because he seeks to enforce his right to the national minimum wage (National Minimum Wage Act 1998), because of the employee's political opinions or affiliations (ERA 1996 s 108(4)) or for bringing a claim against the employer under whistleblowing legislation, there is no qualifying period required before the employee can make a claim of unfair dismissal. In addition, employees working under a fixed-term contract cannot waive their right to claim unfair dismissal and any such clauses will be invalid (ERA 1999 s 18).

The application for unfair dismissal must be made within three months of the contract being terminated. ERRA 2013 now requires that, before making an application to institute proceedings, potential claimants must provide information about the claim to Acas in the first instance and a conciliation officer will be appointed to promote settlement between the parties (Employment Tribunals Act 1996 s 18A). It is hoped that by actively encouraging conciliation in this way, settlement will be reached, avoiding the need for expensive and time-consuming tribunal processes. If settlement is not possible or cannot be agreed within the required time, Acas will issue a certificate confirming the position and only at this point can the employment tribunal application proceed.

In addition, on 25 April 2013 the Government published the Employment Tribunal and the Employment Appeal Tribunal Order 2013 which introduced fees for lodging claims for unfair dismissal. The fees were introduced in an attempt to discourage vexatious, unfounded and inappropriate claims; encourage more mediation and settlement, without need for formal recourse to tribunal; and to make those who use the tribunal system accountable for the cost. Whilst there is a fee remission system for those on a low income, there is an initial fee for issuing an employment tribunal claim, and a further fee for hearing the claim, split into fees for:

- Level 1 claims (simple cases such as unlawful deductions of wages, holiday and redundancy pay) – issuing fee £160 and hearing fee £230;

- Level 2 claims (more complex cases such as unfair dismissal, discrimination and equal pay claims) – issuing fee £250 and hearing fee £950; and

- Employment Appeal Tribunal fees (where the case goes to appeal) – issuing fee £400 and hearing fee £1,200.

Directors should also note that from 25 June 2013, where an employment tribunal finds an employer has breached a worker's rights, it may order the employer to pay a penalty to the Secretary of State of between £100 and £5,000 (Employment Tribunals Act 1996 s 12A).

With effect from 1 February 2014 the statutory limit on a week's pay (relevant for determining the basic award in unfair dismissal cases) is £464 and the unfair dismissal compensatory award limit is £76,574 and may be even higher where an employer refuses to reinstate an employee. In addition the ERA 1999 introduced limitless compensation awards for employees unfairly dismissed or selected for redundancy after they have exercised their rights as whistleblowers on health and safety or public disclosure matters and also where the dismissal is related to unlawful discrimination. As a result the financial burden on a company for unfairly dismissing an employee is potentially considerable and should act as a deterrent against such action.

It should also be noted that in *Leonard v Strathclyde Buses Ltd* [1998] IRLR 693, Ct of Sess the compensation award included the loss in share value that the employee suffered when he was unfairly dismissed and forced to sell his shares.

In the period April 2012 to March 2013 statistics from the Employment Tribunal show 49,036 claims for unfair dismissal were received and accepted for consideration by tribunal; in 2011/12 the maximum award made was £173,408 and the average award was £9,133. Together these give directors an idea of the likelihood of a claim and the severity of financial consequences the company might face where an employee is unfairly dismissed. In addition, the substantial amount of management time incurred investigating and defending a claim is a hidden cost, as is the amount of distraction caused to other employees as facts and information are gathered.

Whilst the list is not exclusive, terminating an employee's employment contract for any of the following reasons will automatically be considered unfair where:

- it is connected with maternity or the taking or proposal to take paternity leave, parental leave, adoption leave or time off for dependants (ERA 1996 s 99);

- it follows a request for flexible working arrangements (ERA 1996 s 104C);

- it arises for reasons connected with the minimum wage (ERA 1996 s 104A);

- the employee attempts to assert a statutory employment right (ERA 1996 s 104) – for example in *Mennell v Newall & Wright (Transport Contractors) Ltd* (1996) 553 IRLB 13 it was ruled that the employee had been unfairly dismissed for refusing consent to allow the employer to deduct the cost of training from his pay;

- there is imminent danger and the employee attempts to take action on health and safety grounds (Trade Union Reform and Employment Rights Act 1993 s 28);

- it follows a transfer of undertaking (subject to meeting the one-year qualifying period);

- it arises by the employee refusing to work on Sundays (ERA 1996 s 101);

- it occurs due to membership or non-membership of a trade union (Trade Union and Labour Relations (Consolidation) Act 1992 (TULR(C)A 1992) s 152);

- it follows an employee having taken part in lawfully organised industrial action lasting twelve weeks or less (TULR(C)A 1992 s 238A);

- the employee carried out activities in relation to his or her role as a representative on health and safety matters (ERA 1996, s 100);

- it occurs due to the employee performing or proposing to perform duties as an employee representative, a workforce representative, or as a trustee of the occupational pension scheme (ERA 1996 ss 103 and 102 respectively);

- it arises for reasons connected with the Working Time Regulations 1998 (ERA 1996 s 101A);

- it is connected with reasons relating to the Tax Credits Act 2002 (ERA 1996 s 104B);

- it is in connection with exercising the right to be accompanied at a disciplinary or grievance hearing (Employment Relations Act 1999, s 12);

- it follows proceedings brought against the employer by a part-time employee or where the employee refuses to forgo a right pursuant to the Part-time Workers Prevention of Less Favourable Treatment Regulations 2000 (SI 2000/1551) (s 7(6), see para **11.70**);

- it arises on grounds relating to the Fixed-term Employees (Prevention of Less Favourable Treatment) Regulations 2002 (SI 2002/2034);

- it occurs after an employee has made a protected disclosure and 'blown the whistle' on wrongdoing at (see para **11.70**). ;

- it arises for reasons relating to the Information and Consultation of Employees Regulations 2004 (SI 2004/3426);

- it arises for reasons relating to the Occupational and Personal Pension Schemes (Consultation by Employers and Miscellaneous Amendment) Regulations 2006 (SI 2006/349);

- it occurs due to jury service (ERA 1996 s 98B).

In addition to a claim for unfair dismissal an employee may also pursue:

- a civil claim for wrongful dismissal where his contract has been terminated with insufficient notice or payment in lieu of notice; or

- a claim for damages for constructive dismissal where, although the employee terminated the employment contract, the employer allegedly gave him no option.

Another important development for directors to note is the Supreme Court's decision in *Ravat v Halliburton Manufacturing and Services Ltd* [2012] UKSC 1 that an employment tribunal had jurisdiction to hear an unfair dismissal complaint made by an employee of a UK company working abroad, on a rotation basis, providing services to a foreign company.

Fair dismissal   **11.42**

However, an employer may dismiss an employee for reasons relating to capability (including skill, aptitude and health), conduct, redundancy, a statutory requirement or any other substantial reason. Of these, the most common reason for dismissal is the employee's conduct, and, for the dismissal to be considered fair, it must be sufficiently concerning to warrant dismissal. For example, in *Denco Ltd v Joinson* [1991] IRLR 63, EAT unauthorised use of a restricted computer file was considered gross misconduct and the resulting dismissal was deemed to have been fair. Another example is *Winful v Whitbread Group plc* ET/1200367/2011 in which it was determined fair for the employer to dismiss an employee who lost the right to work in the UK as a sound procedure had been followed, involving meeting with the employee and exploring what could be done to help resolve the situation. Even where there is a valid reason for dismissing an employee, the directors must ensure that appropriate and reasonable action is taken in the period leading up to dismissal. For example, where an employee's time-keeping or performance has been consistently poor, he must be made aware of the problem and be given an opportunity to improve before dismissal is considered. In *John Lewis plc v Coyne* [2001] IRLR 139, EAT, an employee of 14 years was dismissed for gross misconduct for using a departmental telephone for personal calls despite a circular sent to all staff warning that such action could lead to dismissal. The employment tribunal found the dismissal unfair as the unacceptable behaviour was not raised with the employee individually and there was no prior warning, investigation of circumstances or opportunity for the employee to improve behaviour.

In addition, in *Market Force (UK) Ltd v Hunt* [2002] IRLR 863 the employment tribunal ruled that the employee's dismissal was procedurally unfair. The employee was summarily dismissed when pornographic material was found on his computer and the tribunal considered that, had appropriate investigation been carried out, the employee's claim that it had been stored by mistake might have been substantiated. In such cases where dismissal is considered to be wrongful in terms of not having followed the procedure set out in an employee's contract, an award may be made to compensate for the time it should have taken to correctly follow the disciplinary process.

Disciplinary, grievance and dispute resolution procedures   11.43

Sections 1–7 of the Employment Act 2008 changed the law on disciplinary, dismissal and grievance issues as follows:

- the statutory procedures for dealing with discipline, dismissal and grievance issues, set out in the Employment Act 2002, were repealed;

- employers are encouraged to resolve disputes in the workplace, without need for recourse to an employment tribunal and Acas offers a pre-claim conciliation service for all employment tribunal matters;

- employers are encouraged as a minimum to observe guidance in the Acas Code of Practice on discipline and grievance handling in the workplace (the 'Acas Code') as, whilst it does not prescribe mandatory steps to be followed, it sets out good practice and will be used to determine whether an employer's or employee's actions were 'reasonable'; and

- employment tribunals have discretionary powers to adjust awards (up or down) by up to 25% if employers or employees have failed unreasonably to comply with the Acas Code.

The Acas Code gives employers guidance on handling discipline and grievance situations in the workplace. Whilst failure to observe provisions of the Acas Code would not necessarily render an employer's actions 'unreasonable', observing the Code's principles and procedures could present a strong defence against a claim of unfair dismissal.

Essentially, Acas recommends that the disciplinary procedures:

(1)   are in writing;

(2)   clearly state to whom they apply;

(3)   are non-discriminatory;

(4)   require matters to be dealt with speedily;

(5)   keep proceedings, witness statements and records confidential;

(6)   indicate the disciplinary actions which may be taken;

(7)   specify the levels of management which have the authority to take the various forms of disciplinary action;

(8)   require workers to be informed of the complaints against them and, where possible, of all relevant evidence before any disciplinary meeting;

(9)   allow employees to state their case and be heard in good faith before decisions are reached, without any pre-judgment;

(10) allow workers the right to be accompanied;

(11) except where there has been gross misconduct, ensure no worker is dismissed for a first breach of discipline;

(12) require that no action is taken until the case has been carefully investigated, particularly where the facts are in dispute and need to be determined;

(13) require workers to be given an explanation of any penalties or sanctions imposed; and

(14) provide a right of appeal against a decision;

(15) any suspension is brief and is not used as a sanction prior to a disciplinary meeting.

The disciplinary procedures should apply equally to all employees, regardless of their length of service or status and should be periodically reviewed to ensure that they remain appropriate and in step with current legislation and good practice.

To ensure that all disciplinary matters are treated consistently, it is advisable for the directors to implement and communicate the company's disciplinary and grievance procedures to employees in writing. An example of a disciplinary policy is given in **APPENDIX 26** based upon the sample provided by Acas.

The role played by Acas has been expanded and it now has increased conciliation powers and the time limits for consultation have been removed. It is hoped that Acas will be able to identify those disputes that would benefit from early conciliation, thereby reducing the number of employment tribunal claims that are brought.

Directors should be aware that an employment tribunal will look at whether the employer and employee acted reasonably when they are assessing the merits of a claim. With this in mind, consideration will be given to whether:

- the issues were raised and dealt with promptly with regard to meetings, decisions and confirmation of the decisions;

- employer and employee acted consistently;

- necessary investigation was carried out to establish the facts of the case;

- the employee was informed about the problem and given opportunity to respond and put his or her case before the employer reached a decision;

- the employee was allowed to be accompanied to the disciplinary or grievance meeting; and

- the employee was given the opportunity to appeal the decision.

It is advisable for the disciplinary and grievance procedure, or other employment document policy or handbook, to set out any rules to be observed and standards of conduct expected of employees so there is complete clarity about what is expected. Whilst different companies will have different requirements, these will often cover matters such as timekeeping, absence, health and safety, use of organisation facilities, policies on discrimination, bullying and harassment, quality of work, etc, and also identify matters that would be considered gross misconduct.

Equal opportunities and discrimination   11.50

Discrimination law provides a framework for treating employees and others who fall within its scope fairly. It covers all aspects of the employment cycle, from how a job vacancy is described and advertised, the arrangements made for interviews and the manner in which selection is carried out, to the terms and conditions of employment and the way someone is treated during employment and at work social events. It also applies to termination of employment and can extend to work-related events post-termination, such as the giving of references.

Although progress has been made on discrimination issues in the last 40 years, inequality and disadvantage remain, even at the highest levels within companies. For example, Lord Davies' independent review into Women on Boards, published in February 2011, found that at that time only 12.5% of directors of FTSE 100 and 7.8% of FTSE 250 companies were women; and significant numbers of FTSE 100 and FTSE 250 companies (18% and almost half respectively) had no female directors at all. Whilst progress has been made and, as of March 2013, 17.3% of the directors of FTSE 100 and 13.2% of FTSE 250 companies are women, there is still a considerable way to go in terms of achieving equality at Board level.

In addition, statistics published by the EAT each year reveal that very high, and in many instances growing, numbers of discrimination cases are being accepted for consideration by employment tribunal in all the categories, including age, disability, sex, race, sexual orientation, religious grounds and on the basis of being part-time.

In any event, even if a claim is not accepted, the company will already have incurred substantial costs, in terms not only of legal fees for professional advice but also management time in addressing the matter, which might have been avoided with a bit more thought, communication, discussion, care and caution in the first place.

The Equality Act 2010   **11.50.1**

Discrimination law is now set out in the Equality Act 2010 (EqA 2010), which brings together and restates previous law embodied in a number of different pieces of legislation from the Sex Discrimination and Race Relations Acts to the Employment Equality (Religion or Belief) Regulations. The prior legislation has been repealed or revoked, save where an unlawful act took place before 1 October 2010.

A detailed explanation of the requirements of EqA 2010 can be found in the Equality and Human Rights Commission's Employment statutory code of practice ('the Code'). The Code, together with the more practical guidance for employers published by the EHRC, will help employers understand their responsibilities and avoid disputes in the workplace. Although employers are not legally obliged to follow the Code, doing so may help them avoid receiving a discrimination claim.

Who is protected?   **11.50.2**

The law protects a wide range of individuals, including, among others, agency workers, consultants and directors, as well as employees, from discrimination on the basis of specified protected characteristics.

Protected characteristic	Comments
Sex	Refers to a male or female. A comparator for the purposes of showing discrimination will be a person of the opposite sex.
Sexual orientation	Covers discrimination because someone is gay, heterosexual or bisexual and discrimination connected with manifestations of that orientation, such as appearance or the places they visit.
Gender reassignment	Refers to a personal rather than medical process in which someone moves from their birth sex to their preferred sex. An example given in the EHRC Code is that a person born physically female who decides to spend the rest of his life as a man and successfully passes as a man without the need for medical intervention would have the protected characteristic of gender reassignment.
Marriage or civil partnership	This characteristic does not protect those who are unmarried or those who are divorced or who have had a civil partnership dissolved.

Protected characteristic	Comments
Pregnancy or maternity	It is unlawful for an employer to subject a woman to unfavourable treatment during the protected period set out in the EqA 2010.
Race	Includes colour, nationality and ethnic or national origins.
Disability	Protects people with a physical or mental impairment which has a long-term and substantial adverse effect on their ability to carry out normal day-to-day activities. In most cases protection extends to those who had a disability in the past, even if they no longer have it.
Religion or belief	Includes lack of religion or belief. A religion need not be well-known or mainstream to attract protection but it must have a clear structure and belief system. A belief need not include faith or worship but must affect how a person lives their life or perceives the world and must attain a certain level of cogency, cohesion, seriousness and importance.
Age	Is defined by reference to a person's age group, eg under 40s, over 25s, middle-aged.

Part-time, fixed-term and agency workers **11.50.3**

A part-time worker has the right to be treated no less favourably than a comparable full-time employee, unless there are justifiable reasons for different treatment. This means that those working on a part-time basis are entitled to the same hourly and overtime rates as full-time employees; the same (pro-rated) holiday, maternity and parental leave; to join the company's pension schemes and receive pension benefits; and to be given access to training and development programmes. Directors must therefore make sure that the company's policies and employment contracts reflect these requirements. Where a part-time employee believes he is being treated less favourably, a request can be made for a written statement of the reasons for their treatment. Should the employer fail to comply with the request within 21 days of receipt, or fail to demonstrate justifiable reasons for the employee's treatment, then the employee may present a complaint to an employment tribunal. Where the employment tribunal considers the complaint is well founded, it may make a declaration as to the employee's rights and order payment of compensation and/or corrective action.

Developments in case law and the protection given to part-time workers are also worth noting. For example, in *Preston v Wolverhampton Healthcare NHS Trust*

(No 2); Fletcher v Midland Bank plc (No 2) [2001] ICR 217 the House of Lords confirmed that former part-time employees can backdate their membership of pension schemes to April 1976, or the start of their employment if later, as exclusion of part-time workers constituted sex discrimination as there were proportionately more women working part-time.

Employees working under fixed-term contracts also have the right, unless there is valid justification, to be treated no less favourably than comparable employees with no time limit on the length of their employment. Fixed-term employees can also request a written statement of the reasons for their less favourable treatment (see above). They are also entitled to be notified of permanent vacancies that arise; to protection from dismissal for enforcing a statutory right; and to receive statutory sick pay and notice of termination. In addition, the use of successive fixed-term contracts is limited to four years and any waiver of the employee's right to redundancy payments is invalid.

Similarly, the Agency Workers Regulations 2010 give agency workers, from day one of an assignment, entitlement to use shared workplace facilities, amenities and services such as childcare, transport and catering facilities and to receive information about permanent job vacancies in the company. After 12 weeks in an assignment an agency worker becomes entitled to the same basic pay and working conditions as a comparable employee in the company which means that he will be eligible for paid annual leave, overtime pay, performance-linked bonuses (if paid to others), rest breaks and rest periods and certain maternity benefits, etc.

It is important directors are generally aware of these requirements and ensure their companies' procedures and internal employment practices are regularly reviewed as the time and cost of rectifying mistakes in how part-time employees, fixed-term and agency workers have been treated can be substantial.

Types of discrimination   **11.50.4**

Type	Occurs when	Comments
Direct	An employee is treated less favourably than others because of one of the protected characteristics.	Usually the case must be made by reference to a comparator, save in pregnancy and maternity cases.
Indirect	An employer adopts a rule or policy that seems neutral but actually disadvantages someone with a protected characteristic when compared with others.	Defence exists if the employer can show that the policy or rule is objectively justified, for example on health and safety grounds.

Type	Occurs when	Comments
Harassment	An employee faces unwanted conduct that has the purpose or effect of violating their dignity or creating an offensive, hostile or intimidating environment.	Can be difficult for an employer to defend as they often only learn there is a problem when a claim is made.
Victimisation	A person is treated less favourably because they complain (or intend to complain) about discrimination, or have supported someone else's complaint.	An employee must not be disciplined or dismissed, or suffer reprisals from colleagues, because they have made a harassment complaint.

Someone who is wrongly perceived to have one of the protected characteristics is also protected from direct discrimination, eg a female employee who likes to go to gay clubs to dance as she does not get hassled by men is wrongly thought to be a lesbian could bring a discrimination claim on the basis of sexual orientation.

The law also protects someone who is discriminated against because they are associated with someone who has a protected characteristic (except where the discrimination is cased on the individual's marriage or civil partnership status). This includes, for example, a non-disabled employee who cares for a disabled person.

Preventing discrimination   **11.50.5**

Directors should familiarise themselves with the employment issues and practices that are affected by EqA 2010 and subsequent legislative developments. Some key problem areas which can give rise to discrimination claims are considered below.

- *Recruitment and promotion decisions*: failing to keep good records about how recruitment and promotion decisions were made can leave an employer open to claims of discrimination. Decisions should be made on the basis of strictly objective criteria and, where appropriate, employers should be flexible about arrangements to accommodate applicants' needs.

- *Retirement*: the statutory default retirement age has now been abolished and an employer can only continue to have and enforce a compulsory retirement age of 65 (or over) where it is 'a proportionate means of achieving a legitimate aim'. This is likely to be difficult to determine and demonstrate and should therefore be implemented with caution.

- *Flexible working requests and requests for time off*: refusing to change working hours or denying requests for time off can often constitute indirect discrimination. For example, more women than men making flexible working requests, often to accommodate childcare responsibilities, and turning down a request of this kind would be indirect sex discrimination unless the employer's action can be objectively justified. Problems can also arise where a request to change working hours or to take breaks at specific times is made so that the individual can observe religious requirements during the employer's normal working hours.

- *Dress codes*: When setting dress codes, the most relevant protected characteristics to take into account are gender, religion and disability. A dress code should be fair as regards the requirements for men and women. A conventional dress code requiring employees to dress smartly will normally be appropriate. It is important, however, that a dress code is sensitive to the requirements of different religions, beliefs and disabilities and that reasonable adjustments and exemptions are made to the dress code to accommodate these.

Formal policies which set out clearly the employer's position on equal opportunities and discrimination issues, such as an equal opportunities policy, an anti-harassment and bullying policy or a pregnancy and maternity policy should be put in place and communicated to employees (see para **11.30**). This is essential to make sure that employees know the behaviour expected of them and the consequences of breaching the policies. Such policies should identify the channels an aggrieved employee should use to raise a complaint and the approach the employer will take to try to resolve matters.

Consequences for employers   **11.50.6**

As highlighted elsewhere in this section, a good equality policy will set out the channels an aggrieved employee can follow to bring a complaint of discrimination, harassment or victimisation. If the complaint cannot be resolved internally, the ultimate course of redress for an employee will be to make a formal claim for damages to an employment tribunal but the whole process of initially investigating the matter internally and of any subsequent claim can be time-consuming, expensive and have a damaging negative effect on morale within the organisation. It is worth noting that damages awarded in discrimination claims are not subject to any cap on amount and are therefore unlimited.

Aside from any damages awarded there will also be legal costs incurred in defending the claim which will also take up a significant amount of management time and could result in unwelcome publicity, whether or not the employee's claim is upheld. For example, there was much adverse publicity around the case of *Eweida v British Airways plc* [2010] EWCA Civ 80 where an employee claimed she was disadvantaged by the company's dress code which forbade the wearing of visible jewellery and therefore prevented her from openly wearing a cross and chain as an expression of her Christian faith. It has now been established by the European Court of Human Rights that there must be a genuine reason behind such dress code, such as health and safety grounds and not just corporate branding.

Another consequence to note is that, as well as awarding damages to an aggrieved employee, an employment tribunal can issue recommendations and directions to an employer to improve practices generally (EqA 2010 s 124(3) (b)). In *Stone v Ramsay Health Care UK Operations Ltd* ET/1400762/11 the tribunal awarded the claimant £18,000 for damage to feelings caused by pregnancy and maternity-related discrimination (breach of EqA 2010 s 18) and suggested that the company provide training for its managers and HR team on maternity rights to prevent any recurrence of such poor treatment of an employee.

Transfer of undertakings and employment rights   11.60

The Transfer of Undertakings (Protection of Employment) Regulations 2006 (SI 2006/246) (TUPE 2006) require, amongst other things, protection of employees' rights and the terms and conditions of their employment on the transfer of an undertaking. This occurs when an undertaking, which is an economic entity capable of operating on its own as a going concern, is transferred from one employer to another. Further examples include mergers, a change of licensee or franchisee, the gift of a business through exercise of a will; the sale or transfer of ownership of a business owned by a sole trader or partnership; and situations where functions are outsourced or where outsourced services are to be provided by another contractor, or are taken back in-house. However, for the avoidance of doubt, contracts wholly or mainly for the supply of goods and situations where the services are provided for a single event or a task of short duration are not covered by TUPE 2006.

Before a transfer of undertaking takes place, the directors must ensure that comprehensive and accurate information is provided about the employees being transferred to the buyer under TUPE and the liabilities they will assume as a result. This information must be provided in writing and include details such as the identity and age of the transferring employees and the information contained in their written statements of particulars, together with details of any grievances or legal proceedings brought by them against the seller in the previous two years and details of any disciplinary action taken against them in the last two years. If this information is not provided, the buyer can bring a tribunal claim within three months of the date of transfer and compensation is awarded for each employee about whom information was not provided, or was defective.

Where a company is involved in a transfer of undertaking, the directors must ensure employees are provided with the details of and reasons for the transfer and the legal, economic and social implications for employees as well as any additional changes envisaged, such as relocation.

The employees' rights must be protected, all terms and conditions of employment must be the same with the new employer as with the old (with the exception of pension scheme rights) and dismissal must not occur as a result of the transfer, unless it can be proven necessary on technical, economic or organisational grounds. The employees' representative or the trade union (if appropriate) must be notified about the transfer and any existing trade union must be recognised by the new employer.

In addition, where 20 or more redundancies are planned on a transfer of undertaking, the employer is obliged to consult with employee representatives over the redundancies even where employees are not represented by a union (the Collective Redundancies and Transfer of Undertakings (Protection of Employment) (Amendment) Regulations 1999 (SI 1999/1925); or, where there is a union, TULR(C)A 1992.

The need to observe the requirement to consult with the union is emphasised by the MoD's reported £5 million out-of-court settlement for failing to do so, agreed at the end of May 2012. Prior to this, the case *Cable Realisations Ltd v GMB Northern* [2010] IRLR 42 demonstrated that sufficient time must be allowed in order to adequately discharge the duty to inform and consult employees about a TUPE transfer and allow consultation to take place on an informed basis.

Directors must be aware that failure to observe an employee's rights in respect of a transfer of undertaking is likely to lead to a claim of unfair dismissal, which can be expensive and damaging to the reputation of the company (see para **11.41**). Where a transfer of undertaking is under consideration, directors must ensure that they are fully aware of employees' rights. An increasing number of cases are referred to the courts, examples of which are as follows:

- *Betts v Brintel Helicopters Ltd and KLM ERA Helicopters (UK) Ltd* [1996] IRLR 45, in which it was held that, where the provision for automatic transfer of employment contracts is breached, the remedy is for the employee to take action for compensation for unfair dismissal.

- *TC Cleaning Contractors Ltd v Joy* (1996) IRLB 574, which established that contracts of all existing employees are automatically transferred, whether or not the acquiring employer is aware of the existence of all employees.

- *Rossiter v Pendragon plc* [2001] IRLR 256 which established that whilst a car salesman's resignation took place over a year after the transfer of undertaking, the detrimental changes in his working conditions arising from the transfer were sufficient for his claim of unfair dismissal to be successful.

It should be noted that dismissal following a transfer of undertaking is automatically considered unfair, except where it could not be avoided for reasons requiring economic, technical or organisational change. Where an employee makes application to an employment tribunal for unfair dismissal following a transfer of undertaking and no settlement is agreed with the employer, the tribunal has to determine whether dismissal was reasonable. In the event that the tribunal considers dismissal was unfair, it may make either:

(a)   an unfair dismissal award to an employee for compensation and order reinstatement;

(b)   a detriment award to an employee for compensation; or

(c)   a combined information and consultation award to each employee affected (as opposed to individual awards) which may amount to up to four weeks' pay for each person.

It should be noted that consultation on TUPE and measures to reduce what is increasingly perceived as an unnecessary burden on business closed in April 2013. Changes to the service provision requirement, post-transfer relocation, contract harmonisation and dismissal pre-transfer were proposed in the consultation document and implementation is expected in January 2014.

Other statutory rights   11.70

There is a wealth of legislation primarily devised to protect employees' rights. For example:

(1)   *Pay*. The National Minimum Wage Regulations 1999 came into force on 1 April 1999 and, subject to a small number of exceptions, apply to all workers with contracts of employment, as well as agency workers and some temporary workers. If not conducted already, the directors should ensure that a detailed salary review is carried out to ensure employees are being paid not less than the currently prescribed minimum wage. As at 1 October 2014, the standard rate is £6.50 per hour for employees aged 21 and over, but it should be checked in all cases as it does vary for those on development, young worker and apprentice rates. Employers are required to keep records from which it can be seen that they have paid

employees the national minimum wage. Employers should also check that they are paying the minimum wage to home workers on night shifts and those on standby as it was ruled in *British Nursing Association v Inland Revenue (National Minimum Wage Compliance Team)* [2002] EWCA Civ 494, [2002] All ER (D) 419 (Mar) that employees required to be on call at home to take telephone bookings must be paid the minimum wage for their shift. Also it should be noted that tips, gratuities, cover and service charges cannot be counted towards national minimum wage pay in any circumstances.

There is also an underlying requirement that employees receive equal pay for equal work, regardless of their race, sex, religion, disability, etc. The Equality Act 2010 (Equal Pay Audits) Regulations 2014 (SI 2014/2559) now require a tribunal to order an equal pay audit where it finds there has been an equal pay breach.

(2) *Statutory maternity rights.* Dismissal of a woman for a reason connected with her pregnancy would normally be considered unfair and in breach of provisions of ERA 1996 s 99 and SDA 1975. At present, pregnant women are entitled to:

- time off for antenatal care (ERA 1996 s 55);

- protection from dismissal on maternity-related grounds (see *Halfpenny v IGE Medical Systems Ltd* [1999] IRLR 177, CA in which it was held that an employee had been unfairly dismissed where she exercised her right to return to work but was not permitted to return);

- return to work after their maternity absence (ERA 1996 s 79);

- paid ordinary maternity leave of 26 weeks regardless of length of service. During the ordinary maternity leave period the employees' non-wage contractual benefits must be maintained (in *Gillespie v Northern Health & Social Services Board* [1996] IRLR 214, ECJ, it was held that women on maternity leave are entitled to benefit from any general pay increase during their maternity absence; and in *Caisse Nationale D'Assurance Vieillesse des Travailleurs Salariés v Thibault* [1998] IRLR 399, ECJ, it was held that a female employee on maternity leave was entitled to an annual performance assessment which could qualify her for promotion and refusal to carry out the assessment amounted to discrimination);

- additional maternity leave of 26 weeks, regardless of length of service. Whilst a woman is only entitled to SMP for the first 13 weeks of this additional maternity leave period, she may have a contractual right to receive pay which would need to be observed; and

- adoption leave and pay is available to parents who adopt children. Individuals or one adoptive parent are entitled to up to 39 weeks' ordinary adoptive leave in the same manner and on the same terms as described for maternity leave above.

Directors should note that the Shared Parental Leave Regulations 2014, which took effect on 24 November 2014, allow parents to choose how they manage their rights to maternity leave and pay. From 1 December 2014 mothers retain the right to the first two weeks' compulsory leave, but thereafter can share the remaining 50 weeks' maternity leave and 37 weeks' SMP with the father as flexible parental leave.

(3)   *Statutory sick pay.* Eligible employees are entitled to receive statutory sick pay (SSP) for periods of absence due to sickness exceeding four days and up to 28 weeks. This entitlement is set out in the Social Security Contributions and Benefits Act 1992 (as amended). The rate of SSP payable is determined periodically by statutory instrument. The directors must ensure that SSP is paid to eligible employees regardless of whether the company can recover a percentage of the payment by deducting it from their national insurance contributions, as determined by the Statutory Sick Pay Percentage Threshold Order 1995 (SI 1995/512). Furthermore, directors must ensure that full records of SSP are kept for at least three years including details of dates when an employee is unable to work and the amounts of SSP paid to the employee.

(4)   *Statutory notice periods.* ERA 1996 s 86 contains the minimum period of notice an employee may be given, which increases according to the employee's length of service. The employment contract must provide at least the statutory minimum period of notice and in many cases provides for a longer period of notice.

(5)   *Working Time Directive.* The Working Time Regulations 1998 (SI 1998/1833) provide most categories of employees with the right to:

- a limit of an average 48 hours per week which they can be required to work (averaged over a 17-week period);

- 11 consecutive hours' rest in each 24 hours worked;

- at least one day's rest a week;

- in-work rest breaks;

- paid annual leave of at least 5.6 weeks which cannot be replaced by payment in lieu – this entitlement now accrues from the first day of employment and when employees are on long-term sick leave (*Kigass Aero Components Ltd v Brown; Bold Transmission Parts Ltd v Taree; Macredie v Thrapston Garage* [2002] ICR 697);

- work a maximum of eight hours in each 24-hour period where the work is night work and is carried out between the hours of 11 pm and 6 am; and

- receive health checks, relevant for night workers.

The directors must therefore ensure that all employees' contracts of employment and the company's internal procedures, such as time recording arrangements and provisions for taking rest breaks, are checked to ensure they comply with these provisions. This is important, as EAT statistics show that in the year to March 2012 there were 94,700 claims relating to the Working Time Directive.

At present it is possible for employees to opt out of the limit on the maximum working week by entering into an agreement with the employer, which must be recorded in writing and signed by both parties (reg 5(4)). If no notice period is specified in the agreement the statutory notice period of seven days will apply. An employer cannot force an employee to work in excess of these hours where the employee is not willing to do so and dismissal based on these grounds would most likely be considered automatically unfair. In *Barber v RJB Mining (UK) Ltd* [1999] IRLR 308 a number of employees refused to sign opt-out agreements and it was held that they were entitled to stop work until their average working hours went below the 48-hour limit.

These Regulations, enforced by the Health and Safety Executive (HSE) and the local authority, require employers to maintain and keep a record of hours worked by each employee for at least two years together with details of any health assessments conducted for night workers and the number of hours worked at night. When reviewing the manner in which an employee's time worked is recorded, the directors must ensure the required information is provided. There are no longer any record-keeping requirements for those employees who opt out of the 48-hour week.

However, there has been considerable criticism of the UK over the continuing long-hours culture in the UK and the manner in which employers have implemented the opt out and the European Commission has expressed dissatisfaction with the UK's right to retain the opt out.

(6) *Parental leave.* The Maternity and Parental Leave (Amendment) Regulations 2001 (SI 2001/4010), amended by the Parental Leave Directive allow new and adoptive parents that have one year's completed service with their employers 18 weeks' unpaid parental leave in respect of each child born or adopted. This can be taken up until the child's fifth birthday unless the child is disabled, in which case it can be taken up to the child's 18th birthday. Where adopted, the leave can be taken up to their 18th birthday or the fifth anniversary of their adoption, whichever is sooner. Under the statutory fallback scheme, where no other terms are

agreed by the employer, parental leave can only be taken in blocks of a week at a time, subject to a maximum of four weeks in any year (unless the child is disabled, in which case individual days can be taken) and 21 days' notice of the intention to take parental leave must be given. The employer can postpone, but not refuse, the leave on commercial grounds where the timing would disrupt business or operations..

(7)   *Paternity leave.* EA 2002 entitles working fathers to two weeks' paid paternity leave, paid at the same flat rate as SMP.

(8)   *Flexible working.* EA 2002, as amended by the Flexible Working (Eligibility, Complaints and Remedies) (Amendment) Regulations 2009 (SI 2009/595), provides a parent responsible for bringing up a child with the right, whilst the child is aged under 16 years (or 18 years where the child is disabled), to request more flexible working hours and arrangements to accommodate their responsibilities for looking after the child. The employer needs to give detailed consideration to the request and, where it cannot be agreed, provide clear business grounds for refusal. Directors should be aware that from April 2014 the Children and Families Bill increased the right to request flexible working arrangements to all employees with 26 weeks' continuous employment.

(9)   *Time off.* An employee has the right to take a reasonable amount of time off work in order to deal with specified events affecting a dependant. Dismissal of an employee for exercising this right may constitute unfair dismissal (*Qua v John Ford Morrison Solicitors* (2003) Times, 6 February, EAT).

(10) *Information and consultation.* The Information and Consultation of Employees Regulations 2004 (SI 2004/3426) give employees of companies that employ at least 50 employees the right to be informed and consulted (normally through employee representatives) on an ongoing basis about:

(a)   recent and probable developments in the employing company's activities and economic situation;

(b)   employment prospects; and

(c)   any decisions likely to lead to substantial changes in work organisation or contractual relations, including redundancies and business transfers.

Where a written request is received from 10% of employees, a formal information and consultation procedure must be established. The contents and requirements of the procedure may either be determined by reaching negotiated agreement with employees' representatives or by implementing the statutory procedure. The parties have six months from receipt of a valid request to reach negotiated agreement or, where this is not possible, a further six months to put in place structures necessary to implement the statutory procedure. Under statutory provisions, an information and consultation committee needs to be established, comprising approximately one representative per 50 employees. The committee must be provided with timely information on items listed in points (a) to (c) above.

(11) *Whistleblowing.* The Public Interest Disclosure Act 1998 (PIDA 1998), as amended by the Prescribed Persons Order 1999 (SI 1999/1548), the Compensation Regulations 1999 (SI 1999/1549), gives an employee the right to make a protected disclosure and 'blow the whistle' on wrongdoing at work. These protective provisions apply where an employee discloses to his employer, legal adviser or a government minister, in the public interest and for no personal gain, activities that involve:

- a criminal offence;

- failure to comply with a legal obligation;

- a miscarriage of justice;

- health and safety hazards;

- a risk to the environment; or

- deliberate concealment of any of the aforementioned matters.

The case *Street v Derbyshire Unemployed Workers' Centre* (2004) All ER (D) 377 (Jul) confirmed that the disclosure must be made in good faith. Where an employee is antagonistic to the employer, this may demonstrate bad faith and the tribunal may reduce any award made by 25% where they determine the disclosure was not made in good faith.

Where an employee makes a protected disclosure (ERA 1996 s 43B, amended by ERRA 2013 s 17) about their employer's conduct and they have followed prescribed routes for making the disclosure, dismissal following the disclosure is likely to be considered automatically unfair (see para **11.41**). Similar protections are also in place for workers (ERA 1996 s 47B). There are numerous reports in the press of unfair dismissals being heard at employment tribunal following whistleblowing incidents. For example, in *Sharmila Chowdhury v Ealing Hospital NHS Trust* (*Independent*, 11 July 2010) the tribunal judges ordered that the radiology manager, who reported widespread misconduct and dishonest claims for thousands of pounds by senior doctors, be reinstated on full pay. More recently the decision by price reporting service ICIS Heren to dismiss an employee two months after he raised concerns and blew the whistle on possible price manipulation by large providers in the wholesale natural gas market is subject to appeal (*Guardian*, 18 January 2013). It was obviously felt there was merit in the allegations made as they are now subject to investigation by the FCA and Ofgem. Given the coverage such cases receive and the adverse publicity about the unexpected dismissal responses by the companies concerned, this could cause long-term damage to a company's reputation and perceived integrity from which it is difficult to recover.

To give some idea of scale, one of the largest awards made by a tribunal in a whistleblowing case was £477,600 awarded in the case of *Lingard v HM Prison Service* (unreported, 30 June 2005). In the case of *Virgo Fidelis Senior School v Boyle* [2004] ICR 1210, it was held that 'injury to feelings' suffered by a whistleblower constitutes a serious discriminatory breach, for which a compensation award of £15,000 to £25,000 would be appropriate (ERA 1996 s 103A).

Where a gagging clause is included in an employment contract or in a compromise agreement, reportedly banning protected disclosures, such clause is unenforceable. Again this issue has received much press coverage in recent months and from numerous press releases it is apparent such clauses have been widely used by businesses, the NHS and even charities such as the Royal British Legion.

Directors must therefore ensure their companies stop including such clauses and establish and communicate the procedure to follow and channels of communication through which employees can disclose any concerns they might have (see the example grievance procedure based on the Acas Code in **APPENDIX 26**). An employee is required to follow any internal procedures for bringing malpractice or other wrongdoing to their employer's attention before blowing the whistle externally. However, where the employer fails to determine and communicate an internal policy for whistleblowing an employee would be justified in making a wider, external disclosure, which potentially could be very damaging for the company (*B v ALM Medical Services Ltd* (unreported, 4 May 2000)). An example of a whistleblowing policy is set out in **APPENDIX 27**, which is for a company regulated by the FCA.

(12) *Redundancy.* Directors will doubtless be aware that when an employee is made redundant, for example where the company is struggling and there is a need to reduce staff costs; parts of a business are closing or relocating; or technology and systems have been developed so the role performed by the employee is no longer needed, this is essentially considered a fair reason for dismissal (ERA 1996 s 98(2)(c)). However, to be considered fair, the grounds for the redundancy must be genuine, not engineered, and the employee or employees made redundant must have been treated and selected fairly. The redundancy selection process must be evidence-based, objective, and show the basis on which employees in the redundancy pool were evaluated against measurable criteria to

determine who would be made redundant. In addition, there are formal requirements in terms of employee consultation which vary depending on how many people are affected, consideration must also be given to redeploying employees where possible and, where not, to helping them find alternative employment. Employees with a minimum of two years' continuous service before being made redundant, are entitled to tax-free statutory redundancy pay, calculated against the statutory scale according to the employee's age, length of service and gross weekly wage. As a word of caution, it can be easy for an employer to trip up in the redundancy process as there are many aspects to be considered. For example, in *Capita Hartshead Ltd v Byard* UKEAT/0445/11/RN the employer made the mistake of assuming that because it was mainly work for Ms Byard's clients that had diminished, it was reasonable she was the only person in the redundancy pool. The EAT did not agree and upheld the claim the dismissal was unfair as Ms Byard was one of a number of equally qualified actuaries, all of whom should have been included in the redundancy pool.

(13) *Study or training.* Provided they qualify, employees have a statutory right to request time off for study or training where they can demonstrate it will benefit the employer by achieving improvements in the employee's effectiveness (ERA 1996 s 63D). Only one such request may be made in a 12-month period and, whilst an employer may refuse a section 63D application, this can only be done where there are one or more permissible grounds for refusal. Such grounds might include concern about affordability of course fees and additional costs that would be incurred by reorganising work amongst existing staff or recruiting a temporary replacement, without which performance, quality and the ability to meet customer demands would suffer detriment; insufficiency of work during the employee's training period; or, indeed, that the employer does not consider the employee's effectiveness nor the performance of the business will be improved as a result of the study or training.

Whilst this section only touches on other statutory employment rights, it serves to emphasise the importance and range of employment issues that must be considered by directors and the need for carefully considered employment policies. Directors requiring additional information should refer to the range of advisory handbooks, booklets and information available online from Acas, BIS, GOV.UK and HMRC which cover most employment and pay-related issues.

It is important for directors to note that, with effect from 1 April 2014 and subject to certain conditions, tribunals have power pursuant to ERRA 2013 to issues financial penalties on employers that breach employment rights.

Health and safety requirements 11.80

It makes sound business sense for companies to protect one of their most valuable resources (ie the people who work for them), and all employers have a general duty to employees to ensure their health, safety and welfare at work. This duty emanates from requirements of common law, legislative provisions contained in the Health and Safety at Work etc Act 1974 (HSWA 1974) and subsequent regulations, and the HSE's approved codes of practice ('ACOPs').

However, whilst this basic premise is sensible and obvious, all too often health and safety requirements are reported as being 'over the top', 'ridiculous' or 'gone mad'. This largely stems from a misunderstanding of what is required, which many would say is hardly surprising given the sheer volume of regulation developed over the years and the numerous sources that employers must consult to find out exactly what is necessary. This is being addressed by the legislative review now underway (see para **11.80.1**). Indeed, it appears that in the resulting confusion, common sense can be forgotten and basic measures to protect employees' health and safety overlooked. Consequently there have been a large number of instances where accidents, injuries and fatalities could have been avoided by implementing simple preventative measures.

This misunderstanding has not been helped by those who choose to misinform companies about requirements to their own advantage (by telling them something is needed when it is not, or by preventing them from doing an activity because of their own risk-adverse attitude), or by those companies who blame 'health and safety' for their own failings in customer service. This problem with health and safety myths that have developed is now also being addressed (see para **11.80.1**). Strong leadership for health and safety at Board level is essential, as is the need for visible support by individual directors at all times in order that others within the company follow their lead. This support needs to be demonstrated in what the directors say, their actions and the decisions they make in order that preservation of health and safety becomes embedded in the company's culture. It is very important for those inside and outside the company to see the Board actively and genuinely promoting good health and safety culture and practice (see paras **11.87–11.89**).

As set out in the following paragraphs there are many duties that emanate from health and safety legislation which directors need to ensure are being observed on an ongoing basis at all levels within their companies. In order to achieve this, directors should ensure that:

- responsibility for health and safety compliance is allocated to a specific director, HR manager or health and safety committee;

- health and safety performance is regularly reviewed by the Board;

- they demonstrate high standards in relation to health and safety matters themselves, thereby encouraging a positive health and safety culture within their companies;

- health and safety audits and risk assessments are carried out at appropriate intervals, health and safety performance is routinely monitored and the outcome is reported to the Board;

- there is an accident response investigation plan which can be swiftly activated when needed.

These are expanded upon in the following paragraphs.

Legislative review   **11.80.1**

A number of reviews have been carried out in recent years to address concern that health and safety regulation in the UK is overly complex, lacks clarity about what is actually required and focuses on documenting compliance without achieving any benefits in terms of improved health and safety performance.

Lord Young's report 'Common Sense, Common Safety', published 15 October 2010, recommended changes to update the law and make it more accessible by bringing it into one place; move away from a compliance-driven approach; and simplify requirements for small and medium-sized businesses carrying out low-risk operations. Lord Young's recommendations were supported in the Government's plans for reform entitled 'Good Health and Safety, Good for Everyone'. As a consequence health and safety regulation for Britain's businesses is now undergoing major reform.

Lord Young recommended establishing an Official Occupational Safety and Health Consultants Register, to clamp down on rogue health and safety consultants and ensure businesses have access to competent advice and shifting legislative focus back to high-risk areas and serious breaches of health and safety regulations. The register has since been introduced by government and the shift in focus is also being addressed.

Various government bodies are taking the reforms forward and regular, six-monthly progress reviews are being carried out. Indeed, the review of progress carried out by Professor Lofstedt ('Reclaiming health and safety for all – A review of progress a year on', January 2013) found that 23 of Lord Young's 35 recommendations have been implemented.

In addition in March 2011 the Government established an independent review of health and safety legislation, chaired by Professor Löfstedt, to determine how existing legislation and guidance (comprising some 200 regulations and

53 HSE approved codes of practice) might be improved and simplified, and the burden on small businesses carrying out low-risk activities could be eased.

Professor Löfstedt's report 'Reclaiming health and safety for all: An independent review of health and safety regulation' was published on 28 November 2011, from which it was evident that:

(1)   the sheer volume of regulations was causing confusion amongst businesses about how they are to be interpreted and applied;

(2)   all too often reams of paperwork and lengthy risk assessment documents are generated to demonstrate compliance, which fail to identify and focus on key risks and do not achieve any real benefit or improvement to health and safety outcomes;

(3)   enforcement action is inconsistent, partly as a result of the division of responsibility between the HSE and local authorities; and

(4)   employers are confused by the obligation expressed in much of the legislation for them to take steps to address health and safety issues 'as far as is reasonably practicable', especially given strict liability often placed upon the employer by the civil justice system.

Professor Löfstedt recommended a number of changes to address these issues and ensure the regulatory and legal systems are aligned and focus on addressing risk and achieving proper management of health and safety. These recommendations are set out below, together with an indication of the progress already made by the Government towards addressing them (as reported in Professor Löfstedt's review 'Reclaiming health and safety for all – A review of progress a year on', January 2013):

•   Streamlining and consolidating sector specific regulations, thereby reducing the amount of regulations by up to 35% by April 2015. It is anticipated this will involve revoking some regulations and amending many others including (as identified in Professor Löfstedt's report) those covering first aid, electricity at work, reporting of injuries and dangerous occurrences, working at height, construction and design management, etc, which will be familiar to most readers.

Work is on track and there has already been significant progress towards reducing the volume of regulation. In particular, the Health and Safety (Miscellaneous Revocations) Regulations 2012 (SI 2012/1537) and the Health and Safety (Miscellaneous Repeals, Revocations and Amendments) Regulations 2013 revoke many redundant and outdated statutory instruments. This is a significant step towards making the regulatory framework easier to understand and there has also been significant progress addressing the lack of understanding and misinterpretation of many other regulations, such as the portable appliance testing, working at height, etc by improving information available to employers, particularly on the HSE's website.

- Clarifying regulatory requirements, particularly the distinction between specific duties as opposed to administration concerns, to improve understanding of what is meant by 'reasonably practicable'.

The first part of Professor Lofstedt's recommendation for clarification was addressed in December 2012 when the HSE updated information on its website to make clear the distinction between those regulations that impose specific duties and those that concern administrative requirements.

In addition the 'Health and Safety Toolbox' was added to the HSE's website in September 2012 to help explain what is meant by 'reasonably practicable'. It is interactive and makes practical advice, tools and case studies available in an uncomplicated fashion, particularly with small businesses in mind.

- Improving consistency of enforcement action by one body, the HSE, directing all inspection and enforcement activity.

The HSE is consulting on a National Local Authority Enforcement Code as a means of achieving greater consistency in enforcement but is not, at this stage, proposing to take over the inspection and enforcement action where currently conducted by local authorities.

- Redirecting enforcement activity towards businesses with the greatest risk of injury or ill-health and, indeed, inspectors are now particularly targeting businesses and premises in high-risk sectors.

- By June 2013 reviewing regulatory provisions that impose 'strict liability' on employers and clarifying the content and status of pre-action protocols, to address inconsistency with 'reasonably practicable' requirements.

Again there has been significant progress and s 69 of the Enterprise and Regulatory Reform Act 2013, which received Royal Assent on 25 April 2013, addresses concerns about civil liability for a breach of health and safety duties. Previously there was a right to take civil action where a breach of duty caused damage, but this has changed and the amended HSWA 1974 s 47(2) provides that there shall be no such right unless specifically provided in the legislation. Whilst clarification of the date this change will take effect is awaited, it is expected to be either in October 2013 or April 2014.

The significant progress made in adopting the recommendations made by Lord Young and Professor Lofstedt has already gone a long way towards improving perception and understanding of health and safety requirements and moving the focus back to effective, practical management of risks. In recent years many instances of 'health and safety gone mad' have been reported in the press and the changes now being implemented should help reset the balance as health and safety is not there to make businesses risk averse or stop certain activities, but is about them identifying and managing real risks properly to ensure there are no injuries or accidents. It is also true to say that 'health and safety' often gets the blame and is used as a convenient excuse to stop certain activities going ahead, when it is not the underlying reason why something cannot be done. In response, the HSE has set up the Myth Busters Challenge Panel. Directors should be aware of this as they may contact the panel where they believe health and safety advice they have been given by, say, a safety consultant or insurance company is wrong or disproportionate to the activities. In addition, customers can also contact the panel where they believe the explanation they were given was incorrect. The panel's decisions on complaints are published on their website (www.hse.gov.uk/myth/myth-busting) and a few examples are set out below:

- Case 333: managing agent says garden pond in place for last 25 years needs to be fenced for health and safety reasons – panel decision not mandated by health and safety rules.

- Case 328: customer not allowed coffee with child's meal deal – panel decision not prevented by health and safety rules.

- Case 175: luxury food retailer refused to fill up reusable tea caddy due the 'health and safety' reasons – panel decision not prevented by health and safety rules.

- Case 174: custard pie fight cancelled as organisers unable to get insurance on health and safety grounds – panel decision not prevented due to health and safety reasons and no basis to be uninsurable.

- Case 170: coffee chain could not sell half skimmed and half full-fat milk in coffee due to health and safety – panel decision no health and safety, nor food safety, reasons why milk cannot be served in combination in a drink.

- Case 167: cinema customer refused a glass of tap water at a concession stand on grounds of health and safety and could only buy bottled water – panel decision no valid health and safety grounds as the cinema had a drinking water dispenser to which the customer should have been directed.

These examples demonstrate how misleading, and often ridiculous, explanations given by some companies have helped fuel the health and safety myth to their advantage and how, in many instances, companies hide their real commercial motives and inability to provide good customer service behind an invalid explanation that what has been requested is prevented on health and safety grounds. By publishing the Myth Busters Challenge Panel's decisions on their website, the HSE is using publicity as a way of influencing behaviours and improving public awareness generally.

Cost of health and safety failures   **11.81**

According to statistics published by the HSE, in 2012/13 an estimated two million people suffered from work-related illness, 150 people were killed in work-related accidents and an estimated 28.2 million days were taken off work due to work-related illness and injury.

Many employers misguidedly believe that most incidents will be covered by insurance. Whilst employers' liability insurance will indeed (subject to any excess) meet the cost of serious injury to an employee, it would not usually cover costs incurred through:

- time away from work and loss of the injured person's production;

- payment of sick pay;

- damage to or loss of products, stock and raw materials;

- delays to production;

- arranging temporary cover and/or overtime;

- repairing plant and equipment;

- investigation of the incident and disruption to production;

- imposition of fines;

- legal costs;

- loss of contracts;

- loss of business reputation.

Such uninsured costs can be quite substantial. Indeed, studies by the HSE on the ratio of insurance premiums paid to uninsured losses found that the ratio ranges from 1:8 to 1:36, meaning that for every £1 paid in insurance premiums, a company may have to pay a further £8 to £36 itself to cover uninsured losses arising from an accident. This demonstrates that costs can be substantial, and they are unlikely to be covered by insurance.

Furthermore, employers with a poor record for health and safety claims may find that insurance premiums are substantially increased or, in some instances, that insurance cover is actually refused.

As well as avoiding the hidden costs of health and safety failures, many companies which have adopted high standards for health and safety have benefited from lower insurance premiums, improved levels of productivity and efficiency, improved quality of work, fewer staff absences and lower staff turnover. This is particularly important where investors, suppliers and customers are taking an increasing interest in health and safety performance.

Directors should also be aware that the HSE publishes a list of offenders and the adverse publicity generated by appearing on this list could be very damaging to a company's reputation.

Consequences of breaching requirements   **11.82**

Enforcement action   **11.82.1**

Under HSWA 1974, enforcing authorities (primarily the HSE and local authorities) have power to investigate suspected health and safety offences, which includes the right to make enquiries, search premises, take measurements, test equipment, take photographs, and order disclosure of information, etc. Should the HSE inspector determine from investigation that a company has failed to comply with the requirements of health and safety legislation he may issue an improvement notice or, where the breach may involve serious risk of personal injury, a prohibition notice. The HSE can also apply for a court remedy notice and seize and render harmless articles and substances where deemed necessary. Where an improvement notice is issued a date will be given by which time the contravention must be remedied.

Failure to comply with such notice or order is an offence under HSWA 1974 s 33(1)(g) for which, under s 33(2A), the offender is liable for imprisonment of up to two years, a fine of up to £20,000, or both. Where the case is heard through the higher court the potential fine is unlimited.

To give some idea of scale, in 2013/14, 13,790 enforcement notices were issued by the HSE and local authorities, made up of improvement notices, deferred prohibitions and immediate prohibitions. Details of all enforcement notices issued are available online, which can be damaging for a company's reputation.

Directors should also note that regs 23–25 of the Health and Safety (Fees) Regulations 2012 (SI 2012/1652) put a duty on the HSE to recover the costs of carrying out their regulatory functions from those found to be in material breach of health and safety requirements. Consequently the Fee For Intervention cost recovery scheme ('FFI') took effect on 1 October 2012 since which time those breaking health and safety law have been charged for the HSE's time in making sure they put things right and comply with requirements. Those found to be in material breach will be charged for the HSE inspector's time in conducting visits, inspections and investigations and taking enforcement action, at the current rate of £124 per hour. In two months alone, from implementation to 30 November 2013, the HSE issued FFI invoices for just under £730,000, which is significant, and it is hoped the FFI scheme will encourage compliance in the first place or, failing that, at least ensure fast resolution in putting things right where there has been a breach.

Action for HSWA offence   **11.82.2**

HSWA 1974 s 33 makes clear that it is an offence for a person to fail to discharge a duty contained in HSWA 1974 and other health and safety regulations, for which he might face a term in prison, a fine, or both. The maximum penalties for each offence are detailed in Schedule 3A to HSWA 1974 (as inserted by the Health and Safety (Offences) Act 2008), which also specifies the mode of trial, whether summarily or on indictment. The offences and penalties can be viewed online at www.legislation.gov.uk.

A breach of duty and failure to provide for the health and safety of employees constitutes both a criminal offence in terms of common law requirements and negligence and an offence giving rise to civil liability for breach of statutory requirements of HSWA 1974 and subsequent regulations. At present, the maximum penalty for a breach of HSWA 1974 is £20,000 in the magistrates' court, but higher in the Crown Court where fines are unlimited.

Where an accident or incident has occurred, the enforcing authority may prosecute or recommend prosecution of both the company and its directors as set out below:

(1) *Financial penalty – company.* Failure by a company to meet its obligations under HSWA 1974 s 2(1) by omitting to take reasonable precautions for the health, safety and welfare at work of employees by breaching HSWA 1974 ss 2–6 is a criminal offence by the company and carries a financial penalty. The scale of fines imposed for such breaches will reflect the seriousness of harm caused, how far short of the appropriate standard the employer's performance was and whether action was brought through the magistrates' court, where there is a maximum fine of £20,000, or through the Crown Court, where the fine is unlimited.

The Health and Safety (Offences) Act 2008 now permits more cases to be tried in the Crown Court where the fine for committing an offence is unlimited. In addition, where a breach of duty imposed by health and safety regulations causes damages, the breach may be actionable by civil remedy (HSWA 1974 s 47(2)).

It should be noted that a company can still be liable for a breach of duty at a lower or local management level, even where head office is not aware of the offending actions. This is illustrated in *R v Gateway Foodmarkets Ltd* [1997] IRLR 189, CA, in which it was held that the company was liable for a breach of HSWA 1974 s 2(1) where an employee died by falling down a lift shaft. The lift had not been adequately maintained and when a common fault occurred, without the knowledge of head office, employees repaired it themselves without calling in a lift engineer.

(2)   *Financial penalty – individual.* An individual director, officer or manager of a company can be criminally responsible for health and safety offences where the company has been found guilty of an offence by breach of HSWA 1974 ss 2–6 and the offence was committed with their consent or connivance or where it can be proven to be attributable to their negligence (HSWA 1974 s 37). Where convicted, the same scale of penalties as for companies (described in (1) above) will apply. A director found guilty of a breach of HSWA 1974 s 37 may also be disqualified (see para **5.53**) for up to two years.

The Health and Safety (Offences) Act 2008 has also added a term of up to 12 months' imprisonment as a potential penalty.

Again, to demonstrate scale, HSE statistics for 2012/13 show that 551 offences were prosecuted by the HSE and 88 by local authorities in England and Wales during the year. Indeed a scan through the national press and HSE press releases shows that those who commit breaches are being very actively pursued and the scale of fine imposed for breaches can be significant. The press release area of the HSE website (press.hse.gov.uk) lists the fines imposed for health and safety breaches which occur on an almost daily basis, and makes fairly gruesome reading. Sizeable examples include:

- Balfour Beatty Infrastructure Services Ltd and Enterprise (AOL) Ltd were fined and ordered to pay costs totalling £650k for breaching the Management of Health and Safety at Work Regulations 1999 and HSWA 1974 by providing unsuitable traffic management measures and failing to carry out an adequate assessment of the risks presented by the road works, resulting in a collision and the death of a driver (HSE Release HSE/M/54/12, 22 February 2013).

- UK Power Networks (Operations) Ltd were fined and ordered to pay costs totalling £420k for breaching the HSWA 1974 by not properly assessing the risks, failing to devise adequate work procedures and providing insufficient training to a worker at a substation who was killed when a transformer exploded (HSE Release HSE-E-002/13, 4 January 2013).

- In July 2010 five companies were ordered to pay a total of £9.5m in fines and costs for the Buncefield Oil Storage Depot explosion. The companies were, between them, found guilty of breaches of the HSWA 1974, failing to protect workers and the public, failing to prevent or limit the effects of a major incident under COMAH (see para **12.80**) and breach of the Water Resources Act 1991 for causing pollution to controlled waters.

These represent just a very small selection of offences publicised on the HSE website, which often reach 30–40 each month, but it does give an idea of the scale of penalties that might be imposed and the type of offences committed. One thing that is apparent from these examples is that the accidents could largely have been avoided by carrying out proper assessments to determine what risks were presented by the work and then implementing appropriate preventative measures (see para **11.83**).

Whilst generally this means directors must look after and protect the health and safety of employees in their own companies, they should be aware of the Court of Appeal's decision in *Chandler v Cape plc* [2012] EWCA Civ 525 which established that a parent company can owe a direct duty of care to an employee of a subsidiary where there has been a breach of health and safety requirements resulting in personal injury. Although the circumstances of this case are quite specific and concerned asbestosis suffered by a former employee of the subsidiary, it has set a precedent for a direct line of liability up to the parent company which is worthy of note by directors.

Directors of multinational companies would also be well advised to determine how far they need to go in surveying and controlling what is going on in any overseas subsidiaries in their groups and to implementing safeguards for health and safety and environmental issues. This follows the House of Lords ruling in *Lubbe v Cape plc* [2000] UKHL 41 that they would hear the case against a South African mining company owned by UK domiciled Cape plc brought by 7,500 miners who suffered asbestos-related diseases as a result of their work in South Africa. Whilst the case was settled out of court in December 2001 by payment of £21 million into a trust fund so the full extent of implications for UK companies with subsidiaries overseas is yet to be seen, directors must be mindful that the House of Lords did permit the case to be heard in the jurisdiction of the parent company.

Corporate manslaughter   **11.82.3**

Whilst it has been possible for many years to convict a company of corporate manslaughter, convictions were difficult to secure as, first, a company officer must have been found individually guilty of manslaughter and that person must then be identified as the 'controlling mind' of the company.

It has proved extremely difficult in cases involving larger companies to establish the existence of a controlling mind or interest and consequently there have been only two successful prosecutions for corporate manslaughter since the *OLL Ltd* case, both of which involved relatively small companies (*R v Jackson Transport (Ossett) Ltd* (unreported, 1996) and *R v Roy Bowles Transport Ltd* (unreported, 10 December 1999)). This was certainly a problem following the Herald of Free Enterprise ferry disaster in Zeebrugge where, due to the vast number of employees involved, it could not be established that any person who could be considered as having a controlling interest or directing mind was aware of the operational error and consequently it was only possible to secure a conviction for unlawful killing (*R v P & O European Ferries (Dover) Ltd* (1990) 93 Cr App Rep 72). Similar problems in establishing a controlling mind were experienced in the King's Cross fire in 1987, the Clapham rail crash in 1988, the Piper Alpha oil platform disaster in 1988, the sinking of the Marchioness in 1989, the Southall rail crash in 1997 and the Ladbroke Grove rail crash in 1999. Whilst each of these involved a large number of deaths and casualties, attributed largely to management faults and allowing dangerous working practices to continue, it was not possible to secure a conviction for manslaughter.

However, this has now changed as the Corporate Manslaughter and Corporate Homicide Act 2007 created the statutory offence of corporate manslaughter where a fatality is caused by the gross breach of a duty of care, and where the actions of the company's senior management played a substantial part in the breach. Gross breach will occur where there has been a failure to comply with health and safety law and where an organisation's conduct falls far below what can reasonably be expected.

This makes it easier for prosecutions to succeed, particularly against large organisations, as the prosecution will not have to identify the controlling mind behind the organisation's activities. Instead, the prosecution will focus on the conduct of the senior management, both individually and collectively.

The new offence is directed at the company itself, as opposed to its individual managers or directors, and an organisation convicted under the Act will face an unlimited fine.

However, directors should note that whilst the Act creates a new offence, it does not impose any new obligations on employers. The principal duties of employers are contained in the HSWA 1974 and subsequent regulations and these remain unchanged.

The Sentencing Guidelines Council has issued guidance on the level of fine to be imposed, indicating that fines for organisations and companies found guilty of corporate manslaughter may be in the millions of pounds range, and should seldom be less than £500,000. In determining the appropriate level of fine, account will be taken of a company's turnover and profit, whether risk of serious injury could be foreseen, whether the non-compliance was widespread and a common occurrence and at what levels in the organisation the breach occurred.

However, an individual cannot be prosecuted under the Act and the court cannot impose a custodial sentence, although individuals who commit a serious breach of a duty of care leading to a person's death may still face prosecution and possible imprisonment for the common law offence of gross negligence manslaughter.

The first case brought under the Act was *R v Cotswold Geotechnical (Holdings) Ltd* [2011] All ER (D) 100 (May) in which the company was prosecuted for the death of one of its employees who was taking soil samples from a pit when the unsupported sides of the 3.5m trench collapsed. Cotswold Geotechnical Holdings Ltd was charged with corporate manslaughter under the Act and fined £385,000, representing 115% of annual turnover. In addition there were also other charges made against the company including failing to ensure the safety of an employee as required by HSWA 1974 s 2. The sole director was also charged, initially, with manslaughter by gross negligence and that the breach of duty had been made with his full knowledge. However, the other charges were not pursued given his ill health and the prosecutor's desire to focus on the corporate manslaughter offence. A second case has also been successfully brought against Lion Steel Equipment Ltd which was found guilty of corporate manslaughter and fined £480k plus £84k costs on 20 July 2012. The case concerned death of a maintenance worker who suffered fatal injuries when he fell through a fragile fibreglass rooflight when he went onto the factory roof to investigate a leak. The employee was not given any instruction or training, safety equipment or supervision and no assessment of risk was carried out, nor was any safe system of work determined, which amounted to a gross breach of duty by the company. Whilst three of the company's directors were also originally charged with gross negligence manslaughter and, under HSWA 1974, with failing to ensure safety of employees at work, Lion Steel Equipment Ltd pleaded guilty on the basis that the charges against the directors were dropped, which they were.

In addition, as reported by the HSE in Northern Ireland, on 8 May 2012 JMW Farms Ltd was the first company to be successfully prosecuted in Northern Ireland under corporate manslaughter legislation. The company was fined £187,500 and ordered to pay costs of £13,000 for serious management failings which caused the death of an employee who was struck by an unsecured steel bin as it fell from a forklift driven by one of the company's directors. The Act also provides for courts to impose a publicity order requiring the organisation to publicise details of the conviction and fine which commercially could be very damaging for a company's reputation and serve as a significant deterrent. Indeed, the Sentencing Advisory Panel has recommended that publicity orders should be imposed in virtually all cases and this has been made possible by the Corporate Manslaughter and Corporate Homicide Act 2007 (Commencement No 2) Order 2010 (SI 2010/276). The court may also issue a remedial order, requiring action to be taken to address failures in the organisation that contributed to the employee's death.

Whilst it might appear that progress to secure corporate manslaughter charges is slow, thorough investigation to determine all the facts and unravel events is necessarily complex and time-consuming. In April 2012 the Attorney General indicated there were some 50 cases in which corporate manslaughter was being considered alongside other charges so more cases are, regrettably, on the horizon.

Individual manslaughter   **11.82.4**

An individual may be considered to have committed manslaughter where his gross negligence caused a death. To be found guilty it must be established that:

- the defendant owed a duty of care to the deceased;

- this duty of care had been breached; and

- the breach had caused the death and was so grossly negligent as to be criminal and deserving of punishment.

Directors can be prosecuted personally for manslaughter where they are believed to have committed a health and safety offence or where it can be attributed to their negligence. In the notable OLL case (para **11.82.3**), known as the 'Lyme Bay canoeing disaster', the director was found guilty of manslaughter and jailed for three years for the canoeing accident involving fatality.

Historically, personal prosecutions for health and safety breaches were rare but it is now clear from HSE figures that many more prosecutions have been successfully brought against directors and managers in recent years. A further example is the conviction and imprisonment in 2009 of a director of IC Roofing Ltd on grounds of manslaughter due to gross negligence when a worker, who was not wearing a harness and had not been given adequate training, died by falling through the roof of an industrial unit. He was also disqualified from acting as a director for three years for breaching HSWA 1974 s 37(1).

The forms of action which may be taken for a breach of health and safety requirements emphasise the importance to directors of observing health and safety provisions on behalf of the company. Not only is the company liable to criminal prosecution for a breach, but also the directors personally and, in this context, it is important to note that directors cannot be protected from their own criminal liability by a company's limited liability.

Directors must also ensure the company's insurance policy is sufficient and, where possible, covers the cost of civil penalties under HSWA 1974 and indemnifies the company against defence of a common law manslaughter charge.

Source of health and safety requirements   **11.83**

The HSWA 1974 forms the basis of British health and safety law and, whilst it has been subject to some criticism and changes to refocus emphasis back towards addressing risks and improving health and safety outcomes are underway, no large-scale, radical reform is currently planned (para **11.81**). The Management of Health and Safety at Work Regulations 1999 contain additional and more detailed health and safety requirements, in particular the need for risk assessments. There are also numerous other health and safety regulations made under HSWA 1974, which tend to focus on specific risk areas. These regulations are then supported by many guidance documents and Approved Codes of Practice ('ACOPs') issued by the HSE which provide practical advice on how to comply with the legal requirements.

HSWA 1974   **11.83.1**

The HSWA 1974 sets out, in general terms, the duties employers have to their employees and members of the public affected by their activities, and it requires employers to provide employees with safe conditions and systems of work and with training and supervision to enable them to perform their work safely (HSWA 1974 s 2). It is therefore important that the directors ensure these statutory duties are observed and provisions are made to ensure:

- maintenance of safe plant and systems of work;

- satisfactory arrangements are made for the safe use, handling, storage and transport of articles and substances;

- appropriate communication, instruction, training and supervision are implemented to ensure health and safety (in *Pickford v ICI plc* [1996] IRLR 622, CA (Stuart-Smith, Waite and Swinton-Thomas LJJ) the employer was liable for negligence for failing to communicate to an employee, who contracted repetitive strain injury, the need to take regular breaks from typing, which formed a substantial part of her work);

- conditions in and getting to and from the workplace are safe;

- a safe working environment is provided without presenting any risks to health, including arrangements for welfare of employees whilst at work;

- a written health and safety policy is provided where the company has five or more employees.

Failure to comply with these requirements can have serious consequences for both organisations and individuals. Sanctions include fines, imprisonment and disqualification (para **11.82** and **CHAPTER 5**).

Whilst quite general, the duties set out in the HSWA 1974 taken in totality encompass every aspect of the workplace which has an effect on the health, safety and welfare of employees. When looked at in detail they range from requirements for the employee's method of work and physical design of the workplace, to provision of safety appliances and training and instructions on their use, to procedures for treatment of hazardous substances and provision of welfare facilities all of which need to be addressed.

Some other specific points to note arising from HSWA 1974 include:

- a company is not permitted to delegate responsibility for the health and safety of its employees (see *R v Mersey Dock and Harbour Co* (1995) 16 Cr App Rep (S) 806, where it was held that it can be no defence to claim that health and safety matters were left to other people);

- whilst primary responsibility for an employee's health and safety lies with the employing company, liability for an injury whilst on another company's premises may be apportioned with that other company (*Andrews v Initial Cleaning Services Ltd* [2000] ICR 166). This is particularly relevant where a company employs sub-contractors, in this case contract cleaners;

- HSWA 1974 and other safety regulations require the provision of physical safety devices in certain circumstances. The provision of instructions or a code of practice in their absence would not be considered sufficient;

- HSWA 1974 s 3(1) requires a company to ensure, as far as is practical, that third parties are not exposed to risks to their health and safety caused by negligence of an employee.

Management of Health and Safety at Work Regulations   **11.83.2**

The Management of Health and Safety at Work Regulations 1999 (SI 1999/3242) are more specific in terms of what employers are required to do, the main requirements being to:

(1)   assess the risks presented to employees, customers, partners and any other people affected by the activities of the business (see para **11.85**);

(2)   consult employees about risks at work and the current preventive and protective measures and ensure employees are provided with adequate health and safety training (reg 11);

(3)   appoint a 'competent' employee to provide advice and assistance on health and safety issues in preference to an external adviser and ensure such person has the requisite training, knowledge and experience to carry out the role effectively (reg 7(1)); and

(4)   set up emergency procedures, particularly in terms of first-aid, medical treatment and emergency rescue (reg 9).

It is important for directors to note that reg 21 makes it very clear that an employer cannot hide behind the actions of an employee and avoid their health and safety obligations.

Other regulations   **11.83.3**

There are numerous other regulations made under the HSWA 1974 which impose duties on directors and the companies for which they act. Whilst many of these regulations depend on the specific activities being undertaken by the company and the facilities and equipment provided, there are a number of regulations which have wide application and will need to be observed by most businesses, namely:

(1)   Safety Representatives and Safety Committees Regulations 1977 (SI 1977/500) and Health and Safety (Consultation with Employees) Regulations 1996 (SI 1996/1513) – impose duties on employers to consult their employees on specified health and safety matters. They may either consult directly with employees, via employee-elected representatives, or safety representatives appointed by a recognised trade union (HSWA 1974 s 2(4)), in which case those persons must be given appropriate training, paid time off and facilities to enable them to carry out their functions.

(2)   Regulatory Reform (Fire Safety) Order 2005 (SI 2005/1541) – requires businesses to be responsible for their own fire-risk assessments, implement and maintain a fire-risk management plan (see para **11.85**). Fire certificates have ceased to be provided free of charge by fire authorities and businesses must conduct and record in writing a specific assessment of risks relating to fire and the arrangements that have been made in terms of evacuation procedures, fire exits and fire fighting and fire detection equipment.

(3)   Provision and Use of Work Equipment Regulations 1998 (SI 1998/2306) – require all equipment provided for use at work to be suitable, safe, inspected, maintained, used by people who have appropriate training and instruction and accompanied by suitable safety measures and instructions. The case *Stark v Post Office* [2000] ICR 1013, CA clarified that these regulations impose an absolute liability on an employer to ensure that work equipment is safe to use, and shall apply regardless of whether regular checks and maintenance have been carried out.

(4)   Control of Substances Hazardous to Health Regulations 2002 (SI 2002/2677) (as amended by the 2004 Regulations) – require employers to assess risks to employees from exposure to hazardous substances, prevent or control exposure, ensure control measures are followed, where necessary monitor exposure and introduce health surveillance and ensure employees receive necessary instruction and training.

(5)   Health and Safety (Display Screen Equipment) Regulations 1992 (SI 1992/2792), as amended in 2002 – require employers to assess and reduce the risks to an employee working at a VDU workstation, ensure that such work is interrupted by breaks or alternative tasks and provide employees with eye tests and corrective appliances where necessary (see para **11.84**). In *Conaty v Barclays Bank plc* (unreported, 6 April 2000) a former employee was awarded £243,792 after she developed a work-related upper-limb disorder from processing cheques and accounts.

(6)   Personal Protective Equipment at Work Regulations 1992 (SI 1992/2966), as amended in 2002 and 2013 – require employers to make a formal assessment of what personal protective equipment is needed by employees to carry out their work safely and to provide, maintain and tell them how to use it properly.

(7)   Manual Handling Operations Regulations 1992 (SI 1992/2793), as amended in 2002 – require employers to avoid hazardous manual handling operations where reasonably practicable, assess the risks where such tasks cannot be avoided and reduce risks to employees to the lowest possible level. In *Ghaith v Indesit Co UK Ltd* [2012] EWCA Civ 642, [2012] All ER (D) 205 the employer was found to have breached reg 4 by failing to conduct suitable risk assessment and not allowing the claimant sufficient breaks, resulting in a back injury when clearing out the employer's van.

(8)   Electricity at Work Regulations 1989 (SI 1989/635) – contain requirements relating to the installation and maintenance of all electrical systems and equipment or work activities on or near such systems.

(9)   Smoke-free (Premises and Enforcement) Regulations 2006 (SI 2006/3368) – require employers to ensure all enclosed or substantially enclosed workplaces or public areas, including work vehicles and transport, are smoke-free. No-smoking signs need to be displayed and the ban be actively enforced or an employer could face a fine of up to £2,500.

(10)   Health and Safety (First Aid) Regulations 1981 (SI 1981/917), as amended in 2013 – contain requirements for provision of first-aid equipment and, depending on the size of the company and nature of activities, an appointed person or trained first-aider.

(11)   Reporting of Injuries, Diseases and Dangerous Occurrences Regulations 1995 (SI 1995/3163), with amended reporting and injury classifications – require employers to report major injuries and dangerous occurrences to the enforcing authority. All accidents need to be recorded, and where applicable reported by phone (fatal and major injuries only) and online via the HSE's website, and all reportable work-related accidents, dangerous occurrences and diseases should be investigated to determine how they happened and avoid risk of any reoccurrence. To give some idea of scale,

HSE statistics for 2013/14 show that 77,593 injuries were reported under these regulations.

(12) Control of Noise at Work Regulations 2005 (SI 2005/1643) – require employers to assess the level of noise to which employees are exposed and to take preventative action to reduce exposure and protect the hearing of workers where necessary;

(13) Control of Asbestos Regulations 2012 (SI 2012/632) – require property owners, landlords, tenants, managing agents, builders, etc to find out whether the property contains asbestos and, in so far as it does, to properly monitor and manage the risks it presents. Indeed, in September 2011 Marks & Spencer was fined £1m for failing to protect customers, staff and workers from potential exposure to asbestos during refurbishment work at one of its stores.

(14) Health and Safety Information for Employees (Amendment) Regulations 2009 (SI 2009/606) – require employers to provide certain health and safety information to employees, including the HSE's poster and leaflet.

(15) Workplace (Health, Safety and Welfare) Regulations 1992 (SI 1992/3004) – set out requirements for a wide range of basic health, safety and welfare issues such as lighting, heating, ventilation, seating and washroom facilities, etc.

(16) Health and Safety (Training for Employment) Regulations 1990 (SI 1990/1380) – require provision of such information, instruction and training as is necessary to ensure health and safety of employees, taking into account differing abilities, in particular how vulnerable children and young persons are to accidents.

In addition to the regulations listed above, which have wide application and are relevant to most businesses, there will be additional regulations and requirements which need to be observed, which vary depending upon the activities being undertaken by the company. By way of illustration, these might include:

- Work at Height Regulations 2005 (SI 2005/735) (as amended) – require that all work at height is properly planned and organised, carried out by competent persons and that the risks have been properly assessed and appropriate work equipment and means of control implemented. In *Elizabeth McLachlan v. Early Learning Centre* [2011] CSOH 2 a senior sales assistant was awarded damages for injuries suffered when she fell from a ladder while attempting to retrieve a box from a high shelf in the employer's stockroom as the employer was found to have breached reg 6(2) of the Work at Height Regulations 2005.

- Construction (Design and Management) Regulations 2007 (SI 2007/320) – contain requirements for construction and building projects to ensure the work is being undertaken by capable and competent people and that the construction is safe to build, use and maintain.

- Lifting Operations and Lifting Equipment Regulations 1998 (SI 1998/2307) – require the safe management of risks from lifting equipment and lifting operations.

- Carriage of Dangerous Goods and Use of Transportable Pressure Equipment Regulations 2009 (SI 2009/1348) – regulate the carriage of dangerous goods by road, rail and on waterways and the need for drivers of such vehicles to undergo specific training and examination.

These are just a few examples of an extensive range of other regulations that might apply to the company, depending on the nature of its operations and activities. A company involved in mining, offshore oil or generation of nuclear power, for example, will have many other regulations with which it must comply.

HSE guidance and ACOPs   **11.83.4**

Whilst some health and safety regulations place an absolute and strict liability on employers to meet certain standards, for example to provide safe equipment at work, many regulations require an employer to implement reasonably practicable measures to address risks. This distinction and what constitutes 'reasonably practicable' causes much confusion. To assist employers the HSE has issued guidance notes and ACOPs which contain practical advice on how to comply with the law and give illustrations of what is necessary or might be considered 'reasonable'. The HSE's ACOPs have special legal status and need to be observed as, where an employer is subject to prosecution and it is proved they were not following the ACOP and this was relevant to the accident or injury that occurred, the employer will be found to be in default unless they can show they complied with the relevant regulation by some other means. The HSE is currently considering making changes to its suite of ACOPs by revising, consolidating and withdrawing some, making minor revisions to others and limiting their length all with a view to simplifying and streamlining health and safety regulation as recommended by Lord Young and Professor Lofstedt (see para **11.80.1**).

Health and safety policy   **11.84**

Directors must be aware that where their company employs five or more persons it has a specific statutory obligation to prepare and review periodically a formal written statement of the company's health and safety policy (HSWA 1974 s 2(3)). The policy must be communicated to employees via noticeboards, posters, training and briefing sessions and during induction training for new recruits.

Such policies vary in their size and complexity between different companies but are usually divided into three sections and must contain the following information:

- a general statement of the company's policy on health and safety, outlining the company's overall philosophy on health and safety and the broad responsibilities of management and the workforce;

- organisation for health and safety matters, detailing how responsibility is allocated to individuals for particular aspects of health and safety;

- a statement of arrangements and procedures for health and safety in the workplace, covering practical arrangements and procedures for implementing the policy, such as housekeeping, fire prevention and evacuation, first aid and accident recording, maintenance of equipment and reporting faults, security, training and so forth.

It can be seen that a health and safety policy is the ideal means through which to clearly and publicly explain the Board's responsibilities and commitment to achieving health and safety objectives and to demonstrate how they will be achieved through processes and procedures put in place. Formulation of the policy therefore needs careful consideration.

A further consideration for the Board is that it is becoming increasingly common for customers and suppliers to ask to review a copy of a company's health and safety policy before deciding to engage in business. By using the health and safety policy to demonstrate the company's positive approach towards health and safety performance and the Board's commitment to achieving continuous improvement, the Board may help to establish a competitive advantage and secure new business.

Directors must be aware that it is not enough merely to prepare a health and safety policy and leave it to sit on the shelf gathering dust. It should be a living document communicated to employees, be referred to as decisions are being made and be periodically updated to reflect changes within the company such as technology, processes and staff. Unfortunately experience has shown that it is all too common to find that a company's health and safety policy, efficiently and thoroughly drawn up at the time, is kept in a file somewhere, rarely referred to and was last updated some ten years earlier. Paying lip service to health and safety requirements by having once prepared a policy does not constitute compliance and directors can be personally liable for failing to prepare and implement the health and safety policy.

Risk assessment 11.85

An integral part of formulating a health and safety policy is the conduct of an assessment of conditions and arrangements in the workplace to determine whether there are any risks to employees that need to be addressed in the policy document.

This formal assessment of risks is required by regs 3 and 4 of the Management of Health and Safety at Work Regulations 1992 (SI 1992/2051), as amended by the 1999 Regulations, which require all employers to assess formally risks to employees whilst at work and implement arrangements for protective or preventative measures to reduce risks identified by the assessment. Failure to conduct a risk assessment is an offence.

Essentially, risk assessment involves looking at the work activity and the physical characteristics of the workplace as well as arrangements and procedures in place prescribing how tasks should be carried out, to identify whether any potential hazards exist which could damage an employee's health or cause injury. In so far as hazards and risks are identified by the assessment, an employer should implement preventative and protective measures to assess and combat risks at source; evaluate unavoidable risks and seek to replace dangerous processes or equipment with those that are less dangerous; and provide instructions on work methods and training, focused on the particular hazards and risks presented by the work activity. Much of this will be identified and flow out of the risk assessment process.

This risk assessment process is divided into stages and requires the employer to do the following:

Stages	Reasons
• Examine the workplace and work activity	• To identify possible hazards and the extent of the risk of injury
• Consider and implement appropriate precautions	• To remove hazard or reduce risk of injury
• Identify need for safety equipment	• To reduce or remove risk of injury
• Identify need for training	• To increase employee awareness of risks inherent in their work and ensure that they know how to carry out their job safely in terms of the system of work and any safety equipment to avoid risk of injury

Stages	Reasons
● Formulate a document for a safe system of work and working procedures	● For each employee to consult as part of their health and safety training
● Implement safety measures and procedures	● Must be employed in practical terms
● Control, monitor and review performance under safety constraints	● To ensure that work is carried out in accordance with recommendations and safety equipment is being used

Whilst this list is by no means exhaustive, risks that would typically be examined in the workplace during the assessment include the following:

- Asbestos
- Chemicals
- Confined spaces
- Display screen equipment (VDUs)
- Electricity

- Excavation
- Falling objects/collapsing structures
- Fire and explosion
- Machinery (including guarding)

- Manual handling
- Noise
- Pressure systems
- Radiation

- Slips, trips and falls
- Stress
- Substances hazardous to health (including dust, fumes, etc)
- Temperatures

- Transport (including carrying dangerous substances, and pedestrians in the workplace)
- Vibration
- Violence to staff

- Work equipment
- Work-related upper-limb disorders
- Working alone
- Working at heights
- Working environment

Directors should be aware that, whilst all employers are required to conduct an assessment of risks in the workplace, where five or more persons are employed the risk assessment findings must be recorded in writing. In any event, even where not required to, retaining written records of assessments conducted provides important information for future reference as well as evidence of the serious and responsible attitude adopted by the company, at managerial level, towards the health and safety of its employees.

Failure by employers to carry out adequate risk assessments is often a major cause and contributing factor to accidents and incidents in the workplace, as evidenced by a scan through the offences publicised on the HSE's website (press.hse.gov.uk). Some examples are listed in para **11.82.2**.

Directors should be aware that formal assessment of health and safety risks is important in many decisions that are made and risk assessments often need to be carried out prior to implementation of changes to work practices and the workplace. This recommendation will be far from alien to most Boards, especially those that have adopted recommendations made in the Turnbull Report (now replaced by the FRC's Risk Guidance) for a broad, risk-based approach to internal control. This risk-based approach focuses the Board's attention on the need to actively consider the health and safety implications of changes at the planning stage, in the same way that issues concerning finance, resource allocation, technical requirements, business interruption and regulatory requirements, etc are routinely considered.

An assessment of risk should also be applied when the Board is making decisions about engaging in business with other companies or employing sub-contractors to carry out work, as they should be avoided where they are known to have a poor health and safety record and little or no means of managing health and safety risks. Whilst the initial cost of engaging such companies may be attractive, there is a strong likelihood that this could undermine the company's reputation for high standards of health and safety practice and potentially put the company's own employees at risk, as well as causing irreversible damage to the company's reputation.

Employee involvement and communication   **11.86**

HSWA 1974 s 2(4) requires the company's health and safety policy to be communicated to employees. In addition, as set out in para **11.83.3**(1) above employers are required to consult employees on specified health and safety matters via employee-elected representatives or via safety representatives appointed by a recognised trade union and to give those persons appropriate training, paid time off and facilities to carry out their functions.

With this in mind it is important for the Board to consult employees when devising the health and safety policy and to encourage their participation when tackling health and safety problems and implementing preventative measures. From a practical point it is advisable for Boards to adopt such recommendations, not only to ensure that employees understand the arrangements which affect them and their own responsibilities, but also to include their own often valuable experience and knowledge when determining what procedures, means of communication, reporting and training will work best in practice.

These measures will help encourage a positive health and safety culture throughout the company by generating greater commitment amongst employees to achieving objectives and adhering to health and safety procedures which they themselves helped to put in place. At the same time employees are also likely to have a greater appreciation of the importance of health and safety issues, together with improved knowledge about inherent risks in their workplace, which can only be beneficial.

Health and safety director   **11.87**

One of the best practice recommendations from the HSE's guidance in para **11.89** is that to keep the Board informed about and up to date with all health and safety issues affecting the company and its performance and to ensure that health and safety issues are properly addressed, a member of the Board be appointed health and safety director. This appointment alone will signal that health and safety matters are being taken seriously at the highest level in the company.

It can be seen that the appointment of a health and safety director, in the same way that companies appoint finance directors, operations directors and marketing directors, is very important to ensure that there is one person who will always bring the Board's attention to health and safety issues and ensuring that they are properly considered at this level rather than being left to the operational managers. This should ensure that health and safety implications of all decisions made by the Board are fully considered. In, for example, Board-level discussions on plans for investment in new plant, premises, processes, or products, the health and safety director would raise any relevant health and safety implications in the same way that the finance director would mention finance restrictions or the operations director would raise concerns over business interruption and so forth.

To enable the health and safety director to contribute in a meaningful way, the appointee needs appropriate training and experience to be able to fulfil this role and also to be delegated responsibility to keep the Board up to date with changes in health and safety matters. Similarly, training for some or all of the Board will promote a better understanding of the issues and risks facing their companies.

It can be seen that the requirements of the guidance tie in comfortably with corporate governance recommendations for an ongoing assessment and review of risks facing a company, formalising the need to assess and control health and safety risks. The directors should ensure that health and safety matters are integrated into the governance structure and addressed in terms of monitoring risks and internal controls. This might, for example, involve independent scrutiny of processes by a non-executive director or setting up a risk management or health and safety committee to address key issues.

Reporting performance   **11.88**

Having carried out this process of measurement and review, the guidance requires the Board to report on the company's health and safety performance. Furthermore, the HSE considers it good practice to report on corporate risk and health and safety issues in the company's annual report and has issued guidance on how to do so ('Revitalising Health and Safety: Health and Safety in Annual Reports'). Whilst this guidance is aimed initially at the top 350 companies in the private sector, it will be extended to all businesses with more than 250 employees and other companies would be well advised to adopt the proposals, thereby making the Board publicly accountable for their management of health and safety risks.

The HSE recommends that health and safety information in the company's annual report should include:

- an outline of the health and safety policy;

- the key risks and strategies and systems in place to control them;

- quantifiable goals relating to the policy;

- progress towards achieving these goals;

- short- and long-term plans;

- statistics on health and safety performance, including details of accidents, instances of ill-health, numbers of work days lost through injury and ill-health;

- arrangements for consulting employees and health and safety representatives; and

- details of any health and safety convictions, including the scale of penalties and fines.

Whilst these recommendations are not a legal requirement and do not have to be followed, the benefits in terms of demonstrating the company's commitment to achieving effective health and safety risk management will be evident.

Leading health and safety   **11.89**

Most employers are aware that they have a general duty to ensure the health, safety and welfare of their employees whilst at work as well as a duty to ensure that persons not in their employment but affected by their activities, such as contractors, visitors, members of the emergency services and the general public, are not exposed to risks to their health and safety (HSWA 1974 ss 2 and 3). However, the number of prosecutions brought by the HSE continues to increase each year, indicating that in some instances the importance of health and safety in the workplace fails to be recognised and does not receive the level of attention nor the amount of consideration required.

In recognition that, for a company to achieve a high standard of health and safety management, the process must be led by the Board with ongoing active director involvement, the HSE and the Institute of Directors (IOD) have issued guidance for directors on how to achieve this, entitled 'Leading Health and Safety at Work: Leadership Actions for Directors and Board Members' (www.hse.gov.uk/pubns/indg417.pdf). This guidance highlights to directors the importance of good health and safety practices and procedures in the workplace and identifies three essential principles for successful health and safety leadership and performance, and a four-point agenda to help embed these principles.

Essential principles   **11.89.1**

The guidance identifies three essential principles which must be achieved in order for directors to effectively lead and promote health and safety. The principles are that there must be:

(1)   Strong and active leadership from the top:

- visible, active commitment from the Board;

- establishing effective downward communication systems and management structures;

- integration of good health and safety management with business decisions.

(2)   Worker involvement:

- engaging the workforce in the promotion and achievement of safe and healthy conditions;

- effective upward communications;

- providing high quality training.

(3)   Assessment and review:

- identifying and managing health and safety risks;

- accessing (and following) competent advice;

- monitoring, reporting and reviewing performance.

Achieving these principles is considered fundamental for success, as they underpin all actions taken with regard to management of health and safety.

Four-point agenda   11.89.2

The guidance sets out a four-point agenda identifying what the directors need to do in order to embed the essential health and safety principles within their organisations. The four points are as follows:

(1) Plan: the Board should set the direction for effective health and safety management. Board members need to understand and recognise the significant risks faced by their company and establish a health and safety policy that is an integral part of the organisation's culture, values and performance standards. The Board's own role and that of individual Board members leading on health and safety should be set out in the policy. Health and safety should, as a matter of good practice, be a regular agenda item at Board meetings.

(2) Deliver: there needs to be an effective management system in order to ensure, so far as is reasonably practicable, the health and safety of employees, customers and members of the public. To achieve this the Board must ensure that health and safety arrangements are adequately resourced, competent advice is obtained when needed, risk assessments are carried out and employee involvement is encouraged.

(3) Monitor: monitoring and reporting are vital parts of a good health and safety culture and management systems must allow the Board to receive both routine reports on health and safety performance and reports on particular incidents. Reporting of information to the Board is paramount and must be given sufficient weight and recognition. Periodic audits should be carried out and reported, as should the impact of any proposed changes in the workplace.

(4) Review: a formal boardroom review of health and safety performance is essential. The Board should review health and safety performance at least on an annual basis and ensure that appropriate action is taken when any weaknesses are identified.

The guidance also includes a useful checklist of key questions to enable directors and others leading health and safety to determine how well they are doing (**Appendix 28**). Observing this guidance will help to ensure that not only are the directors doing enough to comply with the law by following best practice, but at the same time they are actively encouraging a positive health and safety culture within their company. Ultimately health and safety considerations would be embedded in the decision-making process and in steps taken at all levels within the company.

Some 19 case studies, on companies ranging from a small brick manufacturer to Rolls-Royce, have been carried out by the HSE. These identify significant benefits to the companies from their investment in health and safety, not only in avoiding fines and imposition of enforcement notices, etc, but also in terms of positive benefits to the businesses as a whole and cost savings made. These might, for example, include:

- reduced costs and reduced risks: employee absence and turnover rates are lower, accidents are fewer, the threat of legal action is lessened;

- improved standing among suppliers and partners;

- a better reputation for corporate responsibility among investors, customers and communities;

- increased productivity: employees are healthier, happier and better motivated.

Almost all the FTSE 100 companies now report publicly on their health and safety management and the HSE's sponsorship of the web-based Corporate Health and Safety Performance Index ('CHaSPI'), which contains rating information to help investors assess the health and safety performance of organisations with over 250 employees in which they are thinking of investing, will doubtless encourage a higher degree of disclosure and increased reporting by many other companies.

Employers' liability insurance   11.90

The Employers' Liability (Compulsory Insurance) Act 1969 (ELCIA 1969), as amended by the Employers' Liability (Compulsory Insurance) Regulations 1998 (SI 1998/2573) (ELCIR 1998) and the 2004 and 2008 amendment regulations, requires employers to effect insurance to cover employees for illness, bodily injury or disease caused during, or arising as a result of, their employment.

Directors should be aware that it is a criminal offence to fail to take out insurance and an employer can be fined up to £2,500 per day they are in default (ELCIR 1998 reg 5). It should also be noted that reg 2 prohibits inclusion of a term in the policy relieving the insurers' obligation to pay the employee's claim where the employer has failed to comply with health and safety requirements or has not kept proper records. It also prohibits inappropriately high policy excesses. Responsibility for maintaining this policy is likely to rest with the directors, who must ensure that they select an approved policy with an FSA approved, authorised insurer and that a copy is visibly displayed at each business premises (which includes display be electronic means). It is important to note that in *Quinn v McGinty* [1998] Rep LR 107 a Sheriff Principal ruled that directors of a company who failed to ensure the company had taken out proper employee insurance as required by ELCIA 1969 could be personally liable to an employee unable to recover from the uninsured company.

Another more recent example was Alina Trade Ltd (HSE Release 254/11, 2 November 2011). Despite two inspections by the HSE, numerous written requests and receipt of formal Notice to Produce from the HSE, the company failed to provide a copy of the ELCI certificate at one of its premises for which it was fined £2,000 for contravening s 1(1) of ELCIA 1969 and ordered to pay costs of £1,567.

Furthermore, to meet the requirements of ELCIR 1998, the policy must be effected to indemnify the employer for a minimum £5 million for a single occurrence.

Typically, terms of the policy would cover the employer for legal liability following:

(1)   negligence in failing to use reasonable care and skill in providing:

    (a)   suitable and safe plant;

    (b)   a safe system of work;

    (c)   a safe place of work; and

    (d)   for selection of suitable and competent employees;

(2)   breach of statutory regulations such as HSWA 1974; and

(3)   employees' negligence causing injury to fellow employees.

Employers are required to display their certificate of insurance at each place of business, either in hard copy or in electronic format. Often the certificate is displayed in common areas such as reception, staff canteen, kitchen or tea points, etc so that it is readily accessible for employees. The maximum penalty for failing to display the certificate is currently £1,000.

Another important consideration is that, due to the period of time that may elapse between the cause of the injury and the onset of the illness or disease, it is essential that records of historic policies are kept to ensure that claims are made under the policy in effect at the time the injury was caused. Retention of past insurance documents must be considered as an essential element of the retention of documents policy, discussed in para **6.40** and **APPENDIX 7**. Whilst the requirement that certificates of insurance be kept by employers for 40 years has been removed, businesses must have regard to their continuing liabilities and ensure appropriate records are retained to allow future claims to be met.

Employers' practices liability insurance   **11.100**

Given the complexity of employment legislation and the vastly increased upper limit for awards of damages in successful claims of unfair dismissal, it may be advisable for directors to consider mitigating potential losses suffered by the company by effecting insurance against employment-related claims. Such employers' practices liability insurance would typically provide cover against a wide range of employment-related issues such as wrongful or unfair dismissal, direct or indirect discrimination, harassment, defamation, etc and protect the company against the cost of arbitration or tribunal proceedings, demands for compensation or reinstatement, punitive damages and defence costs. The policy may be designed to specifically suit the company and type of industry, and it would commonly protect the company as well as individual directors against claims by employees. Commonly the policy will require use of a lawyer from the insurer's approved list and to follow their recommendations of what action to take or the policy will be invalidated.

Employment of immigrant workers   **11.110**

Directors should be aware that it is a criminal offence to employ a person aged 16 years or over who is not entitled to work in the UK. The provisions relate to all full-time and casual workers, and non-compliance can result in action against the company, or the directors, secretary, manager or other officer where they have connived in the offence or if it has been committed as a result of their neglect.

An employer's duties with regard to prevention of illegal working can be found in the Immigration, Asylum and Nationality Act 2006 ss 15–25, which provides for both civil and criminal penalties.

An employer who negligently employs someone who is not entitled to work in the UK is subject to a civil penalty under s 15 of the Act, which currently attracts a fine of up to £10,000 per illegal worker. A defence exists if the employer has checked, made and retained copies of the documents prescribed by the Home Office (such as a birth certificate combined with a document evidencing a UK National Insurance number or a work permit and passport), evidencing entitlement to work. An up-to-date list of the prescribed documents providing evidence of a person's eligibility to work in the UK can be obtained from the UK Border Agency section of the www.gov.uk webiste, as can guidance on the regulations and how to prevent illegal working. There is a sliding scale of penalties that will be considered dependent upon whether full, partial or no checks were carried out before the illegal worker was employed.

A criminal offence arises under s 21 of the Act where an employer knowingly employs someone who is not entitled to work in the UK, and it carries a maximum custodial sentence of two years, or an unlimited fine.

In addition to these penalties, the UK Border Agency now publishes details on its website of any employer issued with notice of liability for employment of illegal workers and the civil penalties imposed on them.

To avoid claims of unlawful race discrimination it is vital that directors carry out entitlement checks for all job applicants, whether they appear to be UK nationals or not. In practice, it is likely that all applicants will be advised that, if successful, they will be required to produce original documents evidencing their entitlement to work in the UK, such as passport, birth certificate or P45. The Home Office has issued a revised Code of Practice to help employers avoid race discrimination in recruitment.

Employment of children and young persons   11.120

There are many rules which govern the employment of children and young persons which, whilst largely consolidated in the Children and Young Persons Act 1933, have since been amended by various enactments and regulations including the Children (Protection at Work) Regulations 1998 (SI 1998/276) and 2000 (SI 2000/1333).

These acts and regulations place various restrictions on employment of children and young persons and set out requirements relating to their health and safety, type of work, hours of work, rest breaks, holiday, pay and time off for training and study, etc. which vary according to the child or young person's age. Directors must ensure that the companies to which they are appointed do not contravene statutory provisions.

Generally, part-time employment of a child who is under 13 years old is not permitted, except where the child is employed for television, theatre or modelling.

Once a child has reached the age of 13 years, he can be employed on a part-time basis provided the employment is not:

- during school hours;
- before 7am or after 7pm on any day;
- for more than two hours on a school day;
- for more than two hours between Sunday and Friday and five hours on a Saturday during term time (increases to eight hours if over 15 years);

- during the holidays for more than five hours each weekday and two hours on Sunday (increases to eight hours if over 15 years) subject to a maximum of 25 hours a week (35 hours if over 15 years); and

- for more than four hours without a one-hour break.

In addition, the child must be allowed at least two weeks where they are not required to work during school holidays. The precise requirements vary according to the child's age and are in age bands. Directors must be aware of these restrictions and ensure that they are observed in the company's employment practices and by those responsible for the child at work. Any breach of these general restrictions renders the employer liable to a fine (Children and Young Persons Act 1933 s 21).

Full-time employment can only start once the child has reached school leaving age and there are additional restrictions which relate to young persons between school-leaving age and 18 years. These are largely embodied in the Working Time Regulations 1998 (SI 1998/1833) and the Working Time (Amendment) Regulations 2002 (SI 2002/3128) as set out below:

- a maximum of 40 hours' work per week;

- daily working time limited to eight hours;

- night work between 10pm and 6am or 11pm and 7am is prohibited;

- must have at least two days off per week;

- a minimum rest period of 12 hours for each 24 hours worked;

- a minimum rest period of 36 hours for each seven days worked;

- a minimum 30-minute break where working more than 4.5 hours;

- a free medical check-up before commencing night work and at regular periods thereafter.

The HSWA 1974 and the Health and Safety (Young Persons) Regulations 1997 (SI 1997/135) set out an employer's duty to ensure that young persons employed by them are protected at work from any risks to their health or safety which are a consequence of their lack of experience and awareness of the potential risks of their work, given their age and lack of maturity. Regulation 13D generally prohibits the employment of young persons where the work:

- is beyond their physical or psychological capability;

- involves exposure to toxic, carcinogenic or mutagenic agents or those which may chronically affect health;

- causes exposure to harmful radiation;

- has a high risk of accidents which the young person, due to his lack of attention, training and experience, is unlikely to recognise; or
- involves risk from extreme heat, cold, noise or vibrations.

In addition, provisions contained in the Management of Health and Safety at Work Regulations 1999 (SI 1999/3242) require employers to assess the health and safety risks to young workers before they commence employment (reg 3(4) and 3(5)). The outcome of the assessment must be notified to parents of school-age children, together with details of the control measures introduced and it should be noted that this also applies to situations where children or young persons are on work experience.

Directors should also be aware that if a risk to the safety, physical or mental health or development of a young person is identified, the monitoring and assessment of their health must be provided at regular intervals.

Furthermore, the Teaching and Higher Education Act 1998 s 32 required employers to permit any employees aged 16 or 17 years not in full-time secondary or further education and who had not attained the prescribed standard of qualification to take time off during working hours to obtain a relevant qualification. This requirement has been enhanced by the Education and Skills Act 2008 which from June 2013 places a duty on all young people in England to participate in education or training until they reach the age of 17 (increasing to 18 in June 2015). It also makes consequential changes in relation to the right young persons have for time off to study and train.

Paragraph **11.83.3**(16) summarises requirements for training, which might need to be tailored and more detailed for children and young persons. Such employees are also likely to need closer supervision at all times.

The Education and Skills Act 2008 (on the UK legislation website) changes the statutory framework placing a duty on all young people in England to participate in education or training until the age of 18.

Finally, following implementation of certain provisions of the Safeguarding Vulnerable Groups Act 2006 in October 2009, employers are also required to obtain enhanced disclosure barring service (DSB) disclosures where relevant and must check whether an applicant's name appears on a statutory list of people considered unsuitable to work with children or vulnerable adults.

Employees and pensions   11.130

In the past, provision by a company of a group pension plan or occupational pension scheme was purely voluntary and many employers provided pension schemes to attract and retain quality staff by making the overall remuneration and benefits package more attractive. The benefits to such companies were improved staff loyalty and reduced staff turnover.

However, amidst tough economic conditions many company pension schemes have closed and there is now growing concern that people are living longer, but failing to make adequate provision for their retirement.

To address this and try to encourage employees to save for retirement the Welfare Reform and Pensions Act 1999 (amended by Pensions Act 2008 s 87) required employers with five or more employees to offer a stakeholder pension scheme to employees. There was no requirement for employers to contribute to the stakeholder pension scheme (merely to make it available) and those with fewer than five employees were exempt from the requirement entirely. Not surprisingly, the initiative had little success in encouraging employees to save for retirement, introduction of the Pensions Act 2008 (PA 2008). This goes much further and requires employers to automatically enrol eligible job-holders into a qualifying scheme and make contributions of at least 3% of an employee's qualifying earnings in the scheme.

This represents a substantive change and it is important that the directors ensure the company's pension provisions are appropriately reviewed to determine not only whether the company's existing scheme satisfies the qualifying criteria but also who will be affected, what process changes are needed, the effect on budgets and forecasts to reflect the additional cost, the timing and what communication is needed with employees and other that will be affected.

Key points to note with regard to auto-enrolment are:

(1)   Whilst all employers will eventually need to comply, the date they need to do this by (the staging date) is calculated by reference to the number of people on the company's PAYE scheme. From 1 November 2013 all those with 500 or more will need to comply.

(2)   All eligible job-holders must be auto-enrolled. These comprise not only employees but also temporary and agency staff, provided they work (or ordinarily work) in the UK, are aged between 22 years and the state pension age, income tax and NICs are deducted by the employer and have gross qualifying earnings of £7,475 or more per annum.

(3)   The company might have a suitable existing workplace pension scheme which already satisfies the qualifying criteria, or it might be suitable provided minor amendments are made to its rules or terms before the staging date. If not, a new scheme will need to be put in place before the staging date. Key requirements are that the scheme does not have any barriers to entry (length of service, age limit, etc) or require employees to make a positive decision to join as it must be automatic.

(4)   The employer must contribute at least 3% of an eligible job-holders qualifying pensionable earnings into the qualifying pension scheme, although this will be phased in so the contribution gradually increases from 1% to 3% over a period of time to ease the financial burden for employers.

Details of the qualifying scheme must be registered with The Pensions Regulator and employers must provide information to employees about the changes and how they will affect them. It is particularly important that employees are made aware of their right to opt out within a month of being auto-enrolled and have any deductions from their remuneration paid back. Even after this an employee has the right to cease inclusion in the scheme. Similarly, an employee has the right to request to join the qualifying workplace scheme even where he has previously opted out and the employee should put in place processes to re-enrol the employee automatically every three years and, each time, advise them of their right to opt out.

It is apparent from The Pensions Regulator that an increasing number of directors are being prosecuted for failing to comply with the Pensions Act 1995 s 49(8) which requires payments by a company into employee pension funds be made at the due date. Directors should be aware that late payment of pension contributions is a civil offence and The Pensions Regulator's powers to fine individuals up to £5,000 and employers up to £50,000 have been extended. The Pensions Regulator can also ban people from undertaking trustees' duties and initiate criminal action for serious failure to comply and fraud. It is important that the pension scheme is properly and effectively administered, that employee contributions are passed to the pension provider and the reason for any delay beyond 19 days from the end of the month in which the deduction was made is communicated to the employee and The Pensions Regulator.

As part of the required payment regime employers must keep a record of payments including identification of employee and employer contributions and any changes made during the scheme year. These must be retained for at least six years. Directors must therefore ensure that the required records are prepared and retained and that the scheme is run efficiently keeping the pension provider fully informed of any changes.

Directors should also be aware that under the PA 2008 an officer, as well as the company to which they are appointed, can be guilty of an offence for failing to comply with requirements under the Act and be proceeded against, for example, for failing to auto-enrol and re-enrol an employee, or not allowing someone who previously opted out to join in. Such penalty might comprise imprisonment for a term not exceeding two years, a fine, or both (PA 2008 ss 45–49).

There are other ramifications from the PA 2008 which also need to be borne in mind, for example that an employer must not give incentives to encourage employees to opt out of the qualifying scheme, unfairly dismiss someone for staying in or give preferential treatment to someone in the recruitment process who indicates he will opt out.

Employment records and data protection   11.140

It is clear that, given the structured nature of employment records, they will fall within the scope of the Data Protection Act 1998 (DPA 1998) and consequently directors must ensure notification to the Information Commissioner includes employment records and that the requirements of DPA 1998 and specifically the data protection principles set out in para **13.102** are observed at all times.

Recognising the complexities in this area, the Information Commissioner has issued the Employment Practices Code ('the Code'), as well as supplementary guidance and a quick guide for small businesses. To help employers to understand requirements of the DPA 1998 in respect of personal information gathered during the employment relationship, from recruitment to termination and beyond, the Code sets out standards or benchmarks for:

- managing data protection;

- recruitment and selection;

- employment records;

- access and disclosure of information, including references;

- monitoring at work (including monitoring telephone, email and Internet use); and

- health records and medical testing (including for alcohol and substance abuse).

Directors would be well advised to observe the recommendations of the Code, as it lays down a bar or marker against which breaches of the DPA 1998 will be judged. The main areas are set out below.

Managing data protection   11.141

The manner in which a company deals with data protection issues in relation to employee records needs to be formally considered, set out and communicated.

The Code sets out the following benchmarks to help employers comply:

(1)   Establish a person within the organisation responsible for ensuring employment practices and procedures comply with DPA 1998 and for ensuring that they continue to do so. Put in place a mechanism for checking that procedures are followed in practice.

(2)   Ensure that business areas and individual line managers that process information about workers understand their own responsibility for data protection compliance and, if necessary, amend their working practices in the light of this.

(3)   Assess what personal data about workers is in existence and who is responsible for it.

(4)   Eliminate the collection of personal data that is irrelevant or excessive to the employment relationship. If sensitive data is collected, ensure that a sensitive data condition is satisfied.

(5)   Ensure that workers are aware of the extent to which they can be criminally liable if they knowingly or recklessly disclose personal data outside their employer's policies or procedures. Make serious breaches of data protection rules a disciplinary offence.

(6)   Allocate responsibility for checking that your organisation has a valid notification in the register of data controllers that relates to the processing of personal data about workers, unless it is exempt from notification.

(7)   Consult trade unions or other workers' representatives, if any, or workers themselves over the development and implementation of employment practices and procedures that involve the processing of workers' data.

To achieve this, responsibility for ensuring collection and use of employee data complies with DPA 1998 needs to be allocated. Depending on the company's size this may be to the human resources or personnel manager, or even the company secretary. Employment procedures must comply with DPA 1998, eg by limiting access to personal and sensitive information, reminding employees of the need for confidentiality, keeping the information up to date, determining how and to whom it can be released, etc. As with any system of control, these procedures must be communicated to line managers and others who regularly process personal data and their actions be periodically checked to ensure they are complying with the requirements of data protection. Employees should know their responsibilities and it be made clear that a breach of data protection policy is a disciplinary offence.

Furthermore, it is important that adequacy of the notification made to the Information Commissioner is assessed from time to time as, for example, there may be changes in the personal information kept or the way it is processed which will need to be notified.

Recruitment and selection   **11.142**

By its very nature, recruitment of staff involves collection and processing of personal data in order to select a suitable candidate. Recognising this, Part 1 of the Code sets out recommendations with regard to:

(1)   Advertising – The name of the company to which an applicant will be providing their personal information and the manner in which it will be used should be clear from the advertisement.

(2)   Applications – It is important for employers to restrict the request for personal information on job applications to that which is necessary as part of the recruitment decision. It must be clear to whom applications are being sent and there must be a secure method of sending them – particularly important where they are submitted electronically, as a secure, probably encrypted, link must be provided.

(3)   Verification – If any checks or verification procedures are to be carried out, such as checking qualifications, contacting previous employers or speaking to an applicant's doctor, the nature of such checks must be explained to the applicant and their consent be obtained. Applicants must also be given the opportunity to explain any inconsistencies in the information supplied, identified by verification.

(4)   Shortlisting – When personal data is used in the process of shortlisting candidates, it must be used objectively and consistently between candidates. If any decision is to be made by automated means, the applicant must be informed of this and be given the opportunity to make representations before a decision is actually made.

(5)   Interviews – In the interview, questions and information obtained must be limited to that which is necessary and relevant to the recruitment decision. It is also important to note that the applicant will normally have the right to see any notes recorded during the interview, including notes and comments scribbled by the interviewer and it must be ensured that these are always justified, professional and relevant.

(6)   Pre-employment checks and vetting – Part 1 of the Code recommends that vetting is used only where the risks to the employer, customers or others affected by the employment are such to justify it and there is no less intrusive method of obtaining information that could be used.

(7)   Recruitment records – Recruitment records should only be retained as long as necessary to achieve a particular business purpose and information obtained by vetting should be destroyed within six months. Personal information of unsuccessful candidates should only be retained where they have agreed to this, ie should other jobs become available or their personal identification details have been deleted.

DPA 1998 and Part 1 of the Code will undoubtedly have far-reaching effects on the way companies recruit staff as together they require a much more formal and predetermined recruitment procedure, especially in terms of deciding in advance what personal information is required, how it is obtained and recorded and the length of time for which it will be kept.

Employment records   11.143

Employers need to keep employees' records, and, to comply with DPA 1998, Part 2 of the Code sets out a number of benchmarks to assist the employer. The benchmarks recommend that the employer should:

(1)   ensure that newly appointed workers are aware of the nature and source of any information kept about them, how it will be used and who it will be disclosed to;

(2)   inform new workers and remind existing workers about their rights under DPA 1998, including their right of access to the information kept about them;

(3)   ensure there is a clear and foreseeable need for any information collected about workers and that the information collected actually meets that need;

(4)   provide each worker with a copy of information that may be subject to change, eg personal details such as home address, annually or allow workers to view this online and ask workers to check their records for accuracy and ensure any necessary amendments are made to bring records up to date; and

(5)   incorporate accuracy, consistency and validity checks into its systems.

Employers must ensure employment records are accurate and not excessive. They must also ensure an employee knows and has agreed to any sensitive data being held and processed (and this would, for example, include sickness records), that information is periodically reviewed and kept up to date and access to employment records is suitably restricted to ensure security.

According to the Information Commissioner, recording the answers to questions asked when conducting reviews or appraisals constitutes processing data. Consequently, to observe the data protection principles it is important that information which is gathered during such interviews and recorded is limited to that necessary for employment decisions, that it is correct and not misleading and is used fairly and lawfully thereafter. Any opinions or comments made by the person carrying out the assessment must be expressed as such and care must be taken that such comments are in no circumstances frivolous as an employee may request a copy of their employment records.

It should also be noted that once an employer has recorded personal information about an employee, they are not free to process it how they want. In many cases the employee's consent must still be sought where, for example, they are to be sent internal marketing or promotions material, before their details are data-matched to prevent or detect fraud or where details are to be transferred outside the European Economic Area (while also observing security measures, see para **13.102**).

It is important to ensure that the outcome of disciplinary proceedings or dismissal of an employee are correctly recorded on the employee's record. For example, where an employee has resigned, requirements of DPA 1998 would be breached where the reason for leaving was recorded as 'dismissed'. It is easy to see that such an inaccuracy on the employee's record could lead to provision of a damaging and misleading reference.

Furthermore, where a disciplinary proceeding has been initiated in respect of an employee, depending on the wording of the policy, record of the proceeding may need to be removed from the employee's record once the period for which it was in force has expired.

Access and disclosure of information   **11.144**

Employees have a right to see the information being held about them by the company and it is therefore important that this information is kept in such a way that it can be collated and passed to the individual on request, as addressed in section 2.8 of the Code.

Furthermore, directors should ensure there is a disclosure policy in place and communicated to staff to ensure that when information about an employee or former employee is requested by a third party, for example a new employer or prospective landlord, the person who receives the request knows how to respond and that the identity of the person making the request and its validity is established before any information is released. Such information must be provided within 40 days of the request.

Employers must also make sure that personal data about employees, both in manual and electronic form, is safely stored and measures are in place to ensure that unauthorised access to the information is prevented. The Code sets out the following benchmarks to help employers to comply with the requirement for security. The employer is required to:

(1)   apply security standards that take account of the risks of unauthorised access to, accidental loss or destruction of, or damage to, employment records;

(2)   institute a system of secure cabinets, access controls and passwords to ensure that staff can only gain access to employment records where they have a legitimate business need to do so;

(3)   use the audit trail capabilities of automated systems to track who accesses and amends personal data;

(4)   take steps to ensure the reliability of staff that have access to workers' records by carrying out background checks, providing training to ensure employees understand their responsibilities for confidential or sensitive information and placing confidentiality clauses in their contracts of employment;

(5)   ensure that if employment records are taken off-site, eg on laptop computers, this is controlled; and

(6)   take account of the risks of transmitting confidential worker information by fax or email and only transmit such information if secure network or comparable arrangements are in place and there is some technical means of ensuring security, such as encryption of data, etc.

It is also important to note that where there is a proposed merger or acquisition, disclosure of information about employees prior to completion should be anonomised as far as possible prior to completion. If this is not possible then an undertaking must be obtained from the party to whom the information is disclosed that the information will not be disclosed beyond the prospective purchaser and its advisers, it will be kept secure and will be returned or destroyed should the transaction not proceed. Where the merger or acquisition takes place, employment records can be transferred but employees should be told this is happening and be given the opportunity to review the accuracy of the information about them that is being transferred. Furthermore the new employer should review the records to make sure that only what is necessary and relevant to the new employment relationship is retained.

Monitoring at work   **11.145**

DPA 1998 does not prevent an employer from monitoring employees but any monitoring must be carried out in a way that complies with DPA 1998, as well as:

●   the Human Rights Act 1998, which requires protection of an employee's right to privacy and to be treated fairly;

●   the Telecommunications (Lawful Business Practice) (Interception of Communications) Regulations 2000 (SI 2000/2699), specifying when employers can listen in to phone calls and intercept emails, etc; and

- the Regulation of Investigatory Powers Act 2000, which restricts access to the actual content of communication.

The main reasons an employer would want to monitor employees would be to check the quality or quantity of work or to check conformity with the employer's rules and standards of conduct required. Monitoring may take the form of surveillance through use of CCTV, intercepting emails, checking use of the Internet and monitoring telephone calls, gathering sales point information, obtaining credit reference details or recording their movements whilst on sick leave, etc.

In so far as such monitoring is recorded, it comes within the scope of DPA 1998 and personal data gathered must be processed in such a way so as to comply with data protection requirements.

Whilst it can clearly be seen why an employer might want to monitor telephone calls, emails and use of the internet by an employee whilst at work, it is important to note that data protection principles must be observed.

Part 3 of the Code recommends that some form of impact assessment is carried out to determine how to conduct monitoring. Where it is decided that monitoring is required as there is no suitable alternative, it is recommended that clear policies are drawn up and communicated to employees setting out what is acceptable to the employer in respect of personal use of these facilities and informing them that monitoring will take place. Given that an email, for example, may contain sensitive data only intended for the recipient, it is important for the employer to have obtained specific consent from the employee to monitor and process it.

The difficulty facing the employer is the need to balance the employee's right to privacy with its own right to determine how much work is being carried out during work time and also to protect its reputation by, for example, ensuring no unsuitable material is being downloaded from the Internet. Directors must be aware of these complexities before instigating employee monitoring.

Part 3 of the Code sets out the following good practice recommendations to help an employer to control monitoring and comply with the requirements of DPA 1998:

(1) Identify who within the organisation can authorise the monitoring of workers and ensure they are aware of the employer's responsibilities under DPA 1998.

(2) Before monitoring, identify clearly the purpose(s) behind the monitoring and the specific benefits it is likely to bring. Determine – preferably using an impact assessment – whether the likely benefits justify any adverse impact.

(3)   If monitoring is to be used to enforce the organisation's rules and standards, make sure that the rules and standards are clearly set out in a policy which also refers to the nature and extent of any associated monitoring and ensure workers are aware of the policy.

(4)   Tell workers what monitoring is taking place and why, and keep them aware of this, unless covert monitoring is justified.

(5)   If sensitive data is collected in the course of monitoring, ensure that consent is obtained.

(6)   Keep to a minimum those who have access to personal information obtained through monitoring. Subject them to confidentiality and security requirements and ensure that they are properly trained where the nature of the information requires this.

(7)   Do not use personal information collected through monitoring for purposes other than those for which the monitoring was introduced unless:

(a)   it is clearly in the individual's interest to do so; or

(b)   it reveals activity that no employer could reasonably be expected to ignore.

(8)   If information gathered from monitoring might have an adverse impact on workers, present them with the information and allow them to make representations before taking action.

(9)   Ensure that the right of access of workers to information about them, which is kept for or obtained through monitoring, is not compromised. Monitoring systems must be capable of meeting this and other data requirements.

(10) Do not monitor workers just because a customer for your products or services imposes a condition requiring you to do so, unless you can satisfy yourself that the condition is justified.

As well as the general recommendations set out above, the Code contains more specific recommendations for monitoring electronic communications, video and audio monitoring, covert and in-vehicle monitoring, and monitoring using a third party.

Health records and medical testing   **11.146**

Medical testing is particularly intrusive and information obtained will comprise sensitive personal data and be subject to requirements of DPA 1998. In the employment context, a company may want to carry this out where, for example, someone is believed to be taking drugs or alcohol and it is having a detrimental effect on their performance or behaviour at work. Alternatively, routine medical testing, screening or surveillance might be required for health and safety reasons to, for example, check exposure to chemicals and biological agents. An employer might also want to carry out medical testing where an employee has been unable to work due to illness for some time, to determine when they might be able to return.

In any event, the Code recommends that medical testing is only carried out where there it is justified by a specific business reason and explicit consent is given freely by the employee or employees concerned.

12 Directors' duties and the environment

12 Directors' duties and the environment

There is an increasing recognition that good environmental performance makes sense for business as environmental factors and the continued availability of natural resources are significant factors in the long-term sustainability of business. Poor environmental performance or the occurrence of a large-scale, high-profile disaster can damage a company's reputation so badly that it is difficult to recover and continue into the future. The expression 'bad news travels fast' has never been more true given the speed with which messages and images can be communicated via mobile phones and the Internet, especially where disasters and catastrophes are concerned.

It is therefore important for a company to fully assess and understand the impact of its operations on the environment and to measure, manage and communicate its performance in this respect. This is necessary not only to ensure that the company does not fall foul of regulatory requirements or have its reputation damaged by environmental incidents, but also to capitalise on the benefits that demonstrating high standards of environmental performance can bring in terms of the positive influence it can have on consumer behaviour and investment decisions.

Directors' duties in relation to pollution and protection of the environment have increased and now, in addition to a company's strict civil liability for environmental damage under common law (established in the case *Rylands v Fletcher* [1861–73] All ER Rep 1), legislation imposes criminal liability where statutory requirements have been infringed. At the same time, directors should be aware that they may be held personally liable for offences committed by the company where they were perpetrated with their consent or connivance, or resulted from their negligence. A company may also be responsible for damage to the environment even if it is not aware of the damage, which is why it is important to fully assess and understand the impact the company's operations might have (*Environment Agency v Brock plc* [1998] Env LR 607).

In response to increasing general awareness of the extent of damage caused by industry to the environment and the major role businesses have to play in helping to sustain, protect and enhance the environment, an expansive range of 'green' legislation has developed worldwide, imposing strict regulations. This legislation covers such issues as gas and dust emissions into the air, odour, smoke, water quality and effluent, solid waste (including toxic and radioactive waste), noise pollution, litter, disposal of waste, environmental labelling and many other matters. Whilst many of the requirements have been consolidated in the Environmental Protection Act 1990 (EPA 1990) and the Environment Act 1995, making it easier for directors to grasp the extent of their duties for environmental protection, there are numerous subsequent regulations that need to be carefully examined for a director to understand the full extent of the organisation's obligations in respect of the environment.

The main provisions of legislation, including the Control of Major Accident Hazards Regulations 1999 (as amended) for the prevention and limitation of the effects of major accidents, are discussed below. However, when considering environmental protection, directors should also bear in mind that requirements of a substantial amount of other legislation are intrinsically linked to protection of the environment and all need to be taken into account. For example, the Control of Substances Hazardous to Health Regulations 2002 (as amended), where the way in which a company obtains, stores, uses and disposes of dangerous substances may have a significant impact on the environment.

CA 2006 s 172 requires directors to have regard to the impact on the community and the environment of any decisions they make (see **CHAPTER 4**) and, as set out in paras **7.13.1** and **7.13.4**, listed companies are also required by CA 2006 to report on significant environmental matters including the quantity of carbon dioxide emitted each year in the business review (being replaced by the strategic report) to the annual report and accounts.

There are also numerous other, non-legislative, developments and initiatives which further increase the need for directors to demonstrate what steps are being taken by their companies to protect and preserve the environment. Amongst these is the FTSE4Good Index Series which measures a listed company's performance in meeting globally recognised corporate responsibility standards to identify those companies which are environmentally and socially responsible. These criteria are increasingly important for investors, fund managers, brokers and the like when making investment decisions as, in some instances, they will only invest in companies which have achieved a best practice grading on the FTSE4Good index. The FTSE4Good Environmental Leaders Europe 40 Index is one element of the index series and it identifies and rates those companies with leading environmental practices that are successfully managing the risks and impacts of their activities and reducing their environmental footprint. High standards need to be achieved to even be included on the index. Whilst this index series is particularly relevant for listed companies, the best practice measures and high standards of environmental performance demonstrated are relevant for companies of all sizes.

The Environment Agency has also launched a number of initiatives and policies to encourage businesses to be more aware of the need to protect and preserve the environment. Various awards are made each year to those demonstrating best practice in relation to the environment. The Greener Business Showcase launched on Twitter and Facebook highlights in a very positive way how organisations lead the way in environmental performance. Similarly, the Greener Business Report provides opportunity for businesses to share best practice ideas by encouraging debate and discussion and identifying those performing well.

There is also an increase in the pressure being put on companies to avoid being named and shamed by inclusion on one of the many publically available lists of environmental offenders. One such example is publication by the Department of Energy and Climate Change of all significant oil and chemical releases notified. Other examples of such lists are available from DEFRA and the Environment Agency. This increasing trend towards openness and transparency needs to be recognised by directors as gone are the days where they might hope few will find out about an environmental incident, and the damage to a company's reputation can be considerable.

Due to the scale of damage caused to the environment the Deepwater Horizon oil spill in the Gulf of Mexico on 20 April 2010 could not go unmentioned in this chapter. It was a catastrophic environmental disaster of unprecedented scale which, as well as causing the death of 11 people in the initial explosion, led to the release of approximately five million barrels of crude oil into the sea, causing extensive damage to marine and wildlife habitats and to fishing and tourism. Given the scale of the disaster and BP's previous record, the prosecutors adopted an aggressive stance in pursuing BP as the designated operator and party ultimately responsible for conducting operations. BP will therefore be held accountable for all clean-up costs and for payment of compensation for damages and is facing civil and criminal prosecution under the Clean Water Act, Oil Pollution Act, the Migratory Bird Treaty Act and Endangered Species Act, amongst others. The US Attorney General's criminal and civil investigation into the spill started in June 2010 and the trial of BP and partners commenced in New Orleans on 25 February 2013. All the claims have been consolidated in the one trial and include action by the families of the workers who were killed, the state's fishing industry, investors, environmental groups, and President Obama's own administration for violation of environmental laws. Action is also being taken against the CEO and COO, some of BP's managers and the well-site managers for manslaughter and environmental violations.

BP's own internal investigations found that they had made mistakes which compromised the standards that should have been exercised and it is evident that there were lapses in their risk management, control and governance processes which should have highlighted potential problems long before the disaster occurred. The formal federal investigation also concluded that the well blowout and oil spill was caused by multiple errors including poor risk management, hurried last minute changes, failure to recognise and respond to critical signs of trouble and insufficient emergency response training. The whole disaster could therefore have been avoided which, whilst of little comfort to those directly affected, is a harsh caution for others to heed.

The Deepwater Horizon catastrophe specifically mentioned because the consequences for BP are immense, not only in terms of potential fines and compensation claims, for which they set aside a $20 billion fund, but also in terms of the company's share price which dropped significantly in the aftermath, the severe and longstanding damage it has done to the reputation of the company and its senior executives and the risk of imprisonment for up to 15 years for any of them found to be directly involved in decisions or failings that led to the disaster.

However, whilst the size of the Deepwater Horizon incident sets it apart, it is only one of many recent incidents involving damage to the environment, a few examples of which are set out below:

(1)   Mr Dixon, sole director of SOS Skip Hire & Haulage, received a suspended 12-month prison sentence, was disqualified as a director and ordered to pay £16,000 of costs on 25 November 2014 for breaching the environmental permit and planning conditions at the waste disposal site operated by his company. Despite having the permit revoked, and receiving enforcement notices and breach of condition notices, Mr Dixon continued to accept waste at the site, in volumes significantly over the amount stated in the permit.

(2)   On 13 November 2014 Southern Water was fined £500,000 by the Environment Agency for discharging untreated sewage into Swalecliffe Brook, polluting the sea and a Kent watercourse.

(3)   On 30 October 2012 Countrystyle Recycling Ltd, FGS AGRI Ltd and the owner and director of both companies pleaded guilty to multiple charges relating to the illegal deposit of waste between January and July 2011 in Kent and East Sussex. As a consequence of the action brought, three waste firms from Kent and one director have been fined a total of £233,670 after pleading guilty to illegally depositing waste on golf courses and farms.

(4)   Three companies, KSV Sussex, Thorn International UK and Ady's Skips and Recycling Services Ltd, and eight men were fined a total of £220,000 for attempting to export hazardous waste (in the form of broken electronic equipment) to developing countries in breach of the Transfrontier Shipment of Waste Regulations 2007 and the European Waste Shipment Regulations 2006 (Environment Agency News, 6 December 2012).

The examples above are, hopefully, a stark reminder to directors of the consequences of failing to fulfil their duties to preserve the environment, which apply whatever the size of the company.

However, improvements in environmental performance are being achieved, as demonstrated in the Environment Agency's 'Sustainable Business Report for 2012' (published in October 2013) which shows an improvement as the number of serious pollution incidents are reducing, more waste is being recovered and there is less air pollution. All of these help to contribute to a cleaner, more sustainable environment. The statistics available in this report show how business environmental performance has fared in England and Wales in 2012 and reveal:

(1)   total fines of just over £1.9m, compared to total fines of £3.6m in 2011;

(2)   an average fine per company of £21,000, compared to £21,600 in 2011;

(3)   there were 504 serious pollution incidents;

(4)   significant improvements are still needed in environmental performance in the waste sector (comprising 33% of fines) and by the water companies (constituting about 40% of fines) and a number of large, high-profile businesses continue to be multiple and repeat offenders; and

(5)   there were no fines in 2012 on businesses in the paper and pulp, textiles, power, refineries and fuel, energy from waste and metal sectors.

Particular industries, such as the water industry, remain a concern, as do the offences of fly-tipping and illegal waste disposal. Obviously the publication of any report by the Environmental Agency in itself is bad publicity for the companies concerned and named in it and the Environment Agency urges Boards to address the problem of environmental pollution and to make the adoption of a 'zero tolerance' policy their objective.

Directors should also note that the Environment Agency has been lobbying for stronger sentencing and an increase in fines, especially for repeat offenders, to act as a greater deterrent for those who might otherwise contemplate committing environmental offences. Consultation on draft Environmental Offences Sentencing Guidelines ended on 6 June 2013 and guidelines were published by the Sentencing Council on 26 February 2014, increasing some of the fines and setting out more consistent treatment of offenders.

The Environment Act 1995   12.10

EA 1995 created the Environment Agency, with statutory power to regulate and control pollution, inspect premises and impose bans where they find that operating methods need to be changed or controls need to be implemented to prevent or minimise pollution. Directors will appreciate that a ban on operations as a result of an inspection will not only have a significant impact on the company's financial results, but may also damage customer relations, attract bad publicity from pressure groups and damage shareholder confidence in the company's management team.

In addition, s 5 of EA 1995 encourages advance planning on environmental issues by requiring companies to assess existing and potential levels of pollution and to identify and implement suitable measures where it is clear that some action is necessary to prevent, minimise, remedy or mitigate pollution.

The Environmental Protection Act 1990   12.20

EPA 1990 consolidated many issues into one piece of legislation and introduced important new controls aimed at limiting and preventing pollution from a wide range of industries. The main features of EPA 1990 which directors need to be aware of are:

- authorisation is needed to operate certain specified processes where there is an inherent risk of harm to the environment (such processes are prescribed in the Environmental Protection (Prescribed Processes and Substances) Regulations 1991 (SI 1991/472). A licence to operate must be obtained before the company commences operations (EPA 1990 s 2(1));

- regulation is through either HM Inspectorate of Pollution (HMIP) or the Local Authority Environmental Health Officer (EHO), depending on the type of pollution and potential for damage by discharging polluting substances into the air, land and water;

- where a company breaches the conditions of authorisation to operate, HMIP and the EHO have authority to issue:

  - enforcement notices requiring immediate remedial action to be taken (EPA 1990 s 13); or

  - prohibition notices suspending authorisation until remedial action has been taken (EPA 1990 s 14);

- certain types of new industrial developments are required to assess and report the likely impact of their operations on the environment as part of the planning application process;

- directors must ensure that emission limits are monitored and adhered to, as they are now legally binding. Similarly, they must be able to demonstrate that they have used the 'best practicable environmental option' for controlling pollution (EPA 1990 s 7(4));

- adequate arrangements for disposal of waste products must be made. Although these arrangements for a manufacturing company which may have to consider treating, storing, transporting and disposing chemical waste may be more complex, they are equally important to an office-based organisation disposing of paper waste. This was reinforced by introduction of the landfill tax, levied on waste disposed of in landfill sites, which penalises those companies that do not attempt to recycle or recover any of their waste;

- Part IIA of EPA 1990 introduced a new statutory regime for identifying and cleaning up contaminated land. Local authorities will establish who caused or knowingly permitted the contamination and serve a remediation notice. Companies that fail to comply with such notice are committing a criminal offence and they could face a fine of up to £20,000 with a £2,000 daily default fine.

Directors have a responsibility to ensure that authorisation to operate is obtained where required and that operations are carried out in accordance with the conditions under which authorisation is granted. Any change in process must be notified before it is brought into effect, and revised authorisation obtained.

Directors should be aware that where authorisation is required and has not been obtained, or where emission limits exceed the stated maximum levels, HMIP or the EHO may take action against the directors as well as, or instead of, the company for the offence under EPA 1990 ss 157(1) and 158 or other environmental legislation, such as the Clean Air Act 1993, the Control of Asbestos in the Air Regulations 1990 (SI 1990/556) or the Radioactive Substances Act 1993, depending on the nature of the pollution.

The penalty for an environmental offence such as the unlicensed depositing of waste, unlawful discharge of trade effluent or illegal storage of substances is punishable by summary conviction, with up to two years' imprisonment and/or an unlimited fine. Similarly, the director may be liable for disqualification as a director under the Company Directors Disqualification Act 1986 (CDDA 1986) s 2. In the case involving a company Pharmacos (Environmental Data Services Report 299, December 1999) a managing director was disqualified from acting as a director for four years under CDDA 1986 for unlawfully operating a prescribed process under Part I of the EPA 1990 and at the same time was fined £2,500 and ordered to pay costs of £3,500.

Similarly on 23 February 2012 the Environment Agency reported that two businesses, BW Riddle and Chungs UK Ltd, which had exported containers of mixed waste to China illegally without observing their duty of care received fines totalling £9,000, including a fine for one of the partners of BW Riddle, and were ordered to pay costs of £6,500. The fines were rendered for their failure to observe regs 23B(2) and 58 of the Transfrontier Shipment of Waste Regulations 2007 and s 34(1)(c)(ii) and (6) of the EPA 1990.

It should also be noted that EPA 1990 redefined 'statutory nuisance' as an offence, and this includes smoke, dust, steam, gas, fumes or other effluents from industrial or trade premises which are either prejudicial to health or a nuisance. Where a statutory nuisance occurs, the EHO will issue an abatement notice to prevent recurrence of the offence and a fine will be imposed for breach of the abatement notice. In addition, the company is liable for criminal proceedings and the court may issue a compensation order under the Powers of Criminal Courts Act 1973 s 35.

Environmental permit   12.30

The Environmental Permitting (England and Wales) Regulations 2010 ('EPR 2010') prohibit operating a regulated facility except under and to the extent authorised by an environmental permit (reg 12). A 'regulated facility' includes an installation that carries out a Schedule 1 activity, mobile plant, waste mobile plant or waste operation carried out by other means (reg 8).

The EPR 2010 (preceded by the EPR 2007) combines the requirements for pollution prevention control and waste management licences so that now only one single environmental permit is required by regulated facilities, thereby improving the effectiveness of regulation by making it easier for companies to understand what is needed.

Directors must be aware of these requirements as it may be necessary to apply for a permit from the environmental regulator (in most cases the Environment Agency or, for less polluting industries, the local authority) before a regulated activity can be carried out. 'Schedule 1' activities are quite broad and include waste management, intensive farming and the food and drink sectors as well as energy, production and processing of metals, minerals and chemicals. EPR 2010 extended the application of the EPR 2007 and now also covers water discharge, ground water activity and regulation of radioactive substances.

In granting a permit, consideration will be given to:

(1)   the management system and what preventative measures there are in place to safeguard against pollution;

(2)   emissions and whether any significant pollution is caused (including odour, heat, noise and vibration);

(3)   minimisation or avoidance of waste production to reduce any environmental impact;

(4)   whether energy is used efficiently;

(5)   whether measures in place to prevent accidents and limit their consequences;

(6)   recovery procedures.

Directors must ensure that, as an operator, the company is able to demonstrate that environmental benefits have been balanced against costs to achieve a high level of protection for the environment from activities carried out overall. Furthermore, operators need to comply with the permit conditions on an ongoing basis and the directors must implement control policies and procedures to ensure these requirements are met.

By way of illustration, on 31 May 2013 Cambridge Magistrates' Court ordered Cambridge University to pay a fine of £28k and costs of £7,363 when it pleaded guilty to causing water pollution on two occasions when slurry from farms run by the University leaked into the river.

Similarly, on 2 August 2011 Universal Beverages Ltd pleaded guilty to seven offences involving water pollution brought by the Environment Agency under s 85(1) of the Water Resources Act 1991 and the Environmental Permitting (England and Wales) Regulations 2007, for which it was fined £36,000 and ordered to pay £20,825. During the investigations several breaches of the conditions of the environmental permit were discovered and an enforcement notice was served on the company requiring improvement of conditions, revised operational procedures and completion of training.

Directors should note that the Environment Agency has made clear that it is placing greater emphasis on investigating and conducting repeated in-depth reviews on businesses which repeatedly demonstrate poor environmental performance and that it will seek prosecution where justified.

Prevention and remediation of environmental damage   12.40

The Environmental Damage (Prevention and Remediation) Regulations 2009 (SI 2009/153) and the Environmental Damage (Prevention and Remediation) (Wales) Regulations 2009 (SI 2009/995) (together the 'Environmental Damage Regulations') came into force on 1 March 2009, implementing requirements of the Environmental Liability Directive (2004/35/EC). They introduce new obligations for preventing and remedying environmental damage and require the polluter to pay for any damage caused.

The Environmental Damage Regulations seek to prevent and discourage environmental damage by forcing polluters to pay remediation and prevention costs. Key features include:

- encouraging prevention of damage by threat of economic liability for repairing any damage that does occur;

- requiring the operator to take preventative measures where there is a threat of environmental damage;

- where environmental damage has already occurred, the operator must restore the damage itself or meet the cost of such restoration.

The Environmental Damage Regulations apply in certain cases where serious damage has been caused. However, existing legislation which contains provisions on environmental liability continues to apply where the threat or occurrence of damage is not covered by the Environmental Damage Regulations or where that legislation goes further in terms of what is required. Such existing legislation includes the Control of Major Accidental Hazards (Amendment) Regulations 2005, 2008 and 2009 ('COMAH'), EPR 2010, Part IIA of the EPA 1990, Water Act 2003, Water Resources Act 1991 and Wildlife and Countryside Act 1981.

'Environmental damage' for the purposes of the Environmental Damage Regulations includes any adverse effects on:

- sites of special scientific interest ('SSSIs') or on conservation of species and habitats protected by the EU;

- surface and ground water, causing a deterioration in quality; and

- land caused by contamination which is a threat to human health.

The regulations also place liability on operators of activities requiring an environmental permit which involve discharges to water and groundwater, water abstraction or impoundment, use of pesticides, biocides or dangerous substances, the use and release of genetically modified organisms and transportation of dangerous goods.

It is therefore important to ensure the directors are fully aware of their responsibilities under the Environmental Damage Regulations and also all other applicable legislation.

In the first instance the company should examine its activities to determine if and what environmental damage could be caused. Once this is known appropriate preventative measures must be put in place to ensure that pollution does not occur. The early signs of an imminent or actual incident must be identified and checks, controls, measures and means of monitoring be put in place to ensure any concerns are acted upon at the earliest opportunity.

Immediate action must be taken as soon as the threat of a pollution incident is identified or where it is apparent that pollution has occurred and the relevant enforcing authority must be informed. The operator must take such steps as necessary to prevent damage and further damage, implement the preventative and remedial measures required by the enforcing authority and pay costs claimed by the enforcing authority in relation to remediation and the environmental damage caused. The enforcing authority may also require certain information to be provided about events leading up to and giving rise to the damage.

When serving a remediation notice the enforcing authority will take into account the remedial measures proposed by the operator when determining what is required.

Environmental reporting   12.50

Coupled with statutory requirements for protection of the environment, directors and those involved in the management of companies are under increasing pressure to account and demonstrate to shareholders, investors, pressure groups, customers and employees what steps the company is taking to fulfil its environmental responsibility. This is an important consideration as, in addition to visible costs of fines following an environmental accident and the clean-up costs to be paid, failure to protect the environment is likely to attract adverse publicity, damage shareholder relations, discourage investors and possibly affect sales for a prolonged period lasting long after the incident occurred.

An increasing number of companies are publishing annual environmental reports in response to pressure for greater disclosure and more public accountability. Indeed, the need for directors to demonstrate how their companies are protecting the environment has further increased as a result of:

- the Companies Act 2006 (Strategic Report and Directors' Report) Regulations 2013, which from 1 October 2013 require all UK quoted companies to report on their greenhouse gas emissions (including carbon dioxide) in the directors' report to the annual report and accounts (see para **7.13.1**(l));

- Financial Reporting Standard FRS 12, which requires the financial impact of certain environmental liabilities to be disclosed in a company's accounts;

- the Turnbull Code on Internal Control (discussed in **CHAPTER 10**) which requires directors of listed companies to identify, manage and evaluate environmental, health and safety and social risks in the company's annual report and accounts and to assess and report on the effectiveness of their control systems;

- the requirement that occupational pension fund trustees in the UK issue a statement of investment policy setting out their approach to social, environmental and ethical matters and consequently their need to assess a company's performance in this respect. As a result a number of large pension fund managers and shareholder voting organisations have indicated that they will vote against annual accounts of any FTSE 100 company that does not include an environmental report as it will restrict their ability to assess these matters.

To assist businesses, on 12 June 2013 the Department of the Environment, Food & Rural Affairs issued 'Environmental Reporting Guidelines: Including mandatory greenhouse gas emissions reporting guidance'. These guidelines help businesses measure and report the environmental impacts of their activities, including greenhouse gas emissions, and set out four simple steps for reporting environmental impacts:

- Step 1 – determine the boundaries of the organisation for environmental reporting purposes (ie which parts are attributed to which company, which is simple for a standalone company, but more difficult where there is a complex organisation structure).

- Step 2 – decide the length of period over which data is collected and measured, which will often correspond with the accounting year.

- Step 3 – identify the key environmental impacts of the business and from these determine key performance indicators ('KPIs') to be measured. These might be impacts in terms of greenhouse gas emissions, water, waste generated, materials and resource efficiency, biodiversity and ecosystem services or emissions into the land, air or water.

- Step 4 – collect data, measure and report performance. Whilst there is no prescribed methodology for this part of the process, there are various widely recognised methodologies and independent standards which could be applied. Disclosure in the directors' report must include details of the methodologies applied, noting in particular the specific requirement for quoted companies to show what methodologies were used to determine greenhouse gas emissions.

To further assist, the Government has also devised various web-based tools to help companies convert activities, such as fuel consumption, vehicle mileage and waste generated, into equivalent carbon emissions. The company could also seek certification under ISO 14031, which concentrates on environmental performance evaluation, to help demonstrate that robust, tested and appropriate measures have been implemented.

It is important to note that surveys of reporting carried out by the Environment Agency have found that whilst environmental disclosures by FTSE All-share companies have improved over the last five years in terms of qualitative information provided, more quantitative data is still needed. This is borne out by statistics for the 2009/10 reporting period which show that although 99% made a qualitative disclosure, only 67% made any quantitative disclosures of performance against KPIs and a much smaller number provided statistics in line with the Government's recommendations. The disclosures made were in a variety of locations in the annual reports including the business review and operating and financial review. 79% of companies in the survey reported on pollution and the most common disclosures were on climate change and energy consumption. It is also important for directors to note that environmental procurement was referred to and considered important by 33% of companies, up from 10% in 2004, demonstrating a sizeable shift of awareness about the needs and requirements of those further along the supply chain. It is believed that further improvements in environmental disclosures will be made as customers, shareholders and investors ultimately attribute greater importance to this information.

Directors of many companies recognise the need to demonstrate to the public their concern for the environment and practical action being taken. That has led to the gradual introduction of environmental policies and, more recently, Environmental Management Systems ('EMS') discussed at para **12.70**.

Environmental policy statements   12.60

There is no legal requirement for a company to have an environmental policy, but increasing pressure from regulators, investors, shareholders, customers, pressure groups and the media has in many ways forced companies to consider the impact of their operations on society and the environment and formalise the steps that will be taken to protect the environment in a policy statement.

There is no standard form or prescribed content for this policy statement. Often it is quite brief and it could, for example, just include details of the company's key environmental objectives, who is accountable for environmental performance, how the objectives will be achieved and by whom. For an office-based services company, the objectives might be for travel and transport; stationery and supplies; to improve efficiency, increase recycling and minimise waste; to deal with other like-minded companies; keep momentum and continuously improve; and to ensure employees and suppliers are committed to achieving the objectives.

Surveys of companies that have implemented environmental policies to improve their environmental performance show that they have experienced improvements in corporate image together with better employee, customer and community relations by having introduced environmental policies, which in some instances is reflected in increased revenues.

Government ministers have, however, expressed dissatisfaction at the number of companies with more than 250 employees which lag behind in implementing environmental policies. They have warned that unless companies do more voluntarily to make their environmental policies public and report on the company's progress under such policies they face imposition of a mandatory standard. In addition, the shareholders' organisation (PIRC) and the Association of Chartered and Certified Accountants have called for a degree of government intervention to ensure consistency in measurement of environmental performance, as it is already difficult to draw comparisons between companies using different ratings, measures and standards.

Ultimately responsibility for formulating, developing, implementing and monitoring the environmental policy will be that of the chairman or CEO in conjunction with the Board. Such policies vary enormously, from single-page statements of intent, to basic guidelines and voluminous policy manuals setting targets and objectives through which improvement can be measured. With this in mind, directors must carefully consider the most suitable policy for their operation, bearing in mind the complexities of their operation and the potential impact on the environment. In many instances separate policies have evolved, each concentrating on single issues such as use of waste material in packaging, raw material recycling, air, water and noise pollution, waste disposal and minimisation and energy conservation.

Furthermore, directors should be aware of the increasing trend amongst organisations where, as a condition of supply, they require suppliers to have and provide evidence of their environmental policy. This further emphasises the importance to directors of their duty to implement environmental policies and take measures to protect the environment.

Environmental management systems 12.70

There has been a tendency over the years for environmental policies to be introduced in a very ad hoc manner, often in response to an environmental concern or disaster reaching the press. The consequence is introduction of separate policies each concerned with different aspects of the environment, such as those for health and safety issues, control of substances hazardous to health, emission limits, noise pollution, disposing of waste, recycling, etc. The volume of separate policies developed in this haphazard manner can be very difficult to manage and performance be difficult to monitor and record given the many interrelated factors which are not addressed by the separate policies.

To produce some conformity, many companies have introduced integrated EMSs to replace standalone environmental policies and introduce a system of data management. The environmental policy is a key element of the EMS, but commonly they extend further to include organisation of personnel and management, details of statutory requirements, clear objectives and targets, operational controls, record systems, audits and reviews.

Again, although there is no legal requirement for implementing an EMS, directors should be aware that such a system can be an advantage by introducing a proactive and informed approach to environmental legislation in the company, most particularly at management level. Similarly, an EMS provides a means of addressing complex and varied environmental issues in a thought out and systematic fashion. Directors should be aware of the following benefits:

- environmental management can pinpoint opportunities for cost savings by, for example, reducing raw materials used, energy consumption, transport and waste disposal costs and by lowering the cost of litigation;

- it ensures a consistent approach to environmental matters;

- an ethical investment is likely to be more attractive to investors;

- lower insurance premiums – an environmental audit may be needed before cover is provided;

- it gains competitive advantage with customers by increasing their confidence in the company's integrity and reducing prices by minimising production costs;

- it improves corporate image with shareholders, employees, pressure groups and the media;

- it improves relations with regulators by being in a better position to display awareness of legislative requirements and the company's approach to meeting them; and

- it provides an opportunity for marketing and provides an edge over competitors.

Having introduced an EMS the company may, depending on the industry sector, gain further benefits by publicly demonstrating a level of attainment, competence and commitment to environmental issues by either:

- achieving certification to ISO 14001:1996, which concentrates on managing the administrative process;

- obtaining registration under the Eco-Management and Audit Scheme (EMAS) EC Regulation No 1836/93; and/or

- implementing the six-phase achievement criteria system recommended by BS 8555, which links into ISO 14001, and requires focused training, auditing and implementation at each level in an organisation and covers the relationship between the company, suppliers and customers.

Independent assessment of the EMS in either manner above will increase credibility of the company's EMS by giving it external validation. From the above, it can be seen that directors' duties in relation to the environment are no longer limited to token gestures. A positive management response is called for, whether through an environmental policy or policies or an EMS.

Control of major accidents   12.80

Where the company's business handles, produces, uses, stores or introduces on any site any of the hazardous substances set out in Schedule 1 to the regulations, the directors will need to ensure the company adheres to the requirements of Control of Major Accidents Hazards Regulations 1999, as amended by COMAH. COMAH builds on existing legislation and require operators of establishments where specified quantities of dangerous substances are present or are likely to be present to take measures to prevent major accidents and limit their consequences to people and the environment.

COMAH mainly applies to the chemical and petrochemical industries but also to some storage activities, explosives and nuclear sites and other industries where threshold levels of dangerous substances are identified.

Notification   12.81

All establishments which come within the scope of COMAH are required to notify the competent authority ('CA', comprising the HSE acting jointly with the Environment Agency) of their operations. New establishments must notify a reasonable time before construction of the establishment, usually three to six months, and existing establishments must notify within one year of becoming subject to the COMAH regulations.

Notification is also required where there is a change in quantities of dangerous substances or their form or where there is a closure or change in operations at the establishment.

Need for compliance   12.82

Regulation 18(1) of COMAH empowers the CA to prohibit bringing into operation any establishment or operation therein where the measures taken by the operator are not considered sufficient to prevent and mitigate major accidents or where the operator has failed to make the required notification.

Furthermore, and of particular importance to directors, failure to comply with any provision of COMAH will constitute an offence under HSWA 1974 ss 33–42.

By way of example, on 13 May 2013 Abbey Metals Ltd was fined £133,000 and ordered to pay costs of £33,000 for failing to take measures to prevent major accidents and limit the consequences to the environment when the river was contaminated with 'a cocktail of hazardous substances' used in metal treatment after a fire at the premises. Charges were brought by the Environment Agency under reg 4 of COMAH. The incident was classed as a major accident and it was judged that the emergency plan had failed as there were inadequate arrangements to contain the water used to extinguish the fire which had become contaminated, and there were no prior arrangements to access the sewerage system for emergency storage or to take contaminated water off site. The company also pleaded guilty to three other charges under the Environmental Permitting (England and Wales) Regulations 2010 by breaching its environmental permit by failing to prevent emissions of contaminated fire water, and failing to meet Environmental Quality Standards for cyanides, copper and cadmium getting into the river.

Duties imposed by COMAH   **12.83**

As well as the need to notify the CA as set out in para **12.81**, operators are required to prepare additional documentation and put procedures in place demonstrating that they are taking all measures necessary to prevent major accidents. The documents and systems such operators are required to prepare depends on whether the quantities of dangerous substances present makes them 'lower tier' or more hazardous 'top tier' sites.

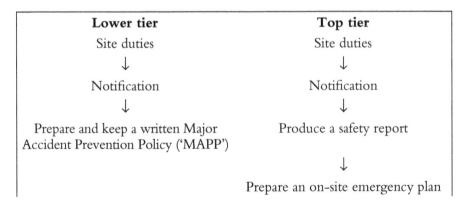

Lower tier	**Top tier**
Site duties	Site duties
↓	↓
Notification	Notification
↓	↓
Prepare and keep a written Major Accident Prevention Policy ('MAPP')	Produce a safety report
	↓
	Prepare an on-site emergency plan

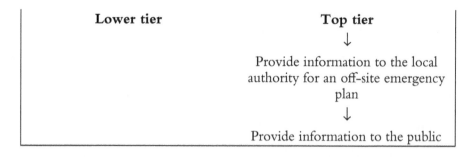

Lower tier duties 12.84

Under reg 5(1), every operator must prepare and keep a written document setting out its policy for prevention of major accidents, although the format of which can vary to suit the operator's circumstances and to fit in with existing health and safety and environmental policies in place.

The content of the MAPP should be proportionate to the potential for major accident hazards at the establishment and demonstrate that the operator has an appropriate safety management system in place setting out the organisational structure, responsibilities, practices, procedures, processes and resources for determining and implementing the major accident prevention policy.

It is important that once the MAPP and integral safety management system have been established, they must be implemented to identify, prevent, control and mitigate the consequences of a major accident (reg 5(5)).

Top tier duties 12.85

Operators of top tier sites must produce a safety report to the CA before starting construction of an establishment. In brief, the purpose of the safety report is to demonstrate that:

- a MAPP and an SMS for implementing the MAPP are in place (see para **12.84**);

- potential major accidents have been identified and that preventative and mitigating measures to limit the consequences to persons and the environment have been taken;

- adequate safety and reliability have been incorporated into the design, construction, operation and maintenance of any installation, equipment and infrastructure linked to its operation;

- on-site emergency plans have been drawn up and information supplied to the local authority to allow an off-site emergency plan to be prepared;

- sufficient information has been supplied to the CA for a decision to be made about siting of new activities or developments close to the establishment concerned.

The form and content of the safety report will vary from operation to operation and it must be reviewed regularly every five years and periodically where there are technical advances about safety matters or a change in the safety management system which could have significant repercussions. Any revisions must be notified to the CA.

In addition, reg 9(1) requires operators of top tier establishments to prepare an on-site emergency plan to be put into effect whenever a major accident occurs which must clearly set out action to take in the event of a major accident. This must also be reviewed and tested at least every three years to ensure the provisions remain adequate and effective.

Furthermore, when instructed by the CA to do so, the operator must supply information on safety measures to people who are likely to be affected by a major accident at the establishment.

Packaging   12.90

In 2010 the UK disposed of approximately 10.8 million tonnes of packaging waste, of which approximately 67% was recovered and recycled compared to 27% in 1998 and 59% in 2007 (www.defra.gov.uk). However, DEFRA is working to improve on this performance by ensuring businesses minimise the packaging they use and recover or recycle a larger proportion of the material it is made from after use. Indeed, DEFRA has some very challenging targets for UK packaging waste, recovery and recycling from 2013 to 2017 which are yet to be achieved.

Directors need to be aware and comply with the packaging regulations set out below if their companies make, fill, sell or handle packaging or packaging materials, as any breach could lead to prosecution and/or a fine.

Quantity and recycling   12.91

The Packaging (Essential Requirements) Regulations 2003 (SI 2003/1941), as amended by the Packaging (Essential Requirements) (Amendment) Regulations 2004, 2006 and 2009 apply to any business that produces packaged goods or places packaging materials on the market. In brief these regulations require:

- packaging to be reduced to the minimum weight and volume possible, subject to safety and hygiene requirements and the specific needs of the packed product and the consumer. To this end a thorough review of packaging is recommended to determine whether any improvements or reductions can be made without risk of damaging products despatched;

- that there are minimal amounts of noxious or hazardous substances in packaging materials. To achieve this, it may be necessary to seek assurance from suppliers concerning the components used in packaging materials. Alternatively, there may be other suitable packaging materials on the market that could be used containing lower levels of such substances;

- packaging to be recoverable through either material recycling, incineration with energy recovery or composting with biodegradation;

- packaging to, as far as possible, be reusable.

There is an additional requirement which may apply, depending on the type of packaging used, setting maximum limits on the heavy metal content in packaging materials. These limits must not be exceeded and it may be necessary to seek assurance from suppliers that packaging materials comply with these limits.

These regulations raise many issues that will require investigation. Most importantly, requirements of the regulations will be enforced by the local trading standards officers who have authority to require a company to provide technical documents to evidence compliance over the previous four years. As a result, any review of packaging should be thoroughly documented to enable the company to demonstrate that:

- the use of packaging has been reduced to the minimum possible;

- materials used in packaging comply with the heavy metal limits;

- the presence of noxious or hazardous substances in packaging materials has been minimised;

- packaging is recoverable through at least one of the recovery processes.

It is important to note that whilst failure to comply with these new regulations may lead to a civil penalty on the company, where the offence is found to have been committed with the consent, connivance or neglect of any director, manager or officer such person or persons shall be considered as having committed an offence also and be liable for a fine or imprisonment.

Registration 12.92

Pursuant to the Producer Responsibility Obligations (Packaging Waste) Regulations 2007 (SI 2007/871) (as amended by the 2010 regulations), companies with turnovers of £2 million or more that handle over 50 tons of packaging per year must register with either the Environment Agency or an approved scheme and contribute to reducing the amount of waste packing they send to landfill sites. 'Handling' includes the manufacture or conversion of raw materials into packaging, putting goods into packaging for sale, leasing or hiring packaging such as crates or pallets, operating a franchise or other licensed business, any import of packaging or packaged materials and bringing transit packaging into the UK which ends as waste in the UK. These activities may be carried out by the company or someone acting on its behalf and all need to be taken into account when calculating the amount of packaging handled for registration purposes.

Where these regulations apply, the director must ensure the company registers and, once registered, pays for the recovery and recycling of certain amounts of packaging waste. Records of this must be kept for at least five years and be provided to the regulator. Compliance can also be achieved by the company registering with a packaging compliance scheme.

Waste 12.100

In addition to responsibilities for packaging and packaging waste set out above, companies that make or import certain electrical products and electronic equipment, batteries and vehicles have responsibilities for those products once they become waste.

For example:

- the Waste Electronic and Electrical Equipment Regulations 2006 aim to reduce the amount of waste electrical and electronic equipment being disposed of and require producers to pay for its reuse, recycling and recovery;

- the Waste Batteries and Accumulators Regulations 2009 require 30% of portable batteries placed on the UK market to be collected for recycling (increasing to 45% by 2016) and prohibit waste industrial and automotive batteries from going to landfill sites or incinerators; and

- the End of Life Vehicle Regulations 2003 and the End of Life Vehicle (Producer Responsibility) Regulations 2005 set certain reuse, recycling and recovery targets for old vehicles and place responsibilities on vehicle producers, including manufacturers and importers, to cover the cost of the 'take-back system' for disposing of vehicles for the last owners and for issuing a certificate of destruction for the vehicle.

These developments explain the expanding trend by retailers to take your old products away when you buy new which, as well as demonstrating very good customer service, is also helping producers to meet their responsibilities for disposal of waste.

Carbon Reduction Commitment ('CRC')   12.110

A mandatory CRC Energy Efficiency Scheme ('CRC Scheme') requires companies that participate to monitor their energy use and report energy supplies each year. The CRC Scheme was brought into effect in the UK to improve energy efficiency and cut emissions in large public and private sector organisations which between them generate some 10% of the UK's greenhouse gas emissions. It is unlikely to apply to small businesses.

When the CRC Scheme first came into effect, it was overly complex, difficult to understand and expensive to administer. However, these issues were addressed when the simplified CRC Energy Efficiency Scheme Order 2013 (SI 2013/1119) came into effect in May 2013.

In essence, all companies that use at least 6,000 megawatt hours ('MWh') of qualifying electricity through settled half-hourly electricity meters during the qualification year must register as participants unless they are specifically exempt.

Participants must monitor their energy use, report their energy supplies annually and purchase and surrender allowances to offset their emissions.

It is expected that some 20,000 organisations, including many companies, will be required to participate. The key obligations that arise for a participant include the requirements to:

- register as a participant;

- produce a self-certified footprint report;

- produce a self-certified annual report about included emissions;

- hold and surrender sufficient allowances to cover their energy use emissions;

- maintain supporting documents and evidence to demonstrate conclusions drawn about the organisation's energy use.

The CRC Scheme is monitored and regulated in England and Wales by the Environment Agency and an annual CRC energy-efficient scheme Annual Report Publication ('ARP') is produced by the Environment Agency ranking organisations in terms of their success at reducing CRC emissions. This is available online, the most recent being for 2013/14. The aim of the ARP is to publicly endorse those organisations that are performing well and, at the same, make sure the public is aware of those that are not. Making information about CRC performance available in this way can influence a participant company's behaviour and give them greater incentive to improve as customers and suppliers are paying much more attention to environmental performance.

Any organisation or company that fails to comply would face a number of civil and criminal penalties, including:

(1)   Failure to register when required – £5,000 fine, £500 daily default fine and non-compliance publicised.

(2)   Failure to disclose required information – £500 fine per half-hourly meter settled.

(3)   Registration incomplete – as above and non-compliance publicised.

(4)   Failure to provide footprint report – £5,000 fine, £500 daily default fine (which doubles after 40 days) and non-compliance publicised.

(5)   Failure to provide an annual report – £5,000 fine, £500 daily default fine and non-compliance publicised.

(6)   Falsifying any records or evidence or make any misleading statements – criminal sanctions including a fine of up to £50,000 and/or imprisonment of up to three months.

(7)   Failure to comply with an enforcement notice or to provide requested information or obstruct an inspection – again criminal sanction and an unlimited fine and/or imprisonment of up to two years.

The CRC Scheme has been described as a 'cap and trade' scheme whereby an organisation that performs well in reducing carbon emissions and implementing energy saving measures can auction or trade the allowances it earns thereby creating a direct financial incentive for improved performance. This is in addition to the desire to avoid any fines or bad publicity for the organisation which might occur as a result of poor performance or non-compliance. Obviously anything that serves to damage a company's reputation is to be avoided and it is expected that in time a company ranked highly in the ARP may be deemed a preferable supplier to one that is not.

Insurance 12.120

All too often good environmental practice is seen only as a cost to a company. However, directors should be aware that it can have important financial benefits, not only by attracting lenders and investors, but also by reducing a company's insurance premiums on the basis of being able to provide evidence of a sound environmental system and good performance.

Public liability policies used to extend cover to all pollution incidents, but in recent years it is more usual for pollution cover to be excluded or limited to pollution caused by 'a sudden, identifiable, unintended and unexpected incident which takes place in its entirety at a specific time and place during the period of insurance' (wording suggested by the ABI). Gradual pollution over a period of time which cannot necessarily be identified would therefore be excluded. Directors need to be aware of this issue and ensure that where pollution risks have been analysed and assessed and gradual pollution has been identified as a risk, then appropriate pollution cover is arranged. This may necessitate the need for a tailor-made environmental policy for the company or site.

13 Duties and the customer

13   Duties and the customer

A substantial amount of legislation to protect the customer has evolved, which directors must observe not only in the interests of reducing potential liability but also to preserve the corporate image. Essentially when offering products or services for sale directors must ensure they are of satisfactory quality, fit for purpose and as described.

HSWA requirements   13.10

The company has a duty to those who are not employed but who may be affected by the way it conducts its undertakings. The duty extends to the general public, and may include customers and contractors, and the company must ensure that their health and safety is not at risk (HSWA 1974 s 3(1) and (2)). As discussed in para **11.80**, action may be taken against the company and the directors for a breach of this duty.

Product safety   13.20

The General Product Safety Regulations 2005 (SI 2005/1803) require that all products placed on the market for consumer use, unless specifically exempt, are safe for normal or reasonably foreseeable use by the consumer. Products must be accompanied by information about any risks from their use which are not immediately apparent and precautions which may be necessary. Contravention of the regulations is an offence and may attract a penalty of up to £5,000, three months' imprisonment, or both.

The Consumer Protection Act 1987 (CPA 1987) introduced the concept of product liability, imposing strict criminal liability on a producer (or any person holding themselves out as the producer, supplier or importer) of a product for damage caused, wholly or partly, by a defect in their product (CPA 1987 s 2(1) and (2)). Whilst some sections of the CPA 1987 have been replaced by the General Product Safety Regulations 2005 (SI 2005/1803) (above), this enactment remains based soundly on the premise that customers have a right to expect that products on sale are safe for them to use. To ensure that this is enforced, the Secretary of State has power to issue prohibition notices prohibiting supply and sale of goods and notices warning purchasers that goods are unsafe (CPA 1987 s 13) as well as suspension notices on the producer (CPA 1987 s 14). Failure to meet the requirements of these safety regulations can result in a fine of up to £5,000 and/or up to three months' imprisonment.

The company producing the product is required to carry out sample tests and investigate genuine complaints to ensure that any risks presented by their product are controlled. This may mean recalling or withdrawing batches from the market where goods are not safe and the Trading Standards' website contains a list of product safety and recall notices (www.tradingstandards.gov. uk). Directors will be aware that, as well as costs in terms of time and money, a product recall could also undermine the company's reputation for high quality, safe and reliable products and erode any competitive advantage gained from this reputation. A few examples of recent recall notices extracted from the Trading Standards website are listed below:

- 24 November 2014: the manufacturer Flymo recalled certain UltraGlide lawnmowers as a potential fault had been identified that could cause them to overheat and combust.

- 1 November 2014: the retailer Aquatix-2U Limited recalled certain leisure scooters when advised by the local Trading Standards office of investigation into use of the front brake alone and how it could cause ejection and injury.

- 5 July 2013: Toys-R-Us recalled a remote control helicopter as the rechargeable batteries inside could overheat and posed a fire and burn risk.

- 27 June 2013: Sabelt recalled its child car seat due to safety concerns about the retention mechanism and risk of failure in an accident.

These are just a tiny sample of the recall notices listed by Trading Standards, the costs of which can be substantial.

The Sale of Goods Act 1979, the Sale and Supply of Goods Act 1994, the Consumer Credit Act 1974 and the Supply of Goods and Services Act 1982 are all concerned primarily with the sale of goods which are not necessarily dangerous but are defective, sub-standard and not of a quality that would reasonably be expected of them. It places minimum standards on products in terms of safety, durability and freedom from defects which directors must ensure are met in products which their companies sell.

In addition, the Sale and Supply of Goods to Consumers Regulations 2002 (SI 2002/3045) imply additional terms into contracts and provide consumers with rights if they are sold faulty goods (in addition to existing consumer protection). The rights include:

- the right to rely on a statement made by any business in the supply chain about the goods, even where it is not included in the formal contract;

- the right to rely on a guarantee, whether or not the retailer or manufacturer intended it to be legally binding;

- where the goods are faulty, the right to request they be repaired or replaced or to request a full or partial refund.

Given the developments in legislation and the potential for claims, directors would be well advised to effect a product liability insurance policy. Whilst certain standard policies are available, the case *Rexodan International Ltd v Commercial Union Assurance plc* [1997] All ER (D) 61, CA emphasised the limitations they can have. In this particular instance Rexodan was only covered in respect of damaged products and unfortunately not the cost of recall, nor packaging purchased in advance which has to be discarded nor loss of future profits. It is very important to ensure that the correct level of cover is obtained and to check the terms and limitations set out in the policy carefully.

It might also be an idea, and indeed a requirement for some products, to have the standard of the company's products externally validated. For example, in the UK, the British Standards Institution (BSI) regulates standards, and products which meet its standards can be marked with the BSI Kitemark. There are also separate standards for the EU which, when met, allow the CE Kitemark to be displayed on packaging and promotional material. Display of these marks can give rise to competitive advantage as it demonstrates that the product conforms to a specific quality standard.

Contract terms   13.30

Directors must be aware of and comply with provisions contained in the Unfair Terms in Consumer Contracts Regulations 1999, which require consumer contracts to be fair and invalidate any unfair terms in such contracts which have not been individually negotiated. Clauses which would be considered unfair may include a provision allowing the supplier to vary or cancel the contract without a similar right for the consumer, or a clause allowing the supplier not to fulfil his obligations fully.

Directors need to review all standard contracts used by the company to ensure that wording is clear and easy to understand and that any unfair terms are removed.

In addition, it should be noted that reg 15 of the Sale and Supply of Goods Regulations 2002 provides that where goods sold or otherwise supplied to a consumer are offered with a consumer guarantee, the consumer guarantee takes effect as a contractual obligation. The enforcement authorities can apply for an injunction in the event of non-compliance.

By way of example, the FCA has issued a statement concerning use of the phrase 'consequential loss' in consumers' general insurance contracts, as it does not consider the term to be in language that is easily understood. It has issued best practice guidance that a statement along the lines of 'you are not covered for any other costs that are indirectly caused by the event which led to your claim, unless specifically stated in the policy' is much easier for a consumer to understand.

Trade descriptions   13.40

Requirements relating to trade descriptions are contained in the Trade Descriptions Act 1968 (TDA 1968) and the CPA 1987 Part III, which attach strict criminal liability for a false description of goods made in the course of a trade or business. A trade description includes any information about:

- quantity, size or gauge;

- method of manufacture, processing or reconditioning;

- composition (what the product is made of);

- fitness for purpose, strength, performance, behaviour or accuracy;

- physical characteristics;

- testing and results;

- approval or conformity, for example with a British Standard;

- place or date of manufacture;

- person by whom made; and

- other history.

The directors, as well as the company, may be personally liable for a trade description offence where it was committed with their knowledge or consent or was due to their negligence. It is therefore essential that they ensure no breaches occur, whether in advertising the goods, packaging and quantities described, or descriptions on fitness for purpose and physical characteristics, etc (TDA 1968 s 20 and CPA 1987 s 2). The penalty for making a false trade description may be a fine of up to £5,000 or two years' imprisonment or both.

Whilst trade descriptions requirements apply equally to small businesses as to large, it is usually the large companies that hit the headlines; for example, the £300k fine imposed on Tesco for misleading customers about a half-price offer on strawberries which it claimed lasted for a longer period of time than it did (*Mirror*, 19 August 2013).

To avoid such penalties, directors would be well advised to implement formal procedures to:

- monitor all advertisements to ensure that any statements made and details given are correct;

- withdraw all sales literature and material describing goods as soon as it becomes out of date;

- frequently check that all statements made on or about goods and services are justified and correct; and

- ensure that employees are giving correct information to customers.

Where it becomes clear that changes in description of the company's goods or services are necessary, the directors will need to check to ensure that they have been made.

It should be noted that these provisions apply not only to goods and services which are, in effect, ready made, but also to those where a specification and quotation are agreed. For example, in *Walker v Simon Dudley Ltd* (1997) 161 JP 224, a supplier was guilty of an offence under TDA 1968 s 1 (now repealed) for failing to supply goods in accordance with the customer's specifications agreed with the supplier.

Consideration should also be given to the requirements concerning consumer practices set out in para **13.50**.

Commercial practice   13.50

The Consumer Protection from Unfair Trading Regulations 2008 (SI 2008/1277) ('the Regulations') prohibit the exercise of unfair commercial practices by businesses, whether directly or indirectly, towards consumers. As well as a general prohibition against unfair commercial practices (reg 3), there are also specific prohibitions on misleading actions (reg 5), misleading omissions (reg 6), aggressive commercial practices (reg 7) and, all matters listed in Sch 1 to the Regulations (see **APPENDICES 11** and **15**).

Directors need to be aware of these regulations and what they require, as any non-compliance by the company might result in an investigation, which would take up a lot of management time and resource, and possibly prosecution and a fine. All of these could cause the company considerable reputational damage, potentially affecting not only customers but also employees and those who have dealings with the company.

General prohibition   13.51

The general prohibition is, intentionally, broad ranging and requires that no act, omission, conduct, representation, or commercial communication (including marketing and advertising) the aim of which is to promote, sell or supply a product to a consumer is unfair, whether such practice is carried out before, during or after the transaction took place.

A commercial practice will be considered unfair where it:

- contravenes the requirements of 'professional due diligence' which would be where it falls below the standard of skill and care that might reasonably be expected by a trader acting honestly and in good faith; and

- materially distorts the economic behaviour of the average customer causing a decision about the product and transaction that would not otherwise have been made.

Where a commercial practice is unfair but is not, necessarily, misleading or aggressive (see paras **13.52** and **13.53**) this general prohibition allows enforcers to take action.

It is also intended that this widely drawn duty will enable any new scams to be addressed without need for further legislation.

Misleading practices   13.52

Regulations 5 and 6 prohibit misleading practices like the giving of false or deceptive messages or leaving out important information where such action or inaction causes, or is likely to cause, the average consumer to make a different transactional decision than would have been made otherwise.

Misleading actions   13.52.1

Directors must ensure that no false or untruthful information is given to consumers about the company's products and that the way the information is communicated and the product is presented is clear, with no risk of being considered deceptive.

Regulation 5 contains a comprehensive list of information which may be considered misleading and includes information about the existence or nature of the product; its main characteristics; the price; any need for service, replacement or repair; the trader's commitments and motives, etc; and the consumer's rights. The list is set out in full in **APPENDIX 11**.

Misleading action also encompasses the manner in which a product is marketed and requires that no information is given or conveyed in such a way as to create confusion with a competitor's products or draw inaccurate conclusions from comparative advertising.

Directors must also ensure that where the company indicates through commercial practice that it complies with a code of conduct, then it must do so, and such compliance must be capable of verification.

Misleading omissions   **13.52.2**

Directors should be aware that a commercial practice would be considered misleading if any material information about the product is omitted; hidden; or is presented in such a way so as to be unclear, unintelligible, ambiguous or untimely, ie delayed. Regulation 5 makes clear that failure to provide consumers with sufficient information to allow them to make an informed choice about a product is a breach where such omissions might cause an average consumer to take a different transactional decision.

Whilst account would be taken of limitations of the communication medium chosen in terms of space and time, no material information should be omitted. At the very least, the consumer needs to be advised of where else further material information is available, as arranged by the company.

Aggressive practices   **13.53**

Regulation 7 specifically prohibits aggressive commercial practices which intimidate or exploit consumers by, for example, the use of harassment, coercion or undue influence which causes them to make a purchasing decision they would not have made in other circumstances.

In determining whether a commercial practice is aggressive, consideration will be given to:

(1)   the timing, location, nature or persistence of the practice;

(2)   whether threatening or abusive language or behaviour has been used;

(3)   whether the trader is exploiting a consumer's misfortune or circumstances to influence his decision;

(4)   whether any onerous or disproportionate barriers are imposed by a trader making it difficult for consumers to exercise their rights;

(5)   whether any threat has been made of action which cannot legally be taken.

It is therefore very important that directors ensure that appropriate information and training is given to any persons selling the company's products to ensure they do not pursue any aggressive practices, as the risk of long-term reputational damage, in addition to the penalties for committing a regulatory office, is significant.

Specific prohibitions   13.54

A commercial practice is unfair in all circumstances if it is one of the 31 commercial practices prohibited by Sch 1 to the Regulations (reg 3(4)(d)). An extract of Sch 1 is set out in **Appendix 15**.

Consequences of non–compliance   13.55

Under Part 8 of the Enterprise Act 2002 enforcers (which include the OFT, Trading Standards services and local weights and measures authorities, etc) may take civil enforcement action for breach of the Regulations. This would involve making an application to a court for an enforcement order, any breach of which could lead to imprisonment for up to two years or an unlimited fine.

The Regulations also contain criminal offences, which can be prosecuted by the OFT or Trading Standards services (not consumers or competitors), the penalties for which are a fine not exceeding the statutory maximum (currently £5,000) on summary conviction or, on conviction on indictment, an unlimited fine or imprisonment for up to two years, or both.

It is important for directors to note that where an unfair commercial practice has been carried out by a company, the Regulations provide that the officers of that company (which includes the directors) with whose consent or connivance the practice was carried out or where the practice was attributable to his neglect shall be liable to prosecution as well as the company (reg 15).

The enforcement authorities have investigative powers and may make a test purchase of a product, inspect goods and enter premises (with or without a warrant), inspect and take copies of relevant documents and, where they have reasonable grounds to believe a breach of the Regulations has been committed, seize and obtain products and documents.

For example, in the year to 31 March 2014, the OFT concluded its formal industry-wide consumer-law investigation into retirement home exit fees, securing voluntary undertakings from a number of retirement home businesses.

Directors will need to ensure that there is complete compliance with any requests or instructions received from the enforcement authorities as it is a criminal offence to intentionally obstruct them or to make any false statements. Any person who does not comply or intentionally obstructs them will be guilty of an offence and, on summary conviction, be liable to a fine (reg 23).

Importantly, with effect from 1 October 2014 the Consumer Protection (Amendment) Regulations 2014 (SI 2014/870) added a new Part 4A to the Regulations introducing a civil right for consumers to seek redress against traders who demonstrate aggressive practices and carry out misleading actions (see paragraphs **13.52.1** and **13.53**). Provided the consumer can show that the misleading or aggressive practice caused him to make a payment or enter a contract, the consumer may seek to unwind the transaction, obtain a discount or obtain damages for harm cause by the prohibited practice. Such damages might be for financial harm or for alarm, distress, physical inconvenience or discomfort.

Competition and consumer protection   13.60

The need to promote healthy competition and prevent practices which are anti-competitive and detrimental to consumers has long been recognised and numerous Acts, regulations and other measures have been developed over the years, imposing penalties as a deterrent. The main regulations include the Enterprise Act 2002 (EnA 2002) which made a number of significant changes to competition law and consumer law enforcement in the UK, with particular regard to the role of the OFT (now replaced by the Competition Markets Authority); and the Competition Act 1998.

Whilst OFT statistics demonstrate that knowledge of competition law held by businesses has increased significantly there is still room for improvement in awareness, particularly amongst smaller businesses which remain less able to identify competition law breaches. A survey carried out by the OFT of approximately 2,000 businesses recorded that whilst 25% of all survey participants felt they knew a considerable or fair amount about competition law, this proportion increased to 45% amongst larger businesses.

To further improve understanding and help businesses and company directors comply with competition law, the OFT issued practical guidance on what is required to ensure compliance. The OFT worked with business groups and consulted on two guidance documents – 'How Your Business Can Achieve Compliance' and 'Company Directors and Competition Law'.

The first of these OFT guidance documents identifies how companies can achieve a compliance culture in relation to competition law matters and suggests a practical four-step risk-based approach to achieving it. Central to this is the Board and senior management demonstrating their commitment to competition law compliance, so it becomes central to and embedded in the company's culture. Once this is demonstrated, the company must:

- identify risks: identification of the company's actual competition law risks, which will vary according to the size and nature of business;

- assess those risks: determine how serious the risks are, what the high, medium and low risks are and which employees are in high risk areas;

- mitigate risks: establish, implement and periodically review the policies, procedures and training to ensure the risks identified do not materialise, or are reported and addressed at the earliest opportunity if they do occur;

- review the process at appropriate intervals, often yearly. There might also be a need for interim reviews based on corporate transactions, operating in new markets, changes in legislation and best practice recommendations, etc.

As well as stating commitment to competition law compliance, the Board must also demonstrate what practical compliance measures it is taking to achieve this. The OFT suggests that, whilst it is for individual Boards and companies to determine what is appropriate, this could be achieved through one director being made responsible for driving compliance, monitoring and reporting to the Board (or, in some instances, audit committee); the Board periodically reviewing and challenging how effective the company's compliance measures are; regular communication amongst directors and senior managers about competition law requirements and the need to identify and address any potential infringement concerns; regular training and information updates; and making clear to employees that a competition law infringement will constitute a breach of the company's code of conduct and a disciplinary offence for which they could face dismissal.

Where a company can demonstrate that it has taken adequate steps to ensure a competition law infringement does not occur, then this may help to mitigate any penalty imposed by the OFT where an offence occurred regardless. Adopting the OFT's four-step process may help to establish that the steps taken were appropriate for the company.

The OFT's second guidance document, 'Company Directors and Competition Law', has been issued to help directors understand their responsibilities under competition law for ensuring their companies do not infringe competition law requirements and the sorts of matters the OFT will take into account when determining the extent of a director's responsibility if an infringement has occurred. It is clear from the guidance document that these would include amongst other things:

(1)   the level of knowledge the director had of the infringement and whether he was directly involved;

(2)   the directors' commitment to competition law compliance and how this can be demonstrated by practical compliance measures and the company's competition law compliance culture;

(3)   what steps had been taken to prevent, detect and address potential infringements, with particular attention to whether the directors have implemented adequate procedures possibly involving the OFT's four-step process outlined above;

(4)   consideration of the director's role, in particular whether executive or non-executive, any specific executive responsibilities within the company (for example for contract negotiations, sales or compliance) and the size of the company or group of companies. The OFT considers these relevant when determining what level of understanding it is reasonable to expect the director to demonstrate and what practical steps he or she could have taken to detect or address the infringement; and

(5)   how frequently and vigorously the directors reviewed and challenged measures implemented to detect and prevent infringements.

In general all directors are expected to be committed to complying with competition law requirements, to understand what the most serious forms of infringement are and that an offence could have serious consequences for the company and for them as directors (see para **5.53.8** for information on competition disqualification orders).

The OFT and now the CMA therefore expects all directors to know that:

●   cartel activity (bid-rigging, price-fixing, production restrictions and market-sharing) is a serious offence; and

●   abuse of a dominant position constitutes infringement.

Those directors with specific executive duties involving compliance and commercial agreements, etc would be expected to have greater, more in depth knowledge of the sorts of activity and agreements that might cause infringement.

Enterprise and Regulatory Reform Act 2013   **13.61**

The Enterprise and Regulatory Reform Act 2013 (ERRA 2013) received Royal Assent on 25 April 2013 and contains important changes to the competition regime in the UK. The main competition reforms are summarised below, the aim being to make it quicker to tackle anti-competitive practices.

The principal change is the creation of an overarching Competition and Markets Authority (CMA) to replace and carry out all the functions of the Competition Commission and the competition functions of the OFT. The CMA's function will be to:

(1)   conduct first-phase and second-phase reviews of mergers (whilst still preserving distinction between the phases) within tighter timeframes;

(2)   carry out whole market studies and, where warranted, conduct second-stage investigations of market practices within tighter timeframes;

(3)   investigate potential breaches of competition rules;

(4)   investigate cartel offences, possibly with enhanced powers in respect of price-fixing;

(5)   investigate all other competition concerns and issues which are in the public interest but not necessarily competition issues.

Directors should note that whilst at present conviction of a cartel offence currently requires a finding of dishonesty, under new provisions in the ERRA 2013 this is to be removed and an agreement where relevant information is not publicised could constitute a cartel offence. This in itself might lead to increased levels of criminal enforcement.

Whilst there was a transition period in 2013, the new competition provisions of the ERRA 2013 came into effect on 1 April 2014, at which point the majority of the OFT's powers transferred to the CMA, with some also being transferred to Trading Standards, Citizens Advice Bureau, the FCA and HMRC.

Enterprise Act 2002   **13.62**

In respect of competition law and consumer legislation, the EnA 2002 has replaced and amended legislation relating to the OFT, merger control, investigation of markets and enforcement of consumer protection legislation, and has introduced provisions relating to the criminalisation of cartels. Consequently, directors need to be aware of the requirements set out in the following paragraphs.

Office of Fair Trading (now replaced by the CMA)   **13.62.1**

Until 1 April 2014 the statutory functions previously possessed of the Director General of Fair Trading were held by the OFT. The OFT's key areas of focus, being enforcement of the requirements of competition and consumer law and the review and study of markets to ensure they are working well for consumers, are now the responsibility of the CMA.

However, from the OFT's annual report for the year to 31 March 2014 and a quick scan through their press releases and summary information about market studies the OFT website it is clear how active and thorough the OFT has been in monitoring and investigating markets and the actions of specific traders through:

(1)   the numerous enforcement cases brought as a result of OFT investigations under consumer law and competition law;

(2)   tackling misleading practices and consumer issues;

(3)   conducting market reviews.

Through its market studies the OFT aimed to identify and address aspects of market failure which caused detriment to consumers. The outcome of a study might have been: confirmation of a clean bill of health; enforcement action by the OFT; referral to the Competition Commission (now replaced by the CMA); recommendations for changes in law and regulation; agreement to self-regulation through, say, a code of conduct; or a campaign to improve information and awareness.

The CMA now has power to apply to the court for issue of an enforcement order where it identifies that a change in practice is necessary (see para **13.62.5**). Before seeking an enforcement order the CMA will usually consult with the business and seek an undertaking from them that they will stop the behaviour giving rise to infringement. Breach of any undertaking given would be drawn to the attention of the court in the event of further infringement.

The CMA (or other designated enforcer) can by notice require a company to provide information and documents either to help establish whether an enforcement order is needed or to monitor compliance with an undertaking or order. Directors should be aware that failure to provide the requested information within the time allowed may result in an application to court for an order requiring its production. The court can award costs against any directors and officers responsible for the information being withheld.

Merger control   **13.62.2**

Pursuant to the EnA 2002 (and amendments in the ERRA 2013), the CMA is required to obtain and review information relating to merger situations, particularly those it considers will or may decrease competition in a UK market and any it considers to fall within the scope of the 'public interest' or 'special public interest' provisions of the EnA 2002.

A merger will only be investigated where the turnover in the merged entity is at least £70 million or the merged entity would have a 25% or more share of the market for the product in a substantial part of the UK.

The CMA will investigate and report the outcome of the investigation to the Secretary of State (usually within 24 weeks of the referral), determining whether the merger situation could result in substantially reduced competition. Where it considers it could, it might recommend that it should not take place or recommend certain remedying or mitigating action to prevent substantial lessening of competition.

It might, for example, require an undertaking or impose an order that:

(1)   the merger is prohibited;

(2)   parties must dispose of certain shares or limit voting powers;

(3)   require break-up of a company or group by sale of assets or subsidiaries; or

(4)   the merged company's conduct be restricted in some way, for example, by regulating prices.

Companies tend to make an informal submission to the CMA about an anticipated merger to ensure that any competition concerns are identified and addressed at the outset. Whilst there were no competition concerns as such, in June 2009 the European Commission fined Electrabel €20m for the acquisition of Compagnie Nationale du Rhone without having received prior approval as required by the EC Merger Regulations. Had the transaction raised competition concerns, the fine may have been higher.

Directors should take care that any information submitted to the CMA is accurate and not misleading which is an offence for which a fine and/or imprisonment of up to two years may be imposed.

Investigation of markets   **13.62.3**

The CMA has authority to inquire into markets where it appears the structure or conduct of suppliers or customers is harming competition (this replaces monopoly enquiries and investigations under FTA 1973) and a recommendation for an investigation will usually be made by the CMA or a sectoral regulator where it suspects one or more features of the market prevent, restrict or distort competition.

Investigations must be completed within two years and where an adverse effect on competition is apparent the CMA may seek undertakings or impose orders requiring a change in practices.

In 2013/14 market studies were carried out on markets in a wide range of sectors including study of competition in banking services for small businesses, competition in the energy market, defined contribution workplace pensions and the quick house sales market.

Criminalisation of cartels   **13.62.4**

EnA 2002 makes it a criminal offence for individuals to engage dishonestly in cartel agreements through which businesses agree not to compete with each other. The criminal cartel offence operates alongside the existing regime in the Competition Act 1998 (and Article 81 of the EC Treaty) (para **13.60**) for the imposition of civil sanctions on the company for operation of cartels and anticompetitive agreements.

Directors should be aware that cartels are the most serious form of anti-competitive behaviour and an individual will be liable to criminal prosecution if he agrees with another person or persons that their undertakings (horizontal in the supply chain) will engage in:

- price-fixing;

- limitation of supply or production;

- market sharing;

- bid-rigging.

The case would be heard in a magistrates' court and the penalty, where convicted, may be up to six months' imprisonment, or a fine up to the statutory maximum or both. Where convicted on indictment, the penalty is a maximum of five years' imprisonment, an unlimited fine or both.

Certain sectors where, for example, there are few competitors, products are very similar, communication between competitors is good and there is excess capacity might be more susceptible to cartel activities. Commonly cartel members agree on pricing, output levels, discounts, credit terms, which customers and which areas will be supplied and who should win a contract.

Directors should be in no doubt from looking at the CMA's website, press releases and newsroom reports that stamping out cartel activities is a priority. Indeed, anyone who blows the whistle on a cartel could be granted immunity from criminal prosecution under the EnA 2002 where they were party to it.

Several high-profile examples help to demonstrate the seriousness with which cartel activity will be treated, not only for the company, but also from the directors' individual perspective:

(1)   In the year to 31 March 2014 the OFT issued a decision finding that four suppliers of certain alarm and access control systems into retirement properties had breached competition law by engaging in collusive tendering arrangements, affecting at least 65 tenders with a combined value of approximately £1.4m. The collusive tendering arrangements were first brought to the OFT's attention by one of the companies which benefited from immunity from financial penalties under the OFT's leniency policy. The OFT imposed penalties on the other companies, totalling £53,410.

(2)   In March 2014 the OFT issued an infringement decision and imposed a £370,000 penalty on three companies – Quantum, Tomm and Lloyd's Pharmacies – for having a market-sharing agreement for prescription medicines to care homes between May and November 2011.

(3)   On 28 November 2011 the OFT fined nine companies (Arla, Asda, Dairy Crest, McLelland, Safeway, Sainsbury's, Tesco, The Cheese Company and Wiseman) a total £49.51m for coordinating increases in the price of milk by conspiring and indirectly exchanging retail pricing intentions with each other.

(4)   In January 2011 RBS agreed to pay a fine of £28.59m after admitting breaches of competition law requirements by disclosing confidential future pricing information about loan products for professional services firms to Barclays Bank which was taken into account by Barclays to determine its own pricing.

(5)   In April 2010 the OFT fined Imperial Tobacco £112m, Gallaher £50m, Co-op and Asda each £14m, Morrisons £8.6m, Safeway £10.9m, Shell £3.3m and Somerfield £3.9m for unlawfully inflating the price of cigarettes and tobacco by price-fixing. Other supermarkets were also involved, including Sainsbury's, which was granted immunity from a fine for alerting the OFT to the infringements.

(6)   The conviction of three former Dunlop executives for dishonestly participating in a cartel by agreeing to allocate markets and customers, restricting supply, fixing prices and bid-rigging since the 1970s (*Guardian*, 12 June 2008). They were sentenced to 30–36 months' imprisonment, disqualified as directors for five to seven years and one was ordered to pay £25,000 costs.

To avoid concern about fines, imprisonment and possible damage to a company's reputation where it is found to be involved in a cartel, it is important for directors to ensure information is given and procedures are in place to ensure business is conducted in accordance with competition law.

Enforcement of consumer legislation   **13.62.5**

The CMA, Trading Standards authorities and any other body designated an enforcer by the Secretary of State have power to enforce consumer legislation by means of enforcement orders against offending businesses where their conduct constitutes, or is likely to constitute, either a UK domestic or an EC Community infringement (EnA 2002 Part 8). The CMA must first consult with the offending business and seek to stop the infringing conduct without the need for a court order but, where this has not been achieved within two weeks, can apply to the court for an enforcement order. The OFT's annual report for 2013/14 shows that numerous enforcement orders concluded in the period, the vast majority were obtained as undertakings rather than needing to obtain court orders.

Super-complaints   **13.62.6**

Consumer groups are entitled to make 'super-complaints' to the CMA and sectoral regulators about market structures or practices which are working against the interests of a significant number of consumers. The CMA then has 91 days in which to determine what action, if any, is necessary.

It is therefore important for directors to determine whether any of the company's actions could be considered anti-competitive and, in so far as they could, to take action to ensure that such behaviour and practices are changed. This is particularly important in the light of the fact the CMA now has power to make application to the High Court for directors to be disqualified for up to five years for competition offences.

Competition Act 1998   **13.63**

When the Competition Act 1998 became law it replaced all existing restrictive trade practices legislation in the UK, including the Restrictive Trade Practices Act 1976, the Resale Prices Act 1976 and the majority of the Competition Act 1980 and brought competition law in this country into line with EU requirements.

This legislation introduced two main prohibitions to improve consumer protection:

- a ban on any anti-competitive agreements (based on Article 81 of the EC Treaty); and

- prohibition on abuse of a dominant position in a market (based on Article 82 of the EC Treaty).

Anti-competitive agreements   **13.63.1**

Directors must ensure that their companies and persons within them do not enter into any agreement (whether formal or informal) that distorts or restricts competition. In particular they must not:

(1) agree to fix prices or terms of trade;

(2) limit production to reduce competition;

(3) agree with a competitor, for example, to split up the market or suppliers;

(4) discriminate between customers by, for example, charging different prices when there is no justifiable reason for doing so.

Whilst the prohibitions are greater for companies and businesses with a significant market share, the practices of even small companies must be such that there is no involvement in anti-competitive agreements such as cartels.

Abuse of dominant market position   **13.63.2**

Abuse of a dominant position in a market is prohibited and companies must not impose unfair prices on customers or suppliers. This prohibition mainly applies to companies with a large market share and, for example, prohibits them from limiting production or technical development to the detriment of the consumer.

By way of recent example, on 19 April 2013 the OFT (now CMA) issued a Statement of Objections to GlaxoSmithKline (GSK) alleging abuse of their dominant market position and acting to delay competition in the drug paroxetine, in the UK. GSK claimed production of the generic drug by other pharmaceutical companies would infringe their patent and secured agreement with each of the other companies to delay supply of the drug for sale in the UK in return for substantial payments from GSK. This is being fully investigated.

Penalties   **13.63.3**

The CMA has power to impose financial penalties of up to 10% of a company's annual, worldwide turnover where it determines that competition or consumer infringements have occurred. In addition, competitors and customers are entitled to seek compensation for damages and the damage to a company's reputation can be considerable. Furthermore, whilst the provisions of the Competition Act 1998 contain civil provisions enforceable against the company, directors should be aware that if they obstruct investigations, they could face unlimited personal fines or up to two years' imprisonment.

Since imposition of the first fine under the Competition Act 1998, the risk to companies who fail to comply with the Act has been quite clearly demonstrated. In 2012/13 Competition Act 1998 investigations carried out included investigations into suspicions of:

- collusive tendering in access controls and alarm systems

- abuse of dominant markets position in respect of bunker fuels;

- price sharing, price coordination and sharing of commercially sensitive information by dealers distributing Mercedes-Benz commercial vehicles (now closed, see below);

- competition infringements by trade associations recommending construction industry training; and

- abuse of a dominant market position by providers of electronic platform services.

In addition investigation might also be carried out by the European Commission, which is currently investigating Shell, BP and Statoil for suspected price-rigging by colluding to distort the published price of oil products and preventing other firms from participating in the price assessment process

The list above is not exhaustive and does not include all investigations, but does give an idea of the scale of work carried out by the OFT. This helps to demonstrate that abuse of competition restrictions must be stamped out as it will most likely be discovered at considerable cost to the company.

The following examples illustrate the potential scale of penalties.

- On 27 March 2013 the OFT issued five infringement decisions and fined Mercedes-Benz and three of its commercial vehicle dealers, Ciceley, Road Range and Enza, £2.8m for infringing competition law by market sharing, price coordination and exchange of commercially sensitive information (in varying degrees in each instance).

- On 16 April 2010 the OFT announced fines imposed on two tobacco manufacturers and ten retailers totalling £225m for having arrangements in force between 2001 and 2003 with retailers restricting the retailers' ability to determine selling prices.

- Six recruitment firms in the UK were fined a total of £39m by the OFT in September 2009 for breaching competition law by collectively refusing to deal with another company which hoped to act as an intermediary in supplying candidates to construction companies in the UK. As well as the collective boycott, they were also engaged in price fixing, by fixing target fee rates.

- In September 2009 fines were imposed by the OFT on 103 parties in the construction sector for widespread cover pricing and bid-rigging from 2000 to 2006. Such fines totalled just under £130m, although a few have since been reduced on appeal.

- Napp Pharmaceuticals Limited of Cambridge was found by the OFT to have breached s 18 of the Competition Act 1998 and abused its dominant market position in the sale of morphine tablets. The company was initially fined £2.92 million for its unfair pricing policy, but this was increased to £3.21 million when, having received notification about the breach, it was evident that it had failed to change its pricing practices.

These cases demonstrate firm action taken by the OFT (and in future by the CMA) against companies that seek to prevent fair competition. Whilst the scale of the fines alone is substantial, the additional costs of bad publicity and damage to a company's reputation as well as the cost and time for preparing defence can be considerable and act as a sizeable deterrent.

In light of these requirements and the substantive fines imposed for misleading practices or anti-competitive behaviour, it is important that directors periodically review agreements with customers, suppliers and competitors to ensure they comply with the requirements of the Competition Act 1998. A comprehensive full legal audit of agreements and practices is recommended from time to time, together with an ongoing staff training and education programme and systems to monitor, review and control compliance.

Bribery and corruption   **13.64**

The Bribery Act 2010 (the 'Bribery Act') came into force on 1 July 2011 replacing offences of bribery at common law and the statutory offences in the Public Bodies Corrupt Practices Act 1889 and the Prevention of Corruption Act 1906 which were widely recognised as being out of date.

In summary, the Bribery Act creates:

- two general offences: bribing another person ('active bribery', s 1) and being bribed ('passive bribery', s 2);

- the offence of bribing a foreign official (s 6);

- an offence for a commercial organisation to fail to prevent bribery by persons working for or associated with them (s 7), although implementation of 'adequate procedures' may prove sufficient defence (s 7(2));

- the ability to prosecute bribery committed abroad in the UK (s 12).

A breach of the requirements of the Bribery Act carries a maximum penalty of ten years' imprisonment or an unlimited fine for any individuals convicted and an unlimited fine for commercial organisations, including companies (s 11). In addition, the directors and senior managers of a company may be prosecuted if an offence was committed by the company with their consent or connivance (s 14).

The Bribery Act is only concerned with bribery, which is defined as giving someone financial or other advantage to encourage them to behave in a certain way and carry out their functions or activities improperly. This could be given to encourage a decision-maker to reach a positive decision, for example to accept a planning application or engage in business, or to desist from acting in a certain way.

It is therefore important for directors to review the company's anti-bribery procedures and internal control and risk management processes to prevent the giving or receiving of bribes by those within, associated with, or working for the company.

Rather alarmingly, research carried out by the Fraud, Investigations and Disputes Services team at Ernst & Young has revealed that a year after enactment, only 56% of British firms had heard of the Bribery Act. Whilst awareness was higher in larger firms (turnover greater than £50m) at 76%, in mid-market firms (£5m–£50m turnover) it was only 36% which is very concerning as the small and medium companies need to address bribery risks and implement appropriate precautions to the same extent, but with a different approach, as large companies. The research also revealed considerable geographic and sector differences and, importantly, that of the firms that had heard of the Bribery Act 52% vet their suppliers to see if they are compliant with Bribery Act.

Adequate procedures   **13.64.1**

As mentioned above, a company might not be found guilty of failing to prevent bribery where it can show that 'adequate procedures' were put in place to prevent it. However, there is no template for such procedures and the Ministry of Justice ('MOJ') is keen to stress that what is adequate will vary according to the nature, size and complexity of the company and its business. The MOJ lists six principles for consideration when determining what procedures might be appropriate, namely:

(1)   proportionality: the action should be proportional to the risks faced;

(2)   top level commitment: a company's Board and senior management must demonstrate their commitment to eliminating bribery, thereby fostering and promoting a culture in which bribery is not accepted;

(3)   risk assessment: periodically assess the nature and extent of bribery risks taking into account factors such as the geographic location of operations and markets, the duration of operations, and people the company is engaging with to promote products, etc;

(4)   due diligence: where considered necessary, carry out due diligence on who you are doing business with to ensure they are honest and trustworthy;

(5)   communication: ensure that the policies and procedures implemented to prevent bribery are communicated to and understood by employees and those engaged to undertake business for the company. Additional training may also be considered necessary given the significance of bribery risks faced;

(6)   monitor and review: periodic monitoring and review of bribery prevention procedures is necessary to ensure they are working as intended and that improvements are made when it becomes clear they are necessary.

It should be emphasised, however, that the procedures adopted should be proportional to the scale of the bribery risk. If that risk is nominal, then extensive documents and policies would be of no benefit and would not be required. However, in a larger organisation which operates in an industry and in overseas jurisdictions where the risk of bribery is prevalent and significant, then detailed polices and procedures would be required.

In any event the directors should periodically review whether the company's procedures are adequate and, as well as determining what is required in terms of a written anti-bribery policy, also assess the implications for other policies that will be affected such as the company's code of conduct, corporate ethics, gifts and hospitality and whistleblowing policies. There may also be a requirement to amend employment, consultant and agency contracts as well as the company's employment handbook to make clear that bribery is prohibited and the consequences if it is discovered.

Implementation of effective anti-bribery and corruption procedures is fundamental to ensuring everyone knows the company's expectations and the restrictions placed upon their behaviour. Effective systems of review and control are also key to being in a position to identify any incidents involving bribery or corruption at an early stage and ensure they are eradicated. Self-regulation and self-referral to the SFO where incidents of bribery or corruption have occurred can be a mitigating factor when penalties are imposed (para **13.64.4**).

Foreign public officials and facilitation payments   **13.64.2**

Bribing a foreign official by offering, promising or giving financial or other advantage with the intention of influencing that person's behaviour in respect of his official functions is a s 7 offence unless the official is permitted or required by the country's applicable written law to be influenced by the advantage.

Examples given by the MOJ to demonstrate where this practice might be acceptable include tenders for publicly funded contracts where those tendering might be asked to provide additional investment in the local community, cost-share, or provide training, etc and the overseas jurisdiction's written laws permit or require the public official to be influenced by such arrangements.

The payment of small bribes to public officials to speed up or facilitate routine actions are prohibited under the Bribery Act, as they were under previous UK legislation.

However, it is widely recognised that this creates a problem where operations take place in some parts of the world and in specific industry sectors where, for example, payments might need to be paid to prevent offices being constantly raided under pretence of an 'investigation'. The need to eradicate facilitation payments is recognised and needs to be supported and promoted by companies as much as possible but it will also require much wider, international collaboration between governments, anti-bribery lobbies and business representatives which will take a longer time to achieve.

In the meantime companies and their directors need to do as much as possible to prevent facilitation payments being made, bearing in mind that even where paid by an agent acting for the company in an overseas jurisdiction, an offence is deemed to have been committed in the UK. It is also important to note that where it can be demonstrated to the Department of Prosecution that the company has a clear policy if facilitation payments are requested and this has been followed or the payment came to light as part of the company's internal monitoring and control process, then the DPP may not be minded to prosecute the offence.

In addition, it is recognised that there might be instances where the failure to make a facilitation payment might cause concern for a person's safety or liberty in which case the payment would need to be made, taking advantage of the common law defence of duress. The DPP is not likely to take action in these circumstances.

In other situations a facilitation payment is not likely to be defensible in which case the DPP may decide to take action for the offence where they consider it is in the public interest to do so. The MOJ makes clear in its guidance on the Bribery Act that the more serious the offence, the more likely it is that prosecution by the DPP will be in the public interest. The DPP will consider each case carefully and has discretion to determine whether to prosecute, which is important for ensuring the Bribery Act is enforced in a just and fair manner.

Corporate hospitality and promotional expenditure   13.64.3

Corporate hospitality, promotional or other business expenditure made in good faith to promote or improve the image of a company and its products and build customer relations is an important part of business and, provided it is proportionate, reasonable and made in good faith, is not prohibited by the Bribery Act. However, it is recognised that it could constitute a bribe in certain circumstances and it is therefore important that the directors ensure clear guidance is given, usually in the form of a corporate hospitality policy, on what is acceptable when giving and accepting hospitality. It is important to demonstrate that there has been no improper performance and there was no intention to influence behaviour. Clearly guidance needs to be given on the acceptable scale, cost and timing of any corporate hospitality accepted or given and an approval process should be determined and periodic monitoring of compliance should be arranged.

Prosecution   13.64.4

There have only been two convictions so far. The first was secured on 18 November 2011 against an administrative clerk, Mr Patel, who was sentenced to six years in prison for accepting a bribe to avoid putting details of a person's traffic summons and motoring offences on the court database. The second case also involved prosecution of an individual, Mr Mushtaq, who attempted to bribe a taxi licensing officer to record him as having passed the driving test for a private hire taxi licence. Mr Mushtaq was convicted of bribery under the Bribery Act s 1 on 4 December 2012 and was sentenced to two months' imprisonment, suspended for 12 months with a curfew restriction. Notwithstanding these two cases, directors should be in no doubt as to the commitment by the Serious Fraud Office ('SFO') to eradicating bribery.

For example, on 25 April 2013 the SFO announced that ENRC had been accepted for criminal investigation in respect of allegations of fraud, bribery and corruption relating to activities of the company and its subsidiaries in Kazakhstan and Africa. This follows ENRC's own internal investigation following allegations made by a whistleblower, the findings of which were reported to the SFO. Developments will be included in future updates of this book.

Similarly, the SFO commenced formal investigation into allegations of bribery and corruption at Rolls-Royce. The claims relate mainly to alleged bribes given by intermediaries to secure contracts in China and Indonesia in the 1980s and 1990s; the level of public interest generated in the allegations alone presents the Rolls-Royce Board with a significant challenge. Rolls-Royce is a highly respected company and mere speculation and uncertainty around these allegations potentially erodes and undermines the company's long-established reputation. As a consequence the whole process needs to be carefully managed and, indeed, Rolls-Royce was swift to commence its own investigation once matters of concern were raised, pass information to the SFO and indicate that it would cooperate fully should formal proceedings be necessary. Through information released it has sought to reassure investors and the market of the thoroughness of the internal review and that current anti-bribery and corruption measures and procedures are robust and appropriate and would prevent any recurrence of events. This has earned Rolls Royce some credibility and, in the absence of further revelations, this positive action taken by the Board to manage the situation and open communication channels may help to preserve the company's reputation in the long term.

In addition there have been a number of high-profile prosecutions successfully brought by the SFO in the High Court. However, because the offences were committed and proceedings commenced before implementation of the Bribery Act, they have been brought under legislation already in existence, namely the Proceeds of Crime Act 2002 (POCA 2002). Examples are set out below.

(1)   In September 2009 on application by the SFO Mabey & Johnson Ltd was sentenced by Southwark Crown Court to pay a total of £6.6m in fines and costs for overseas corruption offences and breaches of UN sanctions. The matter was initially self-referred to the SFO for investigation when first discovered. Pursuant to Part 5 of POCA 2002 in January 2012 the SFO also successfully secured a Civil Recovery Order from the High Court that Mabey Engineering (Holdings) Ltd, Mabey & Johnson Ltd's holding company, pay £130,000 in recognition of sums received through dividends derived from unlawful conduct (SFO, press release, 13 January 2012). The latter is a particularly important development for directors to note where they operate through group subsidiaries, whether in the UK or overseas.

(2)   In July 2012 the SFO secured a Civil Recovery Order from the High Court for Oxford Publishing Ltd ('OPL') to pay £1.89m in recognition of sums it had received by way of dividends from East African subsidiaries as a result of unlawful activity by those subsidiaries involving bribing government officials in those jurisdictions to secure contracts to supply school text books (SFO, press release, 3 July 2012). It should be noted that the decision by the SFO to pursue civil proceedings rather than criminal prosecution was, in part, due to OPL's self-referral of the irregularities to the SFO in the first instance and because no evidence was found that the Board of OPL had any knowledge of the offences. OPL has also since offered to donate an additional £2m to not-for-profit organisations for teacher training and other education purposes in sub-Saharan Africa in

an attempt to demonstrate to the market its recognition that this conduct fell short of expectations and was inconsistent with its overall objective as an organisation, possibly in an attempt to restore its reputation which would have been badly damaged. Another important consequence is the subsidiaries' debarment from participating in future World Bank tenders for a number of years, which will have important commercial implications.

(3)   On 25 January 2012 four men, Messers Rybak, Saunders, Hammond and Smith, received prison sentences of between one and five years for passing confidential procurement information to bidding suppliers involved in a number of high value international oil and gas engineering projects (SFO, press release, 31 January 2012). The offence was 'conspiracy to corrupt' brought under pre-Bribery Act corruption laws. Confiscation orders are also being sought under POCA 2002 s 2 over the individuals' assets to reflect benefit obtained as a result of their offences.

Marketing and selling   13.70

As well as needing to observe the requirements of regulations in terms of how products are described in any marketing material produced (see para **13.40**), consideration also needs to be given to the Privacy and Electronic Communications (EC Directive) Regulations 2003 (amended in 2004) and the Privacy and Electronic Communications (EC Directive) (Amendment) Regulations 2011 (the '2011 Regulations'). These regulations have important implications for the manner in which a company is permitted to carry out marketing activities in an attempt to attract more or new business. Whilst marketing by post is covered by data protection requirements, these regulations apply where direct marketing messages are sent by electronic means including telephone, fax, email, text and video messages and marketing by automated calling systems.

The different rules and requirements that apply to the various methods of marketing are as follows:

(i)   Electronic mail: this includes any electronic message that consists of text, voice, sound or images (such as SMS, messages transmitted in WAP, voicemail and answerphone messages). It is an offence to send unsolicited marketing material by electronic mail to an individual without first obtaining consent from them confirming that they agree to you doing this. This is known as opt-in consent and an individual must have positively indicated their desire to opt in and receive marketing material in this way.

However, where an individual is already a customer and his details have been obtained in the course of business, you do not have to obtain their consent before marketing the company's own products and services to them ('soft opt-in') provided the individual is given the opportunity to opt out from receipt should they so wish. Such requests must be promptly complied with.

Consent is not needed before marketing material is sent to an organisation by electronic mail but the organisation does need to be given the opportunity to opt out and a valid address where such request can be sent. Where an email has been sent this would usually be an email address, and a text reply address where an SMS was sent, etc.

(ii)   Website: in addition to observing the information disclosure requirements and requirements in relation to advertising, trade descriptions and competitive practices (set out in paras **6.52, 13.80, 13.40** and **13.60**) when information about goods or services is given on a company's website and ordering is facilitated, regulations governing the use of internet 'cookies' must be observed. Cookies enable websites to keep track of visitors by storing information about a site visitor and his preferences (often so customised web pages can be presented next time he visits the site). The 2011 Regulations now require all websites using cookies to obtain actual, positive consent from a user prior to the cookie being downloaded. The request must be prominently displayed and the user be made aware of the purpose of the cookie and why it is being used.

(iii)   Telephone marketing and telesales: unsolicited telephone calls cannot be made to individuals or organisations where they have either notified the company direct that they do not want to receive such calls or they have registered with the Telephone Preference Service (corporate telephone service for companies) ('TPS').

(iv)   Automated calls: where pre-recorded phone messages are used to make automated calls, prior consent must be obtained from individuals and organisations before marketing is carried out in this way.

(v)   Faxes: a company must not send an unsolicited marketing fax to an individual unless his prior consent has been obtained. The individual may, at any time, withdraw consent given and can register on the Fax Preference Services so as not to receive marketing faxes.

Whilst prior consent is not required before sending marketing material to an organisation by fax, an organisation can make a request direct to the company that it does not want to receive material in this way or it may register with the Fax Preference Service giving a blanket ban. It is important that material is not sent to any numbers on the Fax Preference Service's list, which must be checked before fax marketing commences, as failure to do so could result in a fine.

Furthermore, to comply with the regulations and regardless of which marketing medium is used, directors must ensure the company is clearly identified in the marketing communication and that details of its address, email and a freephone number are given should the recipient want to contact the company. Contact details are particularly important to enable an opt-out request to be made easily and at little or no cost.

These Regulations have had a significant effect on marketing practices and directors must ensure that everyone involved in marketing within their company is aware of and adheres to the restrictions set out above. It is also important that procedures and processes are in place to keep marketing lists up to date, excluding those who have opted out of receiving unsolicited marketing material.

To illustrate the importance of observing these requirements, in October 2014 the Information Commissioner's Office ('ICO') issued a £70,000 fine to a Devon-based marketing firm, EMC Advisory Services Limited, for failing to make sure that those people registered with the TPS were not called about possible PPI claims, resulting in 630 complaints to the ICO and the TPS between 1 March 2013 and 28 February 2014.

In addition to the regulations detailed above, the Consumer Contracts (Information, Cancellation and Additional Charges) Regulations 2013 (SI 2013/3134) (which replace the amended Consumer Protection (Distance Selling) Regulations 2000 (SI 2000/2334) for contracts entered into on or after 13 June 2014) require all companies that contract with consumers for the sale of goods and services, irrespective of whether the contract is entered into on or off business premises or by means of distance selling, to provide:

(1) clear information about the goods, services or digital content to the consumer;

(2) the supplier's trading name, address and phone, fax and email contact details;

(3) clear explanation of the length of the contract, any minimum duration, renewal requirements, etc;

(4) details of the total price, arrangements for collecting payment and (if applicable) periodic billing;

(5) explanation of delivery charges and arrangements, noting the requirement to supply the goods or services usually within 30 days;

(6) details of the consumer's right to cancel, which has been extended to 14 days, and withdraw from the contract; and

(7)   provide details of the compliant handling policy and how to make a complaint, noting that the use of premium rate telephone customer helplines is now prohibited.

It should be noted that if the contract is completed entirely by electronic means and there is an obligation on the consumer to pay, this must be stated. Also the use of pre-ticked options boxes on contracts to sell extra products and services is prohibited.

The regulations also extend to 'cold callers' who are required to state, at the beginning of their conversation, the purpose of their call and who they represent. They must allow a consumer who enters into a contract during an unsolicited visit to cancel the contract (as above). There is some concern, however, that consumers are generally unaware of their cancellation rights and that some traders are installing goods before the end of the cooling-off period.

As a first step to compliance directors should check whether these regulations apply to their particular business and the goods and services they supply and, if they do, thoroughly review the company's selling process and extent of information given to consumers to ensure it satisfies requirements of the regulations. Failure to do so could result in enforcement action being taken by Trading Standards or the OFT and an injunction against any person considered responsible for the breach.

There may also be additional regulations to be taken into account where, for example, the company is selling financial services (ie the Financial Services (Distance Marketing) Regulations 2004 (SI 2004/2095)) and, in each instance, the directors must ensure the company's own particular circumstances are reviewed to ensure all relevant requirements are identified, understood and satisfied.

As well as addressing marketing correctly, the company's performance through the whole sales process is extremely important. The company's employees and agents will need to be provided with appropriate information and training to ensure they do not fall foul of regulatory requirements or the consequences can be considerable. For example:

- On 3 April 2013 Ofgem imposed its largest fine ever on energy supplier SSE for failures at every stage of the sales process; prolonged and extensive misselling of gas and electricity; severe management failings which meant monitoring and control of sales agents was inadequate; and lack of consideration of the sale process by the Board and senior management. Customers were exposed to misleading statements, inaccurate information on charges and misleading comparisons when sales were conducted by telephone, door-to-door and in store. The £10.5m fine reflected the severity and duration of the offences. SSE also set up a £5m misselling fund from which to compensate affected customers.

- In March 2012, following investigation by Ofgem, EDF Energy agreed to pay £4.5m to vulnerable customers following breaches of marketing rules. EDF were found to have breached some aspects of the licences governing what information is given to customers when selling energy, the information was not always accurate and sometimes promised savings without foundation. As an alternative to receiving a fine, EDF undertook to pay £50 to 70,000 of its 'most vulnerable' customers. It also paid £1m to the Citizens Advice Best Deal campaign.

As well as the financial consequences of such fines and penalties, rulings of this nature can be very damaging to a company's reputation and credibility. In the above instances, public awareness about inaccurate and misleading information given about tariffs and potential savings might make it difficult to secure sales in the future.

Advertising   13.80

The Consumer Protection from Unfair Trading Regulations 2008 (SI 2008/1277) (see para **13.60**) makes clear it is an offence to produce misleading advertising or that which contains unacceptable comparisons. This includes advertisements which contain a false statement of fact, leave out facts, promise to do something when there is no intention of carrying it out and those which create a false impression.

Most complaints about misleading advertisements are handled by the Advertising Standards Authority (ASA) and Trading Standards service as well as the Independent Television Commission, Radio Authority, Financial Services Authority or Medicines Control Agency. The ASA is an independent regulator of all advertising in the UK across all media, including website advertising.

There are some 100 UK statutes, orders and regulations designed to protect consumers which contain provisions on advertising and promotions. In many circumstances they are industry-specific, but others span across industries such as the Business Protection from Misleading Marketing Regulations 2008 (SI 2008/1276), the Consumer Credit (Advertisements) Regulations 2010 (SI 2010/1970), Food Labelling Regulations 1996 (SI 1996/1499), Indecent Displays (Control) Act 1981, Obscene Publications Act 1959 and Weights and Measures Act 1985 (as amended), to name but a few.

As well as needing to comply with the advertising and promotion requirements of these many statutes and regulations, breach of which may give rise to criminal prosecution or civil action, companies advertising the goods and services they sell are required to comply with requirements of the ASA's self-regulatory Codes of Practice and ensure their advertising is legal, decent, honest and truthful. Where the ASA's Council judges an advertisement to be offensive or unjustified contrary to the Codes, everyone responsible for commissioning, preparing, placing and publishing the advertisement will be asked to act promptly to amend or withdraw it.

Should a misleading advertisement or promotion continue to appear after the ASA Council has ruled against it, the ASA can refer the matter to the OFT, which can seek an undertaking from anyone responsible for commissioning, preparing or disseminating it that it will be discontinued. If such undertaking is not forthcoming, the OFT can seek an injunction from the court and anyone who continues to default may be found to be in contempt of court and be liable to be penalised accordingly.

For example, in June 2011 the OFT began investigating MyCityDeal Ltd (trading as Groupon) for possible breaches of consumer protection legislation. Whilst it transpired that the OFT already had concerns about Groupon's trading practices which they were looking into, on 2 December 2011 the matter was referred to the OFT for investigation by the ASA. The ASA was concerned that despite having nearly 50 breaches of advertising regulations in a year, 11 of which had been addressed by formal rulings from the ASA, Groupon continued to fail to conduct promotions fairly, did not provide evidence of the availability of offers and exaggerated claims of savings.

The OFT's investigation concluded in June 2012 following which the OFT announced that it had found specific examples of practices at Groupon which appeared to breach the Consumer Protection from Unfair Trading Regulations 2008, the Unfair Terms in Consumer Contracts Regulations 1999 and the Consumer Protection (Distance Selling) Regulations 2000. The OFT was particularly concerned about Groupon's pricing, advertising, refunds, unfair terms, and the diligence of its interactions with merchants. After consultation, Groupon provided a signed undertaking that it would comply with the law and, if it failed to do so, the OFT would apply to the court for an enforcement order (para **13.62.5**).

Directors should, therefore ensure that those responsible for advertising are aware of the restrictions placed upon them and ensure that the company has controls in place to make sure all advertisements and promotions are accurate, ethical and do not mislead or offend and meet the requirements of legislation and the ASA's Codes of Practice. Having to withdraw advertisements is not only costly but may give rise to bad publicity and harm the company's brand image.

Disability discrimination   13.90

Directors should be aware that the Equality Act 2010 (EqA 2010) requires service providers to take positive steps to make their services available to disabled people and to prevent discrimination on the grounds of a person's disability. Consequently, it is unlawful for a service provider to discriminate against a disabled person by refusing to provide a service which it provides to the public, giving a lesser standard of service, by providing less favourable terms to the disabled person or by failing to make 'reasonable adjustments' (EqA 2010, s 20).

In practical terms this means that:

- service providers are required to take positive steps to make their services accessible to disabled people. This requirement has been addressed in many ways by, for example, service providers visiting disabled people at their own premises to provide services and the provision of services through websites with screen access software to convert written information into speech or Braille, etc; and

- service providers must make reasonable adjustments to physical features of their premises to overcome any barriers to access experienced by a disabled person. Such steps include removing or altering the physical feature impeding access, providing a means of avoiding the physical feature, or providing alternative means of accessing the services. Examples of how this requirement has been addressed include physical improvements made to the access of buildings in the form of ramps, lifts, etc.

The requirement to make reasonable adjustments to physical features of premises has been known for some time and many service providers have already installed means of improving access such as ramps, lifts and signage, etc. Directors should be aware that, if their company is a service provider and provides services, goods or facilities to the public, or a section of the public, an access audit for disabled people should be carried out at all the company's premises to determine whether there are any obstacles to a disabled person's access that need to be addressed. Where obstacles to access are identified in the access audit, the Disability Rights Commission's Code of Practice, 'Rights of Access – Goods, Facilities, Services and Premises', provides some guidance to assist service providers in determining what constitutes a reasonable adjustment. Factors the Code suggests might be taken into account include whether a change would be effective in overcoming the difficulty with access, how practical it is for the service provider to implement the change, the financial cost in relation to the service provider's resources and any financial assistance available, and the extent of disruption that making the change might cause.

In making reasonable adjustments directors should be aware that they are not required to do anything which would compromise a person's health or safety and would, for example, be justified in refusing a person with a severe muscular disorder onto a physically demanding, high speed amusement park ride where refusal is based on genuine concerns for their health and safety.

Directors should also be aware that the company, as the service provider, may be liable to civil action for financial loss and injury to feelings where it has unlawfully discriminated against a disabled person and action may also be brought against a person who has aided the unlawful act. As a first step the Disability Access Rights Advice Service provides an independent advice and conciliation service to resolve disputes. Furthermore, the Equality and Human Rights Commission (EHRC) has been established by the Government to provide advice and assistance, carry out formal investigations and arrange conciliation of disputes.

Data protection   13.100

The Data Protection Act 1998 (DPA 1998) clearly identifies rules for processing personal information which must be observed and gives individuals certain rights over their personal information. DPA 1998 extends data protection to include manual records recorded as part of a 'relevant filing system', which may include paper records stored in files, card indexes, etc and requires companies engaged in processing data to notify their activities to the Information Commissioner. Such notification would include details of the purposes for which data is being processed, who the information is being kept about ('data subjects'), the type of information in terms of its class, ie personal, financial, etc, and any recipients of the information.

It is important that the directors ensure the company complies with the requirements of DPA 1998. Where an offence has been committed by the company with consent or connivance of the directors or as a result of their neglect, they shall be guilty of the offence alongside the company and be liable on summary conviction to a fine not exceeding the statutory maximum (DPA 1998 ss 60 and 61). Depending on the offence, it may be tried in a magistrate's court and subject to a maximum fine of £5,000 or in the Crown Court subject to an unlimited fine. Such offences may include failing to comply with a request from a person about whom personal data is kept to see that information; failure to notify processing of personal data; failing to comply with an enforcement notice or monetary penalty notice and so forth (see para **13.104** for an extensive list). It is a strict criminal offence to process personal data without notification and it carries serious consequences.

Employees and others must be advised that it is an offence under DPA 1998 s 55(1) to knowingly or recklessly obtain, disclose or procure the disclosure of personal information. Furthermore, if a person obtains personal information illegally and offers to sell it, it is a criminal offence (DPA 1998 s 55(3)).

For example, a former manager of a health service based at a council-run leisure centre in Southampton was prosecuted by the Information Commissioner's Office for unlawfully obtaining sensitive medical information belonging to more than 2,000 people. Paul Hedges, who worked as a community health promotions manager, took the information including sensitive medical records of some 2,500 individuals by sending it to his email account for use by his own fitness company after being told that he was being made redundant. He was prosecuted under section 55 of the DPA 1998 on 22 May 2013 and fined £3,000. He was also ordered to pay a £15 victim surcharge and £1,377 prosecution costs.

There has long been a call for tougher penalties, including introduction of prison sentences, to enforce requirements of the DPA 1998 and increase the deterrent on those who choose to ignore them. For many, including the Information Commissioner, the somewhat lenient penalty described above for reckless and intentional abuse, re-energised that call. This being the case, the Government is currently consulting on measures to increase the deterrent for those who commit a section 55 offence by obtaining or disclosing information without the data controller's consent (ICO, news release, 23 May 2013).

Requirement for notification   **13.101**

It is an offence to process personal data unless such data is either exempt or has been notified to the Information Commissioner. Where applicable, the directors must ensure that notification is made which, amongst other things, must include a description of the data to be processed, the purposes and details of any recipient to whom the data is disclosed.

Directors must note that their companies must be fully compliant in terms of notification and observing the data protection principles (para **13.102**). With this in mind companies need to review what data processing is carried out, what information is held, whether it is up to date, what policy and rules are in place for protection of that data and how it is protected when it is sent abroad and so forth. Directors must therefore make sure the following actions are carried out:

- an internal audit to establish what information is collected and stored, how it is processed, and the purposes for which it is used;

- notify these details to the Information Commissioner;

- put a privacy policy in place;

- ensure out of date and irrelevant information is deleted; and

- ensure consent is always obtained from data subjects before transfer to third parties.

Principles   **13.102**

Directors should be aware of the eight data protection principles with which the company, as a data controller processing personal data, must comply. Personal data shall be:

(1) processed fairly and lawfully and at least one requirement of Schs 2 and 3 (the latter only in respect of sensitive personal data such as racial or ethnic origin, political opinions, religious or similar beliefs, health or sexual life, etc) of DPA 1998 must be met principally in terms of consent granted and processing necessary or carried out in the course of legitimate activities;

(2) obtained only for one or more specified and lawful purposes, and shall not be further processed in any manner incompatible with that purpose or those purposes;

(3) adequate, relevant and not excessive in relation to the purpose or purposes for which they are processed;

(4) accurate and, where necessary, kept up to date;

(5) kept for no longer than is necessary;

(6) processed in accordance with the rights of data subjects under the DPA 1998 (see para **13.103**);

(7) kept secure and be protected against unauthorised or unlawful processing and against loss, destruction or damage;

(8) transferred to a country or territory outside the EEA only if there is adequate protection of personal data.

Of particular note is the requirement for specific consent from the data subject for processing of personal or sensitive data to be obtained except where processing is necessary for performance of a contract, required under a legal obligation, for employment purposes, to protect the interests of the data subject or in connection with legal proceedings and so forth.

It is important that directors ensure procedures are in place setting out requirements for processing personal data which comply with the eight principles. To achieve this, responsibilities would need to be delegated to individuals within the company, possibly by means of a data protection policy, so everyone processing data or responsible for determining what is processed is fully aware of what is required of them. Periodic checks should be carried out to ensure compliance and to assist with this, the Information Commissioner has produced an audit manual containing methodology for conducting such audits.

Rights of individuals 13.103

Directors should also be aware that the DPA 1998 has extended individuals' rights in respect of personal data held about them and they have the following rights which must be recognised and complied with by the company, namely the right to:

(1)   access to information held about them – this includes access to information held in paper files;

(2)   prevent processing likely to cause damage or distress;

(3)   prevent processing for direct marketing purposes;

(4)   prevent decisions being taken about them on a purely automated basis;

(5)   take action for compensation for damage suffered by any contravention of DPA 1998 by the data controller (in this case the company);

(6)   take action to rectify, block, erase or destroy inaccurate data;

(7)   make a request to the Information Commissioner where they believe there has been a contravention of the DPA 1998.

Offences under DPA 1998 13.104

Of particular note are the following offences which directors must be aware of to ensure appropriate procedures and training are in place so their companies avoid them:

- processing without notification or before time limits allow;
- failure to notify changes in processing;
- failure to comply with written request for particulars;
- failure to comply with an enforcement, information or special information notice;
- knowingly making a false statement in such notice;
- intentional obstruction or failure to give assistance to a person in execution of a warrant;

- unlawfully obtaining personal data;

- unlawfully selling personal data.

Failure by a company to notify the Information Commissioner that the company is processing personal data is an offence punishable by fine (DPA 1998 s 17).

Furthermore, a person may be entitled to claim compensation for damage caused as a result of a data controller failing to meet requirements of DPA 1998.

The Information Commissioner has legal powers which can be exercised to ensure compliance with the DPA 1998. These include power to:

- conduct assessments to check organisations are complying with DPA 1998;

- serve information notices requiring organisations to provide the Information Commissioner's Office with specified information with a certain time period;

- serve enforcement notices and 'stop now' orders where there has been a breach of DPA 1998, requiring organisations to take (or refrain from taking) specified steps in order to ensure they comply with the law;

- serve a money penalty notice on a data controller of up to £500,000 (ss 55A and 55B); and

- conduct audits to assess whether organisations' processing of personal data follows good practice.

It should be noted that introduction of the Information Commissioner's ability to serve a money penalty notice is relatively new and can be used where the Information Commissioner is satisfied the breach represents a serious contravention, is likely to cause serious damage or distress, was committed deliberately by the data controller or the data controller ought to have known or realised the breach might occur, or where the data controller failed to take reasonable steps to prevent a breach.

From a quick glance it is evident from the Information Commissioner's website (www.ico.org.uk) that the Information Commissioner is very active in monitoring organisations to ensure they comply with DPA 1998, most notably by issue of enforcement notices, monetary penalty notices or by securing formal undertakings from a number of different companies and public bodies following the loss by them of personal data on discs and lost laptops.

A few such examples include:

- In September 2014 the ICO ordered the Council of the Isle of Scilly to implement new data protection policies and training after two breaches involving the disclosure of personal data occurred. The first breach concerned inadvertent inclusion of an attachment to an email which revealed personal data related to a disciplinary hearing and the second concerned two documents containing sensitive personal data ending up in public circulation.

- In August 2014 the ICO served a £180,000 penalty on the Ministry of Justice over serious failings in the way prisons in England and Wales handle people's information following the loss of a back-up hard drive at HMP Erlestoke prison in Wiltshire in May 2013. The hard drive contained sensitive and confidential information about 2,935 prisoners, including details of links to organised crime, health information, history of drug misuse and material about victims and visitors. The device was not encrypted.

- On 24 July 2014 Think W3 Limited, an online travel services company, was served a £150,000 penalty after a serious breach of DPA 1998 revealing thousands of people's details to a malicious hacker.

- On 10 July 2014 a former rogue manager at the car rental company Enterprise Rent-A-Car was prosecuted by the ICO after unlawfully stealing the records of almost 2,000 customers before selling them to a claims management company. He received a £500 fine and was ordered to pay costs of the proceedings.

Press coverage following such incidents is considerable, giving rise not only to damaged reputations but also to a loss of confidence by consumers that their personal data was secure. This could cause a loss of customers and make it difficult to obtain new customers, thereby having a direct impact on turnover and revenue. Where an offence has been committed under DPA 1998, details will be included in the Information Commissioners' Annual Review, which is available online, with possibly damaging consequences for the company in terms of its reputation, customer relations and share price, etc. Directors should be taking action now to adequately address data protection and thereby avoid such bad publicity for the company.

Consequences in relation to customers   **13.105**

Key to compliance with DPA 1998 is the need to be able to demonstrate that the company has obtained consent from data subjects to hold their data for specific uses made clear to them. For example, where a company receives a request to send a brochure to a potential customer and for that purpose captures their details on computer, specific consent must be obtained before using it for any other purpose such as sending newsletters or general marketing information. Otherwise it would be outside the original consent given. Directors therefore need to make sure that suitable procedures are in place to obtain consent to ensure compliance at all times.

Other data protection principles such as the need to keep information up to date and accurate and keep it secure must also be observed, which is important not only from a compliance perspective but also commercially. Having an incorrect address, name or credit details can cause irritation for the customer and similarly, by not protecting customer details from third parties, a very valuable asset for the company could be released into the wrong hands with a damaging effect on sales. Consequently directors must make sure that systems are in place to observe the data protection principles at all times, which can have very positive benefits for the company.

Consumer credit   13.110

Directors must be aware that if their company intends to offer goods or services on credit, or to lend money to consumers, they must observe the requirements of the Consumer Credit Act 1974 (as amended by the Consumer Credit Act 2006) which regulates consumer credit and consumer hire agreements and requires most businesses that offer credit to obtain a consumer credit licence from the FCA. Consideration will also need to be given to observing the requirements of the Unfair Terms in Consumer Contracts Regulations 1999 (para **13.30**) as well as, possibly, the Financial Services (Distance Marketing) Regulations 2004.

A company is likely to need a licence where it:

- sells goods or services on credit (which may include allowing the customers time to pay);
- offers hire purchase terms;
- hires or leases goods for more than three months;
- lends money;
- issues credit cards or trading checks;
- arranges credit for others.
- collects consumer credit debts;
- helps people with debt problems; or
- advises on a person's credit standing.

Directors must be aware of these transactions for which a credit licence is required as it is a criminal offence to enter into such transactions without a licence. The offence is punishable by fine, imprisonment or both. In addition, the company may be left exposed as it is a complex process trying to enforce an unlicensed agreement with a customer and a favourable outcome is by no means guaranteed.

The Consumer Credit Act also sets out certain requirements covering the form and content of agreements, credit advertising, how annual and total credit are calculated and procedures on default, termination and early settlement, etc. The directors must ensure the company complies with these requirements and ensure that, in all cases, credit arrangements are clearly and adequately explained so each borrower is clear about the key facts of the arrangement, the amount of credit being given, the contract period, what payments will need to be made, the costs and consequences of missing a payment or withdrawing, the rate of interest and any other fees payable. There might also be circumstances where the credit arrangement being offered is not considered suitable and this must be made clear to a potential borrower.

In addition, directors of companies that offer goods or services on credit will also need to observe specific requirements set out in the following statutory instruments:

(1)   Advertisements: the Consumer Credit (Advertisements) Regulations 2004 and 2010 which apply to secured credit, such as mortgages, and the Consumer Credit (Advertisements) Regulations 2010, which apply to most unsecured credit, such as loans, hire-purchase and credit cards. In brief, these regulations apply to all types of advertising, whether in newspapers and print media, on the television or Internet and require that advertisements are in plain language and easy to understand, specify the advertiser's name and contact details, use specific criteria for calculating interest rates and the annual percentage rate (if quoted) and state if security is required and the nature of that security.

(2)   Content: the Consumer Credit (Agreements) (Amendment) Regulations 1983 (amended in 2004) which apply to secured credit and consumer hire agreements and the Consumer Credit (Agreements) (Amendment) Regulations 2010 which apply to most unsecured credit including loans, hire purchase, credit cards, overdrafts and some secured credit. These require inclusion of certain specified information in the credit agreement and, in particular, require that the language used is clear, concise and easily to understand. There are also specific requirements about information in the document the borrower signs.

(3)   Disclosure of pre-contract information: the Consumer Credit (Disclosure of Information) Regulations 2004 for most secured loans and the

Consumer Credit (Disclosure of Information) Regulations 2010 for most unsecured credit arrangements. These regulations require pre-contract information to be disclosed to consumers, in most instances, in a standard format and within good time to allow them to fully understand the arrangement, compare different offerings and shop around. Consumers must also be given opportunity to ask questions and, where they do, be provided with further explanation.

(4) Early settlement: the Consumer Credit (Early Settlement) Regulations 2004 and Consumer Credit (EU Directive) Regulations 2010 (amended) which set out requirements for calculating rebates where a borrower decides to settle a credit agreement early, either in full or in part.

Whilst the above provides a brief summary of the requirements of these regulations, it is very simplistic and directors must ensure that where their companies intend to offer goods or services on credit, the regulations are consulted in detail. By way of example, whilst the Consumer Credit (Agreements) (Amendment) Regulations 2010 and the Consumer Credit (Disclosure of Information) Regulations 2010 apply to most unsecured lending, they do not apply to credit agreements secured on land, where credit provided exceeds £60,260 or where they are entered into by a debtor wholly or predominantly for the purposes of his business, unless pre-contract information has been provided (or is purported to have been provided) in compliance with the Consumer Credit (Disclosure of Information) Regulations 2010. This must all be carefully checked.

There is also a requirement to provide certain information and statements during the term of the agreement and to check a consumer's creditworthiness before committing that person to new or an increased level of debt. The latter requirement makes sense not only from a compliance perspective, but also on sound commercial grounds. The company needs to be sure a person can fulfil his repayment commitments, as the cost and time of pursuing non-payment can be considerable. Also, committing or enticing someone into accepting a high level of debt which is really beyond or on the limits of his financial means does not demonstrate any sense of corporate social responsibility and the bad publicity that might arise could be extremely damaging to the company's reputation.

The FCA will investigate concerns about non-compliance and, where they are upheld, can withdraw the company's credit licence. For example, following the compliance review carried out by the OFT of the payday lending sector some 50 payday lenders, accounting for 90% of the payday market, were given 12 weeks to change their business practices or risk losing their licences. This is in response to evidence of widespread irresponsible lending and failure to comply with required standards. Lenders were found to have failed to conduct adequate assessments of affordability before lending or rolling over loans; explain adequately how payments will be collected; and to have used aggressive debt collection practices; and failed to treat borrowers in financial difficulty with forbearance (OFT, press release, 6 March 2013).

Another important reason to ensure compliance, in addition to risk of enforcement action, is that should the regulatory requirements set out above not be observed, it is likely the credit agreement would be unenforceable to the detriment of the company.

14 Directors, creditors and insolvency

14 Directors, creditors and insolvency

The duties directors have to creditors are particularly relevant at the current time given the very difficult trading conditions being experienced by many companies.

Directors' duties to creditors stem from the requirement that the company is able to pay for the goods and services it acquires. If at any time there is a change in the company's ability to meet debts as they fall due, or there is any change in the conditions under which the creditor agreed to trade with the company, such as a change in payment terms or reduction in issued share capital, the directors have a duty to inform creditors.

Provisions in the Insolvency Act 1986 (IA 1986) and subsequent amendment regulations and orders have emerged to deter improper activities by directors when a company is struggling as a going concern and faces inevitable liquidation. Damage to creditors from unpaid debts can be extensive and far-reaching, and duties contained in IA 1986 have been devised to encourage directors to take early action and minimise any loss suffered. Most importantly, IA 1986 introduced personal liability requiring directors to contribute to the company's assets in a winding up where they are found to have committed offences in management of the company, such as misfeasance and breach of duty, fraudulent trading and wrongful trading. Offences under IA 1986 relevant to directors are summarised in **APPENDIX 29**.

Furthermore, directors should be aware that they may be disqualified where they fail to regard the interests of the company's creditors in their management of the company. This was illustrated in the case *Secretary of State for Trade and Industry v Van Hengel* [1995] 1 BCLC 545, where two directors were disqualified for periods of two and six years for fixing their salary levels without consideration of the company's accounts, and there have been many examples since (see **CHAPTER 5**).

The requirement for directors to have regard to fostering business relationships with suppliers, customers and others and maintaining a reputation for high standards of business and conduct when making decisions and seeking to promote success of the company as a stated general duty in CA 2006 s 172(1) has been welcomed as it gives greater emphasis to its importance. Doubtless many directors were already considering these issues but inclusion in the directors' statement of general duties puts the requirement on a more formal footing, which is definitely a step in the right direction (see **CHAPTER 4**).

The Enterprise Act 2002 (EnA 2002) contains a number of provisions which reform and modernise insolvency law. Provisions relating to corporate insolvency include:

- facilitating the rescue of viable companies by reforming the use of administration, which is to be achieved by restricting the use of administrative receivership (where one secured creditor has control) and shifting the balance towards administration to take account of the interests of all creditors;

- streamlining administration and making it more efficient and effective by providing a new out of court route into administration for floating charge holders and companies; and

- removing the preferential status of certain Crown debts whilst retaining such status for certain employee claims and contributions to occupational pension schemes.

The aim of these changes is to make the process more efficient and accessible, making administration a viable means of rescue for a struggling company. EnA 2002 inserted Schedule B1 into the IA 1986, which includes provisions about the administration of companies that need to be observed.

In addition, the Legislative Reform (Insolvency) (Miscellaneous Provisions) Order 2010 permits remote attendance at meetings, use of websites for communication and acceptance of documents in electronic form in place of those in writing.

Directors should also note that the Insolvency Rules 2010 have amended the Insolvency Rules 1986.

Duties to creditors generally   14.10

Directors of any trading company must ensure that at all times they perform the following duties.

(1) Protect the interests of creditors and only enter into contracts with them for provision of goods or services where they believe the company will be able to pay for them. It is an offence for the directors to obtain or induce a supplier to deliver goods when they are aware that there is no reasonable prospect that the company will be able to pay for them, as illustrated in *Re William C Leitch Bros Ltd* [1932] 2 Ch 71.

(2) Inform creditors of any payment out of capital for the purchase by the company of its own shares (CA 1985 s 174). A reduction in capital in this manner might affect the company's ability to repay amounts owing to

creditors in the event of a winding up and has implications on whether the creditors decide to continue to deal with the company (see para **7.22.3.3**). Directors must give notice of the proposed payment out of capital in the London Gazette and a newspaper with national distribution (or by writing to each creditor individually) within a week of members approving the resolution for purchase of shares.

The directors are also required to make a statutory declaration that there are no grounds on which the company could be found to be unable to pay its debts and that the company will, in their opinion, continue as a going concern for at least a year following the repurchase.

(3)   Where the company is a public company, or is a subsidiary of a public company and does not qualify for small or medium company exemptions in the accounts, the directors must ensure that a statement is included in the directors' report concerned with payment of creditors (CA 2006 s 416 and Sch 5 to the Small Companies and Groups (Accounts and Directors' Report) Regulations 2008 (SI 2008/409) and Sch 7 to the Large and Medium-sized Companies and Groups (Accounts and Reports) Regulations 2008 (SI 2008/410)). The report must state the company's standard practice or policy for payment of suppliers and, where this has been formalised, where a copy of the policy is kept. Where no such document exists, the report must be more detailed and set out the precise procedure and terms followed by the company.

Directors should be aware that the Late Payment of Commercial Debts (Interest) Act 1998 as amended and supplemented by the Late Payment of Commercial Debt Regulations 2002 and 2013 makes it particularly important that payment of suppliers' bills is not unduly delayed. All businesses and the public sector irrespective of size now have a statutory right to:

(i)   charge interest (at base rate plus 8%) for late payment, being 30 days after completion of the contracts for their supply; and

(ii)   to claim reasonable debt recovery costs, unless the supplier has acted unreasonably.

It is therefore important that the directors ensure that procedures are in place to pay invoices before such interest is payable.

Duties in relation to the struggling company   14.20

Company voluntary arrangements   14.21

IA 1986 s 1 allows the directors of a company (or where the company is in administration or being wound up, the administrator or the liquidator) to make proposals to the company and its creditors for a compromise or arrangement in satisfaction of its debts (company voluntary arrangement or 'CVA'). Such proposals need to be considered at a meeting of the company's creditors and, where approved by a 75% majority of creditors in terms of value of monies owed, are binding and shall be put into effect unless an application is made to the court challenging the decision. The voluntary arrangement proposal must also be approved by ordinary resolution of the shareholders, following which it shall take effect and bind all those party to it.

The CVA procedure is available to solvent and insolvent companies and involves a proposal being made to members and creditors as a means of avoiding liquidation, with the intention of securing an informal but binding agreement with unsecured creditors about the payment of debts. What is involved in the proposal will vary according to circumstances and any complexities involved but it is not unusual for the CVA for an insolvent company to involve a reduction or rescheduling of debts, for example receipt of £0.10 for each £1.00 of debt owed or a timed payment plan, etc. A person will be nominated in the proposal to supervise implementation of the CVA and, where the company is already in administration or liquidation, this will normally be the administrator or liquidator (as appropriate).

However, a disadvantage with the CVA is there is no automatic statutory moratorium to protect the company from action by its creditors in the interim. This was partly addressed by the Insolvency Act 2000 (IA 2000) which introduced a new voluntary arrangement moratorium for small companies which may provide valuable breathing space and protection for a company at a difficult and vulnerable time (IA 1986 s 1A). Most importantly, whilst the moratorium is in force, the following restrictions apply:

- no petition may be presented for winding up;

- no meeting of the company may be called or requisitioned without consent from the nominee (person monitoring the company's affairs during the moratorium) or leave of the court;

- no resolution may be passed nor order made to wind up the company;

- no petition for an administration order may be presented;

- no administrative receiver can be appointed;

- without leave of the court no landlord or person to whom rent is owed may exercise any right of forfeiture;

- without leave of the court no other steps may be taken to enforce any security over the company's property or to repossess goods;

- without leave of the court, no other proceedings and no execution or other legal process may be commenced.

Where the directors consider it advantageous for the company to obtain a moratorium, they must submit the following documents to the court:

(1)   a document setting out the terms of the proposed voluntary arrangement;

(2)   a statement of the company's affairs, including details of the company's creditors, debts, liabilities and assets, certified by the directors as an accurate, correct and true record;

(3)   such other information requested by the nominee or prescribed;

(4)   a statement that the company is eligible for a moratorium (and there are certain exceptions to eligibility);

(5)   a statement from the nominee confirming consent to act;

(6)   a statement from the nominee confirming that, in his opinion, the proposed voluntary arrangement has a reasonable chance of being approved and implemented, the company has sufficient funds to continue in business during the moratorium and that meetings of the company and its creditors should be summoned to consider the proposed voluntary arrangement.

The moratorium will come into force as soon as the documents listed above are filed with the court and remain in effect until meetings of the company and creditors are held to approve the voluntary arrangement.

Most importantly, whilst a voluntary arrangement is in force, the directors have a duty to ensure that the company complies with the requirements set out in IA 1986 Sch A1, which require that:

(1)   the nominee is notified that the moratorium has come into force;

(2)   the name of the nominee and a statement that the moratorium is in force is noted on all invoices, orders for goods and business letters issued by or on behalf of the company and on the company's website (the Companies (Trading Disclosures) (Insolvency) Regulations 2008 (SI 2008/1897) reg 3);

(3)   the company does not obtain credit of more than £250 from a person who does not know the moratorium is in force;

(4)   the company does not dispose of any property unless approved or by order of the court;

(5)   where the court gives leave for the disposal of property, the directors must send an office copy of the order to the Registrar of Companies;

(6)   the company does not make any payment in respect of any debt or other liability of the company unless approved or pursuant to an order of the court; and

(7) the company does not enter into a market contract, a money market contract or a related contract, give a transfer order, grant a market charge, a money market charge or a system-charge or provide any collateral security.

Failure to comply with these requirements is an offence for which the company and the directors and officers (including shadow directors) may be liable for a fine, imprisonment or both (IA 1986 Sch 10). A detailed list of the offences and penalties is set out in **APPENDIX 30**.

Schemes of arrangement 14.22

CA 2006 Part 26 permits a company to enter into a compromise or arrangement with its members or creditors, often as a means of avoiding insolvency, in the form of a scheme of arrangement. A scheme of arrangement can be used in a wide variety of contexts including but not limited to group reorganisations, mergers and acquisitions, demergers, return of capital, and reorganisation of debt.

The company and its members, creditors and, where applicable, the administrator or liquidator may apply to the court to implement a scheme of arrangement. The proposed compromise or arrangement must then be approved by at least 75% in value of creditors or the members as appropriate to the circumstances (CA 2006 s 899(4)). The notice calling the meeting must be accompanied by a statement explaining the effect of the scheme and state the existence of any material interests held by the directors and how they are affected by the proposed scheme. Failure for a director to disclose a material interest is an offence for which a fine might be imposed (CA 2006 s 898). Where relevant, the statement must also explain how the holders of debentures will be affected. Failure to provide this information may result in the company and its directors and officers being fined (CA 2006 s 897(5)).

Where approved by the requisite majority of creditors or members the court may sanction the scheme of arrangement. Once sanctioned the scheme is binding on all creditors or members (or such classes of them to which the scheme applies) and a copy of the court order must be delivered to Companies House, at which point it becomes effective (CA 2006 s 899(4)).

Administration 14.23

Under IA 1986 Sch B1 para 12, where a company is or is likely to be unable to meet its debts, application may be made to the court by a company's directors, creditors or the company itself for appointment of an administrator to take charge of the company's affairs on behalf of the creditors. An administrator may also be appointed by the holder of a floating charge where such authority is stated in the charge document.

A company is placed in administration normally as a means of averting liquidation and to allow the company 'breathing space' to determine whether, given changes, it can continue trading. Whilst an administration order remains in force, the members cannot pass a special resolution to wind up the company nor can the creditors enforce a claim against the company's assets (unless they have consent from the administrator or leave of court). In addition, once an administration order takes effect, any administrative receiver or receiver shall vacate office (para 41(1)).

Whilst an administration order is in force, the administrator has power to change the directors, convene meetings of the members and creditors and manage the affairs, business and property of the company (IA 1986 Schs 1 and B1). Furthermore, powers of the directors conferred by the Memorandum and Articles and provisions of CA 2006 cannot be exercised in a manner that would interfere with the administrator unless prior consent from the administrator has been obtained.

Every invoice, order for goods or business letter issued on behalf of the company whilst it is in administration must contain the administrator's name and a statement that the order is in force. This information must also be placed on all the company's websites (the Companies (Trading Disclosures) (Insolvency) Regulations 2008 reg 4). Failure to comply with this requirement will render not only the administrator but also the directors liable to a fine (reg 4(2)).

The administrator will require a statement of the company's affairs, containing details of the following:

- the company's assets, debts and liabilities;

- names and addresses of creditors;

- securities held by creditors, and the dates such securities were given; and

- any other information the administrator may require.

This information may be requested from, amongst others, any person who is or has been an officer of the company including the directors and will be required in the form of a sworn affidavit (Sch B1 para 47). Failure to provide the information requested is an offence, resulting in imposition of a fine or daily default fine (Sch B1 para 48).

The administrator will then use this information in preparation of the statement of proposals he is required to make for the company and send a copy to Companies House (Sch B1 para 49). This statement must be made within eight weeks of commencement of the administration order and be presented to the creditors for consideration. The creditors may either approve the administrator's proposals (subject to modification) or reject them.

The administrator may at any time make application to the court for discharge of the administration order where it becomes clear that either the purpose of the order has been achieved, or that it cannot be achieved (in which case the company needs to be placed in liquidation) (Sch B1 para 79).

There has been an increase in recent years in the number of pre-packaged sales of companies in administration, in part due to the economic downturn. This process has been attractive as a purchaser is lined up and terms agreed for them to acquire the company's assets before the company goes into administration. The sale is then effected as soon as the company is placed in administration. The Statement of Insolvency Practice 16 ('SIP 16') provides non-legally binding guidance to insolvency practitioners on the use of 'pre-pack' administrations and the need to provide information to those affected by the administration.

Directors need to be aware that, given most pre-pack administration sales are to the owners or directors of these insolvent companies, there is risk of a lack of transparency and of allegations that the procedure was pursued for the benefit of the purchasers, at the expense of the companies' creditors. Observing the requirements of SIP 16 and providing creditors with critical information regarding the sale will help to overcome these risks from a procedure which, if not abused, provides a relatively quick and inexpensive alternative to formal insolvency proceedings.

According to government statistics (released by the Insolvency Service and BIS) the were 840 pre-pack administrations in 2012 and about 25% of all administrations since 2008 have been by way of pre-pack schemes, 85% of which have been sold to parties already connected with them, usually the directors. Examples include JJB Sport, Dreams and Seymour Pierce.

Whilst those in favour of pre-packs believe they provide a swift solution for struggling companies and preserve jobs, many have expressed concern that the system allows incompetent directors to buy back failing businesses at the expense of unsecured creditors. As a consequence, the Government has announced an independent review of the pre-pack administration process, the outcome of which is awaited.

Administrative receiver 14.24

Where a company is being wound up by the court, application may be made to the court by debenture holders or other creditors for appointment of the Official Receiver to wind up the affairs of a company (IA 1986 s 32). Alternatively, a receiver or manager may be appointed out of court under powers contained in an instrument of charge created over a company's assets (IA 1986 ss 29 and 33). Depending on the nature of the charge, whether fixed or floating, and the powers provided to the receiver or manager in the instrument of charge, the receiver or manager may be either:

- appointed merely to sell the asset over which the creditor has a fixed charge to realise the debt owed to the secured creditor (in which case the receiver's appointment has limited effect on the directors' management functions); or

- appointed as administrative receiver by the holders of debentures secured by a floating charge to take possession of all assets of the company and carry out all actions necessary to realise those assets. Subject to approval by the court, the administrative receiver has authority to dispose of property subject to the charge to discharge unpaid sums secured by it (IA 1986 s 43).

If an administrative receiver is appointed he will require a statement of affairs to be made, showing the same details as those which would be required by an administrator set out in para **14.23** (IA 1986 s 47(2)). This information may be requested from the directors and officers, amongst others, and must be given in the form of a sworn affidavit. Failure to comply with this requirement is an offence and will result in a fine (IA 1986 s 47(6)).

Directors should be aware that when an administrative receiver or manager has been appointed, they have a duty to provide any information requested about the company's affairs and attend interview when required. They must also ensure that all invoices, orders, business letters and other documents on which the company's name appears and the company's websites state the fact an administrative receiver or manager has been appointed (the Companies (Trading Disclosures) (Insolvency) Regulations 2008 reg 2). Failure to show this information is an offence, for which the directors, as well as the receiver, will be liable to a fine (IA 1986 s 39(2)).

Liquidation 14.25

Where the company, for whatever reason, is not able or permitted to continue in operation, application may be made to the court for the company to be placed in liquidation (known as 'winding up'). The directors must ensure that when the company has been placed in liquidation, every invoice, order for goods, business letter or other document in which the name of the company appears and the company's websites all contain a statement that the company is being wound up (IA 1986 s 188).

The company may be wound up voluntarily by the members or creditors, or by the court. The main differences are discussed below.

Voluntary winding up   14.25.1

The members of a company may pass a special resolution to wind up the company in circumstances where the period or purpose of duration determined in the Memorandum and Articles has expired, the company is unable to continue by way of liabilities, or simply where they do not wish to continue and pass a resolution to this effect. The company must cease business once voluntary winding up commences (IA 1986 s 87).

A members' voluntary winding up can only be made where the directors are able to declare that the company is solvent and will remain solvent for at least 12 months following the declaration. Where this declaration cannot be made, the creditors must be notified, and the winding up becomes a creditors' voluntary winding up. The directors' duties in respect of these types of voluntary winding up are as follows:

Type	Directors' duties on appointment of liquidator	Notes
Members' voluntary winding up (s 91)	• Ensure that notice of liquidation is placed in the *Gazette* within 14 days of liquidator's appointment, otherwise liable to a fine (IA 1986 s 85(1) and (2))	• On appointment of a liquidator chosen by the company, all powers of directors cease (IA 1986 s 91)
	• Directors must make a statutory declaration of solvency (IA 1986 s 89 and s 90)	• Directors will be liable to a fine or imprisonment where they make a statutory declaration of solvency when they do not have reasonable grounds to make it (IA 1986 s 89(4))

Type	Directors' duties on appointment of liquidator	Notes
Creditors' voluntary winding up (s 100)	• The directors must summon a meeting of the creditors, to be held within 14 days of approval of the resolution to wind up the company voluntarily (IA 1986 s 98(1))	• On appointment of a liquidator nominated by the creditors, all powers of directors cease (IA 1986 s 103)
	• Directors must preside at the creditors' meeting and provide a statement of affairs to the creditors (IA 1986 s 99(1) and(2))	• Failure to provide a statement of affairs is an offence, for which the directors may be fined (IA 1986 s 99(3))

Directors should be aware that in a creditors' voluntary winding up they have a duty to prepare and lay a statement of the company's affairs before the creditors (IA 1986 s 99(1)). In addition, where a company is insolvent and a liquidator has been appointed, the directors have a duty to cooperate with the liquidator and supply such information concerning the company as required by the liquidator (IA 1986 s 235). Failure to comply and assist the liquidator is a criminal offence, for which a fine may be imposed (IA 1986 s 235(5)).

One change made by the Legislative Reform (Insolvency) (Miscellaneous Provisions) Order 2010 (SI 2010/18) that should be noted is removal of the requirement for the liquidator to hold annual meetings of the member and creditors once the company is in liquidation.

Winding up by the court   **14.25.2**

A company may be wound up by the court, where the company (IA 1986 s 122):

- passes a special resolution to this effect;

- is a public company and has not been issued with a trading certificate within a year of incorporation;

- is an 'old' public company (under provisions of Schedule 3 to the Companies Act 2006 (Consequential Amendments, Transitional Provisions and Savings) Order 2009);

- does not commence business within a year of incorporation or suspends business for more than a year;

- is a public company and has fewer than two members;

- is unable to pay its debts as they fall due;

- in the opinion of the court should be wound up for just and equitable reasons.

When a winding-up order is made, the court will appoint the Official Receiver, who in turn will appoint a liquidator. The liquidator has custody and control of all property of the company and will protect, secure and realise the assets of the company for distribution to the creditors and other persons so entitled.

The directors may be required to provide a statement of the company's affairs by the liquidator or Official Receiver, and failure to comply may result in a fine (IA 1986 s 131). If the directors have given any personal guarantees or security for any debt, they will be required to meet these obligations in the event the company goes into insolvent liquidation.

Duties on appointment of a liquidator   14.30

When a company is placed in liquidation, actions of the directors before and during liquidation will be subject to close scrutiny by the liquidator. Wider issues of wrongful and fraudulent trading are dealt with later in this chapter, but the table below summarises directors' duties, which they must fulfil if they are to avoid claims of malpractice. It should be noted that, whilst these are duties to the liquidator, each of them has evolved to protect the interests of the company's creditors as follows:

Duties to the liquidator	Penalty imposed on directors
(1) Where winding up is imminent, directors must not:	Fine, imprisonment or both for committing any of these offences (IA 1986 s 206).
<ul><li>conceal any company property or debt;</li><li>fraudulently remove company property;</li><li>conceal, destroy, mutilate, falsify or alter company's books or papers;</li><li>make false entries in books or papers relating to property or affairs of company;</li></ul>	

Duties to the liquidator	Penalty imposed on directors
• fraudulently part with, alter or omit information from documents relating to property or affairs; • pawn, pledge or dispose of company property on credit.	
(2) When a company is placed in liquidation, the directors must return all property, books, papers and other documents and items in their possession to the liquidator (IA 1986 s 234).	Fine which will increase over time (IA 1986 s 235(5)).
(3) When the winding-up order has been issued, directors must ensure that they do not: • make a gift of, transfer or create a charge on company property; • conceal or remove property of the company.	Fine, imprisonment or both where these offences are committed (IA 1986 s 207).
(4) During the winding up the directors have a duty to: • discover and disclose to the liquidator all the company's property, any disposals and the value received; • deliver all property, books and papers in their custody to the liquidator; • inform the liquidator of a false debt proved in winding up; • produce all books and papers affecting or relating to the company's property as may be required.	Failure by the directors to fulfil these duties will lead to a fine, imprisonment or both (IA 1986 s 208).

Duties to the liquidator	Penalty imposed on directors
(5) Directors must ensure that all books, papers and documents relating to the company's property or securities remain in their original form and are not destroyed, altered or in any way tampered with.	Falsifying books with intent to defraud or deceive creditors is an offence, resulting in a fine, imprisonment or both (IA 1986 s 209).
(6) Any statement of affairs given to the liquidator by the directors must contain all relevant information.	A material omission is an offence punishable by fine, imprisonment or both (IA 1986 s 210).
(7) All representations made by directors to creditors for their agreement or consent to matters relating to winding up must be correct.	Making a false representation is an offence, for which a fine, imprisonment or both may be imposed (IA 1986 s 211).

Importantly, in *R v McCredie* [2000] 2 BCLC 438 it was held that directors of a company in liquidation owe a duty to the company to cooperate proactively rather than reactively with the liquidators. Consequently the directors have a duty to deliver and disclose company property even where no specific request has been made by the liquidators and they are not aware of the property.

Furthermore, it is fair to assume that directors' conduct and management of the company's affairs and property will be subject to even closer scrutiny where the company is insolvent and is unable to pay its debts.

Duties and winding up   14.40

The liquidator will determine the best and most feasible way to dispose of the company's assets to repay all debts and distribute money to the stakeholders. Obviously this task is much simpler where the company is solvent and all debts can be repaid as well as returning the stakeholders' investment together with any additional sums that they may be entitled to receive.

Where the company is insolvent, the liquidator will be looking very closely at the treatment of creditors, with specific regard to evidence of any preference given or transactions concerned with the avoidance of debt.

Preferential treatment of creditors   14.41

When a company is wound up and funds are distributed amongst creditors, each creditor must be treated equally subject to recognition of any security on their debt ranking them higher in priority to other creditors with unsecured debts.

Any attempt made by the directors to treat any creditor more favourably than another, say, for example, by warning them of impending liquidation and settling their debts in full, is voidable and would be set aside by the court (IA 1986 s 239). In *Re Conegrade Ltd* [2002] EWHC 2411 (Ch), [2003] BPIR 358, the directors had made loans to the company and property was sold to the directors to settle the loans and was leased back to the company. The company later became insolvent and it was held that the company had been influenced by the desire to put the directors in a better position when the transaction had been agreed.

In *Re Corfe Joinery Ltd* [1997] 7 LS Gaz R 29 it was held that payments to directors in the last days before the company ceased trading to repay amounts outstanding on their loan accounts amounted to a preference under IA 1986 s 239, as they put the directors in a better position than they would otherwise have been in.

It was established by the case *Re Living Images Ltd* [1996] 1 BCLC 348 that a director of an insolvent company may be disqualified for giving preferential treatment to a creditor in settlement of debts where it can be proven that the director personally intended the preference to be given.

Furthermore, even where payment to a creditor is not considered a statutory preference under IA 1986, it may nevertheless be found to have been made in circumstances that constitute a breach of the director's fiduciary duties and demonstrate a lack of commercial probity. Where such decision is made, the director may be disqualified on grounds of unfitness, as was held in the case *Secretary of State for Trade and Industry v Richardson* (1997) 141 Sol Jo LB 111.

Restriction on company names following winding up   **14.42**

Directors of a company placed in insolvent liquidation are generally prohibited for a period of five years from trading through a company or business with the same, or a similar, name (IA 1986 s 216). The restriction applies to anyone who was a director or shadow director at any time during the 12 months prior to liquidation. Breach of this prohibition is a criminal offence, and the directors may be personally liable for the debts of the company (see para **5.40**) and be imprisoned for up to two years. By way of example, Christopher Woodhead was convicted of using phoenix companies to steal over £433,000 from companies supplying Yorkshire householders with wall-coating products (SFO, press release, 27 July 2004). He was sentenced on 10 September 2004.

In another example, Stephen Jupe was charged with defrauding investors and creditors and with the illegal use of the name Marshall Wineries Ltd for the phoenix company he created to disguise the fact that Securitised Syndicated Investments Ltd, trading as Marshall Wineries, had failed (SFO, press release, 23 April 2004). On 21 May 2004 he was sentenced to five years' imprisonment for fraudulent trading contrary to CA 1985 s 458 and using a prohibited company name contrary to IA 1986 s 216(4).

Misuse by a director of a liquidated company's name may also be taken into account when determining whether to disqualify a director for unfitness (*Re Migration Services International Ltd* [2000] 1 BCLC 666).

Directors should be aware that, even though they themselves may not have been involved with the insolvent company and are not committing an offence under s 216, they may be personally liable for the company's debts where they take instructions from, or act with, persons they know to be in contravention (IA 1986 s 217). This liability extends to anyone involved in the management of the company who acts on instructions given by a person prohibited from using the name. Furthermore, the offence is one of strict liability whether or not there was any intent to deceive or defraud (*R v Cole* [1998] 2 BCLC 234).

These provisions are designed primarily to prevent directors defaulting on obligations to creditors of one company but immediately setting up a phoenix company of a similar name to carry on the business, exploiting the goodwill and often with the old company's assets obtained at forced sale price. There are certain prescribed exceptions to the rules, designed to make it possible for an insolvency practitioner to realise the goodwill contained in the name. The court may also make exceptions, which are very common in practice.

Transactions at an undervalue 14.43

A transaction at an undervalue occurs where the company confers a benefit without obtaining adequate consideration, at a time when it is unable to pay its debts (IA 1986 s 238). If the transaction is with a connected person such as a director, the onus is on that person to show that the company was not insolvent at the time. The court has power to reverse such a transaction if it took place in the two years before the company went into liquidation, unless it was made in good faith for the carrying on of the business in the reasonable belief that the company would benefit.

Directors should also be aware that transactions made at an undervalue for the purpose of putting assets beyond the reach of creditors will be regarded as transactions defrauding creditors (IA 1986 ss 423–425). The court has the power to set aside such transactions and restore the position of the parties, subject to protection of the rights of innocent third parties. Much depends on the 'intention' of the transaction and, for example, in *Sands v Clitheroe* [2006] BPIR 1000 the judge held that transfer of the family home from a practising solicitor to his wife should be reversed to protect creditors, whereas in *Williams Trustee in Bankruptcy of Jonathan James Taylor v Taylor* [2012] EWCA Civ 1443 application to have the transfer undone was not successful.

Directors responsible for such transactions may be adjudged unfit to hold office and be liable for disqualification proceedings.

Penalties and breach of duty   14.50

Misfeasance and breach of duty   14.51

A director may be ordered to compensate the company if, in the course of a winding up, it appears that he has misappropriated its money or property or been guilty of any misfeasance or breach of duty (IA 1986 s 212). Application for the order may be made by the Official Receiver, the liquidator, a creditor or, with permission of the court, a shareholder.

Misfeasance in the context of insolvency means the improper performance or misconduct by an officer of a task or tasks which he has a duty to perform, resulting in actual loss to the company for which the directors may be required to contribute. In illustration:

- On 29 April 2013 Alex Stone, a director of a motorbike insurance comparison website, Bike Insurer Services Ltd, was disqualified for eight years for paying himself and his American company ahead of other creditors. Mr Stone gave an undertaking that he would not act as a director of a limited company from 9 May 2013 until May 2021 (Insolvency Service, press release, 29 April 2013).

- Stephen Bloch, director of Centenary Holdings III Ltd (previously Seagram Distillers plc), was disqualified for eight years for denuding the company of cash assets of £15m over an 18-month period by making £8m of speculative investments with no financial benefit to the company, paying himself some £1m and declaring a dividend of over £5m to an associated company with no justification or means of payment (Insolvency Service, press release, 1 May 2013).

- In *Re D'Jan of London Ltd* [1993] BCC 646 a director failed to complete and sign a fire insurance form correctly and was held liable to contribute when stock worth £174,000 was destroyed.

- *E D Games Ltd (French & Mummery v Cipoletta)* [2000] EWHC 223 (Ch), which involved the High Court upholding the judgement that a former director of the company be required to compensate the company for the loss caused to the company as a result of withholding VAT payments to HMRC and continuing to trade. The liquidators issued proceedings against the director under IA 1986 s 212 and the High Court considered that the company had been caused loss as a result of being able to continue to trade when it should have stopped due to lack of working capital.

These cases follow investigation by the Insolvency Service and give a clear message that disqualification and financial redress will be sought where funds have been diverted from creditors as a consequence of the director's unfair treatment.

Fraudulent trading   14.52

Where directors have conducted the business of the company with dishonest intent to defraud creditors, or for any other fraudulent purpose, and where it is unlikely that the company's debts will be satisfied, they may be:

(1)   personally liable to contribute to the company's assets in a winding up as determined by the court (IA 1986 s 213); and

(2)   fined, imprisoned, or both (CA 2006 s 993); and/or

(3)   disqualified from acting as directors for a maximum of 15 years (CDDA 1986, s 10).

Directors should note that whilst personal liability to contribute to the company's assets will be required by application of the liquidator in a winding up, criminal action may be instigated (in (2) and (3) above) regardless of whether the company is in liquidation.

The severity of penalties for fraudulent trading is well illustrated by notification in an Insolvency Service press release that, on 3 September 2014, seven former members of Wolstenholmes LLP, which operated a solicitors practice, were disqualified for periods ranging from five to 15 years, a 70-year combined total, for fraudulent trading, misappropriation of some £8m from clients' funds, serious accounting irregularities, failing to keep proper books and accounting records and filing false Stamp Duty Land Transfer returns with HM Land Registry. They misused money entrusted to them, leaving clients with £13m of losses which was paid out of the Solicitors Regulation Authority and the Solicitors Compensation Fund.

Similarly, Mr Nicholas Levene, a city trader, was jailed for 13 years for defrauding investors, false accounting and obtaining money by deception for a prolonged period between 2005 and 2009 (SFO, press release, 5 November

2012). Mr Levene diverted investors' funds into his own personal, business and gambling accounts instead of buying shares for them. To maintain the fraud investors were provided with money described as 'profit' which was, in fact, other investor's money. This deceived investors into believing that he was a successful trader, allowing him to obtain over £250m from investors.

Another example is the Stephen Jupe, Marshall Wineries case set out in para **14.42** above.

Directors should also be aware that obtaining goods on credit when funds are not available to pay the debt constitutes fraudulent trading, as was the decision in *R v Grantham* [1984] QB 675, CA.

Whilst, in accordance with Limitation Act 1980 ss 5 and 21(3), a claim against a director would usually need to be brought within six years of the alleged breach of duty, if the breach of duty is fraudulent there is no such time limit (*DEG Deutsche Investitions und Entwicklungs Gesellschaft mbH v Koshy* [2003] EWCA Civ 1048).

Wrongful trading **14.53**

Wrongful trading applies to circumstances where a director knows, or ought to know, that the company cannot avoid insolvent liquidation, and does not take every step necessary to minimise the potential loss to creditors (IA 1986 s 214). There need be no fraudulent intent on the part of the director.

The liquidator may apply to the court for an order requiring the directors, or any of them, to contribute to the company's assets available to creditors where the company is placed in insolvent liquidation (IA 1986 s 214). The decision by the court in *Re DKG Contractors Ltd* [1990] BCC 903 was that, under the wrongful trading provisions, compensation be paid for all trade debts incurred on or after the date that wrongful trading commenced.

Directors are required to recognise the moment when the company can no longer avoid insolvent liquidation and take immediate and positive action to protect the interests of creditors. In doing so, they will be required to display an objective level of skill and apply it diligently. They will be expected to act not merely as a 'reasonable man' but as a skilled director. To minimise risk of liability, each director must ensure that he is fully informed about the company's cash position and trading profiles, and take a realistic view of the company's future prospects.

However, it should be noted that in order for a director to be liable for wrongful trading, it must be shown that on the date the company went into liquidation it was in a worse position than it would have been had it ceased to trade at an earlier date. If this cannot be shown, claim against the directors for wrongful trading will fail (*Re Marini Ltd (The Liquidator of Marini Ltd) v Dickenson* [2004] BCC 172).

A disqualification order may also be made against the director (see para **5.53.7**) and HMRC may make a claim under tax regulations for the directors to personally pay unpaid PAYE on remuneration.

By way of example, on 30 July 2014 Mr Ofosuhene Ofori-Duah, director of Vintage International Limited, a wine investment services company, was disqualified from acting as a director for nine years for causing the company to trade with undue risk to its clients and creditors who were left owed just over £1m when the company went into voluntary liquidation (Insolvency Service, press release, 12 August 2014). The director failed to ensure proper corporate governance was in place to clearly monitor client orders and the financial position of the company, as a result of which he continued to take new client orders when the company was insolvent and had insufficient funds available to purchase wine stock to meet the orders.

Personal liability of directors   14.60

As discussed in the preceding paragraph and para **5.40**, directors may incur personal liability and be required to contribute to the company's assets in a winding up for misfeasance or breach of duty, fraudulent trading and wrongful trading.

Directors must also be aware that they may be directly liable to creditors when the company is not being wound up for breach of the restrictions on the reuse of company names and acting while disqualified (CDDA 1986 s 15). The directors' liability is joint and several with the company itself and any other person who is liable in the same way. A creditor may take direct action for recovery without the intervention of a liquidator or a government agency. Such actions enable the creditor to recover amounts in full for his own benefit.

Appendix 1 Checklist of matters to include in a director's service contract

1   Names of employer and the director.

2   Job title, brief job description and description of duties required.

3   Date employment commenced (and the period of continuous employment).

4   Place of work or, if the director is required or allowed to work in more than one location and travel to meetings, etc, an indication of this and of the employer's address.

5   Remuneration and details of how and at what intervals it is paid and of any review process.

6   Hours of work and time expected to be dedicated to duties arising from directorship re attendance at Board and committee meetings, etc.

7   Holiday entitlement.

8   Sickness entitlement and disability cover arrangements.

9   Entitlement to other benefits which would often include participation in annual bonus schemes and long-term incentive arrangement schemes; provision of a car or car allowance; mobile telephone and/or other electronic communication device; and medical insurance, etc.

10   Pension and pensions scheme arrangements.

11   Entitlement to notice of termination (both for the employer and the director) and provisions relating to payment in lieu if applicable.

12   Where employment is not permanent, the period for which it is expected to continue or, where it is for a fixed term, the date when employment is to end. Alternatively a statement of retirement provisions.

13   Details of the existence of any relevant collective agreements which directly affect the terms and conditions of the director's employment.

14   The level of travel and other expenses that can be claimed and the required procedure to reclaim.

15   Limitations placed on the director in terms of types and number of other directorships and positions of office held and the need to disclose them and obtain prior approval.

16 Limitations on engaging in business and professional activities other than for the benefit of the company and the need to disclose such activity and obtain prior approval.

17 Suitable termination arrangements to ensure that the executive is not rewarded for failure, but is adequately compensated if the situation in the business changes and his services are no longer required. These should detail how both salary and other benefits will be treated and the requirement to attempt to mitigate loss by both the company and the executive in event of termination, taking into account the ABI/NAPF guidance on severance terms.

18 Any requirement for the director to undergo a medical examination and details of how and to whom the information will be disclosed.

19 Confidentiality of information requirements during and after termination of employment, particularly the need to ensure that price sensitive information is not inadvertently released and making sure that the director is quite clear of the restrictions to be applied.

20 Intellectual property requirements, clarifying who owns any intellectual property created during employment and setting out the company's ownership registration and protection requirements.

21 Details of the company's disciplinary, grievance and whistleblowing procedures.

22 Details of circumstances when termination might occur without notice, for example where there is gross misconduct, negligence, bankruptcy, a criminal conviction, etc or, for an FCA-regulated company, the loss of approved personal status.

23 Restrictive covenants placing restrictions on the directors taking employment or directorship with a competitor, poaching staff or soliciting business from or dealing, either directly or indirectly, with the company's clients, and customers, etc.

24 Restrictions on dealing in the company's own shares and the requirements of the company's share dealing policy and the Model Code.

25 Arrangements and the procedure for approving a director's request to seek independent professional advice.

26 Directors' and officers' indemnity insurance arrangements and requirements.

Appendix 2   Extract from ICSA guidance: a sample non-executive director's appointment letter (Guidance Note 111214)[1]

1   © Institute of Chartered Secretaries & Administrators. Reproduced with the kind permission of ICSA. For the full version of the Guidance Note please see www.icsa.org.uk

Sample letter

I am pleased to confirm that upon the recommendation of the nomination committee, the Board has approved your appointment as [an independent/a non-independent] non-executive director of [name of company] ('the Company'). This letter sets out the main terms of your appointment.

It is agreed that, on acceptance of this offer, this letter will constitute a contract for services and not a contract of employment.

1   Appointment

1.1 Subject to the remaining provisions of this letter, [your appointment is for an initial term of three years commencing on [date]] [your appointment is for an initial term, from [date] until the conclusion of the Company's Annual General Meeting (AGM) occurring approximately three years from that date], unless terminated earlier by either party giving to the other party [one/three] month['s] [s'] written notice.

1.2 Your appointment is subject to the Articles of Association. Nothing in this letter shall be taken to exclude or vary the terms of the Articles of Association as they apply to you as a director of the Company. Your continued appointment as non-executive director is subject to election by the Company's shareholders at the AGM scheduled to be held on [date] and to re-election at any subsequent AGM at which either the articles of association of the Company require, or the Board resolves, that you stand for re-election.

[The Board has resolved to apply Provision B.7.1 of the FRC's UK Corporate Governance Code 2010, whereby all directors will be subject to annual election at the [year] AGM, and expects to do so in subsequent years.]

If the shareholders do not re-elect you as a director, or you are retired from office under the Articles of Association, your appointment shall terminate automatically, with immediate effect and without compensation.

1.3 Continuation of your contract of appointment is also contingent on satisfactory performance and any relevant statutory provisions relating to the removal of a director.

1.4 Non-executive directors are typically expected to serve two three-year terms but may be invited by the Board to serve for an additional period. Any term renewal is subject to Board review and AGM re-election. Notwithstanding any mutual expectation, there is no right to renomination by the Board, either annually or after any three-year period.

1.5 You [will/may] be required to serve on one or more committees of the Board. You will be provided with the relevant terms of reference on your appointment to such a committee. [You also [will/may] be asked to serve as a non-executive director on the Board of any of the Company's subsidiaries or joint ventures, or as Senior Independent Director.] Any such appointment will be covered in a separate communication.

1.6 Notwithstanding paragraphs 1.1–1.5, we may terminate your appointment with immediate effect if you:

(a)   commit a material breach of your obligations under this letter; or

(b)   commit any serious or repeated breach or non-observance of your obligations to the Company (which include an obligation not to breach your duties to the Company, whether statutory, fiduciary or common-law); or

(c)   are guilty of any fraud or dishonesty or acted in a manner which, in the opinion of the Company acting reasonably, brings or is likely to bring you or the Company into disrepute or is materially adverse to the interests of the Company; or

(d)   are convicted of any arrestable criminal offence [other than an offence under road traffic legislation in the UK or elsewhere for which a fine or non-custodial penalty is imposed]; or

(e)   are declared bankrupt or have made an arrangement with or for the benefit of your creditors; or

(f)   are disqualified from acting as a director.

1.7 On termination of your appointment, you shall at the request of the Company resign from your office as a director of the Company [and all offices held by you in any Group company].

1.8 If there are matters which arise which cause you concern about your role you should discuss them with me [or the Senior Independent Director]. If you have any concerns which cannot be resolved, and you choose to resign for that, or any other, reason, you should provide an appropriate written statement to me [or the Senior Independent Director] for circulation to the Board.

2 Time commitment

2.1 You will be expected to devote such time as is necessary for the proper performance of your duties and you should be prepared to spend at least [number of days] days per [month/year] on company business after the induction phase. This is based on preparation for and attendance at:

- scheduled Board meetings
- [Board dinners]
- [the annual Board strategy away-day(s)]
- the AGM
- [site visits]
- meetings of the non-executive directors
- meetings with shareholders
- updating meetings/training
- meetings as part of the Board evaluation process

[Meetings may involve you in some overseas travel.] Unless urgent and unavoidable circumstances prevent you from doing so, it is expected that you will attend the meetings outlined above.

2.2 The nature of the role makes it impossible to be specific about the maximum time commitment, and there is always the possibility of additional time commitment in respect of preparation time and ad hoc matters which may arise from time to time, and particularly when the Company is undergoing a period of increased activity. At certain times it may be necessary to convene additional Board, committee or shareholder meetings.

2.3 The average time commitment stated in 2.1 will increase should you become a committee member or chair, or if you are given additional responsibilities, such as being appointed the senior independent director, or non-executive director on the Boards of any of the Company's subsidiaries. Details of the expected increase in time commitment will be covered in any relevant communication confirming the additional responsibility.

2.4 By accepting this appointment you undertake that, taking into account all other commitments you may have, you are able to, and will, devote sufficient time to your duties as a non-executive director.

3 Duties

3.1 You will be expected to perform your duties, whether statutory, fiduciary or common-law, faithfully, efficiently and diligently to a standard commensurate with both the functions of your role and your knowledge, skills and experience.

3.2 You will exercise your powers in your role as a non-executive director having regard to relevant obligations under prevailing law and regulation, including the Companies Act 2006, the UK Corporate Governance Code and associated guidance[1] and the UK Listing Authority's Listing, Prospectus, and Disclosure and Transparency Rules. [You are also required to comply with the requirements of the [New York Stock Exchange].You will be advised by the Company Secretary where these differ from requirements in the UK.]

3.3 You will have particular regard to the general duties of directors as set out in Part 10, Chapter 2 of the Companies Act 2006, including the duty to promote the success of the company:

> 'A director of a company must act in the way he considers, in good faith, would be most likely to promote the success of the company for the benefit of its members as a whole, and in doing so have regard (amongst other matters) to –
>
> (a)   the likely consequences of any decision in the long term,
> (b)   the interests of the company's employees,
> (c)   the need to foster the company's business relationships with suppliers, customers and others,
> (d)   the impact of the company's operations on the community and the environment,
> (e)   the desirability of the company maintaining a reputation for high standards of business conduct, and
> (f)   the need to act fairly as between members of the company.'

3.4 You will have particular regard to the FRC's UK Corporate Governance Code (the 'Code') and associated Guidance on Board Effectiveness in respect of the role of the Board and the role of the non-executive director.

In your role as non-executive director you will be required to:

- constructively challenge and help develop proposals on strategy;

- scrutinise the performance of management in meeting agreed goals and objectives and monitor the reporting of performance;

- satisfy yourself on the integrity of financial information and that financial controls and systems of risk management are robust and defensible;

- determine appropriate levels of remuneration of executive directors and have a prime role in appointing and, where necessary, removing executive directors, and in succession planning;

- devote time to developing and refreshing your knowledge and skills;

- uphold high standards of integrity and probity and support me and the other directors in instilling the appropriate culture, values and behaviours in the boardroom and beyond;

- insist on receiving high-quality information sufficiently in advance of board meetings; and

- take into account the views of shareholders and other stakeholders where appropriate.

3.5 You will be required to exercise relevant powers under, and abide by, the Company's Articles of Association.

3.6 You will be required to exercise your powers as a director in accordance with the Company's policies and procedures [and internal control framework].

3.7 You will disclose any direct or indirect interest which you may have in any matter being considered at a board meeting or committee meeting and, save as permitted under the Articles of Association, you will not vote on any resolution of the Board, or of one of its committees, on any matter where you have any direct or indirect interest.

3.8 You will immediately report to me your own wrongdoing or the wrongdoing or proposed wrongdoing of any employee or director of which you become aware.

3.9 Unless specifically authorised to do so by the Board, you will not enter into any legal or other commitment or contract on behalf of the Company.

4 *Remuneration and expenses*

4.1 The annual fee rate as at the date of this letter is £[amount] gross per annum, paid [monthly/quarterly] in arrears. This fee covers all duties, including service on any board committee or company subsidiary, with the exception of committee chairmanships and certain additional responsibilities, such as taking on the role of senior independent director. [In your case, a further fee of £[amount] is payable as at the date of this letter for taking on [chairmanship of the [name of committee] Committee] [./and] [the role of Senior Independent Director].]

4.2 All fees will be paid through PAYE and are subject to income tax and other statutory deductions.

4.3 Fees will be subject to an [annual/periodic] review by the Board.

[4.4 [You will comply with the Company's requirements regarding the minimum shareholding level (agreed from time to time by the Board).]

4.5 The Company will reimburse you for all reasonable and properly documented expenses you incur in performing the duties of your office. The procedure and other guidance in respect of expense claims is set out in [name of document].

4.6 On termination of the appointment you shall only be entitled to such fees as may have accrued to the date of termination, together with reimbursement in the normal way of any expenses properly incurred prior to that date.

5 Independence and outside interests

5.1 [The Board of the Company has determined you to be independent, taking account of the guidance contained in B.1.1 of the UK Corporate Governance Code.]

5.2 You have already disclosed to the Board the significant commitments you have outside this role. You must inform me in advance of any changes to these commitments. In certain circumstances the agreement of the Board may have to be sought before accepting further commitments which either might give rise to a conflict of interest or a conflict of any of your duties to the Company, or which might impact on the time that you are able to devote to your role at the Company.

5.3 It is accepted and acknowledged that you have business interests other than those of the Company and have declared any conflicts that are apparent at present. In the event that you become aware of any further potential or actual conflicts of interest, these should be disclosed to me and the Company Secretary as soon as they become apparent and, again, the agreement of the Board may have to be sought.

6   Confidentiality

6.1 You acknowledge that all information acquired during your appointment is confidential to the Company and should not be released, communicated, nor disclosed either during your appointment or following termination (by whatever means), to third parties without my prior clearance.

6.2 This restriction shall cease to apply to any confidential information which may (other than by reason of your breach) become available to the public generally.

6.3 You acknowledge the need to hold and retain company information (in whatever format you may receive it) under appropriately secure conditions.

6.4 You hereby waive all rights arising by virtue of Chapter IV of Part I of the Copyright Designs and Patents Act 1998 in respect of all copyright works created by you in the course of performing your duties hereunder.

7   Price sensitive information and dealing in the Company's shares

7.1 Your attention is drawn to the requirements under both law and regulation regarding the disclosure of price-sensitive information, and in particular to the Disclosure and Transparency Rules of the UK Listing Authority and s 52 of the Criminal Justice Act 1993 on insider dealing. You should avoid making any statements that might risk a breach of these requirements. If in doubt please contact me or the Company Secretary.

7.2 During your period of appointment you are required to comply with the provisions of the Model Code, as annexed to the Listing Rules of the UK Listing Authority, in relation to dealing in the Company's listed securities, and any such other code as the Company may adopt from time to time which sets out the terms for dealings by directors in the Company's listed securities. A copy of the current share dealing code adopted by the Company will be provided to you separately.

8   Induction

8.1 Immediately after appointment, the Company will provide a comprehensive, formal and tailored induction [which will involve travel overseas]. You will be expected to make yourself available during your first year of appointment for not less than an additional [10] days for the purposes of the induction. The company secretary will be in touch with further details.

9 Review process

9.1 The performance of individual directors and the whole Board and its committees is evaluated annually.

10 Training

10.1 On an ongoing basis, and further to the annual evaluation process, we will make arrangements for you to develop and refresh your skills and knowledge in areas which we mutually identify as being likely to be required, or of benefit to you, in carrying out your duties effectively. You should endeavour to make yourself available for any relevant training sessions which may be organised for the Board.

11 Insurance and indemnity

11.1 The Company has directors' and officers' liability insurance in place and it is intended to maintain such cover for the full term of your appointment. You have been informed of the current indemnity limit, on which the Board is updated from time to time. Other details of the cover are available from the Company Secretary.

11.2 You will also be granted a deed of indemnity by the Company.

12 Independent professional advice

12.1 Circumstances may occur when it will be appropriate for you to seek advice from independent advisers at the Company's expense. A copy of the Board's agreed procedure under which directors may obtain independent advice will be provided by the company secretary. The Company will reimburse the reasonable cost of expenditure incurred by you in accordance with its policy.

13 Changes to personal details

13.1 You shall advise the company secretary promptly of any change in address or other personal contact details.

14 Return of property

14.1 Upon termination of your appointment with the Company (for whatever cause), you shall deliver to the Company all documents, records, papers or other company property which may be in your possession or under your control, and which relate in any way to the business affairs of the Company, and you shall not retain any copies thereof.

[15   Non-compete clause

15.1 By countersignature of this letter and in consideration for the fees payable to you under the terms of this letter, you now agree that you will not (without the previous consent in writing of the Company), for the period of six months immediately after the termination of your office, whether as principal or agent and whether alone or jointly with, or as a director, manager, partner, shareholder, employee or consultant of, any other person, carry on or be engaged, concerned or interested in any business which is similar to or competes with any business being carried on by the Company [or any company in the Group.]]

16   Data protection

16.1   By signing this letter you consent to the Company holding and processing information about you for legal, personnel, administrative and management purposes and in particular to the processing of any sensitive personal data (as defined in the Data Protection Act 1998) including, as and when appropriate:

(a)   information about your physical or mental health or condition in order to monitor sick leave and take decisions as to your fitness to perform your duties;

(b)   information about you that may be relevant to ensuring equality of opportunity and treatment in line with the Company's equal opportunities policy and in compliance with equal opportunities legislation; and

(c)   information relating to any criminal proceedings in which you have been involved, for insurance purposes and in order to comply with legal requirements and obligations to third parties.

You consent to the transfer of such personal information to other offices the Company may have [or to a company in the Group] or to other third parties, whether or not outside the European Economic Area, for administration purposes and other purposes in connection with your appointment, where it is necessary or desirable for the Company to do so.

16.2 You will comply at all times with the Company's data protection policy, a copy of which will be provided to you.

17 Rights of third parties

17.1 The Contracts (Rights of Third Parties) Act 1999 shall not apply to this letter. No person other than you and the Company shall have any rights under this letter and the terms of this letter shall not be enforceable by any person other than you and the Company.

18 Law

18.1 Your engagement with the Company is governed by and shall be construed in accordance with the laws of [country] and your engagement shall be subject to the jurisdiction of the courts of [country].

18.2 This letter constitutes the entire terms and conditions of your appointment and no waiver or modification thereof shall be valid unless in writing and signed by the parties hereto.

If you are willing to accept these terms of appointment, please confirm your acceptance by signing and returning to me the enclosed copy of this letter.

Yours sincerely

[name]

Chairman

I confirm and agree to the terms of my appointment as a non-executive director of [name of company] as set out in this letter.

_____

[name]

_____

[date]

1   The FRC's associated guidance comprises: i. Guidance on Board Effectiveness ii. Going Concern and Liquidity Risk: Guidance for Directors of UK Companies iii. Internal Control: Revised Guidance for Directors iv. Guidance on Audit Committees.

Appendix 3 CDDA 1986 Schedule 1: Matters for Determining Unfitness of Directors

Part I – Matters applicable in all cases [relevant to CDDA 1986 s 6 and s 8]

(1) Any misfeasance or breach of any fiduciary or other duty by the director in relation to the company (including a breach of the statutory statement of directors' duties under CA 2006).

(2) Any misapplication or retention by the director of, or any conduct by the director giving rise to an obligation to account for any money or other property of the company.

(3) The extent of the director's responsibility for the company entering into any transaction liable to be set aside under Pt XVI of the Insolvency Act 1986 (provisions against debt avoidance).

(4) The extent of the director's responsibility for any failure by the company to comply with any of the following provisions of the Companies Act 2006:

    (a) s 113 (register of members);

    (b) s 114 (register to be kept available for inspection);

    (c) s 162 (register of directors);

    (d) s 165 (register of directors' residential addresses);

    (e) s 167 (duty to notify registrar of changes: directors);

    (f) s 275 (register of secretaries);

    (g) s 276 (duty to notify registrar of changes: secretaries);

    (h) s 386 (duty to keep accounting records);

    (i) s 388 (where and for how long accounting records to be kept);

    (j) s 854 (duty to make annual returns);

    (k) s 860 (duty to register charges);

    (l) s 878 (duty to register charges: companies registered in Scotland).

(5)   The extent of the director's responsibility for any failure by the directors of the company to comply with the following provisions of the CA 2006:

(a)   s 394 or s 399 (duty to prepare group accounts);

(b)   s 414 or s 450 (approval and signature of abbreviated accounts); or

(c)   s 433 (name of signatory to be stated in published copy of accounts).

Part II – Matters applicable where company has become insolvent [relevant to CDDA 1986 s 6 to s 8 where the company is insolvent]

(6)   The extent of the director's responsibility for the causes of the company becoming insolvent.

(7)   The extent of the director's responsibility for any failure by the company to supply any goods or services which have been paid for (in whole or in part).

(8)   The extent of the director's responsibility for the company entering into any transaction or giving any preference, being a transaction or preference:

(a)   liable to be set aside under s 127 or ss 238 to 240 of the Insolvency Act 1986, or

(b)   challengeable under ss 242 or 243 of that Act or under any rule of law in Scotland.

(9)   The extent of the director's responsibility for any failure by the directors of the company to comply with s 98 of the Insolvency Act 1986 (duty to call creditors' meeting in creditors' voluntary winding up).

(10) Any failure by the director to comply with any obligation imposed on him by or under any of the following provisions of the Insolvency Act 1986:

(a)   s 22 (company's statement of affairs in administration);

(b)   s 47 (statement of affairs to administrative receiver);

(c)   s 66 (statement of affairs in Scottish receivership);

(d)   s 99 (directors' duty to attend meeting; statement of affairs in creditors' voluntary winding up);

(e)   s 131 (statement of affairs in winding up by the court);

(f)   s 234 (duty of any one with company property to deliver it up);

(g)   s 235 (duty to co-operate with liquidator, etc).

Appendix 4   Statutory registers

Type	Statutory requirement	Required location	Notification of location	Disclosure requirements	Use of information
Directors.	CA 2006 s 162	Registered office or other location at which the company keeps records available for inspection (CA 2006 s 1136), as notified to the Registrar.	Notice of location is required unless kept at the registered office (CA 2006 s 162(4)).	(i) Available for inspection by members (no charge) and others (may charge prescribed fee).	● Annual return ● Annual accounts
Secretaries	CA 2006 s 275	Registered office or other location at which the company keeps records available for inspection (CA 2006 s 1136), as notified to the Registrar.	Notice of location is required unless kept at the registered office (CA 2006 s 275(4)).	(i) Available for inspection by members (no charge) and others (may charge prescribed fee).	● Annual return ● Annual accounts

Type	Statutory requirement	Required location	Notification of location	Disclosure requirements	Use of information
Directors' Residential Addresses	CA 2006 s 165	No mention in statute but would expect to keep at office or registered single alternative inspection location.	Protected information and should not be disclosed, save as set out in para 6.11.4.	(i) Protected information and should not be disclosed, save as set out in para 6.11.4.	● Must be kept confidential
Members	CA 2006 s 114	Registered office or other location at which the company keeps records available for inspection (CA 2006 s 1136) as notified to Registrar (s 114).	Form AD02, AD03 and AD04 relating to single alternative inspection location.	(i) Available for inspection by members (no charge) and others (may charge prescribed fee).	● The annual return of a non-traded company must contain an alphabetical list of the names of members. ● The annual return of a traded company must contain the information above plus the name and address of any member holding 5% or more of the issues share capital.

			(ii)	Supply a copy to a member (for no fee) or other person (may charge prescribed fee) upon request. Certain rights exist on the part of the Company under s 116 to ensure that the information is not being used for an improper purpose.	• Share capital details in accounts
Interests in shares (public companies)	CA 2006 s 808 (only where a notice has been issued by a company requiring information about interests in shares under CA 2006 ss 793 or 803).	Registered office or other location at which the company keeps records available for inspection (CA 2006 s 1136), as notified to the Registrar.	Notice of location is required unless kept at the registered office (CA 2006 s 809(2)).	(i)	Available for inspection by any person without charge, subject to the 'proper purpose' test.	• Directors' report to the accounts
				(ii)	Supply a copy to any person upon request, subject to the prescribed fee and satisfaction of the 'proper purpose' test.	

Type	Statutory requirement	Required location	Notification of location	Disclosure requirements	Use of information
Allotments and transfers	N/A (no requirement to keep)	No specified location.	N/A	None	• Annual return
Debenture holders	N/A (no requirement to keep)	Where register is maintained, must be kept at either registered office or other location at which the company keeps records available for inspection (CA 2006 s 1136) as notified to Registrar (CA 2006 s 743).	Forms AD02, AD03 and AD04 relating to single alternative inspection location.	(i) Available for inspection by members (no charge) and others (may charge prescribed fee) subject to the 'proper purpose' test. (ii) Supply a copy to a member or other person subject to the prescribed fee and satisfying the 'proper purpose' test. (CA 2006 s 744).	• Accounts

Record	Statute	Location	Forms	Inspection	Purpose
Charges (comprising copies of instruments creating and revising charges)	CA 2006 s 859P	Registered office or other location at which the company keeps records available for inspection (CA 2006 s 1136) as notified to Registrar (CA 2006 s 743).	Form MR01 and a certified copy of the instrument creating the charge.	(i) Must be available for inspection by any member or creditor without charge while other persons may inspect on payment of fee (CA 2006 s 859Q(4)).	• Accounts and for credit reference purposes
Minute book for minutes of meetings of the directors	CA 2006 s 248	No statutory requirement, would usually be kept at registered or main operating office.	None	(i) Auditors have rights to inspect minutes (CA 1995 s 237 for financial years commencing before 6 April 2008 and CA 2006 s 499 for financial years commencing on or after 6 April 2008).	• Audit and as a formal record of business conducted
Minute book for general meeting minutes	CA 2006 s 355	Registered office or other location at which the company keeps records available for inspection (CA 2006 s 1136) as notified to Registrar (CA 2006 s 358).	Notice of location is required unless kept at the registered office (CA 2006 s 358(2)).	(i) Must be available for inspection by members and auditors without charges. (ii) Supply a copy to members on request and may charge a prescribed fee.	• Audit • Formal record of business conducted and resolutions passed

Appendix 5 Inspection of company records

Company records required to be kept available for inspection include:

- Register of Members (subject to the proper purpose test);
- Register of Directors;
- directors' service contracts;
- directors' indemnities;
- Register of Secretaries;
- record of resolutions;
- contracts relating to purchase of own shares;
- documents relating to purchase/redemption shares out of capital (private company);
- Register of Interest in Shares (public company);
- report to members on outcome of investigation into interests in shares (public company);
- Register of debenture-holders;
- Every instrument creating, amending or varying a charge.

1 Right to inspect company records

A company's records (and any index) must be open and available for inspection by any member of the company without charge, and to any other person on payment of the prescribed fee.

The Companies (Company Records) Regulations 2008 (SI 2008/3006) state that a private company must make its company records available for inspection on any working day for a period of at least two hours upon request, provided either:

(i) Two days' notice is received where the company has issued notice of a general meeting or class meeting, or a written resolution is in circulation; or

(ii) Ten days' notice is received in all other cases.

A public company must make its records available for inspection for at least two hours each working day, between the hours of 9am to 5pm.

The company is not, however, required to change the order or manner in which the information is recorded and, whilst the company must permit a person to make a copy of the record being inspected, it is not required to assist the person doing so.

2 Request for copies of company records

A company must provide a copy of a company record in hard copy form when requested to do so, but is not required to reorder or change the format of that record in any way. When a request for an electronic copy is received, the company must comply with the request but can choose the electronic form in which this is provided. If, however, the records are not kept electronically then a request for an electronic copy can be declined.

3 Prescribed fee

Inspection

The prescribed fee is £3.50 per hour (Companies (Fees for Inspection and Copying of Company Records) (No 2) Regulations 2007 (SI 2007/3535) and the Company (Fees for Inspection of Company Records) Regulations 2008 (SI 2008/3007)).

Copy

The company may charge a prescribed fee for supplying copies of registers as prescribed in the Companies (Fees for Inspection and Copying of Company Records) Regulations 2007 (SI 2007/2612) and Companies (Fees for Inspection and Copying of Company Records) (No 2) Regulations 2007 (SI 2007/3535):

Register of Members, Register of Debentures and Register of Interest in Shares		
• Copies of each of the first five entries	–	£1.00
• Copies of next 95 entries (or part)	–	£30.00
• Copies of next 900 entries thereafter	–	£30.00
• Copies of next 99,000 entries thereafter	–	£30.00
• Remainder of the entries	–	£30.00
• Reasonable costs incurred by the Company in delivering the copies		

Directors' Service Contracts or
Memorandum of Terms of Service

- Copies of each 500 words   –   £0.10 per word
- Reasonable costs incurred by the
  Company in delivering the copies

Appendix 6 Companies Act 2006: statutory forms and filing periods

Functional area	Form	Name of form	Time limit for filing
Accounts	**AA01**	Change of accounting reference date	14 days
	AA02	Dormant Company Accounts (DCA)	
	AA03	Notice of resolution removing auditors from office	14 days
Administration restoration	**RT01**	Application for administrative restoration to the Register	
Annual Return	**AR01**	Annual Return	28 days
	AD02	Notification of single alternative inspection location (SAIL)	14 days
	AD03	Change of location of the company records to the single alternative inspection location (SAIL)	14 days
	AD04	Change of location of the company records to the registered office	14 days
Change of constitution	**CC01**	Notice of restriction on the company's articles	15 days
	CC02	Notice of removal of restriction on the company's articles	15 days
	CC03	Statement of compliance where amendment of articles restricted	15 days

Functional area	Form	Name of form	Time limit for filing
Change of constitution	**CC04**	Statement of company's objects	15 days
	CC05	Change of constitution by enactment	15 days
	CC06	Change of constitution by order of court or other authority	15 days
Change of name	**NE01**	Exemption from requirement as to use of 'limited' or 'cyfyngedig' on change of name	Required with form IN01
	NM01	Notice of change of name by resolution	15 days
	NM02	Notice of change of name by conditional resolution	15 days of the resolution
	NM03	Notice confirming satisfaction of the conditional resolution for change of name	On fulfilment of the condition
	NM04	Notice of change of name by means provided for in the articles	–
	NM05	Notice of change of name by resolution of directors	–
	NM06	Request to seek comments of government department or other specified body on change of name	
Change of registered office	**AD01**	Change of registered office address	14 days
	AD05	Notice to change the situation of an England and Wales company or a Welsh company	14 days
Directors and secretaries	**AP01**	Appointment of director	14 days
	AP02	Appointment of corporate director	14 days
	AP03	Appointment of secretary	14 days

Functional area	Form	Name of form	Time limit for filing
Directors and secretaries	AP04	Appointment of corporate secretary	14 days
	TM01	Termination of appointment of director	14 days
	TM02	Termination of appointment of secretary	14 days
	CH01	Change of director's details	14 days
	CH02	Change of corporate director's details	14 days
	CH03	Change of secretary's details	14 days
	CH04	Change of corporate secretary's details	14 days
Dissolution	DS01	Striking off application by a company	–
	DS02	Withdrawal of striking-off application by a company	–
Incorporation	IN01	Application to register a company	–
Investment companies	IC01	Notice of intention to carry on business as an investment company	–
	IC02	Notice that a company no longer wishes to be an investment company	–
Liquidation	LQ01	Notice of appointment of an administrative receiver, receiver or manager	7 days
	LQ02	Notice of ceasing to act as an administrative receiver, receiver or manager	On ceasing
Mortgage	MR01	Particulars of a mortgage or charge	21 days
	MR02	Particulars of a mortgage or charge subject to which property or undertaking has been acquired	21 days
	MR03	Particulars for the registration of a charge to secure a series of debentures	21 days

Functional area	Form	Name of form	Time limit for filing
Mortgage	**MR04**	Statement of satisfaction in full or in part of mortgage or charge	21 days
	MR05	Statement that part or the whole of the property charged (a) has been released from the charge (b) no longer forms part of the company's property	21 days
	MR06	Statement of company acting as trustee	21 days
	MR07	Particulars of alteration of a charge	21 days
	MR08	Particulars of charge where no instrument	21 days
	MR09	Particulars of a charge subject to which property or undertaking has been acquired and where no instrument	21 days
	MR10	Particulars for the registration of a charge to secure a series of debentures where no instrument	21 days
Opening of overseas branch register	**AD06**	Notice of opening of overseas branch register	14 days
	AD07	Notice of discontinuance of overseas branch register	14 days
Other appointments	**AP05**	Appointment of a manager under s 47 of the Companies (Audit, Investigations and Community Enterprise) Act 2004 or receiver and manager under s 18 of the Charities Act 1993 or judicial factor (Scotland)	

Functional area	Form	Name of form	Time limit for filing
Other appointments	**TM03**	Termination of appointment of manager under s 47 of the Companies (Audit, Investigations and Community Enterprise) Act 2004 or receiver and manager under s 18 of the Charities Act 1993 or judicial factor (Scotland)	
	CH05	Change of service address for manager appointed under s 47 of the Companies (Audit, Investigations and Community Enterprise) Act 2004 or receiver and manager under s 18 of the Charities Act 1993 or judicial factor (Scotland)	
Registrars powers	**RP01**	Replacement of document not meeting requirements for proper delivery	–
	RP02A	Application for rectification by the Registrar of Companies	–
	RP02B	Application for rectification of a registered office or a UK establishment address by the Registrar of Companies	–
	RP03	Notice of an objection to a request for the Registrar of Companies to rectify the Register	28 days of the notice being issued by the Registrar
	RP04	Second filing of a document previously delivered	–
	VT01	Certified voluntary translation of an original document that is or has been delivered to the Registrar of Companies	–

Functional area	Form	Name of form	Time limit for filing
Re-registration	**RR01**	Application by a private company for re-registration as a public company	15 days
	RR02	Application by a public company for re-registration as a private limited company	15 days
	RR03	Notice by the company of application to the court for cancellation of resolution for re-registration	15 days
	RR04	Notice by the applicants of application to the court for cancellation of resolution for re-registration	On notice
	RR05	Application by a private limited company for re-registration as an unlimited company	15 days
	RR06	Application by an unlimited company for re-registration as a private limited company	15 days
	RR07	Application by a public company for re-registration as a private unlimited company	15 days
	RR08	Application by a public company for re-registration as a private limited company following a court order reducing capital	On instruction from Court
	RR09	Application by a public company for re-registration as a private company following a cancellation of shares	15 days

Functional area	Form	Name of form	Time limit for filing
Share capital	**SH01**	Return of allotment of shares	1 month
	SH02	Notice of consolidation, sub-division, redemption of shares or re-conversion of stock into shares	1 month
	SH03	Return of purchase of own shares	28 days
	SH04	Notice of sale or transfer of treasury shares by a public limited company (PLC)	28 days
	SH05	Notice of cancellation of treasury shares by a public limited company (PLC)	28 days
	SH06	Notice of cancellation of shares	28 days
	SH07	Notice of cancellation of shares held by or for a public company	1 month
	SH08	Notice of name or other designation of class of shares	1 month
	SH09	Return of allotment by an unlimited company allotting new class of shares	1 month
	SH10	Notice of particulars of variation of rights attached to shares	1 month
	SH11	Notice of new class of members	1 month
	SH12	Notice of particulars of variation of class rights	1 month
	SH13	Notice of name or other designation of class of members	1 month
	SH14	Notice of redenomination	1 month
	SH15	Notice of reduction of capital following redenomination	15 days

Functional area	Form	Name of form	Time limit for filing
Share capital	SH16	Notice by the applicants of application to court for cancellation of the special resolution approving a redemption or purchase of shares out of capital	15 days
	SH17	Notice by the company of application to court for cancellation of the special resolution approving a redemption or purchase of shares out of capital	15 days
	SH19	Statement of capital (ss 644 & 649)	15 days
	SH19	Statement of capital (s 108)	15 days
	SH50	Application for trading certificate for a public company	No limit but application must be made before the company is permitted to commence trading
Scottish mortgage	466	Particulars of an instrument of alteration to a floating charge created by a company registered in Scotland	–

Overseas companies

Functional area	Form	Name of form	Time limit for filing
Overseas companies	OS IN01	Registration of an overseas company opening a UK establishment	1 month
	OS NM01	Registration of change of name of overseas company as registered in the UK	Within 21 days of receipt of notice of change in UK

Functional area	Form	Name of form	Time limit for filing
Overseas companies	**OS CC01**	Return by an overseas company of an alteration to constitutional documents	Within 21 days of receipt of notice of change in UK
	OS CC02	Return by an overseas company of change of UK establishment relating to constitutional documents	Within 21 days of receipt of notice of change in UK
	OS AA01	Statement of details of parent law and other information for and overseas company	21 days
	OS AA02	Return of alteration of manner of compliance with accounting requirements	Within 21 days of receipt of notice of change in UK
	OS AD02	Notice of location, or change in location, of instruments creating charges and register of charges for an overseas company	14 days
	OS AP01	Appointment of director of an overseas company	21 days
	OS AP02	Appointment of corporate director of an overseas company	21 days
	OS AP03	Appointment of secretary of an overseas company	21 days
	OS AP04	Appointment of corporate secretary of an overseas company	21 days
	OS AP05	Appointment by an overseas company of a person authorised to represent the company as a permanent representative in respect of a UK establishment	21 days
	OS AP06	Appointment of a judicial factor (Scotland) for an overseas company	14 days

Functional area	Form	Name of form	Time limit for filing
Overseas companies	**OS AP07**	Appointment by an overseas company of a person authorised to accept service of documents on behalf of the company in respect of a UK establishment	21 days
	OS TM01	Termination of appointment of director of an overseas company	21 days
	OS TM02	Termination of appointment of secretary of an overseas company	21 days
	OS TM03	Termination of appointment by an overseas company of a person authorised to accept service of documents or person authorised to represent the company in respect of a UK establishment	21 days
	OS TM04	Termination of appointment of judicial factor (Scotland) of an overseas company	14 days
	OS CH01	Return by a UK establishment of an overseas company for change of details	21 days
	OS CH02	Return by an overseas company for a change of company details	21 days
	OS CH03	Change of details of a director of an overseas company	21 days
	OS CH04	Change of details of a corporate director of an overseas company	21 days
	OS CH05	Change of details of a secretary of an overseas company	21 days

Functional area	Form	Name of form	Time limit for filing
Overseas companies	**OS CH06**	Change of details of a corporate secretary of an overseas company	21 days
	OS CH07	Change of details by an overseas company for a person authorised to represent the company in respect of a UK establishment	21 days
	OS CH08	Change of service address for a judicial factor (Scotland) of an overseas company	14 days
	OS CH09	Change of details by an overseas company for a person authorised to accept service of documents on behalf of the company in respect of a UK establishment	21 days
	OS DS01	Notice of closure of a UK establishment of an overseas company	Forthwith
	OS DS02	Notice of termination of winding-up of an overseas company	14 days
	OS LQ01	Notice of appointment of a liquidator of an overseas company	14 days
	OS LQ02	Notice by an overseas company which becomes subject to proceedings relating to insolvency	1. One month if began before registration of UK Establishment 2. 14 days if when UK Establishment registered

Functional area	Form	Name of form	Time limit for filing
Overseas companies	**OS LQ03**	Notice of winding-up of an overseas company	1. One month if began before registration of UK Establishment 2. 14 days if when UK Establishment registered
	OS LQ04	Notice by an overseas company on cessation of proceedings relating to insolvency	14 days
	OS MG01	Particulars of a mortgage or charge by an overseas company	21 days from creation or if outside UK, 21 days from receipt of notice in UK
	OS MG02	Statement of satisfaction in full or in part of a mortgage or charge for an overseas company	–
	OS MG03	Application for registration of a memorandum of satisfaction that part (or the whole) of the property charged (a) has been released from the charge; (b) no longer forms part of the company's property, for an overseas company	–
	OS MG04	Particulars for the registration of a charge to secure a series of debentures for an overseas company	21 days
	OS MG05	Particulars of an issue of secured debentures in a series for an overseas company	21 days

Functional area	Form	Name of form	Time limit for filing
Overseas companies	**OS TN01**	Transitional return by a UK establishment of an overseas company	–

Appendix 7   Schedule of recommended retention periods

Note: recommendations are based upon statutory requirements and principles of best practice for commercial and damage limitation reasons.

Type of document	Statutory minimum retention period	Recommended period of retention
Incorporation documents		
Certificate of Incorporation and certificates on change of name	N/A	Permanently
Certificate to commence business (public company)	N/A	Permanently
Memorandum and Articles of Association (originals and updated copies)	Permanently	Permanently
Printed copy of resolutions submitted to Companies House	Permanently	Permanently
Statutory returns, records and registers		
Annual return (copy)	N/A	At least three years (original at Companies House)
Return of allotments (copy)	N/A	At least three years (original filed at Companies House)
Directors' service contracts	One year after cessation for purpose of inspection	Six years after cessation
Register of directors and secretaries (original)	Permanently	Permanently
Register of directors' residential addresses	Permanently	Permanently

Type of document	Statutory minimum retention period	Recommended period of retention
Register of directors' interests in shares and debentures	Permanently	Permanently
Register of directors' declarations of interest	Ten years after the date of the meeting at which declaration is made	Life of company
Register of interests in voting shares	Permanently	Permanently
Register of charges	Permanently	Permanently
Register of documents sealed (if applicable)	N/A	Permanently
Share registration documents		
Register of members	Permanently	Permanently
Register of debenture and loan stock holders	N/A	Permanently/seven years after redemption of stock
Letters and forms applying for shares, debentures, etc	3.6 years	12 years from issue, with a permanent microfilmed record
Renounced letters of allotment and acceptances	3.6 years	Originals for 12 years from renunciation, with a permanent microfilmed record
Renounced share certificates	N/A	As above
Contracts for purchase of own shares by company	Ten years from the date of purchase of shares	Ten years from the date of purchase of shares
Share and stock transfer forms and letters of request	N/A	20 years after date of transfer, with permanent microfilmed record
Requests for designating or redesignating accounts	N/A	20 years after request, with permanent microfilmed record
Cancelled share/stock certificate	N/A	One year from date of cancellation

Type of document	Statutory minimum retention period	Recommended period of retention
Stop notices and other court orders	N/A	Up to 20 years after order ceasing to be valid
Letters of indemnity for lost certificates	N/A	Permanently
Powers of attorney	N/A	12 years after ceasing to be valid
Dividend and interest payment lists	Three years for a private company or six years for a public company after the audit	Three to six years after audit of the dividend payment
Paid dividend and interest warrants	Three years for a private company or six years for a public company after the audit	Six years after date of payment
Unpaid dividend records	N/A	12 years after dividend declared
Dividend and interest mandate forms	N/A	Six years from when the instruction ceased to be valid
Notification of address change by member	N/A	Two years after notification
Copy of notification for change of name of member	N/A	20 years
Trust deed securing issue of debentures or loan stock	N/A	12 years after stock redeemed
Meetings (Board, committees, general and class)		
Minutes	Ten years after the date of the meeting	Life of company
Written resolutions	Ten years after the date of the resolution	Life of company
Agenda and meeting papers	N/A	Life of company
Notices and circulars	N/A	Life of company

Type of document	Statutory minimum retention period	Recommended period of retention
● proxy forms		
● no poll	N/A	One month after meeting
● poll vote	N/A	One year after meeting (or as directed by court)
Accounting and tax records		
Accounting records (as required by CA 2006 s 388)		
● public limited company	Six years	Ten years
● private limited company	Three years	Ten years
Annual report and accounts (signed)	N/A	Permanently
Annual report and accounts (unsigned)	N/A	Permanently (keep sufficient copies to meet requests)
Interim report and accounts	N/A	Permanently (as above)
Budgets, forecasts and periodic internal financial reports	N/A	Six years
Corporation tax records and tax returns	Inspection possible up to six years after tax/accounting period	Permanently
VAT records and Customs & Excise returns	Inspection may be conducted up to six years after period	Permanently
PAYE records	Three years after end of tax year (payroll records six years after period or expiry of contract)	Permanently
Expense accounts	N/A	Six years
Customer due diligence and verification of identity documents	Five years from date business relationship ends	Ten years from date business relationship ends

Type of document	Statutory minimum retention period	Recommended period of retention
Bank records		
Cheques, bills of exchange and other negotiable instruments		
• public limited company	Six years	Six years
• private limited company	Three years	Three years
Paying-in counterfoils		
• public limited company	Six years	Six years
• private limited company	Three years	Three years
Statements from and instructions to bank		
• public limited company	Six years	Six years after ceasing to be effective
• private limited company	Three years	Three years after ceasing to be effective
Charity donation documents		
Deeds of Covenant	Six years after last payment	12 years after last payment
Documents supporting entries in accounts for donations	Three or six years	Six years
Contracts		
Contracts executed as a deed	N/A	12 years after performance/expiry
Contracts with customers, suppliers, agents or others	N/A	Six years after expiry or contract completion
Rental and hire purchase agreements	N/A	Six years after expiry
Licensing agreements	N/A	Six years after expiry
Contracts relating to building works, maintenance or repairs	N/A	15 years after performance
Employee records		
Job applications and interview records (for unsuccessful candidates)	N/A	Three months to one year after notifying unsuccessful candidate

Type of document	Statutory minimum retention period	Recommended period of retention
Contracts of employment and changes to terms	N/A	Six years after employment ceases for a public company and three years for a private company
Personnel records	N/A	Six years after employment ceases
Senior executive records	N/A	Permanently
Training records	N/A	Six years after employment ceases
Employment agreements	N/A	Permanently
Payroll and wage records (including details on overtime, bonuses and expenses)	Six years	12 years
Salary records	Six years	Six years
Working Time Directive opt-out forms	Two years after opt-out entered into	Permanently
Time records/cards and piecework records	N/A	Two years after audit
Annual leave records	N/A	Six years or longer if able to carry forward
Maternity leave and payment records	Three years after end of tax year in which maternity pay period ends	Duration of employment or three years after end of tax year in which maternity pay period ends if later
Sick leave and payment records	Three years after end of tax year in which payments made	Duration of employment or three years after end of tax year in which payments made if later
Details of benefits in kind	Six years	12 years
Income tax records (P45, P60, P58, P48, etc)	Three years after the end of the tax year to which they relate	12 years

Type of document	Statutory minimum retention period	Recommended period of retention
Annual return of taxable pay and tax paid	Three years after the end of the tax year to which they relate	12 years
Labour agreements	N/A	Ten years after ceasing to be effective
Works council minutes	N/A	Permanently
Consents to the processing of personal and sensitive data	Six years after processing ceases	Six years after processing ceases
Disclosure and Barring Service (DBS) checks and disclosures of criminal records forms	Delete on completion of recruitment process unless relevant to ongoing employment. Delete when conviction spent unless in an excluded profession	Delete on completion of recruitment process unless relevant to ongoing employment. Delete when conviction spent unless in an excluded profession
Immigration checks	Two years after employment ceases	Two years after employment ceases
Employee records from closed units	Some six years	12 years
Health and safety		
Record of consultations and other communications with employees and safety representatives under the Health & Safety (Consultation with Employees) Regulations 1996 and under the Safety Representatives and Safety Committees Regulations 1977	50 years	Permanently
Health and safety policy documents (old and revised copies)	Implied permanently by Health & Safety at Work, etc Act 1994 s 2(3)	Permanently

Type of document	Statutory minimum retention period	Recommended period of retention
Assessment of risks under health and safety regulations (including routine assessment, monitoring and maintenance records for aspects in workplace such as air quality, levels of pollution, noise level, use of hazardous substances, etc)	Management of Health & Safety at Work Regulations 1992	Permanently (old and current copies)
Accident report book and relevant records/ correspondence	Three years from date of last entry (Health & Safety at Work, etc Act 1994 s 7 and The Reporting of Injuries, Diseases and Dangerous Occurrences Regulations 1995 (RIDDOR) (SI 1995/3163 as amended)	Permanently
Medical records (generally):	N/A	12 years
• Radiation accident assessment	50 years	Permanently
• Radiation dosage summary	Two years from end of calendar year	Permanently
• Under Control of Lead at Work Regulations 1998 (replaced 1990 regulations) as amended by the Control of Lead at Work Regulations 2002	40 years from date of last entry to be effective	Permanently
• Under Control of Asbestos at Work Regulations 2002 and the Control of Asbestos Regulations 2006	40 years from date of last entry	Permanently

Type of document	Statutory minimum retention period	Recommended period of retention
● Under Control of Substances Hazardous to Health Regulations 1999 and 2002 (COSHH Regulations)	40 years from date of last entry	Permanently
● Under the Ionising Radiations Regulations 1999	Until the person reaches 75 years of age, but in any event for at least 50 years	Permanently
Insurance		
Public liability policies	N/A	Permanently
Product liability policies	N/A	Permanently
Employers' liability policies	40 years	Permanently
Sundry insurance policies and insurance schedules	N/A	Until claims under policy are barred or three years after policy lapses, whichever is longer
Group health policies	N/A	12 years after final cessation of benefit
Group personal accident policies	N/A	12 years after final cessation of benefit
Claims correspondence	N/A	Seven years after settlement
Intellectual property records		
Certificates of registration of trade/service marks (current and lapsed)	N/A	Permanently or six years after cessation of registration
Documents evidencing assignment of trade/service marks	N/A	Six years after cessation of registration
Patent licences	N/A	Six years after period of licence or life of patent plus six years
Intellectual property agreements and licences	N/A	Six or 12 years after expiry

Type of document	Statutory minimum retention period	Recommended period of retention
Material with copyright protection:		
• Literary, dramatic and musical works	N/A	Life plus 50 years
• Artistic works, recordings, films, photos and broadcasts	N/A	50 years
Pension scheme documents (unapproved schemes)		
Trust deeds and scheme rules	N/A	Permanently for life of scheme
Trustee's minute books	N/A	Permanently for life of scheme
Record of pensioners	N/A	12 years after cessation of benefit
Money purchase details	N/A	Six years after transfer or value taken
Pension scheme investment policies	N/A	12 years after cessation of benefit payable
Pension scheme documents (HMRC-approved and statutory pension schemes)		
Pension fund accounts and supporting documents (including details of monies received, investments and assets, payments made, contracts to purchase lifetime annuities and documents concerning administration of the scheme)	For the tax year to which they relate and six following tax years	Permanently
Actuarial valuation reports	Six years from date report signed	Permanently
HMRC approvals	N/A	Permanently for life of scheme

Type of document	Statutory minimum retention period	Recommended period of retention
Property documents		
Title deeds for property	N/A	Permanently or until sold or transferred
Leases (signed copies)	N/A	15 years after lease and liabilities under the lease have terminated
Licences (signed copies)	N/A	15 years after surrender, expiry or termination
Subletting agreements (signed copies)	N/A	12 years after expiry or termination

Appendix 8 Retention and disposal of records

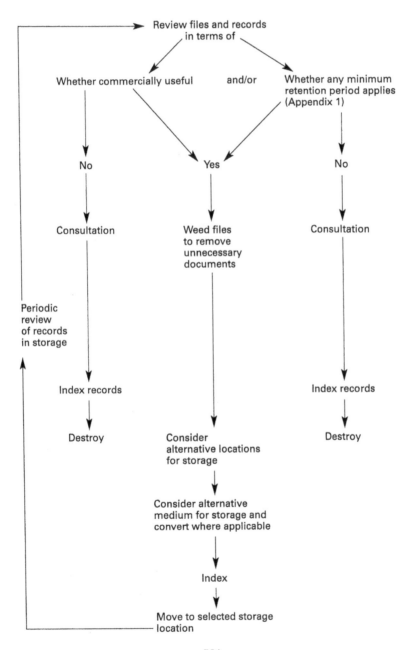

Review files and records in terms of

Whether commercially useful   and/or   Whether any minimum retention period applies (Appendix 1)

No   Yes   No

Consultation   Weed files to remove unnecessary documents   Consultation

Periodic review of records in storage

Index records   Index records

Destroy   Consider alternative locations for storage   Destroy

Consider alternative medium for storage and convert where applicable

Index

Move to selected storage location

Appendix 9   General notice by director of interest in any contract of the company

The Board of Directors

Date: [......]

Dear Sirs

I hereby give notice, pursuant to section 1.7 (duty to declare interest in proposed transaction or arrangement) *or* s 1.2 (declaration of interest in an existing transaction or arrangement) of the Companies Act 2006 **and** [Article [......] of the Company's Articles of Association (for use if the company is a plc)] *or* to Ordinary Resolution passed by the members of the Company on (......)], that I am to be regarded as interested in any contract which may, after the date hereof, be made with any of the under-mentioned companies and firms:

Name of company/firm

Details of interest

Yours faithfully

Director

Appendix 10 Minute recording a director's disclosure of interest

The operations director reported that negotiations had commenced with [......] Limited with a view to them becoming an approved supplier and placing a substantial order for the purchase of [......] from them. At this point, Mr [......] formally declared an interest in the matter by virtue of being a director of [......] Limited. Such interest was duly noted by the board and it was agreed that, by virtue of his interest and in terms of the Companies Act and the Articles of Association of the Company, Mr [......] would not be counted in the quorum present at any meeting or part of any meeting when contract terms or arrangements with [......] Limited were under consideration nor would he be permitted to vote on any resolution to approve or amend the proposed contract.

Appendix 11   Extract from Regulation 5 of the Consumer Protection from Unfair Trading Regulations 2008

(4) The matters referred to in paragraph (2)(a) are:

(a)   the existence or nature of the product;

(b)   the main characteristics of the product (as defined in paragraph 5);

(c)   the extent of the trader's commitments;

(d)   the motives for the commercial practice;

(e)   the nature of the sales process;

(f)   any statement or symbol relating to direct or indirect sponsorship or approval of the trader or the product;

(g)   the price or the manner in which the price is calculated;

(h)   the existence of a specific price advantage;

(i)   the need for a service, part, replacement or repair;

(j)   the nature, attributes and rights of the trader (as defined in paragraph 6);

(k)   the consumer's rights or the risks he may face.

(5) In paragraph (4)(b), the 'main characteristics of the product' include:

(a)   availability of the product;

(b)   benefits of the product;

(c)   risks of the product;

(d)   execution of the product;

(e)   composition of the product;

(f)   accessories of the product;

(g)   after-sale customer assistance concerning the product;

(h)　the handling of complaints about the product;

(i)　the method and date of manufacture of the product;

(j)　the method and date of provision of the product;

(k)　delivery of the product;

(l)　fitness for purpose of the product;

(m)　usage of the product;

(n)　quantity of the product;

(o)　specification of the product;

(p)　geographical or commercial origin of the product;

(q)　results to be expected from use of the product; and

(r)　results and material features of tests or checks carried out on the product.

(6) In paragraph (4)(j), the 'nature, attributes and rights' as far as concern the trader include the trader's:

(a)　identity;

(b)　assets;

(c)　qualifications;

(d)　status;

(e)　approval;

(f)　affiliations or connections;

(g)　ownership of industrial, commercial or intellectual property rights; and

(h)　awards and distinctions.

(7) In paragraph (4)(k) 'consumer's rights' include rights the consumer may have under Part 5A of the Sale of Goods Act 1979 or Part 1B of the Supply of Goods and Services Act 1982.

Appendix 12   Directors' responsibilities: statement for a non-publicly traded company preparing financial statements under UK GAAP

Directors' Responsibilities Statement

The directors are responsible for preparing the Directors' Report and the financial statements in accordance with applicable law and regulations.

Company law requires the directors to prepare financial statements for each financial year. Under that law the directors have elected to prepare the financial statements in accordance with United Kingdom Generally Accepted Accounting Practice (United Kingdom Accounting Standards and applicable law) ('UK GAAP'). Under company law the directors must not approve the financial statements unless they are satisfied that they give a true and fair view of the state of affairs of the company and the profit or loss of the company for that period.

In preparing these financial statements, the directors are required to:

- select suitable accounting policies and then apply them consistently;

- make judgments and accounting estimates that are reasonable and prudent;

- state whether applicable UK Accounting Standards have been followed, subject to any material departures disclosed and explained in the financial statements [save that small and medium-sized companies do not have to state this];

- prepare the financial statements on the going concern basis unless it is inappropriate to presume that the company will continue in business [not needed if a separate statement on going concern is made by the directors].

The directors are responsible for keeping adequate accounting records that are sufficient to show and explain the company's transactions and disclose with reasonable accuracy at any time the financial position of the company and enable them to ensure that the financial statements comply with the Companies Act 2006. They are also responsible for safeguarding the assets of the company and hence for taking reasonable steps for the prevention and detection of fraud and other irregularities.

Each of the directors whose names and roles are listed on pages *[......]* to *[......]* confirm that to the best of his and her knowledge:

- the financial statements, prepared in accordance with UK GAAP, give a true and fair view of the assets, liabilities, financial position and profit or loss of the company; and

- the directors' report includes a fair review of the development and performance of the business and the position of the company together with a description of the principal risks and uncertainties that it faces.

By Order of the Board [*Name, title, signature and date*]

Appendix 13 Summary of companies' accounts filing obligations

Type/size of company	Required information	Comments
Very small 'micro-entity' (accounts prepared under small companies regime and qualifying under micro-entities regime – App 14)	● abridged balance sheet	● must be delivered ● inclusion of an abridged profit and loss account, directors' report, audit report (unless exempt) and abbreviated notes to the accounts is optional or can claim small company exemption (below)
Small (qualifying under small companies regime – App 14)	● balance sheet ● audit report (unless exempt) ● directors' report ● notes to accounts (abbreviated)	● inclusion of the profit and loss account is optional ● where a profit and loss account is not included, the balance sheet must state they are 'abbreviated accounts' prepared under small companies regime
Small (entitled to small companies directors' report exemption)	● balance sheet ● profit and loss account	● inclusion of a directors' report is optional

Type/size of company	Required information	Comments
	● audit report (unless exempt)	
Medium-sized (qualifying under medium-sized companies regime – App 14)	● balance sheet ● profit and loss account (abbreviated) ● directors' report (including business review/ strategic report (see para 7.13.3)) ● audit report (unless exempt) ● notes to accounts (abbreviated)	–
Unquoted	● balance sheet ● profit and loss account ● directors' report (including business review/ strategic report (see para 7.13.3)) ● audit report (unless exempt) ● notes to accounts	–
Quoted	● balance sheet ● profit and loss account ● directors' report (including business review/ strategic report (see para 7.13.3))	–

Type/size of company	Required information	Comments
	<ul><li>directors' remuneration report</li><li>SCGS</li><li>Audit report</li><li>Notes to accounts</li></ul>	
Unlimited	N/A	<ul><li>in most circumstances, no requirement to deliver annual report and accounts</li></ul>
Dormant	<ul><li>dormant company accounts comprising a balance sheet and statement from the directors confirming reliance on the dormant company exemptions</li></ul>	<ul><li>might be able to use Companies House form AA02 to constitute the dormant company accounts</li></ul>

Appendix 14 Qualification as a very small, small or medium-sized group or company

A very small (micro-entity), small or medium-sized *company* is one that meets at least two of the following conditions (CA 2006 ss 382(2), 383(3), 465(2) or 466(3); and Companies Act 2006 (Amendment) (Accounts and Reports) Regulations 2008) and the Small Companies (Micro-Entities Accounts) Regulations 2003 (SI 2013/3008):

Condition (not more than)	Micro-entity	Small company	Medium company
● Annual turnover	£632,000	£6.5 million	£25.9 million
● Balance sheet total	£316,000	£3.26 million	£12.9 million
● Average number of employees	10	50	250

A *group* qualifies as small or medium-sized where it satisfies two or more of the following requirements:

Condition (not more than)	Small group	Medium group
● Aggregate turnover	£6.5 million net (£7.8 million gross)	£25.9 million net (£31.1 million gross)
● Aggregate balance sheet total	£3.26 million net (£3.9 million gross)	£12.9 million net (£15.5 million gross)
● Aggregate number of employees	50	250

Appendix 15 Consumer Protection from Unfair Trading Regulations 2008 Schedule 1 Regulation 3(4)(d)

SCHEDULE 1 Regulation 3(4)(d)

Commercial practices which are in all circumstances considered unfair

1   Claiming to be a signatory to a code of conduct when the trader is not.

2   Displaying a trust mark, quality mark or equivalent without having obtained the necessary authorisation.

3   Claiming that a code of conduct has an endorsement from a public or other body which it does not have.

4   Claiming that a trader (including his commercial practices) or a product has been approved, endorsed or authorised by a public or private body when the trader, the commercial practices or the product have not or making such a claim without complying with the terms of the approval, endorsement or authorisation.

5   Making an invitation to purchase products at a specified price without disclosing the existence of any reasonable grounds the trader may have for believing that he will not be able to offer for supply, or to procure another trader to supply, those products or equivalent products at that price for a period that is, and in quantities that are, reasonable having regard to the product, the scale of advertising of the product and the price offered (bait advertising).

6   Making an invitation to purchase products at a specified price and then—

   (a)   refusing to show the advertised item to consumers,

   (b)   refusing to take orders for it or deliver it within a reasonable time, or

   (c)   demonstrating a defective sample of it,

   with the intention of promoting a different product (bait and switch).

7   Falsely stating that a product will only be available for a very limited time, or that it will only be available on particular terms for a very limited

time, in order to elicit an immediate decision and deprive consumers of sufficient opportunity or time to make an informed choice.

8 Undertaking to provide after-sales service to consumers with whom the trader has communicated prior to a transaction in a language which is not an official language of the EEA State where the trader is located and then making such service available only in another language without clearly disclosing this to the consumer before the consumer is committed to the transaction.

9 Stating or otherwise creating the impression that a product can legally be sold when it cannot.

10 Presenting rights given to consumers in law as a distinctive feature of the trader's offer.

11 Using editorial content in the media to promote a product where a trader has paid for the promotion without making that clear in the content or by images or sounds clearly identifiable by the consumer (advertorial).

12 Making a materially inaccurate claim concerning the nature and extent of the risk to the personal security of the consumer or his family if the consumer does not purchase the product.

13 Promoting a product similar to a product made by a particular manufacturer in such a manner as deliberately to mislead the consumer into believing that the product is made by that same manufacturer when it is not.

14 Establishing, operating or promoting a pyramid promotional scheme where a consumer gives consideration for the opportunity to receive compensation that is derived primarily from the introduction of other consumers into the scheme rather than from the sale or consumption of products.

15 Claiming that the trader is about to cease trading or move premises when he is not.

16 Claiming that products are able to facilitate winning in games of chance.

17 Falsely claiming that a product is able to cure illnesses, dysfunction or malformations.

18 Passing on materially inaccurate information on market conditions or on the possibility of finding the product with the intention of inducing the consumer to acquire the product at conditions less favourable than normal market conditions.

19 Claiming in a commercial practice to offer a competition or prize promotion without awarding the prizes described or a reasonable equivalent.

20   Describing a product as 'gratis', 'free', 'without charge' or similar if the consumer has to pay anything other than the unavoidable cost of responding to the commercial practice and collecting or paying for delivery of the item.

21   Including in marketing material an invoice or similar document seeking payment which gives the consumer the impression that he has already ordered the marketed product when he has not.

22   Falsely claiming or creating the impression that the trader is not acting for purposes relating to his trade, business, craft or profession, or falsely representing oneself as a consumer.

23   Creating the false impression that after-sales service in relation to a product is available in an EEA State other than the one in which the product is sold.

24   Creating the impression that the consumer cannot leave the premises until a contract is formed.

25   Conducting personal visits to the consumer's home ignoring the consumer's request to leave or not to return, except in circumstances and to the extent justified to enforce a contractual obligation.

26   Making persistent and unwanted solicitations by telephone, fax, e-mail or other remote media except in circumstances and to the extent justified to enforce a contractual obligation.

27   Requiring a consumer who wishes to claim on an insurance policy to produce documents which could not reasonably be considered relevant as to whether the claim was valid, or failing systematically to respond to pertinent correspondence, in order to dissuade a consumer from exercising his contractual rights.

28   Including in an advertisement a direct exhortation to children to buy advertised products or persuade their parents or other adults to buy advertised products for them.

29   Demanding immediate or deferred payment for or the return or safekeeping of products supplied by the trader, but not solicited by the consumer, except where the product is a substitute supplied in accordance with regulation 19(7) of the Consumer Protection (Distance Selling) Regulations 2000 (inertia selling).

30   Explicitly informing a consumer that if he does not buy the product or service, the trader's job or livelihood will be in jeopardy.

31   Creating the false impression that the consumer has already won, will win, or will on doing a particular act win, a prize or other equivalent benefit, when in fact either—

(a)   there is no prize or other equivalent benefit, or

(b)   taking any action in relation to claiming the prize or other equivalent benefit is subject to the consumer paying money or incurring a cost.

Appendix 16 Wording of special resolution amending the Articles of Association of a private company to provide power to purchase own shares[1]

'**THAT** the Articles of Association of the Company be amended by the adoption of a new Article

[......] namely:

Subject to the provisions of Part 18 of the Companies Act 2006 the Company shall have power:

(1) Pursuant to sections 684 to 689 of that Act to issue shares which are to be redeemed or are liable to be redeemed at the option of the Company or the shareholder on such terms and in such manner as shall be provided by the Articles of the Company.

(2) Pursuant to sections 690 to 693 of that Act to purchase its own shares (including any redeemable shares).

(3) Pursuant to Chapter 5 of Part 18 of that Act to make a payment out of capital in respect of any such redemption or purchase.

Regulations 3 and 10 in Table A shall not apply to the Company.'[2]

---

1 Companies incorporated on or after 1 October 2009 are not required to insert specific permission into their Articles to enable the purchase of own shares. However, Articles must still be checked to ensure no prohibitions for the purchase of own shares exist.
2 This sentence should be included if the Company has adopted Regulations 3 and 10 of Table A set out in the Companies Act 1948.

Appendix 17   Notice of redemption of shares

Registered Office:

Date:

Dear Sir,

Redemption of preference shares in the capital of the company

In accordance with Article [ ] of the Articles of Association of the Company and pursuant to a resolution of the Board of Directors approved on [.........] 20 […], we hereby give notice of redemption of the whole of the [ ] Preference Shares of £1.00 each in the capital of the Company ('the Shares'). According to our records you are the registered holder of such shares.

The Shares will be repaid at par value in accordance with the terms of issue. Payment becomes due on [.........] 20[…] and to enable payment to be made on the due date, you are requested to complete the attached form and forward it to the secretary at the registered office of the Company, together with the appropriate share certificate(s), by no later than [.........] 20[…].

By Order of the Board

Secretary

Appendix 18　Summary of procedural requirements where resolutions of private companies are passed by written resolution

Procedure	Adaptation: documents to be supplied to members at or before time they receive the written resolution
● Disapplication of pre-emption rights (CA 2006 s 570)	− the written statement of directors required by CA 2006 s 571(7)(a) and described in para 8.11.1(3)
● Authority for off-market purchase of shares (CA 2006 s 693(1)(a))	− a copy of the contract of purchase or a written memorandum of its terms (CA 2006 s 694)
● Approval for payment for purchase of shares out of capital (CA 2006 s 709)	− the directors' statutory declaration and auditors' report required by CA 2006 s 714
● Approval of a director's service contract for more than two years (CA 2006 s 188)	− a written memorandum of the terms of the contract/agreement as required by CA 2006 s 188(5)
● Loans to directors in excess of £10.000 (CA 2006 ss 1.7 and 207)	− a written memorandum disclosing the nature of the transaction, amount of loan and its purpose and the extent of the Company's liability (CA 2006 s 197(4))
● Entering into a credit transaction, give a guarantee or provide security in connection with a credit transaction in respect of a director	− a written memorandum disclosing the nature of the transaction, value of the credit transaction its purpose and the extent of the Company's liability (CA 2006 s 201(5))

Appendix 19   Special notice to company of resolution to remove a director

The Board of Directors

[......] Limited

I hereby give notice pursuant to sections 168 and 312 of the Companies Act 2006 of my intention to propose the following resolution as an ordinary resolution at the next annual general meeting of the Company:

Resolution

THAT [......] be removed from the office of director of the Company forthwith.

Date:

Signature:

Full name:

Address:

Wording in notice to members of a resolution of which special notice has been given

To consider the following resolution which will be proposed as an ordinary resolution, special notice having been given to the Company pursuant to sections 168 and 312 of the Companies Act 2006.

Resolution

THAT [......] be removed from the office of director of the Company forthwith.

Date:

Signature

Appendix 20 Draft format for a written resolution

Number of Company:[.........]

The Companies Act 2006

Company limited by shares

Written resolution[s]
(pursuant to Section 296 of the Companies Act 2006)

[X] LIMITED
('the Company')

We, the undersigned, being [the sole] member[s] of the Company eligible to attend and vote at general meetings of the Company, hereby pass the following resolution[s] designated as [an ordinary] [a special] resolution[s] and agree that the said resolution[s] shall be as valid and effective as if it [they] had been passed at a general meeting of the Company duly convened and held.

Resolution[s]

1. **THAT** [*state wording*]

[2. **THAT** [*state wording*]]

Signed:

[Name]

[Date]

Notes:

1.   These written resolutions have been proposed by the directors of the Company. The purpose of these resolutions is [.........].

2.   The circulation date of these written resolutions is .... 20[...].

3.   Please signify your agreement to those resolutions which you do agree to by signing against your name where indicated, enter the date on which you signed the document and initial those boxes relating to the corresponding resolutions to which you agree. Please then return the document to the Company.

4.   If you sign the document and return it to the Company without indicating whether you agree to all the resolutions or any particular resolution being passed, it will be assumed by the Company that you agree to all of the resolutions being passed.

5.   If you return the document signed, but un–dated, it will be assumed by the Company that you signed the document on the day immediately preceding the day on which it was received by the Company.

6.   If not passed by the requisite majority of the total voting rights of eligible members, these written resolutions shall lapse on the .... 20[...].

7.   As the resolution is [an ordinary] [a special] resolution, the requisite majority needed to pass the resolution is a [simple majority] [three-fourths] of the total voting rights of eligible members.

8.   Once these resolutions have been signed and returned to the Company, your agreement to them may not be revoked.

THE CIRCULATION DATE OF THE RESOLUTION IS THE DATE ON WHICH THE RESOLUTION IS SENT TO MEMBERS, THE LAPSE DATE IS A DATE NOT MORE THAN 28 DAYS AFTER THIS DATE.

WHERE THE RESOLUTION IS AN ORDINARY RESOLUTION A SIMPLE MAJORITY OF THE TOTAL VOTING RIGHTS IS REQUIRED TO PASS THE RESOLUTION.

WHERE THE RESOLUTION IS A SPECIAL RESOLUTION A MAJORITY OF 75% IS REQUIRED TO PASS THE RESOLUTION.

IF PASSED A COPY OF THE RESOLUTION, SIGNED BY EITHER A DIRECTOR OR SECRETARY, MUST BE SUBMITTED TO THE REGISTRAR OF COMPANIES.

Appendix 21 Wording of a directors' responsibility statement

Disclosure and Transparency Rule 4.1.12 requires the declaration to be in the following form:

The Directors confirm that to the best of their knowledge:

(a) the financial statements, prepared in accordance with the applicable set of accounting standards, give a true and fair view of the assets, liabilities, financial position and profit or loss of the [*company name*] and the undertakings included in the consolidation taken as a whole; and

(b) the management report includes a fair review of the development and performance of the business and the position of the [*company name*] and the undertakings included in the consolidation taken as a whole, together with a description of the principal risks and uncertainties that they face.

Signed on behalf of the Board

[*signature*] ......

[*person's name*]

[*title*]

[*date*]

Appendix 22   FCA Handbook, LR 9 Annex 1, The Model Code (R)[1]

1   © Financial Conduct Authority. Reproduced with the kind permission of the FCA. For the full version of the Handbook please visit fshandbook.info/FS/html/FCA

This annex is referred to in LR 9.2 (Requirements with continuing application) and LR 15 (Investment entities).

	Introduction		
	This code imposes restrictions on dealing in the *securities* of a *listed company* beyond those imposed by law. Its purpose is to ensure that *persons discharging managerial responsibilities* do not abuse, and do not place themselves under suspicion of abusing, *inside information* that they may be thought to have, especially in periods leading up to an announcement of the *company's* results.		
	Nothing in this code sanctions a breach of section 118 of the *Act* (Market abuse), the insider dealing provisions of the Criminal Justice Act or any other relevant legal or regulatory requirements.		
	Definitions		
1	In this code the following definitions, in addition to those contained in the *listing rules*, apply unless the context requires otherwise:		
	(a)	*close period* means:	
		(i)	the period of 60 days immediately preceding a preliminary announcement of the *listed company's* annual results or, if shorter, the period from the end of the relevant financial year up to and including the time of announcement; or
		(ii)	the period of 60 days immediately preceding the publication of its annual financial report or if shorter the period from the end of the relevant financial year up to and including the time of such publication; and
		(iii)	if the *listed company* reports on a half yearly basis the period from the end of the relevant financial period up to and including the time of such publication; and

		(iv)	if the *listed company* reports on a quarterly basis the period of 30 days immediately preceding the announcement of the quarterly results or, if shorter, the period from the end of the relevant financial period up to and including the time of the announcement;
	(b)		*connected person* has the meaning given in section 96B (2) of the *Act* (Persons discharging managerial responsibilities and connected persons);
	(c)		dealing includes:
		(i)	any acquisition or disposal of, or agreement to acquire or dispose of any of the *securities* of the *company*;
		(ii)	entering into a contract (including a contract for difference) the purpose of which is to secure a profit or avoid a loss by reference to fluctuations in the price of any of the *securities* of the *company*;
		(iii)	the grant, acceptance, acquisition, disposal, exercise or discharge of any option (whether for the call, or put or both) to acquire or dispose of any of the *securities* of the *company*;
		(iv)	entering into, or terminating, assigning or novating any stock lending agreement in respect of the *securities* of the *company*;
		(v)	using as security, or otherwise granting a charge, lien or other encumbrance over the *securities* of the *company*;
		(vi)	any transaction, including a transfer for nil consideration, or the exercise of any power or discretion effecting a change of ownership of a beneficial interest in the *securities* of the *company*; or
		(vii)	any other right or obligation, present or future, conditional or unconditional, to acquire or dispose of any *securities* of the *company*;
	(d)		[deleted]
	(e)		*prohibited period* means:
		(i)	any *close period*; or
		(ii)	any period when there exists any matter which constitutes *inside information* in relation to the *company*;
	(f)		*restricted person* means a *person discharging managerial responsibilities*; and
	(g)		*securities* of the *company* means any publicly traded or quoted *securities* of the *company* or any member of its *group* or any securities that are convertible into such *securities*.

		Dealings not subject to the provisions of this code	
2		The following dealings are not subject to the provisions of this code:	
	(a)	undertakings or elections to take up entitlements under a rights issue or other offer (including an offer of *securities* of the *company* in lieu of a cash dividend);	
	(b)	the take up of entitlements under a rights issue or other offer (including an offer of *securities* of the *company* in lieu of a cash dividend);	
	(c)	allowing entitlements to lapse under a rights issue or other offer (including an offer of *securities* of the *company* in lieu of a cash dividend);	
	(d)	the sale of sufficient entitlements nil-paid to take up the balance of the entitlements under a rights issue;	
	(e)	undertakings to accept, or the acceptance of, a takeover offer;	
	(f)	dealing where the beneficial interest in the relevant *security* of the *company* does not change;	
	(g)	transactions conducted between a *person discharging managerial responsibilities* and their spouse, civil partner, child or step-child (within the meaning of section 96B(2) of the *Act*);	
	(h)	transfers of *shares* arising out of the operation of an *employees' share scheme* into a savings scheme investing in *securities* of the *company* following:	
		(i)	exercise of an option under an approved SAYE[1] option scheme; or
		(ii)	release of *shares* from a HM Revenue and Customs approved share incentive plan;
	(i)	with the exception of a disposal of *securities* of the *company* received by a restricted person as a participant, dealings in connection with the following *employees' share schemes*;	
		(i)	an HM Revenue and Customs approved SAYE option scheme or share incentive plan, under which participation is extended on similar terms to all or most employees of the participating *companies* in that scheme; or
		(ii)	a scheme on similar terms to a HM Revenue and Customs approved SAYE option scheme or share incentive plan, under which participation is extended on similar terms to all or most employees of the participating *companies* in that scheme; or
	(j)	the cancellation or surrender of an option under an *employees' share scheme*;	

	(k)	transfers of the *securities* of the *company* by an independent trustee of an *employees' share scheme* to a beneficiary who is not a restricted person;
	(l)	transfers of *securities* of the *company* already held by means of a matched sale and purchase into a saving scheme or into a pension scheme in which the restricted person is a participant or beneficiary;
	(m)	an investment by a restricted person in a scheme or arrangement where the assets of the scheme (other than a scheme investing only in the *securities* of the *company*) or arrangement are invested at the discretion of a third party;
	(n)	a dealing by a restricted person in the units of an authorised unit trust or in *shares* in an *open-ended investment company*; and
	(o)	bona fide gifts to a restricted person by a third party.
Dealing by restricted persons		
3	A restricted person must not deal in any *securities* of the *company* without obtaining clearance to deal in advance in accordance with paragraph 4 of this code.	
Clearance to deal		
4	(a)	A *director* (other than the chairman or chief executive) or company secretary must not deal in any *securities* of the *company* without first notifying the chairman (or a *director* designated by the board for this purpose) and receiving clearance to deal from him.
	(b)	The chairman must not deal in any *securities* of the *company* without first notifying the chief executive and receiving clearance to deal from him or, if the chief executive is not present, without first notifying the senior independent director, or a committee of the board or other officer of the *company* nominated for that purpose by the chief executive, and receiving clearance to deal from that director, committee or officer.
	(c)	The chief executive must not deal in any *securities* of the *company* without first notifying the chairman and receiving clearance to deal from him or, if the chairman is not present, without first notifying the senior independent director, or a committee of the board or other officer of the *company* nominated for that purpose by the chairman, and receiving clearance to deal from that director, committee or officer.

	(d)	If the role of chairman and chief executive are combined, that *person* must not deal in any *securities* of the *company* without first notifying the board and receiving clearance to deal from the board.
	(e)	*Persons discharging managerial responsibilities* (who are not *directors*) must not deal in any *securities* of the *company* without first notifying the company secretary or a designated *director* and receiving clearance to deal from him.
5	A response to a request for clearance to deal must be given to the relevant restricted person within five *business days* of the request being made.	
6	The *company* must maintain a record of the response to any dealing request made by a restricted person and of any clearance given. A copy of the response and clearance (if any) must be given to the restricted person concerned.	
7	A restricted person who is given clearance to deal in accordance with paragraph 4 must deal as soon as possible and in any event within two *business days* of clearance being received.	
	Circumstances for refusal	
8	A restricted person must not be given clearance to deal in any *securities* of the *company*:	
	(a)	during a prohibited period; or
	(b)	on considerations of a short term nature. An investment with a maturity of one year or less will always be considered to be of a short term nature.
	Dealings permitted during a prohibited period	
	Dealing in exceptional circumstances	
9	A restricted person, who is not in possession of *inside information* in relation to the *company*, may be given clearance to deal if he is in severe financial difficulty or there are other exceptional circumstances. Clearance may be given for such a *person* to sell (but not purchase) *securities* of the *company* when he would otherwise be prohibited by this code from doing so. The determination of whether the *person* in question is in severe financial difficulty or whether there are other exceptional circumstances can only be made by the *director* designated for this purpose.	

10	A *person* may be in severe financial difficulty if he has a pressing financial commitment that cannot be satisfied otherwise than by selling the relevant *securities* of the *company*. A liability of such a *person* to pay tax would not normally constitute severe financial difficulty unless the *person* has no other means of satisfying the liability. A circumstance will be considered exceptional if the *person* in question is required by a court order to transfer or sell the *securities* of the *company* or there is some other overriding legal requirement for him to do so.		
11	The *FCA* should be consulted at an early stage regarding any application by a restricted person to deal in exceptional circumstances.		
	Awards of securities and options		
12	The grant of options by the board of *directors* under an *employees' share scheme* to individuals who are not restricted persons may be permitted during a prohibited period if such grant could not reasonably be made at another time and failure to make the grant would be likely to indicate that the *company* was in a prohibited period.		
13	The award by the *company* of *securities*, the grant of options and the grant of rights (or other interests) to acquire *securities* of the *company* to restricted persons is permitted in a prohibited period if:		
	(a)	the award or grant is made under the terms of an *employees' share scheme* and the scheme was not introduced or amended during the relevant prohibited period; and	
	(b)	either:	
		(i)	the terms of such *employees' share scheme* set out the timing of the award or grant and such terms have either previously been approved by shareholders or summarised or described in a document sent to shareholders, or
		(ii)	the timing of the award or grant is in accordance with the timing of previous awards or grants under the scheme; and
	(c)	the terms of the *employees' share scheme* set out the amount or value of the award or grant or the basis on which the amount or value of the award or grant is calculated and do not allow the exercise of discretion; and	
	(d)	the failure to make the award or grant would be likely to indicate that the *company* is in a prohibited period.	

	Exercise of options	
14	Where a *company* has been in an exceptionally long prohibited period or the *company* has had a number of consecutive prohibited periods, clearance may be given to allow the exercise of an option or right under an *employees' share scheme*, or the conversion of a convertible security, where the final date for the exercise of such option or right, or conversion of such security, falls during a prohibited period and the restricted person could not reasonably have been expected to exercise it at a time when he was free to deal.	
15	Where the exercise or conversion is permitted pursuant to paragraph 14, clearance may not be given for the sale of the *securities* of the *company* acquired pursuant to such exercise or conversion including the sale of sufficient *securities* of the *company* to fund the costs of the exercise or conversion and/or any tax liability arising from the exercise or conversion unless a binding undertaking to do so was entered into when the *company* was not in a prohibited period.	
	Qualification shares	
16	Clearance may be given to allow a *director* to acquire qualification *shares* where, under the *company's constitution*, the final date for acquiring such *shares* falls during a prohibited period and the *director* could not reasonably have been expected to acquire those shares at another time.	
	Saving schemes	
17	A restricted person may enter into a scheme under which only the *securities* of the *company* are purchased pursuant to a regular standing order or direct debit or by regular deduction from the *person's* salary, or where such *securities* are acquired by way of a standing election to re-invest dividends or other distributions received, or are acquired as part payment of the *person's* remuneration without regard to the provisions of this code, if the following provisions are complied with:	
	(a)	the restricted person does not enter into the scheme during a prohibited period, unless the scheme involves the part payment of remuneration in the form of *securities* of the *company* and is entered into upon the commencement of the *person's* employment or in the case of a non-executive *director* his appointment to the board;

	(b)	the restricted person does not carry out the purchase of the *securities* of the *company* under the scheme during a prohibited period, unless the restricted person entered into the scheme at a time when the *company* was not in a prohibited period and that person is irrevocably bound under the terms of the scheme to carry out a purchase of *securities* of the *company* (which may include the first purchase under the scheme) at a fixed point in time which falls in a prohibited period;
	(c)	the restricted person does not cancel or vary the terms of his participation, or carry out sales of *securities* of the *company* within the scheme during a prohibited period; and
	(d)	before entering into the scheme, cancelling the scheme or varying the terms of his participation or carrying out sales of the *securities* of the *company* within the scheme, the restricted person obtains clearance in accordance with paragraph 4.
Acting as a trustee		
18	Where a restricted person is acting as a trustee, dealing in the *securities* of the *company* by that trust is permitted during a prohibited period where:	
	(a)	the restricted person is not a beneficiary of the trust; and
	(b)	the decision to deal is taken by the other trustees or by investment managers on behalf of the trustees independently of the restricted person.
19	The other trustees or investment managers acting on behalf of the trustees can be assumed to have acted independently where the decision to deal:	
	(a)	was taken without consultation with, or other involvement of, the restricted person; or
	(b)	was delegated to a committee of which the restricted person is not a member.
Dealing by connected persons and investment managers		
20	A *person discharging managerial responsibilities* must take reasonable steps to prevent any dealings by or on behalf of any *connected person* of his in any *securities* of the *company* on considerations of a short term nature.	
21	A *person discharging managerial responsibilities* must seek to prohibit any dealings in the *securities* of the *company* during a close period:	
	(a)	by or on behalf of any *connected person* of his; or

	(b)	by an investment manager on his behalf or on behalf of any *person* connected with him where either he or any *person* connected has funds under management with that investment fund manager, whether or not discretionary (save as provided by paragraphs 17 and 18).
22		A *person discharging managerial responsibilities* must advise all of his *connected persons* and investment managers acting on his behalf:
	(a)	of the name of the *listed company* within which he is a *person discharging managerial responsibilities*;
	(b)	of the *close periods* during which they cannot deal in the *securities* of the *company*; and
	(c)	that they must advise the *listed company* immediately after they have dealt in *securities* of the *company*.
23		A restricted person may deal in *securities* of a *company* pursuant to a *trading plan* if clearance has first been given in accordance with paragraph 4 of this Code to the person entering into the plan and to any amendment to the plan. A restricted person must not cancel a *trading plan* unless clearance has first been given in accordance with paragraph 4 of this Code for its cancellation.
24		A restricted person must not enter into a *trading plan* or amend a *trading plan* during a *prohibited period* and clearance under paragraph 4 of this Code must not be given during a *prohibited period* to the entering into, or amendment of, a *trading plan*. Clearance under paragraph 4 of this Code may be giving during a *prohibited period* to the cancellation of a *trading plan* but only in the exceptional circumstances referred to in paragraphs 9 and 10 of this Code.
25		A restricted person may deal in *securities* of a *company* during a *prohibited period* pursuant to a *trading plan* if:
	(a)	the *trading plan* was entered into before the *prohibited period*;
	(b)	clearance under paragraph 4 of this Code has been given to the person entering into the *trading plan* and to any amendment to the *trading plan* before the *prohibited period*; and
	(c)	the *trading plan* does not permit the restricted person to exercise any influence or discretion over how, when, or whether to effect dealings.
26		Where a transaction occurs in accordance with a *trading plan*, the restricted person must notify the *issuer* at the same time as he makes the notification required by *DTR 3.1.2 R* of:
	(a)	the fact that the transaction occurred in accordance with a *trading plan*; and
	(b)	the date on which the relevant *trading plan* was entered into.

Appendix 23 Extract from ICSA Guidance on Terms of Reference – Remuneration Committee (Guidance Note 101019)[1]

1 © Institute of Chartered Secretaries & Administrators. Reproduced with the kind permission of ICSA. For the full version of the Guidance Note please see www.icsa.org.uk

D Model terms of reference

Note: square brackets contain recommendations which are in line with best practice but which may need to be changed to suit the circumstances of the particular organisation

1 Membership

1.1. The committee shall comprise at least [three] members, all of whom shall be independent non-executive directors. The chairman of the board may also serve on the committee as an additional member if he or she was considered independent on appointment as chairman. Members of the committee shall be appointed by the board, on the recommendation of the nomination committee and in consultation with the chairman of the remuneration committee.

1.2. Only members of the committee have the right to attend committee meetings. However, other individuals such as the chief executive, the head of human resources and external advisers may be invited to attend for all or part of any meeting as and when appropriate and necessary.

1.3. Appointments to the committee are made by the board and shall be for a period of up to three years, extendable by no more than two additional three-year periods, so long as members (other than the chairman of the board if he or she is a member of the committee) continue to be independent.

1.4. The board shall appoint the committee chairman who shall be an independent non-executive director. In the absence of the committee chairman and/or an appointed deputy, the remaining members present shall elect one of themselves to chair the meeting who would qualify under these terms of reference to be appointed to that position by the board. The chairman of the board shall not be chairman of the committee.

2   Secretary

2.1. The company secretary or his or her nominee shall act as the secretary of the committee and will ensure that the committee receives information and papers in a timely manner to enable full and proper consideration to be given to the issues.

3   Quorum

3.1. The quorum necessary for the transaction of business shall be [two].

4   Meetings

4.1. The committee shall meet at least [twice] a year and otherwise as required. [*The frequency and timing of meetings will differ according to the needs of the company. Meetings should be organised so that attendance is maximised, for example by timetabling them to coincide with board meetings.*]

5   Notice of meetings

5.1. Meetings of the committee shall be called by the secretary of the committee at the request of the committee chairman.

5.2. Unless otherwise agreed, notice of each meeting confirming the venue, time and date together with an agenda of items to be discussed, shall be forwarded to each member of the committee, any other person required to attend and all other non-executive directors, no later than [five] working days before the date of the meeting. Supporting papers shall be sent to committee members and to other attendees as appropriate, at the same time.

6   Minutes of meetings

6.1. The secretary shall minute the proceedings and resolutions of all committee meetings, including the names of those present and in attendance.

6.2. Draft minutes of committee meetings shall be circulated promptly to all members of the committee. Once approved, minutes should be circulated to all members of the board unless it would be inappropriate to do so.

7 Annual general meeting

7.1 The committee chairman should attend the annual general meeting to answer any shareholder questions on the committee's activities.

8 Duties

The committee should carry out the duties below for the parent company, major subsidiary undertakings and the group as a whole, as appropriate.

The committee shall:

8.1. Have responsibility for setting the remuneration policy for all executive directors and the company's chairman, including pension rights and any compensation payments. The board itself or, where required by the Articles of Association, the shareholders should determine the remuneration of the non-executive directors within the limits set in the Articles of Association. No director or senior manager shall be involved in any decisions as to their own remuneration.

8.2. Recommend and monitor the level and structure of remuneration for senior management.

8.3. In determining such policy, take into account all factors which it deems necessary including relevant legal and regulatory requirements, the provisions and recommendations of the Code and associated guidance. The objective of such policy shall be to attract, retain and motivate executive management of the quality required to run the company successfully without paying more than is necessary, having regard to views of shareholders and other stakeholders. The remuneration policy should have regard to the risk appetite of the company and alignment to the company's long strategic term goals. A significant proportion of remuneration should be structured so as to link rewards to corporate and individual performance and designed to promote the long-term success of the company.

8.4. When setting remuneration policy for directors, review and have regard to pay and employment conditions across the company or group, especially when determining annual salary increases.

8.5. Review the ongoing appropriateness and relevance of the remuneration policy.

8.6. Within the terms of the agreed policy and in consultation with the chairman and/or chief executive, as appropriate, determine the total individual remuneration package of each executive director, the company chairman and other designated senior executives including bonuses, incentive payments and share options or other share awards.

8.7. Obtain reliable, up-to-date information about remuneration in other companies of comparable scale and complexity. To help it fulfil its obligations the committee shall have full authority to appoint remuneration consultants and to commission or purchase any reports, surveys or information which it deems necessary at the expense of the company but within any budgetary restraints imposed by the board.

8.8. Be exclusively responsible for establishing the selection criteria, selecting, appointing and setting the terms of reference for any remuneration consultants who advise the committee.

8.9. Approve the design of, and determine targets for, any performance-related pay schemes operated by the company and approve the total annual payments made under such schemes (in accordance with the provisions in Schedule A of the Code).

8.10. Review the design of all share incentive plans for approval by the board and shareholders. For any such plans, determine each year whether awards will be made, and if so, the overall amount of such awards, the individual awards to executive directors, company secretary and other designated senior executives and the performance targets to be used.

8.11. Determine the policy for, and scope of, pension arrangements for each executive director and other designated senior executives.

8.12. Ensure that contractual terms on termination, and any payments made, are fair to the individual, and the company, that failure is not rewarded and that the duty to mitigate loss is fully recognised.

8.13. Oversee any major changes in employee benefits structures throughout the company or group.

8.14. Agree the policy for authorising claims for expenses from the directors.

8.15. Work and liaise as necessary with all other board committees.

9   Reporting responsibilities

9.1. The committee chairman shall report to the board on its proceedings after each meeting on all matters within its duties and responsibilities.

9.2. The committee shall make whatever recommendations to the board it deems appropriate on any area within its remit where action or improvement is needed.

9.3. The committee shall ensure that provisions regarding disclosure of information, including pensions, as set out in the Large and Medium-sized Companies and Groups (Accounts and Reports) Regulations 2008 and the Code, are fulfilled and produce a report of the company's remuneration policy and practices to be included in the company's annual report and ensure each year that it is put to shareholders for approval at the AGM. If the committee has appointed remuneration consultants, the annual report of the company's remuneration policy should identify such consultants and state whether they have any other connection with the company.

9.4 Through the chairman of the board, ensure that the company maintains contact as required with its principal shareholders about remuneration.

10   Other

The committee shall

10.1. Have access to sufficient resources in order to carry out its duties, including access to the company secretariat for assistance as required.

10.2. Be provided with appropriate and timely training, both in the form of an induction programme for new members and on an ongoing basis for all members.

10.3. Give due consideration to laws, regulations and any published guidelines or recommendations regarding the remuneration of directors of listed/non listed companies and formation and operation of share schemes including but not limited to the provisions of the Code, the requirements of the UK Listing Authority's Listing, Prospectus and Disclosure and Transparency Rules as well as guidelines published by the Association of British Insurers and the National Association of Pension Funds and any other applicable rules, as appropriate.

10.4. Arrange for periodic reviews of its own performance and, at least annually, review its constitution and terms of reference to ensure it is operating at maximum effectiveness and recommend any changes it considers necessary to the board for approval.

11   *Authority*

11.1. The committee is authorised by the board to obtain, at the company's expense, outside legal or other professional advice on any matters within its terms of reference.

June 2013

Appendix 24   Extract from ICSA Guidance on Terms of Reference – Audit Committee (Guidance Note 101017)[1]

1   © Institute of Chartered Secretaries & Administrators. Reproduced with the kind permission of ICSA. For the full version of the Guidance Note please see www.icsaglobal.com/assets/files/pdfs/guidance/ Guidance%20notes%202010/Terms%20of%20Reference%202010/1010%20Audit%20ToRs%20 FINAL.pdf

D Model terms of reference

Note: square brackets contain recommendations which are in line with best practice but which may need to be changed to suit the circumstances of the particular organisation, or excluded where not relevant to the company or if the company has a separate risk committee.

1   Membership

1.1 The committee shall comprise at least [three] members. [Membership shall include at least one member of the Risk Committee.] Members of the committee shall be appointed by the board, on the recommendation of the nomination committee in consultation with the chairman of the audit committee.

1.2 All members of the committee shall be independent non-executive directors at least one of whom shall have recent and relevant financial experience. The chairman of the board shall not be a member of the committee. C.3.1 of the Code provides that in smaller companies the company chairman may be a member, but not chair, of the committee provided that (s)he was independent on appointment as chairman.

1.3 Only members of the committee have the right to attend committee meetings. However, the external auditor and finance director will be invited to attend meetings of the committee on a regular basis and other non-members may be invited to attend all or part of any meeting as and when appropriate and necessary.

1.4 Appointments to the committee shall be for a period of up to three years, extendable for no more than two additional three-year periods, so long as members continue to be independent.

1.5 The board shall appoint the committee chairman. In the absence of the committee chairman and/or an appointed deputy, the remaining members present shall elect one of themselves to chair the meeting.

2   Secretary

2.1 The company secretary or his or her nominee shall act as the secretary of the committee.

3   Quorum

3.1 The quorum necessary for the transaction of business shall be [two] members

4   Frequency of meetings

4.1 The committee shall meet at least [four] times a year at appropriate times in the reporting and audit cycle and otherwise as required.

4.2 Outside of the formal meeting programme, the committee chairman will maintain a dialogue with key individuals involved in the company's governance, including the board chairman, the chief executive, the finance director, the external audit lead partner and the head of internal audit

5   Notice of meetings

5.1 Meetings of the committee shall be called by the secretary of the committee at the request of any of its members or at the request of external audit lead partner or head of internal auditors if they consider it necessary.

5.2 Unless otherwise agreed, notice of each meeting confirming the venue, time and date together with an agenda of items to be discussed, shall be forwarded to each member of the committee, any other person required to attend and all other non-executive directors, no later than [five] working days before the date of the meeting. Supporting papers shall be sent to committee members and to other attendees as appropriate, at the same time.

6 Minutes of meetings

6.1 The secretary shall minute the proceedings and resolutions of all meetings of the committee, including recording the names of those present and in attendance.

6.2 Draft minutes of committee meetings shall be circulated promptly to all members of the committee. Once approved, minutes should be circulated to all other members of the board unless it would be inappropriate to do so in the opinion of the committee chairman.

7 Annual General Meeting

7.1 The committee chairman should attend the annual general meeting to answer any shareholder questions on the committee's activities.

8 Duties

The committee should carry out the duties below for the parent company, major subsidiary undertakings and the group as a whole, as appropriate:

8.1 Financial reporting

8.1.1 The committee shall monitor the integrity of the financial statements of the company, including its annual and half-yearly reports, interim management statements, and any other formal announcement relating to its financial performance, reviewing and reporting to the board on significant financial reporting issues and judgements which they contain having regard to matters communicated to it by the auditor.

8.1.2 In particular the committee shall review and challenge where necessary—

8.1.2.1 the consistency of, and any changes to, accounting policies both on a year on year basis and across the company/group

8.1.2.2 the methods used to account for significant or unusual transactions where different approaches are possible

8.1.2.3 whether the company has followed appropriate accounting standards and made appropriate estimates and judgements, taking into account the views of the external auditor

8.1.2.4 the clarity of disclosure in the company's financial reports and the context in which statements are made; and

8.1.2.5 all material information presented with the financial statements, such as the business review/operating and financial review and the corporate governance statement (insofar as it relates to the audit and risk management).

8.1.3 Where the committee is not satisfied with any aspect of the proposed financial reporting by the company, it shall report its views to the board.

8.2 Narrative reporting

Where requested by the board, the committee should review the content of the annual report and accounts and advise the board on whether, taken as a whole, it is fair, balanced and understandable and provides the information necessary for shareholders to assess the company's performance, business model and strategy.

8.3 Internal controls and risk management systems

The committee shall

8.3.1 keep under review the adequacy and effectiveness of the company's internal financial controls and internal control and risk management systems; and

8.3.2 review and approve the statements to be included in the annual report concerning internal controls and risk management.

8.4 Compliance, whistleblowing and fraud

The committee shall

8.4.1 review the adequacy and security of the company's arrangements for its employees and contractors to raise concerns, in confidence, about possible wrongdoing in financial reporting or other matters. The committee shall ensure that these arrangements allow proportionate and independent investigation of such matters and appropriate follow up action; and

8.4.2 review the company's procedures for detecting fraud.

8.4.3 review the company's systems and controls for the prevention of bribery and receive reports on non-compliance

8.4.4 [review regular reports from the Money Laundering Reporting Officer and the adequacy and effectiveness of the company's anti-money laundering systems and controls]

8.4.5 [review regular reports from the Compliance Officer and keep under review the adequacy and effectiveness of the company's compliance function]

8.5 **Internal audit**

The committee shall

8.5.1 approve the appointment or termination of appointment of the head of internal audit.

8.5.2 review and approve the charter of the internal audit function and ensure the function has the necessary resources and access to information to enable it to fulfil its mandate, and is equipped to perform in accordance with appropriate professional standards for internal auditors;

8.5.3 ensure the internal auditor has direct access to the board chairman and to the committee chairman, and is accountable to the committee;

8.5.4 review and assess the annual internal audit work plan;

8.5.5 receive a report on the results of the internal auditor's work on a periodic basis;

8.5.6 review and monitor management's responsiveness to the internal auditor's findings and recommendations;

8.5.7 meet with the head of internal audit at least once a year without the presence of management; and

8.5.8 monitor and review the effectiveness of the company's internal audit function in the context of the company's overall risk management system.

8.6 **External audit**

The committee shall

8.6.1 consider and make recommendations to the board, to be put to shareholders for approval at the AGM, in relation to the appointment, re-appointment and removal of the company's external auditor;

8.6.2 ensure that at least once every ten years the audit services contract is put out to tender to enable the committee to compare the quality and effectiveness of the services provided by the incumbent auditor with those of other audit firms; and in respect of such tender oversee the selection process and ensure that all tendering firms have such access as is necessary to information and individuals during the duration of the tendering process;

8.6.3 if an auditor resigns, investigate the issues leading to this and decide whether any action is required;

8.6.4 oversee the relationship with the external auditor including (but not limited to):

8.6.4.1 recommendations on their remuneration, including both fees for audit and non-audit services, and that the level of fees is appropriate to enable an effective and high quality audit to be conducted;

8.6.4.2 approval of their terms of engagement, including any engagement letter issued at the start of each audit and the scope of the audit;

8.6.4.3 assessing annually their independence and objectivity taking into account relevant [UK] professional and regulatory requirements and the relationship with the auditor as a whole, including the provision of any non-audit services;

8.6.4.4 satisfying itself that there are no relationships (such as family, employment, investment, financial or business) between the auditor and the company (other than in the ordinary course of business) which could adversely affect the auditor's independence and objectivity;

8.6.4.5 agreeing with the board a policy on the employment of former employees of the company's auditor, and monitoring the implementation of this policy;

8.6.4.6 monitoring the auditor's compliance with relevant ethical and professional guidance on the rotation of audit partner, the level of fees paid by the company compared to the overall fee income of the firm, office and partner and other related requirements

8.6.4.7 assessing annually the qualifications, expertise and resources of the auditor and the effectiveness of the audit process, which shall include a report from the external auditor on their own internal quality procedures;

8.6.4.8 seeking to ensure co-ordination with the activities of the internal audit function; and

8.6.4.9 evaluating the risks to the quality and effectiveness of the financial reporting process and consideration of the need to include the risk of the withdrawal of their auditor from the market in that evaluation.

8.6.5 meet regularly with the external auditor (including once at the planning stage before the audit and once after the audit at the reporting stage) and at least once a year, without management being present, to discuss the auditor's remit and any issues arising from the audit;

8.6.6 review and approve the annual audit plan and ensure that it is consistent with the scope of the audit engagement, having regard to the seniority, expertise and experience of the audit team; and

8.6.7 review the findings of the audit with the external auditor. This shall include but not be limited to, the following:

8.6.7.1 a discussion of any major issues which arose during the audit;

8.6.7.2 key accounting and audit judgements;

8.6.7.3 levels of errors identified during the audit; and

8.6.7.4 the effectiveness of the audit process

8.6.8 review any representation letter(s) requested by the external auditor before they are signed by management

8.6.9 review the management letter and management's response to the auditor's findings and recommendations

8.6.10 develop and implement a policy on the supply of non-audit services by the external auditor, taking into account any relevant ethical guidance on the matter

9 Reporting responsibilities

9.1 The committee chairman shall report formally to the board on its proceedings after each meeting on all matters within its duties and responsibilities and shall also formally report to the board on how it has discharged its responsibilities. The report shall include:

9.1.1 the significant issues that it considered in relation to the financial statements (required under paragraph 8.1.1) and how these were addressed;

9.1.2 its assessment of the effectiveness of the external audit process (required under paragraph 8.6.4.7) and its recommendation on the appointment or reappointment of the external auditor; and

9.1.3 any other issues on which the Board has requested the Committee's opinion.

9.2 The committee shall make whatever recommendations to the board it deems appropriate on any area within its remit where action or improvement is needed

9.3 The committee shall compile a report on its activities to be included in the company's annual report. The report should include an explanation of how the committee has addressed the effectiveness of the external audit process; the significant issues that the committee considered in relation to the financial statements and how these issues were addressed, having regard to matters communicated to it by the auditor; and all other information requirements set out in the Code.

9.4 In the compiling the reports referred to in 9.1 and 9.3, the committee should exercise judgement in deciding which of the issues it considers in relation to the financial statements are significant, but should include at least those matters that have informed the board's assessment of whether the company is a going concern. The report to shareholders need not repeat information disclosed elsewhere in the annual report and accounts, but could provide cross-references to that information.

10 Other matters

The committee shall

10.1 have access to sufficient resources in order to carry out its duties, including access to the company secretariat for assistance as required

10.2 be provided with appropriate and timely training, both in the form of an induction programme for new members and on an ongoing basis for all members

10.3 give due consideration to laws and regulations, the provisions of the Code and the requirements of the UK Listing Authority's Listing, Prospectus and Disclosure and Transparency Rules and any other applicable Rules, as appropriate.

10.4 be responsible for co-ordination of the internal and external auditors

10.5 oversee any investigation of activities which are within its terms of reference

10.6 work and liaise as necessary with all other board committees

10.7 arrange for periodic reviews of its own performance and, at least annually, review its constitution and terms of reference to ensure it is operating at maximum effectiveness and recommend any changes it considers necessary to the board for approval.

11   *Authority*

The committee is authorised to

11.1 seek any information it requires from any employee of the company in order to perform its duties.

11.2 obtain, at the company's expense, independent legal, accounting or other professional advice on any matter it believes it necessary to do so.

11.3 call any employee to be questioned at a meeting of the committee as and when required.

11.4 have the right to publish in the company's annual report details of any issues that cannot be resolved between the committee and the board.

June 2013

Appendix 25 Basic contents of the written statement of employment

1 Names of employer and employee.

2 Date employment commenced (and the period of continuous employment).

3 Remuneration and intervals at which it is paid.

4 Hours of work (and if on Sunday, nights and/or overtime required).

5 Holiday entitlement (and if it includes public holidays).

6 Sickness entitlement.

7 Pension and pensions schemes.

8 Entitlement to notice of termination (both for the employer and the employee).

9 Job title or a brief job description.

10 Where employment is not permanent, the period for which it is expected to continue or, where it is for a fixed term, the date when employment is to end.

11 Place of work or, if the employee is required or allowed to relocate or to work in more than one location, an indication of this and of the employer's address.

12 Details of the existence of any relevant collective agreements which directly affect the terms and conditions of the employee's employment.

Notes:

- Where the employee is normally employed in the UK but will be required to work abroad for the same employer for a period of more than one month, the statement must also include details of:
  — how long they will be working abroad;
  — currency in which they will be paid;
  — any additional pay or benefits; and
  — terms on return to the UK.

- Where there are no particulars to be given for any of the items listed in 1–12 above, this needs to be indicated in the statement.

- The statement must include details of the employer's disciplinary and grievance procedures and disciplinary rules should cover matters such as conduct, time keeping, absence, health and safety, use of telephones and email, discrimination and performance and behaviour, and should specify the kind of offence that would be considered gross misconduct.

- It must be made clear in the statement whether or not a pensions contracting-out certificate under Pension Schemes Act 1993 is or is not in force for the employment in question.

- Rather than including full details in the written statement, it may refer employees to other accessible documents which the employee must consult for full details of pension schemes, sickness entitlement, disciplinary rules and grievance procedures, etc.

Appendix 26   Sample disciplinary and grievance policy (a modified extract from the Acas guide: Discipline and grievances at work)

Sample disciplinary procedure suitable for any organisation

1   Purpose and scope

This procedure is designed to help and encourage all employees to achieve and maintain standards of conduct, attendance and job performance. The company rules (set out in the employment handbook) and this procedure apply to all employees. The aim is to ensure consistent and fair treatment for all in the organisation.

2   Principles

Informal action will be considered, where appropriate, to resolve problems.

No disciplinary action will be taken against an employee until the case has been fully investigated.

Where formal action is taken the employee will be advised of the nature of the complaint against him or her and will be given the opportunity to state his or her case before any decision is made at a disciplinary meeting.

Employees will be provided, where appropriate, with written copies of evidence and relevant witness statements in advance of a disciplinary meeting.

At all stages of the procedure the employee will have the right to be accompanied by a trade union representative, or work colleague.

No employee will be dismissed for a first breach of discipline except in the case of gross misconduct, when the penalty will be dismissal without notice or payment in lieu of notice.

An employee will have the right to appeal against any disciplinary action.

The procedure may be implemented at any stage if the employee's alleged misconduct warrants this.

3 The Procedure

First stage of formal procedure

This will normally be either:

- *an improvement note for unsatisfactory performance* if performance does not meet acceptable standards. This will set out the performance problem, the improvement that is required, the timescale, any help that may be given and the right of appeal. The individual will be advised that it constitutes the first stage of the formal procedure. A record of the improvement note will be kept for [......] months, but will then be considered spent – subject to achieving and sustaining satisfactory performance; or

- *a first warning for misconduct* if conduct does not meet acceptable standards. This will be in writing and set out the nature of the misconduct, the change in behaviour required and the right of appeal. The warning will also inform the employee that a final written warning may be considered if there is no sustained satisfactory improvement or change. A record of the warning will be kept, but it will be disregarded for disciplinary purposes after a specified period of [......] months.

Final written warning

If the offence is sufficiently serious, or if there is further misconduct or a failure to improve performance during the currency of a prior warning, a final written warning may be given to the employee. This will give details of the complaint, the improvement required and the timescale. It will also warn that failure to improve may lead to dismissal (or some other action short of dismissal) and will refer to the right of appeal. A copy of this written warning will be kept by the supervisor but will be disregarded for disciplinary purposes after [......] months subject to achieving and sustaining satisfactory conduct or performance.

Dismissal or other sanction

If there is still further misconduct or failure to improve performance the final step in the procedure may be dismissal or some other action short of dismissal such as demotion or disciplinary suspension or transfer (as allowed in the contract of employment). Dismissal decisions can only be taken by the appropriate senior manager, and the employee will be provided in writing with reasons for dismissal, the date on which the employment will terminate, and the right of appeal.

If some sanction short of dismissal is imposed, the employee will receive details of the complaint, will be warned that dismissal could result if there is no satisfactory improvement, and will be advised of the right of appeal. A copy of the written warning will be kept but will be disregarded for disciplinary purposes after [......] months subject to achievement and sustainment of satisfactory conduct or performance.

Gross misconduct

The following list provides some examples of offences which are normally regarded as gross misconduct:

- theft or fraud
- physical violence or bullying
- deliberate and serious damage to property
- serious misuse of an organisation's property or name
- deliberately accessing internet sites containing pornographic, offensive or obscene material
- serious insubordination
- unlawful discrimination or harassment
- bringing the organisation into disrepute
- serious incapability at work brought on by alcohol or illegal drugs
- causing loss, damage or injury through serious negligence
- a serious breach of health and safety rules
- a serious breach of confidence.

If you are accused of an act of gross misconduct, you may be suspended from work on full pay, normally for no more than five working days, while the alleged offence is investigated. If, on completion of the investigation and the full disciplinary procedure, the organisation is satisfied that gross misconduct has occurred, the result will normally be summary dismissal without notice or payment in lieu of notice.

Appeals

An employee who wishes to appeal against a disciplinary decision must do so within five working days. The senior manager will hear all appeals and his/her decision is final. At the appeal any disciplinary penalty imposed will be reviewed.

Sample disciplinary procedure suitable for small organisations

1 Purpose and scope

The organisation's aim is to encourage improvement in individual conduct or performance. This procedure sets out the action which will be taken when disciplinary rules are breached.

2 Principles

(a) The procedure is designed to establish the facts quickly and to deal consistently with disciplinary issues. No disciplinary action will be taken until the matter has been fully investigated.

(b) At every stage employees will be informed in writing of what is alleged and have the opportunity to state their case at a disciplinary meeting and be represented or accompanied, if they wish, by a trade union representative or a work colleague.

(c) An employee has the right to appeal against any disciplinary penalty.

3 The Procedure

Stage 1 – first warning

If conduct or performance is unsatisfactory, the employee will be given a written warning or performance note. Such warnings will be recorded, but disregarded after [......] months of satisfactory service. The employee will also be informed that a final written warning may be considered if there is no sustained satisfactory improvement or change. (Where the first offence is sufficiently serious, for example because it is having, or is likely to have, a serious harmful effect on the organisation, it may be justifiable to move directly to a final written warning.)

Stage 2 – final written warning

If the offence is serious, or there is no improvement in standards, or if a further offence of a similar kind occurs, a final written warning will be given which will include the reason for the warning and a note that if no improvement results within [......] months, action at Stage 3 will be taken.

Stage 3 – dismissal or action short of dismissal

If the conduct or performance has failed to improve, the employee may suffer demotion, disciplinary transfer, loss of seniority (as allowed in the contract) or dismissal.

Gross misconduct

If, after investigation, it is confirmed that an employee has committed an offence of the following nature (the list is not exhaustive), the normal consequence will be dismissal without notice or payment in lieu of notice:

- theft, damage to property, fraud, incapacity for work due to being under the influence of alcohol or illegal drugs, physical violence, bullying and gross insubordination.

While the alleged gross misconduct is being investigated, the employee may be suspended, during which time he or she will be paid their normal pay rate. Any decision to dismiss will be taken by the employer only after full investigation.

Appeals

An employee who wishes to appeal against any disciplinary decision must do so to the named person in the organisation within five working days. The employer will hear the appeal and decide the case as impartially as possible.

Sample grievance procedure (small organisation)

Dealing with grievances informally

If you have a grievance or complaint to do with your work or the people you work with you should, wherever possible, start by talking it over with your manager. You may be able to agree a solution informally between you.

Formal grievance

If the matter is serious and/or you wish to raise the matter formally you should set out the grievance in writing to your manager. You should stick to the facts and avoid language that is insulting or abusive.

Where the grievance is against your manager and you feel unable to approach him or her you should talk to another manager or the owner.

Grievance hearing

Your manager will call you to a meeting, normally within five days, to discuss your grievance. You have the right to be accompanied by a colleague or trade union representative at this meeting if you make a reasonable request.

After the meeting the manager will give you a decision in writing, normally within 24 hours.

Appeal

If you are unhappy with your manager's decision and you wish to appeal you should let your manager know.

You will be invited to an appeal meeting, normally within five days, and your appeal will be heard by a more senior manager (or the company owner). You have the right to be accompanied by a colleague or trade union representative at this meeting if you make a reasonable request.

After the meeting the manager (or owner) will give you a decision, normally within 24 hours. The manager's (or owner's) decision is final.

Appendix 27   Example of a whistleblowing policy

If you are concerned about possible wrongdoing at work, the Public Interest Disclosure Act 1998 (PIDA 1998) provides guidance for dealing with these and other whistleblowing issues in a safe and constructive way. It encourages you to raise concerns internally in the first instance.

Internal contacts for whistleblowing

We hope that you will feel able to raise any concerns or suspicions you might have about malpractice internally, confident that it will be dealt with properly and that all reasonable steps will be taken to protect you from victimisation.

Please raise any concerns you have either orally or in writing with the Human Resources Manager or the Chief Executive Officer [insert names and contact details] who have been nominated for this purpose. They will deal with the matter in strict confidence, investigate the matter and provide appropriate advice and action that should be taken in addressing your concerns.

If you feel unable to raise this matter with either the Human Resources Manager or the Chief Executive Officer, then you should raise the matter with [insert name] [Chairman of the Audit and Risk Management Committee] [insert contact details]. In any event, all instances of whistleblowing will be reported to the Chairman and the Audit Committee.

Receipt of your notification will be acknowledged within [5] working days. Preliminary enquiries and investigations will take place and you will be advised of progress, following which, to the extent permissible by law, you will be informed of the outcome and conclusions drawn.

PIDA states that individuals who make qualifying disclosures of information in the public interest have the right not to suffer detriment by any act or omission of their employer because of the disclosure. A qualifying disclosure is one which, in the reasonable belief of the worker, suggests that one or more of the following has been, is being, or is likely to be committed:

- a criminal offence;
- the putting of the health and safety of any individual in danger;

- a failure to comply with any legal obligation;

- damage to the environment;

- a miscarriage of justice; or

- deliberate concealment relating to any of the above.

PIDA 1998 protects you in making a disclosure to your employer where the disclosure meets the requirements set out above is in the public interest and is made in good faith.

External notification

There might be circumstances where you have a reasonable belief that malpractice has been or is taking place and you do not feel comfortable that it is appropriate for you to report your concerns internally. In these instances your concerns should be reported to [name] at [contact details]. You can request that your notification is made in confidence.

[Name] will advise the Chairman of the Audit Committee of receipt of the notification and appropriate internal/external investigation will be commenced.

Receipt of your notification will be acknowledged within [5] working days. Preliminary enquiries and investigation will take place and you will be advised of progress, following which, to the extent permissible by law, you will be informed of the outcome and conclusions drawn.

Advice

If you want free, confidential advice on what is protected by PIDA and how best to raise your concern, you can contact, for example, the independent charity Public Concern at Work on 020 7404 6609 or via the Internet at www.pcaw.org.uk.

Financial Conduct Authority

If you are worried about something at work, it may be that you are concerned about something that is relevant to the functions of the FCA.

If you have disclosed the matter internally but remain concerned either by the response or lack of response, or if you feel unable to talk to anyone internally or pursuant to the external arrangements made by the company for whatever reason, you can contact the FCA.

The FCA's contact details are: telephone number 020 7066 1000, email address is whistle@fca.org.uk and by post at the Intelligence Department (ref PIDA), Financial Conduct Authority, 25 The North Colonnade, Canary Wharf, London E14 5HS.

PIDA 1998 protects you if you contact the FCA where:

- you satisfy the test for speaking to your employer (see above);

- you reasonably believe the information and any allegations in it are substantially true; and

- you reasonably believe the FCA is responsible for the issue in question.

Please note that there are other people and bodies prescribed under PIDA 1998 and subsequent amending legislation to whom concerns can be reported on a range of matters apart from financial services. Details can be found in the List of Prescribed People available from www.gov.uk or from www.pcaw.org.uk.

For example, HMRC if the wrongdoing concerns tax or VAT; the SFO or BIS for concerns about insider dealing or fraud; SOCA about suspected money laundering or financial crime; the Information Commissioner about data protection; and HSE about health and safety concerns.

Appendix 28 HSE's health and safety leadership checklist

To determine status as a *leader* on health and safety:

- How do you demonstrate the board's commitment to health and safety?

- What do you do to ensure appropriate board-level review of health and safety?

- What have you done to ensure that your organisation, at all levels including the board, receives competent health and safety advice?

- How are you ensuring that all staff – including the board – are sufficiently trained and competent in their health and safety responsibilities?

- How confident are you that your workforce, particularly safety representatives, are consulted properly on health and safety matters, and that their concerns are reaching the appropriate level including, as necessary, the board?

- What systems are in place to ensure that your organisation's risks are assessed, and that sensible control measures are established and maintained?

- How well do you know what is happening on the ground, and what audits or assessments are undertaken to inform you about what your organisation and contractors actually do?

- What information does the board receive regularly about health and safety, eg, performance data and reports on injuries and work-related ill health?

- Do you compare your performance with others in your sector or beyond?

- Where changes in working arrangements have significant implications for health and safety, how are these brought to the attention of the board?

- What do you do to ensure appropriate board level review of health and safety?

Appendix 29 Punishment of offences under IA 1986

Note: the following information about offences relevant to the directors and officers of companies has been extracted from Schedule 10 to IA 1986.

Section of Act creating offence	General nature of offence
s 39(2)	Company and others failing to state in correspondence that receiver appointed
s 47(6)	Failure to comply with provisions relating to statement of affairs where administrative receiver appointed
s 53(2)	Failing to deliver to registrar copy of instrument of appointment of receiver
s 54(3)	Failing to deliver to registrar the court's interlocutor appointing receiver
s 64(2)	Company and others failing to state on correspondence, etc that receiver appointed
s 66(6)	Failing to comply with provisions concerning statement of affairs, where receiver appointed
s 85(2)	Company failing to give notice in Gazette of resolution for voluntary winding up
s 89(4)	Director making statutory declaration of company's solvency without reasonable grounds for his opinion
s 89(6)	Declaration under s 89 not delivered to registrar within prescribed time
s 98(6)	Company failing to comply with s 98 in respect of summoning and giving notice of creditors' meeting
s 99(3)	Directors failing to attend and lay statement in prescribed form before creditors' meeting
s 114(4)	Directors exercising powers in breach of s 114, where no liquidator
s 131(7)	Failing to comply with requirements as to statement of affairs, where liquidator appointed
s 164	Giving, offering etc corrupt inducement affecting appointment of liquidator

Section of Act creating offence	General nature of offence
s 188(2)	Default in compliance with s 188 as to notification that company being wound up
s 201(4)	Failing to deliver to registrar office copy of court order deferring dissolution
s 203(6)	Failing to deliver to registrar copy of directions or result of appeal under s 203
s 204(8)	Failing to deliver to registrar copy of court order deferring early dissolution
s 205(7)	Failing to deliver to registrar copy of Secretary of State's directions or court order deferring dissolution
s 206(1)	Fraud etc in anticipation of winding up
s 206(2)	Privity to fraud in anticipation of winding up; fraud, or privity to fraud, after commencement of winding up
s 206(5)	Knowingly taking in pawn or pledge, or otherwise receiving, company property
s 207	Officer of company entering into transaction in fraud of company's creditors
s 208	Officer of company misconducting himself in course of winding up
s 209	Officer or contributory destroying, falsifying, etc company's books
s 210	Officer of company making material omission from statement relating to company's affairs
s 211	False representation or fraud for purpose of obtaining creditors' consent to an agreement in connection with winding up
s 216(4)	Contravening restrictions on re-use of name of company in insolvent liquidation
s 235(5)	Failing to co-operate with office-holder
Sch 7 para 4(3)	Failure to attend and give evidence to Insolvency Practitioners Tribunal; suppressing, concealing, etc relevant documents

Appendix 30   Schedule A1 to IA 1986 – Punishment of offences whilst a voluntary arrangement is in force

Section of Act creating offence	Nature of offence	Mode of prosecution	Punishment
Sch A1, para 9(2)	Directors failing to notify nominee of beginning of moratorium	1. On indictment 2. Summary	Two years or a fine, or both Six months or the statutory maximum, or both
Sch A1, para 10(3)	Nominee failing to advertise or notify beginning of moratorium	Summary	One-fifth of the statutory maximum
Sch A1, para 11(2)	Nominee failing to advertise or notify end of moratorium	Summary	One-fifth of the statutory maximum
Sch A1, para 16(2)	Company and officers failing to state in correspondence etc that moratorium in force	Summary	One-fifth of the statutory maximum
Sch A1, para 17(3)(a)	Company obtaining credit without disclosing existence of moratorium	1. On indictment 2. Summary	A fine The statutory maximum
Sch A1, para 17(3)(b)	Obtaining credit for company without disclosing existence of moratorium	1. On indictment 2. Summary	Two years or a fine, or both Six months or the statutory maximum, or both

Section of Act creating offence	Nature of offence	Mode of prosecution	Punishment
Sch A1, para 18(3)(a)	Company disposing of property otherwise than in ordinary way of business	1. On indictment 2. Summary	A fine The statutory maximum
Sch A1, para 18(3)(b)	Authorising or permitting disposal of company property	1. On indictment 2. Summary	Two years or a fine, or both Six months or the statutory maximum, or both
Sch A1, para 19(3)(a)	Company making payments in respect of liabilities existing before beginning of moratorium	1. On indictment 2. Summary	A fine The statutory maximum
Sch A1, para 19(3)(b)	Authorising or permitting such a payment	1. On indictment 2. Summary	Two years or a fine, or both Six months or the statutory maximum, or both
Sch A1, para 20(9)	Directors failing to send to registrar office copy of court order permitting disposal of charged property	Summary	One-fifth of the statutory maximum
Sch A1, para 22(1)	Company disposing of charged property	1. On indictment 2. Summary	A fine The statutory maximum
Sch A1, para 22(2)	Authorising or permitting such a disposal	1. On indictment 2. Summary	Two years or a fine, or both Six months or the statutory maximum, or both
Sch A1, para 23(1)(a)	Company entering into market contract, etc	1. On indictment 2. Summary	A fine The statutory maximum

Section of Act creating offence	Nature of offence	Mode of prosecution	Punishment
Sch A1, para 23(1)(b)	Authorising or permitting company to do so	1. On indictment 2. Summary	Two years or a fine, or both Six months or the statutory maximum, or both
Sch A1, para 25(6)	Nominee failing to give notice of withdrawal of consent to act	Summary	One-fifth of the statutory maximum
Sch A1, para 34(3)	Nominee failing to give notice of extension of moratorium	Summary	One-fifth of the statutory maximum
Sch A1, para 41(2)	Fraud or privity to fraud in anticipation of moratorium	1. On indictment 2. Summary	Seven years or a fine, or both Six months or the statutory maximum, or both
Sch A1, para 41(3)	Fraud or privity to fraud during moratorium	1. On indictment 2. Summary	Seven years or a fine, or both Six months or the statutory maximum, or both
Sch A1, para 41(7)	Knowingly taking in pawn or pledge, or otherwise receiving, company property	1. On indictment 2. Summary	Seven years or a fine, or both Six months or the statutory maximum, or both
Sch A1, para 42(1)	False representation or fraud for purpose of obtaining or extending moratorium	1. On indictment 2. Summary	Seven years or a fine, or both Six months or the statutory maximum, or both

Appendix 31 Extract from ICSA Guidance on Terms of Reference – Nomination Committee (Guidance Note 101020)[1]

1 © Institute of Chartered Secretaries & Administrators. Reproduced with the kind permission of ICSA. For the full version of the Guidance Note please visit www.icsa.org.uk

D Model terms of reference

Note: square brackets contain recommendations which are in line with best practice but which may need to be changed to suit the circumstances of the particular organisation.

1 Membership

1.1. The committee shall comprise of at least [three] directors. A majority of the members of the committee shall be independent non-executive directors

1.2. Only members of the committee have the right to attend committee meetings. However, other individuals such as the chief executive, the head of human resources and external advisers may be invited to attend for all or part of any meeting, as and when appropriate and necessary.

1.3. Appointments to the committee are made by the Board and shall be for a period of up to three years, which may be extended for further periods of up to three-years, provided the director still meets the criteria for membership of the committee.

1.4. The board shall appoint the committee chairman who should be either the chairman of the board or an independent non-executive director. In the absence of the committee chairman and/or an appointed deputy, the remaining members present shall elect one of themselves to chair the meeting from those who would qualify under these terms of reference to be appointed to that position by the board. The chairman of the board shall not chair the committee when it is dealing with the matter of succession to the chairmanship.

2   Secretary

The company secretary or his or her nominee shall act as the secretary of the committee.

3   Quorum

The quorum necessary for the transaction of business shall be [two] [both of whom must be independent non-executive directors].

4   Frequency of meetings

The committee shall meet at least [twice] a year and otherwise as required.

5   Notice of meetings

5.1 Meetings of the committee shall be called by the secretary of the committee at the request of the committee chairman.

5.2 Unless otherwise agreed, notice of each meeting confirming the venue, time and date, together with an agenda of items to be discussed, shall be forwarded to each member of the committee, any other person required to attend and all other non-executive directors, no later than [five] working days before the date of the meeting. Supporting papers shall be sent to committee members and to other attendees as appropriate, at the same time.

6   Minutes of meetings

6.1 The secretary shall minute the proceedings and resolutions of all committee meetings, including the names of those present and in attendance.

6.2 Draft minutes of committee meetings shall be circulated promptly to all members of the committee. Once approved, minutes should be circulated to all other members of the board unless it would be inappropriate to do so.

7 Annual General Meeting

The committee chairman shall attend the annual general meeting to answer any shareholder questions on the committee's activities.

8 Duties

The committee should carry out the duties below for the parent company, major subsidiary undertakings and the group as a whole, as appropriate.

The committee shall:

8.1 regularly review the structure, size and composition (including the skills, knowledge, experience and diversity) of the board and make recommendations to the board with regard to any changes

8.2 give full consideration to succession planning for directors and other senior executives in the course of its work, taking into account the challenges and opportunities facing the company, and the skills and expertise needed on the board in the future

8.3 keep under review the leadership needs of the organisation, both executive and non-executive, with a view to ensuring the continued ability of the organisation to compete effectively in the marketplace

8.4 keep up to date and fully informed about strategic issues and commercial changes affecting the company and the market in which it operates

8.5 be responsible for identifying and nominating for the approval of the board, candidates to fill board vacancies as and when they arise

8.6 before any appointment is made by the board, evaluate the balance of skills, knowledge, experience and diversity on the board, and, in the light of this evaluation prepare a description of the role and capabilities required for a particular appointment. In identifying suitable candidates the committee shall

8.6.1 use open advertising or the services of external advisers to facilitate the search.

8.6.2 consider candidates from a wide range of backgrounds.

8.6.3 consider candidates on merit and against objective criteria, and with due regard for the benefits of diversity on the board, including gender, taking care that appointees have enough time available to devote to the position

8.7 for the appointment of a chairman, the committee should prepare a job specification, including the time commitment expected. A proposed chairman's other significant commitments should be disclosed to the board before appointment and any changes to the chairman's commitments should be reported to the board as they arise

8.8 prior to the appointment of a director, the proposed appointee should be required to disclose any other business interests that may result in a conflict of interest and be required to report any future business interests that could result in a conflict of interest

8.9 ensure that on appointment to the board, non-executive directors receive a formal letter of appointment setting out clearly what is expected of them in terms of time commitment, committee service and involvement outside board meetings

8.10 review the results of the board performance evaluation process that relate to the composition of the board

8.11 review annually the time required from non-executive directors. Performance evaluation should be used to assess whether the non-executive directors are spending enough time to fulfil their duties

8.12 work and liaise as necessary with all other board committees

The committee shall also make recommendations to the board concerning:

8.13 formulating plans for succession for both executive and non-executive directors and in particular for the key roles of chairman and chief executive

8.14 suitable candidates for the role of senior independent director

8.15 membership of the audit and remuneration committees, and any other board committees as appropriate, in consultation with the chairmen of those committees

8.16 the re-appointment of any non-executive director at the conclusion of their specified term of office having given due regard to their performance and ability to continue to contribute to the board in the light of the knowledge, skills and experience required

8.17 the re-election by shareholders of any directors under the annual re-election provisions of the Code or the retirement by rotation provisions in the company's articles of association, having due regard to their performance and ability to continue to contribute to the board in the light of the knowledge, skills and experience required and the need for progressive refreshing of the board (particularly in relation to directors being re-elected for a term beyond six years)

8.18 any matters relating to the continuation in office of any director at any time including the suspension or termination of service of an executive director as an employee of the company subject to the provisions of the law and their service contract

8.19 the appointment of any director to executive or other office

9 Reporting responsibilities

9.1 The committee chairman shall report to the board on its proceedings after each meeting on all matters within its duties and responsibilities.

9.2 The committee shall make whatever recommendations to the board it deems appropriate on any area within its remit where action or improvement is needed.

9.3 The committee shall produce a report to be included in the company's annual report about its activities, the process used to make appointments and explain if external advice or open advertising has not been used. Where an external search agency has been used, it shall be identified in the annual report and a statement made as to whether it has any connection with the company

9.4 The report referred to in 9.3 above should include a statement of the board's policy on diversity, including gender, any measurable objectives that it has set for implementing the policy, and progress on achieving the objectives.

10 Other matters

The committee shall:

10.1 have access to sufficient resources in order to carry out its duties, including access to the company secretariat for assistance as required

10.2 be provided with appropriate and timely training, both in the form of an induction programme for new members and on an ongoing basis for all members

10.3 give due consideration to laws and regulations, the provisions of the Code and the requirements of the UK Listing Authority's Listing, Prospectus and Disclosure and Transparency Rules and any other applicable Rules, as appropriate

10.4 arrange for periodic reviews of its own performance and, at least annually, review its constitution and terms of reference to ensure it is operating at maximum effectiveness and recommend any changes it considers necessary to the board for approval.

11 *Authority*

The committee is authorised to obtain, at the company's expense, outside legal or other professional advice on any matters within its terms of reference.

June 2013

Appendix 32   ICSA Guidance on Induction of Directors (Guidance Note 120606)[1]

1   © Institute of Chartered Secretaries & Administrators. Reproduced with the kind permission of ICSA. The Guidance Note can be found at www.icsa.org.uk/assets/files/pdfs/guidance/Guidance%20 notes%202012/Induction%20of%20directors.pdf

1   Introduction

1.1 The objective of induction is to provide a new director with the information he or she will need to become as effective as possible in their role within the shortest practicable time.

1.2 In 2003 the 'Higgs Suggestions for Good Practice' stated that the induction process should aim to achieve three things, and these remain relevant today:

(a)   Build an understanding of the nature of the company, its business and the markets in which it operates.

(b)   Build a link with the company's people.

(c)   Build an understanding of the company's main relationships.

This note draws out two further elements: ensuring an understanding of (i) the role of a director and (ii) the framework within which the board operates.

1.3 As well as providing a checklist of topics and documents (section 4) to consider covering in an induction programme, this note makes suggestions for programme design (section 3) because the way in which any induction programme is delivered is an essential factor in its success.

1.4 The time taken to complete an induction will depend on the organisation, its size and complexity, but may take 12 months in order to cover a full board cycle.

2   References to induction in regulation and guidance

2.1   The UK Corporate Governance Code 2010 (the Code), published by the Financial Reporting Council (FRC) [since updated and the 2012 version of the Code applies]

The Code applies to all companies with a Premium Listing of equity shares at the London Stock Exchange.

The Code states (B4) that all directors should receive induction on joining the board and that to function effectively, all directors need appropriate knowledge of the company and access to its operations and staff.

It goes on to state that the chairman should ensure that new directors receive a full, formal and tailored induction on joining the board. As part of this, directors should avail themselves of opportunities to meet major shareholders.

B5 states that the company secretary's responsibilities include facilitating the induction programme under the direction of the chairman.

2.2   The FRC Guidance on Board Effectiveness

This guidance is issued by the FRC as 'associated guidance' to the Code, to assist companies in applying some of the Code's leadership and effectiveness principles.

Paragraph 1.7 reinforces the notion that the chairman should take the lead on induction.

Paragraph 1.12 states that the chairman should make certain that executives are aware of their wider responsibilities when joining the board, and ensure they receive appropriate induction and regular training, to enable them to fulfil the role. It goes on to say that executive directors are also likely to be able to broaden their understanding of their board responsibilities if they take up a non-executive director position on another board.

Paragraph 1.18 states that a non-executive director should, on appointment, devote time to a comprehensive, formal and tailored induction which should extend beyond the boardroom. It states that initiatives such as partnering a non-executive director with an executive board member may speed up the process of him or her acquiring an understanding of the main areas of business activity, especially areas involving significant risk. The director should expect to visit, and talk with, senior and middle managers in those areas.

Paragraph 5.3 states that the outcome of a board evaluation should be fed back, as appropriate, into the design of the induction programme.

2.3 ICSA guidance: a sample non-executive director's appointment letter

The ICSA template letter states that a new director will be expected to make himself/herself available during his/her first year of appointment for an additional number of days. 10 days is suggested in the template letter, reflecting the importance of the induction process.

3 Best practice points and points to consider in the programme design

3.1 Best practice points

3.1.1 Speak to the new director, before devising the programme, to get his/her input on how it should be tailored, in relation to both content and delivery. Previous experience is of course relevant to the induction programme design: it may be that the director is aware of some or most of the non company-specific items and may simply require an update in certain areas.

3.1.2 Plan the timing of the provision of information to avoid overloading a new director with everything all at once. Prioritise and schedule the various induction elements over an extended period. Arrange meetings with employees, advisors, shareholders and other relevant stakeholders over an extended period too. However, let the director see the whole programme plan at the start so he or she has the option to request certain elements earlier, or to have access to certain documents sooner.

3.1.3 Vary the delivery of information, and limit the amount of data presented just as reading material (whether in hard copy or via a board portal/on-line reading room), for example by designating meetings with executives to cover off certain elements, making use of advisors, other stakeholders, external training courses and organising site visits.

3.1.4 Plan the induction programme with reference to the director training and development programme, as one should transition smoothly into the other.

3.1.5 Review the induction with the director mid-way through the process, and after (12/18) months, and seek his/her input on any further induction requirements he or she may have.

3.2 Points to consider

3.2.1 Consider asking an existing non-executive director to bring his/her experience to bear by commenting on the content and design of the draft induction programme intended for an incoming director.

3.2.2 Consider arranging induction meetings/site visits around existing board/committee meetings.

3.2.3 Consider whether it would be appropriate to encourage a new executive director to take up a non-executive role on another board, once he or she has become well-established within their executive role, to broaden their understanding of their responsibility as a member or a unitary board[1].

3.2.4 Consider whether it would be beneficial to partner a new non-executive director with a particular executive director to hasten an understanding of a particular part of the business.

3.2.5 Consider whether any of the outputs of the latest board/director evaluation exercise could be achieved, or partially achieved, by changes to the induction programme.

4 Director induction checklists

The following checklists are not intended to be prescriptive or exhaustive, but to act as an aide-memoire when devising a programme. The expectation is that the programme will be tailored to the needs of the particular director to avoid repeating information the director is already well versed in, and that the content will be delivered using a variety of methods, over an extended period.

Many of the topics listed below will be best conveyed by making the director aware of the source document, while providing an overview/summary of the key points.

4.1 The role of a director

- the role of a director and his/her statutory duties

- UK Listing Authority (UKLA)'s Model Code and details of the company's policies and procedures regarding directors' shareholdings and share dealings, including close period dates

- support role of the company secretary/secretariat

- policies relevant to the director as an individual (independent professional advice, expenses, data protection)

- directors' and officers' liability insurance, deeds of indemnity

- personal development process

- protocol, procedures and dress code (if applicable) for board meetings, general meetings, formal dinners, staff social events, site visits etc, including the involvement of partners where appropriate

4.2 Board issues

4.2.1 Board and committees

- board and committee structure, matters reserved for the board, delegated authorities, committee terms of reference, items requiring approval outside of board meetings

- brief biographical and contact details of all directors of the company, the company secretary and other key executives. This should include any executive responsibilities of directors and their dates of appointment

- schedule of board committee membership

- board composition, board renewal, succession plans and policy on directors' re-election by shareholders

- board support framework: chairman, senior independent director, company secretary

4.2.2 Board meetings

- minutes of recent board meetings

- schedule of dates of future board meetings with pro forma forward agendas of regular items or an indication of when routine business is transacted

- description of board procedures covering details such as when papers are sent out, the method of delivery, the normal location of meetings and how long they last

- training in the use of any board portal or online board paper/reading room facility

4.2.3 Boardroom behaviours

- explanation by the chairman of his/her expectations of the board in terms of its output and behaviours

- culture and values, codes of conduct/ethics etc

4.2.4 Rules, regulation and guidance

- concept of the unitary board
- up-to-date copy of the company's articles of association/constitution
- Companies Act 2006 and legislation in other jurisdictions, as apply to the company
- UKLA's Listing, Prospectus and Disclosure and Transparency Rules
- other jurisdictions' securities and listing rules requirements, as apply to the company
- concept of comply or explain and best practice
- UK Corporate Governance Code and associated FRC guidance (Board Effectiveness, Internal Control (Turnbull), Audit Committees, Going Concern and Liquidity Risk)
- Investors' corporate governance guidelines which the company seeks to follow

4.2.5 Board procedures

- board, committee and individual director evaluation processes
- board training and development programme
- special procedures (accounts sign off, company disclosures)
- treatment and disclosure of price sensitive information
- bid/defence handbook

4.2.6 Current issues

- key governance issues affecting the company
- remuneration policy, trends and issues affecting the company
- voting and shareholder feedback from the last AGM
- most recent board evaluation report

4.3 The nature of the company, its business and its markets

- corporate history, with a summary of significant events (incorporation, acquisitions and divestments, restructurings)
- organisational/business overview/chart, indicating the major domestic and overseas subsidiaries, associated companies and joint ventures

- business model

- products/services

- local, regional/global operations

- strategy

- key performance indicators, including KPIs on which incentive plans are measured

- market analysis, market shares, trading backdrop, recent operational and financial performance, current challenges

- the company's risk profile and tolerance, risk management and internal control procedures and relevant disaster recovery plans

- financial and treasury issues: accounts/interim management statements, audit, management accounts, budgets, funding sources, dividend policy, credit-rating metrics

- significant contracts

- status of company pension plans, including any deficits

- insurance policies

- marketing and branding

- details of any major litigation, either current or potential

- relevant company/group policies, such as health & safety, corporate social responsibility, environmental, ethics and whistleblowing, bribery, diversity, equality, charitable & political donations, etc

- glossary of company-specific jargon/acronyms

- glossary of sector-specific jargon/acronyms

4.4 Building a link with the company's people

- meetings with senior management

- visits to company sites in addition to the head office

- internal company contact list (UK and overseas as applicable)

- employee committees or surveys

4.5 The company's main relationships

- market facing issues: investor relations and media views

- major shareholders (facilitate meetings)

- notices of any general meetings held in the last 3 years

- FRC's Stewardship Code

- recent press cuttings, reports and articles concerning the company

- the company's advisers (lawyers, bankers, auditors, registrars, brokers etc) and the key internal contacts for any external advisers

- key customers

- key suppliers

- key stakeholders (regulators, unions)

5   Board committee induction

Where the director will be joining a committee, he or she should be provided with copies of the committee minutes from the preceding 12 months.

5.1   *For the audit committee*[2]:

- role and remit of the committee

- link between committee policy and the company's strategic objectives

- members of the committee, and those regularly invited to attend meetings

- meeting schedule with pro forma forward agendas of regular items or an indication of when routine business is transacted

- main business and financial dynamics and risks

- regulatory and legal requirements in the UK/relevant jurisdictions

- market practice and current trends

- current issues

- views of investors on current arrangements and potential areas of focus

- meeting(s) with the CFO, external auditors and the head of internal audit

- technical training on key matters, tailored according to level of financial expertise

5.2   *For the remuneration committee:*

- role and remit of the committee

- link between committee policy and company's strategic objectives

- members of the committee, and those regularly invited to attend meetings

- meeting schedule with pro forma forward agendas of regular items or an indication of when routine business is transacted
- regulatory and legal requirements in the UK/relevant jurisdictions
- market practice, current trends and best practice guidelines
- current issues
- views of investors on current arrangements and potential areas of focus
- meeting(s) with the remuneration advisers
- technical training on key matters, tailored according to experience

5.3 *For the nomination committee:*

- role and remit of the committee
- link between committee policy and the company's strategic objectives
- members of the committee, and those regularly invited to attend meetings
- meeting schedule with pro forma forward agendas of regular items or an indication of when routine business is transacted
- board composition, board renewal, succession planning, ongoing recruitment
- internal talent and capability, leadership development programmes
- current issues
- views of investors on current arrangements and potential areas of focus
- recruitment process and recruitment agent(s) typically used

The generic items in 5.1 to 5.3 can be used as the starting point for an induction to other board committees, such as risk or sustainability/CSR.

1 Check the latest regulatory/best practice limits apply to your organisation as regards the number and type of mandates a director can/should hold.
2 See also the FRC Guidance on Audit Committees 2010, in particular paragraphs 1.11, 2.17 and 2.19.

Appendix 33 Extract from ICSA Guidance on Matters Reserved for the Board[1]

1 © Institute of Chartered Secretaries & Administrators. Reproduced with the kind permission of ICSA. For the full version of the Guidance Note please visit www.icsa.org.uk

B Schedule of matters reserved for the Board

1. Strategy and management
1.1 Responsibility for the overall leadership of the company and setting the company's values and standards.
1.2 Approval of the group's strategic aims and objectives.
1.3 Approval of the annual operating and capital expenditure budgets and any material changes to them.
1.4 Oversight of the group's operations ensuring: • competent and prudent management • sound planning • maintenance of sound management and internal control systems • adequate accounting and other records • compliance with statutory and regulatory obligations.
1.5 Review of performance in the light of the group's strategic aims, objectives, business plans and budgets and ensuring that any necessary corrective action is taken.
1.6 Extension of the group's activities into new business or geographic areas.
1.7 Any decision to cease to operate all or any material part of the group's business.
2. Structure and capital
2.1 Changes relating to the group's capital structure including reduction of capital, share issues (except under employee share plans), share buy backs [including the use of treasury shares].
2.2 Major changes to the group's corporate structure.
2.3 Changes to the group's management and control structure.

2.4 Any changes to the company's listing or its status as a plc.

3. Financial reporting and controls

3.1 ★ Approval of the half-yearly report, interim management statements and any preliminary announcement of the final results.
3.2 ★ Approval of the annual report and accounts, [including the corporate governance statement and remuneration report].
3.3 ★ Approval of the dividend policy.
3.4 ★ Declaration of the interim dividend and recommendation of the final dividend.
3.5 ★ Approval of any significant changes in accounting policies or practices.
3.6 Approval of treasury policies [including foreign currency exposure and the use of financial derivatives].
3.7 Approval of material, un-budgeted capital or operating expenditures (outside pre-determined tolerances).

4. Internal controls

4.1 Ensuring maintenance of a sound system of internal control and risk management including: ● approving the company's/group's risk appetite statements ● receiving reports on, and reviewing the effectiveness of, the group's risk and control processes to support its strategy and objectives ● approving procedures for the detection of fraud and the prevention of bribery ● undertaking an annual assessment of these processes ● approving an appropriate statement for inclusion in the annual report

5. Contracts

5.1 Approval of and oversight over execution and delivery of major capital projects.
5.2 Contracts which are material strategically or by reason of size, entered into by the company [or any subsidiary] in the ordinary course of business, for example bank borrowings [above £xx million] and acquisitions or disposals of fixed assets (including intangible assets such as IP) [above £xx million].
5.3 Contracts of the company [or any subsidiary] not in the ordinary course of business, for example loans and repayments [above £xx million]; foreign currency transactions [above £xx million]; major acquisitions or disposals [above £xx million].
5.4 Major investments [including the acquisition or disposal of interests of more than (3) percent in the voting shares of any company or the making of any takeover offer].

6. Communication
6.1 Ensuring a satisfactory dialogue with shareholders based on the mutual understanding of objectives.
6.2 Approval of resolutions and corresponding documentation to be put forward to shareholders at a general meeting.
6.3 ★ Approval of all circulars, prospectuses and listing particulars [approval of routine documents such as periodic circulars about scrip dividend procedures or exercise of conversion rights could be delegated to a committee].
6.4 ★ Approval of press releases concerning matters decided by the board.
7. Board membership and other appointments
7.1 ★ Changes to the structure, size and composition of the board, following recommendations from the nomination committee.
7.2 ★ Ensuring adequate succession planning for the board and senior management so as to maintain an appropriate balance of skills and experience within the company and on the board.
7.3 ★ Appointments to the board, following recommendations by the nomination committee.
7.4 ★ Selection of the chairman of the board and the chief executive.
7.5 ★ Appointment of the senior independent director to provide a sounding board for the chairman and to serve as intermediary for the other directors when necessary.
7.6 ★ Membership and chairmanship of board committees.
7.7 ★ Continuation in office of directors at the end of their term of office, when they are due to be re-elected by shareholders at the AGM and otherwise as appropriate.
7.8 ★ Continuation in office of any director at any time, including the suspension or termination of service of an executive director as an employee of the company, subject to the law and their service contract.
7.9 ★ Appointment or removal of the company secretary.
7.10 ★ Appointment, reappointment or removal of the external auditor to be put to shareholders for approval, following the recommendation of the audit committee.
7.11 Appointments to boards of subsidiaries.
8. Remuneration
8.1 ★ Determining the remuneration policy for the directors, company secretary and other senior executives.
8.2 Determining the remuneration of the non-executive directors, subject to the articles of association and shareholder approval as appropriate.
8.3 ★ The introduction of new share incentive plans or major changes to existing plans, to be put to shareholders for approval.

9. Delegation of authority
9.1 ★ The division of responsibilities between the chairman, the chief executive [and other executive directors,] which should be clearly established, set out in writing and agreed by the board.
9.2 Approval of the delegated levels of authority, including the chief executive's authority limits (which must be in writing).
9.3 ★ Establishing board committees and approving their terms of reference, and approving material changes thereto.
9.4 ★ Receiving reports from board committees on their activities.
10. Corporate governance matters
10.1 ★ Undertaking a formal and rigorous annual review of its own performance, that of its committees and individual directors and the division of responsibilities.
10.2 ★ Determining the independence of non-executive directors in light of their character, judgement and relationships.
10.3 ★ Considering the balance of interests between shareholders, employees, customers and the community.
10.4 Review of the group's overall corporate governance arrangements.
10.5 ★ Receiving reports on the views of the company's shareholders to ensure they are communicated to the board as a whole.
10.6 Authorising conflicts of interest where permitted by the Company's articles of association.
11. Policies
11.1 Approval of policies, including: • Code of Conduct   • Share dealing code   • Bribery prevention policy   • Whistleblowing policy   • Health and safety policy   • Environmental and sustainability policy   • Human relations policy   • Communications policy [including procedures for the release of price sensitive information]   • Corporate social responsibility policy   • Charitable donations policy
12. Other
12.1 The making of political donations.
12.2 Approval of the appointment of the group's principal professional advisers.
12.3 Prosecution, commencement, defence or settlement of litigation [involving above £xx million or being otherwise material to the interests of the group].

12.4 Approval of the overall levels of insurance for the group including directors' & officers' liability insurance [and indemnification of directors].
12.5 Major changes to the rules of the group's pension scheme, or changes of trustees or [when this is subject to the approval of the company] changes in the fund management arrangements.
12.6 Any decision likely to have a material impact on the company or group from any perspective, including, but not limited to, financial, operational, strategic or reputational.
12.7 This schedule of matters reserved for board decisions.

Items marked with ⋆ are not considered suitable for delegation to a committee of the board, for example because of Companies Act requirements or because, under the recommendations of the Code, they are the responsibility of an audit, nomination or remuneration committee, with the final decision required to be taken by the board as a whole.

Matters which the board considers suitable for delegation are contained in the terms of reference of its committees.

In addition, the board will receive reports and recommendations from time to time on any matter which it considers significant to the group.

July 2013

Glossary

The following explanations are not intended to be strict legal definitions.

Abbreviated accounts   A condensed version of the annual accounts which small and medium-sized companies (according to the specified size of criteria) are allowed to file with the registrar of companies. They may not be used as a substitute for the full annual accounts for circulation to members.

Administrator   A person appointed by the court to manage a company in financial difficulties in order to protect creditors and, if possible, avoid liquidation. The administrator has the power to remove and appoint directors.

Agent Someone who is authorised to carry out business transactions on behalf of another (the principle) who is thereby bound by such actions.

Allotment   The issue of shares.

Alternative Investment Market (AIM)   An exchange regulated market operated by The London Stock Exchange.

Annual accounts   The accounts which are prepared to fulfil the director's duty to present audited accounts to members in respect of each financial year. Annual accounts of limited companies must be filed with the registrar of companies. See also *Financial statements. Modified accounts.*

Annual general meeting   A general meeting of the company's members which must, subject to transitional provisions, be held by a public company in each calendar year within six months of the accounts year end.

Annual return   A form filed each year with the registrar of companies containing specified information about the company's directors, secretary, registered office, shareholders, share capital, etc.

Articles of Association   A constitutional document setting out the internal regulations of the company. Unless modified or excluded, the specimen articles in Table A have effect. See also *Table A.*

Audit   The independent examination of, and expression of opinion on, the company's accounts. The auditor must be a chartered or certified accountant (or otherwise specifically authorised by the Department of Trade and Industry).

Authorised share capital   See *Share capital.*

Board (of directors)   See *Director.*

Business Enterprise and Regulatory Reform   The government department responsible for the administration of company law. The Companies Acts confer certain powers on the Secretary of State for Trade and Industry who heads up this department. Now replaced by BIS.

Business Innovation and Skills (BIS)   The government department responsible for supporting sustainable growth and improving skills across the economy and for determining government policy in a wide range of areas including but not limited to company law and regulation, competition, corporate governance, employment relations and insolvency.

Calls   See *Share.*

Capital   See *Share capital.*

Case law   The principles and rules of law established by judicial decisions. Under this system the decision reached in a particular case creates a precedent: that is, it is regarded as exemplifying rules of broader application which must be followed except by higher courts. See also *Common law.*

Certificate of incorporation   A certificate issued by the registrar of companies on receipt of specified constitutional and other documents of the company. The company assumes its identity as a legal person on the date of incorporation shown on the certificate.

Charge A means by which a company offers its assets as security for a debt. A charge is a general term which includes, but is not limited to, a mortgage. A fixed charge relates to a specific asset or assets. A floating charge relates to whatever assets of a specified class are in the company's possession at the time the charge crystallises (if it does so).

Class rights   The rights attached to different classes of shares.

Common law   A body of law based on customer and usage and decisions reached in previous cases. The principles and rules of common law derive not from written legislation but from judgements and judicial opinions delivered in response to specific circumstance. See also *Case law, Statute law.*

Common seal   A seal bearing a company's name for affixing to legal documents which are required to be under seal, such as deeds and share certificates. Depending on the Articles, a director and the secretary usually have to add their signatures to the seal. The requirement that all companies must have a common seal was abolished by the Companies Act 1989 which also set out the procedures to be followed if documents are to have the same effect as if executed under seal.

Company An association of persons which, on incorporation, becomes a legal entity entirely separate from the individuals comprising its membership and which therefore continues unaffected by changes in membership. In the Companies Act 1985, 'company' is restricted to companies registered under that Act or previous Companies Acts. See also *Limited company, Private Company, Public company, Unlimited company.*

Company secretary An officer of the company with a number of statutory duties, such as to sign the annual return and accompanying documents and usually charged with a range of duties relating to the company's statutory books and records, filing requirements, etc. Every company must have a secretary who, in the case of a public company, must meet the qualification requirement laid down in the Act.

Connected person (definition greatly expanded under the provisions of CA 2006 ss 252 and 253) includes the spouse or civil partner, any other person who the director lives with in an enduring family relationship, child or step-child of a director or a person who the director lives within an enduring family relationship who are not yet 18 years of age, the director's parents, a body corporate with whom the director is connected, a person acting on behalf of the director in a capacity as trustee of a trust (excluding a trust in respect of an employee's share scheme or pension scheme) whose beneficiaries also include any person who the director lives with in an enduring family relationship or the director's child or step-child, a person acting in their capacity as partner to the director or any person who the director lives with in an enduring family relationship or the director's child or step-child, a firm which is recognised as a legal person, and which the director is a partner, or where a partner of that firm is the spouse or civil partner of the director, any other person who the director lives with in an enduring family relationship, child or step-child of a director or a person who the director lives with in an enduring family relationship who are not yet 18 years of age, the director's parents, a body corporate with whom the director is connected, a person acting on behalf of the director in a capacity as trustee of a trust (excluding a trust in respect of an employee's share scheme or pension scheme) whose beneficiaries also include any person who the director lives with in an enduring family relationship or the director's child or step-child.

Contract An agreement between two or more persons creating a legally enforceable obligation between them.

Credit transaction A transaction under which the creditor supplies goods or sells land under a hire-purchase agreement or conditional sale agreement, leases or hires land or goods in exchange for periodic payments or disposes of land, goods or services and payment is deferred but remains due.

Crime   An offence against the Crown punishable by a fine or imprisonment or both.

Debenture   A written acknowledgement of a debt owed by a company, often – but not necessarily – secured. It is common practice for a debenture to be created by a trust deed by which company property is mortgaged to trustees for the debenture holders, as security for the payment of interest and capital.

Department of Trade and Industry   The government department responsible for the administration of company law (now reformulated and renamed BERR).

Director   An officer of the company responsible for determining policy, supervising the management of the company's business and exercising the powers of the company. Directors must generally carry out these functions collectively as a Board.

Directors' report   A statement attached to the annual accounts containing certain information laid down in CA 2006.

Disclosure and Barring Service (DBS)   Formerly the CRB, the DBS is a government department responsible for carrying out criminal record and safeguarding checks on individuals applying for jobs or assisting with voluntary work. In most instances a basic disclosure listing spent and unspent convictions, cautions, reprimands and final warnings will suffice.

Disclosure and Transparency Rules   Rules relating to the disclosure of information in respect of financial instruments admitted to trading on a regulated market issued by the FSA in accordance with FSMA 2000, s 73A(3).

Distribution   The transfer of some or all of a company's assets to its members, generally by way dividend or on a winding up.

Dividends   The distribution of a portion of the company's profits to members according to the class and amount of their shareholdings.

Fiduciary   Having a position of trust, such that the power and authority conferred by the position must be exercised solely in the interest of the person with whom the fiduciary relationship exists. Trustees are in a fiduciary position, as are solicitors in relation to their clients. Directors have a fiduciary duty to the company, obliging them to act always in good faith and not to derive a personal profit from their position.

Financial Reporting Council (FRC) An independent regulator in the UK, separate from government, responsible for promoting high-quality corporate governance and reporting. It is responsible for setting, monitoring and enforcing accounting, auditing and actuarial standards and for overseeing the accounting and actuarial professional bodies.

Financial statements The term adopted y the joint accountancy bodies to signify 'balance sheets, profit and loss accounts, statements of source and application of funds, notes and other statements which collectively are intended to give a true and fair view of financial position and profit or loss'. It is thus a description of the form and function of the annual accounts, for which term it is often substituted.

Financial year The period in respect of which the company's profits and loss account is drawn up; it need not coincide with the fiscal or calendar year and in certain circumstances need not be a year.

Floating charge See *Charge.*

General meeting A meeting of the company which all members (subject to restrictions in the Memorandum and Articles) are entitled to attend.

Guarantee A formal agreement under which a guarantor undertakes to meet the contractual obligations of one person to another in the event of default. A company limited by guarantee is on in which the liability of the members is limited to a specified amount in a winding up.

Insider dealing Buying or selling share on the basis of an unfair advantage derived from access to inside information not generally available.

Limited company The most common form of company, in which the liability of members for the debts of the company is limited – either to the amount of share capital for which they have applied (a company limited by shares) or to a specific amount guaranteed in the event of a winding-up (a company limited by guarantee).

Liquidation The process under which a company ceases to trade and realises its assets for distribution to creditors and then shareholders. The term 'winding up' is synonymous.

Listed company A company whose share are dealt on the Official List of The London Stock Exchange.

Listing Rules Rules relating to admission of securities to the official list, issued by the FSA in accordance with FSMA 2000, s 73A(2).

Members The company's shareholders, of which there must be at least two.

Memorandum of Association A constitutional document governing the company's relationship with the world at large, stating its name, domicile, objects, limitations of liability (if applicable) and authorised share capital.

Nominal share capital See *Share capital*.

Objects The purposes for which the company was incorporated, as set out in the objects clause of its Memorandum of Association.

Office-holder Under the Insolvency Act 1986, an insolvency practitioner acting as a company's liquidator, administrator or administrative receiver.

Officer Includes a director, manager or secretary of a company. Not everyone with the title of manager is sufficiently senior to be regarded as an officer, who must have a level of supervisory control which reflects the general policy of the company.

Ordinary resolution A resolution at a general meeting carried by a simple majority of votes actually cast.

Ordinary shares The most common form of share in a company, giving holders the right to share in the company's profits in proportion to heir holdings and the right to vote at general meetings (although non-voting ordinary share are occasionally encountered). See also *Share*.

Persons discharging managerial responsibility Includes a director of a company that has shares traded on a regulated market or a senior executive of the company who has regular access to inside information about the company and power to make decisions affecting the company's future developments and prospects.

PLUS Market A recognised investment exchange operated by Plus Markets Group plc.

Preference shares Share carrying the right to payment of a fixed dividend out of profits before the payment of an ordinary dividend or the preferential return of capital or both. See also *Share*.

Premium listing A listing of equity shares where the issuer is required to comply with higher standards of regulation in chapter 6 of the Listing Rules. A company with a premium listing of securities might also be referred to as a 'primary' or 'premium' listed company.

Private company A company that is not a public company.

Promoter　A person engaged in setting up a company or in raising capital for a newly formed company. A person who acts merely as a professional adviser is not usually a promoter.

Prospectus　Any prospectus, notice, circular, advertisement, or other invitation to the public to subscribe for or purchase a company's shares or debentures.

Prospectus Rules　Rules relating to transferable securities, issued by the FSA in accordance with FSMA 2000, s 73A(4).

Proxy　A person authorised by a member to vote on his behalf at a general meeting.

Public company (plc)　A company which meets specified requirements as to its minimum share capital and which is registered as a public company. Only public companies are allowed to offer their shares and debentures to the public.

Quasi-loan　A transaction under which one party pays or agrees to pay a sum for another or to reimburse expenditure incurred by the other party on the condition that the borrower will reimburse the lender.

Registered office　The address at which legal documents may be served on the company and where the statutory books are normally kept. The registered office need not be the company's place of business and may be changed freely so long as it remains in the country of origin.

Registrar of companies　The official responsible for maintaining the company records filed under the requirements of the Companies Act.

Resolution　A decision at a meeting reached by a majority of members actually voting. See also *Elective resolution, Extraordinary resolution, Ordinary resolution, Special resolution, Written resolution.*

Seal　See *Common seal.*

Secretary　See *Company secretary.*

Serious Organised Crime Agency (SOCA)　Organisation that tackles serious organised crime, including fraud and instances of money-laundering and works to recover assets through obtaining orders for forfeiture, freezing assets and obtaining civil recovery orders.

Share　A unit of ownership of the company, representing a fraction of the share capital and usually conferring rights to participate in distributions. There may be several kinds of shares each carrying different rights. Shares are issued at a fixed nominal value, although the company may actually receive a larger amount, the excess representing share premium. Members may not be required to subscribe the full amount immediately, in which case the shares are partly paid. The members then await calls, which require them to pay further amounts until the share are fully paid.

Share capital   The capital of a company contributed or to be contributed by members. The authorised share capital is the maximum nominal amount the directors are authorised by the memorandum to issue. Issued, or allotted, share capital represents the amount actually contributed.

Share premium   The excess of the price at which shares are issued above their nominal value.

Special Resolution   A resolution which requires approval by at least 75% of the members voting at a general meeting or by written resolution.

Statute law   The body of law represented by legislation, and this occurring in authoritative written form. Statute law contrasts with common law, over which it takes precedence.

Statutory books   The general term applied to the registers and minute books etc that a company is required by the Companies Act to maintain.

Subscriber   A person who subscribes to the memorandum of association and agrees to take up share in the company on incorporation.

Table A   The specimen articles of association for a company limited by shares set out in the Companies (Tables A to F) Regulations 1985. Unless specifically modified or excluded, the version of Table A in force at the time of a company's incorporation automatically applies to the company. A significantly revised version of Table A was introduced on 1 July 1985, but companies incorporated earlier are not affected unless they specifically adopt its provisions.

Tort   A breach of a legal duty that gives rise to a civil action for damages, such as negligence, trespass or libel.

Turnbull Report   'Internal Control; Guidance for Directors on the Combined Code', issued September 1999 by the Turnbull Working Party.

Ultra vires   Outside the powers set out in the company's constitution. Fundamental changes made by the Companies Act 1989 make the rule that a company cannot validly contract to do something outside the scope of the powers specifically granted in its Memorandum, or that directors act ultra vires if they exceed their powers, largely a thing of the past (except for charitable companies). Ultra vires acts may be ratified by special resolution in certain circumstances, following changes made by the Companies Act 1989.

Unlimited company   A company in which the members have unlimited liability for the company's debts in the event of a winding up.

Winding up   See *Liquidation.*

Written resolution   Allows private companies to move any resolution without holding a general meeting. The written resolution must be signed by all members who would have been able to vote.

Index

675